STANDING
ON THE
SHOULDERS
OF GIANTS

Portrait of Isaac Newton by Charles Jervas, probably made when Newton was about sixty, and Halley in his late forties, at a time when both were concerned with comets. (Reproduced by permission of the President and Council of the Royal Society, London.)

EDMVND. HALLEIVS LL.D.
GEOM. PROF. SAVIL. & R.S. SECRET.

Portrait of Edmond Halley by Thomas Murray at about age thirty, when he was Assistant Secretary or Clerk of the Royal Society and at the time when he was editing Newton's *Principia*. The inscriptions were added later and refer to later appointments. (Reproduced by permission of the President and Council of the Royal Society, London.)

STANDING ON THE SHOULDERS OF GIANTS

*A Longer View of
Newton and Halley*

Essays commemorating the tercentenary of
Newton's *Principia* and the 1985–1986 return
of Comet Halley

EDITED BY
NORMAN J. W. THROWER

UNIVERSITY OF CALIFORNIA PRESS

BERKELEY LOS ANGELES OXFORD

University of California Press
Berkeley and Los Angeles, California

University of California Press, Ltd.
Oxford, England

Library of Congress
Cataloging-in-Publication Data

Standing on the shoulders of giants : a longer
    view of Newton and Halley / edited by
    Norman J. W. Thrower.
        p. cm.
    Based on a conference held at the William
Andrews Clark Memorial Library of the
University of California, Los Angeles, Aug.
11–14, 1985.
    ISBN 0-520-06589-1 (alk. paper)
    1. Newton, Isaac, Sir, 1642–
1727. 2. Halley, Edmond, 1656–1742.
3. Newton, Isaac, Sir, 1642–1727.
Principia. 4. Physicists—Great Britain—
Biography. 5. Astronomers—Great
Britain—Biography. I. Thrower, Norman
Joseph William.
QC16.N7S73 1990
509.2′2—dc20   90-10715
                                         CIP

The paper used in this publication meets
the minimum requirements of American
National Standard for Information
Sciences—Permanence of Paper for Printed
Library Materials, ANSI Z39.48-1984. ⊗

Printed in the United States of America
1   2   3   4   5   6   7   8   9

Dedicated to the memory
of Sir Edward Bullard, F.R.S. (1907–1980),
a great admirer of Halley

If I have seen further
it is by standing on the shoulders
of Giants.

Isaac Newton
in a letter to Robert Hooke,
5 February 1675/76

Contents

PART III • HALLEY

PART IV • COMETS

Illustrations

Tables

Preface

The professional relationship between Isaac Newton (1642–1727) and his younger contemporary Edmond Halley (1656–1742) was one of the most fruitful in the history of science. It led to the publication of Newton's *Principia* and the prediction, by Halley, of the return of the comet that now bears his name. These topics are considered in several papers in this collection of eighteen essays. But other achievements beside these spectacular accomplishments resulted from the association of these two great natural philosophers. Other papers in the collection deal with such topics as patronage and institutions as they relate to Newton and Halley. Contributions by these two scientists to astronomy, surveying, mechanics, and mathematics are the subject of several more papers, all considered within a humanistic and philosophical framework.

The timing of the conference "Newton and Halley, 1686–1986" from which these papers were selected was auspicious since it anticipated the year of the tercentenary of the receipt by Halley, in 1686, of Newton's *Philosophiae Naturalis Principia Mathematica,* to give this great work its full title. The circumstances of how the young Halley, then Assistant Secretary or Clerk at the Royal Society and editor of the *Philosophical Transactions,* persuaded a reluctant Newton to write the *Principia* and how Halley edited it and paid for the publication himself are always worth reevaluation. In addition, the conference anticipated by only a few months the recovery of Comet Halley from the Earth on the fourth apparition since its prediction. Viewers on this planet were able to see the comet with binoculars from October 1985 to May 1986 except for a period of a few weeks either side of perihelion, 9 February 1986. Halley's remarkable prediction was based on the calculation of the paths of twenty-four comets, which he accomplished, as he said, with "immense labour." This was the first great application of Newton's law of universal gravitation to an astronomical problem.

These and other matters concerning Newton and Halley were presented at a working conference at the William Andrews Clark Memorial Library of the University of California, Los Angeles, held Sunday, 11 August, to Wednesday, 14 August 1985. The conference was an official post-congress function of the Seventeenth International Congress of the History of Science held at Berkeley, California, 31 July to 8 August 1985. This meeting provided an unparalleled pool of experts on Newton and Halley, who were joined in Los Angeles by scientists who had not, in all cases, attended the Berkeley event.

The conference opened with a public lecture on the UCLA campus, "About Halley's Comet and Others," by Fred L. Whipple, professor of astronomy emeritus at Harvard University and formerly director of the Smithsonian Astrophysical Laboratory (1955–73). This was doubly appropriate because Professor Whipple, one of the world's leading astronomers and cometary physicists, had received his B.A. from UCLA (1927) and his Ph.D. from Berkeley (1933). The introduction to Fred Whipple's illustrated lecture, which was delivered to a capacity audience at UCLA's Arnold Schoenberg Hall, was made by Raymond Orbach, provost at UCLA, himself a distinguished physicist.

The major social event of the conference was a banquet held at the Sheraton Miramar Hotel in Santa Monica for participants and friends. The banquet address was given by Donald Yeomans, mathematician at the Jet Propulsion Laboratory, Pasadena, California, who spoke wittily on dubious achievements in science. Dr. Yeomans was a principal member of the team that made the first recovery of Comet Halley on the recent apparition, 16 October 1982, using the 200-inch Hale telescope at Palomar Observatory in southern California. Neither the lecture by Professor Whipple nor the address by Dr. Yeomans is published here. However, they added immeasurably to the conference and we are most grateful to these distinguished scientists for their contributions.

The sessions in the working part of the conference at the Clark Library were attended by about one hundred invited scholars. Approximately one-third of these were principal speakers or moderators, and the remainder were divided about equally between senior scholars and more junior participants. As the list of individual authors and their institutional affiliations following the preface will attest, the collection is international in scope. Although a majority of the authors are from the United Kingdom and the United States, the geographical representation within these two nations is very wide. Most of the authors are historians or historians of science, but a number are working scientists and scholars from a variety of fields. Similarly, although most of the authors hold appointments in universities, several are from museums and observatories, and one is an independent researcher.

With such a wide representation, we would expect the papers to reflect this diversity. Some ideas that are expressed may seem to conflict with others in the volume; although such points were discussed following the presentations of the papers, these discussions could not be included in the published work. It was with great sorrow that we learned of the untimely death of Professor Eric Forbes, after he had sent in his paper but before the conference began. Professor Forbes's paper was read at the conference.

The sweep of topics covered in the collection is evident from the table of contents. All of the authors are acknowledged authorities on their subjects and, as expected, have contributed new ideas in their presentations. The conference from which the papers were drawn was an exciting event, and it is hoped that the published papers convey some of this excitement. Because little was done officially in the United States to celebrate the 1985–86 return of Comet Halley, this collection is offered, in part, to fill this lacuna.

In order to retain the special character of the conference, a minimum of editorial work has been undertaken on the papers. This collection is not, however, a volume of proceedings of all papers presented; rather, it is a selection of edited essays arising from the conference. Most of the papers are included essentially as they were received but with some light editorial work to convert them from oral to written form in some cases and to give some consistency of style. The order in which the papers were presented has been somewhat rearranged in this published version. Editorial work was greatly facilitated by modern computer technology, which allowed character recognition of the wide variety of typewriter and word processing styles in which the texts of the original papers and abstracts were received.

An undertaking of the scope of the conference "Newton and Halley, 1686–1986" involves many individuals and institutions. As the first major event of the newly-founded (March 1985) Center for Seventeenth- and Eighteenth-Century Studies at UCLA, special thanks go to Sandy Michaels, program development officer of the Center. Supporting the editor of these papers, who organized the conference, was a committee consisting of Roger Hahn of the History of Science Program at the University of California, Berkeley; Robert Westman of the History Department at UCLA; and Donald Yeomans of the Jet Propulsion Laboratory, Pasadena. Sponsors of the event included the Ahmanson Foundation of Los Angeles; Harriet Wynter, Ltd., London; and Zeitlin and Ver Brugge, Booksellers, Los Angeles. Three special exhibits were mounted at the Clark Library at the time of the conference: one of scientific instruments by Harriet Wynter, Ltd.; another of materials from the Clark Library collections, including first and second editions of the *Prin-*

cipia, Halley's Atlantic isogonic chart in the first state, and recent additions from the Bullard estate, curated by John Bidwell; and, finally, a collection of meteorites provided by John Wasson from the Institute of Geophysics and Planetary Physics at UCLA, Leon Knopoff, director.

Some of the meteorites on display were from Canyon Diablo, Arizona; these had been donated to UCLA many years ago by William Andrews Clark, Junior, the founder of the Clark Library. Mr. Clark, who had his own observatory, also gave his Brashear telescope to UCLA. Resources provided by UCLA, the Clark Library, and private sources were matched by Grant #SES 84 19195 from the National Science Foundation, Washington, D.C. The editor is grateful to all those who contributed generously and in different ways to the conference "Newton and Halley, 1686–1986."

Pacific Palisades, California

Contributors

W. R. Albury, Professor, School of Science and Technology Studies, University of New South Wales, Australia

I. Bernard Cohen, Professor, Department of History of Science, Harvard University, Massachusetts, U.S.A.

Sir Alan H. Cook, F.R.S., Professor of Natural Philosophy, Department of Physics, Cavendish Laboratory, and Master of Selwyn College, Cambridge University, England

Suzanne V. Débarbat, Directeur du Département de l'Astronomie fondamentale, Observatoire de Paris, France

B.J.T. Dobbs, Professor of History, Northwestern University, Evanston, Illinois, U.S.A.

Eric G. Forbes, Professor, History of Medicine and Science Unit, Department of History, University of Edinburgh, Scotland

James E. Force, Professor, Department of Philosophy, University of Kentucky, Kentucky, U.S.A.

Gerald Funk, Ph.D., Indiana University–Bloomington, Indiana, U.S.A.

Sara Schechner Genuth, Associate Curator of the History of Astronomy Collection, Adler Planetarium, Chicago, Illinois, U.S.A.

Derek Howse, Lt. Cmdr. R.N. (Ret.), Formerly Keeper and Head, Astronomy and Navigation Department, National Maritime Museum, The Old Royal Observatory, Greenwich, England

David W. Hughes, Senior Lecturer in Astronomy and Physics, The University of Sheffield, England

David Kubrin, San Francisco, California, U.S.A.

Simon Schaffer, University Lecturer in History and Philosophy of Science, Cambridge University, Cambridge, England

F. Richard Stephenson, Senior Research Fellow in Physics, Department of Physics, University of Durham, England

Norman J. W. Thrower, Professor, Department of Geography; Formerly Director, William Andrews Clark Memorial Library; and Founder, Center for Seventeenth- and Eighteenth-Century Studies, University of California, Los Angeles, California, U.S.A.

Albert Van Helden, Professor, Department of History, Rice University, Houston, Texas, U.S.A.

Craig B. Waff, Historian, Project Galileo, Jet Propulsion Laboratory, Pasadena, California, U.S.A.

David W. Waters, Lt. Cmdr. R.N. (Ret.), Formerly Deputy Director, National Maritime Museum, Greenwich, England

Richard S. Westfall, Professor, Department of History and Philosophy of Science, Indiana University–Bloomington, Indiana, U.S.A.

PART I

Newton and Halley

ONE

Newton, Halley, and the System of Patronage

Richard S. Westfall
and
Gerald Funk

In 1691, Edmond Halley sought to obtain the Savilian Professorship of Astronomy at Oxford, which had been vacated by the resignation of Edward Bernard. As a scientist, Halley was eminently qualified: after Newton he was the leading physical scientist in Britain, he was the author of numerous papers in the *Philosophical Transactions,* and after Flamsteed he was the leading astronomer in Britain. As a man who was apparently in financial straits, moreover, he had need of the income attached to the chair.[1] And as an associate of Newton, he had placed the author of the *Principia* under an obligation so extensive that it was beyond both measure and the possibility of repayment.

The obligation began to accumulate when Newton sent the manuscript of Book One of the *Principia* to the Royal Society late in April 1686. At that time, Halley, whose visit to Cambridge a year and a half earlier had precipitated the very idea of the work, was Clerk of the Society. The Society was itself near the nadir of its fortunes and threatening to disintegrate, and three weeks passed without the Council's meeting to take action on the manuscript that Newton had presented to them, or even to acknowledge its receipt. Halley, however, recognizing the epochal dimensions of the work, evidently succeeded in moving the Society—not the Council, which was the body properly constituted for such action, but the miscellaneous collection of members who appeared at the weekly meeting on 19 May—to seize the initiative and order that the work be printed. The Society that so cheerfully issued the order for publication was in fact nearly bankrupt from an adventure in publishing John Ray's *Historia Piscium* the previous year. Hence, when a Council finally did meet on 2 June, it expressed its resentment of the clerk's invasion of its prerogative by summarily instructing Halley to undertake the publication himself. At the end of the year, indeed, the Council nearly voted to replace him as clerk. Although Halley in the end held on to his position, the destitute Society did not in fact pay him again until 1690, even though the clerk, perhaps equally destitute, had apparently accepted the position at least partly because he needed the meager salary.[2] Despite his circumstances, Halley resolved that Newton's masterful work must appear, and without further ado he shouldered the burden imposed on him, engaging a printer and supervising the press. When he finally received the manuscript for Book Two early in 1687, he engaged a second printer to expedite publication as much as possible, and he even considered a third printer for Book Three. There is every indication that, in addition to the effort he poured into Book One, the task of printing the final two books absorbed all his time for most of the first half of 1687, to the extent that he allowed the *Philosophical Transactions*, which was at the time his private venture, to slide so that the *Principia* could receive his full attention.[3]

It seems evident that without Halley's devoted labor, the book that established Newton's reputation for all time would not have been published. Nevertheless, only four years later, when Halley pursued the Savilian chair at Oxford, Newton supported the candidacy not of Halley, but of the Scottish mathematician David Gregory, who ultimately was awarded the appointment. No episode illustrates more clearly the apparent strangeness in the relations of Newton and Halley. This essay examines how far the context of patronage can help us to understand this strangeness.

One possible objection to our enterprise comes immediately to mind. There is a well-known story about Newton's dislike of Halley's free thought in religion. Is there in fact any need to look beyond the religious issue to explain Newton's action in 1691 and what we have called the "apparent strangeness" in the two men's relations? Obviously, we think there is. Indeed, in our opinion the religious issue does not begin to suffice. The story of Newton's reproof to Halley stems from the time when Newton's public image as a devout Christian was almost universally accepted. Today we know better. While there is no doubt about Newton's deep concern for religious questions, neither is there, in light of the evidence contained in his manuscripts, any doubt about the extent of his divergence from received orthodoxy. From what little we know about Halley's religious convictions, it is far from clear that Newton was one whit less advanced a free thinker than Halley. Perhaps Halley was less secretive about his views than Newton, in which case one could argue that Newton feared to be associated publicly with a man known to hold such opinions. Yet we insist immediately that only four years earlier Newton had not feared to be publicly associated with him when Halley assumed responsibility for the *Principia*. No, the religious issue is not adequate—not even close to adequate—as an explanation for the apparent strangeness in their relations.

One other prefatory remark is in order. We are fully aware that the concept of Newton as patron is not original with us. Frank Manuel has employed it extensively in his *Portrait of Isaac Newton*.[4] We see our paper in a dual relationship to Manuel's suggestions. On the one hand, where he has sketched the concept only in the broadest of strokes, we seek to fill it in by supplying detail. On the other hand, in attempting to explicate the relationship of Newton and Halley, we seek substantially to modify the concept as Manuel has presented it.

Patronage has been called the most pervasive characteristic of preindustrial society. Its essence lay in the one-to-one relationship of patron and client, which took the place of a variety of formally defined institutions familiar in the Western world today. As the two words, *patron* and *client,* imply, the relationship was unequal, and the reciprocal goods and services that patron and client supplied to each other differed in kind. Patronage, then, was part and parcel of a hierarchically ordered society in which the distribution of power and wealth was unequal and was accepted as such, and those who were placed above others were in a position to dispense favors of one sort in return for benefits of another.

All of these features characterized the society in which Isaac Newton and Edmond Halley lived. Although Newton himself was born to more than modest means, his elevated position in the social hierarchy did not depend in any significant way on his inherited wealth; rather, it stemmed directly from his intellectual achievement, made public in the *Principia,* which elevated him, by common consent, to the summit of the British intellectual world. His position was largely undefined—another characteristic of patronage, which did not enjoy legal status. Later, Newton would become Warden and then Master of the Mint and President of the Royal Society, but the defined status that derived from these offices was the product of the undefined one, not its cause. We have no doubt whatever that Manuel was right when he insisted on Newton's role of patron, which derived solely from his position as earned through scholarly achievement.

We can trace Newton's role as patron back to the period before the *Principia*. He had, as Lucasian Professor of Mathematics at Cambridge University and the author of some mathematical treatises that circulated among a limited audience, already gained standing as an authority. In the spring of 1682, for example, the governors of Christ's Hospital in London consulted with him regarding the vacant position of master of their Mathematical School, and as a result a young fellow of Trinity received the post.[5] Nevertheless, the publication of the *Principia* expanded

Newton's reputation so enormously that whatever prestige he enjoyed as Lucasian Professor cannot be measured on the same scale. The same year that saw the *Principia* also witnessed Newton's emergence as a political figure when he helped solidify the resistance of Cambridge to King James II's effort to Catholicize the university, and Newton's election to the Convention Parliament may have further enhanced his position. He was never a prominent political leader, however, and even his election to Parliament may not have been entirely independent of the *Principia*. That work, and the position it immediately won for Newton in the British intellectual world, were clearly the foundation on which his function as patron directly depended.

Almost immediately younger mathematicians and natural philosophers in Britain recognized the power of Newton's book and began to enroll themselves under his banner. In the formation of a Newtonian circle we can begin to see various dimensions of the system of patronage. Material advantage was by no means its sole function. From the beginning, the young Newtonians appear to have seen Newton as the prophet of a new order in natural philosophy; thus one of the advantages of being his client was to have access to such a man and to his ideas. When clients talked with Newton, they wrote down all that he said, and at least some of their notes circulated and contributed to the foundation of an incipient school of Newtonian philosophy. The clients learned too of the existence of a considerable body of mathematical manuscripts that promised a revolution in mathematics no less far reaching than that in natural philosophy. A client might hope to have access to these manuscripts, some of which did circulate among a small number of men. And in general terms, a client might aspire to be known as a Newtonian in an age when many were convinced that the future belonged to Newtonian natural philosophy.

If the benefits that a patron could bestow on a client were not solely material, the most important benefits, those without which the system of patronage would never have operated, certainly were material. By the late seventeenth and early eighteenth centuries, a number of university chairs devoted to mathematics and natural philosophy had been created. For a young man interested in such subjects, these chairs were the primary means by which he might hope to support himself while he pursued his work. Inevitably, after the publication of the *Principia*, Newton's voice made itself heard in the all-important granting of appointments.

David Gregory was the first to realize the potential inherent in Newton's new position. Already before the *Principia* he had run into Newton's name among the manuscripts of his uncle, James Gregory, and had written to him in Cambridge.[6] Through John Craig, another young Scottish mathematician, he had even seen some of Newton's work and made use of it in his own studies—excessive use, some thought.[7]

A determined Episcopalian, Gregory soon made himself unpopular in postrevolutionary Scotland, and he decided to seek his fortune in the wider fields of England. Newton's patronage was one specific mean by which he hoped to make his way. Following two unsuccessful attempts at opening a correspondence with Newton, Gregory finally met the great man in London in the summer of 1691 and from that time pursued him relentlessly. When Newton happened to inquire about Scottish universities, Gregory immediately composed a long essay describing them.[8] When Newton left London for Cambridge, Gregory followed him with correspondence and later with visits, taking care that the acquaintance did not languish. He flattered Newton egregiously. "Farewell, noble sir," one letter concluded, "and proceed as you do to advance philosophy 'beyond the paths of Sun and Sky'" (a line adapted from Virgil). Gregory had gone out of his way to include a literary flourish because he intended to publish the letter; when his plans failed to materialize, he dusted the line off and sent it to Huygens a couple of years later.[9] There is no reason to doubt that Gregory truly admired Newton, but in 1691 his efforts had a concrete goal: this was the year of the Savilian appointment, for which Gregory won Newton's endorsement. It would of course be rash to assume that Gregory won the Savilian chair solely because of Newton's endorsement; indeed, the surviving evidence convinces us that that is not the case. For our purposes, however, it matters only that Newton supported Gregory and did not support Halley.

In the years ahead Gregory was ostentatious in playing out his role as client. He kept in constant touch with Newton and when he visited took copious notes on their conversations—no doubt making it quite evident that he was doing so.[10] On such visits, Newton allowed Gregory to peruse his private manuscripts and to copy a number of them. Thus Gregory became the primary conduit through which the growing circle of Newtonians gained access to the realms of Newtonian thought that the master had not exposed in print. He composed a popularization of Newtonian philosophy, further enhancing his own reputation by publishing two hitherto unknown manuscripts by Newton. For a time Gregory nursed an active hope that he might edit a second edition of the *Principia,* and he supported Newton's efforts to force the publication of Flamsteed's observations. Beyond the continuing income from the Savilian chair, he profited from his book and from a temporary appointment in the Edinburgh Mint at the time of union with Scotland. Most of all, he profited from being known as the quintessential Newtonian. It is not going too far to say that his career rested squarely on his position as Newton's client.

The story of Gregory is not unique. A considerable group of young men of Gregory's generation and the following one saw Newton both as their intellectual ideal and as a possible vehicle of preferment. Let us,

however, take Gregory as the model of the client and attempt to understand Newton's relation with Halley by comparing it to that with Gregory.
Almost the first thing that strikes one is the lack of correspondence between Halley and Newton—more precisely, the lack of effort on Halley's
part to cultivate Newton. During the eight years that followed the *Principia,* no exchange between them took place that has survived. (Recall
that during this period Newton and Halley were not resident in the same
city and hence not in direct contact.) In 1695 and 1696 a flurry of letters
passed back and forth. They are the letters of scientific peers discussing
the problem of comets as equals, and not the inherently unequal exchange of patron and client.[11] In 1697 several more letters attended
Halley's tenure as Deputy Comptroller of the Chester Mint, an episode
to which we shall return.[12] Then once again silence: through the rest of
Newton's life he received exactly one more letter that we know about
from Halley, a letter with a calculation about a comet written in reply to a
request from Newton.[13] Letters did not exhaust their relationship, of
course, though it is necessary to remember that for long stretches of time
Halley was not in London. In a word, the surviving correspondence between Halley and Newton presents a decided contrast with that between
Gregory and Newton. So also does the absence of notes in which Halley
set down the *ipsissima verba* of the great man. Even in regard to Newton's
papers a contrast is evident. Although Halley held the highest opinion of
Newton's genius, he did not press Newton as Gregory did to have access
to his manuscripts or to function as editor of them. In short, we cannot
avoid the conclusion that Halley chose not to enroll himself among
Newton's clients, and it is in that choice, we believe, that the essence of
the apparent strangeness in their relations lies.

Concerning Newton's support of Gregory for the Savilian chair in
1691, it may tell us something about Newton that, when no deliberate
demonstration of subservience by Halley was forthcoming, he simply ig-
nored the obligation incurred by the *Principia* and supported Gregory.
If the incident does tell us this, the information is hardly surprising; indeed, it is in keeping with what we know about Newton from other
sources. However, we very strongly doubt that the Savilian election of
1691 should be seen as a comment on Newton personally. More probably, the incident reveals something more generally about the nature of
the patronage system.

We have spoken not of a strangeness per se, but of an *apparent* strangeness in the relations of Halley and Newton, that is, a strangeness apparent to us but not necessarily to them. The Savilian election may thus be
but an indication of the extent to which society in the Stuart Age differed
from our own. It is worth recalling that we have uncovered no hint of
resentment on Halley's part owing to the election, either at the time or in

his subsequent behavior toward Newton. Both men had grown up among the ubiquitous mores of patronage, and it is safe to assume that both understood its unwritten rules. What we take as a debt of Newton's they may not have considered relevant to Newton's recommendation on the Savilian chair, which may have involved a different range of obligations.

Support for the Savilian chair belonged to the realm of patronage. Gregory had clearly appealed to Newton within the categories of that realm. Just as clearly, Halley had not, despite ample opportunity to do so. Halley began to campaign for the appointment in May, three months before Gregory. Although from London he had easier access to Newton in Cambridge than Gregory did, he did not ask for Newton's support. Indeed, he turned to others instead, seeking and obtaining a recommendation from the Royal Society and evidently appealing to Archbishop Tillotson also, with whom he had been acquainted since 1681. Halley's companion on his grand tour, Robert Nelson, was a friend of Tillotson's and had loudly praised Halley in letters to the archbishop. Before long Tillotson had written to Halley as well, by way of Nelson, sending him a friend's observations of the great comet of 1680–81 and receiving a book from Halley in return. Halley also called on this relationship when he was charged with unorthodox religious views in 1691.[14] The fact that Halley did not request Newton's assistance for the Savilian appointment speaks eloquently about their relationship. Both men, we suggest, understood that Halley had no claim on Newton's support for the chair. He had not sought it. As far as the system of patronage was concerned, he had not wanted it.

We should not be too definite in assigning the labels *patron* and *client*. Patronage was a system of nuances, and we will understand it best if we avoid exclusive categories and remember that relations may have varied with time. In 1691, Halley did not seek Newton's patronage. Yet five years later, in 1696, Newton arranged for Halley's appointment as Deputy Comptroller of the Chester Mint, and everything about the proceedings has the odor of patronage. Possibly the odor is misleading—a possibility of which we must take note. Newton had thrown himself into the task of the recoinage, and there had been headaches aplenty in getting the country mints into operation. Halley could have been doing Newton as much of a favor as Newton was doing him. Nevertheless, Halley did speak of owing his employment to Newton's favor, and we should probably accept the apparent meaning of the appointment.[15] Scarcely had Halley arrived in Chester than there was mention of another position, again supported by Newton, to teach military engineering in the army, though Halley himself appeared less than eager to pursue it.[16] Perhaps it is significant that both positions were nonacademic and nonscientific. It is possible that Halley's intent was to deal with Newton as a peer in the realm of science but that, when in economic need—which, regardless of his situation in the mid 1680s, was certainly the case in 1696—he was ready enough to accept assistance in other realms of activity.

In any case, there is again no record that Newton played any role in Halley's eventual appointment in 1704 as Savilian Professor of Geometry at Oxford, whereas he did receive support from the Earl of Nottingham, who was then Secretary of State.[17] During the time that Newton was President of the Royal Society, Halley was elected as Secretary in 1713 and served for several years. In this case, however, the position appears to have been as much a burden as a favor. Halley no longer needed the modest salary, while Newton needed a candidate of stature in his campaign to push Sloane out of the secretary's post. But the situation involved certain ambiguities, which should be recognized. The position did lend its holder standing in the scientific community, and Halley did contrive to hold it until his appointment as Astronomer Royal in 1720 supplied him with another source of prestige. There is, of course, no question that Halley was a Newtonian: the basis of his enduring fame, his treatment of comets, rested directly on a Newtonian foundation. Nor are we calling Halley's estimate of Newton's genius into question or implying any personal tension between them. Our inquiry is directed rather toward the set of mores attached to the system of patronage. We insist on the contrast between Gregory and Halley. Where Gregory was unambiguous in assuming the role of Newton's client, Halley, for the most part, avoided it.

One should not, however, conclude that Halley stood aside from patronage as such. The complicating factor in his relations with Newton, the factor that we take to have been central to his aloofness from Newton as patron, was the presence of other patrons. The first major episode in Halley's scientific career, his expedition to St. Helena nearly a decade before he became acquainted with Newton and involved in the *Principia,* enjoyed the backing of two powerful men, Sir Jonas Moore and Sir Joseph Williamson. Williamson, moreover, arranged for the mandate by which Halley received a degree from Oxford after his return from St. Helena. During the next decade and more, although there is no evidence of similar support, we believe that Halley never lost touch with men of the greatest influence who concerned themselves with naval affairs, to whom the purpose of the catalogue of southern stars, the improvement of navigation, had been a matter of vital concern. Beginning in 1691, anything connected with the Navy that Halley expressed interest in received immediate support. Unfortunately, given the lack of specificity in the sources available to us, we cannot probe beyond the basic fact of support at the highest level, which nevertheless is unmistakable.

In 1691, a Navy frigate was placed at Halley's disposal for his tests with the diving bell. In 1693, together with Benjamin Middleton, he proposed an expedition to explore the variation (or declination) of the magnetic compass as a possible aid in determining longitude at sea. Middleton soon dropped out of the plans, but never mind: Halley was clearly the focus of support for the project, which held sway in both the Treasury and the Admiralty. The Navy had a vessel, the *Paramore*, built especially for the expedition and commissioned Halley, who had no previous experience of command at sea, as its captain. The appointment to the Chester Mint intervened, but the Navy renewed the commission in 1698, and this time Halley did set out. The first expedition in the *Paramore* ended little short of disaster, with Lieutenant Harrison, the principal subordinate officer, and the boatswain in virtual mutiny. Even though a court-martial exonerated Lieutenant Harrison, the Navy renewed Halley's commission, put the *Paramore* back in service, and sent him out again in 1699. Then the following year, after the *Paramore* had again been laid up, Halley suggested a survey of the English Channel; only three days elapsed between his formal proposal and the issue of orders to outfit the *Paramore* anew.[18]

With the survey of the Channel, Halley's activities on the *Paramore* ended, but almost immediately the Navy had further need of his expertise, this time to advise on the fortification of ports of the Holy Roman Empire on the Adriatic so that the Royal Navy could use them safely in the War of the Spanish Succession. In 1702–3 Halley made two official journeys across central Europe for that purpose. Finally we hear the name of a specific patron, the Earl of Nottingham, who two years later, as a trustee of the Savilian Professorship would place Halley in the chair of geometry associated with the astronomy chair he had failed to gain in 1691.[19] In 1720, when Halley replaced the recently deceased John Flamsteed as Astronomer Royal, his appointment was sponsored by the Lord Chancellor, Thomas Parker (later Earl of Macclesfield), and the Earl of Sunderland, who was then Secretary of State.[20] Significantly, the terms of the appointment and Halley's later performance made it clear that the improvement of navigation—that is, a method for determining longitude at sea—was the goal in view, a direct continuation of the naval connection.[21] The Savilian Professorship of Geometry and the office of Astronomer Royal were the two most important positions Halley held during his life, and we do not hear Newton's name mentioned in regard to either one. If Halley did not turn to Newton in these instances, surely it was because he had the support of more powerful patrons.

What the case of Halley and Newton should most teach us about the patronage system in late Stuart England is the position that Newton occupied in the hierarchy of power. By placing himself at the summit of the intellectual world, Newton insured that his voice would be heard in many decisions. Yet his was never the sole voice, and seldom was it the loudest. Manuel's description of Newton as the autocrat of British science could scarcely be more misleading as to the social reality. From sphere to sphere, Newton's power varied. Within the Royal Society it was very high, though even here it was short of absolute: there was always a group that opposed him within the Society, their strength discernible in the size of the vote against Newton year after year in the annual elections. The Society was not solely an organization of scientists; it was also a London club where amateurs from the upper class gathered. Thus the letter that Newton received in connection with the dispute of Woodward and Sloane in 1710 spoke of "some of the greatest Men in the Nation" being ready to enter into the Society.[22] By the nature of life in Augustan England, these were the men who always imposed a limit on Newton's authority.

At the Mint (a locale that has concerned us but little in this essay), Newton was one of the three officers on the Mint board. Because the other two offices were fruits of patronage far too juicy to be left under Newton's control, he always had to contend with others, once again members of the ruling class not readily amenable to his authority. In the realm of academic appointments, his power was more limited yet. The universities of the time were among the largest reservoirs of patronage within Britain. Measured by the scale of royal office the positions were not lucrative, but they were numerous, and the power brokers of the age made it their business to dominate them. Without understanding Newtonian science, these men did understand Newton's position in science, and like patrons everywhere they valued and respected him for it. Newton's very power as a patron was indeed the product of patronage: it sprang from the respect that excellence commanded among the ruling class. As such, however, it was by its very nature always limited.

Patronage was a system whereby the wealthy and the powerful justified their privileges by conspicuously supporting activities deemed to be worthy. The purpose of patronage, of course, was to enhance one's position, not to compromise it. By superb achievement, a Newton might ascend the pyramid of power to a certain level, but he could hardly rise to the top. Newton understood this fact, as did Halley. The apparent strangeness we find in their relations seems to have been largely a reflection of this reality.

NOTES

1. The state of Halley's finances after the death of his father in 1684 is unclear. Although several scholars have assumed that he was left destitute, Colin A. Ronan (*Edmond Halley: Genius in Eclipse* [Garden City, N.Y.: Doubleday, 1969],

82) argues cogently that in the late 1680s, when his small salary from the Royal Society went unpaid, Halley was able to finance the publication of the *Principia* and still provide for his family. That is, he can scarcely have been destitute. Thrower agrees with this conclusion (*The Three Voyages of Edmond Halley in the "Paramore," 1698–1701*, ed. Norman J. W. Thrower, Hakluyt Society Publications, 3d ser., vols. 156 and 157 [London, 1981], 1:24). Without denying the force of their argument, we do want to insist that throughout the 1690s Halley was constantly pursuing salaried positions and even tied himself to a post in the Chester Mint, which he found most uncongenial.

2. Thomas Birch, *The History of the Royal Society . . .* (London: Millar, 1756–57), 4:484–557 passim.

3. See the letters between Halley and Newton in early 1687, in *The Correspondence of Isaac Newton*, ed. H. W. Turnbull et al. (Cambridge: Cambridge University Press, 1959–77), 2:464–81 passim; also Halley to Wallis, 9 April 1687, in *Correspondence and Papers of Edmond Halley*, ed. Eugene Fairfield MacPike (Oxford: Oxford University Press, 1932), 80–82.

4. Frank E. Manuel, *A Portrait of Isaac Newton* (Cambridge, Mass.: Harvard University Press, 1968); see esp. chap. 13, "The Autocrat of Science."

5. Newton to the Governors of Christ's Hospital, 3 April 1682, in *Correspondence* 2:375–76.

6. Gregory to Newton, 9 June 1684, ibid., 2:396.

7. *The Mathematical Papers of Isaac Newton*, ed. D. T. Whiteside (Cambridge: Cambridge University Press, 1967–80), 7:7–11.

8. Gregory to Newton, 8 August 1691, in Newton, *Correspondence* 3:157–62.

9. Gregory to Newton, 7 November 1691, and Gregory to Huygens, 12 August 1693, ibid., 3:179, 278.

10. Notes for 28 December 1691, 4–7 May 1694, and July 1694, ibid., 3:191, 311–15, 327–28, 331–32, 334–36, 340–42, 344–45, 384–86.

11. See the exchange in ibid., 4:165–90 passim.

12. Ibid., 4:213–54 passim and 7:399–403.

13. Halley to Newton, 16 February 1725, ibid., 7:302.

14. See two letters of Tillotson to Nelson, one dated 5 January 1681 and the other simply 1681, in Thomas Birch, *The Life of the Most Reverend Dr. John Tillotson* (London: Tonson, 1750), 82–83, and British Library, MS. Sloane 4236, fols. 227–33; Halley to Hill, 22 June 1691, in Halley, *Correspondence and Papers*, 88.

15. Halley to Newton, 30 December 1697, in Newton, *Correspondence* 4:254.

16. Newton to Halley, 11 February 1697, and Halley to Newton, 13 February 1697, ibid., 4:229–31.

17. A. H. Cook, "The Election of Edmond Halley to the Savilian Professorship of Geometry," *Journal of the History of Astronomy* 15 (1984): 34–36.

18. See the documentation of Halley's three expeditions in the *Paramore* in Thrower, *"Paramore,"* 251–329.

19. Ronan, *Halley*, 183.

20. Martin Folkes's memoir on Halley, published in Halley, *Correspondence and Papers*, 11–12.

21. Thrower, *Paramore*, 76.

22. ? to Newton, 28 March 1710, in Newton, *Correspondence*, 5:17.

TWO

Newton, Halley, and the Royal Observatory

Derek Howse

Telling the full story of Newton, Halley, and the Royal Observatory—or at least the first forty-five years of it—would have to involve an account of the quarrels between Newton and Halley on the one hand and John Flamsteed, director of the observatory, on the other. Because this story has been told elegantly and in detail in at least two recent books,[1] this essay will be confined to the main events in more or less chronological order, with a description of the observatory and its work serving as a background to those events. Unless otherwise stated, dates of observations are recorded in the astronomical fashion, with the day starting at noon; thus, an observation taken at 8:00 A.M. on Tuesday, civil date, would be recorded as occuring on Monday.

THE LONGITUDE PROBLEM

In the mid seventeenth century, one of the most vital problems requiring a scientific solution was to find a method for determining longitude at sea. Solving this problem was of the highest priority in every maritime state, none more so than Britain. When late in 1674, therefore, the Sieur de St. Pierre, a Breton gentleman, called on the Breton Louise de Keroualle, Duchess of Portsmouth and King Charles II's current mistress, claiming "that he hath found out the true knowledge of the Longitude, and desires to be put on Tryall thereof,"[2] the King on 15 December appointed a royal commission to look into the matter.

The circumstances of the foundation of England's Royal Observatory "to find the so-much desired longitude of places"[3] is so well known that it is necessary only to recall that the astronomical solution put forward by

St. Pierre and others before him involved, first, knowing where the so-called fixed stars were relative to one another and, second, being able to predict several years in advance the position of the Moon at any moment relative to those stars and to the Sun.[4] The twenty-eight-year-old Flamsteed, called by the St. Pierre commission as an expert witness, pointed out that the data for doing this were simply not available, but that they could be obtained eventually if the King were to set up a suitably equipped observatory, as the King of France had done some eight years before. King Charles forthwith appointed Flamsteed his "astronomical observator," signing the warrant on Thursday, 4 March 1675.

GREENWICH OBSERVATORY FOUNDED

Only a week later came Flamsteed's first contact with Edmond Halley. "The veneration I have for all who think Astronomy deserves their care . . . was the chief motive that induced me to give you the trouble of these lines," wrote the nineteen-year-old Halley from Oxford on 10 March, "being ambitious of the honour of being known to you, of which if you shall deem worthy I shall account myself exceedingly happy in the enjoyment of the acquaintance of so illustrious and deserving a person as yourself."[5] Flamsteed was delighted, not only with the flattery, but also because he saw that Halley might be of great practical help to him in his new assignment.

Only two days after Flamsteed's appointment, Robert Hooke wrote in his diary that Greenwich Park had been chosen as the site for the new observatory,[6] and Flamsteed tells us that it was Wren who made this swift choice.[7] Flamsteed, meanwhile, had gone to stay with his patron, Sir Jonas Moore, in the Tower of London,[8] setting up an observatory in the White Tower, where on 26 June he observed a lunar eclipse with Halley. Four days later, Hooke, Flamsteed, and Halley went to Greenwich to inspect the site where the observatory was to be laid out, by Hooke to Wren's specifications. On 10 August 1675, Flamsteed laid the foundation stone of the main building (today's Flamsteed House), casting a derisory horoscope to commemorate the event.[9] About this time, too, he moved to a room in the Queen's House at Greenwich, the better to supervise the building work, observing with portable telescopes from the south-facing balcony. Halley himself made several observations when Flamsteed was sick at the end of October and the beginning of November.

The first recorded observation in the new building took place in the Great Room at 8 o'clock in the morning of 1 June 1676 (civil date), when Flamsteed, Lord Brouncker, President of the Royal Society, and Halley (described by Flamsteed in the printed observations as *amicus peritissimus*, "very skilled friend") all made observations of a lunar eclipse with eight- and sixteen-foot telescopes fitted with Towneley's micrometer.[10] Flamsteed and his assistants moved into the house on 10 July.

In the meantime, the first two fundamental instruments for the new observatory—a ten-foot mural quadrant designed by Hooke and a seven-foot equatorially mounted sextant designed by Flamsteed—were being made at Sir Jonas Moore's expense by the blacksmiths of the Tower of London, with the precision parts by the clockmaker Thomas Tompion. The ultimate goal of the observations was the position of each body observed in terms of polar distance and right ascension, celestial coordinates similar to terrestrial latitude and longitude. Although observations made with Hooke's quadrant, mounted on a meridian wall and timed with a clock alongside, would have given these coordinates more or less directly, this instrument unfortunately proved quite unmanageable. For the first twelve years, therefore, Flamsteed had to make do with the sextant alone, measuring angular distances between heavenly bodies and then solving the necessary spherical triangles, basing his final positions on an assumed position for the star Alpha Arietis. He obtained the Sun's position relative to the stars by measuring distances to the planet Venus in the daytime, then from Venus to an appropriate star at twilight. The first recorded observation with the sextant was on 14 September 1676.[11]

Halley made observations at Flamsteed's invitation at Greenwich on more than a dozen occasions following his return from St. Helena in May 1678, and from 11 September to 15 October of that year he took charge of the observatory while Flamsteed was convalescing in Derby. The lunar eclipse of 19 October following was observed by Flamsteed in the Great Room and Halley in the Sextant House.[12] In a letter to William Molyneux of Dublin, Flamsteed describes the lunar eclipse of 11 February 1682, the last observation by Halley at Greenwich of which we have a record before their falling-out: "My friend Mr Halley, a very ingenious person whom I believe you have heard of, was with me. He ordered my business so that he, with my usual assistant, might observe apart [from me] and have no intelligence [of my results at the time of eclipse]."[13]

THE COMET

Meanwhile, Flamsteed had made his first serious contact with Newton, whom he had met briefly when receiving his degree at Cambridge in 1674.[14] During the second half of November 1680 a comet had been observed before sunrise, first in Italy and then briefly in France and England, vanishing into the morning Sun early in December. Some ten days later a comet was seen in the evening sky, soon becoming extremely spectacular, its tail over seventy degrees long just before Christmas.

At that date, comets were thought to be ephemeral bodies that traveled in straight-line paths, and so these apparitions were counted as two different comets. Flamsteed, however, thought otherwise, as he explained to his friend Richard Towneley on 15 December:

> The errand of this [letter] is onely to tell y^u that according as I foresaw & predicted that it would, the late Comet which was seene before sunrise appears again after sunset. I saw it not in ye morneing appearances[15] but looking for it on friday last [9 December] I espyed the tayle riseing up from ye Horizon into ye vertex . . . but its head was too neare the Sun to be seene. On Sunday night the 11th instant I got sight of the head . . . the tayle reaching beyond ye Middle of Sagitta & so being above 35 degrees long.[16]

The same day, he sent a letter to James Crompton at Cambridge, outlining his radical proposal that the two comets were actually one and the same and asking Crompton to pass this theory on to Newton. In subsequent letters he proposed an explanation for this phenomenon, suggesting that comets reverse their direction when close to the Sun owing to magnetic forces. Newton eventually replied through Crompton on 28 February 1681, categorically rejecting Flamsteed's magnetic theory and saying that he was still inclined to believe they were two comets. However, if they *were* one and the same, the only explanation which fitted the observations was that the comet had swung around behind the Sun rather than reversing direction on the near side as Flamsteed had suggested.[17]

Flamsteed wrote again to Towneley on 22 March:

> This has occasioned the change of a letter betwixt my selfe & my brother Mr Newton of Cambridge who was unwilling to allow of my theory. Hee has now an answer to his objections under his hands to which I expect a returne very speedily. What ye end of this amicable controversy shall be I shall not fayle to informe you. On the other side of this page I have pricked of the line which answers my observations best togeather with those I receaved from Rome by ye meanes of Signeur Cassini, transmitted by Mr Halley.[18]

A drawing in this letter shows that Flamsteed now accepted Newton's suggestion that the comet swung around behind the Sun. For his part, Newton likewise eventually came to accept the two comets as being one and the same, though not Flamsteed's magnetic explanation (as he demonstrated in the *Principia*, Proposition XLI, Problem XXI, by observations of the same comet).[19]

FLAMSTEED'S OBSERVATIONS

The death in 1679 of his patron, Sir Jonas Moore, spelled the end of any hope Flamsteed might have had for obtaining financial backing for the fundamental item of equipment he really needed: a meridional instrument to replace the useless Hooke ten-foot quadrant. So, in August 1681, the construction of a seven-foot mural arc—the same radius as the sextant—was started. Although the wooden frame warped and twisted, it was finally mounted on the meridian wall in 1683, and Flamsteed used it for measuring zenith distances until the autumn of 1686 when he abandoned it.[20] His circumstances having been somewhat improved in 1684 by Lord North's presentation to him of the living (i.e., ecclesiastical benefice) of Burstow in Surrey, he could, on 12 February 1687, write to Towneley, "I am at present upon a new meridional arch for taking the declinations of the fixed stars and planets. I have caused it to be formed in wood of the just size and, in a day or two, I expect the workmen down to take care to get it forged in iron. I hope to have it perfect by midsummer, and then I doubt not but one years work with the materials I have by me will give you a better and more accurate [star] catalogue than has yet been published."[21] The new mural arc, of the same dimensions of the "slight" mural arc of 1681 and divided and adjusted by Flamsteed's talented assistant Abraham Sharp, was brought into use in October 1689. It subsequently provided most of the data for Flamsteed's "British Catalogue."

Meanwhile, relations between Flamsteed and Halley had been deteriorating, particularly once Halley became editor of the *Philosophical Transactions* in 1685. In a letter to Towneley dated 4 November 1686, after accusing Halley of plagiarism from the late Peter Perkins, Master of the Royal Mathematical School and Flamsteed's friend, for his compass variation theories and from M. Bardelot for his trade wind and monsoon paper, the prickly Flamsteed has this to say about Halley:

> Hee is got into Mr Hookes acquaintance, has beene his intimate long & from him he has learnt these & some other disingenuous tricks. For which I am not a little concernd for hee has certeinly a clear head, is a good Geometrician and, if hee did but love labor as well as he covets applause, if hee were but as Ingenuous as hee is skillfull, no man could thinke any praises too greate for him. I used him for some years as my freind & I make no stranger of him still but I know not how to excuse these faults even in my freinds, since he ran into Mr Hookes designes and society, I have foreborne all intimacy wth him.[22]

Considering himself the expert on tidal prediction, moreover, Flamsteed was not at all pleased when Halley pronounced on the subject the following year. Nevertheless, Halley himself had no wish to fall out with Flamsteed at this time.[23]

THE LUNAR THEORY AND THE PUBLICATION OF THE OBSERVATIONS

When Newton returned to full health in 1694, he turned his attention to the theory of the Moon's motion, a topic he had not dealt with adequately in the first edition of the *Principia* but which he hoped could be properly explained in the second. On 1 September 1694 he visited Greenwich to ask the Astronomer Royal's help; in particular, he suggested that Flamsteed's observations should be published. Newton left Greenwich with copies of some observations of the Moon, his receipt for which he wrote on the back flyleaf of the mural arc observation book then in use: "Sept.1.1694. Received then of M[r] Flamsteed two sheets MS of y[e] places of the Moon observed & calculated for the years 89 90 & part of 91 w[ch] I promise not to communicate without his consent. Isaac Newton."[24] (Flamsteed extracted this promise because the places of the Moon in the document were in some cases based on star places derived from observations made with the sextant, which was not so accurate as the new mural arc.) "Nevertheless," a biographer of Flamsteed later observed, "he [Newton] imparted what he had derived from them both to Dr. Gregory and Mr. Halley, *contra datam fidem*."[25] Newton's failure to return other observation books was to be a great source of friction in the future.

For a little over a year Newton corresponded with the Astronomer Royal, trying to persuade him to send or publish raw observations of the Moon. This, however, Flamsteed was reluctant to do, because any places derived from those observations must depend ultimately on an accurate star catalogue and an accurate table of refraction, neither of which could be supplied. Newton broke off the correspondence in September 1695.

THE PUBLICATION OF FLAMSTEED'S *HISTORIA COELESTIS*

The complex story of the publication of Flamsteed's observations and star catalogue—and of the many tedious arguments that ensued—has been well told by both Westfall and Christianson.[26] I will therefore confine myself here to summarizing the main events.

Elected President of the Royal Society on 30 November 1703, Newton dined at Greenwich on 12 April 1704, informing Flamsteed that Queen Anne's consort, Prince George of Denmark, might be prepared to fund the publication of the observations, which he, Newton, so badly needed for the projected second edition of the *Principia*. Later that year the Prince visited Greenwich,[27] and on 8 November Flamsteed had a broadsheet printed: "*An Estimate of the Number of* Folio *Pages, that the* Historia Britannica Coelestis, *may contain when Printed*"—1,450 pages in all, plus sixty copper plates for star maps.[28]

On 11 December 1704, Prince George appointed five "referees" from the Royal Society Council to superintend publication. Specimen sheets were printed by Awnsham Churchill, the "undertaker" or publisher, in March 1705, and Articles of Agreement between Flamsteed and the referees on the one part and Churchill on the other, were signed on 10 November 1705. The first sheets were run off in May 1706, and by October 1707 one hundred sheets of sextant observations for the years 1676–89 had been printed and proofread by Flamsteed. On 20 March 1708 he delivered his mural arc observations for 1689–1705 to the referees, although his star catalogue was still not ready. Then, on 28 October 1708, Prince George died—and everything stopped.

On 8 April 1710 the referees submitted an account to the Prince's executors for some £350 miscellaneous publishing expenses paid to Churchill, Flamsteed, and Machin, the manuscript of which is preserved in the Clark Library.[29] (The remainder of the £1,200 asserted by Flamsteed as having been allowed had presumably been spent on paper and printing costs.) On 12 December 1710 the Queen was persuaded to appoint the President and selected members of the Royal Society Council to be constant Visitors to the Royal Observatory, to superintend the work of the Astronomer Royal and the observatory, to purchase and maintain the instruments (which were actually all Flamsteed's own), and to demand copies of the observation results annually. Flamsteed was furious but could not get the order rescinded. Then, to his further chagrin, he was told the following 14 March that, without any consultation with the person most closely concerned—himself—the Queen had given orders that printing should be resumed and that—worse and worse!—Halley had been appointed editor. Halley's edition of *Historia Coelestis* was eventually published in one volume in the spring of 1712[30]—with a star catalogue full of mistakes (according to Flamsteed); a selection of his mural arc observations up to 1705 only, omitting all star observations; and a preface to which Flamsteed took grave exception. Witness these two extracts, the first of which concerns the situation in 1704:

> Flamsteed had now enjoyed the title of Astronomer Royal for nearly thirty years but still nothing had yet emerged from the observatory to justify all the equipment and expense, so that he seemed, so far, to have worked only for himself or at any rate for a few of his friends, even if it was generally

accepted that all these years had not been wasted and that the Greenwich papers had grown into no small a pile.

The second extract concerns 1710:

[Queen Anne] commissioned John Arbuthnot, one of the above delegates, and physician to her Serene Majesty, to appoint the necessary assistants and to resume his work on the edition. As Flamsteed kept his eyes, now less acute at his advanced age, intent upon the ever-increasing phenomena of the stars, the task was given to Edmond Halley LL.D., the Savilian Professor of Geometry and thoroughly experienced in astronomy, of supplying what the rest of the edition lacked and seeing it through to completion.[31]

—which explains some of the not entirely unjustified frustrations of Newton and Halley at this time. Nevertheless, it was Newton's imperious and self-centered behavior that caused most of the difficulties which beset the touchy and sanctimonious Flamsteed.

FLAMSTEED'S LATER YEARS

Having staved off a visitation for nearly three years, the Astronomer Royal finally had to submit when Newton and five fellows—including Halley and Flamsteed's own nephew by marriage, James Hodgson—came to the observatory by appointment on 1 August 1713. He gave them a glass of wine, pleaded gout, and turned them over to two assistants, saying they could go anywhere except his library—probably the small room on the west side of the house which today is the curator's washroom.[32] The only practical result of the visitation was that the Board of Ordnance was persuaded to repair the buildings the following year.

On 20 July 1714, twelve days before her death, Queen Anne signified her royal assent to the Longitude Act authorizing awards of up to £20,000 to the discoverer, of any nationality, of a method of determining longitude at sea under specified conditions. Newton and Halley, but not Flamsteed, had both given evidence before the House of Commons in the debate on the bill. By virtue of their several offices, however, all three became members of the Board of Longitude appointed by the act. The great effect that the Longitude Act had on the later history of the observatory, and of navigation generally, is given in some detail in my book *Greenwich Time*.[33]

King George I's succession brought about a change of government from Tory to Whig, favorable to Flamsteed. Through the Duke of Bolton,

Lord Chamberlain, he succeeded in persuading the Lords of the Treasury, led by Walpole, to give orders that all undistributed copies of
Halley's edition of *Historia Coelestis*—three hundred out of four hundred
printed—should be sent to Greenwich for disposal. In April 1716, thrift-
ily setting aside for use in his own projected edition the 387 pages of
sextant observations that had his approval, Flamsteed burnt the 189
pages that did not[34]—60 pages of star catalogue, 120 pages of planetary
observations with the mural arc, and 9 preliminary pages including
Halley's hateful preface—keeping only a few sets of the latter for distribution to his friends "as evidences of the malice of godless persons."[35]

Flamsteed died at the age of seventy-three on the last day of 1719,
having made his last observation on the mural arc only four days before.
His own edition of *Historia Coelestis*[36]—including the 387 pages Flamsteed
himself saved from the fire in 1716—was eventually published in three
volumes in 1725, seen through the press by his wife and assistants, followed in 1729 by a star atlas that put his star catalogue in graphic form.[37]

HALLEY AS ASTRONOMER ROYAL

Halley was appointed Astronomer Royal on 9 February 1720, but when
he took possession of the observatory and house early in March he
found it devoid of instruments, for Flamsteed's widow had removed
everything. Although the Board of Ordnance threatened legal action,
the case was soon dropped in light of apparently irrefutable proof that
the instruments had indeed been the previous Astronomer Royal's private property. To begin with Halley therefore had to make do with three
of his own telescopes and a borrowed quadrant, all in the Great Room.
In the summer of 1721, having abandoned hope of recovering the original instruments, he pulled down Flamsteed's meridian wall and built "a
little boarded shed between the study and the summer house"[38] (today,
the lobby outside the washroom already mentioned) in which he mounted
a five-foot transit instrument—the earliest in England, the telescope of
which was said to have been made by Robert Hooke—with a clock alongside. His first recorded observation was on 1 October 1721.

That the only instruments in England's national observatory should
have been the astronomer's private property was so obviously unsatisfactory that Halley was able to persuade the government to grant him £500
in 1724 to re-equip the observatory. He forthwith ordered from the
clockmaker George Graham an eight-foot-radius mural quadrant of a
radical new design: made by Jonathan Sisson under Graham's direction,
it was more rigid and more accurate than any previously made; further,
it served as a prototype for a whole series of instruments that contrib-

uted significantly to the flourishing export market achieved by English instrument makers from 1740 on. Mounted facing south on a new stone meridian wall some yards north of Flamsteed's demolished brick one, the first observation with the new quadrant was made on 27 October 1725, and the last, eighty-seven years later in 1812. Halley had intended to have an identical quadrant mounted on the other side of the wall, facing north, but funds ran out, and the second quadrant was not mounted until 1750, eight years after his death.[39]

The lunar method of finding longitude requires the place of the Moon, relative to the Sun or stars at any moment, to be accurately predicted. Newton's theory of the Moon, published in Gregory's *Astronomiae Physicae* of 1702, should have enabled this to be done. Halley, however, said that there was an easier way. As he explained it, every 223 lunations (or eighteen years, eleven days, the so-called saros or eclipse cycle), the relative positions of the Sun and Moon repeat themselves; to find the Moon's predicted place relative to the Sun in say 1700, then, all you had to do was look up the Moon's observed place on the appropriate date in 1682 or 1664, eighteen or thirty-six years earlier. Assuming you could then predict the Sun's place relative to the stars, you could just as easily relate the Moon to the stars. When proposing this method in 1716 as a means of calculating longitude from observed occultations and appulses of stars by the Moon, Halley claimed to have done it successfully during his *Paramore* voyages in the Atlantic in 1698–1700. But this method required regular lunar observations to give the required data, and this, Halley said, Flamsteed had failed to do, having taken none at all in 1716, for example: how sad for the navigator in 1734, said he![40]

When Halley arrived at Greenwich, therefore, he set himself the task of making daily observations of the Moon whenever conditions permitted during one complete eighteen-year-cycle—quite an undertaking for a sixty-four-year-old. He achieved his goal, just, taking his first observation in October 1721 and his last in December 1739. Yet his accuracy left much to be desired, and of all astronomers royal, Halley is the only one whose observations have never been published.

As Savilian Professor at Oxford and later as Astronomer Royal at Greenwich, Halley was ex officio a member of the Board of Longitude from its inception in 1714 and therefore might be expected to be ineligible for any award under the Longitude Act. However, apparently neither he nor others thought this. Flamsteed in 1714 said: "Raymer [his rude name for Halley][41] sets up for a finder of the longitude";[42] Crosthwait, Flamsteed's last assistant, stated in 1730: "Dr. Halley, Mr. Machin, and Mr. Whiston, are all endeavouring to find the longitude in order to obtain £20,000";[43] and he himself, when called on by the Royal Society Council in 1727 (the last one presided over by Newton) to deliver his observations in accordance with the late Queen's orders, reported that "he had hitherto kept his observations in his own custody, that he might have time to finish the theory he designs to build upon them, before others might take the advantage of reaping the benefit of his labours"[44]—which was exactly what he himself had criticized Flamsteed for in the 1710s. Then, in 1731, he republished his 1716 proposals for predicting the Moon's place, adding this comment:

> It remains therefore to consider after what Meanes Observations of the Moon may be made at Sea with the same Degree of Exactness: But since our worthy Vice-President John Hadley Esq: . . . has been pleased to communicate his most ingenious Invention of an Instrument for taking the Angles with Great Certainty by Reflection (vide Transact. N° 420) it is more than probable that the same may be applied to taking Angles at Sea with the desired Accuracy.[45]

Edmond Halley visited the site of the Royal Observatory at Greenwich in 1675, before it was built. Sixty-seven years later, on 14 January 1742, he died there, in his eighty-sixth year. He was buried in the churchyard of St. Margaret's, Lee, but his original tombstone can be seen today in the courtyard of the Old Royal Observatory.

NOTES

1. Richard S. Westfall, *Never at Rest: A Biography of Isaac Newton* (Cambridge: Cambridge University Press, 1980); and Gale E. Christianson, *In the Presence of the Creator: Isaac Newton and His Times* (New York: Free Press, 1984).

2. Warrant appointing Royal Commission, 15 December 1674, Public Record Office SP44/334, fols. 27, 28.

3. Derek Howse, *Francis Place and the Early History of the Greenwich Observatory* (New York: Science History Publications, 1975), gives the early history in detail.

4. Eric G. Forbes, "The Origins of the Greenwich Observatory," *Vistas in Astronomy* 20 (1976): 39–50, discusses St. Pierre's method in detail.

5. Halley to Flamsteed, 10 March 1675, in *Correspondence and Papers of Edmond Halley*, ed. Eugene Fairfield MacPike (Oxford: Oxford University Press, 1932), 37–39.

6. Henry W. Robinson and Walter Adams, eds., *The Diary of Robert Hooke, M.A., M.D., F.R.S., 1672–1680* (London: Taylor & Francis, 1955), 151.

7. Francis Baily, *An Account of the Rev⁴ John Flamsteed* (London, 1835; reprint London, Dawson's of Pall Mall, 1966), 37.

8. Sir Jonas Moore, an astronomer and Surveyor General at the Tower of London, recommended Flamsteed to the commission and to the king. The maintenance and salaries of the observatory remained the responsibility of the Board of Ordnance until 1818.

9. Howse, *Francis Place*, 17–19.

10. Made by or for Richard Towneley in 1667, this micrometer was presented by Sir Jonas Moore to Flamsteed in 1671. Between 1673 and 1687 Flamsteed wrote him many letters giving news of scientific happenings in London because, as a Catholic living in Lancashire, Towneley was unable or unwilling to travel. These letters are preserved at the Royal Society as MS. 243(Fl.).

11. For Flamsteed's instruments, see Derek Howse, *Greenwich Observatory*, vol. 3: *The Buildings and Instruments* (London: Taylor & Francis, 1975).

12. John Flamsteed, *Historia Coelestis Britannica* . . . (London, 1725), vol. 1.

13. Flamsteed to W. Molyneux, 27 February 1682, Southampton City Record Office, D/m.1/3, fol. 11r.

14. Westfall, *Never at Rest*, 392.

15. In a letter to Crompton, 15 December 1680, Flamsteed says that Cuthbert Denton, his unskilled assistant, did see the comet in the morning appearance (*The Correspondence of Isaac Newton*, ed. H. W. Turnbull et al. [Cambridge: Cambridge University Press, 1959–77], 2:315).

16. Flamsteed to Towneley, 15 December 1680, Royal Society MS. 243(Fl.)/50.

17. Newton to Crompton for Flamsteed, 28 February 1681, in *Correspondence* 2:340.

18. Flamsteed to Towneley, 22 March 1681, Royal Society MS. 243(Fl.)/52.

19. *Newton's "Principia": Motte's Translation Revised*, trans. and ed. F. Cajori (Berkeley: University of California Press, 1934), 519.

20. Eric G. Forbes, *Greenwich Observatory*, vol. 1: *Origins and Early History* (London: Taylor & Francis, 1975), 44.

21. Flamsteed to Towneley, 12 February 1687, Royal Society MS. 243(Fl.)/70.

22. Flamsteed to Towneley, 4 November 1686, Royal Society MS. 243(Fl.)/68.

23. Olin J. Eggen, "Flamsteed and Halley," *Occasional Notes of the Royal Astronomical Society* 3 (1958): 211–21.

24. Royal Greenwich Observatory MS. 1/6, fol. 181r (inside back cover). Baily seems to have overlooked this note in Newton's own hand when he examined the Flamsteed MSS. It was brought to my attention some years ago by the late P. S. Laurie.

25. Baily, *Flamsteed*, 62.

26. Westfall, *Never at Rest*, 655–67, 686–96; and Christianson, *In the Presence of the Creator*, 450–60, 484–93.

27. Flamsteed to ?, 24 October 1715, in Baily, *Flamsteed*, 316.

28. A copy of this 1704 broadsheet was found loose in a copy of the 1725 edition of *Historia Coelestis* in the library of the U.S. Military Academy, West Point, New York. Annotations in ink by Flamsteed (though not in his hand) make it likely that it was a copy given by him to the Treasury Office in 1715. In 1905 West Point generously presented the broadsheet to the Royal Society, and it is now kept inside the front cover of the Society's 1712 edition.

29. Derek Howse, "Newton Manuscript Documents: A Celebrated Quarrel," *Clark Newsletter* (UCLA) 6 (Spring 1984): 1–5.

30. John Flamsteed, *Historia Coelestis Libri Duo* . . . (London, 1712).

31. Allan Chapman, *The Preface to John Flamsteed's "Historia Coelestis Britannica"* (Greenwich: National Maritime Museum, 1982), 189–94, gives full translations of the prefaces of both Halley (1712) and Flamsteed (1725).

32. Marked *E* on the plan in Howse, *Francis Place*, 35.

33. Derek Howse, *Greenwich Time and the Discovery of the Longitude* (Oxford: Oxford University Press, 1980).

34. Flamsteed to Sharp, 8 May 1716, in Baily, *Flamsteed*, 322.

35. Flamsteed to Sharp, 29 March 1716, in ibid., 321; see also 101–2. What seem to be two evidence-of-malice copies, containing only those pages suppressed by Flamsteed in 1716, are preserved in the Greenwich Public Library (GPL) and at the Royal Astronomical Society (RAS). Originally bound into these books had been a set of the observatory etchings (as described in Howse, *Francis Place*) that Flamsteed had intended to include in the final work but which, in the event, were omitted from both the 1712 and 1725 editions. The GPL set of etchings are still in the book; those from the RAS copy are now at the Royal Greenwich Observatory.

36. John Flamsteed, *Historia Coelestis Britannica . . .* , 3 vols.

37. John Flamsteed, *Atlas Coelestis* (London, 1729).

38. Crosthwait to Sharp, 1 June 1721, in ibid., 342–44.

39. For Halley's instruments, see Howse, *The Buildings and Instruments*, 6, 21–24, 32–34; and S. P. Rigaud, "Some Particulars respecting the principal Instruments at Greenwich, in the time of Dr. Halley," *Memoirs of the Royal Astronomical Society* 9 (1836): 205–27.

40. Thomas Streete, *Astronomia Carolina*, (London: S. Briscoe & R. Smith, 3d ed. 1716), revised by Halley, who added an appendix giving his method of finding longitude.

41. Nicolaus Raymarus, having been courteously entertained by Tycho Brahe, then proceeded to be very rude about him to others. In letters to Sharp from 1703, Flamsteed started calling Halley "Captain Raymer" or just "Raymer." See Baily, *Flamsteed*, 752.

42. Flamsteed to Sharp, 31 August 1714, in ibid., 311.

43. Crosthwait to Sharp, 29 August 1730, in ibid., 363.

44. Royal Society Council Minute Book, 2 March 1726–27, quoted in F. Baily, "Some Account of the Astronomical Observations made by Dr. Edmond Halley, at the Royal Observatory at Greenwich," *Memoirs of the Royal Astronomical Society* 8 (1835): 188.

45. "A Proposal of a Method for finding the Longitude at Sea within a Degree, or twenty Leagues," *Philosophical Transactions of the Royal Society* 37 (1731–32): 185–95.

THREE

Newton, Halley, and the Paris Observatory

Suzanne Débarbat

Since he never left England, Newton obviously did not visit the Paris Observatory (Observatoire de Paris). Halley, however, who traveled widely, was there twice. Signs of these two Englishmen are still to be found in the venerable Louis XIV–style building, constructed in 1667, and both Newton and Halley inspired a number of French works. Scientists in both Paris and London were interested in knowing what was new on the other side of the Channel. Studying the traces of Newton and Halley in the Paris Observatory, then, can provide an appreciation of the relations between the astronomers of the two countries.

NEWTON'S USE OF FRENCH DATA

The library of the Paris Observatory has a copy of the first edition of the *Philosophiae Naturalis Principia Mathematica* of 1687. On one page (Fig. 3.1) is a dedicatory inscription in Halley's hand to Jean-Dominique Cassini, to whom he presented the book; the facing title page contains the printing license and the name of the author, Newton.

Jean-Dominique Cassini (1625–1712) came from Bologna at the invitation of Louis XIV in 1669. By 1686 he had become the leader of the French astronomers and had a fine apartment on the first floor of the Paris Observatory. After his arrival in Paris, Cassini discovered four satellites of Saturn and the division of the ring now named after him.

An inventory by Taton in 1953 showed that this copy of the *Principia* is one of three (among the ten found in the main Parisian libraries) bearing the inscription "apud plures Bibliopolas" or, more completely, "Jussu Societatis Regia ac Typis Josephi Streater. Prostat apud plures

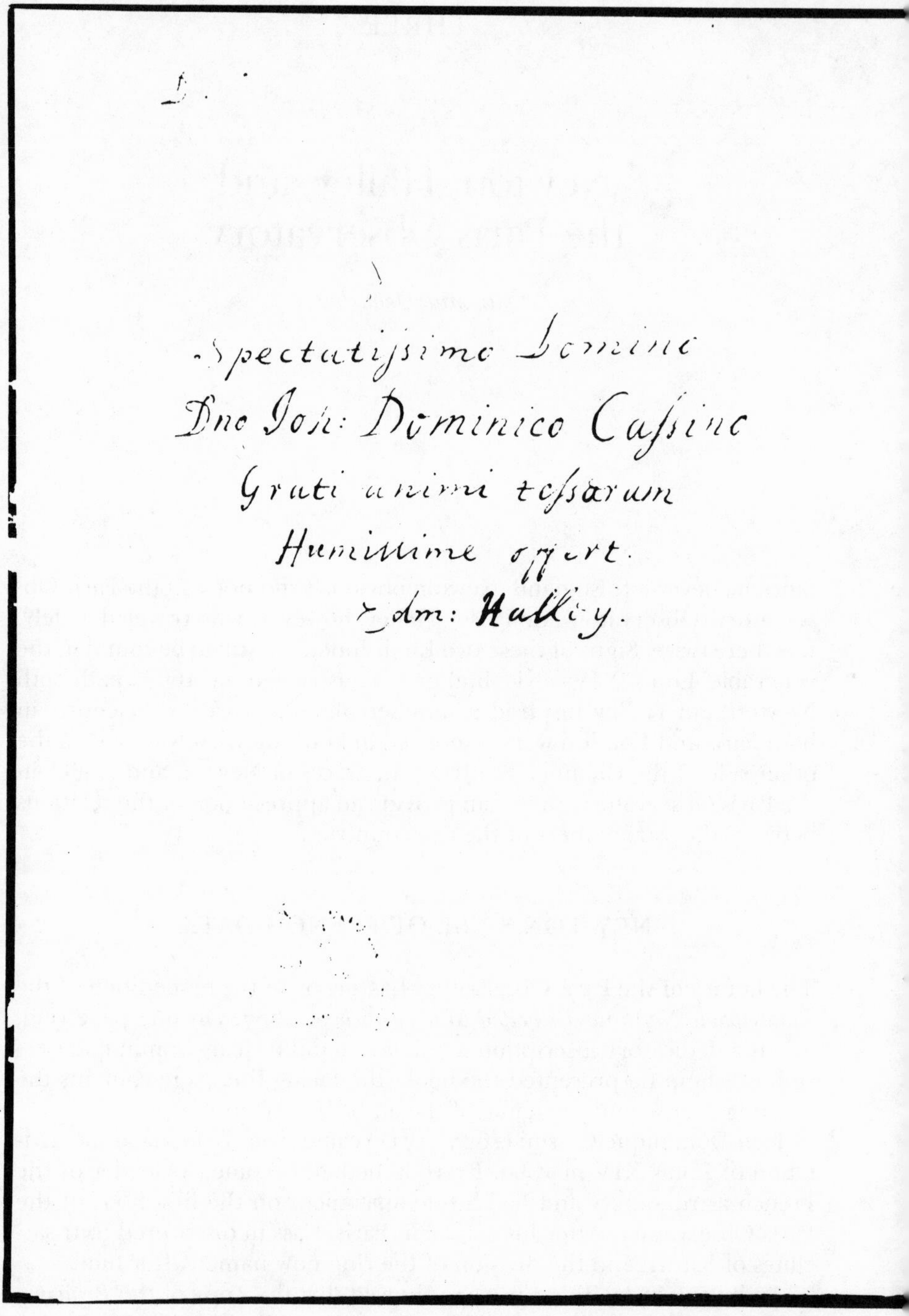
Spectatissimo Domino
Dno Joh: Dominico Cassino
Grati animi tessarum
Humillime offert.
Edm: Halley.

Figure 3.1. The *Principia* of Newton, 1687 edition. Copy in the Paris Observatory with a dedication by Halley to J. D. Cassini. (Collections Observatoire de Paris.)

PHILOSOPHIÆ

NATURALIS

PRINCIPIA

MATHEMATICA.

2͡0053

Autore *J S. NEWTON*, *Trin. Coll. Cantab. Soc.* Matheseos
Professore *Lucasiano*, & Societatis Regalis Sodali.

IMPRIMATÚR·

S. P E P Y S, *Reg. Soc.* P R Æ S E S.

Julii 5. 1686.

20053

LONDINI,

Jussu *Societatis Regiæ* ac Typis *Josephi Streater.* Prostat apud
plures Bibliopolas. *Anno* MDCLXXXVII.

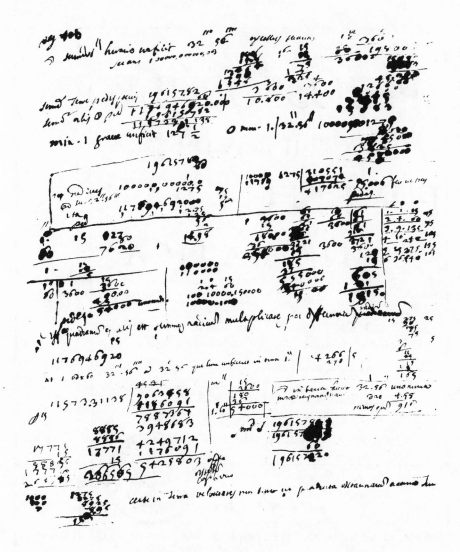

Figure 3.2. Notes by J. D. Cassini on last page of the 1687 *Principia* presented by Halley to Cassini. (Collections Observatoire de Paris.)

Bibliopolas. Anno MDCLXXXVII." Thus, this volume is one of the very first printings of the first edition.[1] The book belonged to Jean-Dominique Cassini and was annotated by him in places: it contains at the end a page of Cassini's calculations (Fig. 3.2)—a testimony of the interest he took in Newton's study of the motion of the Moon (p. 406).[2]

In Book Three, "Philosophiae Naturalis de Mundi Systemate," of this 1687 edition Newton refers several times to French works or results obtained by astronomers of the Paris Observatory. Figure 3.3 lists the main

Distantiæ Satellitum à centro Jovis.

Ex Obfervationibus	1.	2	3	4	
Caffini	5.	8.	13.	23.	
Borelli	5⅔.	8⅔.	14.	24⅔.	
Tounlei *per Micromet-*	5,51.	8,78.	13,47.	24,72.	Semidiam.
Flamftedii *per Microm.*	5,31.	8,85.	13,98.	24,23.	Jovis.
Flamft.*per Eclipf.Satel.*	5,578.	8,876.	14,159.	24,903.	
Ex temporibus periodicis.	5,578.	8,878.	14,168.	24,968.	

atque ambitum Terræ effe pedum Parifienfium 123249600, uti à <u>Gallis</u> menfurantibus nuper definitum eft

Prop. IV, Theor. IV, page 406

Prop.XVIII, Theor.XVII,page 421

Sic Jovis diameter (confentientibus obfervationibus *Caffini* & *Flamftedii*) brevior deprehenditur inter polos quàm ab oriente in occidentem.

Prop. XIX, Prob. II, page 424

Ideoque cùm Terræ femidiameter mediocris, juxta nuperam <u>Gallorum</u> menfuram, fit pedum Parifienfium 19615800 feu milliarium 3923 (pofito quod milliare fit menfura pedum 5000 ;) Terra altior erit ad æquatorem quàm ad polos, exceffu pedum 85200 feu milliarium 17.

Prop.XX, Prob. III, page 425

Quare cum longitudines Pendulorum æqualibus temporibus ofcillantium fint ut gravitates, & *Lutetiæ Parifiorum* longitudo penduli fingulis minutis fecundis ofcillantis fit pedum trium Parifienfium & $\frac{8}{9}$ partium digiti; longitudines Pendulorum in Infulâ *Goree*, in illâ *Cayennæ* & fub Æquatore, minutis fingulis fecundis ofcillantium fuperabuntur à longitudine Penduli Parifienfis exceffibus $\frac{81}{1000}$, $\frac{89}{1000}$ & $\frac{90}{1000}$ partium digiti............................

page 426

.... Jam verò Galli factis experimentis invenerunt quod Pendulorum minutis fingulis fecundis ofcillantium longitudo *Parifiis* major fit quàm in Infula *Goree*, parte decima digiti, & major quàm *Cayennæ* parte octava.

Nam *Flamftedius* collatis fuis cum *Caffini* Obfervationibus Nodos tarde regredi deprehendit.

Prop. XXIII, Prob. IV, page 429

Prop.XXXIV,Prob.XIX, page 472

Exceffus longitudinis penduli, quod in Infula *Goree* & in illâ *Cayennæ* minutis fingulis fecundis ofcillatur, fupra longitudinem Penduli quod *Parifiis* eodem tempore ofcillatur, à *Gallis* inventi funt pars decima & pars octava digiti, qui tamen ex proportione 692 ad 689 prodiere $\frac{81}{1000}$ & $\frac{89}{1000}$. Major eft itaque longitudo Penduli *Cayennæ* quàm oportet, in ratione $\frac{1}{8}$ ad $\frac{8}{10,0}$, feu 1000 ad 712; & in Infula *Goree* in ratione $\frac{1}{10}$ ad $\frac{81}{1000}$ feu 1000 ad 810.

page 473

Caffinus qui Cometam eodem tempore obfervavit, fe declinationem ejus tanquam invariatam manentem parum diligenter definiviffe fallus eft.

Prop. XLI, Prob. XX, page 493

Figure 3.3. Main references to Paris and to French astronomers in the 1687 *Principia*.

Figure 3.4. Dimensions of the Earth in different units of measure, from J. Picard's *La Mesure de la Terre* (Paris, 1671), 23.

Note: 1 *toise* = 6 *pieds*

Earth circumference	20,541,600 *toises* =	123,249,600 *pieds*
Earth diameter	6,538,594 *toises* =	39,231,564 *pieds*
Semi-diameter		19,615,782 *pieds*
Great circle degree	=	57,060 *toises du Chastelet de Paris*

references, based on the index of names from the critical edition by Koyré and Cohen.[3] Newton quoted observations by Cassini on the satellites of Jupiter (p. 403), the flattening of that planet (p. 421), the equation of the nodes of the satellites (p. 429), and the comet of the year 1680–81 (p. 493). French observations on the length of the second-pendulum are given and discussed as well (pp. 425–26, 472–73). Newton does not mention Richer's name, but he knew the results Richer obtained on his two voyages to Cayenne (1672) and the Isle of Gorée (1682), close to Cape Verde. For instance, Newton gives the second-pendulum a length that is, respectively, $\frac{81}{1000}$, $\frac{89}{1000}$, and $\frac{90}{1000}$ *pouce* (p. 425) greater in Paris than in the three places he cites: Gorée, Cayenne, and the equator. As there are 12 *lignes* in a *pouce*, the difference is about 1 $\frac{89}{1000}$ *lignes* on the equator, equivalent to over 2 modern millimeters. This value would indicate that the Earth's shape was not spherical but ellipsoidal.

Among other numerical data, Newton gives the length of the circumference of the Earth as 123,249,600 Paris feet (p. 406) and the value of the semi-diameter of the Earth as 19,615,800 Paris feet (p. 424). These values are derived from measurements made in France in 1669–70 and given in J. Picard's 1671 *La Mesure de la Terre* (Fig. 3.4).[4] Without taking up the debate on the role of Picard in Newton's work (on which the reader should consult the admirable study by A. Rupert Hall),[5] I would simply point out that Newton knew how to make use of the findings he learned of, if only in his writings.

HALLEY AT THE PARIS OBSERVATORY

Halley went to Paris on the occasion of his journey on the Continent during his "Grand Tour."[6] He arrived at the beginning of 1681, and he paid a visit to the Académie des Sciences on Saturday, 10 May.[7] He returned at the beginning of 1682; on 5 January, Cassini wrote in his notebook: "Mr Hallei retourna de Rome et me passa la lettre du P. Eschinard."

Halley's itinerary between April 1681 and January 1682 is to be found in Cassini's notebook,[8] for a list recorded on 15 January of the measurements of latitudes made by Halley (Fig. 3.5) makes it possible to follow his route in France and Italy. With a quadrant in his luggage, Halley left Paris in May. He was at Saumur on 21 May. In August he was in Toulouse (on the 12th), Narbonne (18th), and Montpellier (20th). During September he visited Marseille (on the 3rd), Toulon (19th), and Fréjus (21st) before moving on to Italy to arrive at Genoa on 27 September. From there he went to Livorno (on 7 October), Florence (21st), Siena (23rd), and Rome (28th). Returning to Paris, he met Cassini in January 1682.

A few years later, Halley conceived the plan of measuring one degree of latitude in England, as had been done in France in 1671 by the Abbé Jean Picard (1620–82). Perhaps Halley wanted to check the size of the Earth deduced from Picard's measurements and mentioned by Newton in his *Principia*. On 23 June 1686 he obtained from the Royal Society the

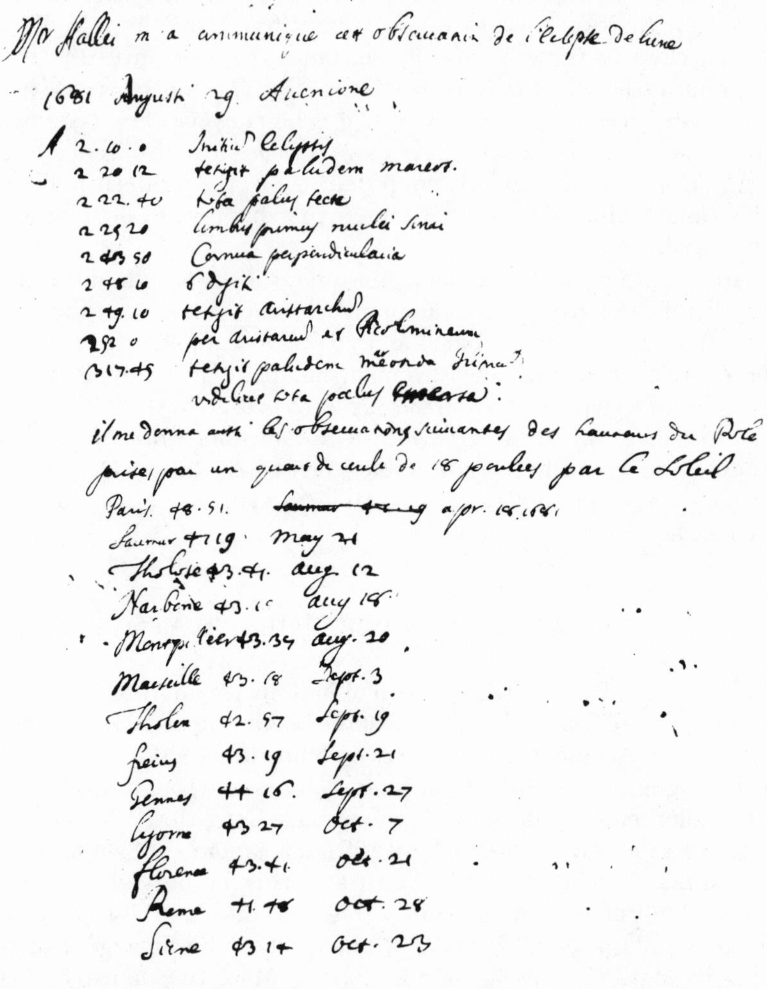
Paris 48.51. apr. 18.1681
Saumur 47.19 May 21
Tholose 43.41 aug. 12
Narbone 43.11 aug 18
Montpellier 43.34 aug. 20
Marseille 43.18 Sept. 3
Tholon 42.57 Sept. 19
Freius 43.19 Sept. 21
Gennes 44.16 Sept. 27
Lyorne 43.27 Oct. 7
Florence 43.41 Oct. 21
Rome 41.48 Oct. 28
Sienne 43.14 Oct. 23

Figure 3.5. Page of Cassini's notebook for 15 January 1682, in which Cassini reported the determination of latitude made by Halley during his journey to France and Italy. (Collections Observatoire de Paris, MS. D1-8, ref. 8.)

necessary funds for this project; Newton, however, submitted the *Principia* for publication without awaiting Halley's results and was granted a publishing license on 5 July.

In the archives of the Paris Observatory is a letter from Halley to Cassini. The address—*A Monsieur / Monsieur Cassini / à l'Observatoire Royal / à Paris*—is in Halley's handwriting, as is the signature: *E. Halley*. The letter itself is by a copyist or a translator (Fig. 3.6). This letter, dated

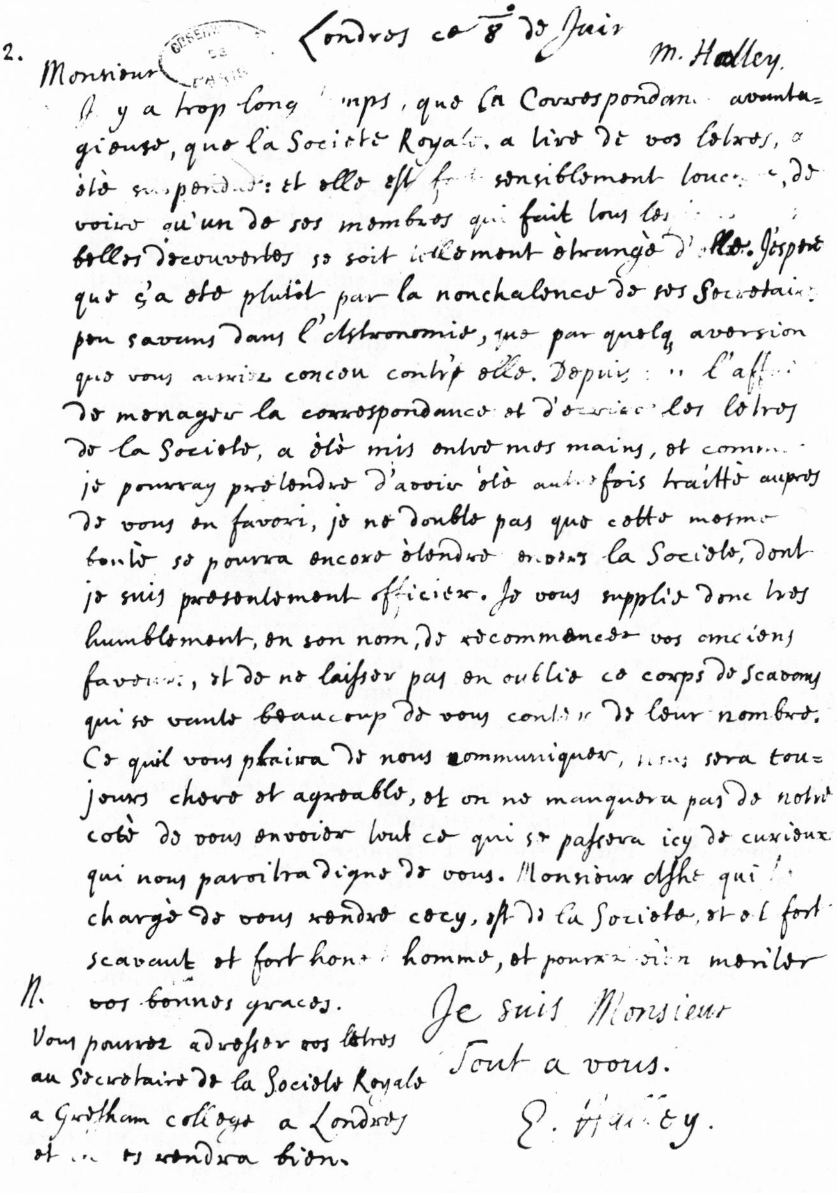

Londres ce 8 de Juin

Monsieur   M. Halley.

Il y a trop long temps, que la Correspondance avantageuse, que la Société Royale, a tiré de vos lettres, a été suspendue: et elle est fort sensiblement touchée, de voir qu'un de ses membres qui fait tous les ... belles découvertes se soit tellement étrangé d'elle. J'espère que ç'a été plutôt par la nonchalance de son Secrétaire peu savans dans l'Astronomie, que par quelque aversion que vous aurieze conceu contre elle. Depuis ... l'aff... de mesnager la correspondance et d'ouvrir les lettres de la Société, a été mis entre mes mains, et comme je pourray pretendre d'avoir été autrefois traitté auprès de vous en favori, je ne double pas que cette mesme bonté se pourra encore étendre envers la Société, dont je suis presentement officier. Je vous supplie donc très humblement, en son nom, de recommencer vos anciennes faveurs, et de ne laisser pas en oubli ce corps de scavans qui se vante beaucoup de vous contre de leur nombre. Ce qu'il vous plaira de nous communiquer, nous sera tous jours chere et agreable, et on ne manquera pas de notre coté de vous envoier tout ce qui se passera icy de curieux qui nous paroitra digne de vous. Monsieur ... qui ... chargé de vous rendre cecy, est de la Société, et et fort scavant et fort honeste homme, et pourra vous meriter vos bonnes graces.

N. Vous pourrez adresser vos lettres au Secretaire de la Société Royale a Gresham colloge a Londres et ... rendra bien.

Je suis Monsieur
Tout a vous.

E. Halley.

Figure 3.6. Letter from Halley to Cassini, with salutations and signature by Halley. (Collections Observatoire de Paris, MS. B4-10.)

only "8 juin," was shown to J. Dudley and N. O'Hora of the Royal Observatory, Greenwich, since an answer from Cassini would enable one to ascertain the year in which it was written. O'Hora determined the year to be 1686, based on the letter and details of Halley's life.[9] At that time Halley was appointed Clerk of the Royal Society in place of Francis Ashton, who had just resigned as secretary of the Society. O'Hora thinks that Halley wrote this letter to resume contact with the French (through Cassini, whom he had met in 1682) and get advice for the measurements he planned to take north of London. This interpretation, which is based on letters among Halley's correspondence, supports the opinion that English astronomers were interested in the measurements made by the French fifteen years earlier while creating geodetic astronomy.[10] This letter also bears testimony to the esteem Halley had for Cassini; he knew his work and discoveries well, which explains why he would write such a flattering letter to him.

THE *PRINCIPIA* AND THE
FRENCH ASTRONOMERS

References to the astronomers of the Paris Observatory vary according to the successive editions of the *Principia* for the years 1687, 1713, and 1726. The Paris Observatory owns no copy of the second edition, despite the fact that "young Monsr Cassini" was on the list of the people to whom the 1713 volume was apparently sent.[11] The copy that I refer to here belongs to the Académie des Sciences.[12] As for the 1726 edition, I use two copies: the 1739 Latin edition with commentary by Le Seur and Jacquier (reprinted 1822) and the so-called Marquise du Chastellet French translation.[13] This French edition of the *Principia* (Fig. 3.7), which is the only translation into French, was published in 1756 and revised by Clairaut (1713–65). Voltaire went over the work and may well have contributed to the commentary interspersed in the translation. The manuscript by Mme du Châtelet and the printed volume have been critically studied by M. F. Biarnais.[14]

Among the three editions (1687, 1713, 1726), that of 1713 contains the most documentation on French works, particularly those of the astronomers of the Paris Observatory. This edition, for example, documents Cassini's tables of the satellites of Jupiter (1668 and 1693) as well as his determination of the periods of revolution of the Saturnian satellites (1712); both the 1713 volume and the 1726 one (p. 391)[15] refer to Cassini for the numerical data (periods and distances) of these satellites. He is also mentioned with regard to the great spot on Jupiter (p. 412) and the differences among the diameters of this planet as measured by

PRINCIPES
MATHÉMATIQUES

DE LA

PHILOSOPHIE NATURELLE,

Par feue Madame la Marquise DU CHASTELLET.

TOME PREMIER.

A PARIS,

Chez { DESAINT & SAILLANT, rue S. Jean de Beauvais.
E T
LAMBERT, rue & à côté de la Comédie Françoise,
au Parnasse.

M. D. C C. L V I.

AVEC APPROBATION, ET PRIVILEGE DU ROI.

Figure 3.7. Title page of Newton's *Principia* (2d ed., 1726), translated into French by feue Mme la Marquise du Chastellet (1756). (Collections Observatoire de Paris.)

various observers (p. 499)—quantities that were given in the 1687 edition but with less precision in the referencing of sources.

The most noticeable differences between the editions of the *Principia* lie in the data presented on the second-pendulum and on the size of the Earth. Newton is particularly prolix in the 1713 edition with respect to French works. Significantly, he even uses French units. For instance, the dimensions of the Earth computed in 1635 by the English astronomer Richard Norwood (ca. 1590–1675) are given in the editions of 1713 and 1726 (p. 412) in English feet; these Newton transformed into *toises de Paris*, setting one degree as 57,300 *toises*. In 1686–87 Newton gave the circumference of the Earth in Paris feet (123,249,600), but without mentioning the unit; in 1713 he added that Picard had deduced the earlier value of the circumference from measurements made between Amiens and Malvoisine, a distance of 57,060 *toises de Paris* (p. 413). In 1713 and 1726, however, Newton also mentions measurements by the Cassinis, father and son.[16] The main thing to be noted here is that Newton became better acquainted with the details of the French works over time.[17] Moreover, Newton's calculation of gravitational acceleration (p. 413) is based on the latitude of *Lutetia*, or Paris (48°50′10″), and he refers to Picard (p. 415) for the semi-diameter of the Earth in Paris feet.

Later Newton undertook other studies on the length of the pendulum (p. 417). The subject is developed in 1687, as previously seen, using measurements from Cayenne and Cape Verde compared with the value obtained in Paris: 3 Paris feet $\frac{17}{24}$ *pouce*. The same value—expressed as 3 Paris feet $8\frac{1}{2}$ *lignes*—is used in 1713 and also in 1726; although less detailed than the 1687 edition, both retain the value given by Huygens in 1673 and by Picard in his *Mesure de la Terre*.[18] The French astronomers mentioned in these editions are Richer (1672), Varin, Deshayes (1682), and Couplet (1697) (p. 419). The observations performed at the Paris Observatory, as Newton points out (p. 420), show a difference from those at Gorée, where the length of the pendulum was 3 Paris feet $6\frac{1}{2}$ *lignes*.

Newton mentions numerous measurements made in several places, and Koyré and Cohen have studied the successive values he used, which are expressed in Paris feet. The French scientists Picard and La Hire are also quoted in relation to the effects of heat (p. 420) on the length of the metal pieces employed for the clock pendulums; the fact that they are longer, because of the increase in temperature, cannot be invoked to explain the "shortening" of the pendulum at the equator. Newton also used Paris feet (p. 465) when he studied the motion of the Moon. Although the English foot was used on rare occasions, for example to describe the orbit of a comet, these observations and calculations are from Flamsteed and Halley. The last Parisian astronomer to be mentioned by

Newton in Book Three of the *Principia* is Auzout (1622–91), for his observations of the comet of 1665. At that time the Paris Observatory had not yet been founded, and in fact, Newton mentions it only in 1726.

Hall and others have given two main reasons for the modifications that Newton introduced in the successive editions of the *Principia* with respect to French astronomers:[19] (1) the quality of their measurements and (2) his misunderstanding with Flamsteed, at that time Astronomer Royal at the Royal Observatory, Greenwich. Since Europe was at the time under the leadership of both England and France, this attitude may also be regarded as either international cooperation or scientific spying, depending on one's point of view.

"HALLEY" BEFORE HALLEY AT THE
PARIS OBSERVATORY

Nowadays it is usual to call Halley's comet "Halley" for short, as in the case of the International Halley Watch. This Halley is also represented in the Paris Observatory archives, not only in the printed papers of Kepler (1571–1630), who observed the 1607 visit of "Halley," but also in manuscripts by Ismaël Bouilliau, Senior, including two drawings of the 1607 comet (Fig. 3.8).[20] At the 1682 return (although it was not recognized as such), "Halley" was observed at the Paris Observatory by, among others, Picard and Cassini, whose notebooks track its progress (Figs. 3.9 and 3.10);[21] also included are angular distances between the comet and some stars. Between 17 August and 11 September Picard and La Hire reported six observations and the distances from the comet to α and β Ursae Majoris, Castor, Pollux, β Lyrae, γ Bootis, and Arcturus. For 23 August–24 September fifteen observations are noted; these provide, in addition to angular distances, the instant at which the comet is in a given vertical together with various stars. Although some of the stars are faint, they were identified by the grandson of Cassini I, Cassini de Thury (Cassini III, 1714–84), who studied the 1682 observations on the occasion of the comet's 1759 return and established agreement with those of Flamsteed (1646–1719) within 3'.

B. Morando, of the Bureau des Longitudes, studied Picard's and Cassini's 1682 observations in 1985.[22] These observations appear to be of low precision compared with those made by Flamsteed in the same period, the latter of which Donald Yeomans, of the Jet Propulsion Laboratory, placed within 30" on an orbit based on the 1607, 1682, and 1759 returns. For the Picard and Cassini observations, the differences from the values of the orbit calculated in those years are approximately 3', the differences in terms of the positions derived from the latest osculatory

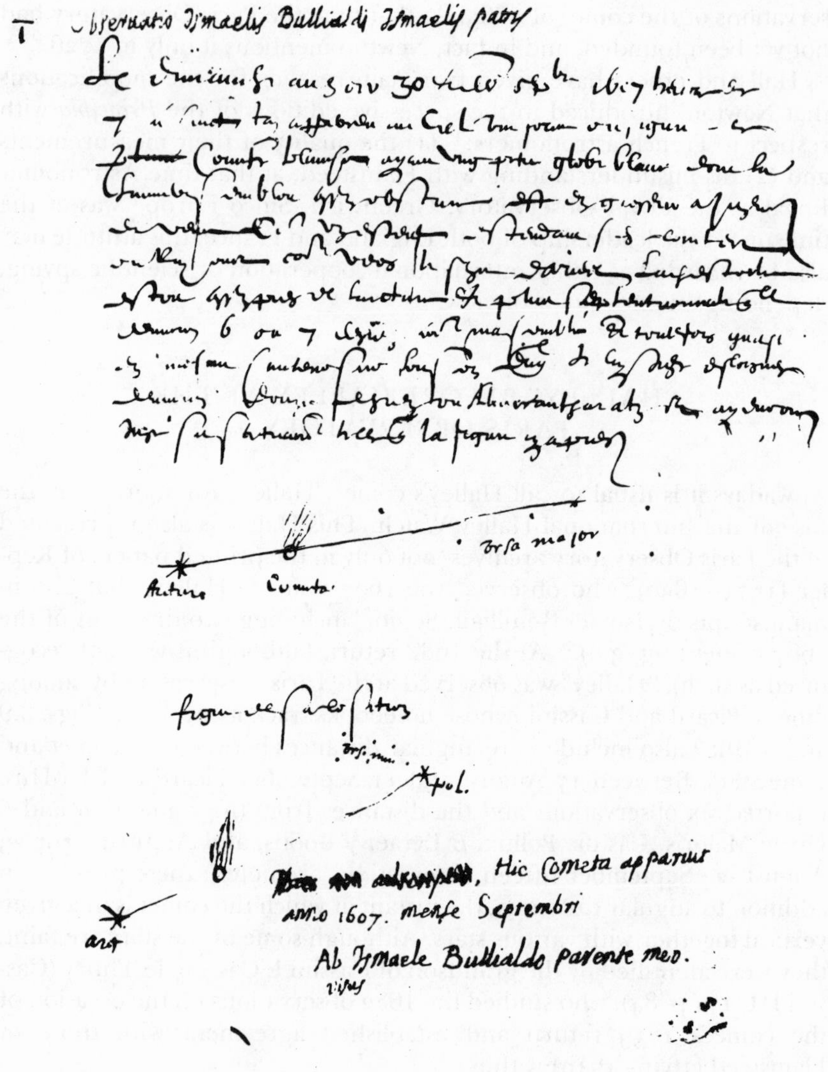

Figure 3.8. A certain comet at its 1607 return. From a manuscript by Ismaël Bouilliau, Senior. (Collections Observatoire de Paris, MS. B3-11.)

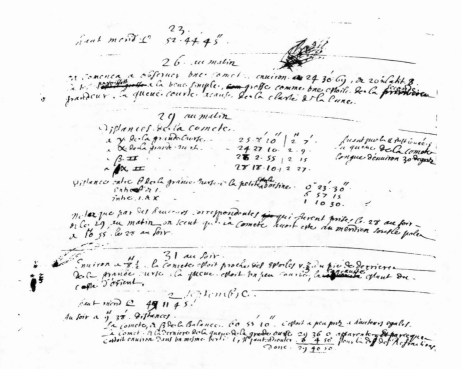

Figure 3.9. Comet "Halley" in Picard's notebook of observations made at the Paris Observatory in 1682. (Collections Observatoire de Paris, MS. D1-16.)

elements published by Yeomans for the return of 1986, using his model for nongravitational forces, are about 20'. This result is not surprising—the model and the initial conditions of this latest return are obtained by using only observations from the 1835 return on.

NEWTON AND HALLEY STILL PRESENT AT THE PARIS OBSERVATORY

The works of Newton and the consequences of his gravitational law had a considerable influence on eighteenth-century French astronomers and mathematicians. Examples include the expeditions to Lapland and Peru under the sponsorship of the Académie des Sciences, with people such as Clairaut and Maupertuis (1698–1759), Godin (1704–60), Bouguer (1698–1758), and La Condamine (1701–74), to mention only a few of those who were seeking to determine the shape of the Earth, as well as published memoirs, articles, and so forth inspired by Halley's prediction

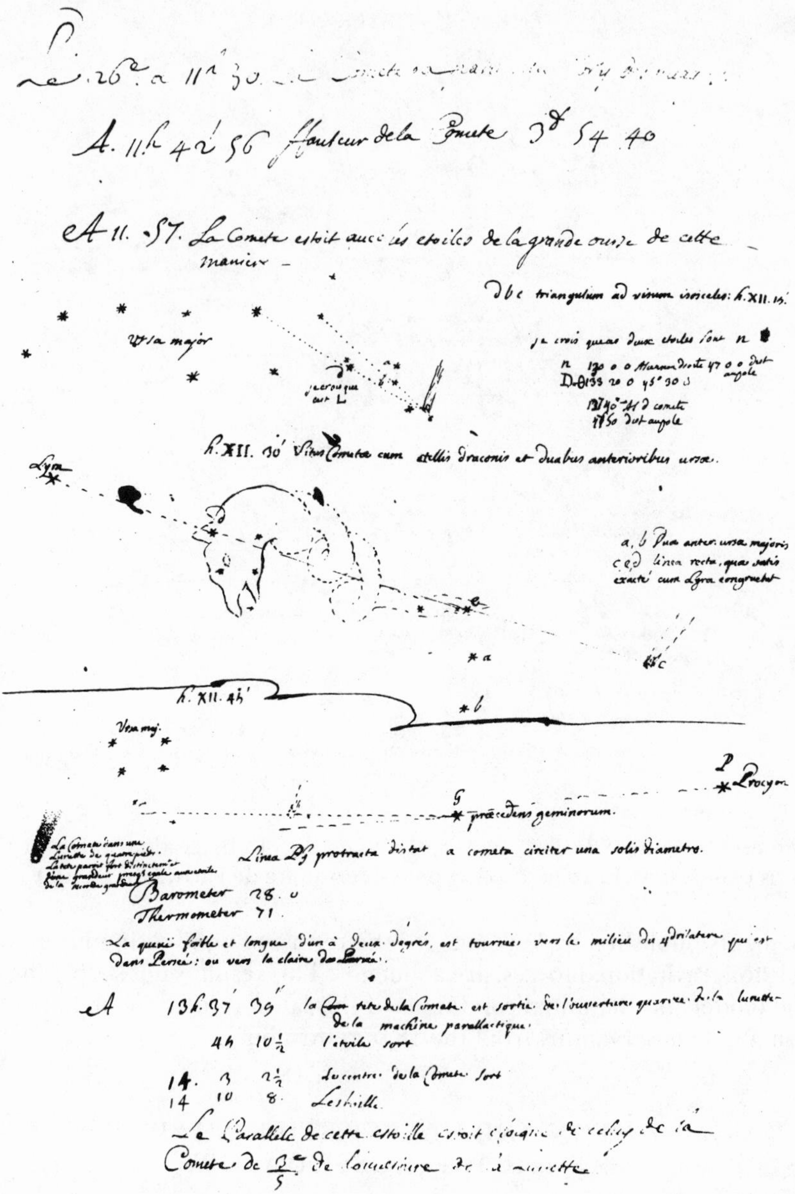

Le 26.ᵉ a 11ᵉ 30 ... Comete ... ...

A. 11ᵉ 42′ 56 ffauteur de la Comete 3ᵈ 54 40

A 11. 57. La Comete estoit avec les etoiles de la grande ourse de cette manier —

D b c triangulum ad vinum isosceles: h. XII. 15.

ut sa major

je crois que ces deux etoiles sont n

h. XII. 30′ Situs Cometæ cum stellis draconis et duabus anterioribus ursæ.

a, b Duæ anter: ursæ majoris, c et d linea recta, quas satis exacte cum Lyra congruebat

Lyra

h. XII. 45′

Ursa maj.

Procyon

G præcedens geminorum.

Linea P G protracta distat a cometa circiter una solis diametro.

Barometer 28. 0
Thermometer 71.

La queue foible et longue d'un à deux degrés, est tournée vers le milieu du ... qui est dans Perseu: ou vers la claire des Perseu:

A   13 h. 37′ 39″   la ... tête de la Comete est sortie de l'ouverture ... de la lunette de la machine parallactique.
      44ʰ 10½   l'etoile sort
14. 3 2½   le centre de la Comete sort
14 10 8   la ...
Le Parallele de cette etoille estoit esloigné de celuy de la Comete de 2/5 de l'ouverture de à lunette

Figure 3.10. Comet "Halley" in Cassini's notebook, 1682. (Collections Observatoire de Paris, MS. D1-8.)

that the 1682 comet would return at the end of 1758 or beginning of 1759. Manuscripts, too, were produced, but these are not well known. J. Alexandre, in an iconographic and bibliographical study of manuscripts kept in the archives of the Paris Observatory, found about twenty documents for "Halley" from 1682 and another twenty for the 1759 return.[23] Among them are the journal of observations made at the Paris Observatory by Cassini III and Maraldi II between 1 and 29 May (Fig. 3.11) and the manuscript copy of Bailly's (1736–93) observations performed between 12 January and 18 May (Fig. 3.12).[24] Messier (1730–1817) watched the comet from the Naval Observatory; the archives contain two manuscripts by him (Fig. 3.13).[25] The "Carte de la route apparente de la célèbre comète de 1759 . . . ," was presented on 5 April to King Louis XV at Versailles, and two days later to the Académie des Sciences (Fig. 3.14). Messier observed "Halley" until 3 June.

The archives of the Paris Observatory have no manuscripts on "Halley" by Clairaut, who, as is well known, made an accurate prediction for the comet's return on the basis of the calculations of Lalande and Mme Lepaute. The error was only one month (thirty-two days exactly) for the return to the perihelion: a tribute to the glory of both Newton and Halley.

Before we leave Halley to focus on Newton and evidence of him at the Paris Observatory, it should be mentioned that in 1835 the famous Arago (1786–1853) was lucky enough to gather a great deal of information on a comet that no doubt was "Halley." In the archives, Alexandre found about fifteen manuscripts about "Halley," with measurements of its diameter made from 22 September to 2 November 1835. The archives also contain drawings and descriptions in letters written to Arago and, among the documents, original drawings by Schwabe (1789–1875), who observed "Halley" between 7 and 30 October 1835.[26]

An item that is perhaps not well known is the portrait ordered by Admiral Mouchez (1821–92) in 1880 for the Paris Observatory Museum, which he had established the previous year. Two octagonal rooms, one on each side of the building, house a portrait gallery; the western one is devoted to French astronomers, the eastern one to eight foreign astronomers. Among these portraits is a not very flattering one of Newton (Fig. 3.15), a copy made from an engraving by Barlow based on the 1689 portrait by Sir Godfrey Kneller and recommended by Airy (1801–92), Astronomer Royal at Greenwich, in a letter dated 12 October 1880. The payment mentioned is 3 guineas, 3 shillings. (The portrait by Kneller, which belongs to the Earl of Portsmouth, is in the same tradition as the one that is the frontispiece of the English translation of the *Principia*.)[27] On the copy, the mention of Isaacus Newtonus is absent, but at the top left there is a mermaid and a red ribbon. This portrait was installed on

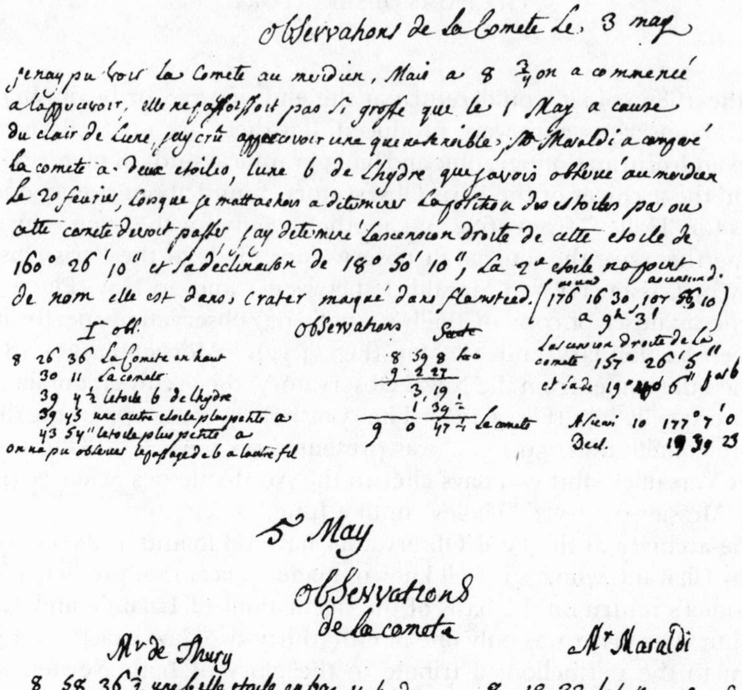

Figure 3.11. Comet "Halley" in 1759, from observations made by Cassini III and Maraldi II. (Collections Observatoire de Paris, MS. D4-16.)

Figure 3.12. Comet "Halley" in a manuscript by Bailly from 1759. (Collections Observatoire de Paris, MS. C5-15.)

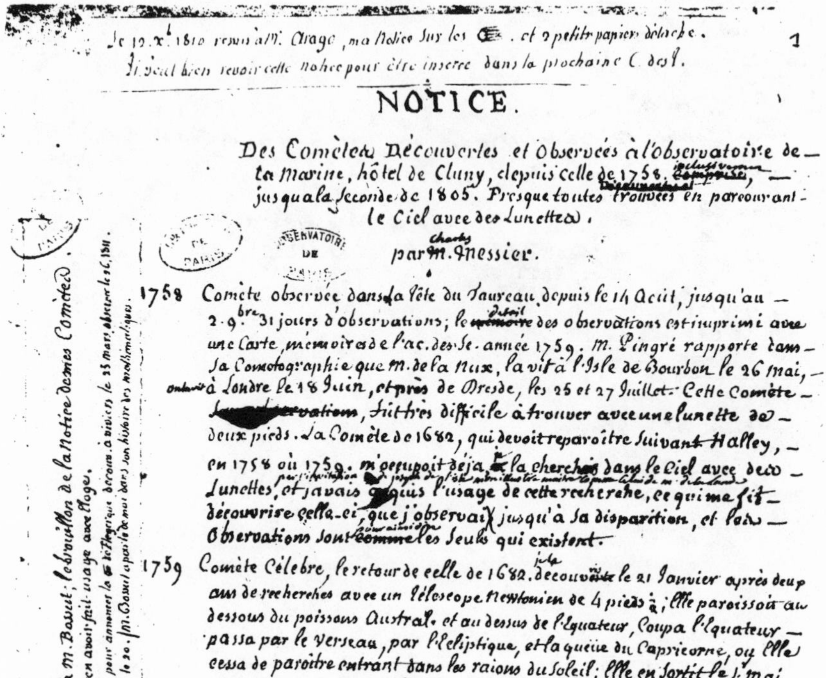

Le 12.x.ͤ 1810 renu à M. Arago, ma Notice sur les ☄. et 2 petits papiers détachés.
Il veut bien revoir cette notice pour être insérée dans la prochaine C.ͣͤ dͤs ͭ.

1

NOTICE.

Des Comètes Découvertes et Observées à l'observatoire de
la marine, hôtel de Cluny, depuis celle de 1758, Comprise,
jusqu'à la seconde de 1805. Presque toutes trouvées en parcourant
le Ciel avec des Lunettes.

par M. Charles Messier.

(left margin, vertical): Lundi 11 Mai 1807 Communiqué à M. Basset, le brouillon de la Notice des Comètes
Rendu le 25 même mois. ma dit en avoir fait usage aux Plages.

1758 — Comète observée dans la tête du Taureau depuis le 14 Août jusqu'au
2. 9.ͧͬͤ 31 jours d'observations; le mémoire des observations est imprimé avec
une Carte, mémoire de l'Ac. des Sc. année 1759. M. Pingré rapporte dans
sa Cométographie que M. de la Nux, l'a vû à l'Isle de Bourbon le 26 mai,
à Londres le 18 Juin, et près de Dresde, les 26 et 27 Juillet. Cette Comète
fut très difficile à trouver avec une lunette de
deux pieds. La Comète de 1682, qui devoit reparoître suivant Halley,
en 1758 où 1759. m'occupoit déjà à la chercher dans le Ciel avec deux
Lunettes, et j'avais acquis l'usage de cette recherche, ce qui me fit
découvrir celle-ci, que j'observai jusqu'à sa disparition, et ces
Observations sont comme les seuls qui existent.

1759 — Comète Célèbre, le retour de celle de 1682. découverte le 21 Janvier après deux
ans de recherches avec un Télescope Newtonien de 4 pieds ½; elle paroissoit au
dessous du poissons Austral. et au dessus de l'équateur, Coupa l'équateur
passa par le Verseau, par l'Écliptique, et la queüe du Capricorne, où elle
cessa de paroître entrant dans les raions du Soleil; Elle en sortit le 1.ͤ mai
au matin, au dessous de l'hydre, traversa l'hydre près de son Noud et
cessa de paroître dans le Sextant; Elle fut observée 13 jours dans la
première branche de son orbite, et 34 jours dans la seconde; le mémoire
des observations avec des planches, se trouve dans le vol. de l'Ac. des Sc.
année 1760. Elle fut découverte, 27 jours avant moi, sans en avoir eu
Connaissance, à Aprohlis, près de Dresde, par un paysant nommé
Palitzch, le 25. x.ͤ 1758. et le 24 Janvier suivant on imprima à
Leipsick, un éphéméride de cette Comète pour la suivre depuis le 28 Janvier,
jusqu'au 13 de mai; Palitzch, se fit connaitre des astronomes par cette
découverte importante; il est mort en 1788. Cette Comète Célèbre, prédite par
Halley depuis plus de 50 ans, pour reparoître à la fin de 1758, où au
commencement de 1759, engagea M. Clairaut à faire beaucoup de Calculs
pour rapprocher d'avantage son retour, fixa son passage au périhélie au
milieu du mois d'avril, et elle y passa le 12 Mars 1759; un mois environ
plûtot que sa prédiction on trouva de grands détails à ce sujet dans l'histoire de l'académie

1760 — Comète, découverte, le 8. Janvier, près de l'Épée d'Orion, observée jusqu'au 30 du
même mois; 6 jours d'observations; Elle fut découverte à la vûe Simple; le
mémoire imprimé avec une Carte, dans le vol. de l'Ac. de 1772. Cette Comète

---

Figure 3.13. Comet "Halley," in a manuscript by Messier (first page). (Collections Observatoire de Paris, MS. C2-19.)

AVRIL 1759

Le 3.

Le ciel couvert toute la journée. Aujourd'hui matin je suis parti pour Versailles avec M. Delisle pour présenter au Roi la Route de la célèbre Comète de 1682 que j'ai découverte le 21 Janvier dernier.

Le 4.

J'étois à Versailles. Le ciel couvert le matin, de même quoique grande partie du reste de la journée avec pluie sur le soir.

Le 5.

Aujourd'hui sur les 5 heures de l'après midi nous avons présenté au Roi et à Mg.r le Dauphin la Carte dont je viens de parler ils l'ont vüe avec plaisir. La journée comme celle d'hier. Sans pluie.

à 15.h 28' 38" Immn: α de Tysmaw. P. Weiss, Oil. Novv. de 4 pieds. Le ciel serein 2.e élevé du 9 degrés.

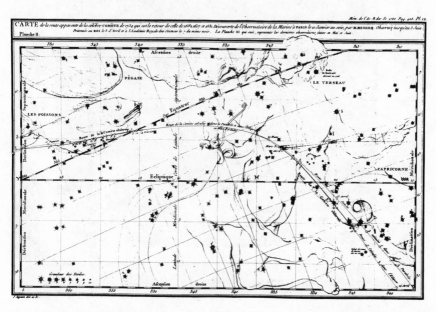

Figure 3.14. "Route de Halley," presented to King Louis XV by Messier. (Top in Collections Observatoire de Paris, MS. C2-19, "Journal des . . . 1759"; bottom in *Mémoires de l'Académie des Sciences.*)

Figure 3.15. Portrait of Newton by one Cartier, ordered by Admiral Mouchez on the recommendation of Airy, Astronomer Royal (Greenwich). (Collections Observatoire de Paris. Photograph Kollar.)

Figure 3.16. Effigy of Halley. Part of an allegory on the 1882 transit of Venus, by Edmond-Louis Dupain, in West Rotunda of the Paris Observatory. (Photograph A. Thévenard.)

29 January 1881 (the artist, Cartier, worked quickly), and Newton remains in the same place today.[28]

Although Halley is not among the English astronomers represented in the gallery, his portrait can be found in an allegory (Fig. 3.16) representing the 1882 transit of Venus across the Sun. This painting, ordered by the Ministry of Arts at the request of Admiral Mouchez, was created by Edmond-Louis Dupain and placed on the ceiling of the west octagonal room in August 1886. In it, Le Verrier (1811–77) watches Delisle (1688–1768) in a silver medallion, and Halley is in a golden one. The painting is an homage to Delisle, who had embraced Halley's suggestion of using the transits of 1761 and 1769 to determine the dimensions of the solar system; but it is a greater homage to Halley, who, in 1716, predicted their usefulness in the first place—a remarkable inclusion in a room devoted to French astronomers, *passage de Vénus oblige!*

FROM NEWTON TO LE VERRIER

Further testimony of the permanence of the relationship between the English and French astronomers may be found in a lock of Newton's hair, which was "part of a large lock in the possession of the present Earl of Portsmouth whose father . . . married Catherine daughter of John Conduitt . . . by Catherine his wife coheiress of Sr Isaac." [29] This lock, presented to Le Verrier in 1847, belonged to Le Verrier's family and was donated by his great-grandchildren to the Paris Observatory in 1965.

The return of Halley's comet in 1759, three-quarters of a century after the publication of the *Principia,* was indisputable proof of Newton's theory. A century later, the announcement made by Le Verrier to Galle (1812–1910) in September 1846 led to the discovery of a new planet, Neptune, confirming the success of Newton's law. Three-quarters of another century was needed for this law to be modified by Einstein (1879–1955)—but Science has not had its last word. In any case, the *Philosophiae Naturalis Principia Mathematica* is still used in many ways, as Newton wished. For example, in 1982 scientists found Halley's comet at the place expected on the occasion of its return, with perihelion passage on 9 February 1986.

CONCLUSION

Works on Newton are numerous. The return of "Halley" has led to the proliferation of books or articles on the astronomer and on the comet named after him. [30] The conference "Newton and Halley, 1686–1986" was an occasion for the Paris Observatory to recall the influence of French astronomers and especially the measurements they made, which were of high precision considering their time and which gave Newton important data on the shape of the Earth. It was also an opportunity to consider the influence of Halley's prediction on French astronomical work in the eighteenth century and the consequences of that work on celestial mechanics during the nineteenth. Less well known are the homages paid by Halley to Cassini, by the English to Le Verrier, and by Admiral Mouchez to Newton. Today we acknowledge the early astronomers of France and Great Britain, the builders of celestial mechanics and of the fundamental astronomy of our day.

NOTES

1. René Taton, "Inventaire des exemplaires des premières éditions des 'Principia' de Newton," *Revue d'histoire des sciences* 6 (1953): 60.
2. Page citations here are to the 1687 copy of the *Principia* housed at the Observatoire de Paris.
3. *Isaac Newton's Philosophiae Naturalis Principia Mathematica*, 2 vols., ed. Alexandre Koyré and I. Bernard Cohen (Cambridge: Cambridge University Press, 1972); hereafter referred to as *Principia* (Koyré-Cohen).
4. Jean Picard, *La Mesure de la Terre* (Paris, 1671), Musée d'Histoire Naturelle, Paris.
5. A. Rupert Hall, "Newton et Picard: Théorie et realité," *Actes du colloque Picard* (Paris: Editions du Centre National de la Recherche Scientifique, 1987), 373–80.
6. Colin A. Ronan, *Edmond Halley: Genius in Eclipse* (London: MacDonald, 1970), 57–68.
7. *Procès-verbaux de l'Académie des Sciences*, vol. 9, fol. 99v.
8. Jean-Dominique Cassini, *Registre des Observations*, Observatoire de Paris MS. D1-8.
9. Nathy O'Hora to author, personal communication.
10. *Correspondence and Papers of Edmond Halley*, ed. Eugene Fairfield MacPike (London, 1937), 30.
11. I. Bernard Cohen, *Introduction to Newton's "Principia"* (Cambridge: Cambridge University Press, 1971), 247.
12. Isaac Newton, *Philosophiae Naturalis Principia Mathematica* (Cambridge, 1713), Académie des Sciences, Paris.
13. Le Seur et Jacquier, *Philosophiae Naturalis Principia Mathematica d'I. Newton. Réédition de 1822 de l'édition latine commentée de 1739* (Glasgow, 1822), Observatoire de Paris; Madame la Marquise du Chastellet, *Principes mathématiques de la philosophie naturelle (I. Newton)* (Paris, 1756), Observatoire de Paris. The Marquise du Châtelet (or Chastellet) (1706–49) was born Emilie Le Tonnelier de Breteuil.
14. Marie-Françoise Biarnais, *"Principia" de Newton et traductions françaises au XVIIIème siecle. Thèse de 3ème cycle*, Cahiers d'Histoire et de Philosophie des Sciences, 2 vols. (Paris, 1982).
15. Page references in what follows are to the 1726 edition of *Principia*.
16. See *Principia* (Koyré-Cohen), 2:876–81, on the various numerical values that Newton includes.
17. Hall makes this point also, in his "Newton et Picard" (published subsequent to the conference for which the present essay was written).
18. Christiaan Huyghens, *Horologium Oscillatorium* . . . (Paris, 1673); Picard, *La Mesure de la Terre*.

19. Hall, "Newton et Picard."

20. Ismaël Boulliau, Sr., *Observatio Ismaelis Bulliadi Ismaelis patris*, Observatoire de Paris MS. B5-12.

21. J. Picard, *Registre de ses Observations*, Observatoire de Paris MS. D1-16; Cassini, *Registre des Observations*.

22. Bruno Morando, "Sur des observations de la comète de Halley faites l'Observatoire de Paris en 1682" (unpublished manuscript).

23. Josette Alexandre, "La comète de Halley à travers les ouvrages et les manuscrits de l'Observatoire de Paris," *Isis* 77, no. 286 (1986): 79–84.

24. César-François Cassini de Thury (Cassini III) and Maraldi II, *Journal des observations faites a l'Observatoire de Paris du 1er mai au 29 mai 1759*, Observatoire de Paris MS. D4-16; Sylvain Bailly, *Observations de la comète de 1759 du 12 janvier au 18 mai*, Observatoire de Paris MS. D5-15.

25. Charles Messier, *Journal des observations . . . du 3 avril au 24 mai 1759* and *Notice de mes comètes (Revue et corrigée par M. de Lalande et M. Arago)*, Observatoire de Paris MS. C2-19.

26. Samuel Heinrich Schwabe, *Dessins de la comète de Halley . . . avec la lunette de Fraunhofer de 6 pieds*, Observatoire de Paris MS. C6-9.

27. The Kneller portrait is also reproduced in Richard S. Westfall, *Never at Rest: A Biography of Isaac Newton* (Cambridge: Cambridge University Press, 1980), 482. For the *Principia* frontispiece, see *Sir Isaac Newton's Mathematical Principles of Natural Philosophy and His System of the World: Motte's Translation (of 1729)*, rev. ed., ed. Florian Cajori (Berkeley and Los Angeles: University of California Press, 1947).

28. *Rapports annuels de l'Observatoire de Paris pour les années 1880 et 1881* (Paris: Gauthier-Villais, 1881–82), Observatoire de Paris.

29. *Certificat authentifiant la mèche de cheveux de Newton*, Observatoire de Paris.

30. See, for example, Peter Broughton, "The First Predicted Return of Comet Halley," *Journal for the History of Astronomy* 16 (1985): 123; David W. Hughes, "The Portraits of Edmond Halley," *Vistas in Astronomy* 27 (1984): 55; Josette Alexandre and Suzanne Débarbat, *La comète de Halley hier, aujourd'hui, demain* (Paris: Observatoire de Paris, 1985).

PART II

Newton

FOUR

"Such an Impertinently Litigious Lady":
Hooke's "Great Pretending" vs. Newton's *Principia* and Newton's and Halley's Theory of Comets

David Kubrin

Few students of Isaac Newton can be unaware of his rivalry with Robert Hooke, or of the episode when Hooke, in response to Edmond Halley's presentation of Newton's *Principia* to the Royal Society, boasted that Newton had taken its key notions from him.[1] It is generally thought that Hooke's claim concerned his priority in discovering the inverse square law of gravitational attraction. Further, most historians would agree that, whatever Hooke's gifts were—and many think they were considerable— his talent was no equal to the "masterly genius" of Newton and none of his works could ever compare to the grand scope of the *Principia*.[2] I do not want to question those judgments; yet before we fully accept them, we should know more accurately just what, in this crucial instance of their lifelong enmity and competition, the two men's dispute really was. For, as I shall argue, neither Hooke's claims in 1686 nor Newton's understanding of his challenge was restricted to Hooke's charge that Newton had taken the idea of the inverse square force law from him. That concept was but one part of a far more extensive system of the world that Hooke had in mind.[3]

An accurate understanding of this dispute will, I believe, shed new light on Edmond Halley's role in the development of Newtonianism. As I shall argue, much of Halley's astronomical career was taken up pursuing the questions that arose in a running debate he engaged in with Hooke for more than a decade after the publication of the *Principia*. Seen in this new light, this rather misunderstood debate will offer us another window onto the ongoing fight between Newton and Hooke, a fight that concerned, among other matters, differing conceptions of the mechanical philosophy as well as divergent interpretations of what has been called Hermeticism. Finally, I shall claim that the issues raised in this particular fight reflect the crucial transformation occurring in the sixteenth and seventeenth centuries in natural philosophers' understanding of the Earth as either a living organism or a dead body, a transformation that, because of the changing political economy in seventeenth-century England, had profound implications for the way early mining and other extractive enterprises treated the land, air, water, forests, and animals.

I

In a lecture delivered to the Royal Society in 1686 at the onset of his fight for priority, Hooke announced: "The Doctrine aimed at, is, the Cause and Reason of the present Figure, Shape and Constitution of the Surface of this Body of the Earth, whether Sea or Land, as we now find it presented unto us under various and very irregular Forms and Fashions and constituted of very differing Substances."[4] He was convinced that his theory of the "Figure, Shape and Constitution of . . . the Earth" formed the inner core of an "excellent System of Nature" he had discovered, a system that revolved around a general theory of the Earth as a dynamic planet.[5] This system included his theories about earthquakes, volcanoes, continent formation, the changes to species down through the ages, and the variation of the Earth's magnetic force, as well as a notion of the Earth's varying fertility over time. In fact, his system amounted to nothing less than a far-reaching formulation of a *history* of the whole of the natural world, in which celestial mechanics was tied to the dynamics of a living Earth.

The inverse square law that Hooke claimed as his idea was an obvious focus of his battle with Newton (it entered into the correspondence between the two men as an explicit formulation in 1679) because for Hooke—as for Newton—a whole system of philosophy rested on this very relationship. If in some areas Hooke's and Newton's systems overlapped, fundamentally they were different in scope, focus, and vision. I believe, moreover, that Hooke's resentment over Newton's "theft" of his ideas was so strong not only because of the praise the *Principia* brought Newton but, more to the point, because the *Principia* quashed any chance that Hooke's own grand synthesis of the universe would ever be properly recognized. Significantly, Newton too saw Hooke's claim as extending beyond mere priority for the inverse square law, and he took the claim quite seriously, as I shall show by examining how he—and Halley, Newton's spokesman in much of this battle with Hooke—responded to Hooke's declarations. In fact, the controversy between Halley and Hooke formed the background against which much of Halley's most fruitful work in astronomy and the physics of the Earth should be viewed.

First, though, I wish to establish that, in response to Halley's 1686 challenge in effect to "put up or shut up," Hooke "put up." I shall follow the parallel emergence of Newton's *Philosophiae Naturalis Principia Mathematica* and what the modern editor of a reprint of Hooke's *Posthumous Works* has called Hooke's most prominent work, his *Lectures of Earthquakes*,[6] without realizing that these lectures represented Hooke's evidence against Newton's theft. In June 1686, a month after the initial presentation to the Royal Society of the manuscript of the *Principia*, Halley wrote Newton that in response to Hooke's boasts Halley had told him that "unless he produce another differing demonstration [of the inverse-square law] and let the world judge of it," no one could believe his claims.[7] Let us look closely at Hooke's activities over the following months.

The press had halted the printing of the *Principia* in the Fall of 1686, with only thirteen sheets printed, possibly as a result of Newton's growing anxiety over the treatise, especially given the controversy with Hooke. On 29 November an attack, quite possibly by Hooke, on Halley's role as Clerk precipitated a crisis at the Royal Society.[8] Two days later Hooke began his lectures on earthquakes, delivering four discourses that month concerning his "excellent System." In January the Royal Society authorized Hooke to provide its meetings with continuous discourses and experiments.[9] Hooke was quite ready. Two lectures on his system followed during that month, and four more in February—as the press, after a hiatus of some months, once more began to print sheets for the *Principia*. March and May each brought another two of Hooke's lectures on his system. From May until November there was no more from Hooke on his theory; in the meantime, however, on 5 July 1687, Halley was able to write to Newton that the printing of the *Principia* was finished.[10] From November 1687 to March 1687/88, Hooke delivered ten more lectures on his subject. (In fact he occasionally discoursed on the same topics until his death—for example in 1690, 1692, 1697, 1698, and 1699—although from 1688 Hooke's health and spirits were visibly declining, and he was said to be in a "wasting condition" for some years before his death in 1702.)[11]

Such an outpouring of sustained work represented a rather uncharacteristic focus for Hooke, who was normally given to rushing pell-mell from topic to topic, the virtuoso par excellence. At the beginning of his first lecture Hooke actually announced that he intended to refute the charges of his minimal accomplishments, as well as similar criticisms of the Royal Society. His following discourse, he said, would vindicate the Society by showing how its years of patient observing and experimenting were able to serve as the scaffolding for a "solid, firm and lasting Structure of Philosophy." It would also provide, as he remarked, an instance of a new methodology for natural philosophy, "but I understand the same thing will now be shortly done by Mr. *Newton* in a Treatise of his now in the Press." [12]

These promises, together with a brief recounting of his principles of methodology, Hooke followed with remarks concerning various fossil remains, some for species that no longer existed.[13] The additional fact that many petrified shells occur on land or even on mountains led Hooke to propose near the end of his first discourse that some of the shells found "differ also from all the known sorts of Shells of that Species of Fishes . . . which are now to be found any where . . . alive . . . in any part of the World." [14] Not only had there been an apparent dying out of some species, he said, but the Earth itself had also undergone huge transformations both as to its shape and to the location of its continents and seas. In fact, Hooke concluded, it was likely that the Earth's very axis of rotation had shifted. In *Lectures of Earthquakes* (most of which was delivered as discourses between 1686 and 1688 but which represented work carried out from 1667 until near the end of his life), Hooke proposed that the Earth was actually a compressed spheroid in shape, with the distance between its poles less than that through the equator.[15]

II

Hooke originally sketched his overall conception of these matters in a far-reaching paper delivered to the Royal Society in 1667–68, in which he focused on both the mysterious variation of the Earth's magnetic force and the puzzling phenomena of seashells found high in the mountains.[16] The puzzle of magnetic variation—and of what some claimed was a variation of the variation—had already given rise to an extensive literature in seventeenth-century England, a topic of particular interest as the nation emerged as a maritime power with increasing colonial interests. Henry Gellibrand, for example, in his *Discourse Mathematical on the Variation of the Magnetical Needle,* proposed in 1635 that the changing of magnetic variation arose because the Earth was not a perfect sphere, citing the suggestion by a Dominicus Maria of Ferraro (mentioned by Galileo) that the axis of the Earth changed over time, and posited magnetic "poles" to help explain this latter phenomenon.[17] Although Maria's suggestion was denied, by William Gilbert among others,[18] others thought the hypothesis plausible. In a letter published in the *Philosophical Transactions* in 1670, the German astronomer Johannes Hevelius

stated that a changing axial inclination was a more credible explanation
for the observed variation of the magnet than the notion either that the
variation arose from the nature of the stone itself or that it was caused by
some kind of aethereal effluvia.[19] To account for the "variation of the
variation," an Englishman named Henry Bond proposed a few years
later that a magnetic sphere circumscribed the physical sphere of the
Earth and lagged behind it during the diurnal rotation; only once every
600 years, he said, would the two spheres return to the same relative
starting point. In this Bond disagreed with Henry Phillippes, who had
written in the *Sea-Mans Kalender* (1669) that the magnetic poles had a
period of only 370 years. Bond also pointed out that since some divines
had suggested 6,000 years as the Earth's likely age when the conflagration came, the end of the present cycle—the tenth—might well signal
the end of the world.[20]

Hooke read Bond and commented on his theories, noting his successful prediction that 1654 would find no magnetic variation and that "it
would afterwards Decline. & vary to the westward as I haue found it to
doe."[21] Certainly Hooke found fault with parts of Bond's theory—he
preferred a 373-year cycle, close to that posited by Phillippes, over
Bond's 600-year cycle, for instance, and he placed the magnetic pole 10°
from the North Pole, in contrast to Bond's 8°30'.[22] Nonetheless, he accepted Bond's conjecture of a magnetic sphere encompassing the solid
Earth and transformed it into his own conception of the Earth's internal
structure. In Hooke's view, the Earth consisted of a series of concentric
shells, one of which contained the magnetic poles—a hypothesis that
would win agreement from his eventual rival, Edmond Halley.

Hooke explained his hypothesis in the 1667 lecture that announced
his concern with the shape and dynamics of the Earth: "The natural
form [of the Earth] produc'd by Gravity would be a multitude of Spherical Shells concreted of the several Substances of which it consists, incom-
passing each other, not unlike the Orbits or Shells . . . of an Onion."[23]
Only during the first days of the Creation was the Earth's form so rational and perfectly spherical, its surface everywhere covered with water,
Hooke explained; soon dry land arose and valleys and mountains
formed, probably as a result of huge earthquakes. In this paper Hooke
sketched in (only "as a hint or memorandum")[24] much of the overview of
his grand scheme of the Earth and cosmos (not including the inverse
square relationship). He stated that earthquakes arose from the internal
dynamics of the Earth and that they in turn could affect the globe's relation to the heavens. He had no doubt that by shifting vast amounts
of material from one spot to another, earthquakes could even cause a
change in the Earth's center of gravity, thus altering its axis of rotation.[25]

To support such notions Hooke cited the variations in magnetic attraction, which to him implied the movement of the magnetic poles, and the suspected changing meridians of the Earth, for which he claimed a multitude of observations: "We know that the direction of these Poles [of the axis of rotation], as to the Heavens, doth vary, for whereas, it pointed at a part of the Heavens many degrees distant from the Star in the top of the tail of the little Bear, now it points almost directly towards it. Besides this, we find that the Points of the Intersection of the Æquinoctial and Ecliptick varies, and possibly even *the motions of all may vary.*"[26] Even though it was but a sketch, Hooke's 1667 lecture does call the "motions of all" into question: the times of the Earth's revolutions may have varied through the ages, he suggested, thus causing time's duration to be different for different periods of history. Additionally, the power of gravity itself and the fertility of the Earth may have varied through the ages.[27] Only years later—in the late 1680s and 1690s, and largely in response to Halley's challenge—would Hooke feel the need to rush to fill in this outline with detailed arguments and a fair ordering of his evidence.

At the heart of Hooke's inquiry, in 1667 as later in the 1680s, were the simple but enigmatic beds of misplaced shells, which Hooke could only conclude now lay on mountain tops because these parts of the Earth had once been beneath the seas. No less puzzling were the fossil records of previous plants or animals, from which Hooke boldly concluded:

> There may have been divers Species of things wholly destroyed and annihilated, and divers others changed and varied, for since we find that there are some kinds of Animals and Vegetables peculiar to certain places, and not to be found elsewhere; if such a place have [*sic*] been swallowed up, 'tis not improbable but that those Animal Beings may have been destroyed with them; and this may be true both of aerial and aquatick Animals: For those animated Bodies, whether Vegetables or Animals which were naturally nourished or refresh'd by the Air would be destroy'd by the Water. And this I imagine to be the reason why we now find the Shells of divers Fishes Petrify'd in Stone, of which we have now none of the same kind. . . . Fourthly, That there may have been divers new varieties generated of the same Species, and that by the change of the Soil on which it was produced; for since we find that the alteration of the Climate, Soil and Nourishment doth often produce a very great alteration in those Bodies that suffer it; 'tis not to be doubted but that alterations also of this Nature [a shift in the axis of rotation] may cause a very great change in the shape, and other accidents of an animated Body.

Hooke, in short, did not doubt that the Earth had suffered quite a number of catastrophic earthquakes, some capable of destroying previous learned ages as well as many species of animals and plants.[28]

Since the focus of this paper is not Hooke but Halley's and Newton's response to Hooke, I shall forgo examining in any detail what happened in 1686–87 and later when Hooke rushed to get his 1667 "memorandum" fleshed out in order to forestall Newton's getting credit for more than was, in Hooke's eyes, his rightful due. One substantial difference between Hooke's earlier and later work is worth noting, however. In a discourse read probably in January 1686/87, Hooke explained that the shape of the Earth's figure would be determined jointly by the gravitating power, which he thought was everywhere equal, and "a contrary indeavour of heavy Bodies to recede from the Axis of its Motion, if it be supposed to be mov'd with a diurnal Revolution upon its Axis, . . . which must therefore most diminish its Gravitation, and consequently the gravity will act the most freely and powerfully under the Poles."[29] Ironically, Hooke cited Halley's observations at St. Helena concerning the length of the pendulum as evidence that the Earth was shaped like a compressed sphere with its greatest distance across the equator.

These explanations in turn allowed Hooke to clarify precisely *how* a shift in the Earth's axis of rotation was likely to wreak absolute havoc on both the interior and surface of the planet. "It may be supposed," he said, "that [if] the poles and axis are moveable, the equinoctial and greatest diameter will be likewise altered, and by consequence the parts of the land, towards which the poles approach, will be raised, and the sea retire; but on the contrary, those parts, from which the poles recede, will sink, and the water rise upon them."[30] Thus, since by 1686–87 Hooke (as well as Newton) understood a lot more about mechanics and dynamics than he had in 1667, now he could, in addition to citing a specific mechanism capable of changing the Earth's surface, provide a quantitative formulation, based on the inverse square law and the measure of centrifugal "force," to derive a precise description of the Earth as an oblate sphere. That is, he could actually show just how extensive any transformation to the Earth's surface would be.

No wonder that Hooke considered his doctrine of the present shape of the Earth to be the key to an "excellent System of Nature"—for the shape itself was a reflection of the dynamic history of the planet, providing a link to the Earth's orientation in space and to the other planets and stars. No less than the formation of the seas and continents, the variation of life-forms over the centuries, and the way the "motions of all may vary" were bound up in the doctrine of the Earth's shape and the inverse square law—contrary to the claim of Richard S. Westfall, Newton's biographer, that for Hooke those two concepts were discrete ideas and not part of an overall system of the cosmos.[31] No wonder either that Hooke raced in 1686 and 1687 to get as much of this system into the public record as possible before Newton's "system" could be published.

III

In 1689, the antiquarian, occultist, and gossip John Aubrey, Hooke's close friend and an enthusiastic partisan in this matter, sent Anthony à Wood a copy of Hooke's theory, along with his own assessment of the treatise: "Mr Wood! This is the greatest discovery in nature, that ever was since the world's creation: it never was so much as hinted by any man before. I know you will doe him right. I hope you may read his hand: I wish he had writt plainer, and afforded a little more paper."[32] Luckily, we do not have to take Aubrey's word alone for the import of Hooke's theory. We can gather that Edmond Halley—and, by inference, Isaac Newton—saw Hooke's discourses as a threat, one to be taken quite seriously. Contrary to what is generally believed, Halley did not limit himself simply to reporting to Newton about Hooke's vain boasts and then reassuring him, encouraging him to keep to his original plans and not retire (as was his constant threat) from having anything further to do with the "impertinently litigious Lady" Newton saw natural philosophy to be.[33] Hooke had begun his new series of earthquake lectures on 1 December 1686; in February 1686/87, in the midst of fighting off the challenge to his position as Clerk of the Royal Society and shepherding Newton's treatise through the press, Halley stepped forward to propose an alternative theory of the Earth to Hooke's.

The key to Hooke's system had been his notion, to which he continually returned, that the axis of the Earth's rotation underwent "certain slow Progressive Motion[s]."[34] Halley accepted Hooke's hypothesis that the Earth's shape was a compressed spheroid, as well as his idea that should the axis of rotation change, "the Equinoctial will so too; and consequently the Water must rise and cover those Parts from which the Poles recede, and fall off and leave bare those Places towards which the Poles approach. By this Means it may be accounted for, how such strange Marine things are found on the Tops of Hills, and so deep under Ground; and scarce any other Way."[35] Any change of the poles would cause the latitude of places on the Earth to change, Halley agreed, increasing it in regions toward which the poles approached and decreasing it in regions from which the poles receded. Comparing recent observations in Nuremburg with ones made two centuries earlier, and contemporary measurements in Alexandria with ones made in the time of Eratosthenes, Hipparchus, and Ptolemy, however, Halley found the differences to be so small as to be wholly attributable either to error or to a motion of the poles that was exceedingly slow—perhaps as little as one degree change in twenty thousand years. Such a rate of change could lead only to gradual flooding; yet both "*Holy Scriptures*, and Pagan Tradition, do unanimously agree, That the last great *Deluge* was brought to pass in a few Days, with no previous Notice."[36] Moreover, Halley pointed

out, since gradual flooding would not have resulted in any significant loss
of life, such changes to the axis were unlikely to have wiped out whole
species, as Hooke supposed.

On the other hand, Halley speculated, the Earth's axis might very well
change suddenly, in a way either brought about directly by "the [intel-
ligent] Powers, that first impress'd this whirling Motion on the Ball [of
the Earth]," or "performed naturally, by the casual Shock of some transient Body, such as a Comet."[37]

Of course, comets were only then coming under the governance of
the Newtonian system, the codification of which Halley was then in the
middle of editing. It was sometime between the summer of 1686 and
April 1687, when Newton sent Book Three of the *Principia* to Halley,
that Newton succeeded in showing how comets, too, followed the laws of
motion and of universal gravitation. Indeed, showing how those errant
bodies conformed to his laws of motion was the crowning achievement
(as well as the conclusion) of his treatise, as Halley well realized.[38] By virtue of their newly discovered predictability, comets were thus able to
serve Halley (and Newton) as a kind of celestial *deus ex machina*. As Newton began to surround himself with a coterie of young followers in the
1690s, he and some of these disciples (notably William Whiston and
David Gregory) were repeatedly to ask the newly established periodicity of comets to carry an increasing burden of explanatory functions,
making it a veritable jack-of-all-trades of Newtonian cosmological speculation, capable of balancing the various harmonies of the solar and terrestrial systems in order to keep everything functioning.[39] Not the least
of the many interesting properties of comets, as Newton noted, was the
ability of their tails—which, because they point *away* from the sun, must
be able to overcome the force of gravitation—to grow in a handful of
months from a speck in the sky to sixty or seventy degrees in angular
length. Whatever formed the tails had to be a most peculiar form of
matter indeed; more than once Newton hinted at a special purpose for
comets, and their extreme properties suggested to him certain alchemical properties.[40]

Halley was the first of the Newtonians publicly to suggest the many
ways in which comets could fulfill certain cosmological and terrestrial
roles, though in his initial paper he only mentioned his idea briefly—like
Hooke, advancing but a "hint or memorandum." Yet as his initial idea
grew and took on flesh, the original proposal on comets soon expanded
to include a number of key questions in astronomy and terrestrial physics. The investigations Halley embarked on as a result of this line of reasoning generated much of his work during the years of his active astronomical career, and help to explain several of his most significant
papers. To these let us now turn.

When he presented his first paper on the subject, in February

1686/87, Halley had only just begun to see how comets could provide an alternative explanation for changing the terrestrial axis. Although Halley spoke against Hooke's theory once at a meeting of the Royal Society in June 1689,[41] the bare skeleton of a theory of a comet's impact, raised at the end of Halley's February 1686/87 paper, had to suffice as long as the publication of Newton's *Principia* proceeded and other matters continued to dominate his attention. In a 1692 discourse, however, he returned to that hint and added more features. Utilizing a 1683 paper on the magnetic variation in which he had proposed "that *the whole Globe of the Earth is one great Magnet, having 4 Magnetical Poles, or Points of Attraction, near each Pole of the Æquator,* and that *in those Parts of the World which lie near adjacent to any of those Magnetical Poles, the Needle is governed thereby; the nearest Pole being always predominant over the more remote,*"[42] he went on to explain how a comet's impact against the Earth could impart different velocities to an outer shell holding one such set of poles and to an inner one holding the other set, the two shells separated by some kind of fluid medium (an internal terrestrial structure rather similar to Hooke's). To skeptics who might argue that such an internal structure was farfetched, Halley pointed to the example of the rings of Saturn. He also claimed that his hypothesis made possible an explanation of why the moon should be denser than the Earth by a proportion of nine to five, as Newton had shown in the *Principia,* by providing for a suitably sized cavity between the inner and outer shells.[43]

Two years later, in 1694, Halley delivered another discourse before the Royal Society concerning a comet's impact against the Earth, hypothesizing that such an impact could have caused the Noachian deluge as well as account for magnetic variation. So, too, could it explain the existence of mountains on the Earth (whose presence on the originally created Earth had been challenged by Thomas Burnet in his influential *Sacred Theory of the Earth* [1681–89]), the seashells found far from any sea, the extreme cold of the Hudson Bay region, and possibly the depressions that formed basins for the oceans. The impact of a comet could readily explain the turmoil of the seas that characterized the deluge.[44] One week after he delivered his discourse, however, Halley admitted that it made more sense to view a comet's impact not as the cause of the Noachian flood but as having brought about, "once or oftner," the destruction of a "former world," reducing it to a "chaos out of whose ruins the present [world] might be formed."[45]

IV

Such notions of "former worlds" were dangerous in 1694—and Halley did not allow them to be printed. They implied a succession of worlds, possibly from all eternity, undergoing periodic dissolution and re-creation, a view closer to Stoic or Epicurean (or even Hindu), than to Christian, cosmology.

Halley had good reason to be cautious. Three years earlier, the position of Savilian Professor of Astronomy at Oxford had fallen vacant and he had sought its appointment. He soon learned that his chances were slim, since the trustees for the position had doubts about his religious orthodoxy. On 22 June 1691, Halley wrote to Abraham Hill, the newly appointed Comptroller to the Archbishop of Canterbury, John Tillotson, asking him to intercede with the archbishop to delay selection so that Halley might use the extra time to "clear myself" of a charge of "asserting the eternity of the world." [46]

Political and social turmoil in England at the time made such a doctrine particularly suspect, especially for someone of Halley's political associations. Ominously, the year 1692 saw large earthquakes hit both the English colony of Jamaica, on 7 June, and London, exactly three months later, occasioning a spate of commentaries on the meaning of these events. [47] That year, too, a plot to assassinate William III and restore the deposed James II to the throne was uncovered; and in April an invasion by James II, in alliance with the French, was rumored, precipitating a preemptive attempt by the English to invade France. [48] Halley, in fact, was known to have Jacobite sympathies. [49] In 1692 and 1693, moreover, books hinting at or declaring the eternity of the Earth were published, including one by the notorious freethinker Charles Blount. [50] To make matters worse, Blount had shortly before published his *King William and Queen Mary Conquerors,* in which he defended their rule solely on the grounds of conquest, thus denying any monarchical principle. [51] Finally, in his important sermon "The Wisdom of Being Religious" (1664), which was placed at the very beginning of his collected works and was often cited by his contemporaries, Archbishop Tillotson had singled out the notion of the world's eternity as one of the most dangerous of heresies. [52]

Tillotson died in 1694, however, the year Halley gave his discourse suggesting that the present Earth was a wreck of a "former world." The implications of this Earth's being but the most recent in a whole series of Creations that might well reach back to all eternity were all too clear, and although Halley delivered his paper, he did not allow it to be printed until decades later. Instead, in late 1692, about a year after his letter to Hill, Halley had begun to give lectures and publish papers that aimed at demonstrating a *finite* age for the Earth. Indeed, these investigations into the question of how old the Earth and moon might be were to dominate much of Halley's astronomical work over the next few decades.

On 19 October 1692, Halley first addressed the question of the world's age directly. Probably owing to the rumors he had complained

about to Hill while seeking the Savilian Professorship of Astronomy
(which he did not get), Halley now stated to the Royal Society that he
could prove the Earth's finite age:

> Halley read a paper, wherein he endeavoured to prove that the opposition
> of the Medium of the Æther to the Planets passing through it, did in time
> become sensible. That to reconcile this retardation of the Motions the An-
> cients and Moderns had been forced to alter the differences of Meridians
> preposterously. . . . Hence he argued, that the Motions being retarded
> must necessarily conclude a finall period and that the eternity of the World
> was hence to be demonstrated impossible. He was ordered to prosecute
> this Notion, and to publish a discourse about it.[53]

At the end of his paper on the cause of magnetic variation that same year
Halley suggested that he could demonstrate that the motions of the
planets were sensibly retarded by the aether. Since resistance to the planets' motion varied as their cross section, while the mass of the bodies and
hence the amount of their motion varied as their volume, smaller bodies
would feel a proportionately greater resistance, and Halley feared that
the satellites of planets, such as our Moon, would tend to fall behind,
eventually leaving their planets altogether. Unless the specific gravities
of Earth and Moon were adjusted proportionately, such might be the
fate of the Earth's Moon.[54] If the Moon did fall behind, that event too
would argue against the eternity of the system.

But as work over the next few years demonstrated, the opposite turned
out to be the case. In 1694 Newton suggested to Halley an alternative
theory, that the Moon *increased* its velocity with respect to the Earth:

> Halley say'd that M[r]. Newton had lately told him That there was reason to
> Conclude That the bulk of the Earth did grow and increase . . . by the per-
> petuall Accession of New particles attracted out of the Ether by its Grav-
> itating power, and he [Halley] Supposed . . . That this Encrese [sic] of the
> Moles of the Earth would occasion an Acceleration of the Moons Motion,
> she being at this time Attracted by a Stronger vis Centripeta than in remote
> Ages.[55]

By systematically comparing the recorded and predicted times of ancient eclipses of the Moon, Halley confirmed Newton's, rather than his
own, hypothesis; this in turn led to Halley's famous theory of the secular
acceleration of the Moon.[56] As with a deceleration, lunar acceleration implied a finite age of the Earth and Moon. Meanwhile, Halley continued
to seek out the evidence for a finite age of the world in other areas. In
1693 he delivered a discourse "concerning a Demonstration of the Contraction of the year, and promising to make out thereby the necessity of

the worlds [*sic*] coming to an end, and consequently that it must have had a beginning, which hitherto has not been evinced from any thing, that has been observed in Nature. Of this he [Halley] was ordered to print a Dissertation."[57]

Perhaps Halley's strategems worked. Except for the discourse in 1694 on the deluge, which he deliberately suppressed, all of Halley's discourses since 1691, when he had written to Hill about clearing himself of the charge of believing in the world's eternity, supported the orthodox notion of the world's having had a beginning. Halley did not get the Savilian Professorship of Astronomy, despite the recommendation he received from the Royal Society; the position went instead to David Gregory.[58] But in 1703, when the Savilian Professorship of *Geometry* became available, Halley's application ultimately proved successful.

When in 1713, however, the much awaited second edition of Newton's *Principia* was published under the editorship of the classicist Richard Bentley, the famous "Ode" by Halley to Newton had been boldly rewritten in a number of places, without Halley's knowledge. The biggest change occurred where Halley had originally written

> . . . until, the origin of things
> He established, the omnipresent Creator, unwilling the laws
> To violate, He fixed the *eternal foundations* of His work. (emphasis added)

This Bentley altered to

> . . . until, the origin of things
> He put together, the all-powerful Creator Himself, His laws,
> Named; and indeed set the foundations of His works.

Bentley, the classicist, was clearly not out to correct Halley's latinity; rather, the *Principia* had to carefully disavow the implication in Halley's "Ode" that the universe could have existed from eternity.[59] Indeed, this was still the case in 1726, when Henry Pemberton edited a third edition:

> Halley told me [wrote John Conduitt] Sir I. N. ⟨promised him⟩[60] made him hope that in Pemberton's edition his verses should be printed from his own copy, but complained they were not, for he made it—
>   Æternique operis fundamenta fixit.   & it is printed
>   Operam quae fundamenta locavit.   & when I said that
> perhaps Sr I. did not care for having any thing appear before his book that seemed to favour the opinion that the world was eternal—Yes said he that is what Pemberton would fix upon me, but aeternum is only aeviternum & I meant no mor[e].[61]

In short, Halley did not believe the world to be eternal and independent of God, but coeternal with God and dependent on Him, but this was a distinction that did not satisfy the Newtonians or most of Halley's contemporaries.[62]

V

One of the historic aims of astronomy has been the search for cycles in the heavens. The philosophical and theological—as well as scientific—implications of any cycle were always carefully considered. For example, Copernicus's student Rheticus commented that

> all kingdoms have had their beginnings when the center of the eccentric was at some special point on the small circle. Thus, when the eccentricity of the sun was at its maximum, the Roman government became a monarchy; as the eccentricity decreased, Rome too declined, as though aging, and then fell. When the eccentricity reached the boundary and quadrant of mean value, the Mohammedan faith was established; another great empire came into being and increased very rapidly, like the change in the eccentricity. A hundred years hence, when the eccentricity will be at its minimum, this empire [i.e., Western Christiandom] too will complete its period. In our time, it is at its pinnacle from which equally swiftly, God willing, it will fall with a mighty crash. We look forward to the coming of our Lord Jesus Christ when the center of the eccentric reaches the other boundary of mean value, for it was in that position at the creation of the world.[63]

A century later the English astronomer Jeremiah Horrocks wrote that through a careful analysis of the motions of the planets "we may hence demonstrate the moment of the stars creation, & consequently of the worlds"; and yet another century later, John Machin, a disciple of Halley, believed that he had found a way "to settle . . . ye time when ye most eminent & ancient Constellations were first formed," using a variation he had observed in the obliquity of the ecliptic.[64] In other words, astronomers have long looked for celestial cycles based on some variation among the stars and planets; whenever the variation reached a minimum, maximum, or some "natural" turning point (a right angle, for instance) would be when the frame of nature would meet its end or, in the past, had had its beginning. At the very least it would be when the frame of nature underwent vast transformations. And if not *the* beginning and *the* end, then *a* beginning or *an* end in an endless series of successive worlds.

It was within the framework of this ancient tradition that debate over

the two rival conceptions, Hooke's mutable axis theory and the Newtonian cometary cosmogony, occurred. It lasted until Hooke's death.
Hooke was no doubt upset when, shortly after he began reading his lectures on earthquakes in 1686, John Wallis, in response to a request by
Halley, sent objections to Hooke's hypothesis to be read to the Royal Society. He had discussed Hooke's ideas with other members of the Oxford
Philosophical Society, Wallis wrote, and they felt no "cogent reason" to
believe what was "but a conjecture, of what may be, without any evidence
from observations that so it is"; the theory, he reported, was "too extravagant for us to admit." [65] To add to the blow, when Wallis's letter was introduced to the Royal Society,

> there was read a paragraph of Mr. NEWTON's mathematical philosophy
> [then in press] concerning the direction and position of the axis of a globe
> turning about itself, and shewing, that by the addition of some new matter
> on one side of a globe so turning, it shall make the axis of the globe change
> its position, and revolve about the point of the surface, where the new
> matter is added. It was thought, that the same translation of the axis might
> be occasioned in the globe of the earth by the blowing up of mountains by
> subterraneous fire.[66]

Halley's next letter to Wallis passed along Hooke's response to the Oxford Philosophical Society's objections and reported that he, Halley, had
received the third and last book of Newton's treatise, dealing with his
theory of the world. Halley recounted the main points it covered and
noted that "he falls in with Mr. Hook and makes the Earth of the shape
of a compressed sphaeroid, whose shortest diameter is the Axis, and determines the excess of the radius of the Equator above the semiaxe 17
miles, and from this quantity shows that the retrocession of the Equinoc-
tiall points does necessarily follow." [67] Thus even to *Halley,* it was Hooke
who had first proposed that the Earth was an oblate spheroid.

For his part, Hooke sniped as he could at Newton, making numerous
passing references in his lectures to "an *Hypothesis* I have formerly acquainted this Society with, somewhat of which Mr. *Newton* hath
Printed." [68] In an abstract of William Whiston's *New Theory of the Earth*
(1696), one of the first treatises based on the new Newtonian principles,
Hooke reported how Whiston thought it was "*NOW evident* that Gravity
(the most mechanicall affection of body) & which seems the most naturall, depends intirely on the constant & Efficatious and if you will the
Supernaturall and miraculous influence of almighty God"; he added pa-
renthetically and snidely to his audience at the Society: "tis well begun
and I conceive he need Say or Solve noe more for this will Solve all, and
all the other Solutio will be in significant & needlesse." [69]

Meanwhile, Hooke spent much of his *Lectures of Earthquakes* discussing what kinds of evidence the natural philosopher could use to determine the present and past shape and structure of the Earth. First, as mentioned above, the most accessible evidence was the beds of shells deposited in locations currently far removed from the sea. Hooke cited instance after instance of such anomalous shells, as well as examples of "figured stones," as they were called, or fossils, from species not native to the places where they were found or, for some, no longer found anywhere on Earth.[70] Second, he firmly believed that mythology often recounted great devastations of the semihistorical past, including much of what is found in Plato, Virgil, and Ovid: "This Mythologick History was a History of the Production, Ages, States and Changes that have formerly happened to the Earth, partly from the Theory of the best Philosophy; partly from Tradition, whether Oral or Written, and partly from undoubted History, for towards the latter end we find accounts of many things our Histories teach, as *Orpheus*, the *Trojan* War."[71]

Third, Hooke proposed a way to determine the rate at which the axis of the Earth did change, admitting, as Halley and others charged, that the inaccuracy of ancient observations made observed differences between ancient and modern latitudinal measurements of specific places (which would vary if the axis were mutable) too small to allow one to say with assurance that such alterations had actually taken place. Even though the changes might be slow and gradual, and any variation tiny, Hooke proposed that if very accurate measurements of the meridians and latitudes of given places were to be made a number of years apart with a long telescope,[72] it would be possible to detect the changes he firmly believed to exist.

Halley, too, sought measurements that would resolve the matter, coming before the Royal Society from time to time to conclude that measurements of the latitude of this location or that, taken two hundred or two thousand years apart, showed no significant difference. In the meantime he became involved in the plans for a naval expedition charged with measuring magnetic variation; by the time the expedition finally set sail in 1698, he was in command of a ship under royal patronage to seek confirmation of a general theory for the variation he had in mind.[73] Eventually Halley was to publish a chart showing curves drawn through all locations having the same variation, but his promised general theory of the variation went no further.[74] Even so, Halley was known to be "very fond" of the Earth's shells hypothesis on which his magnetic theory was based—despite the fact that a quite similar hypothesis had been advanced earlier by Hooke), and he was later to use the same idea to explain the phenomenon of the aurora borealis. Indeed, at Halley's direction, a portrait painted near the end of his life showed him pointing at a diagram of the Earth with six separate shells surrounding an inner core, apparently his proudest achievement.[75]

VI

One is impelled to ask what Newton's role was in all of this. How close were Halley's views to his? And how much of Newton's advice, encouragement, or even planning are we justified in surmising contributed to Halley's work on the internal structure and changing celestial orientation of the Earth? The evidence, though only conjectural, is compelling, and suggests that Newton was quite involved. First is the fact that Halley's initial paper criticizing Hooke's theory and suggesting his own alternative conception was delivered before the Royal Society in February 1686/87, in the middle of his editing the *Principia*. It had been two months since Hooke had begun his own lectures on earthquakes and some ten months since Hooke had first challenged Newton's priority— for Halley, ten very delicate months as he struggled to keep Newton from withholding all or part of the "divine Treatise"[76] from publication in his rage over Hooke's "pretences."[77] It would have been highly unlikely at that time and in such circumstances for the otherwise diplomatic Halley to have opposed Hooke's hypothesis without Newton's encouragement or, at the very least, permission.[78] We do know of at least one visit by Halley to Newton during the ten months after Hooke issued his challenge.[79] At that time, if I may be permitted to conjecture, the two men probably discussed the weaknesses of Hooke's "excellent System." It would have been then that a response could have been planned.

Second, it became Newton's particular style, within a few years of the *Principia*'s publication, to use his growing coterie of young disciples to hint at some of his more speculative notions, at times allowing them to publish these ideas as their own and having them fight his battles with detractors or philosophers who raised rival claims.[80] With two of his closest disciples, William Whiston and David Gregory, men who most self-consciously took on the mantle of propagating a particularly Newtonian approach to natural philosophy, it was, significantly, comets and their cosmic role that Newton specifically discussed at great length; and both men, Whiston in his *New Theory of the Earth* and Gregory in his *Astronomiae Physicae & Geometricae Elementa* (1702), wrote extensively on those strange members of the solar system.[81]

Although Whiston made a point of disagreeing with Halley's "great good Will towards discovering the Age of the World to be greater than the *Bible* gives it,"[82] his *New Theory* bore so much resemblance to Halley's hypothesis of a comet wrecking a former world that when Halley's first paper on the deluge was finally published thirty years after its delivery as a lecture to the Society, a note was appended: "Mr. Whiston's new theory of the earth was not published 'till about a year and half after the date of this paper."[83] Whiston took Halley's hypothesis about the vast changes a terrestrial impact (or even the close passage) of a comet might cause to the Earth and greatly extended it: a comet *was* the primitive chaos out of which, as in *Genesis,* the world arose; a comet no doubt *had* caused the deluge, as Halley initially proposed, and another would bring on the Earth's conflagration, following which the Earth itself would likely become a comet; and additionally, a comet accounted for the physical changes that the Earth had undergone after the Fall, when paradise vanished.[84] Whiston dedicated his book to Newton, whom he had met two years previously and on whose principles the treatise was explicitly based, even to being arranged in sections containing self-described "postulates," "hypotheses," "phenomena," "solutions," and "corollaries"; the younger man had given the manuscript to "Sir Isaac *Newton* himself . . . who well approved of it."[85] A short time later, Newton resigned as Lucasian Professor at Cambridge and named Whiston as his successor.

Gregory has left numerous memoranda of discussions he had with Newton in the 1690s and early 1700s in which the nature of comets figured prominently, many from the period prior to Gregory's publication of his treatise on astronomy.[86] Some of their discussion arose during Newton's work in the 1690s on an abortive second edition of the *Principia,* which Gregory was to edit; for the eventual second edition it was the theory of comets that particularly occupied Newton. When Gregory was preparing his own manuscript for publication, he noted that Newton had wanted some of what he told Gregory about the comet of 1680 to be left out of the work[87]—probably the speculations Newton was later, somewhat reluctantly, to admit to John Conduitt about that comet's falling into the Sun in the future, suddenly increasing the Sun's heat, and so causing a conflagration on Earth. Before he published his book, Gregory talked with Halley about the whole of it; as Thomas Hearne later reported, much of the work had been taken, without acknowledgment, from Halley.[88]

Supporting my thesis that Halley's 1687 critique of Hooke was made with Newton's concurrence, if not actual encouragement, is Newton's own use of comets as cosmogonic wonder-workers. In the first edition of the *Principia,* Newton had suggested that comets carried a kind of cosmic fuel capable of replenishing the life principle on Earth;[89] by the second edition, having clarified his analysis of cometary orbits, Newton speculated that occasionally a comet would fall into a star, thus replenishing its fuel and gravitating principle.[90] Indeed, by positing a kind of cosmic game of billiards involving comets, planets, and moons, with the impact or close approach of a comet being sufficient to change moons into planets or vice versa, Newton formulated an elaborate schema of planetary evolution, which he confided a few years before his death to John Conduitt, expanding on the notions he had previously discussed with Gregory:

> It was his *conjecture* (he would affirm nothing) [wrote Conduitt] that there was a sort of revolution in the heavenly bodies that the vapours & light ⟨gathered⟩ emitted by the sun which had their sediment in water and other matter, had gathered themselves by degrees in to a body & attracted more matter from the planets & at last made a secondary planett (viz one of those that go round another planet) & then by gathering to them & attracting more matter became a primary planet, & then by in creasing still became a comet wch after certain revolutions by coming nearer & nearer the sun had all its volatile parts condensed & became a matter set to recruit & replenish the Sun . . . & that would probably be the effect of the comet in 1680 sooner or later. . . . He could not say when this comet would drop in to the sun it might perhaps have 5 or 6 revolutions more first, but whenever it did it would ⟨occasion⟩ so much encrease the heat of the Sun that this earth would be burnt & no animals in *this* earth could live.[91]

Newton was clearly of the opinion that this Earth was a wreck of a former world that had undergone a devastation and had "visible marks of ruin upon it"—the very basis of Halley's 1694 discourse on the deluge.

VII

I argued above that after Halley lost the Savilian Professorship of Astronomy in 1691, he consciously directed much of his scientific research and writing to demonstrations of the Earth's finite age. I further pointed out that in 1703, when the Savilian Professorship of Geometry fell vacant, Halley succeeded in obtaining the position, but that in 1713, with the publication of the second edition of the *Principia,* suspicions of Halley's belief in the world's eternity resurfaced. In 1715 Halley turned again to the question of the world's duration, trying once more to find evidence in nature for its limited age—this time, however, with a subtle qualification that other unorthodox thinkers had used. Although an outright affirmation of the Earth's eternity was dangerous, much the same effect could be had by referring to the much older chronologies of the Chinese, Egyptians, or Babylonians. Halley wrote this paper, he claimed, "to refute the ancient Notion some have of late entertained, of the Eternity of all Things," but he could not help adding, "though perhaps by [my method] the World may be found much older than many have hitherto imagin'd."[92]

His method was simple, though it would require successive measurements, separated by great intervals of time (centuries perhaps), of the salinity of the seas. All that could be done for the present was to take an initial set of readings. Halley supposed that the seas derived their salinity from minerals carried to them by rivers. Differences in salinity measured over the years, assuming a constant rate of increase and supposing the seas originally to have been salt-free, would enable scientists simply to project back to the beginnings of the seas on the first Earth.[93]

Comparing ancient and modern observations of the declinations of the stars to find a rate for the precession of the equinoxes, Halley reported that he was surprised to find the latitudes of three of the brightest stars, Sirius, Arcturus, and Palieidium, contradicting "the supposed greater *Obliquity* of the *Ecliptick*," which most other stars seemed to confirm. Halley observed that, as the stars were "in all Probability the nearest to the Earth" (given their particular brightness), any motion of the "fixed" stars since the observations made in antiquity 1,800 years before would be discernible first of all in those three. In fact, in the case of Sirius Halley noted a significant change in latitude even since the time of Tycho Brahe, a little more than century earlier.[94] As early as his *Southern Catalogue* (1679), Halley had conjectured about the mutability of the supposedly immutable heavens.[95] What was mutable, his readers knew, could end, and "whatsoeuer shall haue an ende, the same also had beeginying of beeing," as Lambertus Danaeus had observed a century earlier.[96]

In the same year as his paper on oceanic salinity, Halley published a survey of the handful of novas observed in the previous century and a half. This "short history" began with the observation that the very first star catalogue, by Hipparchus, was said to have been prompted by the appearance of a new star. Halley lamented the lack of a record for *that* star, and stated his desire to leave a record of his own age's novas that future astronomers could use when viewing their own skies. Perhaps, Halley suggested, some of the novas of antiquity were identical with those of his own time, their successive appearances being part of another celestial cycle.[97]

Around 1720 rumors of Halley's "little or no Religion" again began to circulate, probably because Halley had renewed his speculations concerning past worlds.[98] He was then sixty-four years old. The next year he resigned as Secretary of the Royal Society and told a friend he hoped to live at least seven years longer, to finish a work he had begun.[99] Although he was actually to live a great deal longer than that, dying only in 1742 at the age of eighty-six, he must have been feeling the tug of mortality. In 1724, apparently feeling secure in his positions as Savilian Professor of Geometry and Astronomer Royal and encouraged by a committee of the

Royal Society, Halley was emboldened finally to publish his 1694 paper on the deluge and on the Earth's rise from the debris of a former world. Should a comet or other large body strike the Earth, readers of the *Philosophical Transactions* now learned, it would "occasion a differing length of the day and year, and change the axis of the globe according to the obliquity of the incidence of the stroke, and the direction thereof in relation to the former axis."[100] Halley published both his initial hypothesis, that such an impact could have caused the Noachian deluge, and his amended thesis, given a week later to the Society, that "a person whose judgment I have great reason to respect" had convinced him that a comet's impact "ought rather to be understood of those changes which might have happened to the earth in times before the creation, and which might possibly have reduced a former world to a chaos, out of whose ruins the present might be formed, than of the deluge."[101] Indeed, "once or oftner" such impacts had befallen the planet, helping "to bury deep from the surface those parts which by length of time are indurated into stony substances, and become unapt for vegetable production . . . : the ponderous matter in such a mixture subsiding first, and the lighter and finer mould remaining for the latter settling, to invest the exterior surface of the new world." It was through such disasters, Halley claimed, that the Earth was made fertile once more.[102] Appended to the published paper was a note explaining that the manuscript of the discourse read to the Royal Society thirty years earlier had been deposited in the archives of the Society, Halley having decided to forgo publication at the time because of apprehension over possible "*Censure of the Sacred Order.*"[103]

Over a period of several decades, I have argued, Halley returned over and over to certain themes and questions, adumbrated in a number of his most significant astronomical and physical papers (most broadly, concerning terrestrial magnetism, the age of the Earth, evidence of stellar cycles, and the role of comets in a vast cosmogonic mechanism regulating the solar system) that arose out of his dispute with Hooke and that constitute a leitmotif through much of what posterity has accepted as Halley's scientific legacy—though how much it is a specifically Halleyean legacy and how much a part of a more general Newtonian worldview that Halley shared remains to be clarified. In any case, it would appear that the publication of Halley's hypothesis about the comet and the deluge rekindled Newton's own speculations, for it was in March 1724/25, during a conversation with John Conduitt—in which, Conduitt later recalled, the aging Newton showed unusual clarity and strength of memory—that Newton gave the fullest explanation of his notion of comets as veritable magical celestial regulators (see above).[104] Newton thought, he told Conduitt, that "there may also be another Effect or Use of a Comet.

Namely, if a Comet passes near a Planet . . . it will so attract it that its
Orbit will be chang'd . . . whence the Planet's Period will also be chang'd.
But the Comet may also by its Attraction so disturb the Satellite, as to
make its Primary Planet and itself become a Primary Planet about the
Sun." [105] In 1694, after recording Newton's belief that comets are "destined [by God] for a use other than that of the planets," David Gregory
went on to note that the moons of Jupiter and Saturn "can take the
places of the Earth, Venus, Mars if they are destroyed, and be held in
reserve for a new Creation." [106] In his *Elements of Physical & Geometrical
Astronomy*, Gregory explained how comets passing close enough to a
planet or moon could drastically change its orbit and period, in some instances even making a moon leave its planet, as Newton was to tell Conduitt, to orbit the Sun as a new planet. [107]

Should a comet fall into the Sun, as Newton believed the comet of
1680–81, after five or six more revolutions, would, it would "so much
encrease the heat of the Sun that this earth would be burnt," killing all
life. [108] Newton thought that the supernovas observed by Hipparchus,
Tycho, and Kepler must have been from comets falling into ordinary
stars. Since the Earth appeared to be built on the ruins of a former
world, such a catastrophe, moreover, had probably happened previously, which meant that the present inhabitants of our planet had resulted from a new creation. [109]

CONCLUSIONS

I hope I have succeeded in showing that Hooke did not shrink from Halley's challenge that he "put up" evidence for his claims against the *Principia*. In fact, he produced a substantial body of work, all aimed at tying
the Earth's shape to a complex cosmogony and general system of nature
involving the mutable axis of the Earth. I have argued that Halley (and
Newton) responded in kind, producing over the next several decades a
rival cometary cosmogony rooted in a mechanism that periodically
rendered more fertile and potent both Sun and Earth.

Having so far constructed the main strands of my paper from an as-
sortment of documents both published and unpublished, I wish to conclude with comments that are necessarily more conjectural. In brief,
what are we to make of these rival conceptions of the Earth? And what
are the final ramifications of Hooke's, as opposed to Halley's and Newton's, theories?

First, it is known that Hooke ran in occult circles (with John Aubrey
and John Beaumont, for example) and that he organized Rosicrucian
groups within the Royal Society. [110] His discourses are filled with refer-

ences to the mystic teachings of the Pythagoreans, to Plato's account of Atlantis, and to Ovid's narrative of pagan traditions.[111] But those were Newton's intellectual haunts as well, as P. M. Rattansi, J. E. McGuire, Richard S. Westfall, and Betty J. Teeter Dobbs have shown so well.[112] While preparing an outline for the preface to his treatise on astronomy, Gregory had many discussions with Halley and Newton, as I mentioned above, focusing on the astronomy, metaphysics, and theology of comets, and the beginning of his outline made the connection of the theory of comets to the central role he gave to the Pythagorean tradition quite clear: "1. The Pythagorean System, 2. the Vniversal gravity of bodys, 3. the [Circulation?] of Comets there ancient opinions lost & now revised."[113] It is apparent as well from Newton's comments to Conduitt in 1724/25 that Atlantis or similar terrestrial disasters were also the basis of his theory of the Earth.

To this degree, for all the differences between Hooke on the one side and Halley and Newton on the other—and I believe those differences were substantial and significant—this debate can be seen as an intramural fight, as two diverging interpretations of what would appear to be, broadly speaking, a common Pythagorean tradition.[114] While this inner dimension of the debate over the Earth may have been clear to the three men's contemporaries, who had just gone through passionate debates over Hermeticism and enthusiasm at the Restoration, it soon became lost; indeed, the magical aspects of Newtonianism—and of the scientific revolution—has only in the past three decades begun to come into the daylight.[115]

Second, I hope that the resemblance of Halley's and Newton's cometary cosmogony to the recent "Nemesis" hypotheses will be readily apparent. In their various forms, these hypotheses all postulate comets periodically raining down on the Earth and causing various terrestrial disasters, possibly including the disappearances of dinosaurs and other species. Traditionally, of course, comets were viewed as harbingers of disaster, and the historic legacy of Halley and Newton, who brought those "blazing stars" under the orderly and predictable governance of the laws of nature, has been seen as the exposure of such "ill-founded" beliefs as nonsense. Halley, for example, wrote that "one of the principal Uses of the Mathematical Sciences" was to undermine the "Superstition of the . . . Vulgar" by showing the true causes of unusual appearances. To this end, in 1715 when a rare solar eclipse occurred in London, he issued a broadsheet chart showing its extent, in order "that the suddain darkness wherein the Starrs will be visible about the Sun, may give no surprize to the People, who would, if unadvertized, be apt to look upon it as Ominous, and to Interpret it as portending evill to our Sovereign Lord King George and his Government, which God preserve."[116] Despite their well-known historical role, however, Halley and Newton themselves believed it quite likely that comets *had* caused worldwide disasters; the only real difference between the traditional view and their own was that with the rigors of Newton's laws and the new calculus that enabled philosophers to fix the elusive "rate of change," just *which* comets were likely to wreck the Earth could now theoretically be calculated. That knowledge, however, as Newton made clear to Conduitt, was to be reserved for a scientific elite. Conduitt wrote:

> I . . . told him I thought he owned there [the *Principia*] what wee had been talking about—viz. that the Comet would drop into the sun, & that fixed stars were recruited & replenished by Comets when they dropt in to them, & consequently the sun would be recruited too & asked him, why he would not own as freely what he thought of the Sun as well as what he thought of the fixed stars—he said that concerned us more, & laughing added he had said enough for people to know his meaning.[117]

The taming of comets thus accomplished, an important ground had been removed from under the "prognosticators," prophets, and other exponents of "enthusiasm." Helping to establish a critical ideological framework for the coming Restoration, Henry More, Newton's friend and teacher,[118] had branded enthusiasm the root cause of the late troubles of the Civil War and Commonwealth periods (when Newton was growing up)—insubordination in the army, regicide, abolition of the Church of England, seizure of property, not to mention group sexual activities—those excesses upon order, propriety, and property that flowered in Europe and England after the Reformation. More considered enthusiasm (literally meaning "filled with gods")[119] to be rooted in overly florid language, in imagination and ecstasy, in lustiness and effeminacy, and in ill-clad prophets hastily claiming divine inspiration for their words and actions. When, in his widely read and influential pamphlet *Enthusiasmus Triumphatus,* he sought out the philosophical foundations for enthusiasm, he found them in Paracelsian alchemy, "*the very prop of ancient Paganism,*" the followers of which believed that they saw God "in every object of their senses." Such "pantheistic" doctrines, however, were not far from Newton's own inner conceptions.[120]

Third, rather significant differences can be identified between the two rival camps I have portrayed, Hooke's (and Aubrey's) versus Halley's and Newton's. Although both sides accepted the possibility of large changes to the Earth's axis, there is an intriguing inversion in the way each imagined those changes to occur. For the Newtonians, clearly, and in this instance true to the dictates of mechanical philosophy, the axis would vary only if an *external* body, a comet or similar object, made an impact against the Earth. Depending on the angle of incidence, then, a cometary impact could result in *either* an Earth that revolved around the same axis as before but was now oriented toward a different place in the heavens *or* a whole new axis of rotation, one not only pointing elsewhere in space but also cutting through a different diameter of the globe than before—and thus, as Hooke had pointed out, giving rise to a new equator and a sudden terrestrial equatorial engorgement. In either case, the change to the axis was sudden, and the Earth itself acted largely as a passive body on which the impact fell.

Hooke's theory was more complex, since it allowed both for sudden transformations and for very slow change spanning eons. Thus in his *Lectures of Earthquakes* he detailed how a sizable earthquake could shift large masses of the Earth from one locus to another and alter the planet's axis in a short time, while at the same time proposing periodical and highly accurate measurements of the meridians and latitudes of locations on Earth to allow natural philosophers to investigate whether, over longer periods, the axis underwent motions not yet recognized, in a rotation whose period could be determined.[121] Most significantly, Hooke's proposed modes for a mutable axis came from events occurring *on* and *within* the Earth. In contrast to axial regulation by Newtonian comets, with Hooke the attention is focused on the dynamics of the living Earth, where overnight oceans might be raised to become continents and the mountains disappear beneath the seas, new species emerging as old ones disappear—a vital planet, whose awesome rumblings, huge eruptions, and wholesale transformations Hooke recounted with great respect in his *Lectures of Earthquakes*.[122] In other words, although Newton too, for most of his life, saw nature and the Earth as alive, Hooke's Earth could act more independently—in a word, was more lifelike—than Newton's entirely passive Earth. For Newton, cosmogonic change came from the sky—where God was.

I have argued elsewhere that the question of whether the Earth is a living organism or a lump of dead matter—the question, that is, that lay at the heart of the mid-seventeenth-century battle between the Hermetic and other magical philosophies on the one hand and the emerging mechanical philosophy on the other—was a crucial social issue for the age, and that it played a particularly critical role in the development of Newton's thought.[123] Economically and socially, vast changes were then occurring in England that entailed wholesale assaults on the land and its "resources"; large-scale mining, deforestation on a massive scale, extensive draining of the fens, and widespread enclosure of the commons in the late sixteenth and seventeenth centuries meant overwhelming changes to the ways people lived and posed profound questions about the use of the Earth and her creatures. Traditional peasant beliefs that the Earth is alive proved formidable barriers to the wholesale exploitation of land, minerals, woods, waters, and animals (including humans) that early English capitalism demanded. Additionally, engaged in the early phase of their drawn-out project of conquering and ruling over most of the rest of the world, Europeans nearly everywhere found cultures based, as in their own peasantry, on the ideology of magic. To "civilize" the non-European lands it was necessary to stamp out wildness both at home and abroad, and for that purpose a mechanical vision of nature was essential. The debates between Hooke and Halley and Newton over the transformations of the Earth's axis, by agents either *internal* or *external,* constitute a major chapter in that larger social history of how the physical world is to be felt or understood—and thus of how the Earth is to be treated. As we know, by the end of the century, with the exception of a few opposing voices such as Leibniz's and Spinoza's, natural philosophers were in close agreement in defining the world in terms of its passivity, just like Newton's Earth. In the arid intellectual soil of the Europe of succeeding centuries, where, owing to the mechanical philosophy, barrenness was seen to be a virtue, the ideas of Spinoza and Leibniz never really took root.

The paradox, of course, is how strikingly the vision of a passive world that emerged from the eighteenth-century Newtonian victory in natural philosophy diverged from Newton's own vision, of a world constituted of "passive" matter that is always closely associated with "active" forces. But we cannot blame the discrepancy on external censorship alone. "Not fit to be printed" reflected, after all, the verdict not just of Dr. Pellet, Newton's literary executor, after he had pored over Newton's alchemical and magical manuscripts [124]—it was also Newton's own verdict regarding this material: a verdict he came to, we should remember, in an England experiencing wide-ranging economic, social, and philosophical controversies.

NOTES

1. The title quotations are from Newton to Halley, 20 June 1686, in *The Correspondence of Isaac Newton,* edited by H. W. Turnbull et al. (Cambridge: Cambridge University Press, 1959–77), 2:437. This episode and the surrounding controversy have been discussed by numerous scholars, among them Philip E. B. Jourdain, "Robert Hooke as a Precursor of Newton," *The Monist* 23 (1913): 353–84; Louise Diehl Patterson, "Hooke's Gravitation Theory and Its Influence on Newton," *Isis* 40 (1949): 327–41 and 41 (1950): 32–45; J. A. Lohne, "Hooke *versus* Newton: An Analysis of the Documents in the Case on Free Fall and Planetary Motion," *Centaurus* 7 (1960): 6–52; A. R. Hall, "Two Unpublished Lectures of Robert Hooke," *Isis* 42 (1951): 219–30; Richard S. Westfall, *Never at Rest: A Biography of Isaac Newton* (Cambridge: Cambridge University Press, 1983), 382ff., 446–52; Alexandre Koyré, "An Unpublished Letter of Robert Hooke to Isaac

Newton," in *Newtonian Studies* (London: Chapman & Hall, 1965); Frank E. Manuel, *A Portrait of Isaac Newton* (Cambridge, Mass.: Harvard University Press, 1968), chap. 8; and Richard S. Westfall, introduction to the 1969 reprint of Robert Hooke's *Posthumous Works . . . Containing His Cutlerian Lectures, and Other Discourses Read at the Meetings of the Illustrious Royal Society. In Which I. The Present Deficiency of Natural Philosophy Is Discoursed Of, with the Methods of Rendering It More Certain and Beneficial. II. The Nature, Motion and Effects of Light Are Treated of, Particularly That of the Sun and Comets. III. An Hypothetical Explication of Memory; How the Organs Made Use of By the Mind in Its Operation May Be Mechanically Understood. IV. An Hypothesis and Explication of the Cause of Gravity, or Gravitation, Magnetism, &c. V. Discourses of Earthquakes, Their Causes and Effects, and Histories of Several, To Which Are Annext, Physical Explications of Several of the Fables in Ovid's Metamorphoses, Very Different from Other Mythologick Interpreters. VI. Lectures for Improving Navigation and Astronomy, with the Descriptions of Several New and Useful Instruments and Contrivances; the Whole Full of Curious Disquisitions and Experiments . . .*, ed. Richard Waller (London, 1705; reprint New York and London: Johnson Reprint Corp., 1967). See also I. Bernard Cohen, "The *Principia*, Universal Gravitation, and the 'Newtonian Style' in Relation to the Newtonian Revolution in Science: Notes on the Occasion of the 250th Anniversary of Newton's Death," in *Contemporary Newtonian Research*, ed. Zev Bechler (Dordrecht: D. Reidel, 1982).

2. The phrase is Bernard de Fontenelle's in his *Elogium of Sir Isaac Newton* (London, 1728), in *Isaac Newton's Papers and Letters on Natural Philosophy*, ed. I. Bernard Cohen (Cambridge, Mass.: Harvard University Press, 1958), 450.

3. It *was* the inverse square law that Halley specified in his letter to Newton of 22 May 1686 announcing Hooke's claims (in Newton, *Correspondence* 2:431).

4. Hooke, *Posthumous Works*, 334; cf. 371.

5. Halley to Newton, 29 June 1686, in Newton, *Correspondence* 2:442.

6. Richard S. Westfall, introduction to Hooke, *Posthumous Works*, xxii.

7. Halley to Newton, 29 June 1686, in Newton, *Correspondence* 2:442.

8. Halley to Newton, 14 October 1686, in Newton, *Correspondence* 2:452; Newton to Halley, 13 February 1686/87, ibid., 464; Halley to Newton, 24 February [1687], ibid., 469; Newton to Halley, 1 March 1687, ibid., 470–71; Westfall, *Never at Rest*, 458, 465–66.

9. Westfall, *Never at Rest*, 465.

10. Halley to Newton, 5 July 1687, in Newton, *Correspondence* 2:481–82; Westfall, *Never at Rest*, 468.

11. I have arrived at these dates for Hooke's discourses by comparing the *Lectures of Earthquakes* in *Posthumous Works* with Thomas Birch, *The History of the Royal Society . . .*, 4 vols. (London: Millar, 1756–57); the *Journal Books* of the Royal Society; Hooke's diary and papers, in R. T. Gunther, *Early Science in Oxford*, vols. 6–8 and 10 (Oxford: private printing, 1930–35); portions of the *Diary*, edited by H. W. Robinson and W. Adams (London, 1935); and Benjamin Martin, *Biographia Philosophia. Being an Account of the Lives* [and] *Writings . . . of . . . Philosophers and Mathematicians . . .* (London, 1764). For Hooke's growing decline, see Iohn Ward, *Lives of the Professors of Gresham College* (London, 1740), 185–88; and Martin, *Biographia Philosophia*, 331.

12. Hooke, *Posthumous Works*, 329, 330. There is some ambiguity over the date of this first discourse; it might have been given on 8 December.

13. Ibid., 331, 337.

14. Ibid., 338.

15. Ibid., 290, 297–98, 313, 343, 345.

16. Ibid., 279–328.

17. Henry Gellibrand, *Discovrse Mathematical on the Variation of the Magneticall Needle together with Its Admirable Diminution Lately Discovered* (London, 1635), 3, 6–7, 20–[22]; and "Halley," in *Biographia Britannica: Or, the Lives of the Most Eminent Persons Who Have Flourished in Great Britain and Ireland, from the Earliest Ages, Down to the Present Times* (London, 1747–66), 4:2501.

18. "Halley" in *Biographia Britannica* 4:2501.

19. *Philosophical Transactions of the Royal Society*, no. 64 (1670): 2060–61.

20. Henry Bond, *The Longitude Found; or, A Treatise Shewing an Easie and Speedy Way . . . To Find the Longitude, Having but the Latitude of the Place, and the Inclination of the Magnetical Inclinatorie Needle* (London, 1676), 5–9.

21. Hooke, "Longitude," Trinity College Library, Cambridge, MS. o.11a 1[8] fol. 6r.

22. Richard Waller, "The Life of Dr. Robert Hooke," in *Posthumous Works*, xix; Ward, *Lives of the Gresham Professors*, 177; and "Halley," in *Biographia Britannica* 4:2500.

23. Hooke, *Posthumous Works*, 326.

24. Ibid., 313–14, 326–27, 328.

25. Ibid., 321–22.

26. Ibid., 322; emphasis added.

27. Ibid., 322, 325–26.

28. Ibid., 327, 328.

29. Ibid., 349.

30. Birch, *The History of the Royal Society* 4:521–22, for 26 January 1687.

31. Westfall, *Never at Rest*, 451. Westfall emphasizes, as well he should, that Newton's was a *mathematical* system, which Hooke's was only to a much more limited degree.

32. John Aubrey and Hooke to Anthony à Wood, 15 September 1689, in Newton, *Correspondence* 3:42. Aubrey took Hooke's theory of the Earth and used it as the basis for the first part of his natural history of Wiltshire. When the naturalist John Ray, who had been sent the manuscript of Aubrey's work, wrote back taking offense at Aubrey's hypothesis of the newly created Earth and calling it "but a Digression, & aliene from your subject," Aubrey wrote on the letter: "This Hypothesis is Mr. Hooks. I say so, and it is the best thing in the Book; it (indeed) does interfere w[it]h y[e] 1 chap. of Genesis" (Aubrey, *The Natural History of Wilts*, Bodleian Library, Oxford, MS. Aubrey 1; and John Ray, *Further Correspondence of John Ray*, ed. Robert W. T. Gunther [London: Printed for the Royal Society, 1928], 169–71: annotation on Ray's letter to Aubrey of 7[br] 22, [16]91).

33. It is tempting to note that Newton's repeated fears of being "seduced" into philosophical controversy, as well as his paranoid suspicions during his breakdown of 1693 that his friend John Locke was trying to "embroil me wth woemen" (Newton to Locke, 16 September 1693, in *Correspondence* 3:280), re-

flect a profound sexual anxiety, for which the adventuresome should consult Manuel's engaging *Portrait of Isaac Newton,* esp. chap. 9.

34. Hooke, *Posthumous Works,* 357: lecture of 9 February 1687.

35. [Halley], "The Obliquity of the Ecliptick and Elevation of the Pole Continue Unaltered," *Philosophical Transactions,* no. 190 (1687), in *The Philosophical Transactions and Collections . . . Abridged . . . ,* ed. John Lowthorp, 5th ed. (London, 1749), 1:*264–65 (hereafter cited as *PTA*).

36. Ibid.

37. Ibid., 1:*263–65; in the version of the paper deposited at the Royal Society, the word *intelligent* was added as an afterthought (Royal Society, *Classified Papers,* vol. 21, no. 19).

38. Westfall, *Never at Rest,* 435, 460–62; Halley clearly saw Newton's treatment of comets to be crucial to his treatise (Halley to Newton, 29 June 1686 and 5 April 1687, in Newton, *Correspondence* 2:443, 474; Halley to Wallis, 9 April 1687, ibid., 475n.4). See also *Isaac Newton's Mathematical Principles of Natural Philosophy and His System of the World,* trans. Andrew Motte, ed. Florian Cajori (Berkeley and Los Angeles: University of California Press, 1960), 491ff.; hereafter cited as *Principia* (Motte-Cajori).

39. See below, as well as my "Newton and the Cyclical Cosmos: Providence and the Mechanical Philosophy," *Journal of the History of Ideas* 28 (1967): 325–46.

40. Halley to Newton, 5 April 1687, in Newton, *Correspondence* 2:474. See, for example, *Principia* (Motte-Cajori), 529–30; Newton, *Opticks, or A Treatise of the Reflections, Refractions, Inflections, and Colours of Light* (New York: Dover, 1952), 369; Kubrin, "Newton and the Cyclical Cosmos," 340.

41. *Correspondence and Papers of Edmond Halley,* ed. Eugene Fairfield MacPike (London: Taylor & Francis, 1937), app. 3, p. 185.

42. Halley, "Theory of the Magnetical Variation," *Philosophical Transactions,* no. 148 (1683), in *PTA* 2:616.

43. Halley, "An Account of the Cause of the Change in the Variation of the Magnetical Needle," *Philosophical Transactions,* no. 175 (1692), in *PTA* 2:618–23.

44. Royal Society, *Journal Book,* 12 December 1692, in Halley, *Correspondence and Papers,* 234; Halley, "Some Considerations About the Cause of the Universal Deluge," *Philosophical Transactions,* no. 383 (1724), in *PTA,* ed. Mr. Reid and John Gray (London, 1733), 6(2):41.

45. Halley, "Farther Thoughts on the Same Subject," *Philosophical Transactions,* no. 383 (1724), in *PTA* 6(2):41; Royal Society, *Journal Book,* 19 December 1694, omitted from *Correspondence and Papers.* For the printing of the discourse, see below.

46. Halley to Abraham Hill, 22 June 1691, in *Correspondence and Papers,* 88.

47. See, for example, Robert Fleming, *A Discourse on Earthquakes, as Supernatural and Premonitory Signs to a Nation Especially as to What Occurred in the Year 1692* (London, 1693); Gerald Straka, *Anglican Reactions to the Revolution of 1688* (Madison: State Historical Society of Wisconsin, 1962), 69.

48. David Ogg, *England in the Reign of James II and William III* (Oxford: Clarendon Press, 1955), 360–63, 366.

49. Halley, *Correspondence and Papers,* app. 18, pp. 268–69.

50. For the tradition in seventeenth-century England of an eternal Earth, see

my 1968 Cornell dissertation, "Providence and the Mechanical Philosophy: The Creation and Dissolution of the World in Newtonian Thought. A Study of the Relations of Science and Religion in Seventeenth Century England," chap. 2. The Blount work referred to was his *Oracles of Reason* (London, 1693). See also Kubrin, "Newton and the Cyclical Cosmos."

51. Straka, *Anglican Reactions*, 60–61.

52. See my discussion of Tillotson in "Providence and the Mechanical Philosophy," 50–52.

53. Royal Society, *Journal Book*, 19 October 1692, in Halley, *Correspondence and Papers*, 229.

54. Halley, "An Account of the Cause of the Change in the Variation of the Magnetical Needle," in *PTA* 2:623; Flamsteed to Newton, 25 October 1694, Letter 14, Cambridge University Library, Add. MS. 2979.

55. Royal Society, *Journal Book*, 31 October 1694; omitted from *Correspondence and Papers*.

56. Halley, "Some Account of the Ancient State of the City of Palmyra; with Short Remarks on the Inscriptions Found There," *Philosophical Transactions* 19 (1695): 160–75; Angus Armitage, *Edmond Halley* (London: Thomas Nelson & Sons, 1966), 106–7. Cf. British Museum Add. MS. 4478b, fol. 146v.

57. Royal Society, *Journal Book*, 18 October 1693, in Halley, *Correspondence and Papers*, 232.

58. S. J. Rigaud, *A Defense of Halley Against the Charge of Infidelity* (Oxford, 1844), 18; Gregory was recommended by Newton. See also Chapter 1, this volume.

59. The different Latin versions of the "Ode" are given in appendix 5 of *Correspondence and Papers;* my translation was aided by Donald Kagan. For a discussion, see my "Providence and the Mechanical Philosophy," chap. 9; and W. R. Albury, "Halley's Ode on the *Principia* of Newton and the Epicurean Revival in England," *Journal of the History of Ideas*, 39 (1978): 24–43. John Keill wrote to Charlett that Bentley had "made bold to emend" Halley's verses, and that the changes "are not near so good as the original: some of them are intolerable" (Halley, *Correspondence and Papers*, 204). It was Bentley, then chaplain to Bishop Stillingfleet, who on behalf of Archbishop Tillotson had questioned Halley concerning his religious beliefs in 1691 (ibid., 264).

60. Words and phrases in angled brackets in this and subsequent quotations indicate expressions crossed out in manuscript version.

61. Memorandum by John Conduitt, King's College Library, Cambridge, MS. Keynes 30, no. 7; *Correspondence and Papers*, 206.

62. A similar distinction was made in the Middle Ages between the eternity of God and the coeternity of the created angels (Ernst Kantorowicz, *The King's Two Bodies: A Study in Medieval Political Theology* [Princeton: Princeton University Press, 1957], 280–81). Following the publication of Francis Baily's *An Account of the Revd John Flamsteed, the First Astronomer Royal . . .* (London: Printed for the Lords Commissioners of the Admiralty, 1835), Halley's reputed infidelity became the subject of a number of books and articles: S. J. Rigaud, *A Defense of Halley;* Anon., "On Whiston, Halley, and the Quarterly Reviewer of the 'Account of Flamsteed,'" *Philosophical Magazine*, 3d ser., 8 (1836): 225–26; S. J. Rigaud, "A

Letter . . . to the Secretary, on the Character of Halley," *Monthly Notices of the Royal Astronomical Society* 6 (1845): 204–5; S. P. Rigaud, "Observations on a Note Respecting Mr. Whewell," *Philosophical Magazine*, 3d ser., 8 (1836): 218–25; William Whewell, "Remarks on a Note on a Pamphlet . . . 'Newton and Flamsteed,'" *Philosophical Magazine*, 3d ser., 8 (1836): 211–18. Much of the material can be found in appendix 18, "Halley's Character and Personality," in Halley, *Correspondence and Papers*. Halley's contemporaries Flamsteed and Thomas Hearne frequently complained about Halley's lack of religion; see, for example, Hearne, *Remarks and Collections (25 May 1710–14 December 1712)*, ed. C. E. Doble (Oxford: Clarendon Press, 1889), 3:472–73.

63. John Wallis to Halley, 4 March 1687, Bodleian Library, Oxford, MS. Ashmole 1813B fols. 327v–28v. Wallis was later to change his mind, writing on 23 May 1702 to Halley that "it is very possible that the *Poles* of the Earth, may, in time, suffer some little Variation" (Royal Society, MS. Letters W.2, no. 67). For some of the correspondence of Wallis, see A. J. Turner, "Hooke's Theory of the Earth's Axial Displacement: Some Contemporary Opinion," *British Journal for the History of Science* 7 (1974): 166–70.

64. Birch, *History of the Royal Society* 4:528.

65. Halley to Wallis, 9 April 1687, in *Correspondence and Papers*, 80.

66. Hooke, *Posthumous Works*, 377. Cf. Hall, "Two Unpublished Lectures," 224.

67. Hooke, "Abstract of Whiston's Theory of the Earth," Royal Society, *Classified Papers*, vol. 20, no. 85. Read on 8 July 1696, this paper hit at the soft white underbelly of the Newtonian ontology—gravitational attraction and the "active principles" Newton saw in relation to that and other forces, those characteristic and problematic constructs on which the Newtonian physical system was built. For most of his life Newton himself believed the forces to arise from a quality of nature best seen in its "lifeful" aspects. "We cannot say that all Nature is not alive," Newton once wrote, his syntax reflecting the hesitancy that caused him to drop this sentence from the published *Opticks* for which it was drafted. The keys to this life force he sought in alchemy, as I believe Westfall's masterful *Never at Rest* shows so clearly. See my discussion in "Newton's Inside Out! Magic, Class Struggle, and the Rise of Mechanism in the West," in *The Analytic Spirit: Essays in the History of Science in Honor of Henry Guerlac*, ed. Harry Woolf (Ithaca, N.Y.: Cornell University Press, 1981); "Newton and the Cyclical Cosmos"; and "Providence and the Mechanical Philosophy." Westfall gives a helpful bibliography; see also Henry Guerlac, "Newton et Epicure" and "Francis Hauksbee: Experimenteur au profit de Newton," in his *Essays and Papers in the History of Modern Science* (Baltimore: Johns Hopkins University Press, 1977), and Henry Guerlac, "Sir Isaac and the Ingenious Mr. Hauksbee," in *Mélanges Alexandre Koyré*, 2 vols. (Paris: Hermann, 1964), 2:22–53; also, Koyré, *Newtonian Studies;* Betty Jo Teeter Dobbs, *The Foundations of Newton's Alchemy, or "The Hunting of the Greene Lyon,"* (Cambridge: Cambridge University Press, 1983); J. E. McGuire and P. M. Rattansi, "Newton and the 'Pipes of Pan,'" *Notes and Records of the Royal Society of London* 21 (1966): 108–43; J. E. McGuire, "Body and Void in Newton's De Mundi Systemate: Some New Sources," *Archive for History of Exact Sciences* 3 (1966): 206–48; J. E. McGuire, "Force, Active Principles, and Newton's Invisible Realm,"

Ambix 15 (1968): 154–208; Ernan McMullin, *Matter and Activity in Newton* (Notre Dame, Ind.: University of Notre Dame Press, 1977). Finally, see Carolyn Merchant, *The Death of Nature: Women, Ecology, and the Scientific Revolution* (San Francisco: Harper & Row, 1980); Morris Berman, *The Reenchantment of the World* (Ithaca, N.Y.: Cornell University Press, 1981); and Starhawk, *Dreaming the Dark: Magic, Sex, and Politics* (Boston: Beacon Press, 1982). I have benefited from conversations with the last three authors as well. I was first introduced to the problem of Newton and the sources of activity in matter in a seminar at Cornell on "Newton's Optics" given by Guerlac.

To solve the problems of the solar system and cosmos, Newton in effect had to begin with the mechanical philosophy of "matter and motion" only to toss it to the winds, thus reanimating the universe which the mechanical philosophy of the Restoration had just succeeded in defining as dead. This contradiction inherent in Newton's physics, which acted almost like a philosophical running sore, was certainly a source of constant puzzlement and creativity throughout his life, from his student notebook *Qu[a]estiones quaedam philosophia* (Cambridge University Library, Add. MS. 3996) to his later letters to Boyle and Oldenburg (in *Newton's Papers and Letters on Natural Philosophy*), "De Gravitatione et aequipondio fluidorum" (in Newton, *Unpublished Scientific Papers*, ed. A. Rupert Hall and Marie Boas Hall [Cambridge: Cambridge University Press, 1962]), and especially his unpublished alchemical papers and the revealing unpublished drafts for the Queries (Cambridge University Library, MS. 3970, fols. 619r–620v, 254r).

Early in the 1690s (when, paradoxically, he was also most caught up in alchemy, according to Westfall), Newton flirted with a mechanical interpretation of gravitational attraction, and was said to have been briefly attracted to the hypothesis of Fatio de Duillier, the Swiss emigré "enthusiast" and an early disciple of Newton, with whom Newton was enamored until shortly before his 1693 breakdown. Newton's return to an ethereal hypothesis in the 1717 *Opticks* has been seen as a second turn to mechancial agents, but J. E. McGuire disputes this in his "Neoplatonism and Active Principles: Newton and the *Corpus Hermeticum*," in *Hermeticism and the Scientific Revolution* (Los Angeles: University of California Press, 1977). See note 112 below. Newton's interest in Fatio's hypothesis, even to the point of considering a second edition of the *Principia* with a preface based on Fatio's conception, is found in a memorandum by David Gregory, in Newton, *Correspondence* 3 : 191—but note that the last line of this memo was added later, for it is written in a different ink and off to the side (28 December 1691, Royal Society MS. Gregory, fol. 71v). Fatio's hypothesis has been reprinted, along with a commentary, by Bernard Gagnebin in *Notes and Records of the Royal Society* 6 (1949): 106–60.

68. Hooke, *Posthumous Works*, 291, 327, 333.

69. Ibid., 384–85, 372, 374.

70. Ibid., 354, 356–59; a sixty- or one-hundred-foot telescope should suffice, Hooke believed (Halley to Wallis, 15 February 1687, in *Correspondence and Papers*, 78, 81; Royal Society, *Journal Book*, 2, 9 February and 9 March 1688).

71. "Halley," in *Biographia Britannica* 4 : 2502; Armitage, *Edmond Halley*, chap. 10.

72. Halley to Burchett, 30 March 1700, in *Correspondence and Papers*, 113.

73. "Edmond Halley," in *Biographia Britannica* 4:2502; see the frontispiece in *Correspondence and Papers*. Halley, "An Account of the Late Surprising Appearance of the Lights Seen in the Air, on the Sixth of March Last; with an Attempt To Explain the Principal Phenomena thereof," *Philosophical Transactions*, no. 347 (1716): 427–28.

74. Halley to Newton, 5 April 1687, in Newton, *Correspondence* 2:473.

75. Newton to Halley, 20 June 1686, ibid., 2:437.

76. For the relations of the two men, see Westfall, *Never at Rest*, 449; and Manuel, *Portrait of Isaac Newton*, 273.

77. The visit was mentioned in a letter from Newton to Flamsteed, 3 September 1686, as having recently occurred (Westfall, *Never at Rest*, 458; and Newton, *Correspondence* 2:448).

78. For Newton's relations with his disciples, see Manuel, *Portrait of Isaac Newton*, 268, 272ff.; and Westfall, *Never at Rest*. The best example of the free rein Newton at times gave his young disciples occurred when Roger Cotes was helping to edit the long-awaited second edition of the *Principia*. After some correspondence regarding Cotes's important preface had gone back and forth, Newton wrote to him: "If you write any further Preface I must not see it, for I find that I shall be examined about it" (*Correspondence of Sir Isaac Newton and Professor Cotes*, ed. J. Edleston [London: Frank Cass & Co., 1969; facsimile of 1850 ed.], 157).

79. David Gregory, *Elements of Physical and Geometrical Astronomy*, 2d ed. (London, 1726), 2:694–713.

80. William Whiston, *Six Dissertations . . .* (London, 1734), 192.

81. Halley, "Farther Thoughts on the Same Subject," 41.

82. William Whiston, *A New Theory of the Earth, from the Original to the Consummation of All Things*, 5th ed. (London, 1737), Book 1, 54–55; Book 2, 73, 85; Book 4, 296–303, 350–51, 373–75, 381ff., 451.

83. *Memoirs of the Life and Writings of William Whiston . . .* (London, 1749), 1:43.

84. For example, memorandum by Gregory, March 1703, in Newton, *Correspondence* 4:402.

85. Memorandum by Gregory, 21 May 1701, ibid., 4:354–55. Royal Society MS. Gregory, fols. 87–88r.

86. Thomas Hearne, in Bodleian Library, Oxford, MS. Rigaud 10, fol. 6r.

87. Newton, *Philosophiae Naturalis Principia Mathematica*, 1st ed. (London, 1687), 506.

88. Newton, *Philosophiae Naturalis Principia Mathematica*, 2d ed. (Cambridge, 1713), 481.

89. Memorandum by John Conduitt, King's College Library, Cambridge, MS. Keynes 130, no. 11. The memorandum has been printed with some changes in Edmund Turnor, *Collections for the History of the Town and Soke of Grantham, Containing Authentic Memoirs of Sir Isaac Newton* (London, 1806), 172–73.

90. Halley, "A Short Account of the Cause of the Saltness of the Ocean and of the Several Lakes that Emit No Rivers; with a Proposal, by Help Thereof, To Discover the Age of the World," *Philosophical Transactions*, no. 344 (1715), in *PTA* 5(2): 218–19.

91. Ibid., 216–18.

92. Rheticus, *Narratio prima,* in *Three Copernican Treatises,* ed. Edward Rosen (New York: Dover, 1959), 121–22.

93. Jeremiah Horrox, *Philosophical Exercises,* Bodleian Library, Oxford, MS. Rigaud 14, fols. 22–24; John Machin, "On the Obliquity of the Ecliptic," read before the Royal Society, 22 February 1733, Royal Society, *Classified Papers,* vol. 8(2), art. 69, fol. 136r.

94. Halley, "Change of the Latitudes of Some of the Fixt Stars," *Philosophical Transactions,* no. 355 (1718), in *PTA* 4(1): 227–28.

95. "Halley," in *Biographia Britannica* 4:2496–97.

96. Lambertus Danaeus, *The Wonderfull VVoorkmanship of the World wherein Is Conteined an Excellent Discourse of Christian Naturall Philosophie, Concernyng the Forme, Knowledge, and Vse of All Things Created: Specially Gathered out of the Fountaine of Holy Scryptures* . . . , trans, T[homas] T[wyne] (London, 1578), 32.

97. Halley, "A Short History of the Several New-Stars That Have Appear'd within These 150 Years," *Philosophical Transactions,* no. 347 (1716), in *PTA* 4(1): 224–25.

98. The description is Thomas Hearne's and is quoted in appendix 18, Halley, *Correspondence and Papers,* 269. See Rigaud, *Defence of Halley,* 28. Halley referred in passing to eternal duration in a 1720 paper, "Of the Infinity of the Sphere of Fix'd Stars," *Philosophical Transactions,* no. 346 (1720): 23.

99. Thomas Hearne, *Remarks and Collections* (Oxford: Printed for the Oxford Historical Society at the Clarendon Press, 1906), 7:242, 305.

100. Halley, "Of the Cause of the Universal Deluge," *Philosophical Transactions,* no. 383 (1724), in *PTA* 6(2): 40–41.

101. Halley, "Farther Thoughts on the Same Subject," 41. It is hard not to suspect that the person whose judgment Halley followed was Newton himself.

102. Ibid. The concern for renewing the Earth's fertility is shared by Hooke and Newton; see Hooke, *Posthumous Works,* 322, 348, 424–27; and Kubrin, "Newton and the Cyclical Cosmos."

103. Halley, "Farther Thoughts on the Same Subject," *Philosophical Transactions,* no. 383 (1724): 125; not in *PTA.*

104. Westfall, *Never at Rest,* 863.

105. Memorandum by John Conduitt, King's College Library, Cambridge, MS. Keynes 130, no. 11; see note 89 above.

106. Memorandum by David Gregory, 5–7 May 1694, in Newton, *Correspondence* 3:336.

107. Gregory, *Elements of Physical and Geometrical Astronomy* 2:853.

108. Memorandum by John Conduitt, King's College Library, Cambridge, MS. Keynes 130, no. 11; cf. the theory announced by the astronomer Thomas Gold in the *London Times* of 27 September 1969.

109. Memorandum by Conduitt, King's College Library, Cambridge, MS. Keynes 130, no. 11.

110. Private communication from Robert Kargon, for whose help I am especially grateful. See also my "Providence and the Mechanical Philosophy"; M. 'Espinasse, *Robert Hooke* (Berkeley and Los Angeles: University of California Press, 1962), 118; and Hooke, *Diary,* 202 (18 December 1675) and 238–39 (24, 29 June and 1 July 1676).

111. Hooke, *Posthumous Works*, 331, 308, 317 (on standing stones), 319–20, 141, 402–3; Manuel, *Portrait of Newton*, 137, 142; and Royal Society, *Journal Book*, 4 January and 29 February 1688.

112. While Westfall has changed from being a skeptic regarding Newton's magical interests to being a believer, McGuire has made the reverse pilgrimage. But the latter's "Neoplatonism and Active Principles" manages to disassociate Newton from the Hermetic tradition only by dubious reasoning and a certain amount of sleight-of-hand—for example, by denying the clear historical connection between the alchemical tradition and Hermetic philosophy, and reverting to the excuse that Newton's alchemical writings were largely reading notes (p. 119). Additionally, arguing that virtually all the important philosophical foundations of Newton's system can be traced to the English Neoplatonic revival, and especially to the ideas of Henry More, McGuire for some reason discusses only the mature More's views, ignoring the younger More's flirtation with magic and minimizing the importance of both More's and Newton's "pantheism." I believe that McGuire's and my disagreement turns partly on how each of us deals with Newton's apparent lack of the radical political and social leanings often associated with seventeenth-century Hermeticism. McGuire seems to want to make such reformist social politics a critical criterion for using "Hermeticism" as a category (p. 100), whereas I would argue that quite a number of Hermeticists, especially after the 1650s fight against enthusiasm got under way (see below), must have had more moderate or conservative political and social leanings—for example, Sir Kenhelm Digby and Sir Robert Moray. Even in its more conservative forms, however, it is clear that Hermetic philosophy was so subversive of established religion that in the seventeenth-century context it should still be seen as essentially having radical social implications—which is why, I have argued, Newton hid so much of his worldview from the public eye. See my "Newton's Inside Out!" and, for More, "Providence and the Mechanical Philosophy." Finally, I think that McGuire's note 84, pp. 140–41, undercuts much of the argument put forth in the text itself.

More generally, I have serious doubts about McGuire's attempt to take the measure of a turbulent intellectual, social, and occultist movement, such as mid-seventeenth-century English Hermeticism was, with rather static and unbending yardsticks, for it was a time when the heady utopian and social forces unleashed by the Civil War brought together in a rich broth a variety of worldviews, ideologies, and religious enthusiasms, when two different Independent sects might go from allies to enemies to friends again in the twinkling of an eye. Thus, some of the distinctions McGuire tries to draw, and the arguments he erects on top of those distinctions, seem inappropriate; particularly when we are dealing with a historical movement like Hermeticism that consistently warned against explicit written material, to impose such rigid criteria for categories seems to be hairsplitting.

113. Memorandum by Gregory, 3 June 1701, Royal Society, MS. Gregory, fol. 79v.

114. See, for example, Edouard Schuré, *The Ancient Mysteries of Delphi: Pythagorus* (Blauvelt, N.Y.: Rudolf Steiner, 1971), 79.

115. I am ignoring the early essay by John Maynard Keynes, "Newton, the

Man," in *Newton Tercentenary Celebrations* (Cambridge: Royal Society of London, Cambridge University Press, 1947); the current discussion of Newton's magic really began with the publication of Frances Yates's *Giordano Bruno and the Hermetic Tradition* (London: Routledge & Kegan Paul, 1964) and McGuire and Rattansi's "Newton and the 'Pipes of Pan.'" That magic formed a significant part of the mature scientific revolution (not the earlier phase, where it can be easily explained away) is still a notion fraught with dangerous implications to many, as Marie Boas Hall, A. Rupert Hall, and Paolo Rossi make clear in *Reason, Experiment, and Mysticism in the Scientific Revolution*, ed. M. L. Righini Bonelli and William R. Shea (New York: Science History Publications, 1975), esp. 73, 265–66, 270, and 277.

116. Halley, "An Account of the Cause of the Late Remarkable Appearance of the Planet Venus, Seen This Summer . . . in the Daytime," *Philosophical Transactions*, no. 349 (1716): 466; Armitage, *Edmond Halley*, 174 and pl. 13; *Biographia Britannica*, 4:2514–15.

117. Memorandum by Conduitt, King's College Library, Cambridge, MS. Keynes 130, no. 11; Kubrin, "Newton and the Cyclical Cosmos."

118. More, of course, was not Newton's teacher in a formal sense, but the young Newton studiously read his publications.

119. Robert M. Pirsig, *Zen and the Art of Motorcycle Maintenance* (New York: Bantam Books, 1974), 296.

120. Henry More, *Enthusiasmus Triumphatus; or, A Brief Discourse of the Nature, Causes, Kinds, and Cure of Enthusiasm* (1st ed. London, 1656). See note 67 above. See the excellent article by P. M. Rattansi, to which my debt is obvious, "Paracelsus and the Puritan Revolution."

121. In the 1690s Hooke turned his attention to the specific mechanisms of earthquakes (*Posthumous Works*, 421ff.).

122. Hooke, *Posthumous Works*, 312–13, for example.

123. See my "Newton's Inside Out!" and "'Burning Times,' Isaac Newton, and the War Against the Earth," to appear in the *Proceedings* of the public symposium entitled "Is the Earth a Living Organism?" held at Amherst, Mass., 1–6 August 1985. See also my *How Sir Isaac Newton Helped Restore Law 'n' Order to the West* (1972, privately printed; a copy has been placed at the Library of Congress); and Paul Deveraux, David Kubrin, and John Steele, *Earthmind* (New York: Harper & Row, 1989), chap. 2.

124. Westfall, *Never at Rest*, 872.

FIVE

Halley's Two Essays
on Newton's *Principia*

I. Bernard Cohen

Edmond Halley's review of Newton's *Principia,* published in the *Philosophical Transactions of the Royal Society,* of which he was the editor and publisher from 1685 through 1692, appeared in issue No. 186 for January, February and March, 1687,[1] a year before the only other major review was published, in the *Acta Eruditorum.*[2] Halley's review was the last item in the issue. Halley observed that "the Publication of these *Transactions* has for some Months last past been interrupted." He desired the reader "to take notice" that the care of seeing Newton's *Principia* through the press had "lain wholly upon the Publisher" of the *Transactions*—i.e., Halley himself—with the result that the *Transactions* "could not be got ready in due time." Now, however, Halley assured his readers, the *Transactions* "will again be continued as formerly, and come out regularly." Halley asserted that he had "been more serviceable to the Commonwealth of Learning" in producing "the Edition of this Book of Mr. *Newton*" than in publishing the *Transactions.* History certainly concurs in this evaluation.

In the opening sentence of his book review,[3] Halley puts on to the public record the fact that historians know well, but which the readers of Newton's book would not have been aware of, that this "incomparable Author" had only "at length been prevailed upon to appear in Publick." This was followed by a tribute of the sort which Halley had put into his introductory poem, printed in Newton's *Principia,* to the effect that Newton had "in this Treatise given a most notable instance of the extent of the powers of the Mind." Newton had not only "shewn what are the Principles of Natural Philosophy," but to the extent that he had derived the consequences from them, "he seems to have exhausted his Argument, and left little to be done by those that shall succeed him." Immediately, this led Halley to state what was obviously for him the most significant aspect of the book—not Newton's codification of the laws of motion, not his definitions (including centripetal force and mass), not the theory of gravity and the explanation of the tides, not the theory of comets, but rather his "great skill in the old and new Geometry." In this context Halley referred specifically to Newton's "own improvements" of the "new Geometry," by which he said "I mean his method of *infinite Series,*" which has "enabled him to master those Problems, which for their difficulty would have still lain unresolved, had one less qualified than [Newton] himself attempted them."

In the second paragraph, Halley briefly describes the structure of the treatise, which—like all Gaul—is divided into three parts (three "Books"). The first two, he observes "are entituled *de Motu Corporum,* the third *de Systemate Mundi.*" Then Halley refers to the definitions (time, space, place, motion) with distinctions made by the author into "absolute and relative, real and apparent, Mathematical and vulgar." Halley also mentions the Laws of Motion and their corollaries, without stating what they may be, and without reference to Newton's having called them "Axiomata." But he does draw attention to the manner in which Newton demonstrates, from these laws and their corollaries, "the composition and resolution of any direct force out of, or into any oblique forces." By this means, Halley says, "the powers of all sorts of Mechanical Engines are demonstrated." A brief mention is given of the principles that govern "the reflection of Bodies in Motion after their Collision."

Following his display of these necessary *"Praecognita,"* Halley opens his discussion of Book One: "our Author proceeds to consider the Curves generated by the composition of a direct impressed motion with a gravitation or tendency towards a Center." We may find this statement extremely interesting, since Newton himself says expressly that in the first two books he is dealing with the mathematical idea of a centripetal force and reserves the introduction of gravitation as a physical example of such a centrally directed universal force until Book Three.[4] But here Halley is apparently using the word "gravitation" in some general sense of a centrally directed or attracted force, rather than the more restricted sense of a specific physical force of universal gravity. Most likely, Halley did not want to use the term "attraction," with its overtones of premechanical physics, and did not choose to use the new term "centripetal force," just introduced by Newton. This becomes apparent when Halley next refers to Newton's demonstration that under the action of any such force the areas described are always proportional to the times. He is evidently fully aware of the generality of Newton's proposition and understands that it is not limited to one kind of centrally directed force: gravity.

Halley lauds Newton's method: "from the Curve described," to find "the Law or Rule of the decrease or increase of the Tendency or Centripetal forces (as he calls it) in differing distances from the Center."[5] He then mentions that there are several examples, referring to the curve produced when the force is "as the fift [i.e., fifth] power or squared-cube of the distance therefrom reciprocally." Another is the spiral that results from a force "reciprocally as the cube of the distance." We may observe, incidentally, that Halley here merely accepts Newton's radical non-Aristotelian formulation of proportion: the spiral results from the force being "reciprocally as the cube of the distance." In the case of "an ellipse" with a force directed toward the center, the force is said to be "directly as the distance." In the case of conic sections, Halley writes, Newton "demonstrates that the *Vis Centripeta,* or tendency toward that *Focus,* is in all places reciprocally as the square of the distance therefrom."

These examples show what a radical step Newton had taken in pioneering the use of "mixed proportions." Only a generation earlier, in the days of Galileo and Kepler, scientists would not have written that a force (or a velocity) is proportional to a distance (or is inversely proportional to the square or the cube of the distance) in the simple and straightforward way that Newton does and that Halley accepts without comment. In the pre-Newtonian age, scientists were constrained to use the old-fashioned logical idiom in which ratios were required to be homogeneous: forces compared to forces, distances to distances, speeds or velocities to speeds or velocities. A typical such expression would read that the distance in one case is to the distance in the other inversely as the square of the speed in the first case is to the square of the speed in the second.

Halley introduces the general topic of orbits that are conic sections by discussing the way in which the "Velocity in the impressed Motion" determines whether the curve will be a hyperbola, a parabola, or an ellipse or circle. He observes that "from this sort of tendency or gravitation it follows likewise that the squares of the Times of the periodical Revolutions are as the Cubes of the *Radii* or *transverse Axes* of the *Ellipses.*" We note once again that Halley has "jumped the gun" on Newton by assuming that the force is an example of "gravitation." He then states that all of this is "found to agree with the *Phenomena* of the Celestial Motions, as discovered by the great Sagacity and Diligence of *Kepler.*" This is a most significant statement, since Halley does not mention the name of Copernicus. Sometimes, the *Principia* was linked with the names of both Copernicus and Kepler, as in the statement that Newton had given a "Mathematical Demonstration of the Copernican hypothesis as amended by Kepler"; these are the words in which Newton's *Principia* was described to the Fellows of the Royal Society, the statement used in the official record to enter the receipt of Newton's manuscript. But in Halley's review, there is no mention of Copernicus.[6]

Halley next points out how Newton elaborates "the consequences of this sort of *Vis Centripeta,*" in particular showing "how to find the *Conick*

Section which a Body shall describe when cast with any velocity in a given Line," it being supposed that the measure of the force is given.[7] Newton, he says, also sets forth "several neat constructions" to determine the orbits, "either from the *Focus* given in two points or Tangents," or "by five points or Tangents or any number of Points or Tangents making together five."[8] Halley also indicates how Newton deals with Kepler's problem: knowing the position of a planet in a conic-section orbit at any given time, to compute the position at some future time. The difficulty arises from the fact that there is no general solution ("in a finite number of terms") of finding a focal sector of a conic section having a given numerical ratio to another focal sector. In an ellipse, for example, there can be no exact prediction of future planetary positions by using Kepler's law of areas. Halley does not go into any details concerning Newton's methods,[9] merely summarizing Newton's methods of computation, saying that Newton "performs [these computations] accurately in the *Parabola,* and by concise approximations comes as near as he pleases in the *Ellipse* and *Hyperbola.*" Newton's methods, Halley insists, are "of the highest concern in Astronomy."

Halley then goes on to describe many other aspects of Book One. He shows how Newton deals with the motion of bodies under the action of a central force, not only "where the tendency thereto is reciprocally as the square of the distance," but also "generally in all other cases, supposing a general quadrature of Curve lines." Here, we may observe, is a public reference to Newton's ability to perform integration. Halley also observes (referring to the propositions around Prop. 41) that Newton "has a general method of discovering the Orbs described by a Body moving in such a tendency toward a Center, increasing or decreasing in any given relation to the distance from the Center." He then discusses Newton's work on the motion of the apsides.

Having dealt with the subject of orbits for a page and three-quarters, Halley next turns to the motion of bodies on given surfaces and the oscillatory motion of pendulums. He describes how Newton treats of the motion of two bodies "drawing or attracting each other" and describing "about the common center of Gravity, Curve Lines, like to those they seem to describe about one another." As an astronomer he particularly stresses Newton's tremendous achievement in initiating the analysis of the motions of "three Bodies, attracting each other, reciprocally as the Square of the distance between their Centers." A number of "Consequences are considered and laid down," says Halley, which are "of great use in explicating the *Phenomena* of the *Moons* Motions, the Flux and Reflux of the Sea, the Precession of the *Equinoctial* Points; and the like." This set of particular applications is not quite so manifest in Newton's text at this point in Book One. The readers of the *Principia* would not as yet have read about such matters in the *Principia* until they had advanced to Book Three.

Halley then devotes almost all of a lengthy paragraph, one that occupies two-thirds of a page, to Newton's analysis of the forces of spheres. Newton, he says, considers the effects that follow "if a sphere be composed of an infinity of Atoms, each of which have a *Conatus accedendi ad invicem*," an expression in which Halley introduces the non-Newtonian notion of an "infinity of Atoms" and a pseudo-Newtonian variant of the Cartesian phrase "conatus recedendi a centro." Newton does use a version of this latter expression in the *Principia* but not in the present context. Halley does not say that the spheres consist of "atoms" which mutually gravitate, but rather atoms which have the aforesaid Cartesian "conatus" which "decreases in duplicate Proportion of the Distance between them." In this case, he reports, Newton has proved that "the whole *Congeries*" will have the same tendency toward the center, that this tendency or "conatus" will decrease toward the center in the inverse square of the distance from that center, and that it will decrease within the surface as the distance from the center directly. He observes also that Newton has a method "to determine the forces of Globes composed of Particles whose Tendencies to each other do decrease in any other *Ratio* of the Distances." Newton carries this "speculation" to "other Bodies not Spherical, whether finite or indeterminate." Clearly, these theorems will be of great significance when Newton will eventually come to deal with the force of universal gravity, in examples of bodies having appreciably large dimensions with respect to the distance through which the gravitating forces act on them. An example is the attraction between the moon and the earth, where the distance between moon and earth is only sixty times the radius of the earth; another is the problem of the falling of an apple to the earth, where the distance from the apple to the earth may be taken to be the earth's radius. Halley, again anticipating Book Three, describes Newton's analysis of the forces in and of solids by saying that this is an example of how "our Author with his usual Acuteness proceeds to examine into the Causes of this Tendency or centripetal Force, which from undoubted Arguments is shown to be in all the great Bodies of the Universe." And indeed, this is related to the preceding discussion of the motion of three bodies, in which Halley says that the consequences of the attractions between three bodies according to the inverse square law leads to "several *Corrallarys* of great use in explicating the *Phenomena* of the *Moons* Motions, the Flux and Reflux of the Sea, the Precession of the Equinoctial Points; and the like."

In the succeeding page and a third, Halley briefly summarizes some aspects of Book Two. In Book One, he says, Newton has dealt with "the Effects of compound Motions *in Mediis non resistentibus*"; now Newton turns to "the consequence of a resistance from a *Medium*." In the midst of discussing the various conditions of resistance and the kinds of motion that occur under these conditions as a result of the actions of various forces, Halley turns to one of Newton's results of the greatest significance for physical thought. That is, he shows how Newton's results link what we call Boyle's law with a particular kind of repulsive force between particles of an elastic fluid. This result, Halley correctly states, is proposed by Newton for "the Contemplation of Natural Philosophers," who must decide "whether the surprising *Phenomena* of the Elasticity of the Air and some other [elastic] fluids may not arise from their being composed of Particles which flie each other." Halley correctly states Newton's position in the summary conclusion that since this is "rather a Physical than Mathematical Inquiry," our "Author forebears to Discuss" it in this place.[10]

There follows a brief discussion of Newton's work with pendulums and the experiments instigated in order to determine the measure of the air's resistance to bodies moving in it. Then Halley summarizes Newton's very original presentation of wave motion. He stresses Newton's great conclusion, toward the end of Book Two, that "the *Cartesian* Doctrine of the *Vortices* of the Celestial Matter carrying with them the Planets of the *Sun,* is proved to be altogether impossible."

Halley then turns to the third and last Book, to which he devotes a whole page. He carefully and correctly paraphrases Newton's own opening declarations, that in this third book "the Demonstrations of the two former Books are applyed to the Explication of the principal *Phenomena* of Nature." Halley says that Newton demonstrates "the verity of the *Hypothesis* of *Kepler,*" by which he seems to mean the system of Kepler's three laws.[11] It is to be observed in this context that in the *Principia* Newton mentions Kepler's name only with respect to one of the three laws of planetary motion, the third. Newton himself believed that Kepler had only guessed at the first two.[12] That is, Kepler had found the elliptical orbit only in the case of Mars and assumed this to be general. Furthermore, Kepler's proof of the area law was imperfect, saved in the proof only by compensating error.

Halley also states specifically that Newton gives a "full Resolution" to "all the difficulties that occur in the *Astronomical* Science." These have proved to be "nothing else but the necessary consequences of the *Sun, Earth, Moon,* and *Planets,* having all of them a gravitation or tendency toward their Centers proportionate to the Quantity of matter in each of them, and whose Force abates in duplicate proportion of the Distance reciprocally." This statement is a quite extraordinary one, because it is without any question the *first appearance* in print of the complete enunciation of Newton's law of universal gravity (in this case applied to the astronomical bodies and the earth). Newton himself, in his own statements in the *Principia,* always discussed the two parts of the law separately, that is, the direct proportionality of the masses or quantities of matter and the inverse proportionality of the square of the distance.[13]

Halley lists the problems which Newton has "indisputably solved." They include the phenomena (Halley says, "the Appearances")[14] of "the Tides," or "Flux and Reflux of the Sea," and the determination of the spheroidal shape of the earth and of Jupiter. This shape of the earth— Halley quite rightly emphasizes—was shown by Newton to be directly related to the "precession of the Equinoxes, or rotation of the Earths axis," as well as "the retrocession of the *Moons* Nodes." It was one of the most profound and unexpected discoveries revealed by the *Principia.*[15]

Halley concludes his discussion of the system of the world of Newton with a half-page devoted to "the Theory of the Motion of the Comets." This is "attempted with such success," says Halley, that in the "Example of the great Comet which appeared in 1680/1," the "Motion thereof is computed as exactly as we can pretend to give the places of the primary Planets." Newton, according to Halley, has succeeded in producing a "general Method," whereby the trajectory of comets may be determined "by an easy Geometrical Construction; upon supposition that those Curves are *Parabolick,* or so near it that the *Parabola* may serve without sensible Error." Halley observes in this connection, however, that "our Author" says "it be more probable . . . that these Orbs are *Elliptical;* and that after long periods Comets may return again." Halley, for the sake of a mathematical reader, explains that "such *Ellipses* are by Reason of the Immense Distance of the *Foci,* and the smallness of the *Latus Rectum,* in the Parts near the Sun, where Comets appear, not easily distinguished from the Curve of the *Parabola.*" He indicates that this is "proved by the Example produced."

In the final paragraph of his presentation, Halley returns to the subject of mathematics. The whole treatise, he says, "is interspersed with *Lemma's* of General use in *Geometry.*" There are also "several new Methods applyed, which are well worth the considering." Then, echoing the sentiments of his introductory poem, he says that "it may be justly said, that so many and so Valuable *Philosophical Truths,* as are herein discovered and put past Dispute, were never yet owing to the Capacity and Industry of any one Man."[16]

There is no question of the fact that this is a rather extraordinary review. Praising Newton for his advances in mathematics, as well as in mathematical physics, he shows how important Newton's abstract discoveries are for physical science, in particular for astronomy, and for our understanding of the system of the world. Furthermore, Halley has called attention to all of the major parts of the *Principia* and has given the reader a very good idea of the chief accomplishments of Newton. In

this presentation, today's scholar will find very few surprises, except perhaps Halley's downplaying of the axiomatization of the principles of motion. Furthermore, although Halley's presentation is distinguished (as I
have mentioned above) for having made the first full presentation of the
law of gravity in relation to planets, Halley nowhere states specifically the
universality of this law.

Only two scientists, other than Newton, are mentioned in the course
of the review: Huygens (the only one of Newton's contemporaries to
whom he applied the adjective "summus")[17] and Kepler. And in referring to the system of the world, it is to be emphasized once again, that
Halley refers to Kepler but not to Copernicus.[18] When introducing Kepler, Halley is to a very slight degree critical of Newton. He states that
Newton's results "agree with the *Phenomena* of the Celestial Motions, as
discoverd by the great Sagacity and Diligence of *Kepler*." A little later, in
the discussion of Book Three, he talks of "the principal *Phenomena* of
Nature," referring primarily to "the verity of the *Hypothesis* of *Kepler*"
which Newton has "demonstrated." This is of interest, as I have mentioned, because Newton strictly limited his references to Kepler so that
Kepler was mentioned only with respect to the third law, not the first
two.[19]

Halley did not rest content with but a single article (or book review)
about the *Principia*.[20] A decade later, in March 1697, he published (in
issue No. 226 of the *Philosophical Transactions*) a second work, headed:
"The True Theory of the Tides, extracted from that admirable treatise
of Mr. Isaac Newton, entituled, *Philosophiae Naturalis Principia Mathematica*." This new article was said to be "a Discourse presented with that
Book to the late King James." This discourse on the tides is particularly
interesting to us, since it was designed for the sake of readers who were
not "knowing in Mathematical Matters" but who were nevertheless "very
curious to be informed of the Causes of Things."[21]

Halley begins by pointing out the way in which "most of the great and
surprising Appearances [Phenomena] of Nature"[22] proceed from no
other principle "than that of *Gravity*, whereby in the Earth all Bodies
have a tendency towards its Centre." This, he asserts, "is most evident."
Halley claims that this "Law of the decrease of Gravity" has been "de-
monstratively proved, and put past contradiction." Newton, Halley says,
has used this law to find "the genuine Cause of the several Appearances
in the Theory of the Moon and Planets," and also to discover "the hitherto unknown Laws of the Motion of Comets and of the Ebbing and
Flowing of the Sea."

Halley then discusses the nature of scientific truths, and their modes
of discovery. This leads him to the question of how "these great Discoveries [of Newton] should have escaped the acute Disquisitions of the best

Philosophical Heads of all past Ages." Why were they "reserved to these our times"? Any wonder in this matter will "soon cease," Halley says, as soon as it is recognized that Newton's discoveries required "great Improvements" in "Geometry," which have been made only in recent times, most notably "the profound Discoveries of our incomparable Author."

Then Halley explains—in a careful, exact, and wholly non-mathematical way—how the curved orbits of planets are produced by a combination of an initial inertial motion and a centripetal tendency decreasing as the square of the distance. He shows how cometary orbits are produced by the gravitating force of the sun. This leads him to the main topic: the action of the sun and of the moon on the oceans of the sea to produce the tides. Eight out of thirteen pages are then devoted to a general exposition of the Newtonian theory of the tides plus specific examples of tidal phenomena and their explanation. Halley concludes with Newton's analysis of the odd "Tides in the Port of *Tunking*" in Indochina.[23] Halley states that "the whole appearance of these tides," deduced "without any forcing naturally . . . from these Principles" is a "great Argument of the certainty of the whole *Theory*."

Whoever reads Halley's articles on the *Principia* will be impressed by his zeal in promoting Newton's ideas. In these two essays he also reveals himself to be a master of scientific exposition. At that time, Halley certainly knew the *Principia* better than any other living person except its author. How fortunate that he was also gifted in being able to explain Newton's principles to those who were not able to follow Newton's mathematics.

SUPPLEMENT: THE OTHER REVIEWS OF NEWTON'S *PRINCIPIA*

When Newton's *Principia* was published, there were four book reviews. We may gain some idea of the merit of Halley's review by comparing it to the other three. Two of these were in French, in the *Journal des Sçavans* and the *Bibliothèque Universelle*, both anonymous; currently scholars attribute the one in the *Bibliothèque Universelle* to John Locke.[24] A third, also anonymous, was printed in Latin in the *Acta Eruditorum*.

The Locke piece is hardly a book review as we ordinarily understand this term. It consists primarily of a translation into French of the Latin headings of the successive sections of Books I and II, followed by the reviewer's own summary of Book III, together with an introductory paragraph. To such an extent is this a brief summary or outline,[25] largely presented in translations of Newton's own words, that the author apologizes for the fact that he could not treat Book III by translating Newton's section headings into French. The reason is that Newton did not divide Book III into sections as he had done in Books I and II. Since Newton did not provide headings which Locke could translate, the reviewer had no other recourse than to fall back on his own meager resources.

The greater part of Locke's presentation of Book III is taken up by a summary of what we now know as the "Phaenomena," even to the extent of reproducing Newton's table of the periodic times and mean distances of the six major planets and of the satellites of Jupiter. In terms of space allocation, this is far out of proportion to either the novelty of this section of the treatise or its importance to the reader.

The reviewer does mention that "there is weight [*pesanteur*] in all bodies, according to the quantity of matter which is in each of them" and he does give Newton's fundamental principle, that "the exertion which the weight makes on all equal particles of a body is reciprocally as the square of the distance of the places of these particles." The summary also states that "the ebb and flow of the Seas proceeds from the pressure [*l'impression*] of the Sun and of the Moon." But I doubt whether any reader of such cryptic and generally misleading sentences would come away with a real insight into Newton's concept of universal gravity as the force which binds the solar system together.

The reader would learn from this review about the relative densities of the planets and the sun, and various odd bits of information—such as Newton's having shown the earth to be an oblate spheroid. But nothing is said about Newton's new technical expression or concept of "centripetal force."[26] Nor is any information given about Newton's amazing and stunning demonstration that Kepler's law of areas is a necessary and sufficient condition for a deviating force to be centrally directed. Nor is there even so much as a hint that Newton had proved that elliptical orbits imply an inverse-square force directed toward a focus.

I do not wish to come down particularly hard on Locke, if he was the author. The fact of the matter is that the mathematical technicalities of Newton's book were far beyond Locke's minimal knowledge. Among the Newtonians there was circulated a story to the effect that Locke was unable to understand the mathematics of the *Principia* and had to limit himself to the physical principles. J. T. Desaguliers reported that the "great Mr. Locke was the first who became a *Newtonian Philosopher* without the help of geometry." Locke, he said, "asked *Mr. Huygens* whether all mathematical *Propositions* in *Sir Isaac's Principia* were true, and being told he might depend upon their Certainty; he took them for granted and carefully examined the Reasonings and *Corollaries* drawn from them."[27] In this way he "became Master of all the Physics, and was fully convinced of the Great Discoveries contained in that book." According to Desaguliers this information concerning Locke and the *Principia* had been given to him "several times by *Sir Isaac Newton* himself."

Was it Locke whom Newton had in mind when he contemplated adding a curious statement to the second edition of the *Principia?* This was to appear in the introductory part of Book III. In the printed version, Newton says that although Book III applies the results of the first two Books to the system of the world, he would not advise his readers to study "every proposition" of the first two Books before turning to the third. This would "cost too much time," he wrote, "even to readers of good mathematical learning." Rather, he says, it is enough for his readers to concentrate on the Definitions, the Laws of Motion, the first three sections of Book I, and then to "consult such of the remaining Propositions of the first two Books, as the references in this, and as occasions, shall require."[28] In his own copy of the *Principia,* Newton then added a sentence reading: "Those who are not mathematically learned can read the Propositions also, and can consult mathematicians concerning the truth of the Demonstrations." Was Newton, in making this explicit contrast between those who are not "mathematically learned" and those who are "of good mathematical learning," thinking about a real person— John Locke—who had actually so consulted a mathematician? The same story was written down by Conduitt, who credited Abraham de Moivre as his source: "Locke took his prop[osition]s for granted on hearing Huygens say that he had proved them."[29]

Far more important than Locke's review was the one in the *Journal des Sçavans.* This was a highly critical review, although the generally derisory comments are made a little more palatable by occasional bits of extravagant praise. It has been suggested[30] that the reviewer was H. Régis, a leading Cartesian philosopher or physicist. The main point of this reviewer, as is well known, is that the *Principia* was a work of "mechanics" rather than "physics." It was, the reviewer declared, "the most perfect Mechanics that one could imagine." But, he added, "one can only regard these demonstrations as if they were 'mechanical,' because the author recognizes himself . . . that he has not considered their principles as Physicist, but only as a Mathematician [or Geometer]." The reviewer recommends to Newton that he now compose the most perfect work that it is possible to create. To do so, Newton has only to give us "a Physics as exact as his Mechanics." He will do this when, finally, he will give us a treatise in which he will have substituted "true movements in place of those which he has supposed." This reviewer obviously did not understand Newton's method, the combination of mathematical considerations later applied to the real world as revealed by experiment and observation.[31] Here is real evidence of the fact that Newton's method, or the "Newtonian style," was indeed revolutionary[32] and thus puzzling to some of the readers of the *Principia,* whose methodological preconceptions it affronted.

There is a very strong possibility that this French review may actually have had some influence upon Newton. The reason is that the System of the World, which Newton presented in Book III, was pilloried by the reviewer for having been based on a set of introductory "hypotheses," that are for the most part arbitrary and hence not to be considered as the basis of a true physics. This opinion was based on the fact that the introductory part of Book III, the section which we know today as comprising the "Phaenomena" and the "Rules of Proceeding in Natural Philosophy" (*Regulae Philosophandi*) were grouped together, with a couple of other propositions, under the general heading of Hypotheses.[33] By the time of the second edition, Newton had altered this presentation by abandoning the general rubric of "Hypotheses" and introducing the categories of "Phaenomena" and "Regulae Philosophandi." Thereafter the objector's interpretation could no longer be valid. We do not have any direct evidence that Newton was influenced in this regard by the reviewer in the *Journal des Sçavans.* But it is difficult to imagine that Newton would not have become aware of this strong criticism, especially the nasty allegation that his book was based upon hypotheses.

The reviewer in the *Acta Eruditorum* was perhaps the editor, but we have no direct evidence on this matter.[34] One cannot easily find words sufficient to praise this great endeavor. It occupies some sixteen pages in print and contains every significant innovation made by Newton in the *Principia,* together with important numerical data. No contemporary reader who gave this review his full attention could have come away without a deep appreciation of Newton's achievement and a recognition of Newton's principal propositions. In some of Newton's later writings— notably discussions concerning Leibniz—Newton shows that he was fully aware that this "epitome" of the *Principia,* to use Newton's own name for it, would have given any reader a very good idea of the contents of the *Principia.* Newton himself says that this "epitome" contains an exposition of "the principal propositions." Newton was particularly concerned about this matter, since Leibniz alleged that he had written an important article just after he had seen this review or "epitome" and long before he had seen the actual book. Leibniz had recognized at once that if he wanted to get any credit for his own ideas he would have to write them up hastily and publish them (as he did in the *Tentamen*), before actually seeing the book itself.[35]

The reviewer in the *Acta* treated the first thirty-five pages of the *Principia* with extreme care. The Definitions, Laws of Motion, Preface, and Section One of Book I are expounded in great detail. From then on, the account is more summary. Clearly, if the author had kept up the original pace, the review would have come to ten or more times the eighteen pages that it occupies.

The tone is generally one of adulation, praise for Newton's main achievements in the *Principia* in pure geometry and other parts of mathematics, in dynamics and general physics, and in celestial mechanics. Thus, it is said that Newton deals with problems of forces, velocities, and mediums, "with a penetration worthy of so great a mathematician." There are lemmas, the reviewer notes, "to no small degree perfecting geometry, especially of conics." From time to time there are "corollaries showing the fullness of topics [that are mathematically] demonstrated." Lest "the exposition should possibly seem sterile," the author, we are told, "introduced scholia illustrating [natural] philosophy."

One can see the deep understanding of the reviewer in the statement he makes about Newton's system of the world. Newton, he says, demonstrates "that the forces by which the circumjovial planets, the primary planets, and the moon, are perpetually drawn off from rectilinear motions, and are kept in their orbits," arise "from their gravitation toward Jupiter, the Sun, and the Earth, and are reciprocally as the squares of the distances from the center of Jupiter, of the Sun, and of the Earth." Here is Newton's great principle admirably expressed. The reviewer also paraphrases Newton when he says that "all bodies gravitate toward each of the individual planets, and that their weights toward any one [and the same] planet, at equal distances from the center of that planet are proportional to the quantity of matter in each one." He then points out that Newton infers from these results "that the weights of bodies do not depend upon their forms and textures," that "gravity occurs in all bodies universally and is proportional to the quantity of matter in each individual one." The detail and exactness of the summary is a source of amazement, even at a remove of some three hundred years. There can be no doubt that this is the best and most important summary of Newton's *Principia* that has ever been written and published.[36]

I have pointed out in my *Introduction to Newton's 'Principia'* that this review might have had an effect upon the later editions of the *Principia*. For the author of the review, referring to page 415 of the first edition of this book, wrote: "from which he concludes that God placed the Planets at different distances from the Sun, so that they would receive heat from the Sun according to the proportion of their densities." This reference to God, accurately paraphrased by the reviewer, perhaps seemed to Newton to be too prominent a statement of a theological position in a book which was notable for lacking discussions of theological matters. Accordingly, Newton canceled this passage in his own copy and altered the text in the second and third editions, so that this reference to God and his providence would be eliminated.[37] We do not know for certain whether the prominence given by the *Acta* to this aside of Newton's was the determining factor in causing Newton to make the change. The consequence, however, has been that some writers, mistakenly believing that the texts of the several editions of the *Principia* were fundamentally identical, and aware that there is no mention of God or Divine Providence in the text proper in the third or final edition, concluded that there was no reference to God or to theological matters in the first edition of the *Principia*. It is all too often thought that God appeared in the *Principia* only in the second and later editions, in the concluding Scholium Generale that Newton composed for the second edition (1713). This contains the famous reference to "this most beautiful System of the Sun, Planets, and Comets, which could only proceed from the counsel and dominion of an intelligent and powerful being." Here too is the lengthy discussion of God: his names, his duration, his omnipresence and his attributes.

NOTES

1. This review is reprinted in facsimile in I. Bernard Cohen, ed.: *Isaac Newton's Papers & Letters on Natural Philosophy* (Cambridge: Harvard University Press, 1958; revised ed., 1978), pp. 405–411, with an introductory essay on "Halley and the *Principia*" by Robert E. Schofield, pp. 397–404.

2. On these reviews, see I. B. Cohen: *Introduction to Newton's 'Principia'* (Cambridge: Harvard University Press; Cambridge [England]: Cambridge University Press, 1971; revised ed., 1978), ch. 6, pp. 145–158. Some aspects of these reviews are discussed in the Supplement to this essay.

3. It is interesting to observe, in passing, that in describing the book at the head of the review, Halley copied the title page word-for-word and line-for-line up to the end of the author's titles: "*Philosophiae Naturalis Principia Mathematica, Autore* Is. Newton Trin. Coll. Cantab. *Soc. Matheseos Professore* Lucasiano, *& Societatis Regalis Sodali.*" Halley even kept the title page's distinction between roman and italic type (reversing them), save that "*Soc.*" of course should have been in roman to go with Trinity College, Cambridge, of which he was a Fellow ("Socius") rather than with the title of Lucasian Professor of Mathematics. Then, instead of giving the imprint to be found on either of the variant title pages, that is, without a mention of either Joseph Streater or Samuel Smith, Halley merely stated the city of publication ("Londini") and then quoted the statement that appeared after Streater's name: "*Prostat apud plures Bibliopolas.*" Readers may be reminded that the title page of Newton's *Principia* appears in two variant states. One contains the name of Streater as printer and the statement (as just quoted) that the book is sold at various booksellers: "*Londini,* Jussu *Societatis Regiae* ac Typis *Josephi Streater.* Prostat apud plures Bibliopolas." The other title page is a cancel, pasted onto the stub of the original; it reads: "Jussu *Societatis Regiae* ac

Typis *Josephi Streater.* Prostant Venales *Sam. Smith* ad insignia Principia Walliae in Coemitario D. *Pauli,* aliosq; nonnullos Bibliopolas." In this context it should be observed that the colophon of the *Philosophical Transactions* reads "*LONDON,* Printed by *J.S. Streater,* and are to be sold by *Samuel Smith* at the *Princes Arms* in St. *Paul's* Church-yard."

4. On this topic see Newton's own statement in the opening and concluding sections of Sect. 11 of Book One of the *Principia.* I have discussed the distinction between Book One and Book Three with respect to the nature of force as an essential aspect of what I have called the "Newtonian style" in my *The Newtonian Revolution* (Cambridge, London, New York: Cambridge University Press, 1980), chapter 3, and in my contribution to the volume *Contemporary Newtonian Research,* edited by Zev Bechler (Dordrecht: D. Reidel Publishing Company, 1982), pp. 21–108, "The *Principia,* Universal Gravitation, and the 'Newtonian Style.'"

5. Halley here conflates the Cartesian "tendency" ("conatus" or "endeavor") and Newton's own new term "centripetal force." Newton introduced the name "vis centripeta" in honor of Christian Huygens, who had written about the oppositely directed force "vis centrifugo"; on this point see my *Introduction to Newton's 'Principia'* (cited in note 2 *supra*).

6. On this description of the *Principia,* see my *Introduction* (cited in note 2 *supra*), p. 130.

7. Halley wholly avoids the question of whether or not Newton had to prove the statement mentioned in corol. 1 to Prop. 13, Book One, to the effect that if a centripetal force acts on a body with an initial component of inertial motion, that body will then move in one of the conic sections, having a focus in the center to which the force is directed. Newton gave an outline of a proof in the second edition (1713) of the *Principia.*

8. These constructions are the subjects of Sect. 4 and Sect. 5 of Book One of the *Principia.*

9. These may be found in Sect. 6 of Book One of the *Principia.* In this context, neither Newton nor Halley mentions Kepler's name. See the commentary in D. T. Whiteside's edition of *The Mathematical Papers of Isaac Newton,* vol. 6 (Cambridge [England]: At the University Press, 1974), esp. p. 302, n. 19.

10. Newton discusses this theorem in Prop. 23, Book Two, and the succeeding Scholium in which Newton contrasts the "physical question" of whether "elastic fluids" are actually composed of particles repelling one another with a force inversely proportional to the distance between their centers and the mathematical "demonstration" of the property of fluids composed of particles having such a force.

11. That is, Newton had mathematically shown the significance of Kepler's area law (Props. 1–3, Book One) and law of elliptical orbits (Prop. 11, Book One), and the harmonic law (Prop. 15, Book One), and then had related these demonstrations to the system of Jupiter's satellites (Prop. 1, Book Three), the planetary system (Prop. 2, Book Three) and our moon (Prop. 3, Book Three). Also, for the first two laws, Prop. 13, Book Three. These results are related to the "Phenomena" at the beginning of Book Three in the second (1713) and third (1726) editions, which—in the first edition—were included among various methodological precepts and improved statements as "Hypotheses."

12. On Newton and Kepler, see my introductory essay, "Kepler's Century: Prelude to Newton's," in *Vistas in Astronomy*, vol. 18, edited by Arthur Beer (Elmsford, N.Y.: Pergamon, 1975), pp. 3–36.

13. In Props. 1, 2, and 3, the force on satellites and planets is shown to vary inversely as the square of the distance; Props. 5 and 6 establish that all bodies gravitate toward planets (according to the inverse square law). The proportionality of gravity to the gravitating masses is the subject of Prop. 7.

Halley was guilty of enthusiastic exaggeration when he referred to Newton's "full Resolution" of "all the difficulties" in "*Astronomical* Science." Newton never even succeeded in dealing analytically (in the Newtonian gravitational manner) with the motion of the moon. See D. T. Whiteside: "Newton's Lunar Theory: From High Hope to Disenchantment," *Vistas in Astronomy*, 1976, vol. 19, pp. 317–328; also Craig Waff: *Universal Gravitation and the Motion of the Moon's Apogee: The Establishment and Reception of Newton's Inverse-Square Law, 1687–1749* (Baltimore: [doctoral dissertation: Johns Hopkins University], 1975); and my edition, with a bibliographical and historical introduction of *Isaac Newton's Theory of the Moon's Motion, 1702* (London: Dawson, 1975).

14. In his review Halley, like other scientists of his day, uses both "phenomena" and its translation "appearances."

15. Prop. 39, Book Three. Halley merely says that Newton's analysis reveals "the Spheroidal Figure of the Earth," but he does not indicate specifically whether Newton concluded that the earth is an oblate or a prolate spheroid.

16. "Nec fas est proprius mortali attingere divos."

17. In a letter to Leibniz, 16 October 1693, Newton referred to Huygens as "vir summus Hugenius," perhaps echoing the phrase used by Leibniz in a letter to Newton, 7 March 1692/3, "summus et ipse Mathematicus, Christianus Hugenius"; *The Correspondence of Isaac Newton*, edited by H. W. Turnbull, vol. 3 (Cambridge [England]: At the University Press, 1961), pp. 257–285.

18. In a survey of the main events of modern astronomy, written for William Wottan, Halley conspicuously omitted the name of Copernicus; see my *Revolution in Science* (Cambridge: The Belknap Press of Harvard University Press, 1985), Supplement 7-2.

19. This reference to Kepler occurs in the discussion of "Phaenomenon IV," Book Three (in the second and third editions of the *Principia*), equivalent to "Hypothesis VII" in the first edition.

20. Even before the *Principia* was published, Halley made a reference to it in an article entitled "A Discourse Concerning Gravity . . . ," published in 1686 in the *Philosophical Transactions*, vol. 16, pp. 3–21. See my *Introduction* (cited in note 2 *supra*), p. 142, n. 27. Halley said his article dealt with the "Affections or Properties of *Gravity,* and its manner of acting on *Bodies falling* . . . discovered, and . . . made out by Mathematical *demonstration* . . . lately by our worthy Country-man Mr. *Isaac Newton,* (who has an incomparable *Treatise of Motion* almost ready for the *Press*)."

21. This article, "The True Theory of the Tides," was published in the *Phil. Trans.,* No. 226, March 1697, pp. 445–457; it is reprinted in facsimile in *Isaac Newton's Papers & Letters* (cited in note 1 *supra*), pp. 412–424. There was an earlier printing in 1687, on the occasion of presenting a copy of Newton's *Principia*

to King James II. Pepys's copy of this printed paper, bound up with a copy of the first edition of the *Principia*, is in the Pepysian Library, Magdalene College, Cambridge; see A. N. L. Munby: "The Distribution of the First Edition of Newton's *Principia*," *Notes and Records of the Royal Society of London*, 1952, vol. 10, pp. 29–31.

22. See note 14 *supra*.

23. Newton (Prop. 24, Book Three) supposes that two tides come together by different channels. Since these differ in length, it may happen that the tides arrive directly in phase (and reinforce each other), or directly out of phase (in which case they annul each other), or in various combinations. Although Newton's ingenious explanation is incorrect, it does apparently constitute the first statement of the principle of interference. See my paper, "The First Explanation of Interference," *American Journal of Physics*, 1940, vol. 8, pp. 99–106.

24. James L. Axtell: "Locke's Review of the *Principia*," *Notes and Records of the Royal Society of London*, 1965, vol. 20, pp. 152–161; see also my *Introduction* (cited in note 2 *supra*), ch. 6, sect. 1. The review was published in *Bibliothèque Universelle*, March 1688, vol. 8, pp. 436–450.

25. There is, however, an introductory paragraph in which some general aspects of the study of mechanics and of God's operation in nature are discussed. Rosalie Colie found this introductory paragraph a sign of Locke's authorship. See her "John Locke in the Republic of Letters," pp. 111–129 of J. S. Bromley and E. H. Kossmann (editors): *Britain and the Netherlands* (London: Chatto & Windus, 1960).

26. In the general introductory paragraph, the author refers to "the general rules of natural Mechanics, that is to say, the effects, the causes, and the degrees of weight, of lightness, of elastic force, of resistance of fluids, and of the virtues [*vertus*] that one calls attractive and impulsive." In his own presentation, in Def. 4, Newton carefully avoided the term "attractive," stating that "impressed force" (*vis impressa*) can have various origins: "a blow, pressure, centripetal force" ("ex ictu, ex pressione, ex vi centripeta").

27. Jean-Théophile Desaguliers: *Course of Experimental Philosophy* (London: A. Millar, ed. 3, 1763), vol. 1, preface, p. viii. See James L. Axtell: "Locke, Newton, and the Elements of Natural Philosophy," *Paedagogica Europaea*, 1965, vol. 1, pp. 235–244.

28. From a new translation of the *Principia* by I. B. Cohen and Anne Miller Whitman, to be published by Harvard University Press and Cambridge University Press.

29. See the edition of the *Principia* with variant readings, prepared by Alexandre Koyré, I. B. Cohen, and Anne Miller Whitman (Cambridge: Harvard University Press; Cambridge [England]: At the University Press, 1972), p. 548.

30. This suggestion was made by Paul Mouy: *Le développement de la physique cartésienne* (Paris: Librairie Philosophique J. Vrin, 1934), p. 256; cf. Alexandre Koyré: *Newtonian Studies* (Cambridge: Harvard University Press, 1965), p. 115. The review was published in the *Journal des Sçavans*, 2 August 1688, vol. 16, pp. 237–238.

31. It is this method that I have called the "Newtonian style"; see my *Newtonian Revolution* (cited in note 4 *supra*), ch. 3.

32. See my *Revolution in Science* (cited in note 18 *supra*), ch. 10.

33. For details see my "Hypotheses in Newton's Philosophy," *Physis*, 1966, vol. 8, pp. 163–184; also my *Introduction* (cited in note 2 *supra*), ch. 2, sect. 2.

34. The review appeared in the *Acta Eruditorum*, June 1688, pp. 305–315. The review was very likely written by the learned editor of the *Acta*, Otto Mencke, to whom Halley had sent a complimentary copy of the *Principia*. See my *Introduction* (cited in note 2 *supra*), p. 155, n. 10; also *The Correspondence of Isaac Newton*, edited by H. W. Turnbull (Cambridge [England]: At the University Press, 1961), vol. 3, pp. 270–271, 291–292.

35. Leibniz said that he composed his *Tentamen*, containing his principles of celestial mechanics, after he had "come across an account of the celebrated Isaac Newton's Mathematical Principles of Nature" in the June 1688 issue of the *Acta*, which he had read in Rome, before he had seen the book itself. The "Tentamen de Motuum Coelestium," originally published in the *Acta Eruditorum*, February 1689, pp. 82–96, is reprinted in *Leibnizens Mathematische Schriften, herausgegeben von C. I. Gerhardt* (Berlin: Verlag von A. Asher & Comp.; Halle: Druck und Verlag von H. W. Schmidt, 1849–1863), vol. 6, pp. 144–161. On Newton's reference to the *Acta* review as an "epitome," see J. Edleston: *Correspondence of Sir Isaac Newton and Professor Cotes . . .* (London: John W. Parker; Cambridge [England]: John Deighton, 1850), pp. 308–309; also my *Introduction* (cited in note 2 *supra*), pp. 152–154.

36. W. W. Rouse Ball was perhaps guilty of chauvinism when he lauded Halley's review while disparaging the one in the *Acta*, which he said "is, and purports to be, little more than a synopsis of the contents." Ball should have known how difficult such a synopsis is, since he himself had prepared an extensive one for his *An Essay on Newton's "Principia"* (London, New York: Macmillan and Co., 1893), pp. 75–112; his comments on the review in the *Acta* appear on p. 68.

37. *Introduction* (cited in note 2 *supra*), pp. 155–156.

SIX

Newton's "Sleeping Argument" and the Newtonian Synthesis of Science and Religion

James E. Force

In this paper I will discuss and interpret a most cryptic reference by Isaac Newton to "yet another argument for a Deity," which lies beyond the standard design argument but which he prefers to "let sleep." I wish to begin, however, by briefly sketching how most contemporary scholars conceive of the relationship between science and religion in eighteenth-century England. Basil Willey speaks for the majority when he states that the "holy alliance between science and religion" has been, from Newton to Priestley in the eighteenth century, "a typically English phenomenon."[1] At the core of this English "alliance" of science and religion is the characteristic eighteenth-century argument of freethinkers and natural philosophers alike—the design argument.

The chief features of this most widely accepted argument consist in its a posteriori and analogical character. It is a posteriori, in the fashion of modern empirical science, because it begins in an accurate description of observed sequences in nature; it is, supremely, analogical because the mechanically or geometrically regular character of the observed natural order is held to be analogous to the mechanically or geometrically regular products of human design. The mainspring of the argument is the principle that "like effects show like causes." By analogy, the orderly processes of nature must also have an intelligent creator, one who is, as Newton phrases it, "very well skilled in Mechanicks & Geometry."[2]

The design argument was around long before Newton's famous "General Scholium" to the second edition of the *Principia*. Especially noteworthy statements of the design argument immediately prior to Newton are to be found in the writings of Robert Boyle and John Ray, to take but two examples.[3] Yet Newton and his *Principia*—even the first edition of 1687, which lacks an actual declaration of divine design—give shape and substance to the most influential form of the argument. Before publishing his Boyle Lectures for 1692, Richard Bentley consulted Newton's great work and corresponded with Newton about adapting its contents to the design argument. Newton responded with the famous words: "When I wrote my treatise about our Systeme I had an eye upon such Principles as might work with considering men for the beliefe of a Deity & nothing can rejoyce me more than to find it usefull for that purpose."[4]

Because no explicit statement of the design argument appears in the first edition of the *Principia,* some scholars have argued that Newton's assertion in this passage of a long-held opinion regarding his scientific work's alliance with natural theology ought not to be taken too literally.[5] But there is no reason to doubt Newton's own words on this point. According to William Whiston, Newton's successor in the Lucasian Professorship of Mathematics at Cambridge, when he inquired directly of Newton why he was so late in publicly professing the religious implications of his "Systeme of the World," Newton replied that "he saw these Consequences; but thought it better to let his Readers draw them first of themselves: Which Consequences however, He did in great measure draw himself long afterwards in the later Editions of his *Principia,* in that admirable *General Scholium* at its conclusion; and elsewhere, in his *Opticks.*"[6]

The design argument dominates the typically English phenomenon of a special "alliance" between science and religion, in large part owing to the triumph of Newton's *Principia.*[7]

DAVID HUME AND THE DOMINION OF GOD

Given the acknowledged importance in the eighteenth century of the design argument, the conclusion of Newton's first and most revealing letter to Bentley (see above) demands attention. After rejoicing over Bentley's use of data from the *Principia* to produce an important expression of the design argument and stating that he himself had long thought his book "usefull for that purpose," Newton mysteriously goes on to say that "there is yet another argument for a Deity wch I take to be a very strong one, but til ye principles on wch tis grounded be better received I think it more advisable to let it sleep."[8]

To what could Newton be referring so cryptically and enigmatically?[9] In what follows, I attempt to elucidate Newton's possible intent as well as to suggest that the nature of the English scientific-religious "alliance" may extend far beyond the boundaries of the conventional design argument.

For its Newtonian proponents, the design argument demonstrates only that God is a supreme Architect-Creator who uses his power to put into effect his beautifully designed plan of natural creation. But Newton also believes that God's continuing dominion over man and nature is revealed in another book, one separate from the "book" of nature. Ultimately, then, our view of this aspect of the Newtonian synthesis of science and religion must be based on a complete reinterpretation of the distinctive manner in which religious, scientific, and political language are integrated in early Newtonian thought. One important element of the Newtonian synthesis of science and religion rests finally on the view that the world contains many languages but that all these languages stem from one original cause. Because the organizing intelligence of these scripts and ciphers is the same (i.e., God), the task of both scientist and Bible interpreter is to demonstrate this fact by revealing their translatability through careful and rigorous scientific procedure. William Whiston best sums up the Newtonian alliance of science with religion, natural and revealed, when he describes the task of the Newtonian biblical scholar:

> Since it has now pleased God, as we have seen, to discover many noble and important truths to us, by the Light of Nature, and the System of the World; as also, he has long discovered many noble and important Truths by Revelation, in the Sacred Truths; It cannot be now improper, to compare these two Divine Volumes, as I may well call them, together; in such Cases, I mean of Revelation, as related to the Natural World, and wherein we may be assisted the better to judge by the knowledge of the System of the Universe about us. For if those things contained in Scriptures be true, and really deriv'd from the Author of Nature, we shall find them, in proper Cases, confirm'd by the System of the World and the Frame of Nature will in some Degree, bear Witness to the Revelation.[10]

Just as God has left the impression of his attributes of power and omnipotence on physical creation in the "book" of nature, so too is abundant evidence of his providential powers to be found in properly interpreted scripture. There is, however, one advantage to the scriptural and prophetic history found in God's other book, the Bible. In contrast to the book of nature, which tells us what sort of architect God is, the prophetic history of scripture shows a God still directly involved in that original creation, a God of special, as well as general or creative, providence. Furthermore, scriptural history contains clues about the course of the future of both the "World Natural" and the "World Politic," in those prophecies that have not yet been brought to fulfillment through God's special providence. God's Lordship continues.

To illustrate the entire providential nature of God—his creative architectural powers as well as his continuing specially provident intervention in and guidance of the affairs of men and nature—design theorists such as Newton and Whiston necessarily become interpreters of scriptural prophecies. There, in the record of miraculous promises made and fulfilled, is revealed the continuously active, specially provident God of Christianity. I label the argument from fulfilled prophecy the "citadel of orthodoxy" in the eighteenth century, by which I mean to suggest that it is not so much a completely separate enterprise from that of the Newtonian design theorists in the first decades of that century as it is a corollary enterprise.[11] The proper interpretation of fulfilled prophecy shows another aspect of God's providence which supplements the general providence of the supreme architect of the design argument. The "holy alliance between science and religion," that "typically English phenomenon" to which Basil Willey refers, consists for Newton and Whiston of both the design argument of natural religion and the properly objective and scientific interpretation of the evidence of God's specially provident intervention in the prophetic history of scripture.

The Scottish religious skeptic David Hume understands better than any other eighteenth-century commentator the true nature of the design argument, recognizing that the sole purpose of the design argument, as Newton and all other design theorists develop it, is to show, in Hume's words, "the *Nature* of that Divine Being; his attributes, his decrees; his plan of providence."[12] The point of the design argument is to illustrate the nature of God's governance of the whole of creation; the crucial problem emphasized, if not invented, is the problem of the nature and extent of God's providential dominion over the world.

Hume grasps the complex nature of this holy alliance between science and religion and attacks it indirectly, saying that the works of man are not clearly analogous to the whole of nature.[13] Hume's criticism of this aspect of God's providential power and dominion over creation is linked to his criticism of the attempt to discover any other aspect of the nature of God's providential dominion in prophetic history. In the first *Enquiry,* his initial critique of the design argument is in fact preceded by his famous essay "Of Miracles," which begins his skeptical attack on the alliance of these two arguments. Hume, along with nearly everybody in the eighteenth century, defines a miracle as a "violation of the laws of nature." Because a miracle is an event that contradicts firm and unalterable experience, the evidence for such an event must be extraordinarily strong. Such evidence is in fact impossible to obtain precisely because it runs counter to our unalterable experience to the contrary. When one goes on to add the possibility of deceit and error in the historical accounts of miracles, the "plain consequence" is that miracles are simply too implausible to be believed.

But, as I have discussed elsewhere at some length,[14] one of the most important elements of Hume's essay "Of Miracles" is his conclusion, where he points out almost in passing that his argument against miracles also undercuts belief in historically fulfilled prophecies, simply because, to be illustrative of divine special providence, true fulfilled prophecies are of necessity miraculous contraventions of natural law and, hence, are simply too improbable to be believed (at least by a skeptical Scot such as Hume).[15] As for the expectation of the fulfillment of those future prophecies, one probably ought not to be surprised that, for Hume,

> when we look beyond human affairs and the properties of the surrounding bodies; when we carry our speculations into the two eternities before and after the present state of things; into the creation and formation of the universe; the existence and properties of spirits; the *powers and operations* of one universal Spirit existing without beginning and without end, omnipotent, omniscient, immutable, infinite, and incomprehensible. We must be far removed from the smallest tendency to scepticism not to be apprehensive that we have here got quite beyond the reach of our faculties.[16]

Hume is one of the few eighteenth-century religious skeptics who understands that the whole point of the alliance between science and religion in the early 1700s is to illustrate all aspects of God's power and dominion over man and nature from the beginning up to the present and into the future. Consequently, Hume attacks both the design argument with its inference to a generally provident, supremely powerful Architect-Creator and the possibility of belief in scriptural histories of a specially provident deity who maintains an active Lordship over his creation through miracles and fulfilled prophecies.

Hume has shown us the false logic of linking the design argument to the supplementary argument from fulfilled prophecy in order to demonstrate the full extent and range of God's dominion over creation, and he has done so in order to destroy belief in such a God. But is there any historical evidence to show that Newton actually makes this linkage? In short, is the argument from fulfilled prophecy, which its adherents utilize to show God's continuing Lordship, Newton's "sleeping argument"?

NEWTON, THE "SLEEPING ARGUMENT" FROM PROPHECY, AND THE DOMINION OF GOD

I believe that Newton *is* referring to the argument from prophecy. He states, to repeat, that "there is yet another argument for a Deity wch I take to be a very strong one, but till ye principles on wch tis grounded be better received I think it more advisable to let it sleep."

Newton's long-standing enthusiasm for the proper principles to be followed in interpreting scriptural prophecy is at least prima facie evidence that it is this argument and the principles on which it depends to which he refers. Newton was a dour, secretive man not given to animated conversation on controversial topics. But when he went to Henry More's rooms in Cambridge in 1680 to discuss a paper by More on the interpretation of the apocalyptic prophecies in the Book of Revelation, More recorded that Newton's "ordinarily melancholy and thoughtful" countenance was "mighty lightsome and chearfull" and that Newton was "in a maner Transported."[17] Newton's discussion with William Whiston in 1706 concerning the proper principles for interpreting the prophecy of the seventy weeks in Daniel was equally animated.[18]

Yet stronger evidence that Newton's "sleeping argument" is the argument from prophecy is his relationship with his onetime protégé, William Whiston. In 1696, Whiston published *A New Theory of the Earth*. Analysts and commentators ever since have tended to focus on Whiston's geological theories, including his radical view that the "choc" of the close passage of a comet may have triggered the events in the Bible literally described in those passages about the Flood of Noah. The theoretical basis for the geological speculations in the main body of the book is contained in a separate, ninety-five-page introduction entitled "Introductory Discourse concerning the Genuine Nature, Stile, and Extent of the Mosaick History of the Creation"—which, Whiston writes, he showed to "Sir *Isaac Newton* himself, on whose Principles it depended, and who well approved it."[19] The principles contained in this introductory discourse become the basis for Whiston's long career as a biblical scholar who reaches heterodox views about everything from the doctrine of the Trinity to the history of the Council of Nicaea and St. Athanasius. The principles in Whiston's book are, I believe, the public proclamations of Newton's privately held views on how to read and interpret scriptural history, and which he states, in 1680 in his letter to Bentley, are so widely *unaccepted* that he prefers to let the argument based on those principles sleep undisturbed.

Soon after the appearance of *A New Theory of the Earth* and its explosive introduction, Newton summoned Whiston from his Lowestoft vicarage to be Newton's substitute in the Lucasian Chair of Mathematics at Cambridge, giving Whiston the full profits of his professorship. When Newton decided to give up the chair to devote himself completely to his duties at the Mint, he insured that Whiston would be his successor by recommending him to the heads of all the colleges.

The principles of interpretation announced first in *A New Theory of the Earth* and applied to geological speculation formed in Whiston's Boyle Lectures in 1707 the basis for an interpretation of how God has given man a record of prophetic predictions that, on being brought to pass, may be used to illustrate God's special providence. This work, which was "originally suggested" to Whiston by Isaac Newton, is entitled *The Accomplishment of Scripture Prophecy.*

Whiston's principles of interpreting the Bible are a threefold set of what, as a mathematician, he calls postulates:

I. The Obvious or literal Sense of Scripture is the True and Real one, where no evident Reason can be given to the contrary.

II. That which is clearly accountable in a natural way, is not without reason to be ascrib'd to a Miraculous Power.

III. What Ancient Tradition asserts of the constitution of Nature, or of the Origin and Primitive States of the World, is to be allow'd for True, where 'tis fully agreeable to Scripture, Reason, and Philosophy.[20]

The second principle shows the general Newtonian sense of discomfort with the notion of miracles; of course, Newton and Whiston accepted "genuine" accounts of miracles, but they tried hard to find natural mechanical explanations for apparently miraculous events related in scripture, for example, the mechanism of comets. And the third principle places Whiston (and Newton) squarely in the taxonomical interpretative tradition of such great Renaissance historians of comparative religion as Gerard Vossius.

Whiston's most basic interpretative postulate, however, is that "the obvious or literal Sense of Scripture is the True and Real one, where no evident Reason can be given to the contrary." Whiston rebels against what he considers to be fanciful interpretations, such as interpreting the Exodus as symbolic of the later Christian doctrine of baptism; the Exodus refers to one and only one historical event, *the* Exodus. In his Boyle Lectures for 1707, *The Accomplishment of Scripture Prophecy,* Whiston applies this first principle to interpreting how God has fulfilled prophetic predictions in the course of human history, arguing that although the language of the prophets may be "peculiar and enigmatical," nevertheless each prophetic prediction points to one, and only one, determinate historical event as its fulfillment. As Whiston states: "If Prophecies are allow'd to have more than one event in view at the same time, we can never be satisfy'd but they may have as many as any Visionary pleases."[21]

Whiston states that his Boyle Lectures, wherein he forthrightly proclaims in public Newton's long-held private views, are based "upon Sir Isaac Newton's original suggestion"[22]—this fifteen years after Richard Bentley gave the inaugural Boyle Lectures, in which the Newtonian design argument received its initial hearing. In the same way that Newton apparently hand-selected Bentley to be his proxy in the first instance, it seems quite likely that Whiston was Newton's chosen instrument for the public proclamation of Newton's "sleeping argument" and the principles underlying that argument.

The purpose of Whiston's lectures is to illustrate a specially provident Lord of creation still active in the daily governance of nature and history. The Architect-Creator of the design argument has not "absconded" after erecting the superbly designed, well-engineered "frame of nature," nor has he remained on station solely to adjust the gravitational mechanism from time to time. God remains active in history; he has made promises to his prophets, and he has kept them. The historical record of this activity reveals, to one who is able to discern it, a God who continues to exercise his Sovereign Lordship over his creation, in the same way that the evidence of design in nature reveals a Sovereign Lord of the physical world.

The nature of God's dominion over his creation is shown in both the book of nature and the book of scripture. Indeed, for the Newtonians the design argument reveals not a skillful or benign clockmaker, but a God of such awe-inspiring physical power that we are moved beyond reverence to fear. As Newton writes, after a lengthy description of how the structure of the eye necessitates the inference of a supremely powerful designer, this argument "ever will prevail with mankind to believe that there is a being who made all things and has all things in his power and who is therefore to be feared."[23] Whiston, too, perpetuates in his natural theology the God of total dominion over the natural realm, writing that "Nature is God's Constitution, and ever subservient to him; and the State of the Natural is always accommodated to that of the Moral World."[24]

Balanced with the Sovereign of the natural world is the Sovereign of human history as revealed to the wise in the prophetic histories. Concerning the "design of God" in providing mankind with so many examples of fulfilled prophetic predictions, and thus of his continuing dominion over the fate of man and his world, Newton writes, in his one published book on prophecy, that "the events of things predicted many ages before, will then be a convincing argument that the world is governed by providence."[25] Whiston, writing twenty years earlier in his Boyle Lectures, states similarly that the many instances of properly interpreted prophecies which show God's many predictions and God's power to fulfill them in history reveals "*the design of God's providence.*"[26]

Perhaps the strongest evidence that Newton's "sleeping argument" is the argument from prophecy, and that by that argument he understands the same thing as Whiston, is found, sleeping, in Newton's unpublished theological manuscripts. These writings show Newton's private concern with rules for interpreting prophetic history and his intention to use these rules to objectivize scripture and to move its interpretation out of the realm of private fancies and idiosyncratic individual hypotheses. Like Whiston, Newton intends his rules to be the tool that illustrates God's dominion over history, just as the "Rules of Reasoning" in the *Principia* become the tools for illustrating his Lordship over nature.

All of Whiston's postulates are repeated in Newton's manuscripts. Whiston's Postulate Three, which asserts the need to compare profane historical sources to sacred ones, and Postulate One, which insists that each prophetic text has only one signification, are integral to Newton's approach. Newton writes:

> John did not write in one language, Daniel in another, Isaiah in a third & the rest in others peculiar to themselves, but they all wrote in one & the same mystical language, as well known wthout doubt to the sons of the Prophets as the Hieroglyphick language of the Egyptians to their Priests. And this language so far as I can find was as certain & definite in its signification as is the vulgar language of any nation whatsoever: so that it is only through want of skill therein that Interpreters so frequently turn the Prophetick types & phrases to signify whatever their fansies & Hypotheses lead them to. He therefore that would understand the Old Prophets . . . must fix the significations of their types & phrases in the beginning of his studies. . . . And as Criticks for understanding the Hebrew consult also other oriental languages of the same root: so I have not feared sometimes to call into assistance the eastern expositors of their mystical writers . . . following herein the example of Mr Mede & other late writers. For the language of the Prophets being Hieroglyphical, had affinity with that of the Egyptian Priests & Eastern wise men and therefore was anciently much better understood in the East then it is now in the west.[27]

As for Whiston's second postulate, concerning the need to seek for a natural or mechanical explanation of events in prophetic history before fixing on God's miraculous suspension of natural laws as the actual cause of that event, Newton advises a similar wariness regarding miracle stories, stating that miracles "are not so called because they are the works of God but because they happen seldom and for that reason excite wonder."[28]

In an important variant of Newton's manuscript entitled "Paradoxical Questions Concerning the Morals and Actions of Athanasius and His Followers" there emerges most clearly Newton's view that, among Athanasius's many other apostasies, he and his followers feigned miracles through the "magical use of the signe of ye Crosse" in order to attract a following:

> These & such like stories sufficiently open the designe of Athanasius & his party in setting on foot this humour of pretending to miracles. They found by experience y^t their opinions were not to be propagated by disputing &

arguing, & therefore gave out that their adversaries were crafty people and cunning disputants and their own party simple well meaning men, and there imposed this law upon the Monks that they should not dispute about ye success of their cause to ye working of miracles and spreading of Monkery.[29]

Newton's private views about the proper method of understanding God's promises and their fulfillment in prophetic history are thus roughly the same as those published by Whiston. Furthermore, their rules have the same purpose: to evade private hypotheses and "fansies" about the nature of God and to show to the world a God who owns, possesses, and uses history in the same way that he owns, possesses, and uses nature.

Newton's Arian Christology is inevitably bound up with his view that God exercises absolute dominion over the whole of creation, including Jesus Christ. In Newton's view, Jesus is not cosubstantial with God the Father but a divine spirit commanded by God to inhabit a human body. Jesus is as much subject to God's dominion as are any of God's other servants. Thus Newton describes how, though Jesus and God are not cosubstantial, Jesus, owing to his special status, shares with God "an unity of Dominion, the Son receiving all things from the father, being subject to him, executing his will, sitting in his throne and calling him God, and so is but one God with the Father as a King and his viceroy are but one king. For the word God relates not to the metaphysical nature of God but to his dominion." [30]

Because of his view that God maintains absolute dominion over nature, history, and even Jesus Christ who is like a viceroy, Newton does not question the power of God to predestine even unborn children to eternal torment. We are all God's vassals and subject to his will: "Shall ye thing formed say to him y^t formed it, why hast thou made me thus? Hath not the potter power over the clay of ye same lump to make one vessel unto honour and another unto dishonour?" [31]

The dominion of God over the Son and past human history is revealed to the scientist-exegete. And even though the passages about the prophetic future are enigmatic and difficult to interpret in advance of their historical occurrence, we may be sure that eventually God's power will be shown to have extended over the future destiny of mankind. God's prophecies of "the last times" are not trifles:

If they are never to be understood, to what end did God reveale them? Certainly he did it for the edification of ye church, if so, then it is as certain y^t ye church shall at length attain to ye understanding thereof. I mean not all that call themselves Christians, but a remnant, a few scattered persons which God hath chosen, such as without being led by interest, education, or humane authorities can set themselves sincerely & earnestly to search after truth. For as Daniel hath said ye wise shall understand, so he hath said also that none of ye wicked shall understand.[32]

Finally, Newton's God controls each of our individual human destinies just as he controls his natural creation. It is because of his absolute dominion over creation as its "Universal Ruler" that we revere and fear him. Newton says: "We reverence and adore him on account of his dominion: for we adore him as his servants; and a god without dominion, providence, and final causes, is nothing else but Fate and Nature."[33]

THE ALLIANCE OF SCIENCE AND RELIGION IN NEWTON'S "SLEEPING ARGUMENT"

I have argued that Newton believes that to demonstrate the complete nature of God's providential dominion over history as well as over nature, over both the "World Politic" and the "World Natural," a supplement to the conventional design argument is necessary. He considers that this supplement is provided by his "sleeping argument," which reveals God's providential hand in history, if only to a remnant few. Just as Newton actively selected Richard Bentley to present the design argument of natural religion in the inaugural Boyle Lectures, so was his instrument for presenting the "sleeping argument" to the public his successor at Cambridge, William Whiston. Furthermore, I have argued that Hume understood the logical connection between design and prophecy because he realized that in both instances theists were attempting to demonstrate different aspects of God's providential dominion and so attacked both arguments. At this point one might well ask what the scripturally based argument from prophecy has to do with science. Scriptural or revelatory religion is based on the text of the Bible and does not, as the design argument does, take root in the observed processes of nature. Michael Hunter, for example, has argued that such Boyle Lectures, presumably, as those of Whiston completely lack any "scientific component."[34]

While I acknowledge that there is no necessary connection between biblical interpretation and the new science of Newton, nevertheless Newton believes in their logical inseparability. In other words, he and his disciple Whiston conceive of the argument from prophecy as a proper scientific argument.

First, in Newton's manuscripts and Whiston's many published books the approach taken to the interpretation of prophecy is founded on a method as rigorous, in its way, as that followed in the *Principia*. The two men seek to fathom the data of prophetic events by following a strict set of rules of procedure. Deductions about a hypothetical interpretation of the fulfillment of some particular prophecy on the basis of "propositions" or "postulates" are the same as the guesses of a physicist about how something works, which he then tries to confirm or disconfirm by experiments. In the case of the interpreters of prophecy, the experiments are the data of sacred, profane, and natural history. This approach to prophetic history yields, for Newtonian exegetes, scientifically respectable accounts of historical events such as the Noachian Deluge or Christ's fulfillment of the prophecies of Isaiah.

Whiston's faith in the extension of the objective methodology of hypothetico-deductive physics into prophetic-historical interpretation is impassioned and touching:

> And if once the Learned come to be as wise in Religious Matters, as they are now generally become in those that are Philosophical and Medical and Judicial; if they will imitate the Royal Society, the College of Physicians, or the Judges in Courts of Justice. . . . And if they will then proceed in their Enquiries about Reveal'd Religion, by real Evidence and Ancient Records, I verily believe . . . that the Variety of Opinions about those Matters . . . will gradually diminish.

But Whiston also understands that this happy result will occur only when and if "the Learned Christians imitate the learned Philosophers and Astronomers of the present Age, who have almost entirely left off Hypotheses and Metaphysicks, for Experiments and Mathematicks."[35]

Not only is the explanatory model for interpreting scriptural prophecies the same as that for interpreting the natural world, but the corollary concept of causality that underlies modern empirical science also underlies the Newtonian approach to prophecy. In modern science, the notion of causality is strongly influenced by the new focus on prediction and control of future events. The essence of the causal connection, as Hume points out, is simply the relationship between two events in our experience, which permits a confident forecast or prediction that any future occurrence of the preceding event or condition will probably be attended by a similar consequence (assuming, of course, that the future resembles the past).

The prediction, of course, is always subject to confirmation or disconfirmation by the actual historical occurrence. Thus, Hume emphasizes, feigned (i.e., a priori) hypotheses about the ultimate cause of all things are, in principle, incapable of experimental verification and so are simply beyond the scope of human knowledge. In this sense, delving into the "two eternities before and after the present state of things" in pursuit of knowledge about some one, infinite, omniscient deity is be-

yond our capacities. But, Hume insists, "so long as we confine our speculations to our morals, or politics, or criticism, we make appeals, every
moment, to common sense and experience, which strengthen our philosophical conclusions and remove (at least in part) the suspicion, which
we so justly entertain with regard to every reasoning, that is very subtle
or refined." [36]

Hume believes that no knowledge can possibly be obtained about the
nature of divine providential causation, because it is empirically inob-
servable. In Newton's and Whiston's view, however, the constancy of the
experienced sequence between cause and effect as discovered in the experimental casebook called the Bible does afford verifiable, experiment-
ally testable predictions enabling one to utilize experiments and avoid
feigned, a priori hypotheses. The Bible is a kind of record book of prophetic predictions communicated by God to man and then miraculously
brought to pass. The constancy of this experienced sequence (Whiston
eventually lists over four hundred fulfilled historical prophecies) affords
a justifiable expectation about those prophecies as yet unfulfilled. Even
though we may not be able to predict exactly when the event will occur,
we may still be confident that the event will in fact happen and that after
it does we will be able to see how it fits into God's providential plan. The
same methodology that leads Newton to the causal agent called gravity in
the "World Natural" leads, in the "World Politic" as discovered in prophetic history, to the demonstration for Newton of the specially provident deity of Christianity. As Newton states, "There is already so much
of Prophecy fulfilled, that as many will take pains in this study, may see
sufficient instances of God's providence." [37]

Newton's and Whiston's alliance of science and religion is based on
their initial assumption that the Bible is as much a book authored by God
as it is the frame of nature. For them, God is similar to college professors
who say the same things over and over again in a variety of talks, books,
and articles, and sometimes in different languages. To ask whether the
Newtonian enterprise of reading both books together for insights into
the nature of divine providence and God's providential plan for the future is in fact "scientific" obscures the historical point, which is that Whiston and Newton *believe* it is. Hume, of course, does not.

CONCLUSION

Why has this aspect of Newtonian thought dropped almost out of sight?
Why is the design argument considered to be *the* eighteenth-century approach to combining science and religion? The main reason, of course, is
that Newton's manuscripts are widely scattered and unpublished. Al-

though Richard S. Westfall's monumental biography and the work of Frank E. Manuel have done much to bring this aspect of Newton's thought to the attention of the learned world, what is necessary is the collection and publication of these papers to the extent possible.

There is, however, another significant factor in the tendency to over-play the design argument at the expense of the argument from proph-ecy in interpretations of the eighteenth-century alliance of science and religion. Religious controversy in England in the 1700s was polarized into two camps. On the one hand we have the lower orders, who were increasingly drawn away from the Church of England by the over-wrought enthusiasms of dissenters; on the other hand are the upper classes, whose members wrote books full of scorn both for the ignorant rantings of their enthusiastic opponents and for the hypocrisy of the fox-hunting politicians of the Church of England, and who were increas-ingly drawn to freethinking religious skepticism. What ultimately came to characterize the Age of Reason, then, was the triumph of deism and the mocking attack on the revealed religion of dissenting enthusiasts and orthodox clergy alike by Hume, Gibbon, and Voltaire, all of whom ac-cept the design argument in some form.

William Whiston realized quite early that Newtonian religious theo-rists were locked in a death struggle with freethinking deists. He points out how readily the freethinkers accepted Bentley's statement of the Newtonian design argument in 1692, but goes on to say that Bentley's persuasive sermons produce an attempt to prize apart natural and re-vealed religion:

> That this is true, I appeal to a certain Club of Persons, not over-religiously dispos'd, who being soberly asked, after Dr. *Bentley's* remarkable sermons at Mr. *Boyle's* lectures, built Sir *Isaac Newton's* Discoveries, and level'd against the prevailing Atheism of the Age, *What they had to say in their own Vindication against the Evidence produc'd by Dr. Bentley?* The answer was, *That truly they did not well know what to say against it, upon the Head of Atheism: but what*, say they, *is this, to the fable of Jesus Christ?* And in confirmation of this Account, it may, I believe, be justly observed, that the present gross *Deism*, or the Opposition that has of late so evidently and barefacedly appear'd against Holy scriptures, has taken its Date in some Measure from that Time.[38]

It is easy enough to tar the eccentric Whiston with the brush of reli-gious enthusiasm. Yet it is not so easy to dismiss Isaac Newton as a zeal-ous ranter. When one puts the excised argument from prophecy, with all its heterodox consequences, back into the historical Newtonian al-liance of science and religion, a more complicated man emerges who be-longs to a more complicated era.

NOTES

The author would like to thank the members of St. Edmund's House, Cambridge, for their hospitality in the spring of 1985, when this paper was written.

1. Basil Willey, *The Eighteenth-Century Background* (Harmondsworth, Eng.: Penguin Books, 1972), 162. See also Robert H. Hurlbutt, *Hume, Newton, and the Design Argument* (Lincoln: University of Nebraska Press, 1965), passim.

2. Newton to Bentley, 10 December 1692, in *The Correspondence of Isaac Newton*, ed. H. W. Turnbull et al. (Cambridge: Cambridge University Press, 1959–77), 3:233.

3. Michael Hunter has argued that John Ray's *Three Physico-Theological Discourses*, first published in 1963, is as influential as the Newtonian design argument presented by Bentley and Newton. This is undoubtedly true, but it is probably also true that though Ray relies most heavily on biological and botanical evidence of design in nature—and so produces a slightly different form of the argument—and that Ray never mentions Newton, Ray is nevertheless a member of the Royal Society and a regular reader of the *Transactions* and so undoubtedly familiar with Newton's natural philosophy. Still, Hunter's point is well taken. See his *Science and Society in Restoration England* (Cambridge: Cambridge University Press, 1981), 35.

4. Newton to Bentley, 10 December 1692, in *Correspondence* 3:233.

5. Henry Guerlac and Margaret C. Jacob have so argued in "Bentley, Newton, and Providence," *Journal of the History of Ideas* 30, no. 3 (1969): 311–12. This article is of special significance because in it the authors show beyond reasonable doubt that Newton actively assisted the executors of Boyle's will in choosing Bentley to deliver the inaugural sermons.

6. William Whiston, *A Collection of Authentick Records Belonging to the Old and New Testament*, 2 vols. (London, 1728), 2:1073–74.

7. For an excellent and persuasive argument of this point, see Hurlbutt, *Hume, Newton, and the Design Argument*.

8. Newton to Bentley, 10 December 1692, in *Correspondence* 3:236.

9. Richard S. Westfall has argued with his usual incisiveness that the greatest interest of Newton's correspondence with Bentley lies in what it illuminates about Newton's natural philosophy. Of this particular Newtonian text, Westfall writes, I believe correctly, that "as far as I know, Newton never explained this reference. He probably had the argument from the providential course of history as foretold in the prophecies in mind" (Westfall, *Never at Rest: A Biography of Isaac Newton* [Cambridge: Cambridge University Press, 1980], 505).

10. William Whiston, *Astronomical Principles of Religion, Natural and Reveal'd* (London, 1717), 133.

11. James E. Force, "Hume and Johnson on Prophecy and Miracles: Historical Context," *Journal of the History of Ideas* 43, no. 3 (1982): 463–75.

12. David Hume, *Dialogues Concerning Natural Religion*, ed. Norman Kemp Smith (London: Thomas Nelson, 1947), 128.

13. Hume is a most astute critic of the design argument. He is well aware of recent scientific theories in astronomy, optics, psychology, geology, microscopy, cosmogony, and electricity and shows how these scientific fields provide fertile new ground both for design theorists and for those, such as Hume himself, who

seek to limit the usual inferences about the nature of God drawn from the evidence of these sciences. Hume is, above all, a philosopher, and he is mainly concerned with the structure of the design argument and not with particular instantiations made on the basis of some particular area of scientific investigation. And the structure of the argument, as declared by Cleanthes in Hume's *Dialogues* (p. 143), is explicitly Newtonian:

> Look round the world: Contemplate the whole and every part of it: You will find it to be nothing but one great machine, subdivided into an infinite number of lesser machines. . . . All these various machines, and even their most minute parts, are adjusted to each other with an accuracy which ravishes into admiration all men who have ever contemplated them. The curious adapting of means to ends, throughout all nature, resembles exactly, though it much exceeds, the productions of human contrivance. . . . Since therefore the effects resemble each other, we are led to infer, by all the rules of analogy, that the causes also resemble, and that the Author of Nature is somewhat similar to the mind of man, though possessed of much larger faculties, proportioned to the grandeur of the work he has executed.

Hume, through Philo, repeats for the sake of clarity that the underlying principle of the design argument is the proposition that *"Like effects prove Like causes"* (p. 165). That Hume recognizes this proposition to be one of Newton's methodological "rules" is virtually certain. In his *Mathematical Principles of Natural Philosophy* (trans. Andrew Motte [1729], ed. Florian Cajori [Berkeley: University of California Press, 1934], 398; hereafter referred to as *Principia* [Motte-Cajori]), Newton phrases the same principle as follows: "Therefore to the same natural effects we must, as far as possible, assign the same causes." This principle is constantly appealed to by such Newtonian scientist-theologians as William Whiston. Whiston writes that this principle underlies the design argument, stating that

> every unbyass'd Mind would easily allow, that like Effects had like Causes; and that Bodies of the same general Nature, Uses, and Motions, were to be deriv'd from the same Originals; and consequently, that the Sun and the fixed Stars had one, as the Earth, and the other Planets another sort of Formation. If therefore any free Considerer found that one of the latter sort, that Planet which we Inhabit, was deriv'd from a Chaos; by a parity of Reason he would suppose, every one of the other to be so deriv'd also. (*A New Theory of the Earth* [London, 1696]; quoted from the separately paginated "Large Introductory Discourse concerning the Genuine Nature, Stile, and Extent of the Mosaick History of the Creation," p. 40)

Whiston is one of many who follow Newton himself in applying this principle to inferences about the nature of God. The nature of this inference and this principle, writes Whiston, is

> the very same by which, from the Contemplation of a Building, we infer a Builder; and from the Elegancy and Usefulness of each Part, we gather he was a skilful Architect; or by which from the View of a Piece of Clockwork, we conclude the Being of the Clockmaker; and from the many regular Motions therein, we believe that he was a curious Artificer." (*Astronomical Principles*, 106)

Whiston also writes that this principle is so "clear, natural, obvious, and sure," that it is grasped "without occasion for a tutor to instruct us in it at first, or for a Logician to improve us in it afterward" (*Astronomical Principles*, 255).

Hume attacks the basic design analogy, of course, arguing at length in the *Dialogues* that the works of man and nature are not clearly analogous. But he also attacks the use made of Newton's second rule in a distinctive and typically ironic manner which suggests that he is thoroughly familiar with all of Newton's "Rules of Reasoning" in the *Principia*. His spokesman in this particular attack, Philo, asks: "But can a conclusion, with any propriety, be transferred from parts to the whole?" (*Dialogues*, 147).

What Hume is really pointing out with this question is that all design theorists, including Newton, ought to be good Newtonians and read Newton's Fourth Rule of Reasoning, which states:

> In experimental philosophy we are to look upon propositions collected by general induction from phaenomena as accurately or very nearly true, notwithstanding any contrary hypotheses that may be imagined, till such time as other phaenomena occur, by which they may either be made more accurate, or liable to exceptions. This rule we must follow that the argument of induction may not be evaded by hypotheses. (*Principia* [Motte-Cajori], 398)

The point of Hume's innocent question about reasoning from the part to the whole is that all design theorists read the principle "Like Effects prove Like Causes" as a hypothetical, metaphysical, a priori assumption about the nature of the real universe. Newton and other design theorists, in their arguments, feign the hypothesis that nature is, in reality, uniform with respect to causes. But, argues Hume, the part cannot be made the rule for the whole in advance of empirical experience. For Hume it is perfectly acceptable to reason from the part to the whole so long as either the scientist or the design theorist recognizes that this principle ought to have the ontological status of a regulative hypothesis adopted as a methodological assumption that is always subject to the checks and revisions of future experience, and not the ontological status given it by Newtonian design theorists, i.e., a feigned a priori hypothesis about the way the world really is. All design theorists, in sum, read the Second Rule of Reasoning without the crucial qualification of Rule Four.

Hume cautiously applauds Galileo's proper and careful methodology. Hume points out that only after the observations with the telescope made evident "the similarity of their nature" did Galileo conclude that the substance of the Moon was similar to or analogous with that of the Earth, enabling us "to extend the same arguments and phenomena from one to the other" (*Dialogues*, 151). For Hume, it really does not matter how much apparent evidence of design and order is turned up by all the new sciences, because the design theorists read that evidence in a false light—as the rule for the whole instead of as a regulative hypothesis or methodological assumption adopted merely to guide future empirical inquiry (*Dialogues*, 166).

Hume's criticism of Newton's own design argument on this head shows his familiarity with Newton's thought; nor is it the last thing we can learn from him about the nature of Newtonian theism.

14. James E. Force, "Hume and the Relation of Science and Religion Among Certain Members of the Royal Society," *Journal of the History of Ideas* 45, no. 4 (1984): 517–36. Besides Hume, Edward Gibbon clearly sees that a fulfilled prophecy is, by definition, a miraculous event. In his famous account "The Prog-

ress of the Christian Religion . . . ," Gibbon discusses the importance of the "mysterious prophecy" of the millennium in the early church, squarely placing the "gift" of "vision and prophecy" into the category of "Miraculous Powers of the Primitive Church," along with the "power of expelling daemons, of healing the sick, and of raising the dead." See *The History of the Decline and Fall of the Roman Empire*, ed. J. B. Bury (London: Methuen, 1909), chap. 15.

15. Hume asserts, "What we have said of miracles may be applied, without any variation, to prophecies; and indeed, all prophecies are real miracles, and as such only, can be admitted as proofs of any revelation" (*Enquiry Concerning Human Understanding*, sec. X, "Of Miracles," last paragraph).

16. Hume, *Dialogues*, 134–35.

17. Henry More to John Sharp, 16 August 1680, in *Conway Letters: The Correspondence of Anne, Viscountess Conway, Henry More, and Their Friends*, ed. Marjorie Hope Nicolson (New Haven: Yale University Press, 1930), 478–79.

18. Whiston and Newton quarreled rancorously in 1706 about the proper interpretation of *Daniel* 9 : 245. Although they ultimately differed on the particular time in biblical chronology to which this particular prophecy refers (and so, consequently, on the nearness of their own day to the millennium), Newton and Whiston shared the same basic methodological approach to interpreting scripture prophecy. See William Whiston, *Memoirs* (London, 1753), 1 : 35–36, 250.

19. Ibid., 1 : 38. See also James E. Force, *William Whiston: Honest Newtonian* (Cambridge: Cambridge University Press, 1985), chap. 2.

20. Whiston, *New Theory*, "Large Introductory Discourse" (separately paginated), 95.

21. William Whiston, *The Accomplishment of Scripture Prophecy* (London, 1708), 15.

22. Whiston, *Memoirs* 1 : 98.

23. Newton, "A Short Scheme of the True Religion," King's College Library, Cambridge, MS. Keynes 7. The material cited here and in notes 27 and 31 is quoted with the permission of the Librarian, King's College, Cambridge.

24. Whiston, *New Theory*, 361.

25. Isaac Newton, *Observations upon the Prophecies of Daniel and the Apocalypse of St. John* (London, 1733), 2, 52.

26. Whiston, *Accomplishment of Scripture Prophecy*, 30.

27. Newton, "The Language of the Prophets," King's College Library, Cambridge, MS. Keynes 5, f. 1.

28. Cited in H. McLachlan, ed., *Newton's Theological Manuscripts* (Liverpool: Liverpool University Press, 1930), 17.

29. Newton, "Paradoxical Questions concerning ye morals & actions of Athanasius & his followers," under the question: "Whether Athanasius did not start false miracles for his own interest" (William Andrews Clark Memorial Library, University of California, Los Angeles). Cf. Newton to John Locke, 16 February 1692, in *Correspondence* 3 : 195.

30. Newton, "History of the Church" (fragment), Jewish National and University Library, Jerusalem, Yahuda MS. 15.1, fol. 154.

31. Newton, "Commonplace Book," under the article "Predestinatio," King's College Library, Cambridge, MS. Keynes 2.

32. Newton, "Treatise on the Apocalypse," Jewish National and University Library, Jerusalem, Yahuda MS. 1, fol. 1.

33. Newton, *Mathematical Principles*, 543.

34. Michael Hunter, *Science and Society in Restoration England* (Cambridge: Cambridge University Press, 1980), 80. Hunter's point here is to argue against Margaret C. Jacob's contention that the Boyle Lectures were in fact crucial for the dissemination of Newtonian philosophy into English society. See also Force, *William Whiston*, 63.

35. Whiston, *A Supplement to the Literal Accomplishment of Scripture Prophecies* (London, 1725), 5–6.

36. Hume, *Dialogues*, 135.

37. Newton, *Observations upon the Prophecies*, 252.

38. Whiston, *Astronomical Principles*, 243.

SEVEN

Newton as Alchemist and Theologian

B.J.T. Dobbs

Our difficulty in understanding Newton as alchemist and theologian has been acute. In large part the widespread incomprehension of Newton's interest in these areas was first engendered by two post-seventeenth-century historical developments: the explicit rejection of alchemical practice and doctrine, and the divorce of science and religion. During the more than two centuries that Newton's papers on alchemy and theology remained virtually unknown, the intellectual climate changed so greatly that the seventeenth-century context of Newton's work was lost to view. At the same time, acclaim for the successful enterprise of modern science swelled to a loud chorus; as praise for Isaac Newton's heroic foundation of modern science was incorporated into the positivist textbook tradition, it became almost inconceivable that Newton could have squandered his great powers on alchemy and theology.

The *locus classicus* for the dismay caused by a survey of Newton's alchemical papers comes from Sir David Brewster's mid-nineteenth-century hagiographic biography: "We cannot understand how a mind of such power, and so nobly occupied with the abstractions of geometry, and the study of the material world, could stoop to be even the copyist of the most contemptible alchemical poetry, and the annotator of a work, the obvious production of a fool and a knave."[1] Brewster's conviction that the core of Newton's personality was really identical to that of a nineteenth-century scientist survived his encounter with Newton's disturbing papers almost intact. John Maynard Keynes, in direct contrast, suggested that our image of Newton the scientist was in some ways erroneous and that we should see him instead as "the last of the magicians."[2] Such ultimately unsatisfactory polarization however, has left those who adhered to neither position with only Wordsworth's enigmatic portrayal of Newton as "a mind for ever / Voyaging through strange seas of Thought, alone."[3]

Diverging from these positions, I will argue here that one needs to see Newton as one whole and historical human being and to realize both that Newton himself saw his diverse studies as constituting a unified plan for obtaining Truth and that his methodology was essentially the same in all his areas of study. Indeed, these arguments for the unity of Newton's thought include the demonstration of a direct connection between his alchemical/theological interests and his work on comets, a connection centered in Newton's understanding of divine providence.

Newton believed Truth to be a unity, guaranteed by the unity and majesty of God; it is thus in a religious interpretation of all of Newton's work that we may find a way to reunite his many strangely divergent but well-polished facets. Blinded by the brilliance of his laws of motion and optics, his calculus, his concept of universal gravitation, and his rigorous experimentation and methodological success, we have seldom wondered whether the discovery of the laws of nature was all that Newton had in mind. Missing the religious nature of his quest, we have often taken the stunningly successful by-products for his primary goal. But Newton wished to look through nature not to study the material world per se, as Brewster thought, or even, as Keynes assumed, to solve the riddle of the universe by tracking down the mystic clues that God has strewn about to challenge the esoteric brotherhood of magicians; rather, he wished to see God. For its own sake the world was of little importance; it was only as a route to the knowledge of God that study of the world gained great significance in Newton's eyes. As he explained in the 1690s, "There is no way $\nearrow$ (wth out revelation) $\swarrow$ to come to y^e knowledge of a Deity but by the frame of nature."[4] The world was God's handiwork, and so nature had direct theological meaning. As one infers something of the character of the artist by studying a work of art, so Newton inferred something of the character of the Deity by studying his creation.

The goal of Newton's work was thus a unified system, one that certainly included natural principles but was to have included divine ones as well. Although he was never fully successful in establishing divine principles, and although his system of natural philosophy came to stand alone and be treated as if it were the whole goal of his life's work, both alchemy and theology had a part in the general plan as Newton himself conceived it. Let us then see what function the study of alchemy and theology had in Newton's grand attempt to establish a system that comprehended all things both on earth and in heaven, and then delineate the connection between those two studies and his work on comets.

THEOLOGY AND ALCHEMY

In theology Newton adhered quite closely to one strand of traditional thought that had been and continued to be very strong in Western Christendom, the doctrine of voluntarism, in which God's will was considered to be his primary attribute. In Newton's papers it is always the will of the supreme God that is put into effect, both in the creation and in its governance. It is not for his essence that God desires to be worshiped, Newton said, but for his actions, the "issues" of his will, especially in "creating preserving & governing all things." To celebrate God for his essence—his eternity, immensity, omniscience, and omnipotence—is very pious and indeed is "the duty of every creature to do it according to his capacity." But those attributes spring not from the freedom of God's will

> but from yᵉ necessity of his nature. . . . And as yᵉ wisest of men delight not so much to be commended for their height of birth strength of body, bewty, strong memory, large fantasy, or other such gifts of nature as for their wise good & great actions the issues of their will: so yᵉ wisest of beings requires of us ⟨chiefly⟩ to be celebrated ↗ not so much for his essence as ↙ for ⟨yᵉ issues of his will which are⟩ ↗ his actions, ↙ the creating preserving & governing of all things ↗ according to his good will & pleasure. ↙. The wisdome power goodness & justice wᶜʰ he always exerts in his actions are his glory.⁵

Newton's heavy emphasis on the will of God thus placed him firmly within the camp of voluntarist theology.⁶ For the voluntarist, the power of God's will is complete, encompassing even the laws of nature, for natural laws—both physical and moral—were ordained by God. Newton, like other voluntarists, was concerned to define the realm of natural law, for that realm represented God's ordained power: although God can abrogate his natural laws whenever he so wills, ordinarily he does not do so because of his goodness and beneficence; rather, he maintains the world in an orderly fashion by his ordinary concourse. But the voluntarist never forgot that God, with the absolute power of his will, could at any time use his laws in an extraordinary way to produce a miracle, abrogate the laws completely, or decree that they be transformed. For the voluntarist the world is always contingent on the will of God.⁷

In an alchemical treatise usually known by its incipit, "Of Natures obvious laws & processes in vegetation," a treatise of his own composition probably written about 1672, Newton entered unequivocally into the lists of the voluntarists with a discussion entitled "Of God." His first point seems to have been that God can do anything that does not involve a logical contradiction:

Of God. Whatever I can conceive wthout a contradiction, either is or may ⟨effected⟩ ↗ bee made ↙ by somthing that is: I can conceive all my owne powers (knowledge, ⟨*illegible word*⟩ activating matter, &c) wthout assigning them any limits Therefore such powers either are or may bee made to bee.

Example. ↗ All the dimensions imaginable are possible. ↙ A body by accelerated motion may ⟨becom infinitly long or⟩ trancend all ⟨space⟩ distance in any finite tim assigned. ↗ also it may becom infinitly long ↙ This if thou denyest tis because thou apprehendest a contradiction in the notion & if thou apprehendest none thou wilt grant it ⟨*illegible word*⟩ ↗ in the ↙ pour of things.[8]

Presumably communing with himself alone as he committed the intimate "thou" to paper in his lonely study, Newton reworked the classical statement of God's absolute power. God can do any conceivable thing as long as no contradiction is involved. Then, exploring the implications of that proposition for God's cosmic creativity, Newton argued that since God could have created any sort of world, our world is as it is not by necessity but by God's "voluntary & free determination y^t it should bee thus":

Arg 2. The world might have been otherwise then it is (because there may be worlds otherwise framed then this) Twas therefore noe necessary but a voluntary & free determination y^t it should bee thus. And such a voluntary [cause must bee a God]. determination implys a God. If it be said ye w^{ld} could bee noe otherwise y^n tis because tis determined by an eternall series of causes, y^{ts} to pervert not to answer ye 1st prop: ffor I meane not y^t y^e ⊕ might have been otherwise notwthstanding the precedent series of causes, but y^t ye whole series of causes might from eterity have beene otherwise here ⟨because they as well as⟩ ↗ because they may be otherwise in other places.[9]

The "whole series of causes" that makes this world what it is could have been different, because God's power is absolute and his choice of any particular set of causes is "voluntary & free," that is, an issue of his unlimited free will.

Newton's purpose in inserting these passages into an alchemical treatise, however, cannot simply have been to rehearse the traditional arguments for a voluntarist theology. On the contrary, he was concerned in the "Vegetation" manuscript to find the laws of vegetable action and to distinguish them from the laws of mechanical action. Mechanical action, by which Newton's predecessors in mechanical philosophy meant action by contact or impact, was readily comprehensible to the human mind, surely one reason for the seventeenth-century popularity of mechanical systems. By reminding himself of God's unlimited power to institute *any* series of causes and not just mechanical ones, Newton was making room within the natural world for the nonmechanical laws of vegetation.

Let us recall the first phrase of his treatise: "Of Natures obvious laws & processes in vegetation." In distinguishing between mechanical and vegetable chemistry in this essay, Newton said that although the mechanical coalitions or separations of particles may explain many changes in common or vulgar chemistry, there is another realm of chemistry, the vegetable one, that operates in all three kingdoms of nature. Within the mineral kingdom, Newton's vegetable chemistry is clearly equivalent to what we know as alchemy. In his fifth distinction between the mechanical and the vegetable realms, Newton argued that some cause other than, and in addition to, mechanical ones must operate in vegetable chemistry:

> 5 So far therefore as ye same changes may bee wrought by the slight mutation of the tictures of bodys in common chymistry & such like experiments many may judg that ⟨there is noe other cause that will⟩ such changes made by nature are done ye same way that is by ye sleighty transpositions ye grosser corpuscles, for upon their disposition onely sensible qualitys depend. But so fast as by ⟨generation⟩ ↗ vegetation ↙ such changes are wrought as cannot bee done wthout it wee must have recourse to som further cause And this difference ⟨is seen clearest in fossile substances⟩ is vast & fundamentall because nothing could ever yet bee made wthout vegetation wch nature useth to produce by it.
> [note ye instance of turning Iron into copper. &c.] [10]

It may consequently be argued that Newton's voluntarism allowed him to rise above the restrictions of seventeenth-century mechanical philosophy. Mechanical causation in the seventeenth-century sense might be more easily understood than nonmechanical causation by limited human minds, but man's mind is not the measure of God's unlimited power. God could have instituted any sort of causal laws he wanted. Since God's laws are contingent on his will and are *not* necessitated by the nature of things, they cannot be formulated by intellectual processes alone. Indeed, the only way human beings have of grasping those laws is empirically to investigate the world as God actually instituted it. That there is thus a close linkage in practice between voluntarism and empiricism has long been recognized.[11] In rehearsing his voluntarist theology in an alchemical context, Newton justified to himself his empirical investigations into the laws of vegetation (i.e., his alchemical experimentation) that so radically contravened the contemporary consensus on mechanical philosophy.

Furthermore, Newton gave us an additional clue to his purpose in inserting the voluntarist doctrine into his alchemical treatise with the following introductory phrases: "Of ye contrivance of vegetables & animalls. Of sensible qualitys. Of ye soules union."[12] None of those topics could be adequately explicated by contemporary mechanical philosophy, and they were to Newton examples of just that sort of natural process for which one must have recourse to some further (nonmechanical) cause and to which his alchemical studies were to provide the key.

Apparently, then, Newton's voluntarist theology had a dual function in his alchemical studies: (1) to free his mind from the shackles of contemporary mechanical dogma enough to allow him to search for nonmechanical causal laws within nature and (2) to encourage an observational/experimental methodology. Since to Newton vegetable chemistry was a part of the natural world (it being *nature's* "obvious laws & processes" for which he searched), one may surely generalize from the theological/alchemical relationship we have just explored. Thus in Newton's natural philosophy in general we find the same emphasis on observation and experiment; and we eventually find a concept of universal gravitation predicated on a nonmechanical causal law.

PROVIDENCE

It is not enough, however, to argue that Newton's theological presuppositions informed his natural-philosophical style. In order to substantiate the claim that Newton's work constituted a unified pattern for him and that he hoped to build a comprehensive system that included both natural and divine principles, one must go further. This we shall begin to do by briefly exploring Newton's attempt to prove conclusively that the world continues under divine, providential guidance.

From the 1660s Newton was troubled by a theological problem regarding God's providential care of the world. Like his older contemporaries Isaac Barrow and Henry More, he was alarmed at the atheistic potentialities of the revived corpuscularianism of his century, particularly of Cartesianism.[13] Although the ancient atomists had not really been atheists in any precise modern sense, they had frequently been so labeled because their atoms in random mechanical motion received no guidance from the gods. Descartes, Gassendi, and Charleton had been at pains to allay the fear that the revived corpuscular philosophy would carry the stigma of atheism that adhered to ancient atomism.[14] They had solved the problem, they thought, by having God endow the particles of matter with motion at the moment of creation. All ensuing activity, then, was due not to random corpuscular action but to the initial intention of the Deity.

Later writers, going further, had carefully instated a Christian providence among the particles, where the ancient atomists had of course never had it. Only providence could account for the particles' obviously designed concatenations. The Stoics had similarly critiqued atomism in antiquity; in the seventeenth century, via Christianity, their critique actually came to be incorporated into the revived corpuscular doctrines. That development was all to the good in the eyes of most Christian philosophers, because it allowed the new mechanical philosophies to support religion: without the providential action of God, the particles could never have assumed the lovely forms of plants and animals so perfectly fitted to their habitats. Though present in Christianity from a very early period, this argument from design assumed unparalleled importance in the seventeenth century, and if the new astronomy had raised doubts about the focus of providence on such an obscure corner of the cosmos, the new corpuscularianism seemed to relieve them.[15]

The difficulty came when one began to wonder how providence operated in the law-bound universe emerging from the new science, and that difficulty was especially severe in the Cartesian system, where only matter and motion were acceptable explanations. Even though Descartes had argued that God constantly and actively supported the universe with his will, in fact it seemed to Henry More and others that Descartes's God was in danger of becoming an absentee landlord, one who had set matter in motion in the beginning but who then had no way of exercising his providential care.

Newton faced this theological difficulty squarely and directly. The mechanical action of matter in motion was not enough. Granted, such mechanical action did exist among the particles and could account for large classes of phenomena, yet it could not account for all. It could not account for the manifold riches of the phenomenal world. All forms of matter, however various, could be reduced to a common primordial matter; but how had they been produced in the first place? The production of variety from unity seems to posit an effect greater than its cause. Newton's problem was similar to but broader than the general problem for the corpuscularian, the origin of forms and qualities. From the particles of a catholic matter with only primary mathematical properties, there seemed to be no "sufficient reason" for forms and qualities to emerge at all.[16] But emerge they did, and in such incredible and well-crafted plentitude that causal explanations based on mechanical interactions seemed totally insufficient. As Newton was finally to say in the "General Scholium" to the *Principia*, "Blind metaphysical necessity [i.e., mechanical action], which is certainly the same always and everywhere, could produce no variety of things."[17] Variety requires some further cause. As Newton argued in his 1670s "Vegetation" manuscript, variety is produced by vegetation, and the agent that activates and guides common matter into the many contrivances "of vegetables & animalls" is a nonmechanical and at least quasi-divine "vegetable spirit."[18]

Newton's distinction between mechanical and vegetable chemistry thus emerges as crucial to his solution of the theological problem posed by his Cartesian inheritance. Mechanical chemistry may be accounted for simply by matter and motion, where only large corpuscles are rearranged. Changes in that realm may seem to be "strange transmutations," but they are "but mechanicall coalitions ↗ or seperations ✓ of particles as may appear in that they returne into their former natures if reconjoyned or (when unequally volatile) dissevered, & y^t wthout any vegetation."[19] Such changes may be explained by contact or impact mechanisms and require no further explanation. But for all that great class of beings that nature produces by vegetation—"All that diversity of natural things which we find suited to different times and places"[20]—we must have recourse to some further cause. Ultimately the cause is God, God who in his wisdom and with his dominion, his providential care, and the final purposes known only to himself, produces all the variety: natural diversity "could arise from nothing but the ideas and will of a Being necessarily existing."[21] Within the realm of vegetable chemistry, where God wills variety to arise, lies one arena of his providential guidance of the world, one area of providential care. Newton's God, although in many ways exceedingly transcendant, was not an absentee landlord.

As the "vegetable spirit" served God as an agent in his providential care of the world, so also did comets. Newton was early convinced by biblical sources that the world would end by fire but would probably be renewed.[22] Surviving evidence suggests also that he was thoroughly familiar with and accepted the Stoic doctrine of *ekpyrosis* that so strongly reinforced the evidence of scripture.[23] As a result Newton searched for a physical agent that would be capable of effecting God's will for the pyrotechnic dissolution of the world, and he thought he had found it in the comet of 1680.

Early in March 1724/25, some two years before his death, Newton explained his conclusion to John Conduitt. "I was on Sunday night . . . at Kensington with Sir Isaac Newton, in his lodgings," Conduitt said. Newton had just emerged from "a fit of the gout" and apparently felt talkative, telling Conduitt "in one continued narration" what he had often hinted at before, "viz. that it was his conjecture . . . that there was a sort of revolution in the heavenly bodies." Newton's idea was that the vapors and light emitted by the Sun, and other celestial matter as well, "gathered themselves by degrees, into a body . . . and [attracting yet more matter] at last made a secondary planet [a satellite such as our Moon]," then a primary planet, and finally a comet, "which after certain revolutions, by coming nearer and nearer to the sun, had all its volatile parts condensed, and became a matter fit to recruit, and replenish the sun (which must waste by the constant heat and light it emitted), as a faggot would this fire, if put into it (we were sitting by a wood fire), and that that would probably be the effect of the comet of 1680 sooner or later."[24]

The comet of 1680 had first been sighted before sunrise early in November, becoming invisible by the end of the month because of its proximity to the rising Sun. In mid December another comet appeared, which moved away from the Sun in the early evening—or at least every astronomer in Europe thought it was another comet, with the one exception of the Astronomer Royal of England, John Flamsteed. Flamsteed thought the two comets were one and the same, a comet that had simply reversed its direction in the vicinity of the Sun. Such an idea was unheard of at the time. Comets had always been alien, erratic, and ephemeral bodies that portended no good for anyone;[25] they were taken to be "signs" of disaster—not causing disaster themselves, for none had ever been known to crash into anything, but rather indicating disruption in the normal course of events as they cut across the customary circular movements of the heavens.

In 1680 this notion of Flamsteed's, though he did not exactly say that the comet was orbiting the Sun, stimulated Newton's interest in comets. Newton, who was then in the earliest stages of applying gravitational concepts to celestial dynamics, argued with Flamsteed for some little while that there were two comets in 1680, but by 1684 he had recognized that comets were subject to the inverse square law of attraction toward a center of gravitation. By the time the *Principia* was published in 1687 he knew that comets described conic sections focused on the Sun.[26] The taming of comets, making them more or less domesticated members of the solar system, was not the least of Newton's achievements in the *Principia,* and it was the comet of 1680 that had provided him with most of the data for his calculations.

If the conic section described by a comet is an ellipse, the orbit will be closed and the comet will make a periodic return. Newton fully realized, however, that his new concept of universal gravitation, in which all bodies *mutually* attract each other, implied disruptions in the regularity of the comet's orbit. Over a long period of time, the comet's motion might very well be sufficiently retarded by its proximity to other heavenly bodies that it would "descend to the sun." In the *Principia* he sounded this note rather positively: "So fixed stars [distant suns similar to our own], that have been gradually wasted by the light and vapors emitted from them for a long time, may be recruited by comets that fall upon them; and from this fresh supply of new fuel those old stars, acquiring new splendor, may pass for new stars."[27] To Conduitt he was more explicit: the comet of 1680 "might perhaps have five or six revolutions more first." He could not say when it might drop into the Sun, "but whenever it did, it would so much increase the heat of the sun, that this earth would be burnt, and no animals in it could live." The Earth already bears "marks of ruin," Newton said, suggesting that a similar conflagration had already taken place in the past. When Conduitt asked how the Earth might in that case have been repeopled, Newton answered: "that required the power of a creator." Indeed, all of the "revolutions of the heavenly bodies" were "by the direction of the Supreme Being."[28]

With comets, then, Newton had found a precise mechanism, described by his mathematical principles, by which the dissolution of this world could be effected. The dissolution would take place through natural law, but this law operated under divine guidance. Newton's ideas had roots in Judeo-Christian texts, as we have seen, and were congruent with the Stoic doctrine of *ekpyrosis;* yet one must in addition recognize that within the rigorous mathematical system of the world for which he is so justly famous, Newton had firmly established a providential God—at least as he himself understood what he had done. His work on the laws of cometary motion was thus of a piece with his work on the laws of vegetation, in that both constituted an effort to demonstrate the operations of divine providence in the created world.

CONCLUSION

Especially after Halley's work popularized the idea that comets return periodically, *regularity* seemed to many to be the most significant aspect of cometary motion. Yet the first formulator of elliptical Sun-focused cometary orbits, Isaac Newton, had not seen the matter thus. Indeed, although Newton recognized natural law and its regular operation in the motion of the comets, always behind the law and giving it meaning was the inscrutable plan of an all-powerful God. It was God's will that this world end in fire; Newton had merely located the natural agent by which God's will would be done. Although that discovery in itself surely constituted some satisfaction for Newton, what really seems to have been important to him was the glimpse through the veil of nature that his discoveries afforded, through nature to God: "There is no way $\nearrow$ (wthout revelation) $\swarrow$ to come to y^e knowledge of a Deity but by the frame of nature." If one accepts the profoundly religious character of Newton's goal as outlined here, then the unity behind all the various aspects of his work becomes apparent, and Newton as alchemist and theologian again becomes one with the Newton of the *Principia*—a Newton who sought to understand and celebrate the "issues" of God's unlimited free will both in vegetating chemicals and in celestial motions.

NOTES

1. David Brewster, *Memoirs of the Life, Writings, and Discoveries of Sir Isaac Newton* (Edinburgh: Thomas Constable; Boston: Little, Brown, 1855), 2:374–75.

2. John Maynard Keynes, "Newton, the Man," in *The Royal Society Newton Tercentenary Celebrations 15–19 July 1946* (Cambridge: Cambridge University Press, 1947), 27–34, esp. 27–29.

3. William Wordsworth, *The Prelude*, book 3, lines 62–63. Cf. Richard S. Westfall, *Never at Rest: A Biography of Isaac Newton* (Cambridge: Cambridge Univeristy Press, 1980), ix–x.

4. Isaac Newton, Jewish National and University Library, Jerusalem, Yahuda MS. Var. 1, Newton MS. 41, fol. 7r. Interlineations in this and subsequent quotations from Newton's manuscripts are indicated by arrows up and down. Cf. Richard S. Westfall, "Isaac Newton's *Theologiae Gentilis Origines Philosophicae*," in *The Secular Mind: Transformations of Faith in Modern Europe. Essays Presented to Franklin L. Baumer, Randolph W. Townsend Professor of History, Yale University*, ed. W. Warren Wager (New York: Holmes and Meier, 1982), 15–34.

5. Isaac Newton, Jewish National and University Library, Jerusalem, Yahuda MS. Var. 1, Newton MS. 21, fol. 2r. Words and phrases in angled brackets in this and subsequent quotations indicate expressions crossed out in manuscript version.

6. The voluntarism expressed in Newton's later papers has been analyzed in J. E. McGuire, "Force, Active Principles, and Newton's Invisible Realm," *Ambix* 15 (1968): 154–208. See also Henry Guerlac, "Theological Voluntarism and Biological Analogies in Newton's Physical Thought," *Journal of the History of Ideas* 44 (1983): 219–29.

7. See Edward Grant, "The Condemnation of 1277, God's Absolute Power, and Physical Thought in the Late Middle Ages," *Viator* 10 (1979): 211–44; idem, *Much Ado About Nothing: Theories of Space and Vacuum from the Middle Ages to the Scientific Revolution* (Cambridge: Cambridge University Press, 1981); Etienne Gilson, *History of Christian Philosophy in the Middle Ages* (New York: Random House, 1955), esp. 387–545; and Francis Oakley, *Omnipotence, Covenant, and Order: An Excursion in the History of Ideas from Abelard to Leibniz* (Ithaca, N.Y.: Cornell University Press, 1984).

8. Isaac Newton, Dibner Library of the History of Science and Technology, Smithsonian Institution, Washington, D.C., Dibner Coll. MSS. 1031B, fol. 4v (formerly Burndy MS. 16). Cf. *Manuscripts of the Dibner Collection in the Dibner Library of the History of Science and Technology of the Smithsonian Institution Libraries*, Smithsonian Institution Libraries, Research Guide no. 5 (Washington, D.C.: Smithsonian Institution Libraries, 1985), 7 (no. 80) and pl. 7 (facing p. 46);

B.J.T. Dobbs, "Newton Manuscripts at the Smithsonian Institution," *Isis* 68 (1977): 105–7.

9. Newton, Dibner Coll. MSS. 1031B, fol. 4v. The symbol $\oplus$ = "world"; the square brackets are Newton's.

10. Ibid.; quote fol. 5v; Newton's square brackets. Cf. B.J.T. Dobbs, "Newton's Alchemy and his Theory of Matter," *Isis* 73 (1982): 511–28.

11. R. Hooykaas, *Religion and the Rise of Modern Science* (Edinburgh: Scottish Academic Press, 1973), esp. 29–53; Daniel O'Connor and Francis Oakley, eds., *Creation: the Impact of an Idea* (New York: Scribner's, 1969), esp. M. B. Foster, "The Christian Doctrine of Creation and the Rise of Modern Science," pp. 29–53, and Francis Oakley, "Christian Theology and the Newtonian Science: The Rise of the Concept of the Laws of Nature," pp. 54–83; Margaret J. Osler, "Descartes and Charleton on Nature and God," *Journal of the History of Ideas* 40 (1979): 445–56; idem, "Providence and Divine Will in Gassendi's Views on Scientific Knowledge," *Journal of the History of Ideas* 44 (1983): 549–60; and idem, "Eternal Truths and the Laws of Nature: The Theological Foundations of Descartes' Philosophy of Nature," *Journal of the History of Ideas* 46 (1985): 349–62.

12. Newton, Dibner Coll. MSS. 1031B, fol. 4v.

13. B.J.T. Dobbs, *The Foundations of Newton's Alchemy, or "The Hunting of the Greene Lyon"* (Cambridge: Cambridge University Press, 1975), esp. 100–105; and Guerlac, "Theological Voluntarism."

14. Robert Hugh Kargon, *Atomism in England from Hariot to Newton* (Oxford: Clarendon Press, 1966), 64, 67–68, 87–89; and Osler, "Descartes and Charleton."

15. Jacob Viner, *The Role of Providence in the Social Order: An Essay in Intellectual History. Jayne Lectures for 1966*, with a foreword by Joseph R. Strayer, Memoirs of the American Philosophical Society, vol. 90 (Philadelphia: American Philosophical Society, 1972), 8–9. For a more extended discussion of the supernatural ontology explicit in some seventeenth-century mechanical philosophies, see Keith Hutchison, "Supernaturalism and the Mechanical Philosophy," *History of Science* 21 (1983): 297–333.

16. Leroy E. Loemker, *Struggle for Synthesis: The Seventeenth Century Background of Leibniz's Synthesis of Order and Freedom* (Cambridge, Mass.: Harvard University Press, 1972), 219–21.

17. *Sir Isaac Newton's Mathematical Principles of Natural Philosophy and His System of the World*, trans. Andrew Motte (1729), ed. Florian Cajori (Berkeley and Los Angeles: University of California Press, 1934; reprint 1966), 2:546; and *Isaac Newton's Philosophiae Naturalis Principia Mathematica: The Third Edition (1726) with Variant Readings*, ed. Alexandre Koyré and I. Bernard Cohen, with the assistance of Anne Whitman (Cambridge, Mass.: Harvard University Press, 1972), 2:763. Hereafter cited as *Principia* (Motte-Cajori) and *Principia* (Koyré-Cohen), respectively.

18. Newton, Dibner Coll. MSS. 1031B passim.

19. Ibid., fol. 5v.

20. Newton, *Principia* (Motte-Cajori) 2:546; (Koyré-Cohen) 2:763.

21. Ibid.

22. J. E. McGuire and Martin Tamny, *Certain Philosophical Questions: Newton's*

Trinity Notebook (Cambridge: Cambridge University Press, 1983), 374–77. Cf., e.g., 2 Peter 3:7, Revelations 21:1, Isaiah 65:17.

23. B.J.T. Dobbs, "Newton and Stoicism," *Southern Journal of Philosophy* 23 (1985): 109–23 (Supplement: Spindel Conference 1984: "Recovering the Stoics").

24. John Conduitt, "Memoirs of Sir Isaac Newton, sent by Mr. Conduitt to Monsieur Fontenelle, in 1727," in Edmund Turnor, *Collections for the History of the Town and Soke of Grantham, Containing Authentic Memoirs of Sir Isaac Newton* (London, 1806), 158–86; quotations p. 172.

25. Westfall, *Never at Rest*, 391.

26. Ibid., 391–97, 402–35.

27. Newton, *Principia* (Motte-Cajori) 2:540–41; (Koyré-Cohen) 2:756–57.

28. Conduitt, op. cit., "Memoirs," 172–73. See also David Charles Kubrin, "Newton and the Cyclical Cosmos: Providence and the Mechanical Philosophy," *Journal of the History of Ideas* 28 (1967): 325–46; and idem, "Providence and the Mechanical Philosophy: The Creation and Dissolution of the World in Newtonian Thought. A Study of the Relations of Science and Religion in Seventeenth Century England" (Ph.D. diss., Cornell University, 1968).

PART III

Halley

EIGHT

Halley and the Dimensions of the Solar System

Albert Van Helden

When Edmond Halley died in 1742, his legacy included not only the prediction of the return in 1758 of the comet of 1682 but also the assurance that, during the 1761 and 1769 transits of Venus, astronomers would be able to arrive at a more accurate figure for the distance of the Sun from Earth. So far astronomers and historians alike have usually assumed that the measurements Halley proposed merely fine-tuned those made of the parallax of Mars by John Flamsteed and Giovanni Domenico Cassini in 1672. An examination of Cassini's and Flamsteed's measurements and calculations, however, and of Halley's comments on them, calls those results into grave doubt. I shall argue here that Halley was entirely correct in his negative assessment of Flamsteed's and Cassini's determination of the parallaxes of Mars and the Sun and that the measurements made during the transits of Venus in 1761 and 1769 were, in fact, the first actual measurements of a parallax other than the Moon's.

TRANSITS BEFORE HALLEY

Transits of Mercury and Venus became important events in astronomy after the invention of the telescope. This is not to say, of course, that transits, or rather their possibility, were entirely unrecognized before the seventeenth century. They were first invoked two millennia earlier by Greek thinkers in the debate about the order of the planets. Whereas in Copernican astronomy the order of the planets follows directly from the planetary models, in geocentric astronomy that order was a matter of convention: Saturn, Jupiter, and Mars could be ordered according to their decreasing sidereal period, but since the mean periods of the Sun,

Mercury, and Venus are the same a different ordering principle was needed for them. Some thinkers put Mercury and Venus below the Sun; others objected that if this were the case Venus and Mercury would occasionally be seen to pass between our eye and the Sun and that since such an event had never been observed, they had to be above the Sun.[1] There is, moreover, some evidence that Venus is in fact visible to the naked eye during a transit.[2] Ptolemy, when he reviewed these arguments, concluded that Mercury and Venus were both below the Sun, ascribing the lack of observed transits to these planets' small size and their departure from the ecliptic.[3]

Once the notion was mentioned in the *Almagest*, the possibility that Venus and Mercury might pass between us and the Sun was never far from the mainstream of astronomy. In 807, during the reign of Charlemagne, a sunspot so large as to be readily seen with the naked eye appeared. The chronicles of the period mention that Mercury was seen on the Sun continuously for eight days![4] Two centuries later, the great Avicenna (980–1037) may have observed Venus on the Sun during the transit of 1032, but all medieval reports of alleged observations of Venus transits are too vague to allow firm conclusions.[5] Following Ptolemy, Copernicus assessed the possibility of a transit of Venus in his discussion of the traditional order of the planets.[6] Finally, in 1607, two years before Galileo and Harriot first turned telescopes to the heavens, Johannes Kepler observed what he thought to be a transit of Mercury with a primitive camera obscura, although a few years later he realized that he had seen not Mercury, but rather a sunspot.[7]

While such observations had always been impractical with the naked eye, the telescope made transit observations possible for the first time. Now all that was needed was a good reason for such observations—and Johannes Kepler provided several. In 1627 Kepler published his *Rudolphine Tables*, from which he went on to calculate ephemerides for the succeeding years. In those for 1631, he predicted transits of both Venus and Mercury, events that he asked all astronomers to attempt to witness. The observations would, of course, give accurate information about the positions of the planets near their nodes, but, more importantly, they would allow accurate measurements of apparent diameters of these planets.[8] The apparent planetary and stellar diameters handed down from Hipparchus and Ptolemy and confirmed by Tycho Brahe were much too large, as Galileo had already discovered.[9] Kepler saw the transits of 1631 as opportunities to correct these errors of the ancients. His own prediction of what the apparent diameter of Venus would be at inferior conjunction, however, was much too large,[10] a miscalculation that caused some observers to use a camera obscura in their observations with negative results.[11]

Kepler was correct in his fear that the transit of Venus would not be visible in Europe, but several observers did manage to witness Mercury's transit.[12] Chief among these was Pierre Gassendi, who was astonished by how small Mercury was compared to the Sun; he had expected it to be much larger, and only with difficulty did he convince himself that he was indeed observing Mercury in transit across the Sun.[13] Unknown to the learned world until two decades later, Jeremiah Horrocks and William Crabtree in 1639 observed a transit of Venus that Kepler had not predicted. In this case, too, the important piece of information derived from the observation was Venus's apparent diameter.[14] During the rest of the seventeenth century one or two observers usually witnessed the more frequent transits of Mercury, and the resulting relatively good measurements of its apparent diameter were put to work chiefly to improve the theory of Mercury.[15] Edmond Halley was to change all that.

THE PROBLEM OF ABSOLUTE DISTANCES

Ptolemy had not only determined the apparent diameters of the planets and the fixed stars, but he also fixed their distances. The result was a complete scheme of absolute sizes and distances of all the bodies in the geocentric cosmos. His main method of fixing distances had been the so-called nesting-sphere procedure, whereby, given no empty spaces in the cosmos, the apogee distance of one planet had to be equal to the perigee distance of the next higher one, starting with the absolute distance of the Moon, determined by other means.[16] This method, though, was impossible in the Copernican scheme, because the Moon had been taken out of the order of the planets; nevertheless, since all the relative heliocentric planetary distances were known, any one absolute distance other than the Moon's would suffice. Over the next two centuries this elusive absolute distance was pursued by means of various methods.

Two other methods for determining absolute distances had been developed in antiquity, both by Aristarchus of Samos. In his book *On the Sizes and Distances of the Sun and Moon*, Aristarchus first showed how the ratio of solar to lunar distance can be found by measuring the angle between these bodies at the moment when the Moon appears exactly half illuminated. Having found that ratio, approximately 19 to 1, he went on to show by means of eclipses how the absolute distances could be found.[17] Hipparchus and Ptolemy both used the eclipse method independently from the method of lunar dichotomy.[18] In both methods, to find the absolute distance of the Sun, the distance of the Moon has to be known. Of the two, the eclipse method remained the preferred one until the seventeenth century.

Tycho Brahe added a third method for finding an absolute distance. In 1582 when Mars was in opposition and at its perihelion, he tried to measure the planet's diurnal parallax, that is, the apparent displacement caused by the distance traversed by the observer during the night because of the Earth's rotation (or rather, its geostatic equivalent). At such favorable oppositions, the distance to Mars is less than half an astronomical unit; its parallax should therefore be two and one-half times that of the Sun, which was traditionally set at about 3'. Tycho was confident that he could measure a parallax of 7' or 8'.[19] As it turned out, he did not succeed in measuring Mars's parallax, but the idea entered the literature at this time. Nearly a century later, observers would take it up again.

During the seventeenth century the eclipse method for determining the distance and parallax of the Sun fell from favor owing to its inherent inaccuracy.[20] For a brief period, the lunar dichotomy method was revived and applied with the help of the telescope. Determining the exact moment of dichotomy was not, however, made easier by the telescope; if anything, it became more difficult. Furthermore, like the eclipse method, the lunar dichotomy method is inherently inaccurate, for a small error in measurement results in a much larger error in the final result.[21] Thus, by about 1660 the only remaining method for determining an absolute distance in the solar system was through measurement of the parallax of Mars. The stage was now set for the celebrated efforts of Giovanni Domenico Cassini and John Flamsteed.

CASSINI, FLAMSTEED, AND THE PARALLAX OF MARS

Cassini began his efforts to improve solar theory when he was appointed to the chair of astronomy at Bologna. Using the huge gnomon in the cathedral of San Petronio, he measured the noon altitudes of the Sun throughout the year, finding the latitude of Bologna and the obliquity of the ecliptic derived from these observations to differ significantly from results obtained by measuring the height of the pole.[22] He guessed that the problem was due to faulty corrections for atmospheric refraction and solar parallax. The traditional solar parallax of 3' had, by this time, been rejected, and Cassini used the figure suggested by Kepler, 1'. He could make the discrepancy disappear by using this parallax in conjunction with refraction tables that varied with the season, or by using a much smaller solar parallax—12" at most—in conjunction with a single table of refraction corrections.[23] The choice between the two options could not be decided in Europe.

When he came to Paris to assume the directorship of the observatory being built for the Académie Royale des Sciences, Cassini had his chance to decide the issue. In 1671 the academy sent Jean Richer, one of its staff astronomers, to Cayenne on the coast of South America, 5° north of the equator, to measure the solar declinations throughout the year. He was also to measure the distances of Mars from fixed stars during the favorable opposition of 1672. Richer's solar declinations showed that only a combination of small solar parallax and better refraction corrections would produce the same obliquity of the ecliptic in Europe as in the tropics. The Sun's horizontal parallax was therefore smaller than 12″.[24] This part of Richer's expedition was an unqualified success, as was the discovery, by means of the pendulum, of the Earth's equatorial bulge. When it came to the parallax of Mars, however, the success of the expedition has been grossly overrated by both astronomers and historians, from Cassini to the present.

While Richer was in Cayenne, Cassini and his colleagues in France were making measurements of Mars's position, to determine the planet's diurnal parallax and to compare with Richer's observations in the hope of finding a parallax caused by the great distance between observers. In England, in the meantime, John Flamsteed was measuring the planet's diurnal parallax with a micrometer.[25] From all these measurements Cassini and Flamsteed teased a horizontal parallax of Mars of the order of 25″, and a consequent horizontal solar parallax of 9.5″ and 10″, respectively.[26] It has generally been assumed that this was the first positive measurement of an actual parallax other than the Moon's, sometimes with the caveat that it was accurate only to a few arcseconds.[27] A careful examination of the measurements and calculations based on them, however, shows that Cassini's and Flamsteed's measurements of Mars's parallax were worthless: the planet's parallax was still confounded by instrumental errors, even after the great revolution in accuracy brought about by the micrometer and telescopic sights.[28]

Given the solar declinations of Richer, however, the Sun's parallax could not be greater than 12″, and thus Cassini and Flamsteed were certainly justified in advocating a slightly smaller value. Although many of their colleagues remained skeptical about this measure, by the end of the century a clear consensus on solar parallax had emerged. Most influential astronomers and philosophers now accepted a solar parallax of about 10″ and a solar distance of something like 22,000 Earth radii.[29] One figure who consciously remained outside this consensus was Edmond Halley.

HALLEY'S OBSERVATION OF THE
TRANSIT OF MERCURY OF 1677

Halley was fifteen years old when Richer set sail for Cayenne, and by the time he became a practicing astronomer himself the consensus figure for solar parallax had already been established. Yet from the start, he struck out on a different path. In 1663 the mathematician James Gregory, in his *Optica Promota,* gave a geometrical demonstration of how, from a conjunction of two planets, or of a planet and a fixed star, the parallaxes of both could be found. This method was already known to Tycho Brahe, but Gregory added in a scholium: "This problem has a beautiful but perhaps laborious use, in observations of Venus or Mercury obscuring a part of the Sun, for from such observations the parallax of the Sun can be found."[30] This was the first explicit, if still cryptic, statement of how transits could be useful in finding parallaxes. It seems reasonable to assume that Halley read this statement, although he may well have arrived at the idea independently. At any rate, he never acknowledged in print that Gregory at least had the idea before him.

Nevertheless, to Halley belongs the credit for developing and advocating this method over the course of his long career. His study of transits began with the Mercury transit of 1677. At the time he was in St. Helena mapping the southern skies. Despite the terrible weather that plagued him during his entire stay there, he managed to observe the transit on 5 November. A month later he wrote to Sir Jonas Moore: "I have . . . had the opportunity of observing the ingress and egress of ☿ on the ☉, which compared with the like Observations made in *England,* will give a demonstration of the Suns Parallax, which hitherto was never proved, but by probable arguments."[31]

Several things in this cryptic account stand out. First, Halley observed both the planet's ingress and egress; indeed, he was the first to observe the ingress. More importantly, he did not even mention the planet's apparent diameter, the determination of which had been the main purpose of all previous observations of Mercury and Venus transits. For Halley, right from the beginning, transits were occasions for determining parallax. Already in 1677 Halley did not believe that Cassini, Flamsteed, or anyone else, had measured a parallax. Thus, he did not advocate the use of transits as just another method for determining parallax: for him it was the only method.

Upon his return to England in 1678, Halley discovered that observers in Greenwich, Paris, and Gdansk had been foiled by the weather. In fact, only two astronomers in Europe had seen Mercury on the Sun: Richard Towneley in Lancashire and Jean Charles Gallet in Avignon. Both missed the planet's ingress but observed its egress. But whereas Towneley got little more than a glimpse of the planet on the Sun, Gallet was able to make a series of measurements, which he forwarded to Paris for publication.[32] Halley compared the St. Helena and Avignon observations in a thirteen-page appendix to his *Catalogus Stellarum Australium* (1679).

Halley had been unable accurately to measure Mercury's position on the Sun because his micrometer was broken. He therefore had only rough estimates of the planet's positions and the times of ingress and egress. Comparing his results with those of Gallet, he found the horizontal parallax of Mercury to be 1'6", and the Sun's 45", which corresponds to a solar distance of about 4,600 Earth radii. Halley realized that because of inaccuracies in the measurements these figures did not merit much faith,[33] but this did not mean that he put any stock in the recent measurements of the parallax of Mars. Referring to the method used by Flamsteed in 1672, Halley argued that even with a very long telescope and an accurately made micrometer one could scarcely hope to succeed in this enterprise.[34] Had he been aware of the much less accurate procedure used by Cassini and Richer, he would certainly have expressed his skepticism about Mars's parallax in even stronger terms.

Attempts to measure the parallax of Mars were thus doomed to failure, according to Halley. Further, the disappointing results of the observations of Mercury's transit of 1677 indicated that this method, too, was incapable of producing the desired result; Mercury's parallax was, after all, only slightly larger than the Sun's. Venus, however, offered more hope, for during a transit this planet's parallax would be much greater than the Sun's. Halley argued therefore:

> There remains but one observation by which one can resolve the problem of the Sun's distance from the Earth, and that advantage is reserved for the astronomers of the following century, to wit, when Venus will pass across the disk of the Sun, which will occur only in the year 1761 on 26 May [O.S.]. For if the parallax of Venus on the Sun is then observed by the method I have just explained, it will be almost three times greater than the Sun's, and the observations required for this are the easiest of all, so that through this phenomenon men can instruct themselves of all they could wish on that occasion.[35]

In the meantime, what was a reasonable figure for the Sun's parallax? Halley was aware that his colleagues made this figure out to be considerably smaller than he had calculated it. As an example of their rationale he cited Thomas Streete's *Astronomia Carolina* (1661), in which the author argued that the Sun's parallax should be between 10" and 20": if it was only 10", Venus, a planet without a moon, would be larger than the Earth, a planet with a moon—an unseemly eventuality; if, conversely, it was as much as 20", Mercury would be smaller than the Moon—and it would hardly be proper for a primary to be smaller than a secondary planet.[36] He himself was persuaded that Mars's parallax could hardly be as large as 1', from which it followed that the Sun's parallax was no larger than 25", a figure that he believed approached the true value closely after all the circumstances had been weighed.[37] This reasoning shows that Halley was not well informed of Cassini's work and the rich mix of ingredients from which Cassini had distilled his figure for the Sun's parallax, even if he had not actually measured it.

Before Halley had his falling out with Flamsteed, he assisted the King's Astronomer on several occasions in attempting to measure Mars's parallax. At these times they used measuring arcs with telescopic sights, presumably because Mars was not sufficiently near fixed stars to use a micrometer.[38] There is no evidence that these attempts did anything but reinforce Halley in his conviction that attempts to measure the parallax of this planet were useless.

HALLEY'S CAMPAIGN

Kepler had been the first astronomer to predict transits of Venus and Mercury. Here his *Rudolphine Tables* were measurably superior to all competitors, including those of Philip van Lansberge. Even so, the *Rudolphine Tables* were not without shortcomings. While Kepler triumphantly predicted the Venus transits of 1631 and 1761, he completely missed that of 1639. Mopping up after Kepler, Jeremiah Horrocks made some adjustments to parameters in the *Rudolphine Tables,* thus improving the theory of Venus enough to predict and observe the transit of 1639. Yet predictions of Venus transits remained problematic until the eighteenth century. Because of Mercury's eccentricity and the difficulty of observing this planet, its orbit was even more problematic, but the more frequent transits of this planet held out hope for improving the theory of its motion.

In England the most influential book on Keplerian astronomy in the second half of the seventeenth century was Thomas Streete's *Astronomia Carolina* (1661), which incorporated the improvements Horrocks had made to Kepler's *Rudolphine Tables*. Streete followed Kepler on the inclinations of the orbits of Mercury and Venus but improved on Kepler's locations of the ascending nodes, which could now be located more precisely because of the transit observations made by Gassendi in 1631 and Horrocks in 1639. Streete himself had witnessed part of the Mercury transit of 1661.[39] Such observations, including Halley's measurement of the transit of 1677, helped refine, over the next century, the parameters of Mercury's orbit. Streete's work was the departure point for Halley's study of Venus and Mercury. Having observed the 1677 transit of Mercury, Halley went on to make a series of daylight observations of that planet between 1682 and 1684, in Islington. As Owen Gingerich has shown, Halley finally managed to measure Mercury's positions near its aphelion, an observation that had escaped observers since antiquity but that the telescope made possible. His observations showed that Streete's elements of the planet's orbit were very accurate and an improvement over Kepler's.[40]

Halley's major conclusions concerning the orbits of Mercury and Venus are contained in a paper entitled "On the Visible Conjunctions of the Inferior Planets with the Sun," which appeared in the *Philosophical Transactions* in 1691. He followed Streete's values with minute modifications and calculated transits of Mercury from the invention of the telescope to the end of the eighteenth century, and transits of Venus for the current millennium.[41] These predictions, however, still left a lot to be desired. Of the eighteen transits between 902 and 1882, Halley predicted only nine correctly, including the three full sets between 1518 and 1769.

Halley ended this first paper ever to be devoted solely to the subject of transits by stating that the chief use of Venus transits was the accurate determination of solar distance and parallax, a quantity that had eluded astronomers who had investigated it by various methods and with the best of instruments. By means of a mediocre telescope and a pendulum clock that kept time accurately for but six to eight hours, observers would be able to time the ingress and egress accurately to the nearest second, thus allowing Venus's and the Sun's parallax to be determined accurately to one part in five hundred.[42]

On this subject Halley attracted at least a few followers. In 1702 David Gregory, in his *Astronomiae Physicae & Geometricae Elementa*, reprinted his uncle James's statement about the usefulness of transits of Venus, concluding that the learned world would have to wait until the 1761 transit of Venus to obtain an accurate measure of the Sun's distance and parallax.[43] At the same time, William Whiston devoted several of his astronomical lectures at Cambridge (printed in several editions beginning in 1707) to transits of Mercury and Venus, taking his material entirely from Halley's 1691 paper.[44]

Although we may be sure that whenever the subject of solar parallax arose Halley advocated the upcoming Venus transits as the only satisfactory way of solving the problem, he did not return to the subject in print until 1716, when he published a paper in the *Philosophical Transactions* entitled "A Singular Method by which the Parallax of the Sun or its Distance from the Earth can be Determined Securely, by means of Observing Venus in the Sun."[45] Halley began with a brief review of the history of the problem of solar parallax, dismissing all measurements attempted so far. Until the time when the measurement he was about to propose could be made, he proposed as a compromise value for the Sun's parallax a value of 12.5″, based, following Streete's reasoning, on harmonic considerations. He scornfully dismissed the authority, however great, of those who had tried to measure the parallax of Mars by means of a pendulum, pointing out that these measurements often produced null or even negative results.[46]

Halley now proceeded to the discussion of transits. During the transit of Mercury of 1677 he had been able to observe both the ingress and egress of the planet. While the exact moment at which the planet made its first or last external contact with the Sun was difficult to determine, through his twenty-four-foot telescope Halley had been able to mark the exact moments of *internal* contact during ingress and egress. Since Mercury's parallax was not much larger than the Sun's, only transits of Venus would give the desired result, but Halley's experience in 1677 did suggest to him a method to use during the upcoming Venus transits. Observers in various parts of the globe would need only diligence and common but good telescopes and pendulum clocks. Exact knowledge of the latitudes and longitudes of the observers was not necessary: all the observers needed to do was to measure the total time of the transit by marking the moment of first and second internal contact. His own experience with Mercury had shown him that these moments could be determined to the nearest second.[47]

The length of time of the transit was a function of Venus's observed latitude on the Sun, ranging from a maximum if the planet passed exactly over the center of the Sun to a minimum when it merely grazed the limb. Comparison of the lengths of the transit as measured by widely separated observers would therefore yield the difference in the planet's closest approach to the Sun's center, a value that was equal to the difference between the parallaxes of Venus and the Sun caused by the separation between the observers. The transit of Venus predicted for 5 June 1761 would start before the Sun had risen in London. To observers in more northern latitudes, however, in Norway and perhaps even in the Shetlands, both the ingress and egress would be visible. At the midpoint of the transit the Sun would be at the zenith for observers near the mouth of the Ganges river or perhaps a bit to the east, so there, too, both ingress and egress would be visible. Around the Hudson Bay in North America, the ingress would come shortly before sunset and the egress shortly after sunrise. Halley urged the English, French, and Dutch to send observers to the various parts of their empires; as many observations as possible should be made, he said, in order to minimize the danger of being foiled by the weather or other circumstances (of which war turned out to be the most dangerous). Halley ended the paper with a complete geometrical analysis of the 1761 transit and a brief mention of the 1769 transit.[48]

Halley's clarion call did not immediately discourage astronomers from continuing their efforts to determine the Sun's parallax by other means. French astronomers made a number of attempts to measure the diurnal parallaxes of Mars and Venus;[49] they also used Mercury transits from 1723 to 1753 for parallax measurements, observations that their British counterparts, in contrast, used only to refine the tables of Mercury. Although the French efforts on Mercury did not produce useful measurements, they served as training exercises for the main event in 1761. The Mercury transit of 1723 was observed by both Halley and Delisle. After Delisle's visit to England in 1724, moreover, he took over the torch from Halley to become the main promoter of the 1761 and 1769 transits—a story that has been well told by Harry Woolf.[50]

CONCLUSION

The Venus expeditions of 1761 and 1769 were among the first successful efforts at international scientific cooperation. Hitherto the astronomical significance of these studies has usually been characterized as a fine-tuning of the parallax measurements in 1672 of Flamsteed and Cassini. If Halley when he started his astronomical career was perhaps less than well informed about best astronomical practice, especially in France, he nevertheless grew into an accomplished astronomer. Yet he never departed from his initial judgment of Flamsteed's and Cassini's measurements. We do well to take Halley seriously in this regard. An analysis of the results of these measurements shows that they can support any parallax one wants, from negative values to several minutes of arc.[51] In retrospect, we know that Halley was entirely correct in dismissing these attempts: the Venus transits of 1761 and 1769 produced the first actual measurements of solar parallax—if not accurate to within one part in five hundred, then at least to the nearest arcsecond. A strong argument can therefore be made that establishing the study of transits as a research subject in its own right and showing astronomers how Venus transits could solve the age-old problem of solar parallax was Halley's most fundamental contribution to astronomy.

NOTES

1. *Ptolemy's Almagest,* trans. Gerald J. Toomer (London: Duckworth, 1984), 419 (Book IX, chap. 1); Bernard R. Goldstein, *The Arabic Version of Ptolemy's "Planetary Hypotheses," Transactions of the American Philosophical Society* 57 (1967): 6.
   2. Bernard R. Goldstein, "Some Medieval Reports of Venus and Mercury Transits," *Centaurus* 14 (1969): 49–50.
   3. *Ptolemy's Almagest,* 419; Goldstein, *Ptolemy's "Planetary Hypotheses,"* 6.
   4. *Annales Laurissensis et Einhardi,* in *Monumenta Germaniae Historica Scriptorum*

(Hanover, 1826), 1:194. See also George Sarton, "Early Observations of the Sunspots?" *Isis* 37 (1947): 69–71.

5. Goldstein, "Some Medieval Reports," 52–53.

6. *De Revolutionibus* (1543), Book I, chap. 10; *Nicholas Copernicus on the Revolutions*, trans. Edward Rosen, vol. 2 of *Nicholas Copernicus Complete Works* (Baltimore: Johns Hopkins University Press, 1978), 18–19.

7. *Phaenomenon Singulare seu Mercurius in Sole* (1609), in *Johannes Kepler Gesammelte Werke* (Munich: C. H. Beck, 1937–), 4:81–98; *Kepler's Conversation with Galileo's Sidereal Messenger*, trans. Edward Rosen (New York: Johnson, 1965), 97–99.

8. Johann Kepler, *Admonitio ad Astronomos* (1630), in *Joannis Kepleri Astronomi Opera Omnia* (Frankfurt, 1858–70), 7:592–93.

9. Albert Van Helden, *Measuring the Universe: Cosmic Dimensions from Aristarchus to Halley* (Chicago: University of Chicago Press, 1985), 65–76.

10. Kepler, *Admonitio ad Astronomos* 7:593.

11. Claude Nicholas Fabri de Peiresc to Pierre Gassendi, 22 December 1631, cited in Pierre Humbert, "A propos du passage de Mercure 1631," *Revue d'histoire des sciences et de leurs applications* 3 (1950): 31. See also W. Schickardi pars Responsi ad Epistolas P. Gassendi . . . de Mercurio sub Sole Viso* (Tübingen, 1632), 4, 14.

12. Van Helden, *Measuring the Universe*, 97–100.

13. Pierre Gassendi, *Mercurius in Sole visus et Venus invisa* (1632), in *Petri Gassendi Opera Omnia* (Lyons, 1658), 4:500–501. See also Albert Van Helden, "The Importance of the Transit of Mercury of 1631," *Journal for the History of Astronomy* 7 (1976): 1–10; and Owen Gingerich, "How Astronomers Finally Captured Mercury," *Sky and Telescope* 66 (1983): 203–5.

14. Jeremiah Horrocks, *The Transit of Venus across the Sun*, trans. A. B. Whatton (London, 1859, 1868), 117–26.

15. Alexandre-Guy Pingré, *Annales célestes du dix-septième siècle*, ed. G. Bigourdan (Paris: Gauthiers-Villard, 1901), 198, 248, 341–43, 475–77, 560–63.

16. Van Helden, *Measuring the Universe*, 15–27.

17. Ibid., 5–9; T. L. Heath, *Aristarchus of Samos the Ancient Copernicus* (Oxford: Clarendon Press, 1913), 351–411.

18. Van Helden, *Measuring the Universe*, 10–13, 15–19; Noel M. Swerdlow, "Hipparchus on the Distance of the Sun," *Centaurus* 14 (1969): 287–305; Gerald J. Toomer, "Hipparchus on the Distances of the Sun and Moon," *Archive for History of Exact Science* 14 (1975): 126–44; and *Ptolemy's Almagest*, 255–57 (Book V, chap. 15).

19. Van Helden, *Measuring the Universe*, 49, 61; Owen Gingerich, "Dreyer and Tycho's World System," *Sky and Telescope* 64 (1982): 138–40.

20. Van Helden, *Measuring the Universe*, passim.

21. Ibid., 79–81, 112–15, 134–35.

22. Giovanni Domenico Cassini, *Les Elémens de l'Astronomie, Verifiés par le rapport des Tables aux Observations de M. Richer, faites en l'Isle de Caienne* (1684), in *Mémoires de l'Académie Royale des Sciences depuis 1666 jusqu'à 1699* (Paris, 1730), 8:55–57.

23. Ibid., 56–61.

24. Ibid., 62–65; Van Helden, *Measuring the Universe*, 139.

25. Ibid., 134–37.

26. Ibid., 136–38, 140–42.

27. Giorgio Abetti, *The History of Astronomy*, trans. Betty Burr Abetti (London: Sidgwick and Jackson, 1954), 127; and Antonie Pannekoek, *A History of Astronomy* (London: Allen and Unwin, 1961; New York: Barnes and Noble, 1969), 284. See also the biographical articles in the *Dictionary of Scientific Biography* (16 vols., ed. C. C. Gillespie [New York: Scribner's 1970–80]) on Giovanni Domenico Cassini by René Taton (3:103) and Jean Richer by Edward Rosen (11:424).

28. Van Helden, *Measuring the Universe*, 137–42.

29. Ibid., 144–54.

30. James Gregory, *Optica Promota* (London, 1663), 130.

31. Halley to Sir Jonas Moore, 2 December 1677, in *Correspondence and Papers of Edmond Halley*, ed. Eugene Fairfield MacPike (Oxford: Clarendon Press, 1932), 40.

32. John Flamsteed, *Historia Coelestis Britannica* (London, 1725), 1:187; Edmond Halley, *Catalogus Stellarum Australium* (London, 1679), appendix (separately paginated): "Mercurii Transitus Sub Solis disco, *Octob.* 28. Anno 1677, cum tentamine pro Solis Parallaxi"; *Journal des Sçavans,* 20 December 1677, 340–48; Pingré, *Annales célestes,* 341–43.

33. Halley, "Mercurius Transitus," 1–3.

34. Ibid., 3–4.

35. Ibid., 4.

36. Ibid.

37. Ibid.

38. *The Gresham Lectures of John Flamsteed*, ed. Eric G. Forbes (London: Mansell, 1975), 99–100.

39. Thomas Streete, *Astronomia Carolina* (London, 1661), 118–19.

40. Owen Gingerich, "Ptolemy and the Maverick Motion of Mercury," *Sky and Telescope* 66 (1983): 11–13; and idem, "How Astronomers Finally Captured Mercury," 205. Halley published his observations in an appendix to the 1710 edition of Streete's *Astronomia Carolina*, prepared by him.

41. Halley, "De Visibili Conjunctione Inferiorum Planetarum cum Sole, Dissertatio Astronomica," *Philosophical Transactions* 17, no. 193 (1691): 511–22, at 521. Halley made only minor modifications in Thomas Streete's parameters for Mercury and Venus. Streete's locations of the nodes of the orbits, especially those of Mercury, were a major improvement over Kepler's.

42. Ibid., 522.

43. David Gregory, *Astronomiae Physicae & Geometricae Elementa* (1702); I have used the second English edition, *The Elements of Physical and Geometrical Astronomy* (London, 1726; reprint New York: Johnson, 1972), 1:482–83.

44. William Whiston, *Praelectiones Astronomica* (1707); I have used the second English edition, *Astronomical Lectures* (London, 1728; reprint New York: Johnson, 1972), 277–97.

45. Halley, "Methodus Singularisqua Solis Parallaxis sive Distantia a Terra, ope Veneris intra Solem conspicienda, tuto determinari poterit," *Philosophical Transactions* 29, no. 348 (1716): 454–64.

46. Ibid., 454–56.

47. Ibid., 456–57.
48. Ibid., 457–64.
49. Van Helden, *Measuring the Universe,* 153–55.
50. Harry Woolf, *The Transits of Venus: A Study of Eighteenth-Century Science* (Princeton, N.J.: Princeton University Press, 1959).
51. Van Helden, *Measuring the Universe,* 136–42.

NINE

Halley, Surveyor and Military Engineer: Istria, 1703

Alan H. Cook

From 1698 to 1703, Halley was occupied almost entirely with navigation and hydrographic survey. His two cruises in the *Paramore* to observe the declination of the Earth's magnetic field occupied him for two years, and he devoted two more to surveys of the tides in the English Channel making use of the same ship. The logs of all those cruises have been published, and a great deal is known of what Halley did and of his methods.[1] It is also known that Halley spent most of the year 1703 making surveys of Imperial ports on the Adriatic, for which he was well rewarded by the Holy Roman Emperor. His visit was an open secret at the time, yet subsequent accounts by MacPike, Armitage, and Ronan do little more than repeat the gossip of the day and give no complete description of his activities.[2] This lack of detail is perhaps not surprising, for his surveys were confidential for the English government of that time. Nonetheless, Halley's own reports of his travels and work survive in the Public Record Office in London, and it emerges from them and other material that Halley possessed a hitherto unsuspected skill: that of a military surveyor and engineer. The surviving records are in fact so complete that it is possible to reconstruct in detail Halley's travels and activities in 1703. These materials thus not only add considerably to Halley's known correspondence but also deepen and extend our understanding of his abilities and character. My purpose in this article, then, is to summarize the results of studies I have made into the records of Halley's visits, extending and to some extent amending several previously published accounts.[3]

Halley's visits to Istria and Dalmatia were made at the beginning of the War of Spanish Succession, in which England, the Netherlands, and the Holy Roman Empire were allied against France and Spain. George Stepney, the English ambassador at Vienna, had proposed in 1701 that an English squadron should be sent into the Adriatic to assist the Imperial forces in their operations against Spanish troops in Italy; when he renewed the suggestion in September 1702, the administration in London adopted it, along with his recommendation that skilled seamen or pilots be sent in advance to examine ports that might harbor a fleet during the winter. The Earl of Nottingham, the secretary of state principally responsible for naval matters, consulted the Board of Admiralty, whereupon Halley was appointed to go and survey possible ports, report on what food and material for ships' stores might be available, and propose fortifications for such ports as he might select.

He left England in December 1702 and, after passing through the Hague and reporting his mission to the Grand Pensionary, traveled on to Vienna, where he arrived at the beginning of January 1703. He spent about three weeks in Vienna awaiting letters of recommendation and passes as well as studying printed maps of the Dalmatian coast that were available there. He fixed on the harbor of Buccari (Bakar) just to the south of Fiume (Rijeka) as likely to be the most suitable for overwintering (Fig. 9.1). He went first to Trieste early in February and secured the help of two local officials, Count Vito di Strasoldo and Count von Herberstein. He surveyed that city's harbor, but found it too open to offer sufficient protection. He continued down the Dalmatian coast as far as Carlopago, close to the border with the Ottoman Empire, and made what must have been a fairly detailed survey of the harbor of Buccari, including in his report recommendations for defensive batteries at the entrance. He returned to Vienna through Graz, from where he sent a rather full account of his findings to the Earl of Nottingham. In Vienna he consolidated his materials and drew up a report and three maps: a general one of the head of the Adriatic, one of the coast of Dalmatia, and one of the harbor of Buccari with the positions of the proposed batteries. After presenting the report, or *Memoriall,* and a set of the maps to the Emperor in an audience, he set out for London; presumably on his arrival he made a full report to Nottingham, and possibly to the Queen. Two copies of the *Memoriall* survive, but none of the maps has come to light, even though references to them appear in later correspondence.

The administration in London expected that the Imperial officials would at once set about constructing the batteries and laying in stores and provender. Soon, however, they came to suspect that little was being done. Stepney made inquiries, but despite reassuring answers, doubts in London were not laid to rest. In June, therefore, Halley was asked to return to Graz and Buccari and see for himself just what was being done. On reaching Buccari early in August he found disappointing progress and sought to urge on the Imperial officers and indeed to direct the con-

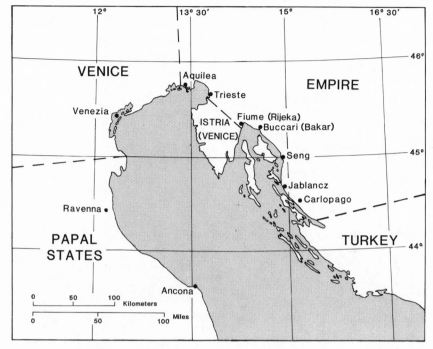

Figure 9.1. General map of the head of the Adriatic.

struction himself. When, at the end of September, the batteries had all been finished, though not provided with cannon, he left Buccari. He was in Vienna in the middle of October and finally arrived back in London at the end of November.

The outcome of Halley's two journeys was inconclusive. Although he saw the batteries finished, the provision of cannon remained a matter of dispute between Vienna and London; indeed, apparently none was ever mounted. The fact was that iron foundries equipped to cast large naval guns did not exist in Austria, or at least not close enough to the coast. An air of unreality therefore seems to permeate the whole scheme of sending an allied fleet in winter to the Adriatic, not to speak of the further idea held in some quarters of developing an Imperial fleet based on Adriatic ports. Naval bases, such as those at Toulon or Portsmouth, were the largest industrial establishments of the day and depended on a well populated hinterland to provide timber, iron foundries, stores, and food, as well as workmen and accommodation for ships' crews. The local townships of Buccari, Buccariza, and Porto Re (Fig. 9.2) were, then as now, poor, sparsely populated places quite incapable of providing the

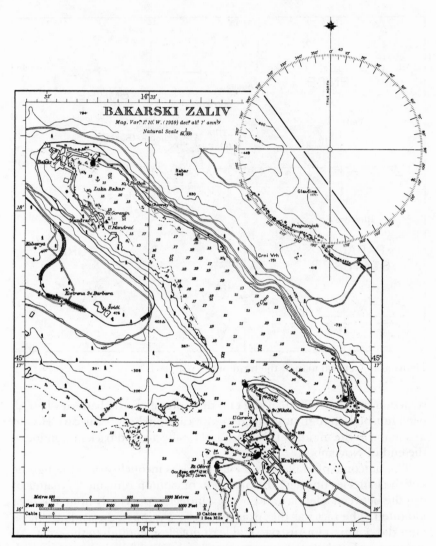

Figure 9.2. The harbor of Buccari at the present (with depths of water in fathoms). (Crown copyright. Reproduced from Admiralty chart 1561 with the permission of the Controller of Her Majesty's Stationery Office.)

support and facilities that a squadron of perhaps ten ships with a total crew of a few thousand would need. In any event, the Adriatic scheme lost its point with the destruction of the French fleet in Toulon and the English capture of Gibraltar and Port Mahon, by which England obtained secure bases in the western Mediterranean, thus rendering the French fleets unable to operate there. For Halley, however, there was a happier personal consequence, for evidently it was as a direct result of his work in 1703 and his dealings with the Earl of Nottingham that he was elected to the Savilian Chair of Geometry in Oxford.[4]

SOURCES

Three sources contain most of the material for the reconstruction of Halley's journeys and his work. Halley wrote regular letters either directly to Nottingham or else to Stepney in Vienna, who then sent on extracts to Nottingham, and that correspondence survives without obvious gaps in the State Papers (Foreign) of the Public Record Office. In addition, the archives of the embassy in Vienna are included in the State Papers, containing both duplicate and supplementary papers, in particular the office copy of the *Memoriall* that Halley presented to the Emperor. This copy, which covers all his actions during his first visit, contains the most complete report on his surveys; it is, however, rather condensed, and in letters Halley indicates that he gave a fuller, oral account to Nottingham and others on his return to London, which would have been in mid April.

The second important source of information, in the Archivio di Stato in Venice, may be found among the dispatches of the Venetian ambassadors in London and Vienna. Although the sea power of Venice was by this time much reduced and no match for France or England, Venice naturally retained an intense interest in the naval situation in the Adriatic and so was very concerned to know what Halley's aims were and what he was doing there. The dispatches from the ambassador in Vienna, Francesco Loredan, show not only that this official found out what he could directly by conversation with Stepney and Halley himself, as well as with the Imperial officers and ministers, but also that he employed devious means, probably bribery, to obtain a copy of Halley's *Memoriall* (collected in Dispacci, Germania) and even managed to view Halley's three maps. Although he was unable to make copies of the maps, his description is the most detailed information we have about them.

The third principal source is housed in the Steiermärkische Landesarchiv in Graz, the repository of the records of the Innerösterreichische Hofkammer, which administered the regions of Istria and Dalmatia from Graz and was directly responsible to the Emperor independently of the ministers in Vienna. A great deal of correspondence describes how the authorities in Graz and their subordinates on the coasts responded to the Emperor's wishes that they assist Halley in every way, but apart from a valuable account of the survey of Trieste, not much exists on the details of Halley's first visit. Subsequent correspondence concerns the steps taken in Graz to construct batteries at Buccari and to arrange food supplies and stores, including a contract with one Simon Milesi. The correspondence about Halley's second visit, when he effectively took over from the Imperial officials supervision of the batteries' construction, is more informative and, taken with other material, enables the positions of those batteries to be determined with some confidence.

While the material in London, Venice, and Graz is the most important for gaining firsthand knowledge, other relevant, though not contemporary, documents are available as well. For instance, the archives in Vienna contain a few scattered references to Halley, although they lack, in particular, any account of his audiences with the Emperor. About thirty years after Halley's visits, moreover, an Imperial surveyor, M.-A. Weiss, surveyed a route for a road from Trieste to Fiume, Buccari, and on to Carlstad close to the Ottoman border, and the extensive set of maps, diagrams, and views that he made are now in the Finanz und Hofkammer Archiv, Vienna.[5] Among other features they show fortifications possibly constructed by Halley. Some of the background to Halley's visits is also supplied by correspondence in the Stepney papers (British Library) and the Finch-Hatton papers (British Library and Northamptonshire Record Office).

THE SURVEY OF TRIESTE

Halley's own account of his survey of the port of Trieste is brief; he considered the harbor too open to both storms and enemy attack for it to be worth consideration as an overwintering ground. Orders had, he reports, been received by Count Strasoldo, the governor of the castle, and by Count von Herberstein, the military governor, "to furnish all that I shall desire for the service." He goes on to say that he has "been oft at sea and surveyed this bay," continuing: "Here are the remains of an ancient Mole, which seems once to have had a Fort on a native rock at the head of it; since converted into a church, which being again made a fort would contribute much to the security of the port." He comments also on the depth of the water and the condition of the bottom.[6]

Many details of Halley's survey of Trieste are supplied in the report that Strasoldo submitted to the Hofkammer at Graz.[7] He says that he took Halley to sea in his own barque to measure water depths, whereupon he gives the soundings at different distances from the shore as well as in the neighborhood of the mole mentioned by Halley (the Zucco) and on the other side of the harbor by a point called Musiella. He also comments on the possibility of fortifying the mole. Finally, he says that after completing his work at Trieste Halley hurried off to Fiume, followed by

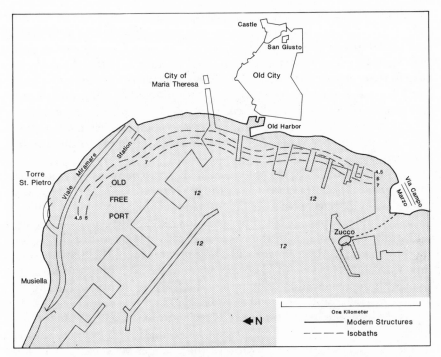

Figure 9.3. The harbor of Trieste, as surveyed by Halley (showing modern quays).

a certain Sig. Andreassi, who accompanied Halley to Buccari and who was intended to be the inspector general of an Imperial fleet, should one be formed.

The port of Trieste has been greatly altered since Halley's day by the construction both of the old free port and of the railway station on reclaimed land; there is consequently little point in trying to relate Halley's survey to modern charts. The Zucco does still exist, but in greatly modified form, and the old shoreline is traceable in the neighborhood of the Musiella, where the present coast road runs at what appears to be the foot of the low cliffs shown in sketches of Halley's time.[8] Figure 9.3 shows the harbor of Trieste according to Strasoldo's description and the 1735 map of Weiss; superimposed are the outlines of the modern port. Weiss's map and his sketch view of the harbor probably represent what Halley saw.

One problem in interpreting Strasoldo's account is that he gives both distances and depths in *passi*. Although the length of the *passo* varied from place to place, in the Adriatic the common one seems to have been that of Venice, with a value of 1.74 m. Trieste, too, had a *passo* of its own, but since in this account measures are specified in terms of the "Italian *passo,*" most likely the Venetian unit is meant. Whether Strasoldo was correct in giving the depths of water as measured by Halley in *passi* rather than in English fathoms, however, is more doubtful. In the next section I argue that at Buccari Halley probably measured depths in fathoms; he may therefore also have used fathoms at Trieste, in which case his results were misreported in *passi* by Strasoldo. In view of the rather small difference between the fathom and *passo,* nonetheless more significant for the deeper water at Buccari, it seems pointless to pursue the issue further.

As already indicated, the 1735 sketch and map of Weiss seem to show the port of Trieste much as it was thirty years earlier when Halley was there. Later in that century the first of major changes occurred when salt marshes and salt pans situated between the old city (which to a large extent still exists, along with the castle and cathedral) and the site of the railway station were built over with the construction of the new city during Maria Theresa's reign. Thereafter came the free port and the railway, with the obliteration of almost all the features mentioned in the accounts of Halley and Strasoldo.

Aside from the general interest in trying to see Trieste as Halley saw it, there is the more technical interest in attempting to estimate the accuracy of Halley's surveys. In view of the changes between his day and ours, however, it seems that little can be done at Trieste. Buccari, in contrast, seems to have altered little over the centuries, and there a clearer idea of Halley's precision can be gained.

THE SURVEY AND FORTIFICATION OF BUCCARI

Halley gave his own account of Buccari in a letter to the Earl of Nottingham, in which he summarized the features of the harbor, the possibilities for fortification of the entrance, and the availability of food and stores in the surrounding regions.[9] He promised to send Nottingham maps of the harbor and coast, with proposals for possible positions of defensive batteries. It seems, though, that he did not send the material but instead brought it back himself to London to present to Nottingham and the Queen. Although the maps have disappeared, the *Memoriall* that Halley presented to the Emperor on his return to Vienna from the coast survives in two copies.[10] The information in this document is essentially the same as that in the letter to Nottingham, and we have no further records from Halley's own hand of his surveys and proposals.

As has already been said, however, Loredan managed to see Halley's maps, and even though he was unable to make copies of them, as he evidently attempted to do, he did send a description of them on to Venice.[11] He considered that the general maps of the coast contained no new information, in contrast to Halley, who evidently thought that his surveys added to or corrected existing maps. The two opinions are not necessarily inconsistent, for the maps available in Venice and known to Loredan were likely more reliable than those Halley could have seen in Vienna. Halley speaks only of seeing printed maps in Vienna, whereas in Venice, apart from printed maps, the archives of various Venetian offices contained many manuscript maps, some of which certainly give a good delineation of the Dalmatian coast in Halley's day.

Loredan did, however, recognize the map of the harbor of Buccari as depicting essentially new information. The dimensions of the harbor, its length, greatest breadth, and least width of the entrance are those of Halley's letter and *Memoriall* and do not differ greatly from those shown on the modern Admiralty chart. The additional information that Loredan gives us consists of marked water depths at various places, both in the entrance, where it was about 25 units, and in the harbor itself, where a range of 20 to 16 units is described. But what units were these? Loredan himself calls them *passi*, which would be natural enough for a Venetian given no other indication; yet if we look at the modern chart (Fig. 9.2), we see figures in fathoms that (allowing for the fact that the map locations are far more definite than those in Loredan's description) in effect duplicate those given by Loredan. We do not know exactly where Halley made his soundings, but where the depths do not vary greatly from place to place, the figures reported by Loredan may reasonably be compared with modern values. The depths vary least in the entrance and in the deepest part of the harbor, and there the difference between *passi* and fathoms is sufficient to show that Halley's figures are most probably fathoms also, and not *passi* as Loredan thought. I conclude similarly that the depths Strasoldo gave for Trieste are also in fathoms. If I am right, Halley's chart of the harbor of Buccari differs little from the modern one, discounting manmade changes since 1703. Indeed, most of those changes have occurred only in quite recent times, for a nineteenth-century description of the harbor seems just as applicable to what Halley saw and to the harbor as mapped and drawn thirty years later by Weiss: until the 1870s or so tuna fishing was the main activity around the harbor; and subsequently, although first coal and then oil-handling plants were built, the topography remained largely unchanged, unlike at Trieste.[12]

These comments are more pertinent, however, in relation to the batteries that Halley laid out. We read in his own letters from his second visit to Buccari that little had been done to build the batteries he had laid out on his plan, and those letters, together with letters from an Imperial

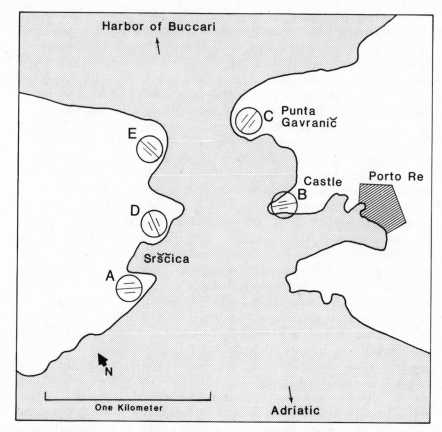

Figure 9.4. Entrance to the harbor of Buccari showing probable sites of batteries erected by Halley.

officer, Endres, to the Hofkammer in Graz, indicate that he not only insisted on the prompt completion of the works but also took over himself as site engineer and saw that the project was finished.[13] Before he left Buccari at the end of September Halley saw built (but not armed) the structures of the four masonry batteries that he had set out on his original maps, and a fifth earthwork battery as well.

Where were the batteries? I found no relic of them on a visit to Bakar in 1983 in company with Professor D. Munič of Rijeka. Halley and Endres describe their locations in rather general terms (Fig. 9.4), one just under Porto Re, one on the bay of Srščica, and one on the Punta Gavranič; and they speak of a fourth one, even less definitely located, apparently on the headland opposite the last. Louis Salvator Habsburg describes the ruins of batteries in the second and third of those places, although it is quite possible that these are the remains of some later works that obliterated Halley's.[14] Weiss, however, gives the most detailed description of batteries that might be Halley's. He shows, on a map of the entrance, batteries in the positions of those already mentioned at Porto Re (B on Fig. 9.4), Srščica (D) and Punta Gavranič (C). He indicates neither an installation in position (A), nor anything that might be an earthwork (which might have been at E).[15] He also has a pen-and-wash sketch of the entrance to the harbor as seen from a point near an earlier fort at Srščica,[16] which shows clearly the same three batteries. It is plain from this sketch why today nothing of those works is to be seen—houses have been built on the site at Porto Re, oil installations at Srščica, and a road around Punta Gavranič lies over the site of the battery there. An inconsistency may obtain, however, between the description of Habsburg and the sketch of Weiss, in that the latter shows the Gavranič battery as well above the shore, whereas Habsburg speaks of the waves washing over its ruins.

There is no difficulty in accepting that the installations depicted by Weiss, those that Louis Salvator Habsburg saw, and those constructed by Halley are all one and the same. Halley, for example, indicates that the batteries were designed to take sixty cannon, and he outlines how the guns were to be distributed, in both numbers and caliber. The Weiss sketch shows batteries of about the right size, which could accommodate up to twenty guns each; nor is Habsburg's description of the ruins inconsistent. Yet we have no documentary evidence to prove this identity. Moreover, references in other literature suggest that Buccari may have received additional fortifications after Halley—all the more reason to use caution in making such an identification. Nonetheless, even if the Weiss map and sketch do not show Halley's works per se, it is perhaps true enough that they give a good idea of where these batteries were and how they probably looked.

CONCLUSION

Halley, as the logs of the *Paramore* cruises remind us, was a skilled navigator who thought deeply about the basis and problems of that craft. He was also adept at onshore survey in the confined waters of the English Channel. The accounts assembled here of his activities in Trieste and Buccari show him to be just as at home surveying a harbor as abroad in the Atlantic. At Buccari, further, he seems to have produced a chart that can stand against a modern production, even though he apparently took only two or so days to make the survey. No doubt in these surveys he established his positions at sea by the same resection procedure that he described in a letter to Southwell.[17]

We also know that Halley had thought about gunnery, and here we see him laying out batteries and providing them with cannon of large enough caliber and in sufficient numbers to defend the entrance to Buccari harbor against the attack of an enemy fleet taking advantage of a strong wind from the sea. Indeed, Halley emphasized in his *Memoriall* the need to have sufficient guns of heavy caliber, because it would not be possible to reload if ships were coming in quickly. The guns would no doubt be trained to dismast ships, for damage to the wooden hulls would do little to stop them.

The *Paramore* logs show Halley to be a masterful man in command at sea. His letters of 1703 reveal similar characteristics. He writes impatiently and somewhat sardonically of the Imperial administration's slow methods and, from Buccari, trounces the venality of the three Imperial commissioners who, instead of getting the batteries constructed, rested content to draw their substantial daily allowances for days idly spent. He was asked by the Queen and her ministers in London to report on progress with the batteries, but he went still further, taking on himself the responsibilities of a site engineer and urging the Imperial officers and their workmen on to get the building done before winter put a stop to the work.

To the government at home Halley appeared as technically highly skilled, but more important, as Nottingham wrote at the time of Halley's election to the Oxford professorship, he was found to be both responsible and zealous in public service. Stepney, too, praised his ability and responsibility and told Nottingham how well he was regarded in Vienna. At the end of this study of a year in Halley's life, I find myself impressed not so much with Halley's achievements in survey and construction, important though I think those are, as with his character. Edmond Halley comes through in his Adriatic dealings as forceful and attractive, energetic and dependable; clear-sighted in his view of the inadequacies of others, he was nevertheless respected and admired by all he met in Vienna.

NOTES

As an amateur historian I am greatly indebted to the many scholars who have guided me to archives and made them available to me. Dr. Albert Hollaender of the Public Record Office in London told me of the Stepney correspondence there and also advised me of the Vienna records, introducing me to Dr. Christiane Thomas of the Staatsarchiv, who opened those collections to me. With the help of Dr. Nicholas Rogers and Miss Katherine Houston of the Public Record Office I came across maps from the English Consulate in Venice, which led me to the Archivio di Stato in Venice. There, with the help of the Director, Dr. Tiepolo, and of Signora E. Zolla, I found the accounts of Halley housed in that archive. The director and members of the staff of the Steiermärkische Landesarchiv in Graz have likewise been most helpful. I have had helpful conversations and correspondence with Professor M. Legovič, Professor D. Munič, and Dr. Danilo Klen, all of Rijeka, and also with Professor John Hattendorf of the U.S. Naval War College, who generously shared with me his knowledge of the War of Spanish Succession.

1. Norman J. W. Thrower, ed. *The Three Voyages of Edmond Halley in the "Paramore," 1698–1701,* Hakluyt Society Publications, 3d ser., vol. 156 (London, 1981).

2. *Correspondence and Papers of Edmond Halley,* ed. Eugene Fairfield MacPike (Oxford: Oxford University Press, 1932); Angus Armitage, *Edmond Halley* (London: Nelson, 1966); Colin A. Ronan, *Edmond Halley: Genius in Eclipse* (London: MacDonald 1970).

3. See my "Halley in Istria, 1703: Navigator and Military Engineer," *Journal of Navigation,* 37 (1984): 1–23; "An English Astronomer on the Adriatic: Edmond Halley's Surveys of 1703 and the Imperial Administration," *Mitteilungen der Oesterreichischen Archiven* 38 (1985): 123–62; and idem, "Surveys of Istria and Dalmatia at the Beginning of the War of Spanish Succession," *Problemi svernog Jadrana* (in press).

4. A. H. Cook, "The Election of Edmond Halley to the Savilian Professorship of Geometry," *Journal of the History of Astronomy* 15 (1984): 34–36.

5. Marc-Antonio Weiss, Collection of Maps and Plans (1735), Vienna, Finanz und Hofkammer Archiv, C. 16.

6. Halley to Stepney, 4 February 1703 (Trieste), London, Public Record Office, SP 80/20, fol. 109.

7. Count Vito di Strasoldo to Hofkammer, Graz, 11 February 1703 (Trieste), Steiermarkisches Landesarchiv, HK 1703-1-53, fols. 10–13.

8. Weiss, Maps and Plans, Finanz und Hofkammer Archiv, C. 16, fols. 26, 35.

9. Halley to the Earl of Nottingham, 25 February 1703 (Graz), London, Public Record Office, SP 80/20, fols. 145, 157.

10. The first copy is in the archives of the English embassy in Vienna, London, Public Record Office, SP 105/67, fols. 418, 419; the second, that sent by the Venetian ambassador in Vienna, Loredan, to the Senate in Venice, is in the Archivio di Stato, Venice, Senato, Dispacci Germania, filza 185, fols. 17, 318.

11. Venice, Archivio di Stato, Dispacci Germania, filza 185, fols. 309–16.

12. Anon. [Louis Salvator, Archduke of Habsburg], *Der Golf von Buccari–Porto Re: Bilder und Skizzen* (Prague, 1871).

13. Halley to Stepney, 5 August, 11 August, 8 September, Public Record Office, SP 105/69; 15 September, Public Record Office, SP 105/70, fol. 29. Also Endres to Hofkammer, 1 September 1703, Graz, Steiermärkisches Landesarchiv, HK 1703-IX-11.

14. Louis Salvator Habsburg, *Der Golf von Buccari,* 10, 106–7.

15. Not all the maps and views in the Weiss collection are by Weiss himself. The Trieste plan is signed by Weiss, but that of Buccari is not; there is a second version, also unsigned, in the Kriegsarchiv in Vienna as well (Kartensammlung, G.I.h.62). The views of Trieste and Buccari are similar in style, but neither is signed. In each case, the date can only be put at before 1735.

I have come across further maps in my research that establish the positions of four batteries at sites A, B, C, and D of Figure 9.4 by about 1730. There is, beside the map and sketch of Weiss (see notes 5 and 9 above) a map by Antonio di Vernada of 1733 (Vienna, Mappa Ignografica Kriegsarchiv, B. IX b. 89), which shows the traces of four batteries, and one by P. G. Capello of 1732, reproduced by Danilo Klen in *Pomorski Zbornik* (Rijeka) 17 (1979): 487–511 and in *Dometi* (Rijeka) 4 1986: 89–98. More a perspective view than a map, the latter also shows four batteries on the same sites. Klen also states in his 1986 article that he has himself seen ruins of Srščica.

16. Weiss, Maps and Plans, Vienna, Finanz und Hofkammer Archiv, C. 16 fols. 41–42.

17. Thrower, *"Paramore,"* 338–40.

TEN

Captain Edmond Halley, F.R.S., Royal Navy, and the Practice of Navigation

D. W. Waters

Edmond Halley, Fellow of the Royal Society, Astronomer Royal (1720–42), is rarely thought of or mentioned as a sea captain or a scientific seaman. Yet his shiphandling in the course of three voyages in command of Their Majesties' Pink *Paramore* (1698–1701) in the North and South Atlantic Oceans, in fine and in foul weather, and amid the towering icebergs of Antarctica as in the tide-torn, tempestuous English Channel is in itself proof that his seamanship was of the highest order. Similarly, the practical innovations that he made in the arts of navigation and pilotage, in the form of printed sea charts and sailing directions, were fundamentally scientific and therefore remain relevant today.

Captain Halley, Royal Navy, the scientist, helped the mariner at sea to answer with greater confidence the perennial questions in the mind of every shipmaster or captain from the moment he casts off from the quayside or weighs anchor in the stream to put to sea, until the moment when, the ship being safely moored, anchored, or secured with shore lines in his intended haven, he can finally go below and write in his logbook precisely where he is—as Captain Halley did himself in October 1701 at the end of his third and last voyage: "10 We came to Deptford, and I delivered the pink into the Custody of Capt Wright, Master of Attendance. 16 The pink was paid off at Broad street."[1]

The questions seamen ask are seemingly very simple, such as "Where am I?" "Whither am I bound?" "What are the course and distance to make good?" "What allowance should I make: for the tidal stream, its speed and direction—for the state of the tide—the depth of water—to clear the bar with safety—to clear the sunken rocks in the offing?" "How far from the land as charted am I?" "How can I proceed in safety down the English Channel?" "What allowance should I make for the magnetic variation?" "How can I safely make the Channel from the ocean?" "How can I measure distance sailed in the ocean east or west in terms of longitude from my prime meridian (if any is shown) on my chart?"

Captain Halley the seaman applied science to seamanship and published the results to help shipmasters answer such questions more confidently than ever before. His nautical contributions were among the very few examples of science being successfully applied on a wide scale during the Scientific Revolution in order to improve man's control over nature. Outside the esoteric worlds of astronomy, horology, meteorology, and microscopy it is difficult to find improvements that were not technological and empirical in origin, rather than derived from scientific observation and theory, as Halley's were. It is to be remarked that those improvements of an astronomical or horological nature made were chiefly for the improvement of positional astronomy, so that navigation at sea might be perfected. The sea influenced English science profoundly.

On the occasion of the tercentenary of the foundation in 1675 of the Royal Observatory at Greenwich (Fig. 10.1), E. G. Forbes observed concerning the Gresham Lectures of John Flamsteed (the first Astronomer Royal, 1675–1719), perhaps hopefully, that

> the present generation of scientifically minded historians is much more eager to gain a deeper insight into, and clearer understanding of, the problems confronting practical astronomy in the very decade when Newton conceived his *Principia Mathematica Philosophiae Naturalis* [London, 1687]. This interest alone justifies the publication of these manuscript lectures which are designated as R.G.O.MSS. 38 in the Public Record Office's system of classification [for Flamsteed dealt in them with the problems confronting him as a practising astronomer of the late seventeenth century]. A further justification for the publication of these lectures is that recent philosophically orientated writings on the seventeenth-century astronomical revolution have completely ignored the contributions of the inventions of telescope, screw-micrometer, and pendulum clock; the gradual refinement of observational methods; and the application of new instrumental techniques.[2]

Thus I justify consideration of Halley as a seaman because he made some of his most important contributions to science and society as a practical seaman, and specifically in an effort to solve scientifically the most mundane problems of the art of navigation. Also, in his later role as Astronomer Royal, many of his scientific activities, inquiries, and efforts were similarly devoted to developing the art of navigation into a science. Indeed, even his earlier scientific interests, inventions, and experiments are difficult, if not impossible, to isolate also from the demands of the sea.

PROSPECTUS SEPTENTRIONALIS.

Figure 10.1. The Royal Observatory, Greenwich: the first official scientific institution in England, 1675. Engraving by Francis Place, 1676. (Courtesy of the Trustees of the National Maritime Museum, Greenwich.) The Observatory was founded in 1675 by King Charles II for "the finding out of the longitude of places for perfecting navigation and astronomy," in the words of the Royal Warrant of 22 June authorizing its construction. Edmond Halley succeeded the first Astronomer Royal, the Reverend John Flamsteed, in January 1720, and like Flamsteed held the office until his death, in January 1742. The building was designed by Sir Christopher Wren, Gresham Professor of Astronomy (1657–60) and Savilian Professor of Astronomy (1660/61–1673). Since 1669 Wren had been Surveyor General. In his inaugural address at Gresham Wren reminded his audience that "the whole Doctrine of Magneticks, as it was of English Birth, so by the Professors of this Place was augmented."[1] As Surveyor General he had been one of the commission, set up by the King in December 1674, to inquire into the lunar distance method of finding longitude proposed by the Sieur de St. Pierre, protégé of Louise de Keroualle, Duchess of Portsmouth, whose findings led to the founding of the Royal Observatory. Twenty years before, at Oxford, Wren had pioneered in making and using the telescope as a device for making astronomical measurements, previously it had been useful only for qualitative observations. He was thus singularly well qualified to design an observatory dedicated to positional astronomy for finding the longitude at sea. "Former Industry," he wrote, "hath hardly left anything more glorious to be aim'd at in Art."[2]

1. J. A. Bennett, "Christopher Wren: Astronomy, Architecture, and the Mathematical Sciences," *Journal for the History of Astronomy* 5, pt. 3 (October 1975): 149–84; quotation p. 164.
2. Ibid., 169; quoting from *Parentalia* (London, 1750), 217.

For to the obverse of the "medallion in the mind" of Halley as scientist there should be—for there is—a reverse: Halley as seaman. The former, by general consent, hangs in our imaginary English "Gallery of Scientific Fame" after that of Newton, but after him alone. Where in any imaginary national "Gallery of Famous Sea Captains" should the medallion of Captain Halley hang? I think that question has never been asked. Yet it was as a sea captain that Edmond Halley made some of his most original scientific contributions.

Is such an appraisal important? I think so, because it is relevant to the pragmatic view of history, by which the facts of history are treated with reference to their practical lessons. Assessing and appreciating Halley as a seaman should contribute to a better understanding of the Scientific Revolution in England. For Halley is acknowledged to have been one of the two most important (Newton being the other), but also the most versatile, of the English Scientific Revolutionaries. Moreover, while Newton lies with the nation's illustrious dead under a splendid monument in Westminster Abbey, Halley lies beneath an obscure slab in the neglected graveyard of the parish church of Lee, in what is now a London suburb. This disparity of treatment in death of the nation's two most gifted scientists is, when called to mind, continuing visible and tangible evidence of the malevolence of established religion in that age against those thought not to conform or not seen demonstrably to conform. Such persons could be penalized, if not always when living, at least after they were dead. So Halley, branded by clerics in 1691 "a sceptick, and a banterer of religion," and successfully turned down for the Savilian Professorship of Astronomy at Oxford, was eventually punished for achieving, despite clerical disapproval, the Savilian Professorship of Geometry in 1704.[3] The fact is that, in that age of patronage, Halley had all his life the patronage of the highest persons in the land—always that of the king or queen, or both. And deservedly so, for he was a practical man of commanding appearance, genial character, and great charm, as well as of many and brilliant talents which he used to the nation's benefit. Thus in 1702 and 1703 he was employed successfully by Queen Anne on delicate diplomatic missions to the Emperor in Vienna, using in Istria his nautical expertise.[4] He was abroad when, on the death of Dr. Wallis in October 1703, the coveted Savilian Professorship of Mathematics fell vacant; but Captain Halley's extraordinary talents and zeal in the public service were nevertheless further rewarded, and the position was his.

With death, however, patronage ceased. Obscurity was all that the church would accord the suspect Halley's mortal remains and reputation. I shall therefore try to do justice to Halley (of whom no full life study has ever been written—was he too versatile and brilliant for his achievements to be appraised and penned by any one person?) as a seaman, as England's first and greatest scientific sea captain.

The seventeenth century is the century of the Scientific Revolution. This era is commonly thought of as starting in England in 1600 with the publication of Dr. Gilbert's *De Magnete*, which is usually called the first scientific book by an Englishman. But I confer this distinction on the book that was its inspiration: *The New Attractive*, by the seaman and sea-compass maker Robert Norman, published in London in 1581. In this book Norman describes his discovery of magnetic dip using scientific methods. From this seminal work of the Scientific Revolution in England came Gilbert's electricity . . . and much else!

We generally think of the Scientific Revolution as ending in 1700 and, as it began, with a seminal scientific—and again nautical—publication, the first-ever isogonic chart, "the first published isoline map of any kind."[5] This chart of the Atlantic Ocean, showing lines of equal magnetic variation in degrees from geographical north, was compiled that year by Captain Halley, Royal Navy, and published early in 1701 for the use of seamen. Yet just as the century of the Scientific Revolution extends, in fact, back into the 1580s, so it extends forward into the 1710s—to the year 1714, to be precise, the year of the passing by Parliament of the first scientific legislation, the Longitude Act, "An Act for Providing a Publick Reward for such Person or Persons as shall Discover the Longitude at Sea." The act was passed expressly to insure "the Safety and Quickness of Voyages, the Preservation of Ships and the Lives of Men." It provided for "some Publick Reward to be Settled as an Encouragement for so Useful and Beneficial a Work" and to meet the cost of "Trials and Experiments necessary" to bring "Inventions or Proposals . . . to Perfection."[6]

The passing of the Longitude Act manifests more clearly than any other public, organized social activity that the belief was now firm that, given the material resources, through reason man *was* able to master the forces of nature for the good of mankind, as had long been supposed. Moreover, the inspiration and the stimulus of this first official acknowledgment of the power of reason to overcome and exploit by "trials and experiments" the forces of nature (especially the sea) was the "Safety of the Navy, and Merchant Ships, as well as Improvement of Trade."[7] Thus, the extension of the Scientific Revolution into the eighteenth century demonstrates factually the reality of the belief in the power of reason and invention, combined with "trials and experiments" involving unprecedented manipulative skill. Reason based on science, not faith, was to be encouraged financially and officially, so that the "so much-desired longitude of places for the perfecting the art of navigation"—to use the words of the Royal Warrant of 4 March 1674–75 appointing John Flamsteed the first Astronomer Royal—might be found.[8]

Though the beginning and ending of the Scientific Revolution are imprecise, their dates debatable, the cause of the commencement in England of the Scientific Revolution was nautical—the scientific study of magnetism in connection with the manufacture of sea-compasses and dip-dials (to give but two examples)—just as its continuance was officially fostered from the last quarter of the seventeenth century with nautical aims in mind by the founding of the Royal Observatory "for the perfecting the art of navigation." Similarly, it culminated with the passage through Parliament of the act awarding unprecedented and fabulous prizes to the discoverer of practical means to measure a ship's position at sea. Thus, what started the Scientific Revolution in England was something very practical.

The manufacture of Flamsteed's optical and horological instruments for precision astronomical and time measurement also influenced critically the growth of the scientific instrument trade and chronometry in England, as well as the consequential expansion and refinement of scientific observation and measurement that ensued. When Newton began to contemplate preparing a second edition of his epoch-making *Principia* (1687), he recognized that one of its chief weaknesses, for which he desired to compensate, was that he had not included a general theory of the Moon's motion, which would lead to a better understanding of tidal phenomena. At his request, in 1694 Flamsteed supplied him with the necessary lunar observations; these were obtainable from no other astronomer, and as Newton acknowledged in his letter of thanks, dated 16 February 1695, "all the world knows that I make no observations myself."[9] Thus, one of the most important sections of Newton's *Principia* is concerned with the tides and their causes, another subject of perennial practical importance to seamen. The phenomenon was also of absorbing interest to Halley. When Francis Davenport of the East India Company described in the 1684 *Philosophical Transactions of the Royal Society* observations he had made of the peculiar course of the tides at the port of Batsha, in the Gulf of Tonkin, however, Halley was struck by their scientific theoretical interest; Davenport, however, had used them merely to draw up detailed instructions to enable large East Indiamen to cross the bar of the river safely.[10]

The year 1684 saw the beginning of the fruitful cooperation between Halley and Newton, which culminated in Halley's undertaking the publication of the *Principia* at his own expense in May 1687. He collected much of the material for Book Three, including tidal information. This is the book in which Newton explained the principle of the phenomena of the solar system: the motions of the planets according to Kepler's laws;

the spheroidal shape of the Earth; the inequalities of the Moon's motions; the tides; the precession of the equinoxes; and comets.[11] When, in 1687, an advance copy of the work was presented to King James II, it was accompanied by a paper in the form of a letter to the king in which Halley gave a brief account of the contents, with special reference to Newton's theory of the tides, that King James, a noted seaman, was most likely to find of particular interest. This paper was also printed as a tract (London, 1687) and, ten years later, in the *Philosophical Transactions*. Designed for the reader curious as to the causes of the tides but unequal to the mathematical demands of Newton's treatise, it was invaluable in elucidating for seamen tidal phenomena and soon found its way into the principal manuals published to enable seamen to learn the art of navigation. In this explanation Halley followed the doctrine of the *Principia* fairly closely (Book Three, Prop. 24); he reproduced Newton's suggested explanation of the anomalous tides at Batsha. Hitherto Halley had thought these inexplicable. Now he declared, "the whole appearance of these strange Tides, is without any forcing naturally deduced from these Principles, and is a great Argument of the certainty of the whole Theory."[12] Thus the inclusion of the purely nautical phenomenon of the tides was crucial for the acceptance of Newton's theory of universal gravitation.

It was while he was a pupil at St. Paul's School in London that, in 1672, Halley measured the magnetic variation that he subsequently published in the *Philosophical Transactions* (1683).[13] By the time he left for Oxford University in 1673, Halley had, according to John Aubrey, become such a keen astronomer that Joseph Moxon, the distinguished London book, map, chart, and globe seller, averred: "if a star were misplaced in the globe he would presently find it."[14] In correspondence with Flamsteed on the latter's appointment as first Astronomer Royal, Halley was soon in the older man's company and observed with him two eclipses in 1675. Flamsteed's warrant appointed him "to apply himself with the most care and diligence to the rectifying the tables of the motions of the heavens, and the places of the fixed stars, so as to find out "the so much-desired longitude of places for the perfecting the art of navigation."[15] Sited as he was at Greenwich, in latitude $51\frac{1}{2}°$ North, it was impossible for Flamsteed to rectify "the places of the fixed stars" visible in the southern hemisphere above latitude $38\frac{1}{2}°$ South. Hence, and presumably in consultation with Flamsteed, "the ingenious youth, Edmond Halley," to use Flamsteed's words, decided that he would prepare a catalogue and planisphere of the southern constellations for the benefit of mariners plying the southern seas.

The star catalogue in current use, Kepler's *Rudolphine Tables* (1627), was based on the observations of Tycho Brahe and of the Dutch pilot

Pieter Dirckszoon Keyser, made in Madagascar in 1595. Although Keyser died in Sunda the following year, his catalogue, comprising the twelve original southern constellations, was published in 1603 by his fellow sea captain, Frederick de Houtman. Johannes Bayer immediately incorporated the new material into his *Uranometria*, published the same year,[16] and Kepler included in his *Rudolphine Tables* 136 southern star places based on Bayer's charts.

Inevitably, these pretelescopic star positions were inaccurate and in need of correction by the use of "large and accurate [optical] instruments, so as to be able to make a most accurate sphere of fixed stars, and complete our globes throughout," as Halley put it in a letter to Henry Oldenburg, Secretary of the Royal Society, in July 1676. The site chosen for Halley's proposed observatory was to be the "island of St Helena the southernmost of all territories under English rule, where the south celestial pole is moderately elevated above the horizon."[17] The island had been taken from the Dutch as recently as 1673, in the course of the Second Dutch War, as a watering and provisioning place for East Indiamen homeward bound and was, in fact, the only English possession in the southern hemisphere at that time.

Approved by the Secretary of State, the project was drawn to the attention of King Charles II, as founder of the Royal Observatory, by the indefatigable Sir Jonas Moore, Flamsteed's patron. The king also approved. It was a matter in which he was genuinely interested, for it concerned the welfare and safety of his seamen; also, the undertaking would entail no expense to him if he commended it to the Court of Committees of the Honorable East India Company, which forthwith he did. The court complied with what was, in effect, a royal command. Thus the Company conveyed young Edmond Halley, together with his assistant James Clark (or Clerk), free under royal patronage to and from the Island in two of their East Indiamen and accommodated them there free (except for their board). Halley's father defrayed his other expenses.

Halley and Clark sailed in November 1676 in the *Unity*, arriving at St. Helena the following February. On completing their observations—Halley determined the places of 341 stars, most of them not visible from Europe—they departed in March 1678 in the East Indiaman *Golden Fleece;* they reached England before the end of May. Halley thus spent about six months at sea. During this time he must have lived in the close company of most of the officers, certainly of those concerned with the navigation of the ship. For a young and enthusiastic astronomer and gifted mathematician, as Halley was, it must have been of great professional interest to see how the ship was navigated, and for an intelligent young man, how life aboard was organized and disciplined.

In order to understand seventeenth-century English intellectual life, it is essential to keep in mind the paramount importance to the English of ships, shipping, and everything pertaining thereto for their safety and prosperity. In brief, maritime affairs dominated the English scene. In the seventeenth century every responsible Englishman was aware of the benefits as well as the dangers of being an islander, an awareness that since the 1650s had shaped the nation's economy and defense.

Politically, in both home and foreign policy, this awareness of ships and the sea was given reality by the Navigation Acts. These acts, first framed in 1650 in the time of the Commonwealth, were specifically designed to make and then keep the nation self-sufficient in ships and seamen for both trade and defense against invasion and to facilitate affairs in case of war. They were also designed to develop and exploit commercially the raw materials of the colonies, on the one hand, and the manufactures and agricultural products of England, on the other, and to build up and maintain a fleet of merchant ships numerous enough to carry imports and exports of all these goods. To this end the carriage of such products, both inward and outward, was rigorously confined (with rare exceptions) to English ships manned predominantly by Englishmen.

In terms of defense the Navigation Acts were aimed deliberately at building up enough seamen to man the Royal Navy fully and efficiently in time of war and at the same time to enable trading by sea to continue. By the last decades of the century, when the population of England and Wales was about 5.5 million, there were about 55,000 seamen, and at least as many again were involved with the building and maintenance of some 4,300 ships, totaling 340,000 tons.

In the City and port of London were concentrated virtually all the printers and publishers licensed in England to trade in books, maps, and charts, all the makers of navigational and scientific instruments, and all the teachers of the art of navigation. Here, too, in the City, close to the Thames, young Edmond Halley and the East Indiamen's officers bought their books, charts, and instruments, learned the art of navigation, and, in the now numerous coffee houses, discussed its problems. About half the English merchant tonnage and one-third of the ships were London-based, most of them deep-sea traders. The East Indiamen, Blackwall-based (opposite but downriver of Greenwich), worked from the Thames only, a dozen ships a year making the two-year round-trip voyage to the East Indies, some as far as China for its increasingly popular tea. The several hundred smaller West Indiamen and North American traders made one round-trip voyage a year. These ships, like the Baltic and White Sea timber ships, were big ships, 150- to 600-tonners, but still tiny by modern standards.

It is virtually certain that the East Indiamen's pilots used Mercator charts for the oceanic passages, as they had done for the past sixty years.

Halley, to whom the mathematics would have been child's play, could not have gone to sea in better instructional ships, navigationally speaking. Their homeward-bound cargoes were among the most valuable in the world, and the directors of the Honorable Company endeavored to ensure their safety in every way, for in those goods lay their wealth. The use of the best navigational practices and aids was the cheapest form of insurance.

In 1676 there were seventeen map and chart sellers—all in London—but of these five specialized as well in publishing charts: William Fisher, Robert Morden, Joseph Moxon, John Seller, and John Thornton. Seller not only sold instruments but, unusual for the period, taught their use also. He was the Navy Board contractor for sand-glasses and sea-compasses and the best-known nautical instrument maker and hydrographic publisher. Along with Moxon, Seller was Hydrographer to the King and was in the process of compiling and publishing his ambitious "Sea Waggoner for the Whole World, with Charts and Draughts of particular places, and a large Description of all the Roads, Harbors and Havens, with the Dangers, Depths and Soundings in most parts of the World" (Fig. 10.2).[18] *The English Pilot*, as it was called, comprised various, appropriately subtitled volumes covering different seas, as well as a *Sea Atlas* depicting all the seas of the world. It was Seller, moreover, who had finally settled by experimentation that compass needles touched by any of several lodestones always pointed—contrary to popular belief—in the same direction.[19]

The East Indiamen in which Halley took passage almost certainly carried waggoners, probably English ones as well as Dutch. Since the publication of the first one by Lucas Waghenaer (whence the name) in 1585, the Dutch had monopolized the world market for them by publishing waggoners in translation in English, French, German, Italian, and Spanish. The genius behind this enterprise had been William Blaeu (1571–1638), whose large, lavishly charted, and detailed sailing directions in *The Sea Mirrour* (to give its English title) of 1623 had become the pattern for all waggoners. These waggoners covered the coasts and seas of the northern, eastern, and western European navigations of the Dutch (and other European) seamen, as far south on the coast of Barbary as Cape Verde, and west to the Azores. It is highly probable that, if none of the officers in the *Unity* had bought a copy of Seller's *English Pilot. The Third Book. Describing . . . the Oriental Navigation*, first published in 1675, at least Halley had. Although Seller had ended the sailing directions peremptorily off the coast of Siam, *The English Pilot. Oriental* was invaluable, as it was the only Far Eastern waggoner in print. Of greatest importance was "The First Part," which was devoted to "shewing the Nature and Properties of the Winds and Moussons between England and the East-Indies."

Figure 10.2. John Seller, *Practical Navigation* (London, 1672), title page of the second edition. (Courtesy of the Trustees of the National Maritime Museum, Greenwich.) This title page was used, with changes in typography, for all later editions of the book (that of the first [1669] lists the contents), the last being that of 1738. It illustrates virtually all the navigational instruments in use during Captain Halley's lifetime and sold by Seller. Against the symbolic background of the Sun, Moon, and stars are, from left to right and downward: celestial globe, equinoctial compass, terrestrial globe; vellum or paper single-sheet sea chart; single-handed dividers; (a chain of) single-handed dividers, sea-compass, rule, sinical quadrant, cross-staff with three crosses, armillary sphere, sea-astrolabe, quadrant, Gunter's Scale, sea-compass, single-handed dividers; single-handed dividers; nocturnal, sinical quadrant; two navigators holding, respectively, a cross-staff and a Davis backstaff; between them, azimuth compass, quadrant, equinoctial compass, plow, sea-compass; on Seller's *English Pilot* (bound, printed charts and sailing directions) dividers and single-handed dividers; in front, Plain Scale and twelve-inch rule.

This section occupies four folio pages of print and is an entirely original compilation, admirably organized and methodically treated. Halley's treatise and chart of the wind distribution in the tropics, published in the 1686 *Philosophical Transactions,* would seem to be deeply indebted to Seller's work. Because copies of Seller's *Oriental Pilot* of 1675–1701 are today exceedingly rare, it is perhaps correct to speculate, the originality and importance of his work on winds have lain hitherto unrecognized.

Halley, it is true, acknowledged the use of other writers' descriptions of winds and sailors' observations in addition to his own observations at St. Helena in composing his "Historical account of the trade winds, and monsoons, observable in the seas between and near the tropicks, with an attempt to assign the physical cause of the said winds." [20] Yet an appreciation of Seller's originality in producing the first fundamental work on the winds and monsoons of the oceans (for there is none comparable in any other language), which he himself compiled and published for seamen, is long overdue. Such acknowledgment in no way detracts from the scientific originality of Halley's treatise in seeking to explain the mechanics of the trade winds and monsoons, or from Halley's originality in constructing and publishing his "Chart of the Trade Winds and Monsoons," the first meteorological chart ever published. However, while it is doubtful whether many seamen ever saw either of Halley's works as originally published, Seller's account of the seasonal distribution and behavior of the trade winds and monsoons was certainly read and used by generations of English seamen, for it continued to appear for close on a century in later editions of *The English Pilot. Oriental.* Moreover, this work was shortly to be supplemented by reproductions of the main features of Halley's chart of the winds, for arrows representing prevailing wind direction were soon a standard feature of terrestrial globes, world maps, and charts published by London globe, map, and chart sellers, and have remained so ever since.

Halley's 1678 catalogue and planispheres of the southern and northern stars can be seen as two more of the wedges being driven by the English into the cultural and nautical dominance of the Dutch at this time. The catalogue was brought out with great speed at the end of 1678 (though dated 1679) as a quarto entitled *Catalogus Stellarum Australium sive Supplementum Catalogi Tychonici.* This was accompanied with a chart of the southern stars and a companion one of the northern stars, both engraved by Jacob Clark. The southern one Halley dedicated to King Charles II, the northern one to Sir Jonas Moore, who, with the king, had been instrumental in making his voyage possible; they were the two most influential patrons of nautical science in England at the time.

Soon afterward Halley supplied the star positions for a map of the zodiac published in 1679 by John Seller, who bound Halley's southern planisphere into issues of his *Atlas Maritimus*. He also used Halley's as a model for a southern planisphere map of his own.[21]

Meanwhile, Halley had been elected a fellow of the Royal Society in November 1678. During the next fourteen years Halley, besides touring the Continent and marrying (1682), occupied himself with studying and writing, as noted above, about magnetic variation (1683 and 1692) and the tides (1684);[22] he also wrote on the winds of the oceans (1686), busied himself with the publication of Newton's *Principia* (1687), and provided a nonmathematical explanation of the tides.

Of particular relevance to Halley's nautical interests is his development between 1689 and 1691 of an efficient diving bell and suit (apparently for use on a Guineaman wrecked in Pagham Bay, on the coast of West Sussex), an undertaking that involved the use of a frigate lent by the Admiralty. Consequently, he now experienced life aboard a Royal Navy ship, becoming acquainted with the handling of a warship and the organization and discipline of the crew. In 1689 he had presented before the Royal Society his "Sea draught of the Mouth of the River of Thames, wherein he saith, that he hath corrected severall very great, and considerable faults in all our Sea-Charts hitherto published," as the Society's *Journal Book* records. This chart of the Thames, together with that (noted on 15 November 1693) "of the West Coast of Sussex between Selsey and Arundell with the line form and situation of the dangerous sholes called the Owers," further illustrates his active participation in sea affairs and his preoccupation with the dangers of the sea, with practical measures for reducing those dangers, and with methods for recovering wrecked treasure from the depths.[23]

The Thames estuary was the entrance not only to the chief mercantile port of the realm but also to the chief naval dockyards: Deptford and Woolwich on the River Thames, and Sheerness and Chatham on the River Medway. Similarly, the Owers shoal flanked the main approach channel to Portsmouth dockyard. This was the only dockyard on the Channel coast that William III had then, the decision to create a dockyard at Plymouth having been taken only on 29 July 1692, after the crushing victory over the French fleet at La Hogue that had established him and his Stuart queen, Mary II, on the throne.

Halley's survey of the Owers, which he was to repeat in 1701 while in command of a ship of the Royal Navy, also suggests a naval connection. It seems likely that Halley's Owers surveys were incorporated in the inset chart of the Isle of Wight included in the large Channel chart published in 1702 with Halley's tidal and magnetic observations on it. However that may be, on 12 July 1693 the Queen had directed the Admiralty to set up and build in the Royal Yard at Deptford "a Vessell of about Eighty Tuns Burden" for Mr. Halley "to endeavour to gett full information of the Na-

ture of the Variation of the Compasse over the whole Earth, as Likewise
to experiment what may be expected from the Severall Methods proposed for discovering the Longitude at Sea." Nine months later the vessel was launched and "named the Paramour & entered on the List of the
Royall Navy by the same name."

On completion, however, the *Paramore* was laid up. The death of
Queen Mary in December of that year, 1694, may have put an end to the
scheme for the time being. By authorizing the project she had inevitably
been its chief patron, just as she had been responsible for fostering the
establishment of a Naval Hospital for seamen, which after her death
William III created in their joint names at Greenwich in her memory.

The shelving of the projected voyage was probably all to the good. As
a result of the *Paramore* being "Rigged and brought afloat" by order of
King William III, "in Ordr to make Some Experimt about her sayling
. . . in such manner as the Czar [Peter the Great, early in 1698, was
studying shipbuilding in Deptford yard] shall desire," she was found to
be "very Crank." It was therefore decided "to cause her to be Girdled
[made beamier by additional planking] in such manner, as shall be
thought most proper for making her Carry ye Better Saile" (see Fig.
10.3).[24]

The Treaty of Ryswick ending the war was signed on 20 September
1697. Halley's Mint duties ceased in early 1698, and by 9 August the *Paramore* was being sheathed (planked from the waterline downward as a
protection against the burrowings of the teredo worm) and fitted for a
voyage of twelve months under the command of Captain Halley, whose
commission from the Lords of the Admiralty was delivered ten days
later. Two azimuth compasses were issued to him, at his request, in mid
September, no doubt of Seller's make. The *Paramore* was armed, against
Salee rovers and pirates in the Atlantic and buccaneers in the West Indies, with six 3- and two 1-pounders.

On 15 October Captain Halley received his orders to proceed

with her on an Expedition, to improve the knowledge of the Longitude
and variations of the Compasse . . . with all the accuracy you can, as also
the true Scituation both in Longitude and Latitude of the Ports where you
arrive . . . and . . . you are to stand soe farr into the South, till you discover
the Coast of the Terra Incognita, supposed to lye between Magelan's
Streights and the Cape of Good Hope . . . to visit the English West India
Plantations . . . to lay them downe truely in their Geographicall Scituation . . . of which you are to keep a Register in your Journall . . . conforming your selfe to what is directed by the Generall Printed Instructions
annex'd to your Commission, with regard . . . to the Government of the
Shipp under your Command.[25]

Figure 10.3. An English merchantship, last half of the seventeenth century, by T. Flessier (d. 1665?). (Courtesy of the Trustees of the National Maritime Museum, Greenwich.) In rig and build not dissimilar to, though perhaps bigger than, Captain Halley's *Paramore*. She is leaving harbor under mizzen, foresail, fore-topsail and main-topsail. She is certainly a typical merchantman of the times during which Halley was actively engaged in sea affairs.

If Halley felt a need to brush up on his navigation, he could now consult titles that were not in print when he first voyaged into the Atlantic twenty years before: Captain Daniel Newhouse's *The Whole Art of Navigation*, first published in 1685, was republished in 1698; James Atkinson's *The Seaman's New Epitome* had come out in 1686; and in 1695 Samuel Newton, Mathematical Master at Christ's Hospital, had published his ponderous *An Idea of Geography and Navigation*. What Halley had no need to consult was *Idea Longitudinis: being, a brief Definition of the best known Axioms for finding the Longitude* (1696). Dedicated to the Commissioners of the Admiralty, *Idea Longitudinis* had been written by and printed for a Lieutenant Edward Harrison of the Royal Navy, and was sold by John Seller, Richard Mount, and Philip Lea, the principal nautical booksellers. Halley had already read and reported on the work to Their Lordships, informing them that it contained nothing new; since then he had evidently forgotten about it. Certainly, when the lieutenant he had requested to improve discipline arrived on board the *Paramore*, Halley did not associate the Lieutenant Harrison appointed with the author of that book. Today the importance of Harrison's book lies in its anecdotes and reminiscences of navigational practice in East Indiamen and in ships of the Royal Navy, in which he had served some ten years by 1698.

Halley probably had a copy of the latest, 1690, edition of Seller's *English Pilot. Southern,* with its charts and sailing directions for the Atlantic islands—the Madeiras, Canaries, Cape Verdes, and Azores—for he was to call in, as was customary, at the Madeiras for wine and at the Cape Verdes before proceeding westward into the ocean. But to go down the Channel safely, with the possibility of being forced to call into Portsmouth or Plymouth, he had probably bought a copy of the latest English "pilot," Captain Greenville Collins's folio *Great Britain's Coasting Pilot* of 1693, which had taken Collins seven years of survey work and included by far the best charts available of the English Channel and of the main ports on the English south coast. It also had the only up-to-date printed chart of that notorious hazard to shipping, the Isles of Scilly at the mouth of the Channel. This chart derived from the survey made of the islands by two master mariner Elder Brethren of Trinity House when that authority had established a lighthouse on the southernmost of the inhabitable islets, St. Agnes, in 1680.

Because Captain Halley's orders directed him (as, later, Lieutenant James Cook's did as well) to explore the South Atlantic in search of the supposed southern continent, "Terra Incognita," he probably had the latest *Atlas Maritimus,* recently published by Fisher and Mount. Moreover, since his orders (which he had himself originally drafted based on his scientific nautical activities) directed him to the West Indies after his southern explorations were complete, he would have been rash indeed not to have purchased a copy of Thornton and Mount's *English Pilot. The Fourth Book [America and the West Indies],* which came out that very year, in 1698; of course, had he been unable to buy this version, he would, no doubt, have obtained a copy of the 1689 edition by Fisher and Thornton.

It is virtually certain that Halley had a copy of *A New Voyage round the World; describing particularly the . . . Islands in the West Indies, the Isles of Cape Verd, the Passage by Terra del Fuego . . . and Santa Helena. . . ,* by Captain

William Dampier, of which the third edition had come out in February 1698 (the first having been published only in February 1697). But Halley would have had to wait for his copy of Dampier's *Supplement of the Voyage round the World*, with its *A Discourse of Trade-Winds, Breezes, Storms, Seasons, Tides, and currents of the Torrid Zone throughout the World . . . with Maps and Draughts . . .*, as this work was not published until 1699.

Halley's bos'n was also the gunner (as was usual in small ships), but knowing that the *Paramore* would be armed, Halley may have read up on technicalities of which he should be aware in Thomas Binnings's *A Light to the Art of Gunnery*, which had come out, appropriately, in 1689, at the start of the recently ended war.

Halley was careful to ask that a naval surgeon be appointed to the *Paramore*—a position that such small ships usually did not require—and the surgeon George Alfrey was duly brought on. This foresight displays Halley's appreciation of the fact that the success or failure of his expedition hinged on the health of his crew. It is to be expected that both Halley and Alfrey knew of the latest work on diseases of the sea, William Cockburn's *Account of the nature, causes, symptoms . . . distempers . . . incident to seafaring people*, published in 1696. When it came to injuries from battle, Moyle's *Chirurgus Marinus* (Sea Surgeon), of which the first edition had come out in 1693, was the best. Moyle wrote from the experience of attending the wounded in the dimly lit cockpit of a ship in action, describing the blood-stained scene vividly. Halley's son, born this very year, 1698, was to become a sea surgeon when he grew up.

In this diet-conscious age, only a few words need be said about scurvy, the greatest scourge of seamen engaged on long voyages, who subsisted on the official ration of salted beef, pork, and fish, with twice-baked ship's biscuits, butter, and cheese and washed down with weak beer, wine, or rum. The cause of scurvy was unknown, just as no certain cure had been discovered for it. On such a diet the first manifestations of the disease appeared after some forty days, and the full clinical picture of fatigue, depression, bleeding gums, painful opening of old wounds, and incapacitating swellings of joints developed between eighty-four and ninety-seven days, that is, within three months.[26] The best preventive of scurvy is the juice of lemons, but this fact was not widely appreciated, although some naval surgeons and naval commanders apparently did ship lemons aboard at this time. There is no evidence that Halley knew of this preventive; however, one of the most remarkable accomplishments of Captain Halley's two long-at-sea Atlantic voyages (he made a second in 1699–1700) is that he kept his crew, it seems, free from sickness. Indeed, he lost only one of his crew (on the second voyage), "my poor Boy Manley White . . . drowned, by falling overboard."[27]

During the first three months of the first voyage few, if any, of the

crew went ashore; only Halley did, and evidently he obtained no fresh
provisions on these excursions, not even when he landed at Paraíba (now
João Pessoa), in Brazil. He reported to Josiah Burchett, Secretary to the
Admiralty, from Barbados on 4 April 1699: "Twas the last of November
before we left the coast of England [they had sailed from Deptford 20
October], wch considering the Uncertainty of the Winds was I find two
months too late. . . . We watred in the river of Paraibo . . . [but] I refused all commerce with them [the Portuguese]. . . . Having gotten our
water we arrived here in three weeks. . . . Our whole shipps company is
hither in perfect health and our provisions proves very good."[28]

The crew were apparently still healthy when the *Paramore* anchored
in the Long Reach in the Thames on 8 July, for he had already reported
from Plymouth, "I this day arrived here . . . in 6 weeks from the West
Indies, having buried no man during the whole Voiage"—an exceptional achievement in those days.[29] Halley had had problems getting
water and fresh provisions in the islands as he worked his way north
across the prevailing trade winds. But at the end of April he could log
that at St. Christopher's there was excellent water, which, unlike at previous watering places, was easily got. On 9 May, at anchor in the Road of
Anguilla, he had logged: "I provided Myselfe with hens and other re-
freshments,—such as the place afforded, and on Tuesday afternoon set
saile for England I steered away North between Dog Island and Turpen-
tine Island, and about 7 Dog Isle bore West about halfe a League off; I
reckon Myselfe to depart from Latitude 18°.20' Long 62°.50' west from
London."[30] This, too, is remarkable—Anguilla lies in latitude 18°20'
North, longitude 63°00' West from Greenwich!

This longitude might be regarded as a lucky coincidence, given the
observational limitations of contemporary nautical astronomical tables
and instruments. But I think it also reflects good navigation by Halley,
based on his determination of the longitude of Barbados (at Bridge-
town) by an eclipse of the first satellite of Jupiter, a method long advocated by Flamsteed. Halley had used Cassini's tables, probably those published in the *Philosophical Transactions* as recently as 1694 as "New and
Exact Tables for the Eclipses of the First Satellite of Jupiter reduced to
the Julian Stile and the Meridian of London."[31] The conditions had not
been ideal, and he had gotten a longitude about twenty-five miles short
of the correct longitude. Halley knew the longitude to be "about 59° to
the Westward of London," a fact he had thus confirmed. He also confirmed that in sailing from Paraíba in latitude 7° South he had "been sett
about 3° to the Westwards . . . beyond [his] reckoning."[32] Indeed, they
had sighted the peaks of Barbados on the evening of 1 April.

They had prudently been running down the latitude of Barbados for
the past two days, with the northeast trade on their starboard quarter
taking them along, as they thought, at a comfortable five knots, making

good 120 miles a day. It must have been quite a surprise, therefore, to sight the island a day and a half sooner than expected, for by the reckoning they were in longitude 56° West. The cause, of course, lay in, successively, the South Equatorial and North Equatorial Currents, which in these latitudes sweep along westward at from eighteen to fifty-two miles a day.[33]

Halley had already had this sort of experience before. Sailing from the Cape Verdes on 6 January 1698/99, he had made the island of Fernando de Loronha on 19 February in search of water (they found none) and to scrub the ship clean of weed. Two days before, he had observed a transit of the Moon and a star, from which he had logged: "concluded myself 160 leagues more westerly than our account." When he reached the island, he fixed its position "in Latt. 3°57′ South, and Longit by reckoning from London 23°40′ West." It actually lies in 4° South 33°10′ West. On the strength of his Moon sight Halley corrected his longitude to 34°, thus making his error in longitude under 1° west, as compared to 9°30′ east by reckoning.

A few days later, on approaching the coast of Brazil, again in search of water, they fell in with the coast unexpectedly, at three in the morning and in the dark. Captain Halley prudently anchored until daylight, "fearing foul ground." According to his five charts, they had not yet made half their westing. That night he took another Moon sight for longitude, as before at sea, and a few days later, at Paraíba, he observed the end of an eclipse of the Moon, "from both which observations I conclude the Longitude of this coast full 36° to the Westward of London," he entered in his journal. The actual longitude is 34°53′ West, so again, his error by observation was only about 1° west. This accuracy is comparable with that attainable typically by the lunar distance method when it became practicable at sea from the 1760s.

In 1731, Halley explained how he had recorded observations of the Moon and stars in the 1680s, "From whence, at all Times, under the like Situation of the *Sun* and *Moon,* I might . . . have the Effect of exact *Lunar Tables* capable to serve at Sea, for finding the *Longitude* with the desired *Certainty.*" He used this method for finding the longitude at sea, he explained, "having by my own Experience found the impracticability of all other Methods proposed for that Purpose, but that derived from a perfect Knowledge of the *Moon's Motion.*" He then went on to reveal how he took these observations on board ship:

I had found it only needed a little Practice to be able to manage a five or six Foot Telescope, capable of shewing the Appulses or Occultations of the *Fix'd Stars* by the *Moon,* on Shipboard, in moderate Weather; . . . Whereas the Eclipses of the *Satellites* of *Jupiter,* how proper soever for *Geographical* Purposes, were absolutely unfit at Sea, as requiring Telescopes of a greater

Length than can well be directed in the rolling Motion of a Ship in the Ocean. . . . So in the remote Voyages I have since taken to ascertain the *Magnetick Variations* [1698–99 and 1699–1700], they have been of signal Use to me, in determining the *Longitude* of my *Ship*, as often as I could get Sight of a near *Transite* of the *Moon* by a known *Fix'd Star:* And thereby I have frequently corrected my *Journal* from those Errors which are unavoidable in long Sea-Reckonings.

Then, as an experienced mariner should, he warned anyone using his method: "you may, without sensible Error, from thence pronounce in what *Meridian* your *Ship* is; taking Care in so operate a Calculation, to commit no Mistake; and, notwithstanding the Direction the Moon gives you, not confiding so much therein as to omit any usual Precautions to preserve a Ship when she approaches the Land."[34] By this advice he meant, in particular, establishing the ship's latitude, sounding with the lead, and keeping a sharp lookout.

It is not surprising to find Halley recording one of his Moon sights for longitude on his voyage home in 1699 when north of Bermuda, before he altered course to the northeastward for the Soundings, or recording when he reached latitude 48° North: "The Collour of the Sea begun to Change the 12th. in the Morning the Moon apply'd to a Starr in Line piscium by which I find my Selfe 25 Leagues more Westerly than my Reckoning"; or, on the eighteenth: "At Sunn Sett Struck ground at 80 Fath:, and on the 20th, at Sunn Sett had ground at 60 Fath Scilley Seene."

The next morning he wrote: "The North part of Scilley was seen bareing East halfe South about 3. Leagues distant: at noon the sd. North part bore due East, Variation allowed; so haveing a very good observation I make the Lattitude thereof 49°57′." His reckoning, however, was 144 miles (48 leagues) "before the Shipp." This miscalculation he attributed to his log line being too short, following the customary safety measure— probably a correct assumption, given that he was sailing by a Mercator chart. The islands were not passed until sunset, when, knowing that ahead in the darkness the mainland lay, Halley, with the prudence of the born seaman, "stood away first SE, then ESE" into mid Channel. The weather was thick and hazy when, at daylight, he hauled into the northeast. By noon their hoped-for landfall, the Lizard, was in sight and safely passed, bearing to the west. Having another good sight, Halley made "the Lattitude of the Lizard no more than 49°54′." His position was thus, remarkably, a mere 3 minutes south of the true latitude of 49°57′ North. No doubt Captain Halley recorded this observation because some of his charts would have shown the Lizard somewhere between 50°00′ and 50°12′ North—that is, from 2.5 to 15 miles north of its true geographical position. The Scillies, it will be recalled, were often similarly displaced; Captain Halley, however—and even more remarkably—correctly observed their northern latitude to be 49°57' North. Still, decades would pass before the Lizard and the Scillies would be charted in their correct latitudes.

"The principal thing in a pilot or coaster of our coast is to know where he is," declared that experienced early Stuart sea commander, Sir William Monson, around 1625; and to drive the message home, he added: "The skill of a coaster is to know the land as soon as he shall descry it."[35] There is a very interesting early entry in Captain Halley's "Journall of the Voyage in his Majesties Pink the Paramore entended for the Discovery of the Variation of the Magneticall Compass," which he opened on 20 October 1698. On 30 October he wrote: "The Wind blew so hard at North that we were forced to hand our Top sailes, about 2. the Isle of Wight bore from us NNW the body of it, but it being cover'd with Snow, Some that ought to have known it better, tooke it for portland," forty-five miles to the westward. Did Captain Halley's "Some" include his lieutenant? Who else besides the lieutenant and the bos'n—the two watchkeepers—would express an opinion? He, of course, had the advantage of knowing the coast well in all weather (which can change the appearance of even a well-known coast most deceptively) from his diving and surveying activities in the area. It must have been very satisfying to be proved a competent coastal pilot so early in the voyage, despite being for only a short while and for the first time commander of a ship, particularly one of His Majesty's with an experienced lieutenant on board as second in command.

I have devoted considerable attention to the latter part of Halley's first Atlantic voyage because its successful outcome (he came to an anchor in Plymouth Sound on 23 June 1699, giving his "people leave," after eight months aboard, "to divert themselves on Shore") proved crucial to his career as a seaman and, hence, as a scientist. On 5 June Lieutenant Harrison had affronted his captain grossly—the culmination of a long series of insults and subversive activities—telling him before the other officers and the men on deck that he "was not only uncapable to take charge of the Pink, but even of a Longboat," whereupon Halley relieved him of his duties and informed him: "I would take the charge of the Shipp myself, to shew him his mistake: and accordingly," he informed the Secretary to the Admiralty, "I have watcht in his steed ever since, and brought the Shipp well home from near the Banks of Newfound Land, without the least assistance from him."[36]

Captain Halley supposed that the cause of his lieutenant's disrespectful behavior was that "perhaps I have not the whole Sea Directory so perfect as he." Seamen have—and in the days of sail especially, they

had—a virtual language all their own. It was essentially a technical language, the words mostly monosyllabic, at most of two syllables, terse,
precise, the phrases explicit, as they had to be for orders shouted at the
height of a storm to be heard, understood, and acted on instantly, without error or hesitation, either of which failings could risk the entire ship
herself; "for there is no dallying nor excuses with stormes, gusts, over-
growne Seas and lee-shores," as Captain John Smith expressed it so well
in his first of all English marine grammars, *A Sea Grammar*, published in
1627 and last republished in 1692.[37] In fact the cause was nothing of the
sort, as came out at the "Court Martial held ab[oar]d his Majties Ship the
Swiftsure in the Downes the 3d July 1699 . . . The Honble Sr Clowdsly
Shovell Kt Admll of the Blew. President."

After the court martial Captain Halley advised the Secretary to the
Admiralty: "My Lieutenant has now declared that I had signally dis-
obliged him, in the character I gave their Lopps [Lordships] of his Book,
about four years since, which therfor, I know to be the cause of all his
spite and malice to me, and it was my very hard fortune to have him
joyned with me, with this prejudice against me." The court and, when
they had perused its proceedings, Their Lordships, evidently thought
the same: they severely reprimanded the erring officers and resentful
Lieutenant, who left the Navy and rejoined the merchants' service. Captain Halley they reemployed. Thus, after paying off his ship on 20 July
at Deptford, Captain Halley was recommissioned on 23 August 1699 "to
be Master and Commandr of his Matt Pink the Paramour"—with a one-
armed bos'n, and four men in place of the missing arm! The orders were
similar to those for the first voyage, of which this was for all practical
purposes a continuation, the misconduct of his lieutenant and bos'n
being merely an interruption. Today this incident is often regarded as a
reflection on Captain Halley's competence as a commanding officer of a
ship of the Royal Navy. This, however, is clearly not how his contemporaries in the service saw it. To Admiral Sir Cloudisley Shovell and the
eleven other members of the court—three admirals and eight captains—
such "grumbling" was "generally in Small Vessels under such Circumstances."[38] The Admiralty, as we have seen, retained and reemployed the
commanding officer (Halley) to continue the expedition without the of-
fending officers. And less than two years later they reemployed him to
command a third expedition in the same ship. It is, perhaps, appropriate
to remind the present generation that the Naval Discipline Act, under
which the Admiralty acted, was designed primarily to enable disciplinary
control to be exercised over the *officers* of the Royal Navy, frequently an
unruly lot, not the men.

We should also remember that, on 6 May 1701, "In obedience to His
Mats Commands"—that is, to the orders of King William III—the Navy

Board paid over to Captain Halley the then very substantial award of £200, "in consideration of his great Paines and care in the late Voyage he made for discovering the Variation of the Needle"; and, moreover, that, on 20 April 1702, it was Queen Anne's "Royl Will and pleasure that the Summ of two hundred pounds shall be payd to Capt Edmd Halley (over and above his Pay as Captain of her Pink the Paramour) as a reward to him for his Extraordinary pains and care he lately tooke, in observing and setting down the Ebbing, and Flowing, and setting of the Tydes in the Channell as also and bearing of the head-Lands on the Coasts of England and France." Finally, when in 1729 Queen Caroline, the consort of King George II, paid the first royal visit to the Royal Observatory, she obtained, through the King, the grant to Captain Halley of the half-pay of a post captain of the Royal Navy, which he received, as became a captain of the Royal Navy, until his death on 4 January 1742 in the eighty-fifth year of his life.[39] But perhaps the last word lies with John Flamsteed, who had known and worked with Edmond Halley for nearly thirty years when he wrote to his former assistant, Abraham Sharp, a week before Christmas of 1703, that "Mr. Halley . . . now talks, swears, and drinks brandy like a sea captain." Halley was then forty-seven.[40]

The details of Captain Halley's second Atlantic (16 September 1699–9 September 1700) and Channel voyages (14 June 1701–16 October 1701) I shall leave to the curious to read in his recently published journals, without which I, for one, could never have studied Captain Halley the seaman. Of his skill as a ship handler, as a coaster, and as a deep-sea navigator during his first voyage there can be no question. It is my considered opinion that the unqualified success and originality of the other two voyages simply endorse his outstanding seamanship in temperate, tropical, and Antarctic seas as well as in the notoriously most dangerous and treacherous coastal waters in the world, the English Channel.

Also, I must reemphasize that no other seaman had ever undertaken such voyages, voyages dedicated—on the initiative of the one who undertook them—to the scientific discovery of navigational aids "of generall use to all Shipping, especially such as," to use Captain Halley's own words, "is wanting towards the compleating the Art of Navigation."[41] Neither had any other seaman ever made and published so many new, diverse, rationally organized, elegantly presented, and lucidly expounded observations tending "towards the Security of the Navigation of the Subjects of his Majtie or other Princes tradeing into the Channell"[42] and over the known oceans of the world, or made such voyages without losing one man through sickness. The difference between Captain Edmond Halley, Royal Navy, F.R.S., and Captain James Cook, Royal Navy, F.R.S., is, I think, one of publicity: the journals of the former lay unpublished for generations, whereas those of the latter received immediate and worldwide publicity in print, enriched visually by the handiwork of gifted artists, his shipmates on the various voyages of exploration that he made.

There was, of course, one fundamental difference: Captain Cook during his first Pacific voyage (1768–71) found his longitude within about 1° frequently, by means of lunar distances, using the annual *Nautical Almanack*, a reliable pocket watch, and a hand-held reflecting quadrant capable of giving any navigator angular readings of the requisite accuracy—that is, to within 1 minute of arc and his longitude to within sixty miles. On his second (1772–75) and third (1776–79/80) Pacific voyages he also used chronometers, which yielded positions reliably and consistently within 3 minutes of longitude. For all these scientific nautical devices and methods, Cook was indebted either directly or indirectly to the innovating scientific imagination, brains, energy, and skill of Captain Edmond Halley, who had had none of these navigational aids on his pioneer voyages of scientific nautical inquiry and exploration. In their stead he had used his own lunar saronic tables, which he developed himself to determine the longitude of a ship at sea. By his method he determined longitude to within about 1°, an accuracy that was seldom bettered by lunar distances from the time, when they became practicable for seamen in the mid 1760s. It was Halley who first explained, in the *Philosophical Transactions* of 1692, the correct moment in the Sun's rising at which to measure its amplitude for determining magnetic variation.[43] By 1718, if not earlier, this method was included in Seller's *Practical Navigation* as follows: "because the Refraction . . . causeth the Sun to appear in the Horizon, when indeed he is about 30 minutes below it, and consequently seems to make him rise further to the Northward in North Latitude (and the contrary) than really it doth . . . let the Center of the Sun be about 30 minutes . . . almost half his diameter above the Horizon."

That Halley took his amplitudes with azimuth compasses we can deduce from the Navy Board minutes of 14 September 1698, where a note was made to "Send a Warrant to the Officers at Deptford to supply the Parramore Pink with two Azimouth Compasses." This instrument should have made his observations the most accurate practicable, but when he demonstrated "the variation of the needle" before the Royal Society on 7 May 1701 "using the two needles which he had with him on this late voyage, by the one the Variations was 7°40′ and by the other 8°00′ W."[44] In short, they differed by 20 minutes of arc. Nevertheless, his observations were, with very little doubt, the most accurate of any made at sea up to this time; after all, he was probably the first seaman to make amplitude observations (to measure magnetic variation) at the correct moment of the Sun's rising. He thus contributed to greater accuracy in course steering, in position fixing by compass bearings, and in longitude estimation based on magnetic variation. Halley also constructed, and had published commercially, magnetic variation charts—in 1701 for the Atlantic and in 1702 for the Atlantic and Indian Oceans as well as the English Channel. The charts were sold by the leading hydrographic and navigational publishers of the day, the partners William Mount and Thomas Page, and had the inestimable virtue of making visible, as it were, magnetic variation, that inexplicable invisible phenomenon which affected compasses in varying amounts and at various places and which misdirected seamen, particularly when out of sight of land, who then in ignorance ran onto unexpected shores, wrecking their ships.

Halley's isogonic lines not only showed seamen for the first time the amount and direction of variation experienced at any given place but also systematized the overall distribution of variation for the year 1700; an accompanying description, which warned that that variation was not static, gave its annual change for future guidance. Henceforth, a navigator knowing where he was could, by visual inspection alone, find the variation needed to correct his compass course and bearings. Where the lines ran north and south, as near the western and southern coasts of Africa, he could get a check on his estimated longitude by measuring the variation himself and comparing that with the isogonic lines on the chart. Halley's charts thus helped the navigator to safeguard himself against a surprise landfall in thick weather or in hours of darkness when running down the latitude to round the Cape of Good Hope, whether outward or homeward bound.

These were the chief uses of Halley's two oceanic charts, the originality of which, insofar as the isogones were concerned, is beyond dispute. What charts he used to derive the coastlines, which at various points he corrected from his own observations, as well as at what points or places specifically he observed latitudes and longitudes, has as yet not been determined. The origin of the coastlines of Halley's Channel chart also remains to be identified, as do the positions of the headlands shown on it, compared to those currently shown in Channel charts: for his orders of 12 June 1701 instructed him "to take the bearings of the Principle headlands on the English coast one from another and to continue the Meridian as often as conveniently you can from Side to Side of the Channel, in order to lay down both Coasts truly against one another."[45] Noticeably, determination of neither the latitudes nor the longitudes of headlands is mentioned.

These orders had been originated by Halley in a letter of 11 June addressed to the secretary of the Admiralty, a letter that once again reveals Halley's extraordinary ability to see the need to synthesize and render visually comprehensible a complex mass of uncoordinated observations, in this instance tidal. He had asked, in a letter of 23 April, to be provided with "a small vessel" in order that their Lordships should have "an exact account of the Course of the Tides on and about the Coast of England, so taken as at one View to represent the whole." Such a single representation of the complex tidal pattern of the Channel would be of great advantage in that it would prove "of general use to all Shipping, especially such as have occasion to turn [tide] to Windward"—to use his explanation.[46] By this he meant that by knowing the times of the ebbing and flowing of the tides in the Channel, the master of a ship wishing to work his way up (or down) Channel against a contrary wind would be able to do so by tiding over—anchoring while the tidal stream (and wind) is adverse, then getting under way when the tidal stream will carry a ship to windward up (or down) Channel until it turns, whereupon the ship is again anchored to await the next turn of the tide. This maneuver Captain Halley logged several times in the *Paramore*, for instance on 31 August 1700.[47]

This ability to tide over could be of crucial strategic importance in time of war, particularly now that France and the French Navy threatened to exercise control over shipping in the Channel and, with the recently developed naval bases outside the Channel fronting the Bay of Biscay, to control shipping in the south western approaches also. Hitherto, ships without pilots or masters not intimately familiar with the Channel tides through long apprenticeship in Channel waters were often windbound for weeks, or even months, in one or another of the Channel ports or anchorages. Great developments were currently in hand to make Portsmouth and Plymouth main fleet dockyards, in place of those on the Thames facing the North Sea and the Dutch and so difficult of access for fleets operating in the Channel, the Soundings, or overseas against the French, whose new and powerful fleets were now the main threat to England herself and her shipping. Captain Halley's tidal survey and tidal chart of the Channel (incorporating also the variation) was therefore certainly seen as of the utmost importance to naval as well as mercantile shipping.

After the Channel chart was published, English fleets of both warships and merchantmen, in time of war convoys especially, had mobility in place of immobility, for Captain Halley had given them exploitable organized scientific tidal facts in place of gleanings of customary and uncoordinated (though accurately recorded) tidal lore. I have not the slightest doubt that King William III and the Lords of the Admiralty were acutely aware of the strategic significance of Halley's tidal, magnetic, and hydrographic proposals. Indeed, this awareness is implicit in his final orders, for besides those cited (which included observing "the Precise Times of High and Low waters") Halley was instructed "to be very carefull in the taking notice" of any other matters "the observing and Publishing whereof may tend towards the Security of the Navigation" of seamen "tradeing into the Channel."[48]

How conscientiously Captain Halley discharged his duties is evidenced not only by the various Channel charts published with tidal and magnetic variation information engraved on them, but also by the anonymous 1701 broadside "by a Fellow of the Royal Society" entitled *An Advertisement necessary to be observed in the Navigation Up and Down the Channel of England*,[49] subsequently included in the later editions of *The English Pilot. Southern*, published by Mount and Page frequently until 1792. Custom was very powerful in "Channeling"—sailing into, out of, and in the English Channel. Magnetic variation changed only about 1 degree in seven years, of which even the cumulative effect was hardly noticeable in the lifetime of a seaman using a common sea-compass. Around 1657, the variation that, when measurable at sea, had always been easterly, became nil. Thereafter it began to increase, but so slowly as for years to be imperceptible with the ordinary ship's compass; moreover, it was now westerly. As a consequence, for generations a course by ship's compass of East (090°), uncorrected for variation, had brought a ship safely into the Channel from the ocean, provided she was not north of latitude 49°40′ North. Similarly, a compass course of Southwest by West (236°15′), uncorrected for variation—customarily called the "Channel course"—had taken a ship outward bound from Dungeness (some twenty-five miles west of the Strait of Dover) safely down the Channel, passing it north of the vicious reefs of the Casquets that extend westward from Alderney, the northernmost of the Channel Islands. The variation when the Channel course was adopted was about 7°30′ east; the true course steered had thus been 7°30′ north of the compass "Channel course," or about 244° True.

By 1700, when the variation had changed to about 7°30′ west, a ship entering the Channel from the west on a compass course of East (uncorrected for variation) actually steered 7°30′ north of East (082°30′ True). If she persisted on this course until she met land, she would find herself carried into the low-lying Isles of Scilly or onto the rocky cliffs of north Cornwall or Devon. Similarly, outward-bound ships proceeding down Channel on the customary Channel course now actually steered south of it by 7°30′ (about 229° True) and so straight onto the Casquets, if visibility was poor or if the watch were not keeping a sharp lookout for dangers ahead.

Captain Halley's *Advertisement* for the first time explained these facts and gave the safe courses to follow when entering the Channel from east or west, in 1700 and in the future (that is, what to allow for the changing variation). He thus corrected Captain Greenville Collins who, in his *Great Britain's Coasting Pilot* of 1693, had attributed wreckings on the northern coasts of Devon and Cornwall to a tidal stream that ran nine hours northward and only three hours southward in the Western Approaches. But Captain Halley had noticed the recent outward-bound wreckings on the Casquets also. Being thoroughly conversant with the Channel, and having an inquiring as well as an observant scientific mind, he perceived that these seemingly disconnected and widely separated events had a common cause, namely, westerly magnetic variation. He appreciated that when a ship was outward bound this variation had the effect of deflecting the westerly points on the compass card 7°30′ *south* of west, or if she were inward bound, the easterly points 7°30′ to the *north* of east, so that if she were following either of the customary Channel courses uncorrected for variation (as was usual practice), wrecking was almost inevitable. All this he explained. His *Advertisement* is thus a scintillating example of applied science, and of Captain Halley's professional ability as a seaman to improve the practice of navigation. In this broadside Captain Halley also pointed out that the Scilly Islands—whose northernmost and southernmost latitudes, like that of the Lizard, he had observed at sea with good Sun sights—were in most charts "laid down too far Northerly by near 5 leagues," that is, fifteen miles. Masters relying on such charts, therefore, would believe themselves to be south and well clear of the Scillies and the north Cornish coast when, in reality, they were steering directly toward them.

In the Channel, visibility can close down and obscure sea and coast literally in minutes; also, visibility by day as well as by night is often so poor so that, to be sure of sighting his intended landfall, a master must venture his ship to within a few miles of the shore. This eventuality combines with the effects of the tidal streams and the rocky coastlines to make the waters of the English Channel among the most dangerous in the world. Captain Halley's broadside was thus timely in more ways than one in warning of the dangers of the Channel and in suggesting seamanlike precautions to avoid them. For instance, he "recommended to all Masters of Ships . . . that they come in, out of the Sea, on a Parallel not more Northerly than 49°40′, which will bring them fair by the *Lizard*." [50]

The value of this recommendation was brought home dramatically on the night of 22 October 1707, when Admiral Sir Cloudisley Shovell, now commander-in-chief of the Mediterranean Fleet, returning with twenty-one of his ships, was lost with four of them and some two thousand men on the Scillies, the northern jawbone of the Channel. Yet he had held a council with the masters of his ships but a few hours before in order to establish his fleet's latitude. The majority had believed themselves to be in that of Ushant, the southern jawbone of the Channel (latitude 48°25′ North). As these officers were among the most experienced seamen of the age, the admiral had accordingly proceeded on a rising gale and in poor visibility on a northeasterly course into the Channel mouth. This loss was a major national disaster, for England was in the midst of the War of the Spanish Succession (1702–13), and Admiral Shovell was an illustrious and able sea commander.

Captain Edmond Halley was not only the first seaman who could log that he had determined "the *Longitude* of my *Ship*" astronomically as often as he could, thereby frequently correcting his "*Journal* from those Errors which were unavoidable in long Sea-Reckonings," but also the first to take thermometers and a marine barometer to sea to give warning of changes in the weather. This barometer was an invention of Robert Hooke's; Hooke had described it to the Royal Society on 2 January 1667/68, but thereafter it appears to have been neglected for over thirty years, until Captain Halley took one to sea on his second Atlantic voyage. When he returned to England Hooke was ill, so Halley himself gave a description of it in the *Philosophical Transactions* of 1700–1701,[51] explaining: "I had one of these Barometers with me in my late Southern Voyage, and it never failed to prognostick and give early Notice of all the bad Weather we had"—proof indeed that he understood how to use theoretical science to improve the practice of seamanship. Again he was decades ahead of other seamen, this time in the use of a barometer and of thermometers at sea.[52]

As Savilian Professor of Geometry, Halley was one of the commissioners of the Board of Longitude from its creation in 1714. As such he advised the suspicious and reluctant John Harrison, who visited him in 1728 to find out the board's attitude toward a "longitude machine" that he proposed, to explain the principles of his idea to Mr. George Graham, F.R.S. The result for Harrison was a loan from Graham to complete his first marine timekeeper (H1) for testing at sea, which he did in 1735. Harrison then received the first of several loans from the Board of Longitude, on which Halley still played the key role. Halley did not live, however, to see the vindication of his judgment of Harrison, the horological genius, by the successful testing of his fourth marine timekeeper (H4) at sea in the 1760s and the belated award to Harrison of the Longitude Prize.[53] Similarly, it was Captain Halley who first saw the potential of John Hadley's invention of a reflecting quadrant or octant for taking accurate lunar distances at sea, as happened in the 1760s.

Captain Halley had what all good seamen have: sound judgment. This he used faultlessly all his life, at sea and ashore. The basis of his sound judgment, moreover, was scientific. Edmond Halley was the first and remains to this day the greatest scientific seaman.

NOTES

1. Norman J. W. Thrower, ed., *The Three Voyages of Edmond Halley in the "Para-more," 1698–1701*, Hakluyt Society Publications, 2d ser., vols. 156–57 (London, 1981), 247. Subsequent quotations from or relating to Halley are generally from this work (vol. 156 text) unless otherwise indicated.

2. Eric G. Forbes, ed., *The Gresham Lectures of John Flamsteed* (London: Mansell, 1975), xiii.

3. Thrower, *"Paramore,"* 28, 74. This injustice to his memory was "corrected" when a memorial to Halley was unveiled at Westminster Abbey on 13 November 1986.

4. A. H. Cook, "Halley in Istria, 1703: Navigator and Military Engineer," *Journal of Navigation* 37 (1984): 1–23. (It is to be observed that although Halley is in this article distinguished as a military engineer, sea officers of that time were expected to be thoroughly conversant with laying out marine fortifications—it was, after all, an age of combined operations and naval bombardments of shore fortifications. Thus, Captain Samuel Sturmy's *Mariners Magazine* of 1669 [last edition, 1700], a storehouse of nautical knowledge, included "A Compendium of Fortification" by Philip Staynred. Half a century later John Robertson's encyclopedic *Elements of Navigation* [2 vols. (1754)] similarly included *A Treatise of Marine Fortification*. *Elements* was prepared "For the Use of the Royal Mathematical School at Christ's Hospital [where boys were educated in navigation], and the Gentlemen of the Navy," and was still being published in the nineteenth century.)

5. Norman J. W. Thrower, *Maps and Man: An Examination of Cartography in Relation to Culture and Civilization* (Englewood Cliffs, N.J.: Prentice-Hall, 1972) 65, 68.

6. 12 Queen Anne Ch. 15. The (first) Longitude Act is printed in full as Appendix 1 in Humphrey Quill, *John Harrison: The Man Who Found Longitude* (London: John Baker, 1966), 225–27.

7. "A Petition of several Captains of her Majesty's Ships, Merchants of *London*, and commanders of Merchantmen . . . ," *House of Commons Journal*, no. 17 (25 May 1714): 641–42.

8. Eric G. Forbes, *Greenwich Observatory*, vol. 1: *Origins and Early History (1675–1835)* (London: Taylor & Francis, 1975), 19.

9. Ibid., 67.

10. "An Account of the Course of the Tides at Tonqueen in a Letter from Mr. Francis Davenport July 15, 1678; with the Theory of them, at the Barr of Tonqueen, by the learned Edmund Halley Fellow of the Royal Society," *Philosophical Transactions of the Royal Society* 14 (1683–84): 677–84; "A theory of the tides of the bar of Tung King," ibid., 685–88.

11. Angus Armitage, *Edmond Halley* (London: Nelson, 1966), 67.

12. "A true Theory of the Tides, extracted from that admired Treatise of Mr.

Isaac Newton, intituled, *Philosophiae naturalis principia mathematica;* being a Discourse presented with that Book to the late King James," *Philosophical Transactions* 19 (1697): 445–57.

13. "A Theory of the Variation of the Magnetic Compass," *Philosophical Transactions* 13 (1683): 208–21.

14. John Aubrey, *Brief Lives*, 2 vols., ed. Andrew Clark (Oxford: Clarendon Press, 1898), 282.

15. Forbes, *Origins*, 19.

16. Armitage, *Halley*, 27; and Deborah J. Warner, *The Sky Explored* (New York: Alan R. Liss, 1979), 18–19, 20 (plate of southern polar region).

17. Armitage, *Halley*, 25.

18. John Seller, *Practical Navigation* (London, 1669), British Library C. 175.i.24.

19. "Answer to some Magneticall Inquiries, proposed Numb. 23 of these Transactions, Pag. 423, 424 . . . Mr Seller returns this Answer," *Philosophical Transactions* 1–2 (1667): 478–79.

20. "An historical Account of the Trade Winds, and Monsoons, observable in the Seas between and near the Tropicks, with an Attempt to Assign the Phisical cause of the said Winds," *Philosophical Transactions* 16 (1686): 153–68. George Hadley first correctly explained the deflection both of the trade winds and of the westerly winds in temperate latitudes on kinematic principles in 1735, during Halley's lifetime, in "Concerning the Cause of the General Trade-Winds: by Geo. Hadley, Esq.: F.R.S. No. 437. p. 58 April &c. 1735," *Philosophical Transactions (From the year 1732, to the year 1744) Abridged and Disposed under General Heads* 8, pt. 1 (1747): 500–502. See Armitage, *Halley*, 83–86n.11.

21. Warner, *The Sky Explored*, 107, 109, 130, 233, 236–37.

22. See note 13 above, and "An Account of the Cause of the Change of the Variation of the magnetical Needle; with an Hypothesis of the Structure of the internal Parts of the Earth," *Philosophical Transactions* 17 (1692): 563–78; also note 10 above (tides at Batsha in the Gulf of Tonkin).

23. Thrower, *"Paramore,"* 26, 62n.; and Armitage, *Halley*, 118–22.

24. Thrower, *"Paramore,"* 252, 255, 261.

25. Ibid., 262–63.

26. *Problems of Medicine at Sea*, Maritime Monographs and Reports, no. 12, National Maritime Museum (Greenwich, 1974): Surgeon Vice-Admiral Sir James Watt, "The Burns of Sea Battles," 4; and Surgeon Commander G. J. Milton-Thompson, "The Changing Character of the Sailor's Diet and Its Influence on Disease," 21–24.

27. Thrower, *"Paramore,"* 130, 281.

28. Ibid., 280.

29. Ibid., 281.

30. Ibid., 110.

31. "Monsieur Cassini, his New and Exact Tables for the Eclipses of the First Satellite of Jupiter, reduced to the Julian Stile, and Meridian of London," *Philosophical Transactions* 18 (1694): 237–56.

32. Thrower, *"Paramore,"* 106–7. Longitude is measured by difference of time. The difference in time between the predicted time of the eclipse at London (given in the tables) and the time at which it was observed to occur by Halley at

Barbados gave him the longitude of Barbados from London (00°05′ East of
Greenwich, the modern longitude Zero).

33. Admiralty, Hydrographic Department Chart no. 5211, "North Atlantic
Ocean," 1960 edition.

34. "A Proposal of a Method for finding the Longitude of Sea within a Degree,
or twenty Leagues," *Philosophical Transactions* 37 (1731): 185–95. The lunar distance method of finding longitude required the place of the Moon, relative to
the Sun or stars at any moment, to be accurately predicted. This was not possible
in Halley's lifetime; only in the 1760s did it become feasible, when it was based
on Newton's theory of the Moon, published in Gregory's *Astronomiae Physicae* of
1702. Halley's method, which he claimed was easier, was based on the fact that
every 223 lunations (18 years 11 days, the so-called saros or eclipse cycle) the
relative positions of the Sun and Moon repeat themselves. Therefore, if you
wanted the Moon's predicted place relative to the Sun in, say, 1698, all you had to
do was look up the Moon's *observed* place in 1680 or 1662, eighteen or thirty-six
years earlier. Then, by predicting the Sun's place relative to the stars, the Moon's
place could be related to the stars. Halley used the method successfully by observing occultations (cutting off from view by passing in front) and appulses
(near approach) of stars by the Moon during his Atlantic voyages.

35. M. Mason, B. Greenhill, and R. Craig, eds., *The British Seafarer* (London:
Hutchinson/BBC in association with the National Maritime Museum, 1980), sec.
5, p. 3.

36. Thrower, *"Paramore,"* 281–82.

37. K. Goell, ed., *A Sea Grammar Captain John Smith* (London: Michael Joseph,
1970), 96.

38. Thrower, *"Paramore,"* 286.

39. Ibid., 77, 321, 345.

40. Ibid., 74.

41. Ibid., 317.

42. Ibid., 329.

43. "An Account of the Cause of the Change of the Variation of the magnetical Needle."

44. Thrower, *"Paramore,"* 265, 321.

45. Ibid., 328–29.

46. Ibid., 317.

47. Ibid., 211–12.

48. Ibid., 329.

49. Ibid., 64–65, where the broadside is reprinted in full.

50. Ibid., 65.

51. "An Account of Dr. Robert Hook's Invention of the Marine Barometer,
with its Description and Vses, published by order of the R. Society, by E. Halley,
R.S.S.," *Philosophical Transactions* 22 (1701): 791–94. One of Hooke's barometers
is in the Museum of the History of Science, Oxford.

52. For Halley's use of thermometers, see Thrower, *"Paramore,"* esp. 42n.1.

53. Quill, *Harrison*, is the standard account.

ELEVEN

The Royal Patrons
of Edmond Halley, with
Special Reference to His Maps

Norman J. W. Thrower

Although the name Edmond Halley is more likely to evoke associations with comets[1] than with cartography, Halley, Haley, or Hawley, as his name is variously spelled (and pronounced),[2] was in fact a great contributor to the development of graphic expression.[3] As Halley stated his thoughts on this subject, some phenomena "may be better understood" by the use of maps "than by any verbal description whatsoever."[4]

It was said of Halley "that he flourished under six crowned heads and received favors from each of them which were the pure effects of his singular merit [which was] as well known abroad as at home."[5] Actually, he was a citizen under, or subject of, nine British rulers: two lords protector, five kings, and two queens regnant (if we count William and Mary separately). In addition, he had significant contact with several British consorts and a number of foreign royal personages.

Halley was born in Haggerston about three miles northeast of Saint Paul's Cathedral, London, on 29 October 1656 (o.s.). This was during the Commonwealth, when Oliver Cromwell was Lord Protector of England (1653–58), subsequently to be succeeded by his son Richard, who was Lord Protector until 1659. Halley was thus less than four years of age when the monarchy was restored and Charles II came to the throne. Crowned on 23 April 1661 and married to the Portuguese princess Catherine of Braganza on 21 May 1662, Charles II reigned until his death in 1685, a period of over two decades during which Halley grew from infancy to manhood.

Halley's father, also Edmond Halley, was a successful merchant in the City of London who owned a considerable amount of rental property. Although much of this property was destroyed in the Great Fire of London (1666), the family business, concerned with soap and salt, continued to flourish. One of his father's apprentices taught the young Edmond Halley writing and arithmetic before he was sent to St. Paul's School. It was while at school that Halley, in 1672, made his first recorded scientific observation, measuring the variation (declination) of the magnetic compass.[6] During this time, too, he familiarized himself with the use of the celestial sphere and is said to have accompanied the party, which included the architect Sir Christopher Wren, charged with selecting the site of the Royal Observatory at Greenwich.[7]

When he entered Queen's College, Oxford, in the summer of 1673, Halley took with him "a curious apparatus of instruments," with which he continued his observations.[8] While still an undergraduate Halley published his first scientific paper.[9] During summer holidays he assisted the Reverend John Flamsteed, whom in 1675 Charles II had appointed "Astronomical Observer" (first Astronomer Royal) at Greenwich.

Before taking a degree, Halley approached the newly founded Royal Society of London[10] with a proposal for observing the stars in the southern hemisphere in order to produce a catalogue of the southern hemisphere constellations similar to that already available for the northern hemisphere. Halley's project was brought to the attention of King Charles II by the Secretary of State, Sir Joseph Williamson, at the beginning of October 1676. In response, the King sent a letter to the East India Company recommending that Halley and a friend, James Clark (or Clerk), who would serve as his assistant, be given free passage to the South Atlantic island of St. Helena, the most southerly Company possession at which its ships often called. Halley received a generous allowance from his father, and he and Clark left London in the *Unity* on November 1676. They arrived in February 1677 at St. Helena, where they set up an observatory near the highest point of the island, Mount Actaeon.

After a difficult year of observing, Halley returned to England where, within a few months, he had published a catalogue of telescopically determined star positions and a large celestial planisphere (star chart),[11] on which he named a constellation, *Rober Carolinum*, in honor of the reigning monarch (Fig. 11.1). The chart is dedicated to the king, who on 18 November 1673 ordered that Halley be awarded the degree of Master of Arts *per literas regius* and "without performing any previous or subsequent exercises for the same";[12] the degree was granted on 3 December. In the previous month Halley had been elected a fellow of the Royal Society, and from that time until the end of his life his work was very closely tied to the Society. He traveled widely on the Continent at this time, visiting Hevelius at Danzig (Gdansk) on the Society's behalf. In 1680 he went on the Grand Tour, during which travels he saw a comet; this event excited his interest in the phenomena, which he discussed with Jean-Dominique Cassini in Paris (see Suzanne Débarbat's essay, Chapter 3).

CAROLO II. D.G.MAG.BRIT.FRAN.&HIB.REGI SEMPER AUG.

Hanc A U S T R A L I S H E M I S P H Æ R I I *tabulam*
Superis obfervationibus juffu Regio fufceptis, reſtitutam,
Plurimifq stellis nondum Globo afcriptis locupletatam,
submiſse offert

Subditus Humillimus EDMUNDUS HALLEIUS *c Coll: Reg. Oxon.*

Figure 11.1. Halley's southern hemisphere star chart (1678), dedicated to King Charles II. The constellation *Rober Carolinum* (Charles's Oak) is to the right center of the planisphere.

The first of his two important papers on terrestrial magnetism was published in the *Philosophical Transactions* in 1683. Three years later he gave up his fellowship in the Royal Society to become Clerk to the Joint Secretaries, partly because he wished to immerse himself more fully in the affairs of the Society. On 16 June 1686, after a trial period, Halley became

editor of the *Philosophical Transactions*, in which he eventually published
some eighty articles on a wide range of scientific topics. One of these articles, on the winds in the lower latitudes, has appended to it a map that
has been called the "first meteorological [really, climatological] chart." [13]
Unlike other of Halley's major maps, this chart of the trade winds has no
title, scale, or dedication; it arose from Halley's royally sponsored journey to and from St. Helena and residence on that island, and is a thematic map of great originality.

King Charles II died on 6 February 1685 and was succeeded by his
brother James II, who reigned for only three years before abdicating the
throne. It was during this period that Isaac Newton's *Principia* was published. The reluctant Newton wrote this work on Halley's urging, whereupon, in 1686, it was delivered to Halley, who edited it and saw it
through the press; moreover, because there was no money at the Royal
Society for the purpose, Halley also paid for its publication. It has been
said that without Halley the *Principia* "would not have been thought of,
nor when thought of written, nor when written printed." [14] Halley prepared an explication of the contents of the *Principia* for the monarch,
with special emphasis on those parts having to do with the tides. It begins:

> May it please Your most Excellent Majesty.
>
> I could not have presumed to approach Your Majesty's Royal presence
> with a book of this nature, had I not been assured, that when the weighty
> affairs of your government permit it, Your Majesty has frequently shown
> yourself inclined to favour mechanical and philosophical discoveries. And
> I may be bold to say, that if ever book was worthy the favourable accep-
> tance of a Prince, this, wherein so many and so great discoveries concern-
> ing the constitution of the visible world are made out, and put past dispute,
> must needs be grateful to Your Majesty; being especially the labours of a
> worthy subject of your own, and a member of that Royal Society founded
> by Your late Royal brother for the advancement of natural knowledge, and
> which now flourishes under Your Majesty's most Gracious Protection.
>
> But being sensible of the little leisure which care of the public leaves to
> Princes, I believed it necessary to present with the book a short extract of
> the matters contained, together with a specimen thereof, in the genuine
> solution of the cause of the tides in the ocean, A thing frequently at-
> tempted but till now without success, whereby Your Majesty may judge of
> the rest of the performances of the author.

The body of the letter follows, and then concludes with these words:

> If by reason of the difficulty of the matter there be anything herein not
> sufficiently explained, or if there be any material thing observable in the
> tides that I have omitted wherein Your Majesty shall desire to be satisfied, I
> doubt not but if Your Majesty shall please to suffer me to be admitted to

the honour of Your Presence, I may be able to give such an account thereof
as may be to Your Majesty's full content:
I am great Sr. Your Majesty's most dutiful & obedient subject

Edmond Halley[15]

Although the above statement does not concern cartography per se, it
well illustrates Halley's thoughts on royal patrons and patronage in general. After the abdication of the king in 1688, James's eldest daughter,
Mary, and her husband, William of Orange, were proclaimed joint sov-
ereigns as King William III and Queen Mary II. During the convulsive
period known as the Glorious Revolution (1688), Halley, like other
prominent men, was investigated concerning his loyalty to the new mon-
archs, but since he was "continually employed at his telescope," it was
decided "not to disturb his speculations"; moreover, he was soon (unlike
Samuel Pepys) given further naval appointments (see the essay of D. W.
Waters, Chapter 10, for further information on this matter).[16]

In 1692 Halley published his second important article on geomagnetism in the *Philosophical Transactions,* and now he wished to test his theories at sea.[17] He may have been led to this endeavor by his being refused
the Savilian Professorship of Astronomy at Oxford (see the essay by
Richard Westfall and Gerald Funk, Chapter 1). In any case, in March
1693 an application was made to the Royal Society "to Obtaine of their
Majesties a vessell" for this purpose, and by 12 July of the same year the
Navy Board reported that

> a vessell of about eighty tuns burthen fitted out for the said voyage, and
> maintained therein at their Majesties charge . . . which petition having
> been laid before the Queen [Mary] Her Majesty is graciously pleased to
> encourage the said undertaking. And in pursuance of her Majesty's plea-
> sure signified therein to this Board, we do hereby desire and direct you
> forthwith to cause a vessell of about eighty tuns burthen to be set up and
> built in their Majesties yard at Deptford as soon as may be.[18]

The small ship, of the type known as a pink, was ready for launching
in the spring of 1694, when the Navy Board directed that the vessel be
launched "and that she be named the *Paramour* and entered on the List
of the Royal Navy by the same name."[19] The ship was ready and Halley
received his commission on 4 June 1694. Only some seven months later
Queen Mary died, on 28 December, and thereafter William ruled alone
until his death on 8 March 1702.

There was a long delay in Halley's departure owing to his employment at the Mint at Chester by Newton, then Master of the Mint in London. Halley was also employed in instructing Czar Peter (later known as
the Great) in the "new science" during Peter's visit to England. Halley

was apparently happy to teach the Czar, as indicated by the following account attributed to Martin Folkes, who knew Halley personally and was later (1741–52) President of the Royal Society.

> Halley . . . possessed all the qualifications necessary to please princes who were desirous of instruction, great extent of knowledge, and a constant presence of mind; his answers were ready, and at the same time pertinent, judicious, polite and sincere. When Peter the Great, Emperor of Russia, came into England (1698) he sent for Mr. Halley, and found him equal to the great character he had heard of him. He asked him many questions concerning the fleet which he intended to build, the sciences and arts which he wished to introduce into his dominions, and a thousand other subjects which his unbounded curiosity suggested; he was so well satisfied with Mr. Halley's answers, and so pleased with his conversation, that he admitted him familiarly to his table, and ranked him among the number of his friends, a term which we may venture to use with respect to a prince of his character; a prince truly great, in making no distinctions of men but that of their merit.[20]

The Czar asked for permission to sail the new vessel on the Thames and thus became the first captain of the *Paramore,* as recounted in correspondence contained in the Royal Navy Lords' Letter Book for 16 March 1697:

> Gentlemen:
>
> The Czar of Muscovy having desired that his Majesty's Pink the Paramour at Deptford may be rigged and brought afloat in order to make some experiment about her sailing. We do therefore hereby desire and direct you in pursuance of His Majesty's pleasure signified to this Board, forthwith, to give the necessary orders for rigging and bringing afloat the said vessell and employing her in such a manner as the Czar shall desire, so we remain.
>
> Yours, etc.
> O., H.P., G.R.[21]

By the fall of the year everything was ready for what turned out to be the earliest of three voyages, called "the first sea journey taken for a purely scientific purpose."[22] Twenty men—Halley as captain, a regular Royal Navy lieutenant, and a crew of eighteen—left Deptford on 20 October 1698. The little ship traveled in convoy with the squadron of Rear Admiral John Benbow, which was going to the West Indies. After separating from the admiral at Madeira in late December, the *Paramore* continued on along the African coast to the Cape Verde Islands. Here she was fired on by an English merchant vessel whose captain thought she was a pirate ship. After this problem was resolved, Halley steered across the Atlantic to the island of Fernando de Noronha (4°S), of which Halley made a sketch map; he then sailed on to the coast of Brazil, reaching the Paraíba River (7°S) on 23 February 1699.

The Portuguese were hospitable, and Halley was invited to visit the Governor, Dom Manuel Soarez Albergaria, at the town of Paraíba (now João Pessoa). The Governor allowed Halley to replenish his water supply and take on provisions for the continuation of his voyage. Halley, who had been delayed initially in England, took longer to reach the southern hemisphere than expected and had experienced trouble with his crew, especially his lieutenant. He now decided to go to the West Indies to try to find a flag officer, possibly Benbow, so that he could have the lieutenant court martialed. When no flag officer could be found, Halley decided to return to London, which he reached in July. A court martial was held, but the lieutenant, to Halley's dissatisfaction, was only reprimanded. Halley pointed out that, despite certain difficulties, he had carried out his instructions concerning the collection of scientific data, including the recording of compass variation. He also asked that he might go again, this time without a lieutenant, so that he could complete his work. This request was soon approved.

Thus Halley set out a second time, on 16 September (a month earlier than on his previous voyage), with a total of twenty-four persons but no lieutenant. He followed more or less the same route as before, reaching Rio de Janeiro, Brazil, on 14 December. Again the Portuguese authorities were cooperative; he took on supplies for his intended southward journey, and on the twenty-ninth the *Paramore* left Rio. A little over a month later, on 1 February 1700, Halley reported his farthest southward point (52°24'), where the *Paramore* narrowly escaped being wrecked in iceberg-infested waters. Halley managed to extricate himself, however, and he sailed to St. Helena (where he had spent a year previously) and on to the island of Trinidada (20°30'S). Halley, as he states in his journal, "took possession of the island in His Majesties name . . . leaving the Union flag flying"; [23] he also left a pair of guinea fowl and breeding stock of goats and hogs.[24] Upon landing, Halley climbed to the highest point and then rowed around the island, in order to make a detailed map. He thought Trinidada would make a useful place for replenishment of ships because of its plentiful water supply.

Halley now sailed again for the coast of Brazil, which he reached at Pernambuco (Recife) on 21 April. Again the Portuguese (after some initial difficulties with the resident English consul) were cooperative, the Governor allowing Halley to reprovision his ship. He decided to return to England by way of the West Indies, at several of which islands he anchored. He continued by way of Bermuda, where the *Paramore* was careened and painted, and then on to Newfoundland, where they were once more fired on by an English ship whose captain mistook the *Paramore* for a pirate ship. She reached London on 18 September 1700, a year almost to the day since she had started out on the second voyage. If the promoters had questions concerning the first voyage, there were no criticisms of the second. Halley had brought back a healthy ship with only one person lost, a cabin boy who had accidentally fallen overboard at Madeira. He had also brought back a great deal of scientific data, which were soon put into publishable form. On 30 October, Halley showed the assembled fellows of the Royal Society what may have been a manuscript map of his Atlantic chart.

Early in the new year, on 5 February 1701, Halley displayed before the fellows a map on which the *Paramore's* route in the Atlantic had been delineated and magnetic variation plotted. Of the latter phenomenon he now had 150 observations, with which he was able to make an isoline map. Published in early 1701, this map, commonly known as Halley's Atlantic Chart of Magnetic Variation, is the first printed map showing what we now call isogones; it is also the first published map of isolines of any kind. The dedication for this chart, one of the most important maps in the history of cartography, was received by King William III (Fig. 11.2). In consideration of his accomplishments on his two Atlantic voyages, Halley, in addition to his pay as a captain in the Royal Navy, was given a special gratuity. This grant was recorded in the Letter Book of the Lords of the Admiralty, 6 May 1701, as follows:

Gentlemen:

In obedience to His Majesty's commands signified to this Board, we do hereby desire and direct you to cause to be paid unto Captain Edward [Edmond] Halley, out of the money in the hands of the Treasurer of the Navy, upon account of the tenths of prizes the sum of two hundred pounds in consideration of his great pains and care in the late voyage he made for discovering the variation of the needle.
We are

Yours, etc.
P., DM., GC.[25]

Upon King William's death on 8 March 1702, his deceased wife's sister, Anne, came to the throne. Anne had married Prince George of Denmark in 1683, and soon after her accession she made him Generalissimo of all Her Majesty's Forces and Lord High Admiral of England. These titles are given in the dedication of the next important map of Halley's composition (Fig. 11.3), a world map on which the isogones are extended from the Atlantic to the Indian Ocean—but not to the Pacific, because, as Halley notes, "I durst not presume to describe the like curves

Figure 11.2. Cartouche from Halley's Atlantic Chart of Magnetic Variation (1701), with dedication to King William III.

in the South Sea wanting accounts thereof." This map, generally known as Halley's World Chart of Magnetic Variations (1702), also contained two poems, in Latin, presumably of Halley's own composition. One of these lauds the unknown inventor of the magnetic compass, and the other (Fig. 11.4), Queen Anne as the patroness of Britain's expanding maritime interests. They are contained in special and separate insets; the poem concerning the Queen has been translated as follows:

> To our Lady the Queen
>
> Most like those impious giants he contends
>   Who in Jove's empire his own sway extends
> Where the Assyrian ruled, where Persian reigned,
>   There Oxus' flood and Indus' there restrained.

Figure 11.3. Cartouche of Halley's World Chart of Magnetic Variation (1702),
with dedication to Prince George of Denmark, Lord High Admiral of England.

In vain the Macedonian sheds his tears
  Because to him too small the world appears.
Even to Rome a water bound was set
  Where Danube here and Tigris here she met.
But wider the blue wave to Britain bows
  Where'er the breezes waft her mighty prows.
ANNA the sea's bright queen, Jove's ally thou,
  Don thou thine armour, crown thy royal brow.
Pallas herself who grants thee all her aid,
  All men will think thee, in her image made.[26]

Halley's development of the isoline, as drawn on his world and Atlantic
magnetic charts, has been greatly praised by later scientists, including
Alexander von Humboldt (1769–1859), who invented the isotherm; Sir
George Airy (1801–92), Astronomer Royal, who, like Halley, was interested in geomagnetism; and Sir Edward Bullard (1902–80), a physicist
who contributed to modern geomagnetical theory and oceanography.

Soon after completing his second Atlantic voyage, Halley asked if he
might use the *Paramore* again, this time to investigate the tides in the
English Channel. Permission for this undertaking was speedily granted,
and so, in the spring of 1701, we find him enlisting a crew for three

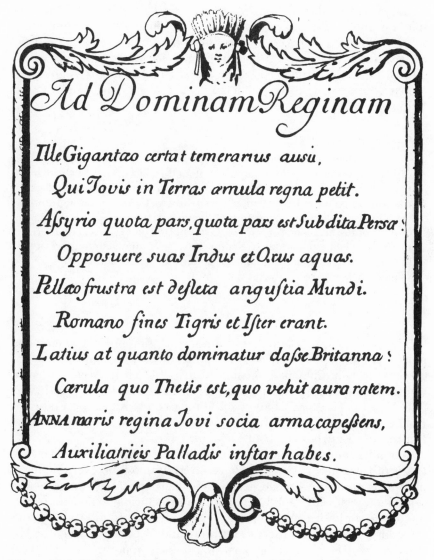

Ad Dominam Reginam

Ille Gigantæo certat temerarius ausu,
Qui Jovis in Terras æmula regna petit.
Assyrio quota pars, quota pars est Subdita Persæ:
Opposuere suas Indus et Oxus aquas.
Pellæo frustra est defleta angustia Mundi.
Romano fines Tigris et Ister erant.
Latius at quanto dominatur dasse Britanna:
Cærula quo Thetis est, quo vehit aura ratem.
ANNA maris regina Jovi socia arma capessens,
Auxiliatricis Palladis instar habes.

Figure 11.4. Inset from Halley's World Chart of Magnetic Variation, with a poem in Latin, presumably by Halley, lauding Queen Anne.

months of investigation in waters close to home. The published result of this voyage was also principally cartographic, "A New and Correct Chart of the Channel between England and France . . . with the Flowing of the Tides and the Setting of the Current." This map, which resulted immediately from Halley's survey of the Channel but also reflects his long-term interest in tidal phenomena, is as original as his earlier charts. For the first time a formula was provided for estimating the height of the water in the Channel according to lunar position; it is considered the earliest true tidal chart.[27] Although the map has no dedication, Halley's efforts did not go unnoticed by the monarch. Queen Anne's appreciation is expressed in correspondence in the Royal Navy Lord's Letter Book, 20 April 1702, as follows:

Gentlemen:

It being her Majesty's Royal will and pleasure that the sum of two hundred pounds shall be paid to Captain Edmond Halley (over and above his pay as Captain of her pink the Paramour) as a reward to him for his extraordinary pains and care he lately took, in observing and setting down the ebbing and flowing and setting of the tides in the Channel as also and bearing of the headlands on the coasts of England and France. I do therefore in obedience to her Majesty's commands hereby desire and direct you, to cause the said sum of two hundred pounds to be paid unto him the said Captain Halley accordingly.

I am yours, etc.

P[28]

The Queen's appreciation also found expression in Halley being employed in special service abroad on her behalf. In 1702 and 1703 he was engaged in two diplomatic missions, during which he visited Vienna, where he met Emperor Leopold and Prince Eugene of Savoy, and Istria (see Alan Cook's essay, Chapter 9). On a second visit to the Emperor, Halley went by way of Hannover, where he dined with the Electoral Prince, later King George II of England.

When he returned from Vienna, Halley was appointed Savilian Professor of Geometry at Oxford. He received this position over the objections of Flamsteed, who had been increasingly critical of Halley, whose reputation was rising rapidly. In addition to lecturing on and contributing to the study of mathematics at Oxford, Halley found time to continue his astronomical observations there and in London, which he visited frequently. In 1710 he was awarded an honorary doctorate at Oxford, where he built a small observatory on the top of his house.

Queen Anne died on 1 August 1714 without an heir, thus ending the House of Stuart. (Her husband, Prince George, had predeceased her in 1708, and her only child of seventeen pregnancies to survive infancy, William, Duke of Gloucester [born 1689], had died in 1700.) According to the Act of Settlement, Anne was succeeded by the Elector of Hanover, who became George I of England and to whom Halley is said to have taken an oath of allegiance at Westminster. Some nine months later, on

25 April 1715, Halley was in London to observe the total eclipse of the Sun. He had predicted this phenomenon and, before the event, to use his own words, "caused a small map of England, describing the track and bounds thereof to be dispersed all over the Kingdom."[29] This map, "a description of the passage of the shadow of the moon over England," which has no dedication, well illustrates not only Halley's concern with the entire cosmos but also the highest attribute of science, so well shown by Halley's work on comets, transits, and so forth: the ability to predict.

Upon the death of Flamsteed, on the last day of 1719, Halley became his logical successor at Greenwich, and on 9 February 1720 King George appointed Halley the second "Astronomical Observer" or Astronomer Royal. Although now sixty-four years of age, Halley remodeled Greenwich Observatory and embarked on a great series of lunar observations, which would take eighteen years to complete. It was at Greenwich that one of the most touching events concerning Halley and his royal patrons occurred.

King George I died on 11 June 1727, to be succeeded by his son George II. In 1705 George had married the attractive and clever Caroline of Ansbach, who came to England with her husband when her father-in-law became King of England. Caroline, first as Princess of Wales and later as Queen of England, took an active interest in the affairs of state and wielded considerable influence. In 1729, Queen Caroline visited Halley at Greenwich. She had learned that the salary of the Astronomer Royal had not been increased since Flamsteed had taken the position over fifty years earlier. When Halley heard that she wished to improve his pay he said, "Pray your Majesty do no such thing, for if the salary should be increased it might become the object of emolument to place there some unqualified needy dependent, to ruin the institution."[30] The Queen found a way around these objections by obtaining for Halley, through the King, a grant of half pay as post captain in the Royal Navy, which he received until the end of his long life.

Halley died on 14 January 1742 and, at his request, was buried in the churchyard of St. Margaret at Lee near Greenwich beside his wife of fifty-five years, who had died six years previously. His son, also Edmond Halley, predeceased him by about two years. His two daughters and a son-in-law were later interred in the same tomb as Halley. The tomb was restored in 1845, with the original stone let into the wall of the Old Royal Observatory (Fig. 11.5). The Latin inscription on the tablet can be translated (in part) as follows:

Under this marble peacefully rests, with his beloved wife, Edmond Halley, LL.D., unquestionably the greatest astronomer of his age. But to conceive an adequate knowledge of the excellencies of this great man, the reader

Figure 11.5. The Royal Observatory, Greenwich; detail showing the capstone of Halley's tomb, with inscription, let vertically into the wall at foreground, covering a window opening.

must have recourse to his writings, in which all the sciences are in the most beautiful and perspicacious manner illustrated and improved. As when living he was so highly esteemed by his Countrymen, gratitude requires that his memory should be respected by posterity. To the memory of the best of parents their affectionate daughters have erected this monument in the year 1742.[31]

As this inscription suggests, Halley's publications, including his maps, for some of which royal dedications were received, are his best memorial. It is a great tribute to Halley, "a man of prodigious versatility and most attractive personality," as Sir Edward Bullard has called him, that he continued to enjoy royal patronage through nearly seventy years of rapid political change.[32] In contrast to Samuel Pepys, who fell from royal favor with the abdication of James II, Halley, for whom Pepys had a great admiration, flourished through seven reigns.[33]

NOTES

This essay first appeared in *Vice-Almirante A. Teixeira da Mota: In Memoriam*, vol. 1 (Lisbon: Academia de Marinha/Instituto de Investigação Científica Tropical, 1987).

1. On its current approach to the Sun, Halley's Comet was first observed by astronomers of the Jet Propulsion Laboratory, California Institute of Technology, Pasadena, using an advanced electronic detector system and the 200-inch Hale Telescope at Palomar Observatory, California, on 16 October 1982. The comet was brightest as seen from the Earth between March and April 1986. This event gave rise to a flurry of literature of a scientific and popular nature. An example of the first is Donald K. Yeomans, *The Comet Halley Handbook: An Observer's Guide* (National Aeronautics and Space Administration/Jet Propulsion Laboratory, California Institute of Technology, Pasadena, 1981), and of the second, Nigel Calder, *The Comet Is Coming* (New York: Viking Press, 1980).

2. The name was entered on his marriage certificate and his will as Edmond Halley (*Notes and Queries*, ser. 11, 4 (1911): 85, 198, ser. 13, 155 (1928): 24–25). He also used this form in the rare instances where he wrote his full signature. Usually he used the abbreviation Edm. for his Christian name, which some have interpreted as Edmund. The surname has been spelled in a variety of ways.

3. Angus Armitage, *Edmond Halley* (London: Nelson, 1966), and Colin A. Ronan, *Edmond Halley: Genius in Eclipse* (New York: Doubleday, 1969), are two general biographies on Halley including information on his mapping endeavors. In addition, several articles have appeared on specific aspects of his work, with the following on his cartographic accomplishments: Sydney Chapman, "Edmond Halley as Physical Geographer and the Story of His Charts," *Occasional Notes of the Royal Astronomical Society*, no. 9 (1941): 1–15; Norman J. W. Thrower, "Edmond Halley and Thematic Geo-Cartography," in *The Terraqueous Globe* (Los Angeles: William Andrews Clark Memorial Library, 1969), and idem, "Edmond Halley as a Thematic Geo-Cartographer," *Annals of the Association of American Geographers* 59 (1969): 652–76.

4. Edmond Halley, "An Historical Account of the Trade Winds, and Monsoons, observable in the Seas between and near the Tropicks; with an attempt to assign the physical cause of the said Winds," *Philosophical Transactions of the Royal Society* 16 (1686): 153–88, esp. 155.

5. Royal Society, *Collectanea Newtoniana* (comp. Charles Turnor), no. 4, (1837): pp. 25–27, fols. 28–42.

6. By "variation" Halley meant "the deflection of the magnetical needle from the true meridian" (i.e., the difference between magnetic north and true north). This observation was later published as "A Theory of the Variation of the Magnetical Compass," *Philosophical Transactions* 13 (1683): 208–21.

7. The Royal Observatory, founded by King Charles II, was built in 1675 on the highest ground at the Royal Park at Greenwich to the east of London, where a castle formerly stood.

8. *Biographia Britannica* 4 (1757): 2494–2520. Information for this account of Halley's life was supplied, in part, by his son-in-law, Henry Price.

9. Edmond Halley, "Methodus directa & geometrica, cujus ope investigantur aphelia . . . ," *Philosophical Transactions* 11 (1676): 683–86.

10. The Royal Society was founded formally in 1660, but it had existed informally for at least fifteen years prior to this time.

11. Edmond Halley, *Catalogus Stellarum Australium, sive Supplementum Catalogi Tychonici,* 1679. See Sir Edward Bullard, "Edmond Halley (1656–1741), *Endeavour* 15 (1956): 189–99. Bullard was a great authority on Halley and collector of Halleyana.

12. Armitage, *Halley,* 36; Ronan, *Halley,* 42.

13. Chapman, "Halley," esp. 3–4.

14. Ronan, *Halley,* 88, quoting Augustus de Morgan.

15. *Correspondence and Papers of Edmond Halley,* ed. Eugene Fairfield MacPike (Oxford: Oxford University Press, 1932), 268–69; spelling, punctuation, etc. have been modernized for clarity. The body of this letter, which occurs between the two introductory and final closing paragraphs quoted here, was later printed in the *Philosophical Transactions* 19 (1695–97): 445–57.

16. *Correspondence and Papers,* 269.

17. Edmond Halley, "An Account of the Cause of the Change of the Variation of the Magnetical Needle; with an Hypothesis of the Structure of the internal Parts of the Earth," *Philosophical Transactions* 17 (1692): 563–78.

18. Norman J. W. Thrower, ed., *The Three Voyages of Edmond Halley in the "Paramore," 1698–1701,* Hakluyt Society Publications, 2d ser., vols. 156–57 (London, 1981), 250, 252.

19. Ibid., 253. There has been only one ship of this name in the Royal Navy. Halley spelled it *Paramore* in the titles of his three journals and elsewhere, hence this usage in this volume. The various other spellings of the name of this vessel include *Parrimore* and *Parramore.* She was the first ship of the Royal Navy to be built expressly for the purpose of scientific investigation.

20. *Correspondence and Papers,* 261.

21. Thrower, *"Paramore,"* 262. The initials are those of Admiral Edward Russell (created Earl of Orford, 7 May 1697), First Lord of the Admiralty; Henry Priestman; and Admiral Sir George Rooke. In the quotation, spellings, punctuation, etc. have been modernized for clarity.

22. Chapman, "Halley," 5. Chapman seems to have thought of Halley's first and second Atlantic voyages as one.

23. The Union flag at this time consisted of St. George's Cross of England on St. Andrew's Cross of Scotland; it had been used, with interruptions, since the union of the crowns of England and Scotland in 1603, which occurred when Queen Elizabeth I died leaving no heirs and James VI of Scotland became James I of England. Thus the Tudor dynasty was extinguished and the Stuart dynasty in England began.

24. Richard H. Eyde and Olson L. Storrs, "The Dead Trees of Ilha da Trinidade," *Bartonia,* no. 49 (1983): 32–51. Perhaps the domesticated animals set loose on the island in 1700 by Halley might have contributed to the deforestation of the island, as this paper suggests.

25. Thrower, *"Paramore,"* 321. The initials are those of Thomas Herbert,

Earl of Pembroke and Montgomery, First Lord of the Admiralty; Vice Admiral Sir David Mitchell; and George Churchill.

26. Chapman, "Halley," 9; Chapman's wife translated the verses. Halley was a considerable classical scholar, having been a pupil at St. Paul's School during the highmastership of Thomas Gale, who had given up the Regius Professorship of Greek at Cambridge University to take the appointment. In line one of the poem, Otus and Ephiates are referred to, and in line five, Alexander the Great.

27. J. Proudman, "Halley's Tidal Chart," *Geographical Journal* 100 (1942): 174–76.

28. Thrower, *"Paramore,"* 4. The initial is that of Thomas Herbert, Earl of Pembroke and Montgomery, soon to be replaced as Lord High Admiral by Prince George of Denmark. In this quotation, spellings, punctuation, etc. have been modernized for clarity.

29. Edmond Halley, "Observations of the late Total Eclipse of the Sun . . . ," *Philosophical Transactions* 29 (1715): 245–62. On the map legend Halley includes the following statement: "I thought it not improper to give the Publick an Account thereof, that the suddain darkness wherein the Starrs will be visible about the Sun, may give no surprise to the People, who would, if unadvertized, be apt to look on it as Ominous, and to Interpret it as portending evill to our Sovereign Lord King George and his Government, which God preserve."

30. MacPike Papers, Newberry Library, Chicago; and Thrower, *"Paramore,"* 77–78.

31. Thrower, *"Paramore,"* 79.

32. Bullard, "Halley," 189.

33. Samuel Pepys, Secretary of the Royal Navy and diarist, wrote of Halley, "Mr. Hawley—May he not be said to have the most, if not to be the first Englishman (and possibly any other) that had so much, or (it may be) any competent degree (meeting in them) of the science and practice (both) of navigation" (*Samuel Pepys's Naval Minutes,* ed. J. R. Tanner [London: Navy Records Society, 1926], 420).

TWELVE

Halley and the Barometer

W. R. Albury

During the last half of the seventeenth century, according to W. E. Knowles Middleton, "more attention was paid to the barometer in England than in any other country."[1] Edmond Halley's contribution to the investigation of the barometer during this period consisted of only one serious theoretical paper, published in 1686, and two minor notes on matters of application and design, published in 1697 and 1701, respectively—the latter being a description of an instrument invented by Robert Hooke in 1668.[2] Yet despite the apparent meagerness of Halley's work in this area, especially in contrast to that of the prolific Hooke,[3] it seems that during the first two decades of the eighteenth century Halley's countrymen regarded him as the leading scientific authority on the barometer and its phenomena. Let me offer three examples in support of this claim.

First of all, in volume one of John Harris's *Lexicon Technicum*, published in 1704, the article on the barometer relies for its meteorological discussion of the instrument entirely on Halley's 1686 paper, which it describes as "an Excellent Discourse upon the Reasons of the Rise and Fall of the Mercury in Fair or Foul Weather."[4] In addition to presenting an extensive summary of this theoretical paper, the article also reports the substance of Halley's technical papers of 1697 and 1701. Second, a short book entitled *An Historical and Philosophical Account of the Barometer, or Weather-Glass*, published by Edward Saul in 1730 but written in 1710, when Saul was tutor to the Duke of Rutland, follows Harris in repeatedly invoking Halley's account of the barometer as authoritative.[5] According to Saul, the barometric discoveries of Halley, together with those of Robert Boyle, have left others little to do in this area but to follow their well-trodden path.[6]

Finally, even a critic of Halley's barometric theory, the virtuoso and essayist Roger North, writing in the period 1710–15, expressed his high regard for the 1686 paper: "Of all the accounts in print concerning the *barometer* that I have met with, Dr *Halley's* . . . is the most candid and philosophical, and shows a spirit ambitious of truth." While not sharing Saul's view about the definitive nature of Halley's barometric ideas, North nevertheless considered Halley's work on the subject a model for others to follow: "I cannot but lament, that no great genius, such as hath been named, if there be one so great, after the example of his discourse, hath taken the hint, and pursued a subject so comprehensive and critical as that of the barometer."[7]

In view of the considerable reputation Halley's barometric work achieved early in the eighteenth century, it is worthwhile to look at the single paper on which that reputation seems almost entirely to have been built. What was the intellectual context within which the barometric paper of 1686 was written, and what was the intellectual content of its theory? How was this paper initially received, and what factors made it prominent some twenty to twenty-five years after it was first presented? I shall try to provide an answer to each of these questions in turn.

In April 1685 the Royal Society received from the Oxford Philosophical Society a paper on the weather and barometric phenomena written by George Garden of Aberdeen.[8] This paper had been sent to the Oxford Society in response to that group's letter of September 1684 seeking to open a philosophical correspondence with the Scottish universities.[9] Accompanying Garden's paper was a second paper on the same topic, written by the President of the Oxford Society, John Wallis, replying to and extending Garden's ideas on the relationship between the weather and the weight of the air.[10] These two papers were read and discussed at consecutive meetings of the Royal Society in April 1685,[11] and were published together in the *Philosophical Transactions* for that same year. In September 1685 Garden sent the Oxford Society a further discussion of the weather, concentrating on the connection of winds and air pressure; this too was transmitted to the Royal Society and published in the 1685 volume of the *Philosophical Transactions*.[12]

These papers provided the background for Halley's meteorological discussion of the barometer in 1686. I say his "meteorological discussion," because his paper on the barometer published in the *Philosophical Transactions* of that year actually combined two different talks he had given before the Royal Society in June and July 1686, respectively.[13] In the first talk, corresponding to the first half of his paper, he was concerned with the use of the barometer as an instrument for measuring heights, especially of mountains.[14] This interest, like his interest in meteorological aspects of the barometer, was stimulated by correspondence with the Oxford Society, one of whose members, John Caswell, had been measuring the heights of mountains by both trigonometric and barometric means.[15] But I shall not pursue this aspect of Halley's interest in the barometer, to which Hooke's early 1686 experiments measuring the specific gravity of mercury also contributed.[16] Instead I shall concentrate on the second half of Halley's barometric paper, that relating to meteorological concerns, since it is this aspect of this work which is most relevant to Halley's eighteenth-century reputation as a barometric theorist.

Halley's meteorological interest in the barometer is linked to the papers of Garden and Wallis by another paper of his own on the trade winds. Although Halley's discussion of this topic appeared in the *Philosophical Transactions* after the barometer paper, Halley's discourse on trade winds at the Royal Society took place in May 1686—about two months before he presented his meteorological theory of the barometer.[17] Garden in his second paper, on the relationship between winds and air pressure, had argued that the constant and generally easterly winds between the tropics of Cancer and Capricorn were caused by the greater heat of the sun in this region; as the earth turned eastward, he reasoned, the warmer and more rarefied air of the tropical region tended to be left behind and was thus displaced from east to west.[18] Halley's reply, at least in its published version, did not mention Garden by name, but it specifically criticized Garden's theory and offered an alternative explanation of the trade winds based on the same physical causes Garden had used—the heat of the sun and the diurnal rotation of the Earth. Rather than the warmer tropical air being displaced westward as the Earth turned, Halley said, it was the westward displacement of the point directly beneath the Sun that caused the trade winds. This point—always between the tropics—would be the place of maximum atmospheric heat and rarefication at any given moment, toward which denser air would tend to flow. As this point moved from east to west with the daily rotation of the globe, the constant easterly flow of the trade winds between the tropics was set up. This theoretical explanation was accompanied by Halley's famous world map of the trade winds, showing some exceptions to their generally easterly flow, which Halley accounted for by the nature and location of various land masses.[19]

The meteorological portion of Halley's discussion of the barometer followed the same argumentative strategy vis-à-vis Garden as did his paper on trade winds: first he presented a more comprehensive empirical survey of the phenomena in question; then he offered an explanation which he claimed could account for these phenomena more adequately than did Garden's. Thus Halley enumerated eight generally observed relationships between barometric and meteorological phenomena and proposed that the "Theory that can well account for all these

Appearances, will in all Probability approach nearer the true Cause of the *Barometers* Variations, than any thing hitherto offered; and such an one I am bold to believe, is that which I here lay down."[20] Whereas Garden had held "that 'tis more easie and intelligible to account for the falling of rains and the impetuosity of Winds by the change of the Atmosphere's gravity, then to explicate the change of the Air's weight from the rain and Winds," Halley argued "that the principal Cause of the Rise and Fall of the *Mercury*, is from the Variable Winds, which are found in the *Temperate Zones.*"[21] Winds blowing together from opposite directions, according to Halley, heap up the air and thus make it heavier, while winds blowing in opposite directions away from the same region deplete the air and make it lighter.[22] This process is completely different from the rarefaction and condensation of air by heat and cold, which Halley did not believe could produce significant barometric effects, "for when the *Air* is rarified by Heat, the Vapours are raised most copiously, so that tho' the *Air*, properly so called, be expanded and consequently lighter, yet the *Interstices* thereof being crouded full of Vapours of much heavier Matters, bulk for bulk the weight of the *Compositum* may continue much the same." Finally, Halley stated that rainfall occurs when the air is made lighter by the outflowing of winds, "for the *Air* being light, the Vapours are no longer supported thereby, being become specifically heavier than the *Medium* wherein they floated; so that they descend towards the Earth, and in their fall meeting with other aqueous Particles, they incorporate together and form little Drops of Rain."[23]

It was this rather incoherent theory that was later seen as Halley's major contribution to the understanding of the barometer. Judging from Birch's *History*, Halley's presentation of this theory provoked no significant discussion in the Royal Society, although John Wallis did write to Halley from Oxford in November 1686 saying that he liked the version published in the *Philosophical Transactions.*[24] Later Wallis and Halley exchanged several more letters, in which Wallis criticized and Halley defended the trade winds paper;[25] within a few months, however, the correspondence between London and Oxford broke down, largely because of the political troubles that eventually led to the flight of James II and his replacement in 1688 by William and Mary. Lacking the provincial stimulus, the Royal Society seemed to lose interest in the barometer as a meteorological instrument, thus giving Halley the last word on this topic for the time being. From 1688 until the early 1700s, attempts to relate barometric phenomena with changes in the weather were pursued mainly by commercial manufacturers of the instrument in order to make their products more attractive to the public.[26]

In the first decades of the eighteenth century the barometer, like the microscope, had become largely a philosophical toy. Edward Saul reports that at this time the barometer was "in most houses of figure and distinction hung up as a philosophical or ornamental branch of furniture," and its main function lay in "supplying often matter of discourse upon the various and sudden changes of it." Hence Saul's 1730 book on the barometer was presented not as a technical research treatise but as a discourse written "for the satisfaction of many of my inquisitive countrymen; who having given themselves and their parlours an air of philosophy, by the purchase of a *Barometer,* may be willing to know the Meaning of it, and desirous of exerting now and then a superiority of understanding, by talking clearly and intelligibly upon it."[27]

It is apparent that for such an audience what counted was not the technical adequacy and coherence of a barometric theory but its intelligibility and veneer of scientific authority—and at this period a veneer of scientific authority was most easily obtained by some association with the work of Newton. Now, the meteorological portion of Halley's 1686 paper suited these requirements perfectly, so when the impecunious clergyman and former Boyle lecturer John Harris compiled his *Lexicon Technicum* as a commercial venture in 1704,[28] it was to this paper that he turned for his article on the barometer. Halley at this time was at the height of his career, being clearly identified with Newton since the publication of the *Principia* (1687), having completed three celebrated voyages in command of a naval vessel (1698–1701),[29] and having just been appointed successor to John Wallis in the Savilian Chair of Geometry at Oxford (1704). Thus he combined scientific authority with the sea captain's reputation for practical mastery of weather lore; and Harris did not hesitate to refer to him in both these capacities, speaking of "the Learned and Ingenious Capt. *Halley,* now *Savilian Professor* of Geometry in *Oxon,*"[30] whose work is cited in many articles in the *Lexicon.*

Now, Harris's *Lexicon* was to all indications a great commercial success,[31] and Halley—who was not above self-promotion and commercial entrepreneurship—brought out in the following year (1705) the first volume of his *Miscellanea Curiosa,* presented anonymously to "inquisitive Gentlemen" as a collection of the most interesting and authoritative papers published in the *Philosophical Transactions.*[32] In this volume over half the papers reprinted were by Halley himself, with nearly every one of his papers referred to by Harris in the *Lexicon* included. Thus Halley not only had, as it were, the last word in the barometric discussions of the 1680s, but he also had editorial control over which papers arising from these discussions were reprinted in 1705.

It was through the combination of the *Lexicon Technicum* and the *Miscellanea Curiosa,* then, that Halley achieved something of a monopoly position as a barometric theorist in early-eighteenth-century Britain. Apart from giving prominence to his barometric paper of 1686, both these collections also featured Halley's work on winds, vapors, rainfall, the origin of springs and fountains, and other meteorological phenomena. Hence Halley's barometric theory appeared as just one element in a comprehensive meteorological doctrine—so comprehensive, in fact, that Roger North was moved to call Halley "our proto-naturalist" in this domain, and James Jurin at about the same time described him as a "man perfect in meteorology."[33]

After the first decade of the eighteenth century, as the rivalry between Newton and Leibniz intensified, Halley's position as Britain's leading barometric theorist was further solidified by polemical considerations. Although the 1686 paper had none of the conceptual apparatus characteristic of Newton's work, it became, for the physicists at the Royal Society such as J. T. Desaguliers, "almost a part of the Newtonian canon."[34] When a barometric theory proposed by Leibniz was published by the Paris Academy, it was Halley's alternative that Desaguliers championed in his reply; and when James Jurin attempted once again, in 1723, to organize systematic meteorological observations in Britain and on the Continent, Halley's barometric theory was singled out as the most suitable for empirical testing.[35]

From a consideration of the factors listed above, it is evident that Halley's status in the early eighteenth century as the leading British theorist of barometric phenomena derived from his overall scientific reputation; from his association with Newton, even though the theory had no specifically Newtonian conceptual elements; from his broad range of meteorological interests, including seamanship; and from the commercial exploitation of his 1686 paper (especially in the *Lexicon Technicum* and the *Miscellanea Curiosa*)—rather than from any intrinsic qualities of the 1686 paper itself. Whatever his other scientific merits, and they were many, Edmond Halley was not a major contributor to the theory of the barometer.

NOTES

1. W. E. Knowles Middleton, *The History of the Barometer* (Baltimore: Johns Hopkins University Press, 1964), 55.

2. Edmond Halley, "A Discourse of the Rule of the Decrease of the Height of the Mercury in the Barometer, according as Places are Elevated above the Surface of the Earth; with an Attempt to Discover the True Reason of the Rising and Falling of the Mercury, upon the Change of Weather," *Philosophical Transactions of the Royal Society* 16 (1686–87): 104–16; idem, "A Letter from Mr Halley of June the 7th. 97. concerning the Torricellian Experiment tryed on the top of Snowdown-Hill and the Success of it," *Philosophical Transactions* 19 (1695–97): 582–84; and idem, "An Account of Dr Robert Hook's Invention of the Ma-

rine Barometer, with its Description and Uses," *Philosophical Transactions* 22 (1700–1701): 791–94.

3. For an indication of the scope of Hooke's work on the barometer, see R. T. Gunther, *Early Science in Oxford* (Oxford, 1923–25), vols. 6–7: *The Life and Works of Robert Hooke*, passim. See also the many references to Hooke in Middleton, *History of the Barometer*, as listed in the index of that volume.

4. John Harris, *Lexicon Technicum; or, an Universal English Dictionary of Arts and Sciences* . . . (London, 1704–10), vol. 1, art. "Barometer" (unpaginated).

5. Edward Saul, *An Historical and Philosophical Account of the Barometer, or Weather-Glass* . . . (London, 1730).

6. Ibid., p. 2 of "Dedication" (separately paginated).

7. Roger North, "Essay of the Barometer," British Library Add. MSS. 32541, fols. 175r, 175v–176r. For a review of North's scientific interests, see F.J.M. Korsten, *Roger North (1651–1734), Virtuoso and Essayist* (Amsterdam: APA/Holland University Press, 1981), chap. 2.

8. George Garden, "A Discourse Concerning Weather, etc.," *Philosophical Transactions* 15 (1685): 991–1001.

9. Gunther, *Early Science in Oxford* 4:92–93.

10. John Wallis, "A Discourse Concerning the Air's Gravity, Observed in the Baroscope, Occasioned by that of Dr. Garden," *Philosophical Transactions* 15 (1685): 1002–14.

11. Thomas Birch, *The History of the Royal Society* (London, 1756–57), 4: 393, 395.

12. George Garden, "Extracts of Two Letters, Written by Dr. Garden of Aberdeen; One Concerning the Causes of Several Winds . . . ," *Philosophical Transactions* 15 (1685): 1148–56.

13. Birch, *Royal Society* 4:488, 494.

14. On this point see Florian Cajori, "History of Determinations of the Heights of Mountains," *Isis* 12 (1929): 482–514, esp. 505.

15. Birch, *Royal Society* 4:472–73; and Gunther, *Early Science in Oxford* 4: 180–81.

16. Compare Hooke's experiments, reported to the Royal Society in February 1686, with those of Halley reported in April of that year. See Gunther, *Early Science in Oxford* 7:683–86; and Birch, *Royal Society* 4:472–73.

17. Birch, *Royal Society* 4:485.

18. Garden, "Extracts of Two Letters."

19. Edmond Halley, "An Historical Account of the Trade winds, and Monsoons, Observable in the Seas Between and Near the Tropicks, with an Attempt to Assign the Physical Cause of the Said Winds," *Philosophical Transactions* 16 (1686–87): 153–68.

20. Halley, "A Discourse of the Barometer," 111.

21. Garden, "A Discourse Concerning Weather," 997; Halley, "A Discourse of the Barometer," 111.

22. Halley, "A Discourse of the Barometer," 111–12.

23. Ibid., 109, 111.

24. John Wallis to Edmond Halley, 8 November 1686, in Gunther, *Early Science in Oxford* 12:112–14.

25. This correspondence is reprinted in ibid., 4:193–98 and 12:121–27.

26. Nicholas Goodison, *English Barometers, 1680–1860: A History of Domestic Barometers and Their Makers and Retailers* (Woodbridge: Antique Collectors' Club, 1977), chaps. 2–3.

27. Saul, *An Historical Account of the Barometer,* 1, 2.

28. Douglas McKie, "John Harris and His *Lexicon Technicum,*" *Endeavour* 4 (1945): 53–57.

29. The ship's log kept by Halley on these voyages has recently been published as *The Three Voyages of Edmond Halley in the "Paramore," 1698–1701,* ed. Norman J. W. Thrower, Hakluyt Society Publications, 2d ser., vols. 156–57 (London, 1981).

30. Harris, *Lexicon Technicum,* vol. 1, "Preface" (unpaginated).

31. McKie, "John Harris," 55.

32. Edmond Halley, *Miscellanea Curiosa, Being a Collection of Some of the Principal Phenomena of Nature, Accounted for by the Greatest Philosophers of This Age* (London, 1705–7), vol. 1, "To the Reader" (unpaginated).

33. Roger North, "Physica," British Library Add. MSS. 32544, fol. 245r; James Jurin, quoted in J. L. Heilbron, *Physics at the Royal Society During Newton's Presidency* (Los Angeles: William Andrews Clark Memorial Library, 1983), 29.

34. Jurin, in Heilbronn, *Physics at the Royal Society,* 110.

35. J. T. Desaguliers, "Remarks on the Second Paper in the *History of the Royal Academy of Sciences,* for the Year 1711, Concerning the Cause of the Variation of the Barometer: to Shew that the Way of Accounting for It in that Paper is Insufficient, and that the Experiment Made Use of to Prove What is There Asserted, Does No Way Prove It," *Philosophical Transactions* 30 (1717): 570–79; James Jurin, "Invitatio ad Observationes Meteorologicas Communi Consilio Instituendas," *Philosophical Transactions* 32 (1723): 422–27.

PART IV

Comets

THIRTEEN

The Ancient History
of Halley's Comet

F. Richard Stephenson

The history of Halley's Comet, the only known bright periodic comet, is well established as far back as 12 B.C. P/Halley (the prefix denoting the periodic nature of the comet) typically becomes visible to the unaided eye for two to three months at intervals of seventy-five to eighty years, at which times it has frequently attracted widespread interest. In his pioneering investigation of 1705, Halley demonstrated that the comets of A.D. 1531, 1607, and 1682 were one and the same.[1] Little further progress was made in tracing the comet's history until J. R. Hind in 1850 compared Far Eastern observations with the calculated motion of P/Halley.[2] In making the necessary orbital calculations, Hind worked backward one step at a time, with each step representing some seventy-five years. Despite his semiempirical procedure, Hind managed to correctly identify records of almost every return of P/Halley back to 12 B.C. His analysis was considerably improved upon by P. H. Cowell and A.C.D. Crommelin in 1907–8, who developed the present-day technique of integrating the equations of the comet's motion backward in time, taking into account planetary perturbations.[3] They were able to rectify several errors of identification made by Hind and also suggested that comets seen by the Chinese in both 87 and 240 B.C. might be references to Halley's Comet. At the earlier epoch, however, they had to assume an error of some eighteen months in their calculated date of perihelion.

More recently, T. Kiang in 1971 made a much more thorough numerical integration of the past orbit of P/Halley.[4] He carefully compared theory with observation, placing special emphasis on East Asian sightings, and considerably refined the solution of Cowell and Crommelin. Kiang's work may be regarded as the definitive study of the history of the comet back to 12 B.C. For the era before that date he was unable to make much

231

progress, since the available observations proved to be vague and of doubtful reliability. Although he gave some support to Cowell and Crommelin's identification of the Chinese records in 87 and 240 B.C., he could find no trace of the intermediate apparition, the calculated date of which is 164 B.C. The recent discovery of Babylonian sightings of Halley's Comet in 164 and 87 B.C. by F. Richard Stephenson, K.K.C. Yau, and H. Hunger in 1985, as well as directly extending the history of the comet by two further returns, has also enabled much more confidence to be placed in the Chinese observation of 240 B.C.[5] Nevertheless, as I shall consider below, the more ancient history of this famous comet seems likely to remain obscure.

This paper has three main objectives: (1) a detailed investigation of the Chinese observations made at the apparition of 12 B.C.; (2) discussion of the Chinese and Babylonian observations made at the returns of 87, 164, and 240 B.C.; and (3) examination of the problems that prevent the successful identification of still earlier records.

THE ACCURACY OF ORBITAL PARAMETERS

Various long-term numerical integrations of the motion of Halley's Comet have been made in recent years. Y. C. Chang in 1979, Donald K. Yeomans and T. Kiang in 1982, J. L. Brady in 1982, and W. Landgraf in 1984 independently computed sets of osculating orbital elements for every perihelion passage back to well before 1000 B.C.[6] Although the present investigation does not include a further numerical integration, it makes use of the results obtained by these authors. Because Stephenson, Yau, and Hunger considered in some detail the agreement among these solutions, both with one another and with observation, only a brief summary of these investigators' findings seems necessary here.

The apparent motion of a comet across the celestial sphere is only weakly dependent on small changes in such orbital parameters as eccentricity, inclination, and perihelion distance. However, this motion is very sensitive to variations in the precise date of perihelion passage (T). Of the various numerical integrations cited above, the T values computed by Chang tend to be in poor accord with those deduced from observation, with errors of a month common except in recent centuries. Hence, I will not consider his solution further. For the other three investigations, the computed dates of perihelion are well supported by observation as far back as A.D. 374; discrepancies do not exceed about five days. Before this date, Chinese observations in A.D. 141 and 66 closely confirm the T values calculated by Yeomans and Kiang and by Landgraf, but in each case Stephenson, Yau, and Hunger found Brady's result to be some

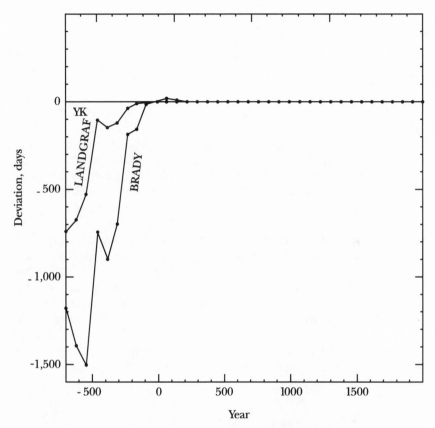

Figure 13.1. Plot of the deviations between the calculated dates of perihelion passage for Halley's Comet according to J. L. Brady and W. Landgraf relative to the results of Donald K. Yeomans and T. Kiang for the period since 700 B.C.

twenty days in error. The explanation may be the cumulative effect of unusually large perturbations of the motion of P/Halley caused by occasional close approaches to the Earth, notably in A.D. 837 when the separation was only 0.035 astronomical units (AU). Whereas Yeomans and Kiang and Landgraf incorporated several of the more accurate Chinese observations in order to rectify the comet's computed motion, Brady preferred to use a continuous integration.

All three solutions are once more in good agreement for 12 B.C., the computed dates of perihelion ranging over only about five days. In the period before 12 B.C., however, the relative discord among Brady, Yeomans and Kiang, and Landgraf becomes a serious barrier to successful identification of past records of Halley's Comet. This is illustrated by Figure 13.1, which shows the mutual discrepancies in the dates of perihelion passage; here the data of Yeomans and Kiang have arbitrarily been adopted as the standard. While the spread of T values deduced by the three authors is a tolerable forty-five days in 87 B.C., by 164 B.C. it has reached almost five months, and by 240 B.C. roughly six months; for all previous returns even the year in which perihelion occurred is in dispute.

Difficulties in identifying sightings of P/Halley in more ancient times are further exacerbated by both the inferior quality of early cometary records and the likely appearance of bright comets other than P/Halley. From the catalog of Far Eastern sightings of comets and "new stars" compiled by Ho Peng Yoke in 1962 and 1970 it is apparent that on average a comet becomes visible to the unaided eye every five years or so.[7] In 1910, for example, a daylight comet of very long period appeared only about three months before P/Halley itself. Similar double events are not infrequent in earlier centuries, as Stephenson, Yau, and Hunger show. Hughes in 1984 pointed out that a comet observed by Apian, and illustrated in several of his works, had at its return in A.D. 1531 been incorrectly regarded as Halley's Comet.[8] This object was instead, Hughes demonstrated, a long-period comet that appeared a year after P/Halley's return. He makes the telling comment: "Far from 'punctuating history every seventy-six years like an exclamation mark,' P/Halley is often overshadowed." Clearly, if only a brief report of a comet is available for ancient times, it may prove impossible to decide if Halley's Comet is indeed the object alluded to.

THE APPARITION IN 12 B.C.

Cassius Dio in his *Roman History* (Book 54) mentions the occurrence of a bright comet shortly before the death of Agrippa in 12 B.C. The date can be only approximately deduced, though, and no useful astronomical details are provided. We can only be confident that Halley's Comet is referred to on account of a careful Chinese description of the same event. The latter record is in the *Han-shu*, the official history of the Former Han dynasty (206 B.C.–A.D. 9), with the actual entry found in the *Wu-hsing-chih*, or "Treatise on the Five Elements" (chap. 27). The Chinese record is in two parts: a rather lengthy positional description, followed by an imperial edict that gives interesting background information regarding the motive for observation. The observational record is as follows:

> In the first year of the Yüan-yen reign period, the 7th month, on the day hsin-wei (Aug. 26) there was a "Bushy Star" at Tung-ching (in Gemini); it was treading on Wu-chu-hou (also part of Gemini). It appeared to the

north of Ho-shu (the stars Procyon and Castor) and passed through Hsüan-yüan (in Leo) and T'ai-wei (a large star group in Coma Berenices, Leo and Virgo). Later it travelled at more than 6 deg daily. In the morning it appeared at the eastern direction. On the evening of the 13th day (Sept. 7) it was seen at the western direction. It trespassed against Tz'ŭ-fei (Regulus), Ch'ang-ch'iu (eta Leonis), Pei-tou (in Ursa Major) and Saturn. Its "swarming flames" again penetrated within Tzŭ-wei (the region of sky near the north pole), with Ta-huo (Antares) right behind. It reached T'ien-ho (The Milky Way), sweeping the region of Hou and Fei (eta and gamma Leonis). It moved southwards, crossing and trespassing against Ta-chüeh (Arcturus) and Shê-t'i (eta and zeta Boo). When it reached T'ien-shih (a large star group in Hercules, Ophiuchus, etc.), it moved slowly at a regular pace. Its "flames" entered T'ien-shih. After a further ten days it went towards the west. On the 56th day (Oct. 20) it went out of sight together with Ts'ang-lung (in Scorpius).[9]

The term *Hsing-po* is here translated "Bushy Star." In the medieval period the Chinese usually described a comet without an obvious tail in this way, but in more ancient times both Bushy Star and the more common expression "Broom Star" (Hui-hsing) were probably used indiscriminately to denote comets in general. Apart from the above account in the *Wu-hsing-chih*, there is also a very brief mention of the same object in the *Pên-chi* (Basic Annals) of the *Han-shu*, but this provides no independent details. It is regrettable that our main text gives few precise dates; those that are included relate only to discovery, reappearance after conjunction with the Sun, and final disappearance. A list of dates when the comet passed the various asterisms mentioned in the text would have been of great value for establishing the precise date of perihelion passage, and although such information was in all probability reported by the imperial astronomers, presumably it was omitted when the present account was inserted in the *Han-shu*. Despite these criticisms, the recorded motion agrees well with calculation, apart from a few obvious discrepancies noted by Kiang in 1971.[10] There can thus be no doubt that Halley's Comet is indeed the object described in the text.

As already mentioned, Brady, Yeomans and Kiang, and Landgraf agree on the date of perihelion in 12 B.C. to within five days. The various T values (mean October 8.5) are in excellent agreement with the date of perihelion deduced from the observed conjunction with the Sun—i.e., close to 8 October.[11] It is thus possible to make confident calculations of the motion of the comet through the constellations. Figure 13.2 shows the computed motion of P/Halley during the autumn of 12 B.C. for the adopted mean date of perihelion of October 8.5. The motion through most of the asterisms is in excellent accord with observation, but neither the head nor tail of the comet can have passed near eta Leonis, Saturn,

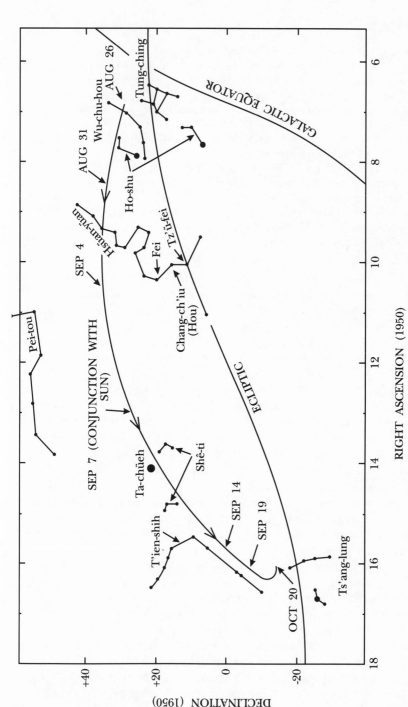

RIGHT ASCENSION (1950)

Figure 13.2. The computed motion of Halley's Comet (i.e., the nucleus) in 12 B.C. between 26 August (discovery) and 20 October in relation to the various asterisms mentioned in the *Han-shu* text. Note (a) the rapid eastward motion in early September; (b) the close approach to Arcturus (Ta-chüeh); and (c) the very slow motion, becoming retrograde, in late September and October. Calculations are based on a mean date of perihelion of 8.5 October. The planet Saturn is mistakenly mentioned in the text, but this lies considerably to the east of the area shown.

Antares, or the Milky Way. Possibly these positional descriptions were originally part of the record of some other object and have been included in the extant text by mistake.

CHINESE REFERENCES TO COMETS
AROUND 87 AND 164 B.C.

The two apparitions of Halley's Comet immediately preceding 12 B.C. (i.e., 87 and 164 B.C.) also occurred during the Former Han dynasty. Only sparse astronomical records have survived from either period. Table 13.1 lists the observations (apart from the solar eclipses) that are reported in the *Han-shu* around this time. (Solar eclipses are not included since the records of these events tend to be much more systematic than for any other astronomical phenomena.) In the table, years are given as B.C. for ease of identification; otherwise dates are in their original form.

The picturesque terms translated "Long Star" (Ch'ang-hsing), "Celestial Magnolia" (T'ien-ch'an), and "Tangle Star" (P'êng-hsing) all usually relate to comets. Only the reign period (Chih-yuan) in which the last of these objects appeared is known, hence the exact year is uncertain; it could have been any time between 86 and 81 B.C. Although Tsu Wen Hsion in 1934 suggested a possible identification of this comet with P/Halley,[12] neither the recorded date range nor the observed motion agrees with modern calculation. The *T'ien-wên-chih* (Treatise on Astronomy) of the *Han-shu* states that the comet "was first seen at the west in the eastern door of T'ien-shih (in Aquila), passed Ho-ku (also in Aquila) and entered Ying-shih (in Pegasus)." The computed dates of perihelion

TABLE 13.1. *Astronomical Observations Recorded in Chinese History*
ca. 164 and 87 B.C.

Year B.C.	Month	Cyclical Day	Summary of Observation
172	(Summer)	—	"Long Star" at E
162	1	jen-yin	"Celestial Magnolia" at SW
158	4	i-szu	Conjunction of 3 planets
158	8	—	Fall of a meteorite
89	4	ting-yu	Fall of two meteorites
87	7	—	"Bushy Star" at E
86–81	—	—	"Tangle Star" (detailed account)
77	—	—	"Guest Star" at N

for Halley's Comet lie between 10 July and 23 August 87 B.C., which corresponds to the late summer or early autumn of the second year of the Hou-yuan reign period. In addition, the calculated path of P/Halley (based on the above T values) did not come within about sixty degrees of the region of sky indicated in the text. Hence, the record of the Tangle Star must allude to another comet. As will be discussed later, the Bushy Star of 87 B.C. is a much better candidate for being P/Halley.

There is no Chinese record of a comet seen in 164 B.C., an omission that has led various investigators, most recently Chang in 1979, to identify the comet of 162 B.C., which is recorded, as P/Halley.[13] Assuming an error in the year—reading first rather than second year of the Hou reign period in the *Han-shu* text—Chang found that the observation seemed to agree satisfactorily with his own calculations for P/Halley (the recorded date would now correspond to 11 February 163 B.C.). However, Chang's suggestion is obviated by the rather careful Babylonian account of Halley's Comet in the autumn of 164 B.C. (discussed below), which enables the date of perihelion to be fixed within about a week of 16 November 164 B.C. By the following February the comet would have long since faded from sight. Hence, there is no good reason for assuming a dating error in the *Han-shu* text, and the original year can be restored. It is apparent that the Chinese observation must relate to a comet other than P/Halley.

From the above discussion we may conclude that there is no extant Chinese record of Halley's Comet in 164 B.C. and at best only a brief mention in 87 B.C. In order to offer an explanation for this deficiency we must examine the statistics of astronomical observations throughout the Former Han dynasty. Figure 13.3 is based on a count by decades which I made of astronomical phenomena other than solar eclipses noted in the *Han-shu*. These observations, which relate mainly to planetary phenomena and comets, are taken from three sections of the history: the "Imperial Annals" (chaps. 1–10), the "Astronomical Treatise" (chap. 26), and the "Treatise on the Five Elements" (chap. 27). Presumably the main source of information was the reports of the court astronomers.

As can be seen in Figure 13.3, only in a single decade (160–150 B.C.) is there an average of more than one observation per year. Clearly much data must have been missing by the time the *Han-shu* was compiled (A.D. 58–76), a conclusion that is supported by the highly irregular form of the histogram. Survivals appear to be particularly low around the time when Halley's Comet appeared in 87 and 164 B.C., so that the lack of an extant record in the earlier year need cause no surprise.

Moreover, only in two discrete periods during the Former Han dynasty—roughly 160–140 B.C. and after 75 B.C.—are dates frequently

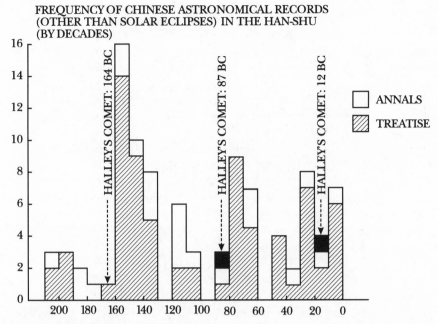

Figure 13.3. The frequency by decades of Chinese astronomical records (other than solar eclipses) in the *Han-shu*. Data obtained from the "Astronomical Treatise" and "Treatise on the Five Elements" are indicated by the shaded regions to distinguish them from the material in the "Annals." The black squares indicate the sightings of Halley's Comet in 12 B.C. and (less reliably) in 87 B.C.

given to the nearest day (Fig. 13.4). At all other times, no more than the month is specified. This possibly suggests that when the *Han-shu* was compiled, the astronomical material was taken from two main sources, one of which contained little detail. The brief account of the comet of 87 B.C., for example, is fairly typical for its period in noting only the month of observation.

COMETARY RECORDS FROM ANCIENT CHINA

Prior to the Former Han dynasty, Chinese cometary records are in general infrequent and lacking detail. About half of the little that survives, amounting to only about ten observations, dates from the Chan-kuo or Warring States period (ca. 480–221 B.C.) and subsequent Ch'in dynasty (221–206 B.C.). That there was originally much more material is evident from a silk manuscript discovered recently in a tomb dating from 168 B.C.

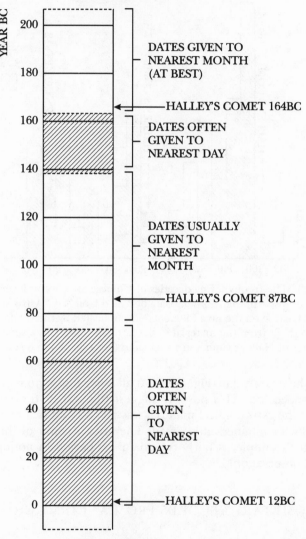

Figure 13.4. The accuracy of recording dates of astronomical events in Chinese history during the Former Han dynasty.

on which twenty-nine separate drawings of cometary tails, each with a separate astrological interpretation, are shown (unfortunately, all are undated).[14] Another silk manuscript contains hitherto unknown records of planetary phenomena. No doubt numerous ancient astronomical records were destroyed both at the systematic "burning of the books" in 213 B.C. and a few years later when the capital was sacked by rebels (207 B.C.). The former event was a deliberate purge of historical and other literature at the command of the first emperor, Ch'in Shih-huang. Possibly the later disaster was even more serious, since most of the remaining copies of the proscribed books, which had been carefully preserved in the imperial palaces, now perished.[15]

Apart from this silk manuscript, virtually all of the extant astronomical records from the Warring States period are found in the *Shih-chi* (Historical Record) compiled by Grand Historian Szu-ma Ch'ien between 104 and 87 B.C. These records are mainly located in the *Piao* (Chronological Tables) and consist almost exclusively of observations of comets and solar eclipses. Because it is the style of the *Piao* to give only brief summaries of major historical events, Szu-ma Ch'ien may have even further condensed the meager astronomical information to which he had access from this period. Practically all of the observations that he cites are from the history of the state of Ch'in, which ultimately—in 221 B.C.—became the ruling house.

Table 13.2 summarizes the cometary records contained in the *Shih-chi* for the Warring States period and Ch'in dynasty. A further comet, whose date is equivalent to 433 B.C., is cited in medieval works, but there is no surviving ancient report. Of the observations in Table 13.2, only in two examples is even the month given, and in several instances we know nothing whatsoever about the position or motion of the object. The "bright star" seen in the west during 214 B.C. is identified as a Broom Star in the commentary on the *Shih-chi*.

According to calculation, in the time range covered by the table Halley's Comet should have appeared around the years 240, 316, 392, and 467 B.C. As will be discussed below, the evidence for a sighting of P/Halley in 240 B.C. is fairly good. Since there is nothing to suggest that the two previous returns were noted, we must go back to 467 B.C. to have any prospects of a further identification. The comet that was seen in—or near—467 B.C. has been frequently linked with P/Halley, as Chang, Brady, and Landgraf indicate.[16] Apart from the complete lack of any descriptive details that might offer confirmatory evidence, however, the recorded year itself may well be in error.

In order to check the general accuracy of dates in the *Shih-chi* during the fifth century B.C., I have investigated the three earliest records of

TABLE 13.2. *Cometary Records from the Shi-Chi During
the Warring States Period and Ch'in Dynasty*

Year B.C.	Ch'in Reign Year	Month	Summary of Observation
470	Li 7	—	"Broom Star" (no details)
467	Li 10	—	"Broom Star" (no details)
361	Hsiao 1	—	"Broom Star" at W
305	Chao 2	—	"Broom Star" (no details)
303	Chao 4	—	"Broom Star" (no details)
296	Chao 11	—	"Broom Star" (no details)
240	Shih-huang 7	5	"Broom Star" at E, then N; seen at W for 16 days
238	Shih-huang 9	—	"Broom Star" at W, then N; south of Pei-tou; seen 80 days
234	Shih-huang 13	1	"Broom Star" at E
214	Shih-huang 33	—	Bright star at W

solar eclipses in this work, with years corresponding to 443, 435, and 410 B.C. (thirty-fourth year of Duke Li of Ch'in, eighth year of Ch'ao, and fifth year of Chien). On the first of these occasions the text states that there was darkness by day and stars appeared, while on the second both the Sun and the Moon were eclipsed in the sixth month. I have carefully computed the local circumstances of all eclipses in China around these times, using as a guide a detailed study of past variations in the Earth's rotation.[17] The results of this investigation are as follows. Around 443 B.C. there were two large eclipses, having calculated dates of 24 October 444 B.C. and 11 March 442 B.C.; either date could be correct, and it is difficult to decide between them. In the vicinity of 435 B.C. only the following pair of dates is possible: 16 May 436 B.C. (lunar eclipse) and 31 May 436 B.C. (solar). Finally, around 410 B.C. only the eclipse of 1 June 409 B.C. would reach a significant magnitude. Clearly then, an error of a year in the date of an event noted in the *Shih-chi* is quite typical at this period.

Returning to the cometary sighting in question (ca. 467 B.C.), the available evidence suggests the correct year to be probably between 468 and 466 B.C., but we cannot be more definite than this. Taking into consideration the fact that different numerical integrations yield dates of perihelion ranging between July 468 B.C. and July 466 B.C. for the return of P/Halley around this time, no firm conclusions can be drawn regarding the nature of the comet recorded in the *Shih-chi*.

Going back still further in time, the *Shih-chi* notes Broom Stars in years corresponding to 481, 482, 500, 516, 525, 532, and 613 B.C. Because the computed dates of return for Halley's Comet in this period are close to 540 and 618 B.C., all these observations must relate to other objects. Nevertheless, the 613 B.C. record deserves special mention as probably the earliest reliable sighting of a comet from anywhere in the world. The *Ch'un-ch'iu* (Spring and Autumn Annals) gives a relatively detailed account of this event, as it does also for the comets of 482 and 525 B.C. This work, the only survivor of the ancient state chronicles, covers the period 722–481 B.C. and is reputed to have been edited by Confucius; although it contains few astronomical records other than solar eclipses, there are as many as thirty-seven eclipse observations, the dates of which in most cases agree exactly with modern calculation. The account of the comet of 613 B.C. in the *Ch'un-ch'iu* reads as follows: "In autumn, during the 7th month (August) of the 14th year of Duke Wen of Lu, a Bushy Star entered Pei-tou (i.e., the Plough)."

Before 613 B.C., Ho Peng Yoke, who made a careful search of the available ancient literature, could trace no more than three allusions to comets;[18] all of these are of dubious reliability and are cited only in late works. The oracle bone fragments from the Shang dynasty—ca. 1500–1050 B.C.—contain several likely references to comets, but none are datable and there are no observational details.[19] Hence, during the whole of the period before 12 B.C., only in 87 and 240 B.C. do we find Chinese records that are worthwhile investigating as possible sightings of Halley's Comet. These will be discussed below, following some general remarks on Babylonian observations of comets.

LATE BABYLONIAN COMETARY RECORDS

The Late Babylonian astronomical diaries in the British Museum originally covered the period from about 750 B.C. to A.D. 75, but only about 5 percent of this once vast corpus of material is now extant. Whereas the Babylonian astronomers mainly concentrated on lunar and planetary phenomena, the occasional comet was also carefully followed. The typical diary had two types of entry—a daily record and, at the end of each month, a summary of important events—with cometary records found in both. The Babylonian term for a comet was *sallammu* (or *sallummu*); although no etymology of the word is known, evidence points to a cometary interpretation. For example, the diaries frequently note that *sallammu* remained visible for several days or weeks, which rules out a meteoric interpretation (H. Hunger, personal communication). Additionally, the dates of Babylonian reports of *sallammu* in 234, 157, and 138 B.C. agree well with those of comets sighted in China. Thus no viable alternative interpretation seems to suggest itself.

In all, Babylonian observations of nine separate comets are extant, with dates of 234, 210, 164, 163, 157, 138, 120, 100, and 87 B.C. It is quite likely that cometary records initially extended much further back in time, possibly to around 750 B.C. (the likely starting date of the diaries); if this is so, however, all earlier texts are now lost. Even the existing descriptions are fragmentary, but they still enable us to infer the characteristic features of a typical Babylonian cometary account. Whether in the daily reports or the monthly summaries, records of comets were apparently entered only on the following occasions: (1) first sighting; (2) heliacal setting; (3) heliacal rising; (4) any stationary points; and (5) last visibility. On each of these dates (apart from the first) it was customary to provide a retrospective summary for reference. The following illustrations, the contexts of which are all discontinuous because of textual damage, are taken from diaries for the years 174, 192, and 202 of the Seleucid Era (SE) (respectively 138, 120, and 110 B.C.): (a) "That month (Month II) the comet which had set in Libra reappeared on the night of the 20th in the west in the area of. . . ." (b) "Night of the 26th (of month III), beginning of the night, the comet which had set in the east, on the 29th (of the previous month) in Aries in the path of Anu. . . ." (c) "(Month IX, day 1, a comet) in the east, its tail toward the west in the path of. . . . (Days 10 to 12) the comet which on the 1st had appeared in the path of Enlil to the north. . . ." (trans. H. Hunger, personal communication).

In these examples, Enlil and Anu, along with a third "path" named Ea, denote the major regions into which the Babylonian astronomers divided the sky, Enlil being the northern sky, Anu the equatorial zone, and Ea the southern sky. All were named after deities. That these divisions, which are never found in planetary records, were used to describe the locations of comets suggests that the Babylonians were well aware of the highly wayward movements of comets. Text (c) mentions the direction of the tail (*mishu*) of a comet, and there are several similar references in other texts.

Clearly, the Babylonian astronomers recognized that the same comet could be visible both before and after conjunction with the Sun. Yet in view of the fragmentary nature of the texts and also the generally poor quality of ancient Chinese cometary records, it is impossible to assign priority for this discovery to either civilization.

Comparing the computed dates of perihelion of P/Halley with the list of Babylonian cometary observations given above, it is clear that any Babylonian records of either the 240 B.C. and earlier or the 12 B.C. and A.D. 66 apparitions are now lost. Yet as Stephenson, Yau, and Hunger, show, accounts of the apparitions in both 164 and 87 B.C. are still preserved, the former on two separate tablets. These observations will be considered in the immediately following sections.

THE APPARITION OF 87 B.C.

The computed dates of perihelion passage at this return range from 10 July to 23 August, an acceptably small range of time. As discussed above, only a brief Chinese record of a comet remains from this year, in the "Imperial Annals" of the *Han-shu* (chap. 7) and reading as follows: "In autumn, during the 7th month (of the 2nd year of the Hou-yuan reign period), there was a Bushy Star at the E direction." The recorded date corresponds to the interval between 10 August and 8 September 87 B.C., according to oriental calendar tables.[20]

As translated by Stephenson, Yau, and Hunger, Babylonian tablet WA 41018 in the British Museum gives the following report (rev. 8'–10'): "On the 13th (?), the interval between moonrise and sunset was 8 degrees, measured; first part of the night, a comet . . . which in month IV day beyond day one cubit . . . between north and west its tail 4 cubits. . . ."

As with so many other tablets, the date (both year and month) is broken away. However, the obverse of the text makes mention of the city of Seleucia, which was founded around 300 B.C. and replaced Babylon as the royal city ca. 275 B.C. This sets a useful upper age limit to our text. From the planetary and lunar information recorded on the same tablet, Abraham Sachs in an unpublished note (communicated to me by H. Hunger) was able to calculate a unique date of somewhere between June and August in 87 B.C.; using chronological tables, the equivalent date on the Seleucid calendar was then identified as the lunar months II, IV, and V of the year SE 225. This calculation was fully confirmed by Stephenson, Yau, and Hunger in a more detailed investigation. The cometary entry above is shown to be included in the observations for the fifth lunar month, and, as a check on the measured interval between moonrise and sunset shows, the date of this entry is exactly equivalent to 24 August 87 B.C. Following the usual practice, much of the text is retrospective.

Brief though the surviving Babylonian account is, it contains appreciably more details than the Chinese version; we shall therefore consider it first. For any date of perihelion in or near the computed range of 10 July to 23 August, Halley's Comet would be fairly prominent (approaching magnitude 0) in the late summer of 87 B.C. Figure 13.5 shows the apparent daily motion of P/Halley calculated for a date of perihelion

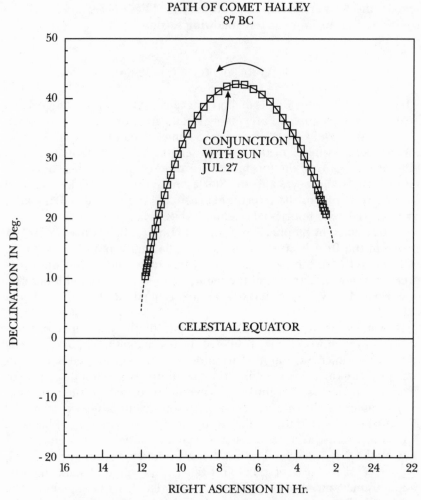

Figure 13.5. The apparent daily motion of Halley's Comet around the time of perihelion passage in 87 B.C. The location on July 27 (conjunction with the Sun) is shown for reference. Note the fairly regular motion in a general eastward direction. Calculations are based on a date of perihelion of 6 August, as derived by Yeomans and Kiang. (After K.K.C. Yau, private communication.)

of 6 August; this is the date deduced by Yeomans and Kiang and represents a good mean of the other two results, 10 July (Brady) and 23 August (Landgraf). The comet's high declination (between about +20 and +45 degrees) would place it well for northern observers. Both the weather records in the Babylonian diaries and modern meteorological data show that cloud cover during the summer months in this part of the world is negligible, so there can be little doubt that P/Halley would be seen by the Babylonian astronomers. Our text does not suggest that more than one comet was visible, while the regular motion of Halley's Comet at this apparition—between one and six degrees daily for at least a month—would fit in well with the recorded "day beyond day one cubit." (Analysis of a number of lunar and planetary observations by Stephenson, Yau, and Hunger indicates that the angular equivalent of a cubit was roughly 2.5 degrees.) The case is thus strong for identifying the Babylonian *sallammu* with P/Halley.

Stephenson, Yau, and Hunger showed variously that to obtain the most satisfactory accord between theory and observation, a date of perihelion for Halley's Comet between about 25 July and 15 August 87 B.C. is required. The phenomenon reported on 24 August is interpreted as the last sighting in the west. The date range deduced provides support for the calculations of Yeomans and Kiang (T = 6 August) but is somewhat at variance with the results of Brady (10 July) and Landgraf (23 August). The Chinese record alleges visibility in the eastern sky sometime between 10 August and 8 September. Because this cannot be reconciled with the Babylonian observations, and either the month or direction in the Chinese account must be erroneous as Kiang in 1971 independently suggested.[21] Such a mistake is not unreasonable, for the Chinese text represents only a brief summary written up more than a century after the event and possibly based on deficient material. In contrast, the Babylonian text is part of a detailed report, presumably compiled from observing notes within months of the events described.

THE APPARITION OF 164 B.C.

Two fragments of Babylonian astronomical diaries in the British Museum contain the only known records of the 164 B.C. return. Translations of the relevant texts by Stephenson, Yau, and Hunger are as follows: (a) WA 41462 (obv. 16–17) "The comet which had previously appeared in the east in the path of Anu in the area of Pleiades and Taurus, to the west . . . and passed along in the path of Ea." (b) WA 41628 (obv. 9′) "[In the path of] Ea in the region of Sagittarius, 1 cubit in front of Jupiter, 3 cubits high towards the north. . . ."

Once again, the year and month are missing from both tablets. By calculating the lunar and planetary information, Sachs in 1955 deduced identical Julian dates for each: the end of 164 B.C. and the beginning of 163, equivalent to SE 148, months VIII, IX (obverse), and XII, XII/2 (reverse).[22] The most effective dating evidence is provided by a lunar

eclipse described on the reverse of both tablets.[23] This same eclipse is also
reported in a third diary (WA 34037), which fortunately provides an
exact date for the event: the fifteenth of month XII/2 in the year 148 SE,
corresponding to 30–31 March 163 B.C.[24] and exactly confirmed by calculation. WA 41462 and WA 41628 duplicated several additional observations, and these prove beyond any doubt that the two existing fragments are copies of the same diary and that the cometary texts (a) and (b)
indeed overlap. Both texts are found in the summaries at the end of
month VIII (21 October–19 November 164 B.C.).

The calculated range of T is between 22 June and 12 November.
Stephenson, Yau, and Hunger showed that merely by allowing the date
of perihelion to vary between these limits, the computed motion of Halley's Comet can be readily brought into excellent agreement with the
record itself. This remark applies both to the first appearance in Taurus
and to the subsequent conjunction with Jupiter while in Sagittarius. In
particular, the conjunction with Jupiter, although on an unspecified day,
enables the date of perihelion passage for P/Halley to be fixed confidently between about 6 and 24 November. Hence, the range of T may
be reduced from the calculated interval of nearly five months to only two
weeks. It is noteworthy that the T value derived by Yeomans and Kiang
(12 November) lies within this range, while that of Landgraf (30 October) is only a little outside it. By contrast, Brady's date (22 June) is seriously in error. There is a fragmentary Babylonian record of a comet
seen in September 163 B.C. This apparition, however, is almost a year
too late and cannot be brought into association with P/Halley. As already
implied, both Yeomans and Kiang and Landgraf incorporated early observations in their solution, whereas Brady preferred a purely numerical
integration. This latter technique would therefore appear to be unsatisfactory for investigating the more ancient apparitions of Halley's
Comet, owing to the accumulation of large errors.

Figure 13.6 shows the computed daily motion of Halley's Comet in
the autumn of 164 B.C., based on a date of perihelion of 12 November.
This date, derived by Yeomans and Kiang, lies well within the range indicated by observation.

THE APPARITION OF 240 B.C.

As already noted, any Babylonian observation of this return is now
lost and we have to rely on a brief Chinese record. In the "Annals" of
the *Shih-chi* (chap. 6), the following account is given: "In the 7th year
(of Ch'in Shih-huang), a Broom Star first appeared at the northern

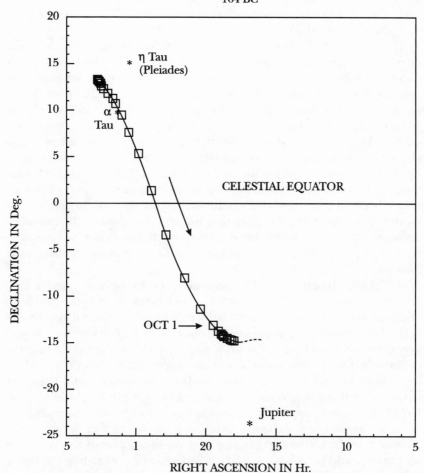

PATH OF COMET HALLEY
164 BC

Figure 13.6. The apparent daily motion of Halley's Comet around the time of perihelion passage in 164 B.C. The Babylonian astronomers first sighted the comet in the Pleiades/Taurus area, and they probably last observed it near Jupiter. The location on 1 October is shown for reference. Note the rapid motion for a few days in late September when the comet passed rather close to the Earth—only about 0.1 AU away. Calculations are based on a date of perihelion of 12 November, as derived by Yeomans and Kiang. (After K.K.C. Yau, private communication.)

direction. During the 5th month (24 May–23 June) it was again seen at the western direction. General Ao died (while at war). . . . The Broom Star remained visible at the western direction for 16 days. In the summer, the Empress died."

The *Shih-chi* appears to make no attempt to link the comet with the deaths of either General Ao or the empress; these events are merely noted in historical sequence. The most useful observation is that during the month equivalent to 24 May–23 June the comet, having passed conjunction with the Sun, reappeared in the west and remained visible for sixteen more days. The computed dates of perihelion are respectively 30 November 241 (Brady), 28 April 240 (Landgraf), and 25 May 240 (Yeomans and Kiang). According to Brady's solution, there is no possibility of the comet of 240 B.C. being linked with P/Halley, but the limitations of his technique when applied to more ancient returns have already been noted. Landgraf's solution would require an error of a month in the recorded date (reading fourth for fifth), but the results of Yeomans and Kiang, which better satisfy the Babylonian observation in 87 and 164 B.C., are in close agreement with the existing report in the *Shih-chi*.

Calculation based on the T value deduced by Yeomans and Kiang (25 May) shows that Halley's Comet would probably become visible in mid May and would then be seen before dawn in the eastern sky. By the end of the month, the declination would be so high (close to +40 degrees) that it would be visible in a north-northeast direction, roughly confirming the statement that the comet appeared at the north. Following conjunction with the Sun around 2 June, the comet would reappear in the western sky after dusk, but by the end of June its brightness would have faded considerably. This is perhaps as good a representation of observation as we might expect, bearing in mind the lack of details in the *Shih-chi* text. Nevertheless, because of a possible error in the recorded month, it would be unwise to make any deductions regarding the range in T as indicated by this observation.

The computed daily motion of P/Halley during the summer of 240 B.C. is shown in Figure 13.7 (as before, based on the date of perihelion deduced by Yeomans and Kiang).

CONCLUSION

Using both Chinese and Babylonian observations, we can trace the history of Halley's Comet with some confidence back to 240 B.C. Of the various numerical integrations of the comet's past orbit, that of Yeomans and Kiang is found to give results closest to observation. Yet in the absence of

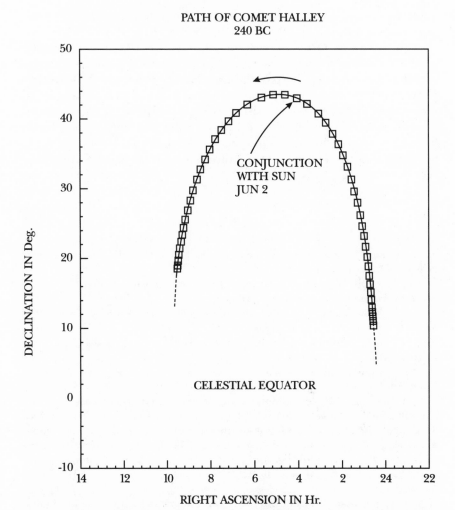

Figure 13.7. The apparent daily motion of Halley's Comet around the time of perihelion passage in 240 B.C. The location on 2 June (conjunction with the Sun) is shown for reference. The comet was probably observed in China both before and after conjunction and would be well placed for northern observers. Calculations are based on a date of perihelion of 25 May, as derived by Yeomans and Kiang. (After K.K.C. Yau, private communication.)

useful earlier records and the increasing discrepancies between the various computed values of T, there would seem to be little hope of extending this investigation further back in time. Yeomans and Kiang computed the orbital elements of P/Halley as far back as 1404 B.C., while both Brady and Landgraf continued their numerical integration well beyond 2000 B.C. The evidence discussed here indicates that integration over such a long time scale was both unjustified and misleading. Although 240 B.C. is rather late in world history, the Chinese observation in that year will probably have to stand as the earliest identifiable sighting of Halley's Comet. Despite the fact that the history of P/Halley appears to begin rather abruptly, we may express considerable satisfaction that since 240 B.C. each successive apparition of the comet has been reported in the chronicles of at least one civilization. More than 2,200 years of unbroken history represents a remarkable achievement on the part of both astronomers of antiquity and modern authorities on orbital theory.

NOTES

1. Edmond Halley, "Astronomiae Cometicae Synopsis," *Philosophical Transactions of the Royal Society* 24 (1705): 1882–99.
2. J. R. Hind, "On the Past History of Halley's Comet," *Monthly Notes of the Royal Astronomical Society* 10 (1850): 51–58.
3. P. H. Cowell and A.C.D. Crommelin, *Monthly Notes of the Royal Astronomical Society* 67–68 (1907–8), five papers.
4. T. Kiang, "The Past Orbit of Halley's Comet," *Memoirs of the Royal Astronomical Society* 76 (1971): 27–66.
5. F. Richard Stephenson, K.K.C. Yau, and H. Hunger, "Records of Halley's Comet on Babylonian Tablets," *Nature* 314 (1985): 587–92.
6. Y. C. Chang, "Halley's Comet: Tendencies in Its Orbital Evolution and Its Ancient History," *Chinese Astronomy* 3 (1979): 120–31; Donald K. Yeomans and T. Kiang, "The Long-Term Motion of Comet Halley," *Monthly Notes of the Royal Astronomical Society* 197 (1982): 633–46; J. L. Brady, "Halley's Comet: A.D. 1986–2647 B.C.," *Journal of the British Astronomical Association* 92 (1982): 209–15; and W. Landgraf, "On the Motion of Halley's Comet," ESTEC EP/14.7/6184 *Final Report* (1984).
7. Ho Peng Yoke, "Ancient and Medieval Observations and Novae in Chinese Sources," *Vistas in Astronomy* 5 (1962): 127–225; and idem, "Chinese Astronomical Records on Comets and 'Guest Stars,'" *Oriens Extremus* 17 (1970): 63–99.
8. David W. Hughes, "Apian's Woodcut and Halley's Comet," *International Halleywatch Newsletter* 5 (1984): 24–25.
9. F. Richard Stephenson and K.K.C. Yau, "Far Eastern Observations of Halley's Comet: 240 B.C. to A.D. 1378," *Journal of the British Interplanetary Society* 38 (1985): 195–216.
10. Kiang, "Past Orbit," 56.
11. Stephenson and Yau, "Far Eastern Observations," 201–2.
12. Tsu Wen Hsion (= Chu Wên-hsin), "The Observations of Halley's Comet in Chinese History," *Popular Astronomy* 42 (1934): 191–201.

13. Chang, "Halley's Comet," 127.

14. Xi Ze-zong, "The Cometary Atlas in the Silk Book of the Han Tomb at Mawangdui," *Chinese Astronomy and Astrophysics* 8 (1984): 1–7.

15. H. H. Dubs, *The History of the Former Han Dynasty,* vol. 1 (Baltimore: Waverly Press, 1938), 7.

16. Chang, "Halley's Comet," 129; Brady, "Halley's Comet," 212; Landgraf, "On the Motion of Halley's Comet."

17. F. Richard Stephenson and L. V. Morrison, "Long-Term Changes in the Rotation of the Earth," *Philosophical Transactions A* 313 (1984): 47–70.

18. Ho Peng Yoke, "Ancient and Medieval Observations," 141.

19. Xu Zhentao, K.K.C. Yau and F. Richard Stephenson, "Astronomical Records on the Shang Dynasty Oracle Bones," *Journal for the History of Astronomy* 20 (1989): S562–S571.

20. Tung Tso-pin, *Chronological Tables of Chinese History* (Hong Kong: Hong Kong University Press, 1960).

21. Kiang, "Past Orbit," 56.

22. Abraham J. Sachs, *Late Babylonian Astronomical and Related Texts* (Providence, R.I.: Brown University Press, 1955), xvi.

23. F. Richard Stephenson and C.B.F. Walker, *Halley's Comet in History* (London: British Museum 1985), 36.

24. R. A. Parker and W. H. Dubberstein, *Babylonian Chronology: 626 B.C.–A.D. 75* (Providence, R.I.: Brown University Press, 1956).

FOURTEEN

Halley, Delisle, and the Making of the Comet

Simon Schaffer

HALLEY'S TABLES AND THEIR USES

In 1728 Henry Pemberton set out a summary of the English consensus on the achievements and methods of the cometography of Halley and Newton. Pemberton, editor of the third edition of the *Principia* (1726), argued that "comets move in elliptical orbits, tho' of a very oblong form," and had an eccentricity so large that "they approach so near parabolas that they may be taken for such without sensible error." Pemberton spelled out the implications of these facts: comets would return, but the only way of predicting returns was to use a "historic" method: construct a parabola, and hence the elements of an orbit; look for similar elements in previous observed transits, and hence derive a period. "The comparing together different appearances of the same comet is the only way to discover certainly the true form of the orbit." Pemberton also observed that Halley's claim about the return of the comet of 1682, announced at the Royal Society in June 1696 and published in 1705, was by no means a secure one. Perturbation by the major planets would easily change the period Halley had guessed.[1] Each component of Pemberton's summary was a skillful simplification of the work performed by Halley and Newton from 1684 until the 1720s. The claims that all comets would return, that parabolas would be a useful approximation, and that some effect would result from planetary perturbation were all contested and revised during the first half of the eighteenth century. The fragile consensus in cometography that finally was established by 1759 was, in short, a result of strenuous efforts to understand and clarify these claims.

Newton had assumed that comets moved in closed orbits some time before he had any evidence of this belief. In late 1684 his tract *De Motu*

carried the statement that comets' paths were elliptical and that from the
"magnitude, eccentricity, [peri]helia, inclinations to the plane of the
ecliptic and nodes of the orbits compared with one another, we may
know whether the same comet returns time and again."[2] Yet as late as
September 1685 Newton had failed to compute any cometary orbits;
soon thereafter he completed his "System of the World," in which the assumption of closure was reiterated.[3] The work that Halley performed in
the autumn of 1695 resulted in the conviction that the orbits of both
1680–81 and 1682 were ellipses, the former having a period of over five
hundred years and the latter a period of "about 75 years." As early as
April 1687 Halley had proposed working on many comets, and by June
1698 he was able to tell David Gregory that he had completed the elements of at least fourteen or twenty; his table of 1705 included those of
twenty-four.[4] The second (1713) edition of the *Principia* included Halley's predictions for the 1682 comet and a vague statement about that of
1680–81; by the third edition this statement had been amplified to identify the 1680–81 comet with those of 44 B.C. and A.D. 531 and 1106.[5]

The context of the statements about comets in the *Principia* linked
their return firmly with functional considerations about their cosmological role, such as the cause of cataclysms and the restoration of terrestrial and stellar activity. Evidently it was these considerations that
prompted Newton's very early commitment to an elliptical model.[6] Thus
in 1738 Voltaire argued that "it would not only be a considerable fault to
prolong the parabolical Motion beyond the distances in which Comets
are visible, but we should moreover deprive ourselves thereby of ever
seeing them again."[7] Maupertuis, citing the work of David Gregory, emphasized that comets were now "re-established in all their reputation of
terror which they used to have," and stressed that the "historic" method
was still, in 1742, the only way of predicting their frightful returns: "they
can bring dire changes to our Earth and to the whole economy of the
heavens, against which only habit reassures us."[8]

Such views connected the idea of cometary returns with specific notions of cometary function and structure. Natural philosophers did not
separate their speculations about the matter of which comets were composed from statements about their function in the production or destruction of planets and stars, and thus about the forces that might act on
them. In 1717, when Halley completed a revision of the *Synopsis*, he
added to his tables of comets and of parabolic elements a more detailed
analysis of the 1682 comet. As Rigaud has shown, Halley's confidence in
the virtue of this prediction had markedly weakened. Whereas in 1705
he had undertaken "confidently to predict," by 1717 this was qualified to
"I think I may venture to foretel."[9] He reminded his readers that the
difference between the orbits of 1682, 1607, and 1531 "seemed to me a

little too large."[10] Borrowing a technique from Kepler's *Rudolphine Tables*, Halley computed a table for an ellipse of period 75.5 years (the average of the two previous periods), from which the mean motion and true anomaly could be derived. From this table he worked out thirteen positions for the 1682 comet, showing that this method gave errors as small as 8 minutes in longitude and 10 minutes in latitude for 1607 and 1531, though the error increased near the end of the transit, in October 1607.

But this pleasing accomplishment did not remove Halley's major trouble. As he put it, the inequality in successive periods "is much larger than those which we observe in the revolutions of any single planet, since one of these periods exceeds the other by more than a year . . . while the inclination of the Comet of 1682 is 22′ larger than that of the Comet of 1607."[11] To cope with this difficulty, Halley appealed to Proposition 13, Book Three, of the *Principia*, where Newton discussed disturbances in Saturn's orbit due to the pull of Jupiter. At the two planets' conjunction in February 1683, the period of Saturn could be altered by over one month. Newton observed that this disturbance would produce great changes in the mean motion of the planet and urged that Saturn's orbit should be focused in the center of gravity of Jupiter and the Sun. Halley had raised this problem for comets with Newton in a letter of October 1695, but they had concluded that observations by Hevelius and Cassini and others were too vitiated to serve as reliable data, and in any case such a method was not practicable for cometary paths. Therefore, in 1717 Halley relied on a vague order-of-magnitude guess for the perturbation: Jupiter, he concluded, would probably accelerate the comet, and thus he could guess at a return for late 1758 or early 1759. He commented, however, that "all this is nothing but a light trial, and we leave the effort of making this matter deeper to those who survive until the event justifies our predictions," closing his conjecture with a patriotic flourish: "Posterity will not forget that *it is to an Englishman that it owes this discovery*."[12]

Astronomers' response to this timorous and confused publication concentrated on the obscurity of the technique Halley had used and on the dubious character of the real presumptions he had made. Le Monnier made a characteristically bitter comment in his own translation of Halley's tables in 1743: "What was once clear is now become almost unintelligible."[13] Delambre, in his survey of eighteenth-century astronomy (1827), managed to derive Halley's equations directly from the general equation of an ellipse, but castigated Pingré's remark that Lacaille, Lalande, and others had faithfully followed Halley's method. In fact, Delambre observed, "the method was completely unknown to us, save in the general table of parabolic motions, entirely changed by Lacaille, and . . . Pingré himself extended the latter table in preference to that of Halley."[14] Delambre summarized the condition of cometography at the time of Lacaille's initial work in 1746: "This indifference had as its principal cause the obscurity of the method and the few details given by Halley in the section of his book which would have most particularly interested calculators."[15]

Of course, most of the obstacles Halley himself encountered when dealing with perturbations and reliance on the "historic" method still obtained in the 1740s. Star catalogues were still inaccurate, early observations were unreliable, and there was no good way of determining an orbit from three or more observations taken in one transit. As late as 1766, according to Delambre, Pingré observed that "an error of a few seconds would often be sufficient to change the ellipse into a parabola or an hyperbola"; indeed, planetary attraction might make this change: "the comet would distance itself to infinity, might pass from one system to the neighbouring system. What would be served by this communication?"[16]

There were also very specific charges to be laid against Halley's own published utterances. He had guessed at the return of comets in 1759, 1789, and 2255. Although the last, as Delambre put it, "cannot in any way interest the present generation,"[17] the prediction did draw fire from the Cambridge mathematician Richard Dunthorne. In a paper of November 1751 he showed a wide disagreement between the comet of 1106 and that of 1680, which "must very much lessen, if it does not quite overbalance, the force of the arguments brought by Dr. Halley to prove the identity of these two comets."[18] This error in Halley's work was worrying for those astronomers concerned with the 1759 return. If he could be so wrong about 1680, why not about 1682? Later in the century Maskelyne, Mechain, and their colleagues also were to demolish Halley's prediction that the comet of 1660 would return in 1789; although Bailly and Messier painstakingly watched for it, its failure to appear was already an established assumption of cometography.[19]

This problem was combined with that of the details of the 1682 comet's return. The inequalities in period were so large that Thomas Stevenson suggested in the London Magazine in 1758 that there were in fact two comets, each with a period of 151 years.[20] In his own edition of Halley's tables, Lalande went into the details of Halley's error about the perturbation due to Jupiter. First, an acceleration of the comet would increase the period only if the orbit's position were invariable, which it manifestly was not. Second, when the comet passed near Jupiter in 1683 the acceleration it experienced in 1681 would be canceled out exactly, not overbalanced as Halley had supposed. Last, what really disturbed the comet's path was not momentary approaches to Jupiter but, for example, the shift in the Sun owing to Jupiter's pull, a computation that was certainly beyond the accomplishments of the celestial mechanics of

Halley's time. Lalande concluded that when the return finally came due "the time when the Comet should appear was absolutely unknown, and, from the year 1757, everyone was waiting for it and looking for it."[21]

Certainly many astronomers used the return of the comet in 1759 to sustain rival stories about the success of cometography. On 25 April 1759, for instance, Lalande gave a carefully prepared statement to the Académie. His tone balanced affirmation of the triumph of the research program initiated by Halley with an emphasis on the woeful insufficiencies of Halley's actual work, thus effectively propagandizing for the accomplishments of French celestial mechanics. This statement entailed giving an exact definition of what Halley had done, as well as an equally exact definition of the distinguishing features of a comet. Thus Lalande had to work hard to show that the comet of 1759 was indeed the same as that of 1682, despite differences in both period and appearance. "Let us therefore put away as an absurdity any reflection which might tend to produce the belief that this Comet cannot be that of 1682." Lalande had to cope with the consideration that the comet of 1759 lacked a tail. It lacked a tail, he now suggested, because of its distance from the Sun and because "the comet could not be found this year in any of those favourable circumstances." He also noted the remarkable inequality in successive periods, demolished Halley's account of perturbations, and dismissed Euler's suggestion of 1744 that ether resistance might accelerate the comet's motion: "I have demonstrated in a memoir on the secular equations that this system of universal acceleration had no reality in it."[22]

Lalande was also forced to emphasize the need for a fine choice between elliptical and parabolic orbits. Thus, on 21 May 1759 the comet was, at $102°45'42''$, in true anomaly whichever path it was viewed in, but the distances would have been 1.4596 astronomical units (AU) in an ellipse and 1.4978 AU in a parabola. This difference depended critically on the choice of period: "For May 21 the true anomaly in the parabola is smaller than in the ellipse by $44'50''$, when taking the largest period . . . and only $2'$ if one takes the period between 1607 and 1682. . . . Thus one sees the necessity of examining which period to use."[23]

To summarize: astronomers such as Lalande strove hard to assure their public that the comet was the same, that they were using the criteria of identity for a comet, based on its position, and hence that the comet had indeed returned—thus making this return count as a triumph for their celestial mechanics. This strategy demanded a careful appraisal of Halley's own accomplishment. His methods were obscure and often unexploited, and his assumptions questionable. Nor was everyone convinced that comets would return, or that Halley's guesses about perturbation were adequate. Apparently, then, the presentation of the return as a success for Newtonian cometography, as represented by Halley's

Synopsis, was itself a finely balanced and deliberate accomplishment of the astronomers who dominated the Paris ceremonies in 1759.

This picture of a triumphant celestial mechanics was very difficult to make. In Paris, d'Alembert claimed that all the important work had already been done by Halley in 1705, thereby depriving his enemies, including Clairaut and Lalande, of the credit they sought.[24] In Cambridge, the astronomy professor Roger Long repeated Newton's views on the close link between cometary function and their return. Perturbations were a function of the forces to which comets were subject, the appearance of their tails a consequence of their cosmological role; teleological considerations thus provided support for the insistence that the comet must return, and had indeed done so. Long attacked Lalande's deprecation of Halley's achievements, insisting that Halley should be credited with identifying the 1607 and 1682 comets, with observing the perturbing effects of Jupiter, and with foretelling the comet's retardation.[25]

In Britain, furthermore, the return of comets could not be divorced from their role as agents of divine power and restoration. Newton's views on this question were widely disseminated through the *Principia* and a host of English commentaries. In 1728 Pemberton had given them a long exposé. In 1742 the Scottish antiquarian Sir John Clerk, trained at Oxford by Halley and Gregory, nevertheless wrote to the eminent mathematician Colin Maclaurin arguing that the prediction of cometary returns was a hopeless task, simply because of the activity of various powers in the heavens. Two years later, following a spate of cometary appearances, the *Gentleman's Magazine* publicized Maupertuis's views about the terrible effects of a cometary transit, to which Richard Yate replied that since comets were merely "solar meteors," "who can but smile that sees the ingenious Dr. Halley employed in describing the orbit and calculating the periodical revolution of a meer *Ignis Fatuus* or *Jack with a Lanthorn?*"[26] Theologians, too, found comets to be valuable commodities. In 1755, when commenting on the recent earthquake at Lisbon, John Wesley confused the comets of 1680 and 1682 in his efforts to warn his flock of imminent disaster when the comet returned. Such views were not laid to rest by the return of 1759, and indeed were strengthened by the successes claimed as a result of that event.[27]

Furthermore, there was little consensus about the right way to view comets as objects of celestial mechanics. Lalande, in 1759, decried any appeal to final causes but also suggested that their tails were designed to "sweeten the aridity experienced on them, to maintain and promote circulation, fluidity, motion and life."[28] During the 1740s Euler, reiterating views developed by Halley in the early 1690s, suggested that aether resistance would have marked effects on the motion of comets, planets, and satellites; he proffered this phenomenon as a "proof, purely physical, that the World, in its present state, must have had a Beginning, and must have an End."[29] Euler and Clairaut also suggested important modifications to the exact inverse square law, while d'Alembert, Buffon, and, later, Euler, all referred to magnetic action between celestial bodies as a possible supplementary force.[30]

So the preservation of a pristine version of celestial mechanics was fraught with problems, whether involving force laws, the role of comets, or the natural philosophy of comets' appearances and tails. The construction of the 1759 return as a vindication of a Newtonian program in celestial mechanics involved a complex process of negotiation by astronomers, who were compelled to clarify the precise achievements of the past half century of cometography and then to show that the predictions generated by that program had now triumphed.

CASSINI'S DEFENSE

The specific problems associated with this task of defining and clarifying the 1759 return as a "success" are dramatized in a memoir of César-François Cassini (III) published in that year. As head of the team at the Observatoire de Paris, Cassini III took on himself the responsibility of defending the tradition of astronomical research that had flourished there under his father, Jacques, and grandfather, Jean-Dominique. His defense was explicitly directed against claims that the 1759 return implied a decisive victory for the celestial mechanics of supposedly Anglophile astronomers. In his memoir, Cassini III made three comments. First, he pointed out that both his father and grandfather had reported substantial errors in Newton's cometary theory; indeed, in 1737 Jacques Cassini (II) had announced a difference of 32 minutes in longitude in the position of that year's comet. The Observatory data, therefore, allegedly "astounded Astronomers by their conformity with observations." Second, Cassini III noted that there was nothing unusual in the "historic" method Halley had used to develop his prediction; on the contrary, "I say that this idea was that of all the Astronomers of his [Halley's] time; it is on this foundation that my grandfather announced the return of several Comets." Finally, Cassini III insisted that although Newton's theory indeed "put Halley in a state where he was able to construct his Table of observed Comets," by itself this fact should not compel any contemporary astronomer to accept the full implications of Newtonian celestial mechanics.[31]

Cassini III's remarks had much to commend them. In 1681 Jean-Dominique Cassini (I) had published a detailed analysis of the motion of the great comet of that year, sketching its orbit as a great circle around the Earth with a period of two and a half years. He gave a copy of his book to Halley, in Paris in the spring of 1681. Halley subsequently told Hooke that Cassini I had tried to show that the comet of 1680–81 was the same as both that of 1577 observed by Tycho and that of 1665. Halley expressed skepticism of Cassini I's model, but was unable to develop one of his own. For example, Halley failed to construct an adequate straight-line path; and he told Hooke that "'tis very remarkable that 3 Cometts should soe exactly trace out the same path in the Heavens and the same degree of velocity."[32] This was Halley's earliest contact with cometography, and it must have played a significant role in his own views on cometary returns.

Cassini I developed and revised his understanding of cometary returns in the first decade of the eighteenth century. He violently rejected the opinion of De la Hire that comets were merely meteorological phenomena. In 1699 and in 1702 he published analyses of further similar cometary elements, and he also encouraged Maraldi to compare contemporary comets in the same way. Cassini I argued in 1702 that "the work which we have begun to perform in this century on the comparison of comets has already had the consequence of closely predicting the path which a comet must follow after having observed it two or three times."[33] The programs of the Observatoire and of the English cometographers thus had made many close similarities. Like Halley, Cassini I pointed out that unknown physical causes beyond the Earth-Sun system might cause massive deviations of cometary paths. Like Halley and Lalande, too, Cassini I observed that comets' tails were accidents and thus capable of considerable changes that might prevent the same comet being recognized twice: "because of all these reasons, even when one had found the period of a Comet, one would not be able to answer by seeing it on its return."[34] Thus Cassini I's program of cometography was quite plausibly interpreted as effectively equivalent with that of Newton and Halley.

This attempt to establish an equivalence between French and English cometography became difficult only after the death of Cassini I in 1712. Troubles emerged precisely when French astronomers were faced with the detailed propaganda efforts of the English exponents of Newtonian cometography. The astronomers at the Observatoire, however, together with their ally Bernard de Fontenelle, found many ways of saving their own program from the English challenge. There seemed little reason considerably to modify a program that still bore striking resemblances to Halley's method. Even those most active in the promotion of Newton's optical theories in France, such as Malebranche's disciple Pierre Rémond de Montmort, remained perfectly satisfied with traditional cometography. Montmort visited England in 1700, when he met both Newton and Gregory, and again in 1715, when he witnessed Desaguliers's demonstrations of the optical trials and visited Halley's observatory. He also encountered the Cambridge mathematician Brook Taylor, to whom he sent hampers of champagne on his return to France. Nevertheless, in 1719 Montmort emphasized his loyalty to Cassini's program. The allies of Newton in Great Britain had heard that Montmort was writing a long manuscript attacking Newtonian astronomy. John Keill suggested to Taylor that the retrograde motions of comets, and their return in ellipses focused in the Sun, were key arguments against the theory of vortices. Taylor tried these arguments against Montmort, who, relying on the status of Cassini's views, answered bluntly: "I know with certainty that our best Astronomers, and those who are most involved in making observations, regard these assertions as dreams."[35]

Cassini II, for his part, by 1725 was prepared to contemplate cometary paths focused on the Sun, but he was not prepared to accept that retrograde comets argued against vortices. Cassini II suggested instead that such comets were actually orbiting around other stars; the comet of 1737, for example, which appeared to be orbiting the Earth, was possibly focused in some planet more distant than Saturn. Thus, all thirty-nine comets that Cassini II could list as being observed since 1472 might actually have a direct motion, in the same direction as the solar vortex: "This direction of motion is an invariable rule of nature," he argued in 1731.[36] Fontenelle wrote approvingly that "to make all the celestial bodies move in a vacuum in order to disembarrass oneself of the difficulty of cometary motions, is an expedient itself subject to terrible difficulties."[37] Even committed disciples of Newton's celestial mechanics, such as Bouguer, were still using rectilinear methods for saving cometary appearances in the 1730s.[38] It was therefore quite possible for Cassini III to state in 1759 that the career of French cometography over the previous sixty years revealed a continuous development of theories of motion that not only used the historic method of predicting returns but also had come to accept that orbits were focused in the Sun, and that this had been the commonsense approach at the Observatoire with no commitment whatsoever to Newtonian celestial mechanics being needed. Given this version of the history of cometography as it had been pursued at the heart of the French astronomical establishment, severe obstacles remained to be overcome before Lalande and his colleagues could present that history as a triumphant one for Newtonian celestial mechanics.

DELISLE AND THE
PARIS ASTRONOMERS

The propaganda work of 1759 was itself a consequence of the formation of the astronomical community in Paris. A key aspect of this formation had been the early contacts established with England and the communication of techniques and attitudes by such Anglophile savants to their followers in France. The dissemination of Newtonian techniques in France during the first half of the eighteenth century has been analyzed by Brunet and Metzger and, more recently, by Hall, Guerlac, and Greenberg.[39] Much of this work has emphasized the importance of early knowledge of Newton's optical theories and the significance of the debate on the figure of the Earth. Perhaps as a consequence, the means by which celestial mechanics emerged despite the opposition of the Observatoire and Fontenelle is less well understood.

Most commonly, the traditional view of the role of Maupertuis and his allies, notably the young Clairaut, in the expeditions to Lapland and Peru, has limited attention to the problems of geodesy and terrestrial gravitation.[40] Equally important, however, were early contacts with England on cometography and solar and lunar theory, by which means Halley's texts on comets were publicized in France. Detailed contacts with and visits to London were always crucial. In this respect, Maupertuis was typical rather than unique. He published a paper on differential calculus in the *Mémoires* for 1726, a paper that revealed the worth of his training by Guisnée, himself a pupil of Varignon. In 1728, apparently "already a Newtonian," Maupertuis went to London to see Maclaurin and Pemberton about the applications of fluxional analysis in mechanics. The key texts of 1732–33, together with anonymous reviews in the influential *Journal Historique*, which opened the campaign against the geodesic program of the Cassinis, were among the consequences of this early set of contacts with Britain. During the 1740s Maupertuis published extensively on the analysis of cometary motion and on the cosmological significance of comets, displaying a detailed grasp of a specific brand of cometography closely allied to and often publicized by English astronomy.[41]

Maupertuis was by no means alone in this career or in this level of commitment. In the 1740s, for example, Lalande's teacher, Le Monnier, worked unsuccessfully to propagandize for English cometography and celestial mechanics. Clairaut sent Euler copies of Le Monnier's definitive observations of the comet of the winter of 1743–44, though he warned Euler that cometary theory remained rudimentary at the level of computational technique.[42] Le Monnier imported Graham's transit instruments in 1741; he also issued editions of John Keill's *Institutions of Astronomy* (1746) and Halley's *Synopsis* (1743). In 1748 he went to London, subsequently traveling to Scotland to observe a solar eclipse with Short and Macclesfield. In his *éloge* for Le Monnier, Lalande commented acidly on his teacher's inveterate hostility to Lacaille and Delisle, and recalled that Le Monnier had broken off contacts with him when he, Lalande, went to work with Delisle in Paris. Nevertheless, Lalande also

recorded Le Monnier's very early work, in order to "dissipate the prejudice which still reigned in France about comets,"[43] even though the
effects of this work were blunted by Le Monnier's controversies with his
colleagues and by his insistence on the incompleteness and inaccuracy of
the tables Halley had provided.[44]

Similar problems were encountered earlier in the century by the
chevalier de Louville, a close ally of Delisle, whom he employed as an
instrument maker. Delisle and Louville were made members of the Académie in the same year, the former as a student and the latter as an associate astronomer. In 1715 Louville was a member of the key delegation
to London that witnessed Desaguliers's experiments on optics and visited
Halley, a crucial visit to Newtonian theory's subsequent career, since it
led to the propagation of optical theory in France. Louville was also the
first academician to print a memoir on Newton's celestial mechanics, in
1720, though, as Hall has pointed out, he found it necessary to attribute
the views of the English astronomers to the creative genius of Kepler
alone. Guerlac has also suggested that Louville was the anonymous
"chevalier" who as early as 1718 expressed his support for Halley's
cometography.[45]

Louville's colleague and Le Monnier's great rival, Joseph-Nicolas Delisle, was the chief proponent of this cometography, being in a position
in 1759 to rewrite the history of this research program and thus to assure its triumph. Like Louville, Le Monnier, and Maupertuis, Delisle
had early and important contacts with the English and, also like them,
paid an impressive visit to Britain at a key moment in his career. Delisle
committed himself to astronomy following the observation of a solar
eclipse at Paris in 1706, when he was eighteen years old. By 1712 he had
established his own observatory at the Palais de Luxembourg, and following his election to the Académie he was, in 1718, made professor at
the Collège Royale, where he lectured on the system of the world, succeeding De la Hire. The most significant aspect of his research program
before his departure from Paris for St. Petersburg in the summer of
1725 was his commitment to the construction of astronomical tables in
which the celestial mechanics of Newton would be compared directly
with the best existing observations.[46] Throughout these years, therefore,
Delisle sought to collate such observations from astronomers across Europe, to maintain the closest contact with the English, notably Halley,
and to distribute these tables to his correspondents. The network that
Delisle established was highly significant in the construction of a European-wide astronomical community, which was soon to become dominated by his own concerns for celestial mechanics and cometography.
This project, therefore, is the key to an understanding of the events of
1759, when Delisle and his colleagues Lalande, Clairaut, and Messier
dominated the proceedings at the Académie.

Delisle's initial work on this research program seems to have developed from Louville's 1715 trip to London. Soon after, Louville gave Delisle information about the endeavors of Halley, who completed the revision of his astronomical tables, including a new version of the *Synopsis,* in 1717. Delisle also closely read the second edition of the *Principia* (1713) and was given, by Louville, a copy of a "perpetual Ephemerides of the motions of the Moon in the same position with respect to the Sun."[47] In the summer of 1716, therefore, Delisle worked hard to complete his own version of a lunar and solar theory derived from this edition of the *Principia.* He wrote that he was convinced of the need for "physical hypotheses" for astronomy and dissatisfied with the English strategy of propagandizing for Newtonian celestial mechanics, since these investigators did not try to match theory with observations, "which has meant that our Astronomers have not been willing either to take the trouble to test it." As a preliminary, therefore, Delisle decided to calculate solar and lunar tables "uniquely using the conclusions which Mr Newton took from the observations following his theory of gravity"; these he completed by early 1717.[48]

He was also occupied in arguing against the French view that the optical distortions seen around planets were due to their atmosphere, suggesting instead, on the basis of Newtonian optics, that the distortions were diffraction effects. "This understanding seems to me to be very useful indeed for the perfection of astronomical observations and to make us more cautious in the use we make of these observations for the establishment of astronomical hypotheses."[49] The chief hypothesis he wished to promote was that contained in the *Principia* and extended by Halley, and he strenuously sought support from the government, including Bignon and the duke of Orleans. He told Teinturier in February 1717 that the duke had now agreed to subsidize his campaign, and that he had completed his astronomical tables with considerable difficulty. In April Delisle sought further help from Réaumur, a dominant figure at the Académie and, usefully, no ally of the Cassini group. In a manner that prefigured Maupertuis's appeal over the head of the Observatoire to the government for support for the Lapland expedition, Delisle lobbied Bignon and Réaumur by sending them copies of his tables and of his glosses on the virtues of English celestial mechanics.[50] "These are merely tables calculated following Newton's determinations. It is true that I needed to study his theory, which is fairly difficult, but, after all, I have done nothing but follow him." Once this support was secured, Delisle told Bignon, his astronomical program would yield rich results.[51]

Delisle was rewarded with the astronomy chair at the Collège Royale on De la Hire's death in 1718. He immediately began to establish contacts with Halley and Newton in London, and to open an assault on the power of Cassini II at the Observatoire. He asked correspondents such

as the army officer Chardeloup and the Königsberg astronomy professor Rast, who were visiting London to talk with Halley, to check
whether he had published observations of the eclipse of 1715 and to find
out "in what state is his abacus of the apparent motions of the Moon and
what else one can expect of the work of this indefatigable Astronomer."[52] Rast told Delisle that Halley had now finished and printed his
astronomical tables and had included in them a new version of the *Synopsis*. While Delisle did not propose to suppress his own tables, he waited
impatiently to see Halley's.[53] News of these tables also reached Antonio
Conti from Pierre des Maizeaux during 1720, who wrote that they "furnish a very beautiful demonstration of the principles of Mr Newton," including those of cometography. Des Maizeaux echoed Delisle's argument that it was now more important to investigate the astronomical
worth of these data than to indulge in "metaphysical speculations or lose
oneself in finding the cause or the nature of that attraction, which will
perhaps always be unknown, while it is only a question of effects, which
are visible and palpable." Both Delisle and Des Maizeaux saw their campaign as a hard struggle against "the force of prejudice and of habit."[54]
Louville's extraordinarily timorous essay on celestial mechanics of the
same year and Delisle's April 1720 manuscript on geodesy, an explicit
but private set of memoirs directed at Bignon to gain support for a survey that would replace that of the Observatoire, were utterly unsuccessful attempts in this arena,[55] as the Observatoire and the Académie
remained under the control of what Delisle considered his chief opponents. As early as autumn 1721, in fact, Delisle was already contemplat-
ing a journey to St. Petersburg, and he wrote to the czarina's chief physician outlining his plans for a Russian tenure of office, where he might
join Bernoulli, Euler, and Hermann.[56]

During the mid 1720s, however, Delisle remained in western Europe
and worked actively in propagandizing the English version of celestial
mechanics. He told the Dutch astronomer Nicolaus Struyk that Halley
was "as great a Geometer as an Astronomer."[57] Struyk answered that at
that moment (the spring of 1722) he was engaged on correcting the
more spectacular errors in the cometary sections of the *Principia*, since
his colleague 'sGravesande was about to print a new edition of the mas-
terwork. Struyk also told Delisle of the common complaint that Halley's
original version of the *Synopsis* had contained no indication of the methods used in the arithmetic calculus for computing the elements of the
parabolic path. Struyk and Delisle both hoped that the 1717 version
would be an improvement.[58] Struyk himself worked continuously on this
problem and in the spring of 1749 printed an extended table of eighteen
further cometary elements to add to those in the *Synopsis:* in this task the
extended network Delisle had established, which included the Jesuit

astronomers in Peking and elsewhere, was an invaluable resource. Delisle's own need for Halley's new work and the observations performed by many astronomers during the 1723 transit of Mercury, prompted Delisle's decision to travel to London in the summer of 1724.[59] This journey was crucial to his own astronomical program and, ultimately, to cometography.

The hopes that Delisle and his correspondents, such as Struyk and Rast, expressed about Halley's new printed tables, together with English cometography's comparative lack of impact in the first two decades after the appearance of the *Synopsis,* clearly demonstrate the insufficiencies of this initial version of Halley's work. For example, there is no indication that Halley's predictions of cometary returns drew any significant attention in this period. This is striking because, as we have seen, the astronomers at the Observatoire were taking such predictions seriously, and also because for protagonists such as Keill, Taylor, Montmort, and Des Maizeaux cometography was a vital resource in the establishment of Newtonian astronomy. Furthermore, the woeful lack of detail in Halley's presentation of his own techniques sustained these difficulties in confronting English astronomy. The excellent new instruments produced by Graham and his colleagues among the London instrument makers was also important: such instruments embodied many of the new astronomical techniques, and their availability in France would be a key advance for Newtonian celestial mechanics. This astronomy did pose a new set of questions for the French, including the need for an adequate lunar theory and for systematic observations of such events as the transit of Mercury. Delisle pointed out in February 1717 that "since Newton recognized more irregularities in the motions of the Moon than other astronomers accept, and attributes these irregularities to physical causes, such calculation reveals itself to be very lengthy and very complicated."[60] When he began direct contacts with Newton and Halley in the spring of 1724, Delisle soon impressed them with the accuracy of his calculations and data and quickly gained a fellowship in the Royal Society. As Newton told him in April 1724, "your own merits . . . impelled me to move your election into our Society."[61] In June 1724 Delisle, sending further observations of the total solar eclipse, announced his intention of visiting London. He left France at the end of August.[62]

DELISLE AND THE
ENGLISH ASTRONOMERS

While in London, Delisle toured the principal astronomers and instrument makers. He met Pound and Bradley, to whom he gave copies of his

observations of the Mercury transit. He went to the shops of Hadley and
of Senex, where he purchased an excellent planisphere. He asked Halley
to send him copies of any observations of Rooke and Towneley, and the
latest version of Flamsteed's *Historia Coelestis*. He was able to supply Halley with the fruits of his astronomical network, including eclipse observations by Louville, Laval, Kirch, and many others from Germany and
Italy. Most significantly, Delisle established close links with the Royal Society's bookseller Innys, acting as an intermediary between him and the
French. Delisle arranged to send Halley and Newton copies of the *Mémoires,* he promised to dispatch a copy of Varignon's *Nouvelle mécanique,*
and he hoped that when Halley's tables were ready for distribution he,
Delisle, could send copies to the French.[63]

Delisle's promotion of the work of both Halley and Varignon was
among the most important consequences of his visit. Varignon had lectured on mathematical physics at the Collège Royale until his death in
1722. Following 1713, via De Moivre, Varignon established very close
links with Newton and, like Delisle, was made a fellow of the Royal Society on Newton's direct nomination. This correspondence was an important aspect of the early mathematical and optical links with the English, and, so Guerlac has suggested, Varignon played a key role in the
production of a Paris edition of the *Opticks* in 1722.[64] During his journey
to London in 1724, then, Delisle proposed that the French and English
jointly produce an edition of the Newton-Varignon correspondence.
This was a bold but well-chosen suggestion. Fontenelle became involved
in the scheme on the French side, while Newton told Delisle that he
trusted him and Fontenelle to "publish what he thinks proper."[65] On Delisle's prompting, too, the Paris bookseller Claude Jombert sent the *Mémoires* and the works of Varignon and asked Newton himself to use his services to print any further tests "which have won you the admiration of
Europe."[66]

Delisle's talks with Halley were equally fruitful for the development of
exchanges with the English astronomers. There had been a rumor, according to Louville, that Halley himself would come to Paris in May
1724. Delisle himself corrected this notion, expressing his own admiration of the English reception: "throughout my life," he told Newton, "I
will keep the memory of the favorable welcome which you gave me when
I had the honor to see you in London."[67] On his return to Paris in October 1724, Delisle set about energetically propagandizing for Halley
and his colleagues. He received observations made by the Jesuit astronomers at Peking of the great comet of 1723 and immediately sent them to
Halley with the comment that "you will have no trouble making them fit
the path which Mr. Bradley gave for this comet, following his own obser-

vations. I am waiting impatiently for this occasion to make the theory of
Mr. Newton prevail over the prejudices of this country."[68]

In the same month as his return from England, Delisle set out the superiority of the work of Halley and of Bradley, "a young astronomy professor at Oxford who gives great hopes of what he will perform in astronomy some day."[69] He explained to the mathematics professor at
Ingolstadt the great virtues of English celestial mechanics. Cassini's
tables were nothing but "a great mystery," and those of Delisle's prede-
cessor De la Hire, being constructed on a purely empirical basis, were
worthless. Delisle wrote of his own attempts, which were "better than all
those which have yet appeared. . . . I have also taken care to construct
my tables upon a regular and uniform theory, as geometrical as it is
physical, which is that of the English." Delisle said he had gone to England to find out personally about the state of Halley's own tables and
having seen them in print had now abandoned the effort of printing his
tables of 1716, since Halley's, which included tables of the moons of
Jupiter and of Saturn and a revised version of the *Synopsis*, were "just
what I had expected."[70] Innys sent him an authoritative copy of these
tables in December 1724, and Delisle worked hard to publicize them and
to suppress the competition. He told Innys that he had successfully dissuaded the Paris booksellers from reissuing the tables of De la Hire, so
as not to damage the sales of Halley's. Jombert, for example, ordered
several copies of these invaluable texts. Delisle's endorsement of Halley's tables was nothing short of ecstatic: he told Nicasius that "the tables
of Mr. Halley represent the observations very exactly, and perhaps as
exactly as it is possible to represent them at the moment without making new discoveries or admitting new hypotheses, whence you can see
what advantage Astronomy might gain from the publication of these
tables, which will furnish Astronomers with means to make such new
discoveries."[71]

During the winter and spring of 1724–25, therefore, Delisle had
available to him in Paris the key text from England which he had sought,
as well as close contacts with Newton, Halley, and De Moivre about the
Varignon correspondence and the astronomical tables of planets, satellites, and comets. He argued forcefully against the views of astronomers
such as the Dane Horrebow, who, together with Observatoire theorists, still espoused the hypothesis of vortices.[72] Delisle gently deflated
Horrebow's proud boast that his *Clavis Astronomiae* used "physico-
mathematical causes" to demonstrate the "truth and the nature of vortices." By February 1725 Delisle was entirely prepared to construct a new
research program on the motions of the Moon, the planets, and the comets that would use the emblematic status of Halley's tables to win converts

to English celestial mechanics. However, before the end of the year Delisle had been dispatched to St. Petersburg, and all these plans were
suspended.[73]

THE RUSSIAN EXILE

Delisle's sojourn in Russia has normally been interpreted as the voluntary and comfortable exile of a discontented French Newtonian.[74] There
is little indication that Delisle was content to leave Paris, however, and he
was always keen to return. His absence from Paris obviously did have important consequences for the career of celestial mechanics and cometography there. The principal resource, Halley's *Synopsis* and tables,
was certainly not widely distributed in France, despite Delisle's sterling
efforts in 1724–25—which explains Delambre's much later comment
that in the 1740s Halley's methods were still almost unknown.[75] The key
debates of the 1730s centered on geodesy, not cometography, and there
was little response to the treatises of Le Monnier and Chéseaux produced on the occasion of the comets of 1742–44, or to the new French
edition of Halley. Thus only *after* Delisle's return to Paris in the summer
of 1747 did Halley's cometography again receive detailed attention in
France, notably from Clairaut, Delisle himself, and the other commentators on Bevis's Latin edition of Halley's tables, which finally appeared
in 1749. We shall see that Delisle himself played a very important role in
the French response to Bevis, also producing the decisive *Lettres sur les
Tables astronomiques de M. Halley* in the same year.[76]

During his stay in Russia, however, Delisle did attempt to develop the
program in celestial mechanics and cometography he had outlined in
1717–24 in Paris. He directed the construction of the observatory at the
St. Petersburg Academy, coordinated observations of eclipses and transits with observers in Germany and Russia, and supervised a regular
set of lectures at the Academy on celestial mechanics. For example, in
March 1728 he debated in public with Daniel Bernoulli on the relation
of observational astronomy to the proof of the Earth's motion. Delisle
told his audience of the problems of parallax observations and reassured
them of the theological propriety of the heliocentric system: "Scripture
itself teaches us that God gave the world as a subject for disputes
amongst men."[77] He also reminded them of the significance of English
accomplishments in astronomy. As Boss has pointed out, Delisle played a
leading role in (unsuccessful) Russian efforts to emulate the French expeditions to determine the figure of the Earth during the 1730s; he has
also noticed that Delisle "appears to have lost faith in vortices at a remarkably early date."[78] In fact, the evidence suggests that Delisle never

placed any faith in such views of astronomical theory and practice. He told the Academy of Halley's demolition of the claims made by Cassini I about parallax observations, "This is a right of reply which the English astronomers exercise over the French."[79]

Despite these exercises in campaigning for English celestial mechanics, Delisle by no means occupied a secure or a welcome place in St. Petersburg. It is misleading to suggest, as a recent historian has stated, that in Russia Delisle "was accorded all the scope and all the money he needed for his research."[80] On the contrary, Delisle's initial task in Russia was as an expert delegate and informant for the French state. Most of his work in Russia was devoted to extensive surveys of the empire, involving cartography, geodesy, and natural history. He was the son of a geographer and he employed his brother, Louis, on several expeditions into the north, work that resulted in the completion of the great Russian Atlas in 1745.[81]

His letters back to Paris sent soon after his journey to St. Petersburg reveal the character of the difficulties Delisle encountered in reconciling the projects in the Russian survey and in astronomy. In May 1729 he told the navy minister Maurepas of the enormous difficulty in procuring instruments for his observatory. By January 1730 Delisle had still heard nothing of his detailed instructions from France. He had already experienced severe conflicts with the academic chancellor, Schumacher, who was later to lead real organized opposition to Delisle. Now Delisle heard that Maraldi, head astronomer at the Paris Académie, had died. Delisle had always been ambitious for this post and had even suggested to his ally Louville that Louville should become an honorary academician there so that Delisle himself could become a pensionary academician. He was now furious to learn that Maurepas and Bignon had dissuaded the Académie from replacing Maraldi with himself on the grounds of his absence in Russia. Delisle told Bignon that he had gone to Russia only on the orders of the government and on condition that he would not have to stay longer than four years. He reminded Bignon that he was in Russia purely for the interests of the French government and that the government had promised to preserve Delisle's place at the Collège Royale and to pay the residue of his salary to his family. "Now that because of the death of M. Maraldi there is a vacant astronomy place at the Académie, it is no longer convenient for me to remain in this country beyond the four years of my engagement";[82] this was especially true since Delisle said he had had considerable difficulty in switching from his program in astronomy to that which the French required. Bignon answered tactfully that Maraldi had in fact been replaced by the seventy-year-old Jacques Lieutaud, who would in any case probably die before three years were out, and he reminded Delisle that he was still committed to a further three-year term in Russia. Lieutaud did die in 1733, but Delisle did not return.[83]

Delisle received a series of orders to remain in Russia, and he struggled there until he left in 1747. When he went to Siberia to observe the Mercury transit in May 1740, for example, Schumacher and others led violent attacks on his work. In April 1743 Struve told Euler in Berlin that Delisle believed Euler was trying to attract astronomers away from Russia to Berlin. Euler denied this charge, but the following September, after the establishment of a committee to reform the St. Petersburg Academy, Delisle was still trying to leave. Schumacher attacked him because he had communicated astronomical observations to foreign observers, and Delisle was to receive no salary from 1742 onward. His efforts to leave were ambiguous and frustrated and his relationship with his correspondents irregular and disrupted.[84] In February 1744, Euler told Delisle that it would be splendid if he could come to Berlin from St. Petersburg to help handle the reestablishment of the observatory there, for which the Prussians had ordered "excellent instruments from England." But Euler thought it unlikely that Delisle would be released, since "under your care the St. Petersburg Observatory has acquired such a great reputation that one cannot expect you will be given permission to leave, until your place is filled by a worthy successor, which will be a very difficult and perhaps completely impossible matter."[85]

Meanwhile, however, Delisle was careful to limit the distribution of his own crucial observations, notably those of the comets of 1742 and 1744. Delisle told Euler not to show these observations to anybody "until I have corrected them and calculated them more exactly, and until I have myself derived the consequences which can be deduced from them."[86] Euler agreed: "I promise you in good faith that I will conceal your observations from everyone and above all from those you warn me about," the latter being the colleagues of Delisle in St. Petersburg, including the German astronomer Heinsius, with whom Delisle had broken contact at least three years before.[87] His contacts with Paris were also unreliable, partly because of his difficulties with the ministry and partly, so he complained to Euler in the summer of 1742, because he relied on his sister for information (for example, about Clairaut's work on Bradley's theory of aberration), and Delisle's sister "does not understand these matters at all."[88] Indeed, when Delisle left St. Petersburg in the summer of 1747, the Academy's president Razumovsky banned all academicians from communicating by any means with the obstreperous Delisle. Because this ban applied even to Euler, it completely disrupted Delisle's crucial communciation network.[89]

It is therefore a caricature to portray Delisle's sojourn in Russia as a triumphant success for status and patronage or a propaganda victory for Newtonian celestial mechanics. Instead it represented little more than a failed intelligence mission on behalf of the French government and a series of bitter struggles with the authorities at St. Petersburg to establish an autonomous program in astronomy. Even so, Delisle did retrieve some work from the wreckage, which most notably involved a significant exchange with Euler and, indirectly, with Clairaut, after the appearance of the comet of 1742. These exchanges showed clearly that any consensus in celestial mechanics, at least as represented by the views of Euler and his colleagues at Berlin, by no means accepted or perhaps comprehended the character of Halley's work and his techniques. In contrast, Delisle persistently clarified, refined, and policed what he took to be a Newtonian orthodoxy—an undertaking with considerable implications for the subsequent career of cometary theory, since it resulted directly in the contemplation of reasons for the perturbation of comets' paths and the massive refinement of methods for their computation.

DELISLE AND EULER IN THE 1740S

The comets of 1742 and 1744 aroused much discussion of cometography across Europe. Chéseaux's *Traité de la comète* and Le Monnier's *Théorie des comètes* were among the texts produced on the occasion. In the summer of 1742 Delisle sent Euler and Bevis observations of the comet that had appeared at St. Petersburg during February and March of that year. He used Flamsteed's *Atlas*, obtained from England, to calculate longitude and latitude, and he told Euler that he had tried the rectilinear method based on three closely spaced observations which Bouguer had propounded in 1733. Yet Delisle was extremely dissatisfied with this approach, even though it might enable a model to be constructed for all nineteen days that the comet was visible. "Since this theory cannot be true," he wrote, "I have begun to seek the true trajectory of this comet following the method and principles of Mr. Newton." Delisle soon discovered, though, that the texts by Halley and Newton contained insufficient information for this calculation to be completed with any ease. Delisle therefore asked Euler "if you could find the means of resolving this problem more easily, by employing either a greater number of observations or else observations taken under peculiarly favourable circumstances."[90] With such a new method, Delisle would be able to deal with comets left out of the *Synopsis* and then predict their return, "which as you know we have not been able to do with as much certainty as we can predict the return and appearance of the planets after their exit from the rays of the Sun." On this occasion, Delisle also demanded news of Clairaut and the expeditions to Peru and Lapland. He wanted to know whether any French astronomers had been working on the comet.[91]

Euler answered swiftly that he had heard little from Paris or Clairaut. He also commented gratifyingly that Delisle's were the only observations he had received on which a calculation of the comet's path could be based. All current German observations were worthless. Most importantly, however, Euler sent Delisle the rudiments of a method he would present at the Berlin Academy in September 1742, in which he derived both a means of getting an approximate path from three observations and also a theorem that would give the time of motion through a parabolic orbit in terms of two radius vectors and the chord linking them.[92] There immediately followed a bitter dispute with Heinsius and Schumacher at the Academy. Delisle presented Euler's method and his own work at the St. Petersburg Academy in two sessions in August 1742 and May 1743. Heinsius apparently used the work presented there to make his own machine for a graphical calculation of the true path. Schumacher now charged that Delisle had been illegitimately reporting his work to foreign savants before presenting it to his colleagues in Russia, and in the autumn of 1743 broke off payments of Delisle's salary.[93]

Despite these battles, Delisle persisted in his efforts to work out an improved method of cometography, even while quite deliberately separating himself and the resources of his observatory from other astronomers at St. Petersburg. The dispute prompted the departure of Georg Krafft for Tübingen and of Heinsius for Leipzig, both in 1744. Delisle told Euler that he himself continued to "look at the sky almost always when it is clear to see if anything new appears."[94] In January 1744 this devotion paid off. Euler wrote to Delisle to tell him of a great comet visible in Berlin from 3 January as a third-magnitude star. The comet was approaching perihelion, and Euler expected much from Delisle's observations when it returned: "It is to be hoped that the astronomers, and above all you, Monsieur, will observe it most carefully, it will be possible for them to do this, since I flatter myself that I have carried the method of calculation so far as by its means to be able to determine its orbit, as long as I have four good observations."[95] Delisle replied to Euler's request on 3 March. He enclosed high-quality observations of the comet as seen from the observatory and graphically described the circumstances of its first sighting: on the evening of 16 January "the servant of M. Heinsius, whom he had sent into the city, told him on his return in the evening that he had noticed something extraordinary in the sky, upon which M. Heinsius realized that it was a comet and arranged for the discovery to be announced in the *Gazette* as having been made by him at $5^h\frac{3}{4}$ in the evening."[96] Because Delisle had waited until the stars were clearer, he saw the comet later but more accurately than his rival. In fact, Delisle commented waspishly on all his colleagues, noting Heinsius's erroneous calculation that the comet was moving toward the ecliptic as well as that printed at Hamburg about its perihelion. He also pointedly commented on Euler's reliance on low-quality observation at Berlin: "whatever state the Berlin Observatory is in, that could not prevent one determining with some precision the motion of the comet during the month it lasted." Delisle recommended a simple telescope of small size such as he used at St. Petersburg.[97]

Delisle spelled out his recommendations for improving observations of comets in a letter sent to Euler in July: "If there were a greater number of people who observed the sky, without doubt we would discover a greater number of comets, which, however feeble, would not fail to contribute to the progress of astronomy; this has made me think of constructing a kind of glass which, by covering a space of 3 or 4 degrees in the sky, could serve to run over the whole visible extension of the heavens in very little time."[98] This remark, together with Euler's response to Delisle's observations, represents the initiation of a new phase in cometography. Delisle's proposal eventually culminated in the sustained cometographic program of his student and collaborator Messier from 1758, whereas Euler's work began the transformation of Halley's vague techniques into an analytic method for computing cometary paths.[99] Unlike Delisle, Euler was able to maintain direct links with the French. While Delisle complained to Euler that he had received no observations from Paris, Euler was in close touch with Clairaut, receiving from him observations made by Cassini II and by Chéseaux, collated for Clairaut by Le Monnier. In April 1744 Euler sent Clairaut the theory of the comet's motion he had already sent Delisle, and Clairaut arranged for it to be read at the Académie.[100] Clairaut and Delisle both heard of the completion of Euler's great *Theoria Motuum Planetarum et Cometarum*, the first analytic treatment of cometary motion. Although Clairaut was intrigued by Euler's remarks on the possible perturbations of the comet's motion by the planets, Delisle was more anxious than ever to forestall others learning of the new analytic technique Euler had developed for handling four observations of the comet. Euler identified planets with comets, distinguishing them solely by the shape of their orbits. Delisle claimed that this technique was entirely due to his own initial suggestions, and he hoped that Euler would now extend this program to larger numbers of comets.[101] Euler and Delisle, however, soon encountered fundamental problems in their alternative interpretations of cometography.

These problems centered on three vital issues of technique and theory, all derived from varying assumptions about the character of comets. First, Delisle argued—against Euler—that Halley's use of a parabolic orbit for all comets was merely an approximation and a preliminary to the application of the "historic" method. Second, Delisle implied that no approach based on observations made in one passage of a comet would as yet allow astronomers to determine any definite shape for the orbit. Finally, he suggested the urgent need for a radical improvement in the quality and number of cometary observations performed across Europe. Delisle presented all three issues, which were of key importance in the work of 1758–59, in a lecture at the St. Petersburg Academy in December 1744, extracted from a memoir entitled *Nouvelles considérations sur la théorie des comètes* (later included in expanded form in Delisle's lengthy commentary on Halley's astronomical tables, which was published in France in 1749).[102] Euler, in contrast, had his attention focused on cometary perturbations and hence the likely errors to which successive passages would be subject. This work, as we shall see, was then incorporated into his research on aether resistance in the heavens. Such resistance was an obstacle to cometography that both Delisle and his allies such as Lalande worked hard to remove.

The debate with Euler began in September 1744, soon after Delisle received information about Euler's new *Theoria*. Delisle asked Euler for the observations by his colleague at Berlin, the astronomer Johann Wagner, made of the comet of the winter of 1742–43.[103] After some confusion on Euler's part about the identity of this earlier comet, Euler told Delisle that Wagner's observations, just like those he had made at Berlin in January 1744, were of rather low quality because of the terrible state of the Berlin Observatory. Nevertheless, Euler felt confident enough to apply his new method to Wagner's data, deriving an extremely divergent hyperbola for its orbit. Euler then told Delisle, significantly, of the consequences of this result for Halley's research program: "Those English gentlemen, who in their method suppose that the orbits of all comets are parabolic, would be able to discover nothing. While most comets move in orbits closely approaching parabolas, nevertheless I see no impossibility in there being some which move in hyperbolas or ellipses very different from the parabola, and I suspect that Mr. Halley fairly detectably deceived himself with respect to certain comets, which he calculated on the parabolic hypothesis."[104] Euler told Delisle that his new method allowed one to tell conclusively from one transit which conic was followed by a given comet. He referred to the work of Johann Kies, a mathematics professor at Tübingen, who as a loyal disciple of Euler had begun applying this single-transit method to all the comets of the century. For the comet of the summer of 1729 observed by Cassini, Kies derived an ellipse of period just over twelve years and a perihelion distance of as much as 3.4AU. Euler boasted that with data from a second passage of such a comet he would calculate its ellipse "as well as in the case of a planet."[105] Delisle treated Euler's claims as crass misunderstandings of Halley's strategy, and he replied swiftly to correct what he saw as Euler's errors.

Delisle's main concern was to establish the parabolic hypothesis as a necessary assumption for the use of the historic method, *not* as a statement about the real paths comets followed. Halley, Newton, "and those who follow them only use the parabolic hypothesis for greater convenience, not believing that they can distinguish by one sole appearance of a comet if it is describing a section of a parabola or an ellipse." Delisle made two further remarks: first, he pointed out that Halley had "assured us that no one had ever seen a comet" in a hyperbolic path and said that Halley's words should be trusted, since they came from "such a great geometer and astronomer";[106] second, he insisted that all existing cometary observations were too vitiated to be adequate for assessing a path from one passage. Thus it was entirely conceivable, as Euler had maintained for the one of 1743, that this comet followed a hyperbolic path.

Nevertheless, Delisle used this point to challenge all previous models of cometary paths. Kies made the 1729 comet travel in an ellipse, while Bouguer had given it a hyperbolic track; Kies had suggested a period of over twelve years, while Cassini II had estimated ten years and Nicasius six and one-half. Delisle himself had also worked on this comet, assuming a parabolic approximation, as he believed the true Halleyan approach demanded. Any residual errors resulting from this approximation Delisle attributed to errors in star tables and in observations. "I believe that my calculations prove that this Comet described a parabola, or a curve so approaching it that one could not distinguish it from these observations alone."[107] Delisle showed that the same problem had troubled Euler and Wagner's work on the comet of 1743. He quoted work he had received from Olof Hjorter and Anders Celsius in Sweden, who had applied a parabolic model to this comet "without one minute's error,"[108] and that of Bradley and Halley performed on the comets of the previous century and of 1723. With all this evidence that a parabola could always be used for a single passage, Delisle now insisted that "I have trouble believing that at the moment anyone can demonstrate, from the observations of a single appearance, that it described an ellipse or a hyperbola rather than a parabola."[109] Once a parabolic orbit had been constructed, moreover, the historic method could then be applied.

Euler was only partly impressed by these strictures. With regard to the specific observations, he told Delisle in October that Wagner had detected massive errors in the path for the 1743 comet, that Kies now agreed the orbit of the 1729 comet was a parabola, and that the initial model for that comet was false because he had used insufficiently accu-

rate figures for a comet so displaced from the Sun. However, Euler repeated his claim about the practicality of using observations taken from a
single transit, and he referred Delisle to the copy of the *Theoria* he had
just sent to Schumacher. Most importantly, Euler insisted that the parabola could be accurate if and only if the *latus rectum* of the orbit were
exactly four times greater than the perihelion distance. The 1743 comet
could not be parabolic, therefore, since for that comet this ratio was
more than ten.[110]

Delisle answered in January 1745, enclosing a copy of his treatise presented to the St. Petersburg Academy in the autumn. He still insisted on
the need for greater numbers of truly accurate cometary observations,
and he cited as an example the worrying differences between the parabolic orbits he and Kies had now derived for the comet of 1729. So he
remained skeptical about Euler's approach, which, he held, "may not always be sufficient in practice because of the small number of terms you
use." Euler had not "proceeded with sufficient precision in performing
the other astronomical and trigonometric calculations." Delisle repeatedly affirmed the virtues of the strategy he learned in England: it was
always better to use "the general tables calculated by Mr. Halley 40 years
ago which give all the necessary precision with all possible ease."[111]

The 1742–45 exchange between Euler and Delisle had dramatic
effects. Not only did it show Delisle how much remained to be achieved
before the combination of the parabolic hypothesis, the historic method
of retrodiction for elliptical paths, and a European-wide network of
cometography could be established, but it also allowed Euler to integrate
the problems of comets into his existing research program in celestial
mechanics. Delisle had convinced him that the fundamental problem for
comets was in fact that of predicting returns by estimating successive
cometary appearances through application of the parabolic hypothesis.
But Euler realized at once that such a strategy was intimately connected
with his work on perturbing factors, variables that might affect all celestial motions and that, as he began to argue in the mid 1740s, would destroy the exactitude of Newton's original scheme. Euler's claim was dramatically evinced in his analysis, initiated following Euler's contacts with
Clairaut in 1744, of aether resistance and its application to the comet of
1682.

In August 1744 Clairaut told Euler that he was proposing to extend
his analysis of Newton's celestial mechanics to cope with troubles that
plagued the results of the Lapland and Peru expeditions. In particular,
Clairaut wrote of severe difficulties in the treatment of the motion of the
lunar nodes in the *Principia*.[112] Euler presented his remarks on Clairaut's
work at the Berlin Academy in October 1744, and as Waff has shown,

the two men began a long-drawn-out exploration of the difficulties of solar and lunar theory as analyzed by Newton.[113]

Just as Delisle began his exchanges with Euler on the problems of the parabolic hypothesis for comets, Euler was also starting his project to test the validity of the Newtonian theory in the mechanics of planets and satellites. Between the spring of 1745 and early 1746, Euler and Kies worked together to produce a revised set of lunar and solar tables, which they printed in December 1745.[114] Thus when Delisle pointed out the considerable differences between the parabolic models derived for the comet of 1729, Euler responded at once that these might well be due to his use of these new tables: "I believe that the difference in our results comes mainly from the theory of the Sun; I have made use of tables that I have established myself, in which I have taken account of the effects of the Moon, which according to Newton's theory must a little disturb the motion of the Earth."[115] Delisle wanted to know whether these tables were those Euler had used in his *Orbitae Solaris Determinatio,* printed at St. Petersburg in 1740, and expressed his doubt whether these revisions could have a measurable effect on the positions of comets.[116] But Euler answered in May that the new tables were very different and that his successes in lunar theory and in establishing the Earth's orbit had shown that the Earth's eccentricity and period had changed considerably. These changes were particularly relevant for comets with long periods and whose returns would take place over very long times. Euler announced that the computation of exact cometary paths was a matter of urgency. Yet, Euler also gave Delisle a significant warning: the resistance of the interplanetary aether, he now suggested, "could bring some changes to the motion of planets and comets," thus shortening the periodic times of planets and comets and altering their eccentricities. The most "convincing" demonstration of these changes, according to Euler, was precisely that derived from the shortened periods of the comet of 1682: "the time from its first appearance to the second exceeds by almost one year that from the second to the third."[117] Euler's comment made aether resistance and the change in successive periods a powerful threat to the cometography Delisle and his allies sought to develop.

Euler was preoccupied by the failure of Newton's celestial mechanics throughout the period from 1745. So was Clairaut, as well as his inveterate enemy d'Alembert.[118] In the spring of 1746, Euler told Delisle of the imminent appearance of a collection of his memoirs, including detailed assaults on Newtonian optics and celestial mechanics. The most significant of these texts was an analysis that showed a progressive diminution in the length of the mean tropical year and argued forcefully that this change was an effect of aether resistance. "So in the case of comets it must be the case that this effect is very considerable, and this is actually found in Halley's tables of comets."[119] Euler also reminded Delisle of Halley's work of the early 1690s demonstrating the secular acceleration of the Moon, an effect Halley himself had privately attributed to aether resistance.[120]

Although Delisle still believed that this change and resistance would be difficult to demonstrate from unreliable ancient data, by the summer of 1747, when Delisle left Russia, both Clairaut and Euler were ready to announce publicly their deliberate challenges to the exact validity of an inverse square law. In June, then, Euler presented his argument in a public session at the Berlin Academy, suggesting a range of factors that could perturb the law and commenting that since gravity had a mechanical cause it could neither follow this law exactly nor extend to great distances.[121] In September Clairaut deposited his own memoir on this problem in Paris, which he was later to publish as *Du système du monde dans les principes de la gravitation universelle*.[122] Clairaut told Euler that he was "charmed to see that you think as I do about Newtonian attraction. It seems to me to be demonstrated that it does not suffice to explain the phenomena."[123]

The relevance for the theory of comets was that both Clairaut and Euler doubted whether the inverse square law extended accurately as far as Jupiter or Saturn, let alone the enormous distances of cometary aphelia—and Euler certainly worked hard to establish the reality of major physical perturbations for the unimpeded motion of comets through space. At the end of September he told Clairaut that, given the secularly demonstrated perturbations of the motion of the lunar nodes, the motion of Saturn and Jupiter, and the change in the tropical year, "I do not doubt that a certain disturbance of the forces which are supposed in the theory must be the cause. This circumstance makes the vortices or some other material cause of these forces very probable to me." Thus, too, the disturbances of the superior planets and indeed the comets would be very considerable.[124] Even though Clairaut was not convinced by this argument for the vortices, both he and Euler were now to argue for a significant change in the principles of celestial mechanics. This action led to the notorious exchange between Clairaut and Buffon in Paris during 1748–49, and ultimately to a violent priority dispute with d'Alembert. Not until May 1749 was Clairaut able to show that the lunar theory could be saved, along with the exact inverse square law; nor was Euler convinced of this result until April 1751.[125]

The results of these researches of the late 1740s did not, however, dampen Euler's commitment to a series of supplementary physical causes, principally ethereal, which could have manifest effects on the periods of celestial bodies. His interest in this fluid was sustained by his independent research in optics and meteorology, which demonstrated to him that the aether transmitted light, that the Sun was responsible for the vibration of such an aether, and that phenomena such as auroras and comets' tails were effects of these actions. Such claims were published by Euler throughout the 1750s and 1760s, including the *Letters to a German Princess* of 1760.[126]

Euler's exchanges with Tobias Mayer in 1751–55 also showed the strength of his commitment to aether resistance, not to mention his inveterate hostility to English celestial mechanics. Euler insisted, and Mayer agreed, that gravity could not be an innate force. Euler claimed it to be magnetic in origin; d'Alembert had told him in the summer of 1748, during discussions of lunar theory, that the magnetic force that produced the variation of the compass might also trouble the Moon's motion.[127] While Mayer's work showed Euler that the Ptolemaic data on which his argument for secular acceleration was based could not be trusted and that magnetism was surely no adequate cause of gravitation, since there could be no active magnetic matter between the planets, Euler remained convinced that the inertial homogeneity supposed by the English was but a tendentious hypothesis, and in February 1754 he still told Mayer that "the resistance of the aether still appears to me to be well established and necessary."[128] Since Mayer had removed the evidence Euler was using from the changes in the periods of the Moon and the Sun, this belief must have relied primarily on just those cometary problems Euler had raised with Delisle ten years earlier.[129] This negative view of English cometography indicated Euler's overall attitude to English savants. In May 1755 he congratulated Mayer on the success his lunar tables had experienced in London at the longitude commission, commenting that "this nation is very late in giving foreign discoveries their proper right, yet because all tables constructed on the Newtonian theory have for so many years erred by over 5′ from the truth, English self-complacency could not stretch to such a point that the superiority of your tables could remain unknown."[130]

Euler's attitude was typical of the criticisms leveled at English celestial mechanics in the period between 1744 and 1755. His memoirs on cometary paths certainly influenced Johann Lambert, who read them in detail during 1755–57, before his crucial visit to Paris in the summer of 1758 to discuss the imminent return.[131] Euler also persuaded his Berlin colleague Franz Aepinus of the reality and power of the aether, as evidenced by Aepinus's August 1757 question "If the comet of 1682 were to approach the Sun in a straight line, could it be retarded a whole year because of the resistance of the aether?"[132] Aepinus still argued for such views when he went to St. Petersburg in 1757, and Condorcet and Bossut discussed similar consequences of aether resistance as late as 1766.[133] On

his return from Russia in 1747, Delisle began at once to campaign at the
Collège Royale and the new observatory at Cluny to transform the prediction of the return of the comet of 1682 into a crucial test for the worth
of his program in celestial mechanics. For this cause he recruited the
young astronomers Lalande and Messier.

PREPARATIONS FOR COMET HALLEY

During the winter of 1748–49 Delisle heard from Bevis of the imminent
publication of Halley's astronomical tables, together with precepts for
their use composed by Bevis himself. Bevis described the range of
troubles he was experiencing with Halley's executors and with the bookseller Innys. He was also involved in a dispute with Bouguer and La
Condamine over the publication of a translation of their report on the
expedition to Peru, which had been sent to Halley in 1738. Bevis was
furious when he discovered in August 1749 that Innys had issued Halley's tables, together with the new edition of the *Synopsis*, but without the
necessary accompaniment of Bevis's own *Uranographia*.[134] Delisle expressed his sympathy in a letter of 22 October in which he warned Bevis
not to trust his enemy Le Monnier with care of the French edition of
Halley: "It appears to me that it would be most convenient if I did this
rather than anyone else; not only because Mr. Halley when giving me his
tables 25 years ago explained to me how to use them, but also because
since that time I have made continual use of them and have added to
them several tables which are necessary." Le Monnier, by contrast, was "a
man to take on anything, although often with less basis than others."[135]
By December, Delisle had completed a commentary on Halley's tables
and was preparing to send a copy to London for Bevis and a full edition
in Paris to preempt Le Monnier's plans. Thus Delisle's commentary was
designed both to clarify and improve Halley's method and to establish
his own rights of control over the proper interpretation of Halley's
methods and data.[136]

　　Delisle's *Lettres sur les Tables astronomiques de M. Halley* appeared in late
December 1749. Delisle commented in detail on the importance of these
tables for the career of celestial mechanics. He listed previous efforts, including those of Horrebow and Nicasius, which he had learned of during the 1720s, and explained that the delay in the appearance of Halley's
text was due partly to the disputes between Bevis and Halley's heirs but
principally to Halley's wish to incorporate corrections after the transit of
Mercury and further observations of the Moon.[137] Delisle condemned
his colleagues who had not deduced their tables from a theory such as
that of Newton, and he pointed out the extreme importance of the com-

ments Halley had made on the changes in the mean motions of Jupiter and Saturn due to their mutual gravitation. Delisle reported that Halley estimated an acceleration of Jupiter by 57' and a deceleration of Saturn by 2°19' in one thousand years. Halley, "the greatest astronomer of his time as Newton was its greatest Geometer," had also worked on the secular acceleration of the Moon, and on Newton's suggestion had added $1\frac{1}{2}'$ to the Moon's longitude to compensate for this effect.[138] Delisle repeatedly referred to his own privileged access to Halley in 1724, when Halley had given him copies of the uncorrected data on condition that it be given to no other French astronomer or used by them. Delisle also recalled his own 1716 tables, the very first, he claimed, that were calculated "in exact conformity with the theory of Mr. Newton."[139] He also pointed out the intense significance of the changes in motion of the major planets and the Moon for the debates raging in the Académie about Newtonian celestial mechanics. Delisle saw no reason to use Euler's notion of aetherial resistance, but he did draw attention to the relevance of the mutual attractions of the superior planets for the computation of any perturbing force acting on other planets or the comets.[140]

Delisle's gloss on the new version of the *Synopsis* was his first public pronouncement on the key role he believed the return of the 1682 comet would play in the career of Newtonian astronomy. "What is most interesting is that in this way we can approach the hope of seeing this comet again in 8 years from now; which will be the greatest proof one could have of the certainty of the theory of Mr. Halley about comets."[141] This pronouncement was in stark contrast, for example, to the views printed by Chéseaux in 1744 that the comet might conceivably be mistaken for two such bodies, both having periods of about 151 years. Delisle now claimed that Halley had had the resources to produce a perfectly accurate prediction but had had insufficient opportunity. He therefore announced his own intention of so doing: "by this means Astronomers will be better prepared to observe it at its next appearance in order to confirm by their observations one of the most beautiful parts of our knowledge of celestial motions."[142]

We have already noted Euler's continuing commitment to the effects of aethereal resistance on the period of the 1682 comet. As Waff has argued, however, there was no consensus whatsoever on the character of the prediction Halley had made. Euler's model of secular acceleration prompted the view that the comet would return in 1757, and indeed the comet of September 1757 was at one stage assumed to be that of 1682. In England, Thomas Stevenson in 1758 suggested that astronomers might in fact be dealing with two comets of periods of about 151 years.[143] Thus Delisle perceived his own task as the organization of French astronomers around a view of the comet that would act as a key test for Halley's prediction and, equally important from his own point of view, unambiguously preempt all other rivals in confirming this prediction. Delisle supervised the work of his assistant Charles Messier, first at the Navy-run Cluny Observatory and later, after the end of March 1759, at the Collège Louis-le-Grand, carefully suppressing his team's early observations of the comet's first appearance.[144] His other student, Jérôme Lalande, worked as calculator, together with Mme. Lepaute, to help Clairaut derive a precise version of the cometary prediction.[145] Delisle remained as faithful as he could to his version of Halley's method. In Messier's words, Delisle "thought he must proceed in a different manner from what other astronomers had done, to find out in what part of the heavens it must be sought. He considered that it was not necessary to know its place throughout its whole course, but only at the first moment of its appearance."[146] It was therefore crucial for Delisle to establish, by an ingenious application of the historic method, just when the comet would be first visible and to direct Messier to look in that part of the sky.

This project demanded yet another thorough review of all previous sightings of the comet. Delisle compiled such a survey in the summer of 1757, wherein he pointed out that Halley and Newton had used eleven observations made by Flamsteed at Greenwich between 30 August and 19 September 1682. Halley had initially handled these observations with his parabolic hypothesis, then corrected the apparent places when he introduced an ellipse. Delisle therefore reworked all of Halley's original calculations based on Flamsteed's data as he found them in the two versions of the *Synopsis*, in the *Principia*, and in Flamsteed's *Historia Coelestis*, whereupon he sought to reconcile these data with the observations of Cassini I, De la Hire, Picard, and Kirch, which he had amassed from his correspondents in Germany and France. Delisle concluded that since in 1682 the comet had become visible twenty-four days before perihelion, and in 1607 thirty-three days before perihelion, he should calculate parabolic paths for the comet on the assumption that it would be visible twenty-five or thirty-five days before perihelion. He prepared a star chart of the northern hemisphere with an exterior and interior oval for these two respective assumptions, which he handed to Messier to guide his watch.[147]

Although Delisle reported on this project in the *Journal de trévoux* in November 1757, he revealed his chart to no one save Messier and forbade Messier to disclose his observations. When a comet finally appeared near λ-Pisces on the evening of 21 January, however, it was very far from Delisle's proposed place in Capricorn. Nevertheless, what was important was the dispute over the meaning of the comet's return.[148]

In the autumn of 1757 Lalande and Delisle had already worked hard to initiate a campaign that would make the comet's return count as a success for their celestial mechanics. Lalande, in a letter written on 15 October, published an estimated ephemerides for the comet in the same journal as Delisle; he also completed a paper on the secular equations of the planets. Lalande sneered at the suppositions of Euler and others about the spiraling of the Earth into the Sun and the effects of aether resistance on the superior planets, saying that "this acceleration of the Earth should already have led to a deadly consequence for humanity, in letting us know almost the time and the manner in which it must end."[149] Lalande then repeated these results when he addressed the Académie on the occasion of the comet's return in April 1759. Again he referred to Euler's unnecessary supposition and to the need for a deliberately analytic approach to the inequalities in periods due to the effects of the superior planets and the Sun. This analysis was achieved by Clairaut, whose celebrated prediction that the comet would reach perihelion in mid April 1759 was announced in November 1758 and published in the *Journal des sçavans* in January 1759.[150]

THE MAKING OF THE COMET

The events of the first months of 1759, as well as the controversy that followed, can only be understood in the light of the previous decades of interpretation and struggle for the legacy of Halley's cometography. Delisle believed it crucial that he establish his group's ownership of the successful prediction, which must count as a mark against his rivals in Paris. He prevented Messier from publicizing the observations made from Cluny during January and February. Clairaut and Lalande were equally committed to this view of the return and emphasized even more than Delisle the specific accomplishments of their own calculations as opposed to those vague guesses available in Halley's tables. Their enemies such as d'Alembert and Le Monnier, already hostile to Delisle and Clairaut since the 1740s, continued this campaign when the comet appeared after perihelion on 1 April.[151] Messier and Delisle observed the comet from the observatory of Merville in the Collège Louis-le-Grand, since Cluny was too low to see the comet in the morning. The same day, Delisle heard from Heidelberg about the now-famous observation of the comet on Christmas Day 1758 by Palitzsch in Saxony. Others in Paris heard of this same sighting via a pamphlet by Delisle's old enemy Heinsius, printed at Leipzig in January 1759.[152] At the meetings of the Académie on 4 and 7 April, therefore, Pingré, Delisle, and Messier presented their version of the path and the discovery of the comet—which Delisle prudently delivered at Versailles on 5 April. By 18 April Delisle had drafted a long memoir on the comet that triumphantly displayed its return as a victory for his own research program. Lalande and Clairaut worked equally hard to spell out the character of this victory.[153]

Both Delisle and Clairaut were extremely careful, therefore, about the publicity they gave of the return and the prediction, and they both encountered severe problems in presenting this work as a success. Clairaut told Daniel Bernoulli on 10 April that some believed that Delisle and Messier had only known where to look because of the early news from Germany; as he put it, "there remain some large clouds over his report."[154] Clairaut himself had pondered whether or not to release the details of his prediction method when he made it the previous November, but apparently he believed it would be more effective propaganda for the "important and new verification of the Newtonian system" if he, together with Lalande and Lepaute, were to make a bold prediction without revealing the method they had used in estimating the perturbations due to the Sun-Jupiter and Sun-Saturn systems.[155]

Le Monnier insisted in an article in the *Mercure de France* that Clairaut's prediction had actually drawn observers' attention away from a search for the comet's first appearance in Pisces in December and January 1758–59, while Le Monnier and d'Alembert both argued that Clairaut had added little and Delisle nothing at all to Halley's original and vague conjecture.[156] Clairaut presented two long memoirs in his own defense at the Académie in 1758–59, and Lalande produced an entirely new edition of the *Synopsis* and Halley's other tables in the autumn. Lalande told his readers that, against the views of his critics, Clairaut was owed "the most beautiful proof which remained to us to provide for universal gravitation."[157] What was an error of thirty days in an interval of more than 151 years, of which less than $\frac{1}{200}$ part had been observed? Lalande printed extracts from these comments in the *Journal encyclopédique* in the summer.[158]

The debate initiated by the bold claims of Delisle and Clairaut was also connected with the politics of the *Encyclopédie*, since its opponents used the attacks on d'Alembert as ammunition against their enemy. D'Alembert and his allies alleged that Clairaut's prediction had been too vague and that Delisle's program had been shown to be ineffective. Clairaut answered that Halley's *Synopsis* had utterly failed to compute perturbations adequately or to tell the difference between the moment when the comet would be first visible and the moment when it would be reaching perihelion. The work of Delisle and Clairaut had made this distinction clear. Clairaut said that although he had given Halley credit for what was his, it was ludicrous to give him "the glory of having done everything and of having said everything about the Comet."[159] Only in September 1762, when Clairaut shared with Johann Euler a St. Petersburg prize for an essay on cometary perturbations, did d'Alembert relent in his offensive.[160]

What is genuinely revealing about the disputes that clouded the 1759 return, however, is the consensus they revealed. In the 1730s and 1740s, as Delisle and his colleagues had found, there was little comprehension and even less approval of Halley's cometography; most of its assumptions were questioned and some were utterly rejected, as the views of Euler, Bouguer, and Chéseaux illustrate. But in 1759, those who believed that Halley's program represented major and important advances stood ranged only against those who now stood convinced that all the triumph of cometography should be Halley's alone. This consensus was by no means a natural consequence of the appearance of the comet in January 1759. On the contrary, it had required painstaking and strenuous propagandizing and argument by astronomers such as Delisle during the previous half century.

NOTES

I acknowledge the generous research support of the British Academy. I would also like to thank John Greenberg and Craig Waff, whose comments were of invaluable help to me in preparing this paper.

1. Henry Pemberton, *View of Sir Isaac Newton's Philosophy* (London, 1728), 191, 192, 193, 194.

2. Isaac Newton, *De Motu Corporum in Gyrum*, in *Unpublished Scientific Papers of Isaac Newton: A Selection from the Portsmouth Collection in the University Library, Cambridge*, ed. A. R. Hall and M. B. Hall (Cambridge: Cambridge University Press, 1962), 283–85; *The Mathematical Papers of Isaac Newton*, ed. D. T. Whiteside (Cambridge: Cambridge University Press, 1967–80), 8:57–61, 58–60n.79.

3. Newton to Flamsteed, 19 September 1685, in *Correspondence of Isaac Newton*, ed. H. W. Turnbull et al. (Cambridge: Cambridge University Press, 1959–77), 2:419; "System of the World," in *Sir Isaac Newton's Mathematical Principles of Natural Philosophy and His System of the World*, trans. Andrew Motte (1729), ed. Florian Cajori (Berkeley: University of California Press, 1934), 615, 619, 629 (hereafter cited as *Principia* [Motte-Cajori]; Newton, *Mathematical Papers* 6:483 n.7, 485n.10, 498–504.

4. Halley to Newton, 28 September, 15 October 1695, in Newton, *Correspondence* 4:171–72, 176–78; *Correspondence and Papers of Edmond Halley*, ed. Eugene Fairfield MacPike (London: Taylor & Francis, 1937), 238; Royal Society, Gregory MSS 247, fol. 62.

5. *Isaac Newton's Philosophiae Naturalis Principia Mathematica: The Third Edition (1726) with Variant Readings*, ed. I. Bernard Cohen and Alexandre Koyré (Cambridge: Cambridge University Press, 1972), 721, 733, 756 (hereafter cited as *Principia* [Cohen-Koyré]).

6. Sara Schechner Genuth, "Comets, Teleology, and the Relationship of Chemistry to Cosmology in Newton's Thought," *Annali dell'Istituto e Museo di Storia della Scienza di Firenze* 10 (1985): 31–65; Simon Schaffer, "Newton's Comets and the Transformation of Astrology," in *Astrology, Science, and Society: Historical Essays*, ed. P. Curry (New York: Longwood, 1987), pp. 219–43.

7. Voltaire, *Elements of Sir Isaac Newton's Philosophy* (London, 1738), 329.

8. P.L.M. de Maupertuis, *Lettre sur la comète qui paroissoit en 1742*, in *Oeuvres* (Lyon, 1768), 3:241, 247.

9. Edmond Halley, "Astronomiae Cometicae Synopsis," *Philosophical Transactions of the Royal Society* 24 (1705): 1897; S. P. Rigaud, *Some Account of Halley's "Astronomiae Cometicae Synopsis"* (Oxford: Private printing, 1835), 3–23; P. Broughton, "The First Predicted Return of Comet Halley," *Journal for the History of Astronomy* 16 (1985): 125.

10. David Gregory, *Elements of Physical and Geometrical Astronomy* (London, 1715), 2:901. For the dating of these statements, see M. A. Hoskin, "The First Edition of Halley's 'Synopsis,'" *Journal for the History of Astronomy*, 16 (1985): 133.

11. Edmond Halley, *Astronomical Tables with Precepts Both in English and Latin* (London, 1752), sigs. Llll3–Tttt4. See Jérôme Lalande, *Tables astronomiques de M. Halley* (Paris, 1759), 39–40, 54–56.

12. Halley to Newton, 7(?) October 1695, in Newton, *Correspondence* 4:173–75; *Principia* (Cohen-Koyré), 588; Lalande, *Tables astronomiques*, 105; Halley, *Astronomical Tables*, sig. Ssss.

13. P. Le Monnier, *La théorie des comètes ou l'on traite du progrès de cette partie de l'astronomie* (Paris, 1743), 85.

14. J. B. Delambre, *Astronomie théorique et pratique* (Paris, 1814), 3:202; J. B. Delambre, *Histoire de l'astronomie au dix-huitième siècle* (Paris, 1827), 673.

15. Delambre, *Histoire de l'astronomie*, 466.

16. Ibid., 677; N. Lacaille, *Leçons élémentaires d'astronomie* (Paris, 1746), 243.

17. Delambre, *Histoire de l'astronomie*, 196, 757.

18. Richard Dunthorne, "Letter Concerning Comets," *Philosophical Transactions* 47 (1751): 281–88.

19. S. L. Chapin, "The Academy of Sciences During the 18th Century: An Astronomical Appraisal," *French Historical Studies* 5 (1968): 388n.52, discusses the work of Bailly and Messier.

20. Thomas Stevenson's letter is printed in *London Magazine* 27 (November 1758): 564; it is cited in Craig B. Waff, "The First International Halley Watch," Chapter 18 this volume.

21. Lalande, *Tables astronomiques*, 105–8.

22. Ibid., 104, 103, 108; Euler's work is attacked by Lalande in "Mémoire sur les équations séculaire," *Mémoires de l'Académie Royale des Sciences*, 1757 (pb. 1762): 413.

23. Lalande, *Tables astronomiques*, 114–15, 121.

24. See R. Taton, "Clairaut et le retour de la comète de Halley," in *Arithmos-Arrythmos: Skizzen aus der Wissenschaftsgeschichte*, ed. K. Figala and E. Berninger (Munich: Berninger, 1979), 253–74; T. L. Hankins, *Jean d'Alembert: Science and Enlightenment* (Oxford: Oxford University Press, 1970), 30–42.

25. Roger Long, *Astronomy* (Cambridge, 1764), 2:562–63.

26. Pemberton, *View of Newton's Philosophy*, 243–46; Richard Yate, "A New Theory of Comets," *Gentleman's Magazine* 13 (1744): 193–95; Sir John Clerk to Roger Gale, 8 April 1742, in *Family Remains of the Reverend William Stukeley, M.D.*, ed. W. C. Lukis (London: Surtees Society, 1882–87), 3:435–36; Colin Maclaurin to John Clerk, 23 March 1742, in *Collected Letters of Colin Maclaurin*, ed. S. Mills (Nantwich, Eng.: Shiva, 1982), 87; Long, *Astronomy*, 563; James Hill, *Urania* (London, 1754), s.v. "Comets"; J. L. Cowley, *Discourse on Comets* (London, 1757), 36; Richard Turner, *A View of the Heavens* (London, 1765), 20.

27. Craig B. Waff, "Comet Halley's First Expected Return: English Apprehensions 1755–1758," *Journal for the History of Astronomy* 17 (1986): 1–37, discusses Wesley; see also *Gentleman's Magazine* 47 (1777): 133n. and Simon Schaffer, "Authorized Prophets: Comets and Astronomers After 1759," *Studies in Eighteenth Century Culture* 17 (1987): 45–74.

28. Lalande, *Tables astronomiques*, 102.

29. Leonhard Euler, "A letter . . . Concerning the Gradual Approach of the Earth to the Sun," *Philosophical Transactions* 46 (1749–50): 205.

30. Ibid.; also Euler, "A Letter Concerning the Contraction of the Orbits of the Planets," ibid., 356–59, original in Euler to Wettstein, 20 December 1749, in *Die Berliner und die Petersburger Akademie der Wissenschaften im Briefwechsel Leonhard Eulers*, ed. A. P. Juskevic and E. Winter (Berlin: Akademie Verlag, 1959–76), 3:286–88. Euler's work on aether resistance is discussed in C. Wilson, "Perturbations and Solar Tables from Lacaille to Delambre," *Archive for History of Exact Sciences* 22 (1980): 93–103. Halley's work on the acceleration of lunar motion is discussed in Simon Schaffer, "Halley's Atheism and the End of the World," *Notes and Records of the Royal Society* 32 (1977): 33. See Craig B. Waff, "Universal Gravitation and the Motion of the Moon's Apogee: The Establishment and Reception of Newton's Inverse Square Law 1697–1749" (Ph.D. diss., Johns Hopkins University, 1975), chap. 2 and the texts in n. 140.

31. César-François Cassini, *Observations de la comète de 1531 pendant le temps de son retour en 1682 faites par Jean-Dominique Cassini* (Paris, 1759), 12–13; Jacques Cassini, "De la comète qui a paru aux mois de février, de mars et d'avril de cette année 1737," *Mémoires de l'Académie Royale des Sciences*, 1737 (pb. 1740): 176.

32. Halley to Hooke, 29 May 1681 in *Correspondence and Papers*, 51. Cf. Jean-Dominique Cassini, *Observations et réflexions sur la comète qui a paru au mois de décembre 1680 et aux mois de janvier, février et mars de cette année 1681* (Paris, 1681), 19–25; Halley to Hooke, 15 January 1681, in *Correspondence and Papers*, 48–50.

33. Jean-Dominique Cassini, "Comparaison des premières observations de la comète du mois d'avril de cette année 1702," *Mémoires de l'Académie Royale des Sciences*, 1702 (pb. 1704): 128. See Jean-Dominique Cassini, "Réflexions sur les observations [de Maraldi]," *Mémoires de l'Académie Royale des Sciences*, 1702 (pb. 1704): 111.

34. Jean-Dominique Cassini, "Du retour des cometes," *Mémoires de l'Académie Royale des Sciences*, 1699 (pb. 1702): 40.

35. On Montmort, see H. Guerlac, *Newton on the Continent* (Ithaca, N.Y.: Cornell University Press, 1981), 134–35; Taylor to Keill, 29 April 1719, in Newton,

Correspondence 7:37; Conti to des Maizeaux, 1 April 1718, in ibid., 6:441*n*.8; Brook Taylor, "Réponse à la dissertation de M. Montmor," *Europe Savante* 9 (1719): 83–134, cited in ibid., 7:150*n*.10.

36. Jacques Cassini, "Du mouvement véritable des comètes à l'égard du soleil et de la terre," *Mémoires de l'Académie Royale des Sciences*, 1731 (pb. 1733): 346.

37. Bernard de Fontenelle, "Histoire," *Mémoires de l'Académie Royal des Sciences*, 1725 (pb. 1727): 97.

38. Pierre Bouguer, "De la détermination de l'orbite des comètes," *Mémoires de l'Académie Royal des Sciences*, 1733 (pb. 1735): 332.

39. P. Brunet, *Introduction des théories de Newton en France* (Paris, 1731); H. Metzger, *Newton, Stahl, Boerhaave et la doctrine chimique* (Paris: Felix Alcan, 1930); A. R. Hall, "Newton in France: A New View," *History of Science* 13 (1975): 233–50; Guerlac, *Newton on the Continent;* J. Greenberg, "Mathematical Physics in Eighteenth Century France," *Isis* 77 (1986): 59–78.

40. See S. L. Chapin, "Expeditions of the French Academy of Sciences, 1735," *Navigation* 3 (1952): 120–22; C. J. Nordmann, "L'expédition de Celsius et Maupertuis en Laponie," *Cahiers d'histoire mondiale* 10 (1966): 74–97; Harcourt Brown, "From London to Lapland: Maupertuis, Johann Bernoulli I, and *la Terre Applatie*," in *Literature and History in the Age of Ideas*, ed. C.G.S. Williams (Columbus, Ohio: Ohio State University Press, 1975), 69–94; R. Taton, "Sur la diffusion des théories newtoniennes en France: Clairaut et le problème de la figure de la terre," *Vistas in Astronomy* 22 (1978): 485–509.

41. Maupertuis, *Discours sur les differentes figures des astres* (Paris, 1732); idem, "Sur la figure de la terre, et sur les moyens que l'astronomie et la géographie fournissent pour la déterminer," *Mémoires de l'Académie Royale des Sciences*, 1733 (pb. 1735): 153–64. See J. L. Greenberg, "Geodesy in Paris in the 1730s," *Historical Studies in Physical Science* 13 (1983): 239–60; idem, "Degrees of Longitude and the Earth's Shape," *Annals of Science* 41 (1984): 151–58.

42. Clairaut to Euler, 19 February, 12 May 1744, in Leonhard Euler, *Opera Omnia*, ser. 4A, ed. A. P. Juskevic and R. Taton (Basel: Birkhäuser Verlag 1980), 5:152, 155.

43. Jérôme Lalande, *Bibliographie astronomique* (Paris, 1803), 821.

44. Le Monnier, *Théorie des comètes*, 85.

45. On Louville, see Hall, "Newton in France," 239–41; and Guerlac, *Newton on the Continent*, 132–34. The key text is Jacques-Eugène, chevalier de Louville, "Construction et théorie des tables du soleil," *Mémoires de l'Académie Royale des Sciences*, 1720 (pb. 1722): 35–84.

46. For Delisle's biography, see J. P. Grandjean de Fouchy, "Eloge de M. de l'Isle," *Mémoires de l'Académie Royale des Sciences*, "Histoire," 1768 (pb. 1770): 167–83; H. Woolf, *The Transits of Venus: A Study of 18th Century Science* (Princeton: Princeton University Press, 1959), 23–32; R. Jacquel, "L'astronome français J. N. Delisle et Christfried Kirch," *Actes du 97ᵉ congrès national des sociétés savantes, section des sciences* (Paris: C.N.R.S., 1976), 1:407–32; N. I. Nevskaia, "J. N. Delisle (1688–1768)," *Revue de l'histoire des sciences* 26 (1973): 289–313. For his early work on geodesy, see Paris Observatory MSS A7.7 ("Mémoire sur la grandeur et la figure de la terre"), discussed in Greenberg, "Geodesy in Paris," 243–46, 259–60. Delisle's career at the Collège Royale is summarized in R. Hahn, "Les

observatoires en France au dix-huitième siècle," in *Enseignement et diffusion des sciences en France au dix-huitième siècle*, ed. R. Taton (Paris: Hermann, 1964), 653–58.

47. Delisle to Rast, 16 July 1718, Paris Observatory MSS B1.103; Delisle to Teinturier, 7 February 1717, ibid., B1.55; Delisle to Réaumur, 27 April 1717, ibid., B1.58.

48. Delisle, "Tables du soleil et de la lune suivant la théorie de Mr Newton dans le 2ᵉ édition de ses Principes calculées en 1716," Paris Observatory MSS A2.9, no. 23. These claims are discussed in Craig B. Waff, "Newton and the Motion of the Moon: An Essay Review," *Centaurus* 21 (1977): 64–75.

49. Delisle to Teinturier, 7 February 1717, Paris Observatory MSS B1.55; cf. Delisle, "Expériences sur la lumière et les couleurs," in *Mémoires pour servir à l'histoire et au progrès de l'astronomie* (St. Petersburg, 1738), 205–66.

50. Delisle to Teinturier, 7 February 1717, Paris Observatory MSS B1.55; Delisle to Réaumur, 27 April 1717, ibid., B1.58.

51. Delisle to Bignon, 11 June 1717, ibid., B1.59; cf. Delisle to Bignon, Bibliothèque Nationale MSS Fr. 22227 fols. 214–17, on the cost of instruments for the observatory.

52. Delisle to Chardeloup, 3 October 1718, Paris Observatory MSS B1.62; cf. Delisle to Rast, 19 June, 16 July 1718, ibid., B1.94, B1.103.

53. Rast to Delisle, 1 July 1718, ibid., B1.97.

54. Des Maizeaux to Conti, 11 September 1720, in Newton, *Correspondence of Newton* 7 : 100.

55. Louville, "Construction et théorie des tables du soleil"; Delisle, "Mémoire sur la figure de la terre."

56. Delisle to Blumentrost, 8 September 1721, Paris Observatory MSS B2.26. Cf. Euler to Blumentrost, 9 November 1726, in *Berliner und die Petersburger Akademie* 3 : 28. Blumentrost was first president of the St. Petersburg Academy of Sciences, 1725–33; see A. Lipski, "The Foundation of the Russian Academy of Sciences," *Isis* 44 (1953): 349–55.

57. Delisle to Struyk, 8 March 1722, Paris Observatory MSS B2.33.

58. Struyk to Delisle, 4 April 1722, ibid., B2.34; 'sGravesande to Newton, 24 June 1718, in A. R. Hall, "Further Newton Correspondence," *Notes and Records of the Royal Society* 37 (1982): 26.

59. Delisle to Struyk, May 1722, Paris Observatory MSS B2.39; Delisle, "Histoire et détails de ma correspondance avec les missionaires (astronomes) de la Chine et des Indes orientales," ibid., E1.13. Struyk's new table of comets is "Viae cometarum, secundum hypothesin quae statuit illos curso suo Parabolam circa Solem describere," *Philosophical Transactions* 46 (1749–50): 89–92. For the transit of Mercury, see Delisle to Halley, 27 December 1723, Paris Observatory MSS B2.79; Delisle, "Sur le dernier passage attendu de Mercure dans le Soleil," *Mémoires de l'Académie Royale des Sciences*, 1723 (pb. 1725): pp 105–10; Woolf, *Transits of Venus*, 28–30.

60. Delisle to Teinturier, 7 February 1717, Paris Observatory MSS B1.55.

61. Delisle to Newton, 22 March 1724, and Newton to Delisle, April 1724, in Newton, *Correspondence* 7 : 269–70, 271.

62. Delisle to Halley, 5 June 1724, Paris Observatory MSS B2.110.

63. Delisle to Halley, 21 December 1724, ibid., B2.131; Delisle to Newton, 10 December 1724, ibid., B2.130, and Newton, *Correspondence* 7:296–97. Delisle's notes on comets, using the maps of Senex and Flamsteed's catalogue, are preserved as Paris Observatory MSS A4.8, no. 42a.

64. For Varignon, see Guerlac, *Newton on the Continent,* 147–63; E. J. Aiton, *The Vortex Theory of Planetary Motions* (London: Macdonald, 1972), 196–200; A. R. Hall, *Philosophers at War: The Quarrel Between Newton and Leibniz* (Cambridge: Cambridge University Press, 1980), 239–41. For early contacts with the Royal Society, see Varignon to Newton, 7 November 1714, in Newton, *Correspondence* 6:187–88.

65. Newton to Delisle, January 1725, in *Correspondence* 7:301.

66. Jombert to Newton, 12 September 1725, ibid., 332–33; Delisle to De Moivre, 21 December 1724, Paris Observatory MSS B2.132.

67. Louville to Delisle, 23 May 1724, Paris Observatory MSS B2.102; Delisle to Newton, 10 December 1721, ibid., B2.130.

68. Souciet to Delisle, September 1724, ibid., B2.126; Delisle to Halley, 21 December 1724, ibid., B2.131.

69. Delisle to Nicasius Grammaticus, October 1724, ibid., B2.128.

70. Ibid.

71. Ibid.; Delisle to De Moivre, 21 December 1724, ibid., B23.132; Delisle to Innys, 21 December 1724, ibid., B2.133; Jombert to Newton, in Newton, *Correspondence* 7:332–33.

72. Delisle to Horrebow, 1 January 1725, Paris Observatory MSS B2.137; Horrebow to Delisle, 12 February 1725, ibid., B2.142.

73. J. Marchand, "Le départ en mission de l'astronome J. N. Delisle pour la Russie," *Revue d'histoire diplomatique* 43 (1929): 1–26.

74. Nevaskaia, "Delisle," 292; V. Boss, *Newton in Russia: The Early Influence, 1698–1796* (Cambridge, Mass.: Harvard University Press, 1972), 133.

75. Delambre, *Histoire de l'astronomie,* 673.

76. Le Monnier, *Théorie des comètes;* J. P. Löys de Chéseaux, *Théorie de la comète qui a paru en décembre 1743 jusqu'en mars 1744* (Paris, 1745); John Bevis, *Edmundi Hallei Astronomi dum viveret Regii Tabulae Astronomicae* (London, 1749); Delisle, *Lettres sur les Tables astronomiques de M. Halley,* (Paris, 1749). For the errors in these tables, see Woolf, *Transits of Venus,* 52–53. For Delisle's compilation of data on Comet Halley, see J. Alexandre, "La comète de Halley à travers les ouvrages et manuscrits de l'Observatoire de Paris," *Isis* 77 (1986): 81–82.

77. Delisle, *Discours lu dans l'assemblée publique de l'Académie des Sciences le 2 mars 1728* (St. Petersburg, 1728), 2. For Delisle's continuing warfare with the French geodesy program, see Delisle, "A Proposal for the Measurement of the Earth in Russia," *Philosophical Transactions* 40 (1738): 27–49; Greenberg, "Geodesy in Paris," 255–56. For Delisle and the academy, see N. I. Nevskaia, "Joseph Nicolas Delisle i Petersburgskaia Akademia Nauk," *Voprosy istorii astronomii* (Moscow: Nauka, 1974), 61–93.

78. Boss, *Newton and Russia,* 133.

79. Delisle, *Discours lu . . . le 2 mars 1728,* 13. During 1727 Delisle began some calculations on the path of the 1682 comet using Halley's elliptical and parabolic models; for these trials and worksheets, see Paris Observatory MSS A4.11, no. 42d.

80. Nevskaia, "Delisle," 292; cf. Lipski, "Foundation of the Russian Academy of Sciences."

81. Jacquel, "Delisle et Kirch," 412; M. H. Omont, "Lettres de J. N. Delisle au comte de Maurepas et l'abbé Bignon," *Bulletin de la section de géographie de la Comité des Travaux historiques et scientifiques* 32 (1917): 130–64; V. F. Gnucheva, *Geograficheskii Departament Akademii Nauk XVIII veka* (Moscow: Nauka, 1966), 77ff.

82. Delisle to Bignon, 3 January 1730, in Omont, "Lettres de Delisle," 157.

83. Bignon to Delisle, 25 June 1730, ibid., p. 158.

84. Euler to Delisle, 23 April 1743, in *Relations scientifiques russo-françaises*, ed. A. T. Grigorian and A. P. Juskevic (Moscow: Nauka, 1968), 162–63 (Paris Observatory MSS B8.78); Delisle to Euler, 25 February 1743, ibid., 159–60 (B8.74); Delisle to Euler, 7 September 1743, ibid., 165–66 (B8.89); Heinsius to Euler, 22 January 1743, in Leonhard Euler, *Opera Omnia*, ser. 4A, ed. A. P. Juskevic, V. Smirnov, and W. Habicht (Basel: Birkhäuser Verlag, 1975), 1:175, and in *Berliner und Petersburger Akademie* 3:80. Euler's contacts with Delisle are discussed in N. I. Nevskaia, "Euler als Astronom," in *Leonhard Euler: Beiträge zu Leben und Werk* (Basel: Birkhäuser Verlag, 1983), 363–71.

85. Euler to Delisle, 13 February 1744, in *Relations scientifiques russo-françaises*, 172–74 (Paris Observatory MSS B8.105).

86. Delisle to Euler, 3 March 1744, ibid., 176–80 (B8.109).

87. Euler to Delisle, 8 September 1744, ibid., 190–93 (B9.8).

88. Delisle to Euler, 23 June 1742, ibid., 139–43 (B8.48).

89. For Delisle's troubles at St. Petersburg, see Euler to Schmettau, 13 December 1748, ibid., 274–78 (B10.49); Euler to Schumacher, 30 July 1748, in *Berliner und Petersburger Akademie* 2:139; d'Anville to Razumovsky, 5 August 1751, in Gnucheva, *Geograficheskii Departament*, 169. The controversies involving Schumacher and Delisle are discussed in L. Schulze, "The Russification of the St. Petersburg Academy of Sciences and Arts in the Eighteenth Century," *British Journal for the History of Science* 18 (1985): 316–17; James E. McClellan, *Science Reorganized: Scientific Societies in the Eighteenth Century* (New York: Columbia University Press, 1985), 79–80, 242.

90. Delisle to Euler, 23 June 1742, in *Relations scientifiques russo-françaises*, 139–43 (Paris Observatory MSS B8.48).

91. Ibid.; cf. Delisle to Bevis, 12 June 1742, Paris Observatory MSS B8.38. See Nevskaia, "Delisle," 298; and Bouguer, "De la détermination des orbites des comètes," *Mémoires de l'Académie Royale des Sciences*, 1733 (pb. 1735): 331–50.

92. Euler to Delisle, 21 July 1742, in *Relations scientifiques russo-françaises*, 148–53 (Paris Observatory MSS B8.52); Wagner to Delisle, 5 August 1742, ibid., B8.53. For the distribution of Euler's method in Germany, see Euler to Krafft, 11 August 1742, in *Berliner und Petersburger Akademie* 3:142–43. For Euler's cometography, see Leonhard Euler, "Determinatio orbitae cometae qui mense Martio hujus anni 1742 potissimum fuit observatus" (1743), in *Opera Omnia*, ser. 2, ed. L. Courvoisier (Zurich, 1959), 28:29–32. For his use of Delisle's observations, see ibid., 43, 90: "When, however, observations of the comet were sent by the most celebrated Delisle, all the others scarcely seemed to approach this degree of perfection, and I decided to use four of them to illustrate this method, which, if sufficiently accurate, would reveal the true orbit of the comet."

93. Delisle to Euler, 7 September 1743, in *Relations scientifiques russo-françaises*, 165–66 (Paris Observatory MSS B8.89); cf. Heinsius to Euler, 29 September, 20 October 1742, summarized in Euler, *Opera Omnia*, ser. 4A, 1 : 174, and in *Berliner und Petersburger Akademie* 3 : 74–76. Heinsius's drawing of his machine, sent 30 June 1742, is reproduced at ibid., 69, and in *Leonhard Euler: Pisma k Uchenym*, ed. T. N. Klado, Y. Kopelevic, and T. A. Lukina (Moscow: Akademia Nauk, 1963), 83.

94. Delisle to Euler, 3 March 1744, in *Relations scientifiques russo-françaises*, 176–80 (Paris Observatory MSS B8.109). For the troubles at the academy, see Krafft to Euler, 27 October 1742, Euler to Kantemir (the Russian ambassador in Paris), 5 January 1743, and Heinsius to Euler, 17 December 1743, 4 February 1744, in *Berliner und Petersburger Akademie* 3 : 144, 126, 87.

95. Euler to Delisle, 1 February 1744, in *Relations scientifiques russo-françaises*, 172–74 (Paris Observatory MSS B8.105). On 21 March 1744 Euler sent data about the comet both to Krafft and to Heinsius; in *Berliner und Petersburger Akademie* 3 : 88, 151.

96. Delisle to Euler, 3 March 1744, in *Relations scientifiques russo-françaises*, 176–80 (Paris Observatory MSS B8.109).

97. Ibid.; see Heinsius to Euler, 19 May 1744, and Euler to Heinsius, 26 May 1744, in Euler, *Opera Omnia*, ser. 4A, 1 : 177, and in *Berliner und Petersburger Akademie* 3 : 89–92. In late 1745 Heinsius received several British observations of the 1744 comet, including those of Peter Collinson and Nathaniel Bliss; see Heinsius to Euler, 1 January 1746, ibid., 101.

98. Delisle to Euler, 11 July 1744, in *Relations scientifiques russo-françaises*, 185–86; (Paris Observatory MSS B9.1).

99. See, for example, the comments of the Königsberg professor Martin Knutzen in B. Erdmann, *Martin Knutzen und seine Zeit* (1876; reprint Hildesheim: Georg Olms, 1973), 123; Knutzen to Delisle, 13 April 1744, Paris Observatory MSS B8.117; Knutzen to Euler, 22 May 1744, in Euler, *Opera Omnia*, ser. 4A, 1 : 206. Messier's comments are in "Notice de mes comètes," Paris Observatory MSS C2.19, fol. 1.

100. Delisle to Euler, 11 July 1744, in *Relations scientifiques russo-françaises*, 185–86 (Paris Observatory MSS B9.1); Euler to Delisle, 8 September 1744, ibid., 190–93 (B9.8); Clairaut to Euler, 12 May 1744, in Euler, *Opera Omnia*, ser. 4A, 5 : 155.

101. Euler, "Theoria motuum planetarum et cometarum" (1744), in *Opera Omnia*, ser. 2, 28 : 106–7; Clairaut to Euler, 12 May 1744, in Euler, *Opera Omnia*, ser. 4A, 5 : 155; Delisle to Euler, 22 September 1744, in *Relations scientifiques russo-françaises*, 196–99 (Paris Observatory MSS B9.10).

102. Nevskaia, "Delisle," 298–300. See Delisle, "Rechercher ce que Mr Euler a remarqué sur l'effet de la résistance de l'ether," Paris Observatory MSS A4.8, no. 42a; and idem, "Calculs pour l'établissement de la théorie de la comète de 1682 suivant les considerations de 1745," Paris Observatory MSS A4.11, no. 42d.

103. Delisle to Euler, 11 July 1744, in *Relations scientifiques russo-françaises*, 185–86 (Paris Observatory MSS B9.1); Delisle to Wagner, 22 September 1744, Paris Observatory MSS B9.12.

104. Euler to Delisle, 8 September 1744, in *Relations scientifiques russo-françaises*, 190–93 (Paris Observatory MSS B9.8).

105. Ibid.

106. Delisle to Euler, 22 September 1744, ibid., 196–99 (Paris Observatory MSS B9.10).

107. Ibid.

108. Ibid., and Hjorter to Delisle, 15 August 1744, Paris Observatory MSS B9.4.

109. Delisle to Euler, 22 September 1744, in *Relations scientifiques russo-françaises*, 190–93 (Paris Observatory MSS B9.8).

110. Euler to Delisle, 31 October 1744, ibid., 202–5 (Bibliothèque Nationale MSS N.acq.fr. 6197 fols. 89–90); Euler to Schumacher, 10 November 1744, in *Berliner und Petersburger Akademie* 2:75. Euler discussed these conditions on the *latus rectum* (parameter) of the orbit in a letter to Heinsius 11 August 1742, ibid., 3:61.

111. Delisle to Euler, 16 January 1745, in *Relations scientifiques russo-françaises*, 208–10 (Paris Observatory MSS B9.20).

112. Clairaut to Euler, 23 August 1744, in Euler, *Opera Omnia*, ser. 4A, 5:156–59; Clairaut, "De l'orbite de la lune dans le système de M. Newton," *Mémoires de l'Académie Royale des Sciences*, 1743 (pb. 1746): 17–32, read at sessions between 13 June and 5 December 1744; Euler to Delisle, 8 September 1744, in *Relations scientifiques russo-françaises*, 192 (Paris Observatory MSS B9.8). See Waff, *Universal Gravitation and the Motion of the Moon's Apogee*, 66n.20, 72n.30.

113. Euler, "De motu nodorum lunae" (1744), in *Opera Omnia*, ser. 2, ed. L. Courvoisier and J. O. Fleckenstein (Basel: Birkhäuser Verlag, 1969), 23:11–48; Waff, *Universal Gravitation and the Motion of the Moon's Apogee*, 55.

114. Euler, "Tabulae astronomicae solis et lunae" (1746), in Euler, *Opera Omnia*, ser. 2, 23:1–10; Euler to Delisle, 8 May 1745, in *Relations scientifiques russo-françaises*, 224–26 (Bibliothèque Nationale MSS N.acq.fr. 6197, fols. 91–92). For the publication of these tables in late 1745 and their revision in 1746 in Berlin, see Waff, *Universal Gravitation and the Motion of the Moon's Apogee*, 56n.8.

115. Euler to Delisle, 13 March 1745, in *Relations scientifiques russo-françaises*, 212–14 (Paris Observatory MSS B9.28).

116. Delisle to Euler, 27 March 1745, ibid., 216–19 (Paris Observatory MSS B9.30); Euler, "Orbitae solaris determinatio" (1740), in Euler, *Opera Omnia*, ser. 2, 28:17–25.

117. Euler to Delisle, 8 May 1745, in *Relations scientifiques russo-françaises*, 224–26 (Bibliothèque Nationale MSS N.acq.fr. 6197, fols. 91–92). In the summer of 1746 Euler told a London correspondent that he knew the defective tables prepared by the English astronomers Charles Leadbetter and Charles Brent, and that he had seen the tables in LeMonnier's 1745 edition of John Keill's *Introductio ad Veram Astronomiam;* see Euler to Wettstein, 16 July, 10 December 1746, in *Berliner und Petersburger Akademie* 3:260, 264.

118. On d'Alembert's work on the errors in celestial mechanics, see Hankins, *D'Alembert*, 30–42; Waff, *Universal Gravitation and the Motion of the Moon's Apogee*, 87–93. On aether resistance to planetary and cometary motion, see Wilson, "Perturbations and Solar Tables," 92–104.

119. Euler to Delisle, 15 February 1746, in *Relations scientifiques russo-françaises*, 236–39 (Paris Observatory MSS B9.55); Euler, "De Relaxatione Motus Planetarum," in *Opuscula (Varii Argumenti)*, (Berlin, 1746), 1:246–76, for the

mathematical treatment of aether resistance; and Delisle, "Rechercher ce que Mr Euler a remarqué sur l'ether," for Delisle's response.

120. Edmond Halley, "The Ancient State of the City of Palmyra," *Philosophical Transactions* 19 (1695–97): 174; Schaffer, "Halley's Atheism." Early references to Halley's work are in the second edition of the *Principia* (Cohen-Koyré, 758–59) and in Pemberton, *View of Newton's Philosophy*, 203.

121. Euler, "Recherches sur le mouvement des corps célestes en général" (1747), in *Opera Omnia*, ser. 2, ed. M. Schurer (Basel: Birkhäuser Verlag, 1971), 25:1–44; Delisle to Euler, 21 June 1746, Paris Observatory MSS B9.64. See Waff, *Universal Gravitation and the Motion of the Moon's Apogee*, 50–60.

122. Clairaut, "Du système du monde dans les principes de la gravitation universelle," *Mémoires de l'Académie Royale des Sciences*, 1745 (pb. 1749): 353–64 (a revision of papers read on sessions from 28 June 1747 to 20 January 1748).

123. Clairaut to Euler, 11 September 1747, in Euler, *Opera Omnia*, ser. 4A, 5:173.

124. Euler to Clairaut, 30 September 1747, ibid., 176.

125. On the Clairaut-Buffon dispute, see Craig B. Waff, "Alexis Clairaut and His Proposed Modification of Newton's Inverse Square Law of Gravitation," in *Avant, avec, après Copernic* (Paris: C.N.R.S., 1975), 281–88; Waff, *Universal Gravitation and the Motion of the Moon's Apogee*, 128–74; Wilson, "Perturbations and Solar Tables," 133–45; P. Chandler, "Clairaut's Critique of Newtonian Attraction," *Annals of Science* 22 (1975): 369–78. Clairaut's retraction is in "Avertissement de M. Clairaut au sujet des mémoires qu'il a données en 1747 et 1748," *Mémoires de l'Académie Royale des Sciences*, 1745 (pb. 1749): 577–78. Euler's agreement is in Euler to Clairaut, 10 April 1751, in *Opera Omnia*, ser. 4A, 5:206–7.

126. For Euler's subsequent commitment to an aether, see Euler, "Lettres à une princesse d'Allemagne" (1760–62), in *Opera Omnia*, ser. 3, ed. A. Speiser (Zurich: Birkhäuser Verlag, 1976), letters 17 (6:41), 20 (47), 59 (130–31) and 75 (164). This work is interpreted as a Newtonian text in R. Calinger, "Euler's *Letters to a German Princess* as an Expression of His Mature Scientific Outlook," *Archive for History of Exact Sciences* 15 (1976): 211–33, and as a defense of the undulatory theory of light in D. Speiser, "The Distance of the Fixed Stars and the Riddle of the Sun's Radiation," in *Mélanges Alexandre Koyré*, ed. R. Taton and I. B. Cohen (Paris: Hermann, 1964), 1:541–51.

127. Eric G. Forbes, *The Euler-Mayer Correspondence, 1751–55* (London: Macmillan 1971). For the analogy with magnetism, see d'Alembert to Euler, 17 June 1748, in Euler, *Opera Omnia*, ser. 4a, 5:288; Euler, "Dissertatio de Magnete," in *Opuscula (Varii Argumenti)* (Berlin, 1751), 3:16–18; cf. Mayer to Euler, 15 November 1751, and Euler to Mayer, 25 December 1751, in Forbes, *Euler-Mayer Correspondence*, 42, 44.

128. Euler to Mayer, 26 February 1754, in Forbes, *Euler-Mayer Correspondence*, 79. See Mayer to Euler, 22 August 1753, ibid., 73–76.

129. For the subsequent career of Mayer's tables, see Eric G. Forbes, *Tobias Mayer, Pioneer of Enlightened Science in Germany* (Göttingen: Vandenhoeck und Ruprecht, 1980), 134–50, 196–205.

130. Euler to Mayer, 27 May 1755, in Forbes, *Euler-Mayer Correspondence*, 97.

131. R. Jacquel, "J. H. Lambert et l'astronomie cométaire au dix-huitième siè-

cle," *Comptes rendus du 92ᵉ congrès national des sociétés savantes, section des sciences* (Paris, 1969), 1:27–56, 33–35; J. Levy, "Lambert et la mécanique céleste: Le problème des comètes," in *Colloque internationale et interdisciplinaire J. H. Lambert* (Paris: Ophrys, 1979), 279–83.

132. R. Home, *Aepinus's Essay on the Theory of Electricity and Magnetism* (Princeton: Princeton University Press, 1979), 72–73; cf. S. Gaukroger, "The Metaphysics of Impenetrability: Euler's Conception of Force," *British Journal for the History of Science* 15 (1982): 149, for Aepinus's subsequent views on aether and magnetism. In September 1757 Aepinus told Euler that Swedish observers claimed that the comet then visible might be that of 1682: see Aepinus to Euler, 30 September 1757, in *Berliner und Petersburger Akademie*, 3:25.

133. Condorcet to Bossut, 3 September 1766, in J. Pelseneer, "Lettres inédites de Condorcet," *Osiris* 10 (1952): 322–27; and abbé Bossut, "Recherches sur les altérations que la résistance de l'éther peut produire dans le mouvement moyen des planètes," *Receuil des pièces qui ont remporté les prix de l'Académie Royale des Sciences en 1762* (Paris, 1771; published independently 1766), 1–50.

134. Delisle to Bevis, 8 November 1748, Paris Observatory MSS B10.28; Bevis to Delisle, 13 January 1749, ibid., B10.53; Delisle to Bevis, 1 March 1749, ibid., B10.81; Bevis to Delisle, 3 April 1749, ibid., B10.69; Bevis to Delisle, 8 September 1749, ibid., B10.102. See R. Wallis, "John Bevis," *Notes and Records of the Royal Society* 36 (1982): 211–25; and W. Ashworth, Jr., "John Bevis and his *Uranographia*," *Proceedings of the American Philosophical Society* 75 (1981): 52–73.

135. Delisle to Bevis, 22 October 1749, Paris Observatory MSS B10.105. Cf. Delisle's earlier "Calculs de la comète de 1682 dans l'orbe elliptique suivant les élémens donnés dans les tables astronomiques de M. Halley," ibid., A4.11, no. 42d.

136. Delisle to Bevis, 3 December 1749, ibid., B10.115. Halley's tables were awaited, for example, by Euler: see note 117.

137. Delisle, *Lettres sur les Tables astronomiques de M. Halley* (Paris, 1749), 1:33–34, 2:11–12.

138. Ibid., 1:5, 2:22.

139. Ibid., 2:11.

140. Ibid., 38–45.

141. Ibid., 43.

142. Ibid., 44. For Delisle on Chéseaux, see also "Hypothèses de M. de Chéseaux sur le retour de la comète de 1682," Paris Observatory MSS A4.11, no. 42d.

143. Stevenson, in *London Magazine* 27 (November 1758): 564; cf. Broughton, "First Predicted Return," 127–28; Waff, "First International Halley Watch," Chapter 18 this volume.

144. Delisle, "Avis aux astronomes sur la comète prédite par M. Halley," Paris Observatory MSS A4.11, no. 42d and "Lettre sur le retour de la comète de 1682," *Mercure de France*, July 1759, 146–75; Messier, "Journal des observations astronomiques, 3 avril–24 mai 1759," Paris Observatory MSS C2.19, and "Histoire et observations du retour de la comète de 1682," *Mémoires de mathematiques et physique*, 1759 (pb. 1765): 380–90.

145. Lalande, *Tables astronomiques*, 99–129; idem, "Mémoire sur le retour de

la comète de 1682," *Mémoires de mathematiques et physique*, 1759 (pb. 1765): 1–40; idem, *Bibliographie astronomique*, 676–81 (on Lepaute).

146. Messier, "A Memoir Containing the History of the Return of the Famous Comet of 1682," *Philosophical Transactions* 55 (1765): 297. See Messier, "Histoire et observations," plate 2, also preserved in Paris Observatory MSS B4.8.

147. Messier, "Histoire et observations," 385–86; Delisle, "Lettre sur le retour," 148–56; idem, "Liste des ouvrages où sont raportées les observatións de la comète de 1682," Paris Observatory MSS A4.3, fols. 2–3.

148. Delisle's announcement is in *Mémoires de Trévoux* (November 1757), 2867; see Messier, "History of the Return," 298, and "Journal des observations."

149. Lalande, *Tables astronomiques*, 107. See Lalande, "Mémoire sur les équations séculaires," 413. Lalande's announcement is in *Mémoires de Trévoux* (November 1757), 2850–63.

150. Clairaut, "Mémoire sur la comète de 1682," *Journal des sçavans*, January 1759, 38–45.

151. Waff, "First International Halley Watch"; Taton, "Clairaut et le retour de la comète."

152. Messier, "History of the Return," 302–4, and "Journal des observations"; Delisle, "Lettre contenant la découverte du retour de la comète de 1682," *Journal des sçavans*, June 1759, 356–64. Waff, "First International Halley Watch," points out that Heinsius was the source of the announcement of the recovery of the comet in Saxony. See Heinsius to Euler, 21 April, 9 May 1759, in *Berliner und Petersburger Akademie* 3:120–21.

153. Delisle, "Lettre contenant la découvert du retour de la comète"; Taton, "Clairaut et le retour de la comète," 257.

154. Clairaut to Bernoulli, 10 April 1759, in Taton, "Clairaut et le retour de la comète," 265.

155. Ibid.

156. Le Monnier, "Suite de l'apparition de la comète," *Mercure de France*, July 1759, 140–45. D'Alembert's comments are in *L'observateur littéraire*, August 1759, 181.

157. Lalande, *Tables astronomiques*, 111. See Clairaut, *Théorie du mouvement des comètes, par laquelle on a égard aux altérations que les orbites éprouvent par l'action des planètes* (Paris, 1760) (read 8 August 1759), and *Réponse à quelques pièces, la plupart anonymes, dans lesquelles on a attaqué le Mémoire sur la Comète de 1682* (Paris, 1759) (read 14 November 1748).

158. Lalande's comments are in *Journal encyclopédique*, June 1759, 41–50.

159. Clairaut, *Réponse à quelques pièces*, 7–8. See Hankins, *Jean d'Alembert*, 38–41.

160. Clairaut to Müller, 31 December 1760, in Euler, *Opera Omnia*, ser. 4A, 5:239; Clairaut, *Recherches sur la comète des années 1531, 1607, 1682 et 1759* (St. Petersburg, 1762) (sent 3 December 1761).

FIFTEEN

Newton and the Ongoing Teleological Role of Comets

Sara Schechner Genuth

In an era in which the periodicity of comets was commonly affirmed, Malthus opened his famous essay on population with an astronomical metaphor: "Like a blazing comet," he wrote, "[the French Revolution] seems destined either to inspire with fresh life and vigour, or to scorch up and destroy the shrinking inhabitants of the earth."[1] As this apt metaphor of Malthus indicates, the periodicity of comets did not preclude their teleological significance.[2] A century earlier, by 1687, Newton and Halley had concurred that each comet was a sort of planetary body which followed a prescribed orbit throughout the solar system.[3] On one level, these scholars transformed unpredictable and monstrous comets into the flotsam of the solar system; on another level, though, they strengthened the monstrous character of comets by giving them both invigorating and devastating roles in the cosmos.

The cometary theories espoused by Newton, Halley, and many eighteenth-century natural philosophers share an attitude that was rooted in traditional comet lore and reveal how that lore was assimilated into astronomy. In this multistep process, comets were transformed from prodigious signs of calamitous events into natural causes of those events. To set these theories into context, I would like to sketch the increasing naturalization of comet theory in the preceding centuries.

Aristotle believed comets to be signs and not causes of natural events. In particular, comets forecast severe wind, drought, earthquakes, tidal waves, and storms. Yet he also suggested an underlying cause for the observed correlation between the two sets of phenomena: both were symptoms of excessive amounts of hot, dry exhalations.[4] In this sense, a comet signified drought in the way a barometer's falling mercury today signifies an impending storm. Nevertheless, this natural correlation between comets and meteorological disasters was subsequently forgotten. Roman authors such as Manilius, Pliny, Seneca, and Ptolemy emphasized the portentous character of comets, warning that they heralded blighted crops, sickness, civil discord, insurrection, war, and murder, and downplayed the symptomatic relationships.[5]

From antiquity to the Renaissance, men contended that bearded stars, as comets were often called, participated in a grand design of menacing and prodigious events. Comets kept company with fiery meteors; rains of blood, stones, or frogs; earthquakes; celestial apparitions of battling armies; multiple suns; and monstrous births.[6] Like the other signs in this lamentable list, comets began to be seen by medieval authors as extraordinary creations. God formed comets at his discretion to herald his punishment of the wicked.[7] Aquinas pointed out that comets had apocalyptic associations, that they presaged world reformation and the vindication of the elect.[8] At the local level, comets forecast imminent events like the death of princes, political or religious revolutions, plague, or bad harvests.[9] Although these views have been labeled as "popular superstitions" by modern authors, until the seventeenth century they were as commonplace in the astronomical observatory as they were on the street corner, being advocated, for example, in 1578 by Tycho Brahe and in 1619 by Johannes Kepler and John Bainbridge, who later became the first Savilian Professor of Astronomy at Oxford.[10]

In the Middle Ages, a second view of cometary influences began to achieve popularity. Albertus Magnus and others argued that comets were not merely portentous, astrological signs; generated through the influence of Mars and Mercury, rather, comets signified events that these planets caused or "inclined" to occur.[11] Authors in the fourteenth and fifteenth centuries extended and fortified this argument, shifting the primary causes from the planets to the comets and their constituent exhalations. They upheld comets and exhalations to be the natural, local causes of the cataclysmic events comets were thought to presignify.[12] Their arguments followed a standard recipe: composed of hot, dry, burning exhalations, comets would heat the air and dry out the earth. Barrenness, poor harvests, and famine would follow. Noxious comet steams would further infect the air, engendering disease and pestilence. Princes, of course, were the first to die, because their dissipated eating habits, luxurious life-styles, and great cares weakened them and made them less robust than the vulgar peasant stock. The death of princes often led to religious unrest and political upheaval. Moreover, as cometary exhalations heated the air, they kindled anger and inflamed human spirits, with brawling, fighting, seditions, bloodshed, wars and victories, and ultimately changes in the civil and religious order the likely results. In the sixteenth and seventeenth centuries, this naturalized view of cometary effects gained increasing support,[13] coming to exist side-by-side with the persistent older position that saw comets strictly as signs.[14] While many pamphleteers debated the merits of each position, both sides certainly agreed that comets signaled important events.

Although Newton never linked comets to specific worldly crises like the authors just discussed, he still assigned them purposive roles in the cosmos.[15] According to David Gregory, Savilian Professor of Astronomy at Oxford, Newton remarked that "the great eccentricity in Comets in directions both different from and contrary to the planets indicates a divine hand: and implies that Comets are destined for a use other than that of the planets."[16] What was this special use? Or, as Newton himself raised the question, "To what end were comets framed?"[17] I wish to argue that Newton's views on the teleological design of comets have much in common with the traditional comet lore.

My account of Newton begins with his views on transmutation. In 1687 Newton believed that an aqueous fluid was a universal substrate capable of being transmuted into all the manifold forms of gross matter.[18] The transmutation of this fluid was necessary for the healthy workings of the Earth. The process was, however, a unidirectional one by which the bulk of the solid Earth was continually increased. Fluid transmuted was fluid lost. Without an extraterrestrial means of replenishing the aqueous fluid, all planetary activity would cease.[19] The magnificent Earth would decay. In the *Principia,* Newton boldly suggested that comet tails likely replenished the planetary fluids consumed in mundane operations. After diffusing throughout the solar system and eventually mixing with planetary atmospheres, comet tail vapors condensed and were converted into the substances of animals, vegetables, and minerals. Moreover, Newton suspected that comets also furnished a vital spirit in our air required to sustain life.[20]

In the 1687 edition of the *Principia,* nothing refueled the Sun and stars; these simply wasted away gradually by emitting light and heat for long periods of time. In the revised 1713 edition, Newton presented a natural instrument by which God could conserve the stellar bodies. Once again the instrument was a comet. Orbital calculations for the 1680 comet had revealed its extreme proximity to the Sun at perihelion. Indeed, it seemed to have passed through the solar atmosphere, where its motion must have been resisted and retarded. Every subsequent revolution would slow it further, Newton reasoned. Eventually it would fall into the Sun and then rekindle that wasting star. From this fresh supply of comet fuel, an old star would acquire new brightness and perhaps pass for a new star. The so-called novas that had puzzled Hipparchus, Tycho, and Kepler were probably, according to Newton, old stars suddenly refueled by comets falling into them.[21] Thus comets replenished the Sun, stars, and planets and so renovated the cosmos and preserved world order.

Nonetheless, this stocking of the celestial cupboards was routine housework compared to the cataclysmic reformations Newton envisioned in private. According to Gregory and Newton's nephew, Conduitt, Newton intimated that there was what he called "a sort of revolution in the heavenly bodies." Vapors and light emitted by the Sun would gravitationally collect into a moon, which would attract more and more matter until it became a planet. After the planet grew sufficiently in bulk, it became a comet, which ultimately dropped into the Sun, thereby recharging the whole cyclical system.[22]

This mechanism made possible the succession of worlds predicted in Scripture.[23] In the Apocalypse, the Earth could be destroyed by impact and by fire: According to Newton, a comet could strike the Earth,[24] or else the newly stoked flames caused by a comet's falling into the Sun might scorch the Earth. In fact, Newton determined that the 1680 comet was designed for that blazing end.[25] Given the roles assigned to comets in effecting these apocalyptic reformations, it is not surprising that Newton also considered it possible that a comet had a role in causing the Deluge.[26] Finally, when God saw fit to start again he would direct a comet to disturb a moon from its orbit around a primary planet and make this moon itself into a new planet fit for a new creation. Newton reasoned that the satellites of Jupiter and Saturn were even now being held in reserve for such new creations.[27] Newton's theory thus implied a succession of earths, a series of creations and purgations. Historical periods were punctuated by cometary catastrophes,[28] with comets serving as divine agents to reconstitute the entire solar system, to prepare sites for new creations, and to usher in the millennium.

In advocating both salutary and apocalyptic roles for comets, Newton assimilated traditional cometary functions into his natural philosophy. Rather than denude comets of their local religious, political, and agricultural significance, Newton just enlarged the scope of their effects. In his scheme, comets engaged respectively in religious reformations of the solar system, in revolutions in the heavenly order, and in the circulation of matter vital for vegetation.

Many natural philosophers followed Newton's lead. Edmond Halley deferred to Newton in discussions of the composition of comet tails and so presumably subscribed to Newton's theory of the tails' replenishing roles.[29] Yet in 1694 Halley proposed his own ideas on the salutary effects of comets. Like Newton, Halley suggested that the surface materials of the Earth would, over time, become hard and stony, unfit for vegetation and animal life. If a comet collided with the Earth, these stony materials would be buried deep within the globe, while a lighter, finer soil would settle on the surface. Although this collision would kill all inhabitants of the globe, it would be necessary to prepare the Earth for future races and new creations. Deadly in the short term but healthful in the long run, cometary collisions allowed for the succession of worlds.[30]

Indeed, Halley had a long-term interest in such collisions as an explanatory device to account for major terrestrial upheavals. In 1687 (the same year that Halley was reading Newton's page proofs on the periodicity of comets), Halley noted the possibility of a past comet's striking the Earth, altering its axis and orbit, and causing the biblical Flood.[31] Halley elaborated on this point in 1694 at a meeting of the Royal Society.[32] The comet's collision would have reduced the Earth to its "old Chaos"; the sea would have rushed violently toward the site of the blow, and great waves would have recoiled back, furiously raking up the sea bottoms and burying marine animals beneath the mountain chains that were heaped up where opposite waves crashed together. Present-day evidence of this comet shock included the crater of the Caspian Sea, the unusually cold climate in North America near the unthawed, icy site of the prediluvian North Pole, fossilized marine animals, and the figure of the Earth, which seemed "new made out of the Ruins of an old World."[33] Yet Halley remained puzzled about how Noah's ark could have survived the cataclysmic event, and a week later he amended his theory, suggesting that this cometary impact more likely happened before creation and would have reduced a former world into a chaos from whose ruins the present world was formed.[34] In his famed *Astronomiae Cometicae Synopsis* (1705), Halley again raised the specter of a comet striking the Earth, and in the revised posthumous version (1752) he indicated that a near approach of the 1680 comet could perturb the Earth's orbit, whereas a collision would reduce the Earth to its "ancient chaos" and destroy it.[35]

A sampling of eighteenth-century natural philosophers quickly shows that many shared Halley's and Newton's penchant for giving comets teleological roles, both salutary and apocalyptic. It became commonplace to assert the replenishing capacity of comets. Kant, for instance, believed that comets refueled the Sun, as did Maupertuis, Buffon, Wright, and Herschel.[36] Citing Newton's hypotheses as authoritative, many others also believed that comets replenished planetary fluid, humidity, and vital spirit.[37]

Among those who implicated comets in the classic religious reformations of creation, deluge, and conflagration and in major reorganizations of celestial hierarchy were Whiston, Buffon, Maupertuis, and Kant. In 1696 Whiston argued that the Earth had been formed by a comet, the Flood had resulted from the near approach of a comet, and the final conflagration would be ignited by a return of the comet.[38] Buffon in 1749 proposed that a comet, in sideswiping the Sun, had sheared off solar matter that, with the comet, had coalesced to form the planets and satellites, while the near approach of a comet to the Earth at a later date could also alter the Earth's axis—though to what end Buffon did not say.[39] His countryman Maupertuis agreed that comets might be the physical cause of extraordinary events. Citing Halley and Whiston, he did not preclude a comet's role in the deluge and conflagration.[40] Near approaches of comets might, he said, drown the Earth in a torrent of vapors, alter its axis, kick the planet into a cometary orbit, or steal its moon, with other comets later taking up residence as new planets or satellites. Cometary impacts could also rearrange land masses, change climate, or utterly smash the planet to pieces, while a comet tail could wrap a planet in a decorative ring.[41]

A connection between comet tails and Saturn's ring also impressed Kant. Believing that there was a gradual transition between comets and planets, and citing Saturn's ring as evidence of that planet's former cometary status, Kant proposed that Earth once had a watery cometary ring, which, perhaps disrupted by another passing comet, precipitated to cause the Flood. Kant further maintained that the solar system would ultimately be consumed by fire fueled largely by comets (and planets) falling into the Sun.[42]

Herschel, too, asserted that comets could be transformed into planets. In words that echoed Newton's, he described "revolutions" in the heavenly bodies by which nebulous comets became consolidated into planets.[43] Record of the astronomical revolutions undergone by the once cometary Earth could be found partly in the terrestrial evidence of parallel geological revolutions.[44]

Lambert, however, emphasized the permanence of celestial bodies and decried theories in which planets became comets and comets became planets.[45] Following the "principle of plenitude," he believed that the primary function of comets was to pack the universe with as many creatures as possible. Yet while Lambert certainly claimed cometary catastrophes to be very rare exceptions, he did not wholly preclude them, arguing instead that they served "the purpose of preparing the system of each fixed star to future changes."[46]

In fact, natural philosophers who took pains to disagree with outright features of Newton's and Halley's comet theories continued to advocate teleological roles for comets. Wright in his later work, for example, rejected the periodicity and planetary character of comets.[47] As eruptions from celestial volcanoes, however, he believed that comets circulated a salutary, providential fire throughout the universe, thereby purifying the aether and nourishing the central suns in his system; they also reminded man of the ultimate dissolution of nature, for they could destroy worlds by impact and disturb planetary orbits by near approach.[48] Another textbook author in 1840 disparaged Newton's theory that comets refueled the Sun and planets, yet deemed it plausible that comets replenished the electrical fluid that planets required.[49]

Despite the variations in the arguments presented, their tenor is the same. Although comets were depicted as natural bodies following routine courses throughout the heavens, they remained apparitions of God's design. God used comets as a natural means to conserve, renovate, and reform the cosmos. What distinguished Newton and Halley from their predecessors, and defined discourse for their successors, was the level of activity that they assigned to the comets. Whereas Newton and many eighteenth-century natural philosophers never linked comets to specific European political revolutions, religious reformations, or health and agricultural problems, they did use comets to incite apocalyptic revolutions in the cosmic order and to transport life-sustaining materials to the planets and fuel to the Sun. The scope of cometary effects had become global, indeed cosmological, but in their extended field of action comets continued to fulfill traditional teleological functions.

NOTES

1. Thomas Robert Malthus, *An Essay on the Principle of Population* (London, 1798), 2.

2. Halley's comet made its predicted return in 1758–59.

3. Isaac Newton, *Philosophiae Naturalis Principia Mathematica* (London: 1687), 474–510; translated as *Isaac Newton's Mathematical Principles of Natural Philosophy and His System of the World*, trans. Andrew Motte (1729), ed. Florian Cajori (Berkeley: University of California Press, 1934; reprint 1962), 491–542 (hereafter cited as *Principia* [Motte-Cajori]). Edmond Halley's efforts in getting Newton to publish this section of the *Principia* are well known. Halley celebrated Newton's transformation of comets into planetary bodies in his "Ode to Newton," which prefaced the *Principia*.

4. Aristotle, *Meteorologica*, Book 1, chap. 7.

5. Manilius, *Astronomica* [ca. A.D. 9–15], Book 1, lines 874–918; Pliny, *Naturalis Historia* [A.D. 77], Book 2, chaps. 22–23, 25–27; Seneca, *Naturales Quaestiones* [ca. A.D. 62–65], Book 7; Ptolemy, *Tetrabiblos* [ca. A.D. 150], Book 2, chaps. 9, 13. The widely read *Centiloquium*, ascribed to Ptolemy but spurious, also associated comets with the death of kings, economic and political changes, foreign invasion, sickness, and death; see *Claudii Ptolemaei Alexādrini astronomorum principis centum sententiae, interprete Georgio Trapezuntio. Lucae Gaurici oratio de inventoribus, utilitate et laudibus astronomiae* (Rome, 1540), para. 100. For discussion of other ancient authors, see Clarisse Doris Hellman, *The Comet of 1577: Its Place in the History of Astronomy* (New York: Columbia University Press, 1944), 13–41.

6. Tacitus, *The Annals* [ca. A.D. 70], Book 15, chap. 47; and Ambroise Paré, *De Monstres et Prodiges*, 3d ed. (Paris, 1579), published in English as *On Monsters and*

Marvels, trans. Janis L. Pallister (Chicago: University of Chicago Press, 1982), 150–53. Two broadside ballads include "A Lamentable List, of certaine Hidious, Frightfull, and Prodigious Signes" (London, 1638), in *The Pack of Autolycus, or Strange and Terrible News of Ghosts, Apparitions, Monstrous Births, Showers of Wheat, Judgements of God, and Other Prodigious and Fearful Happenings as Told in Broadside Ballads of the Years 1624–1693*, ed. Hyder E. Rollins (Cambridge, Mass.: Harvard University Press, 1927; reprint 1969), 21–25; and "The Englishmans Advice" (London, 1680), in *The Pepys Ballads*, ed. Hyder E. Rollins (Cambridge, Mass.: Harvard University Press, 1929–32), 3:47–50. On monstrous phenomena, see Katharine Park and Lorraine J. Daston, "Unnatural Conceptions: The Study of Monsters in Sixteenth- and Seventeenth-Century France and England," *Past and Present* 92 (1981): 20–54.

7. An early statement of this position is found in John of Damascus, *De Fide Orthodoxa* [742–49], chap. 21; reprinted as Book 2, chap. 7, of *Exposition of the Orthodox Faith*, trans. Rev. S.D.F. Salmond, in *A Select Library of Nicene and Post-Nicene Fathers of the Christian Church*, 2d ser. (New York: Scribner's, 1899), 9:24.

8. Aquinas cited St. Jerome's view that comets would be one of fifteen signs to precede the Day of Judgment. He also believed that the star of Bethlehem had a cometary significance, since it portended that "the heavenly kingdom of Christ *shall break in pieces, and shall consume all the Kingdoms of the earth, and itself shall stand for ever* (Dan. ii. 44)" (Thomas Aquinas, *Summa Theologica* [1267–1273], trans. Fathers of the English Dominican Province [New York: Benziger Brothers, 1911–25], Part 3, Question 36, Art. 7, in 16:142; and Part 3 [supplement], Question 73, Art. 1, in 20:88).

9. See the works of Origen, Synesius of Cyrene, John Laurentius Lydus, Isidore of Seville, Bede, John of Damascus, Peter Abelard, William of Conches, Michael Scot, William of Auvergne, Vincent of Beauvais, Albertus Magnus, Roger Bacon, Leopold of Austria, Robert of York, Geoffrey of Meaux, John of Legnano at Bologna, Jacobus Angelus, and Matthew of Aquila. They are discussed in Hellman, *The Comet of 1577*, 41–73; Theodore Otto Wedel, *The Mediaeval Attitude Toward Astrology, Particularly in England* (New Haven: Yale University Press, 1920), 28–29; Lynn Thorndike, *A History of Magic and Experimental Science*, 8 vols. (New York: Columbia University Press, 1923–58), vols. 1–4 passim.

10. Tycho Brahe, *De Cometa Anni 1577* [German work, 1578], in *Tychonis Brahe Dani Opera Omnia*, ed. J.L.E. Dreyer et al. (Copenhagen: 1913–29), 4:379–96; Johannes Kepler, *De Cometis* (Augsburg, 1619), Books 2, 3; John Bainbridge, *An Astronomical Description of the late Comet from the 18. of Novemb. 1618. to the 16. of December following. With certaine Morall Prognosticks or Applications drawne from the Comets motion and irradiation amongs the celestiall Hieroglyphicks* (London, 1619). Also see Hellman, *The Comet of 1577*, 122–36; Thorndike, *A History of Magic* 6:69–71, 7:23; Charles Webster, *From Paracelsus to Newton: Magic and the Making of Modern Science* (Cambridge: Cambridge University Press, 1982), chap. 2; J. R. Christianson, "Tycho Brahe's German Treatise on the Comet of 1577: A Study in Science and Politics," *Isis* 70 (1979): 110–40; Clarisse Doris Hellman, "Kepler and Comets," *Vistas in Astronomy* 18 (1975): 789–96; Robert S. Westman, "The Comet and the Cosmos: Kepler, Mästlin, and the Copernican

Hypothesis," *Studia Copernicana* 5 (1972): 7–30; and Edward Rosen, "Kepler's Attitude Toward Astrology and Mysticism," in *Occult and Scientific Mentalities in the Renaissance,* ed. Brian Vickers (Cambridge: Cambridge University Press, 1984), 253–272.

11. Albertus Magnus [ca. 1200–1280], *De Meteoris,* Book 1, Tractatus 3, chap. 11; and Aegidius of Lessines, *De Essentia, Motu et Significatione Cometarum* [ca. 1264]; both in *Latin Treatises on Comets between 1238 and 1368 A.D.,* ed. Lynn Thorndike (Chicago: University of Chicago Press, 1950), 62–76, 87–184; see esp. 75–76, 101–3, 160. Cf. Ptolemy, *Tetrabiblos,* Book 2, chap. 9. Also see Lynn Thorndike, "Aegidius of Lessines on Comets," in *Studies and Essays in the History of Science and Learning Offered in Homage to George Sarton,* ed. M. F. Ashley Montagu (New York: Henry Schuman, 1946), 403–14.

12. John of Legnano at Bologna, *Tractatus de Cometa* [1368], in *Latin Treatises on Comets,* 234–59, esp. 247–49; and Matthew of Aquila, *De Causis Atque Natura Comete et Terremotus* [1456], discussed in Thorndike, *A History of Magic* 4:416–17, and Hellman, *The Comet of 1577,* 60–61, 72–73. Cf. The writings of Albertus Magnus and Aegidius of Lessines (note 11), where, for example, Mars aroused heat and wrath and consequently provoked animosity between hot-tempered individuals and ultimately war.

13. Girolamo Cardano, *De Rerum Varietate* (Basel, 1557), Book 1, chap. 1; Georgius Busch, *Beschreibung von zugehörigen Eigenschafften und natürlicher Influentz des grossen und erschrecklichen Cometen welcher in diesem 1577. Jahre erschienen* (Erfurt, 1577); Hellman, *The Comet of 1577,* 94–95, 233. William Fulke, *Meteors; or, A Plain Description of all kinds of Meteors, as well Fiery and Ayrie, as Watry and Earthly* ([1563] London, 1654), 33–34; John Edwards, *Cometomantia. A Discourse of Comets* (London, 1684), 61–73; Increase Mather, *ΚΟΜΗΤΟΓΡΑΦΙΑ, or a Discourse Concerning Comets* (Boston, 1683), 21–22, 132–34. David Gregory also considered the noxious effects of comet tails in his *Astronomiae Physicae & Geometricae Elementa* (Oxford, 1702), 408.

14. Authors with a scientific background who believed comets to be portents included Girolamo Cardano (*De Subtilitate*), Paul Fabricius, Valentin Steinmetz, Robert Recorde, Leonard Digges, Conrad Dasypodius, Nicolaus Bazelius, Thaddaeus Hagecius, Bartholomaeus Scultetus, Andreas Nolthius, Michael Maestlin, Cornelius Gemma, Helisaeus Roeslin; all are discussed in Hellman, *The Comet of 1577,* and Thorndike, *A History of Magic* 6:67–98. A sample of portent-oriented political and religious pamphlets includes Francis Shakelton, *A blazyng Starre or burnyng Beacon* (London, 1580); William Lilly, *Lillies New Prophecy; or, Strange and Wonderful Predictions, relating to the Year, 1678. As well from the late Blazing-Star* ([London], 1678); John Hill, *An Allarm to Europe: By a Late Prodigious Comet* (London, [1680]), W[illiam] G[reen], *Memento's to the World; or, An Historical Collection of divers Wonderful Comets and Prodigious Signs in Heaven,* bound with William Knight, *Stella Nova; . . . or, An Account of the Natural Signification of the Comet* (London, 1680/81); C[hristopher] N[ess], *A Full and True Account of the Late Blazing-Star: With some probable Prognosticks upon what may be its Effects* (London, 1680); idem, *The Signs of the Times* (London, 1681); Democritus [pseud.], *The Petitioning-Comet* (London, 1681). For a late account, see William Whiston, *The Astronomical Year; or, An Account of the many remarkable Celestial Phaenomena of the Great Year*

MDCCXXXVI. Particularly of the Late Comet, Which was foretold by Sir Isaac Newton, and appeared at its Conclusion (London, 1737).

15. Sara Schechner Genuth, "Comets, Teleology, and the Relationship of Chemistry to Cosmology in Newton's Thought," *Annali dell'Istituto e Museo di Storia della Scienza di Firenze* 10, no. 2 (1985): 31–65. Also see David Kubrin, "Newton and the Cyclical Cosmos: Providence and the Mechanical Philosophy," *Journal of the History of Ideas* 28 (1967): 325–46. On Newton's analyses of cometary orbits, see James Alan Ruffner, "The Background and Early Development of Newton's Theory of Comets" (Ph.D. diss., Indiana University, 1966).

16. David Gregory, "Annotations Physical, Mathematical, and Theological from Newton" (memoranda), 5, 6, 7 May 1694, in *The Correspondence of Isaac Newton*, ed. H. W. Turnbull et al. (Cambridge: Cambridge University Press, 1959–77), 3:336.

17. "Quem in finem facti sunt Cometae?" Query 20, *Optice* (London, 1706), 314.

18. Draft preface and conclusion to the *Principia* (Spring 1687), University Library, Cambridge, MS. Add. 3965, fol. 620, and 4005, fols. 25–28, 30–37, respectively in *Unpublished Scientific Papers of Isaac Newton: A Selection from the Portsmouth Collection in the University Library, Cambridge*, ed. A. R. Hall and M. B. Hall (Cambridge: Cambridge University Press, 1962), see esp. 306–7, 341. Also see Query 22, *Optice*, 319–20. Newton's views on transmutations are discussed in Genuth, "Comets"; Michael T. Walton, "Boyle and Newton on the Transmutation of Water and Air, from the Root of Helmont's Tree," *Ambix* 27 (1980): 11–18; J. E. McGuire, "Transmutation and Immutability: Newton's Doctrine of Physical Qualities," *Ambix* 14 (1967): 69–95; Betty Jo Teeter Dobbs, *The Foundations of Newton's Alchemy, or "The Hunting of the Greene Lyon"* (Cambridge: Cambridge University Press, 1975); Richard S. Westfall, "The Role of Alchemy in Newton's Career," in *Reason, Experiment, and Mysticism in the Scientific Revolution*, ed. M. L. Righini Bonelli and William R. Shea (New York: Science History Publications, 1975), 189–232; Arnold Thackray, *Atoms and Powers: An Essay on Newtonian Matter-Theory and the Development of Chemistry* (Cambridge, Mass.: Harvard University Press, 1970).

19. *Principia* (1687), 506; *Principia* (Motte-Cajori), 530. On the increasing bulk of the planets, see Isaac Newton, *Philosophia Naturalis Principia Mathematica*, 2d ed. (Cambridge, 1713), 481; and Halley's report to the Royal Society of Newton's view, *Journal Book* of the Royal Society, 31 October 1694 (in Edmund Turnor, *Collections for the History of the Town and Soke of Grantham. Containing Authentic Memoirs of Sir Isaac Newton* [London, 1806], 184).

20. *Principia* (1687), 506, and additional material in the second edition, *Principia* (1713), 481; *Principia* (Motte-Cajori), 529–30, 542. See also the draft revision of Book 3, Proposition 41, *Principia*, University Library, Cambridge, MS. Add. 3965, fol. 152v; in I. Bernard Cohen, "Isaac Newton's Principia, the Scriptures, and the Divine Providence," *Philosophy, Science, and Method: Essays in Honor of Ernest Nagel*, ed. Sidney Morgenbesser, Patrick Suppes, and Morton White (New York: Saint Martin's Press, 1969), 531, 537.

21. *Principia* (1713), 480–81; Isaac Newton, *Philosophia Naturalis Principia Mathematica* 3d ed. (London, 1726), 525–26; *Principia* (Motte-Cajori), 541–42;

John Conduitt, Memorandum, March 1724/25, King's College, Cambridge, Keynes MS. 130, no. 11 (in Turnor, *Collections for the History of Grantham,* 172–73).

22. Conduitt, Memorandum, of March 1724/25, in Turnor, *Collections for the History of Grantham,* 172–73. See also Gregory, "Annotations Physical, Mathematical, and Theological from Newton" (memoranda), 5, 6, 7 May 1694, in Newton, *Correspondence* 3 : 336.

23. Newton's student notebook of 1664–65 reveals his early interest in these matters (*Questiones Quaedam Philosophicae,* University Library, Cambridge, MS. Add. 3996, fol. 101r, p. 27; in *Certain Philosophical Questions: Newton's Trinity Notebook,* ed. J. E. McGuire and Martin Tamny [Cambridge: Cambridge University Press, 1983], 374–77). See also "De Millenio ac Die Judicij," in "A Com^n Place Book of S^r Is: Newton," King's College, Cambridge, Keynes MS. 2, no. 21; in Newton, *Theological Manuscripts,* ed. Herbert McLachlan (Liverpool: Liverpool University Press, 1950), 134–35.

24. Gregory, Memorandum, March 1702/3, in Newton, *Correspondence* 4 : 402.

25. Conduitt, Memorandum, of March 1724/25, in Turnor, *Collections for the History of Grantham,* 172.

26. Gregory, Memoranda, ? July 1698, in Newton, *Correspondence* 4 : 277.

27. Gregory, "Annotations Physical, Mathematical, and Theological from Newton" (memoranda), 5, 6, 7 May 1694, ibid., 3 : 336; idem, *Astronomiae Physicae & Geometricae Elementa,* 481.

28. According to Conduitt, Newton also believed that the Earth had visible marks of ruin on it. Wrought by a comet, a dramatic terrestrial upheaval had occurred prior to the present creation; another upheaval would occur when the 1680 comet fell into the Sun (Conduitt, Memorandum of March 1724/25, in Turnor, *Collections for the History of Grantham,* 172–73).

29. Edmond Halley, "A Synopsis of the Astronomy of Comets," in *Astronomical Tables with Precepts both in English and Latin for computing the Places of the Sun, Moon, Planets, and Comets* (London, 1752), Ssss2.

30. Halley, "Some Considerations about the Cause of the universal Deluge, laid before the Royal Society, on the 12th of December 1694" and "Some farther Thoughts upon the same Subject, delivered on the 19th of the same Month," *Philosophical Transactions of the Royal Society* 33 (1724–25): 118–25, esp. 124.

31. Halley, "An Account of some Observations lately made at Nurenburg by Mr. P. Wurtzelbaur, shewing that the Latitude of that Place has continued without sensible alteration for 200 years last past; as likewise the Obliquity of the Ecliptick; by comparing them with what was observed by Bernard Walther in the year 1487," *Philosophical Transactions* 16 (1686–87): 403–6, esp. 406.

32. Journal Book of the Royal Society, 12 December 1694; in *Correspondence and Papers of Edmond Halley,* ed. Eugene Fairfield MacPike (New York: Arno Press, 1975), 234. The paper delivered was printed in the *Philosophical Transactions* in 1724 (see note 30).

33. Halley, "Some Considerations about the Cause of the universal Deluge," 172.

34. Halley, "Some farther Thoughts," 123–25. Also see Halley's paper read to the Royal Society in 1697, British Library MSS Add. 4478b, fols. 142–50;

quoted in part by Margaret C. Jacob, *The Newtonians and the English Revolution 1689–1720* (Hassocks, Eng.: Harvester Press, 1976), 135–36. Cf. Conduitt, *Memorandum of March 1724/25*, in Turnor, *Collections for the History of Grantham*, 172–73. Jacob suggests that Halley might have been reporting Newton's views, but given the chronology of publications and reported conversations, it seems quite possible that Newton had the ideas from Halley. For further discussion of Halley's views on the end of the world, see Simon Schaffer, "Halley's Atheism and the End of the World," *Notes and Records of the Royal Society of London* 32 (1977): 17–40.

35. Halley, "Astronomiae Cometicae Synopsis," *Philosophical Transactions* 24 (1704–5): 1882–99, esp. 1898–99; idem, "A Synopsis of the Astronomy of Comets," Tttt4.

36. Immanuel Kant, *Allgemeine Naturgeschichte und Theorie des Himmels* [Leipzig, 1755]; in *Kant's Cosmogony, as in His Essay on the Retardation of the Rotation of the Earth and His Natural History and Theory of the Heavens*, trans. W. Hastie, introduction by Gerald Whitrow (New York: Johnson, 1970), 99–100, 153. Pierre Louis Moreau de Maupertuis, *Lettre sur la comète* ([Amsterdam?], 1742), 103–5; Georges Louis Leclerc, Comte de Buffon, *Natural History, General and Particular*, trans. William Smellie, 3d ed. (London, 1791), 1:66–67; Thomas Wright of Durham, *Second or Singular Thoughts upon the Theory of the Universe* [ca. 1771], ed. M. A. Hoskin (London: Dawsons of Pall Mall, 1968), 35–36, 41, 43, 76; William Herschel, "On the Nature and Construction of the Sun and fixed Stars," *Philosophical Transactions* 85 (1795): 46–72 (in *The Scientific Papers of Sir William Herschel*, ed. J.L.E. Dreyer, [London: The Royal Society and Royal Astronomical Society, 1912], 1:470–84, see esp. 478).

37. John Harris, *Lexicon Technicum*, 2d ed. (London, 1708), s.v. "Comets"; Henry Pemberton, *A View of Sir Isaac Newton's Philosophy* (London, 1728), 244–46; Colin Maclaurin, *An Account of Sir Isaac Newton's Philosophical Discoveries* (London, 1748), 374–75; James Ferguson, *An Idea of the Material Universe, Deduced from a Survey of the Solar System* (London, 1754), 27; idem, *Astronomy Explained upon Sir Isaac Newton's Principles*, 4th ed. (London, 1770), 39; Benjamin Martin, *The Theory of Comets* (London, 1757), 11–12; John Winthrop, *Two Lectures on Comets* (Boston, 1759), 41; John Hill, *A New Astronomical Dictionary, or, A Compleat View of the Heavens; Containing the Antient and Modern Astronomy* (London, 1768), s.v. "Comets"; Bartholomew Burges, *A Short Account of the Solar System, and of Comets in General: Together with a Particular Account of the Comet That Will Appear in 1789* (Boston, 1789), 15; and Maupertuis, *Lettre sur la comète*, 101–3.

38. William Whiston, *A New Theory of the Earth, from Its Original to the Consummation of all Things* (London, 1696).

39. Buffon, *Natural History* 1:64–82, 95.

40. Maupertuis, *Lettre sur la comète*, 55–56, 69–76, 83–86. See John A. Schumaker, "Pierre de Maupertuis and the History of Comets," *Scripta Mathematica* 23 (1957): 97–108.

41. Maupertuis, *Lettre sur la comète*, 65–69, 79–86, 95–99, 99–101; idem, *Discours sur les différentes figures des astres* (Paris, 1732) (in *Oeuvres de Maupertuis* [Lyons, 1768], 1:154–60).

42. Kant, *Cosmogony*, 66–67, 95, 101–2, 113–16, 129–31, 152–54. See Simon Schaffer, "The Phoenix of Nature: Fire and Evolutionary Cosmology in Wright and Kant," *Journal for the History of Astronomy* 9 (1978): 180–200.

43. William Herschel to Sir William Watson, 7 July 1817, Royal Astronomical Society, Herschel Papers W 1/1, fols. 298–99. Cf. Conduitt, Memorandum of March 1724/25, in Turnor, *Collections for the History of Grantham*, 172–73. William Herschel, "Astronomical Observations relating to the Construction of the Heavens," *Philosophical Transactions* 101 (1811): 269–336; idem, "Observations of a Comet, with Remarks on the Construction of its different Parts," *Philosophical Transactions* 102 (1812): 115–43; and idem, "Observations of a second Comet with Remarks on its Construction," *Philosophical Transactions* 102 (1812): 229–37 (all in *The Scientific Papers of Sir William Herschel* 2:459–519; see esp. 480–88, 513–14, 519). Also see Simon Schaffer, "'The Great Laboratories of the Universe': William Herschel on Matter Theory and Planetary Life," *Journal for the History of Astronomy* 11 (1980): 81–111; and idem, "Herschel in Bedlam: Natural History and Stellar Astronomy," *British Journal for the History of Science* 13 (1980): 211–39.

44. Herschel to Watson, 7 July 1817, Herschel Papers W 1/1, fols. 298–99.

45. J. H. Lambert, *Cosmologische Briefe über die Einrichtung des Weltbaues* (Augsburg, 1761); in *Cosmological Letters on the Arrangement of the World-Edifice*, trans. Stanley L. Jaki (New York: Science History Publications, 1976), xiii–xiv, 9–11, 22–24, 67, 100–101, 114 (pagination as in the 1761 edition). On Lambert's cosmology, see M. A. Hoskin, "Lambert's Cosmology," *Journal for the History of Astronomy* 9 (1978): 134–39; and idem, "Lambert and Herschel," *Journal for the History of Astronomy* 9 (1978): 140–42.

46. Lambert, *Cosmological Letters*, xii, xv, 2, 17, 73–74, 95–96, 168; quotation p. 17.

47. Wright, *Second or Singular Thoughts*, 22, 26, 29–38, 77. On Wright's cosmology, see M. A. Hoskin, "The Cosmology of Thomas Wright of Durham," *Journal for the History of Astronomy* 1 (1970): 44–52; and Schaffer, "The Phoenix of Nature."

48. Wright, *Second or Singular Thoughts*, 29, 31–32, 35–36, 38–39, 41–46, 53, 76.

49. Samuel D. M'Cullough, *Picture of the Heavens* (Lexington, Ky., 1840), 101. Also see [Charles Burney], *An Essay towards a History of the Principal Comets That Have Appeared since the Year 1742* (London, 1769), 100–103; Hugh Hamilton, Bishop of Ossory, *Philosophical Essays* (Dublin, 1766) (in *The Works of the Right Rev. Hugh Hamilton, D.D., Late Bishop of Ossory*, ed. Alexander Hamilton [London, 1809], 2:159–274, esp. 213–47); and S. Vince, *The Elements of Astronomy*, 4th ed. (Cambridge, 1816), 253–55.

SIXTEEN

The Comet of 1680–1681

Eric G. Forbes

Prior to the appearance of the comet of 1680–81, cometary theory was speculative, empirical, and closely linked with astrology and superstition. Only afterward did it become scientific, being founded on reliable astronomical observations and rigorous mathematical demonstrations. The instrumental reason for this transformation was the introduction of micrometer eyepieces on telescopes and quadrants, while those generally credited with providing new conceptual insights into the theory of cometary motion are Georg Samuel Dörffel, Johann Hevelius, Isaac Newton, and Edmond Halley. Although John Flamsteed supplied reliable observational data for this purpose, his views on cometary motion have tended to be undervalued. Due recognition must also be given to Robert Hooke for his stimulating speculations concerning cometary appearances and his role in prompting Newton to give serious attention to gravitation as the cause of orbital motions in the heavens. In this paper, I shall attempt to define and evaluate the importance of the various contributions by those individuals to our knowledge both of the comet of 1680–81 in particular and of comets in general.

Dörffel's claim to fame rests on the priority of his discovery, announced in an anonymous tract published in 1681, that the orbits of comets are parabolae with the Sun at the focus.[1] The illustration accompanying his text strongly suggests that his adoption of the Copernican hypothesis of the Earth's annual motion around the Sun, despite his religious misgivings regarding the physical validity of such activity, influenced his belief in the identity of the apparitions observed in November 1680 and in January 1681.[2] Although Dörffel's superimposition of his calculated values for the celestial latitudes on the ecliptic projection of the resulting motion in celestial longitude does give the appearance of a parabolic shape, with the Sun stationed in the neighborhood of the focus, the poor-quality radius used in the measurement of the angles between the comet and the Sun on which his diagram was based was too crudely constructed to yield the accuracy required to substantiate this interpretation.

My own opinion is that Dörffel's assertion was little more than a lucky guess, triggered by his having observed the comet of 1680–81 both before and after its conjunction with the Sun, and perhaps also by his having read Hevelius's *Prodromus Cometicus* (1666), where Kepler's discovery that a planet moves in a conic section with the Sun at one focus is suggested as a possible model for cometary motion. His specific choice of a parabola as the orbital path, as opposed to a circle or elongated ellipse, can likewise be ascribed to the influence of Johann Hevelius's *Cometographia* (1668). In this comprehensive work, Hevelius cleverly reconciled the traditional Aristotelian belief in the meteorological nature of comets with Tycho Brahe's discovery that they do not exhibit diurnal parallax and hence are more distant than the Moon; this he did by regarding them not as spherical bodies but as disc-shaped conglomerations of atmospheric vapors that have spun off tangentially from axially rotating planets.[3] The rectilinear motion thus imparted was then assumed to be modified by a force acting throughout the planetary system, causing the comet to face into the Sun just as a magnetic needle points toward magnetic north. The resistance of a celestial aether was supposed to act both as a brake and as a rudder, reducing the comet's natural motion while at the same time steering it away from its inertial trajectory—these effects being greatest at more remote distances from the Sun.[4] This ingenious (though fanciful) pre-Newtonian explanation of cometary motion thus combined a magnetic with a nautical analogy and invoked the idea of a resisting medium in space.

Hevelius's writings on this and other aspects of astronomy were well known to John Flamsteed, too, who dismissed them as incapable of explaining the details of his Greenwich observations of the comet of 1680–81.[5] As I have shown elsewhere, however, some of these "details" resulted from computational errors he made in developing his own theory of this comet's motion.[6] Flamsteed's rejection of the widespread belief that comets move in straight lines in favor of the assumption that they follow great-circle arcs was based not on his own or contemporaries' observations, but on Giovanni Battista Riccioli's account of what earlier astronomers—particularly Regiomontanus and Apianus—had written on this subject.[7] His views on the nature and formation of comets were also drawn mainly from Riccioli, as well as from contemporary descriptions of cometary appearances printed in the Royal Society's *Philosophical Transactions* for 1665, 1668, 1672, and 1677.[8] Yet it was his own micrometric measurements of the new comet's position relative to neighboring bright stars made between 12 December 1680 and 5 February 1681 that gave rise to the "philosophical thoughts" he communicated shortly afterward to his young protégé Edmond Halley.[9] These observations also fueled his "amicable controversy" with Isaac Newton on the subject (see below).[10]

Halley was destined to be Flamsteed's personal link with both Hevelius and Newton. Despite his youth, he had already undertaken an expedition to St. Helena to observe the southern skies; he had also spent two months working with Hevelius in Danzig in order to gain firsthand experience of the German astronomical instruments and observational techniques and thereby settle the controversy between Hevelius and Flamsteed regarding the accuracy of telescopic vis-à-vis naked-eye sights.[11] When the comet of 1680–81 was first observed on 13 November in Coburg by the Saxon astronomer Gottfried Kirch, Halley was in Rome.[12] He subsequently sent Flamsteed a copy of rather coarse observations made there in his presence by Jean Charles Gallet and Marc' Antonio Collio, along with those of Giovanni Domenico Cassini and his associates at the Paris Observatory.[13] (The French observations were of lesser significance, since the times of observation overlapped with those at Greenwich.) This information convinced Flamsteed that the comet observed by Gallet and Collio in November and that observed by the Paris astronomers in December were identical. It appeared to be attracted by the Sun and move toward it while in the east and to be repelled by the Sun when in the west, after having been carried around by what Flamsteed calls the solar vortex. Flamsteed's conclusion that the comet's appearances were affected by the Earth's motion—there was no other way to explain them—echoed Hevelius's belief that "without the annual Motion of the Earth, no rational Account can be given of any Comet, but that all is involved with perplexities, and deform'd by absurdities."[14]

In an interesting exchange of correspondence with James Crompton in Cambridge regarding the comet of 1680–81, Flamsteed assumes it to have been *repelled* by a magnetic action emanating from the Sun, which caused it to turn backward, and ascribes the shortening in the length of its tail to the weakening of this force with increasing distance from the Sun.[15] When Newton was informed by Crompton of this hypothesis, he proclaimed a preference for attraction rather than repulsion and queried the assumption that the force was magnetic in origin, since all terrestrial bodies exhibiting this property lose it when heated to temperatures far lower than that of the Sun.[16] Flamsteed did not accept the premise that the constitution of the Sun was similar to that of iron. Although not opposed in principle to Newton's suggestion that the presence of a constant, centrally attracting force in the Sun could impel the comet to depart from a rectilinear path, swing around the Sun, and continue its motion in the opposite direction, he recognized that this required the comet to undergo a considerable acceleration, which seemed inconsistent with the rates of motion calculated from the contemporary observations (including his own) he had been analyzing. Newton, replying through Crompton, subsequently acknowledged that the solar magnetism could both direct and attract the comet and hence be the causal agent of its observed motion.[17]

The reasons for this change of opinion can be inferred from two statements made in a draft intended for Flamsteed but not included in the letter that was actually sent four days later, on 16 April.[18] One of these statements reveals Newton's continued skepticism of Flamsteed's belief in the existence of only one comet. This belief would have been strengthened by a diagram sent by Flamsteed to Crompton, showing that the comet's changing orbital position as witnessed by Abraham Hill of Canterbury on 11 November 1680, by the Rome and Paris observers, and by Flamsteed himself at Greenwich can be well represented by two straight lines.[19] The other statement indicates that Newton now believed himself to be in possession of a method for determining the paths of comets to as great a degree of exactness as the orbits of the planets, provided that reliable enough observations were at hand.[20] Taken together, these remarks imply that Newton was relying at this time upon the graphical method invented by Christopher Wren in the early 1660s, in which the motion of the comet is assumed to be uniform and rectilinear and that of the Earth uniform and circular and in which at least four entirely reliable observations are required to define the comet's changing heliocentric position.[21] The truth of this inference is confirmed by two worksheets published in an appendix to volume five of Newton's mathematical papers;[22] one has been chosen from among several extant calculations to reveal the practical shortcomings of this graphical method, while the other provides a comparison with the equivalent synthetic presentation in Problem 52 of Newton's *Arithmetica*.[23]

Essentially, the practical shortcomings arise, on the one hand, from the inaccuracy inherent in the observations themselves and in their reduction to ecliptic coordinates and, on the other, from the fact that every comet near the time of its conjunction with the Sun alters its speed considerably over even a relatively short period of time. It was Newton's failure to account satisfactorily for the motion of the comet of 1680–81 by Wren's method, I believe, that encouraged him to apply his theory of fluxions to the problem. In this approach he possessed a ready-made analytical tool for investigating both the changes in position and the variations in these changes. What he needed was a general theory for investigating the properties of curved lines capable of a wider application to what Newton still regarded as the fundamentally different problem of planetary motion.[24]

A manuscript Latin treatise that seems very like a vain attempt to answer this need, for which "an intensive search of contemporary sources has not only brought to light any comment on its purpose or adequacy but has also failed to unearth any reference to its existence," was published along with its English translation in Whiteside's fourth volume of Newton's mathematical papers.[25] Whiteside refers to this "Geometry of Curved Lines" as a "refined method of fluxions" and claims that it was never completed because Newton became "diverted" by the comet of 1680–81.[26] Could it be that this "diversion" really provided the raison d'être for the larger work on the comet? Such an interpretation would entail only a slight adjustment to the tentative dating of circa 1680 for this obscure treatise and provide at least a partial explanation of why it came to be written at that time. Newton's lack of success with his endeavors to frame new geometric elements to measure quantities generated by continuous flow according to a precise law ultimately obliged him to simplify the problem of *planetary* motion by accepting Kepler's first law and the hypothesis of a centripetal force directed toward the Sun (previously shown to be equivalent to Kepler's second law of areas) as the two postulates for his demonstration of the inverse square distance dependency of that force.[27]

For the purpose of his calculations, it was of course immaterial whether magnetism or gravitation was taken to be the causal agent. In presenting "A Discourse on the Nature of Comets" to a meeting of the Royal Society soon after Michaelmas in 1682, Hooke drew attention to the analogy between gravitational attraction and magnetic action.[28] He referred to the well-known phenomenon in static electricity that when a plate of glass is rubbed with a piece of cloth, some light bodies, such as pieces of paper, are attracted upward toward it. (Interestingly, he ascribed this experiment to Newton rather than to William Gilbert or other seventeenth-century experimental scientists.) The inference which he then draws is that the internal vibrative motion of the particles of electric bodies can attract other bodies; hence, if such internal motions, or pulses, were to occur in the Earth's core, everything on the surface of the Earth would experience an attraction toward its center. As with light and sound, that power would, he believed, increase inward in reciprocal proportion to the area of the sphere of propagation of the pulse and consequently to the square of the distance from the center. A propagated pulse of electricity could therefore be the fundamental cause of the observed descent of bodies toward the Earth. If this pulse were to be experienced outside the confines of our planet and be the cause of planetary motion, a universal aether had to be invoked as the agent of transmission.

Although Newton himself was reluctant to accept that the inverse-square law of gravitation operated throughout the solar system, when in early August 1684 he was finally persuaded by Halley to do so, he began also to accept the possibility that a comet might likewise be controlled by this force and to regard its path as approximating a highly elongated hyperbolic or parabolic orbit with a focus in the Sun.[29] His own observations of the comet of 1680–81—taken from 25 February to 9 March 1681 with a seven-foot refracting telescope with a micrometer and threads at the focus—had yielded seven positions relative to seventeen bright stars in the zodiacal constellations of Taurus and Gemini identifiable with the aid of Bayer's star chart.[30] From these he had deduced the comet's corresponding celestial longitudes and latitudes, using a mixture of ruler-and-compass constructions and arithmetic calculations. Plotting these coordinates on a large sheet of paper, he confirmed that they could be well represented by a parabola. Knowing also that previous comets had been confined mainly to the region of the zodiac, with speeds through the heavens that were compatible with calculations based on the assumption of a parabolic trajectory, he began to develop a new method for calculating the elements of a parabolic trajectory from three accurate observations that he obtained from Flamsteed.[31]

Newton's attempt to improve the accuracy of his calculations by taking account of other observations by Joseph Dionysius Ponthaeus in Rome, Jean Charles Gallet in Avignon, Pierre Ango in La Fleche, Geminiano Montanari in Venice, Robert Hooke in London, Johann Jacob Zimmermann in Nuremberg, Arthur Storer in Maryland, and other astronomers in Boston and in Ballasore (East Indies) was also to no avail—principally because of their limited accuracy and the lack of information about the nature of the instruments and methods of reduction employed. With the exception of Hooke's unimportant visual sightings at dawn on 22 and 23 November 1680, the data he had used were extracted by Newton from Halley's copy of a special tract collated by Cassini and presented to Halley shortly before his departure from Paris at the end of his continental tour.[32] Discouraged by this investigation, Newton reverted for a short time to Wren's method, but that too failed to yield a viable approximation.[33]

Perhaps it was the receipt from David Gregory in June 1684 of a fifty-page tract by his recently deceased uncle James Gregory anticipating certain ideas in the still-unpublished *De Analysi* that led Newton to develop an alternative computational method for a parabolic curve linking the notion of fluxions to that of series expansions and involving a summation of first-, second-, third-, and fourth-order differences, and so forth.[34] His further efforts during the winter of 1685–86 are recognized as a fitting climax to his previously unrewarded labors in this field.[35]

Soon they were to culminate in the revised method for constructing the elements of a parabolic orbit for the comet of 1680–81 from three selected observations of its celestial longitude, published as Proposition 41 of the third book of the *Principia* (1687).[36]

The merits of this theory have been praised by A. N. Kriloff, who has elaborated and amended it, expressed it in modern notation, explained the lemmas by which Newton justified his construction and interpolated intermediate positions of the comet, and applied it to compute the orbits of more recent comets.[37] As presented by Newton, the geometrical construction was supposed to relate to the plane of the ecliptic; strictly, though, it ought to be projected onto the plane of the comet's orbit, in which case the Sun would not remain exactly at the focus of the projected parabola and there would be a slight discrepancy in the calculated positions. Although he may not have been conscious of the fact, this was why Newton's comparisons of the calculated positions with those plotted from his own observations and those deduced from the other eleven Flamsteed observations yielded errors in the celestial latitudes several times larger than those anticipated from the internal accuracy of the micrometric measurements (viz. ± 1′).

Subsequently Halley employed this same theory to calculate the elements of a further twenty-three comets from the even less reliable nontelescopic and nonmicrometric measurements of earlier observers. His results, tabulated in his forty-two-page *Synopsis Astronomiae Cometicae* (1705), reveal the close similarities in orbital elements that led him to infer that certain comets had been seen at more than one epoch. The idea of a comet's returning to Earth instead of vanishing forever into the cold dark regions of outer space was a comforting one, and does indeed apply to the comet of 1682 which has come to bear Halley's name. He was nevertheless mistaken in his belief that the comet of 1680–81 had a period of 575 years and could be identified with three others that had appeared 44 B.C., A.D. 531, and A.D. 1106.[38] William Whiston, Newton's successor as Lucasian Professor of Geometry at Cambridge, was misled by this erroneous result. Indeed, it was his extrapolation of this fictitious period backward in time to 28 November 2349 B.C. that led him to blame that comet for the biblical Flood! Whiston's remarks on this subject in the appendix to the second edition of his *New Theory of the Earth* constitute an excellent example of the danger in attempting to extrapolate too much from too small a statistical sample of descriptive data and in giving too little weight to the errors inherent in theoretical calculation and observational practice.[39]

The nature and purpose of Newton's corrections and addenda to the later editions of the *Principia* may now be conveniently studied in the modern variorum edition prepared by the late Alexandre Koyré and Bernard Cohen.[40] As Cohen remarks in the separately published introduction to this text, the fact that Newton had not fully solved the trajectory of comets in the first edition of the *Principia* was one of three reasons for producing a second edition.[41] By the time of its publication in 1713, his relationship with Flamsteed had deteriorated to such an extent that Newton removed the earlier reference to the latter's "outstanding observations" of comets. He also substituted Halley's improved reductions of the originally published cometary data and added James Pound's own observed and reduced star-positions as well as a great deal more descriptive material showing the comet's path and tail.[42]

For the purpose of precise orbital calculations, only those observations made with a telescope and focal-plane micrometer (e.g., by Picard, Newton, and Kirch) or with an astronomical quadrant fitted with telescopic sights and a micrometer eyepiece (e.g., by Flamsteed, Cassini, Picard, Marchetti, and Ponthaeus) were in principle reliable.[43] Yet even from among those a further selection had to be made, since adequate information was not always given about the observations or the instruments used and many were clearly inaccurate. When Johann Franz Encke turned his attention to this matter in the early nineteenth century, he carefully examined the plethora of data and narrowed down the field to fourteen observations by Flamsteed, six by Newton, five plus four incomplete (right ascensions only) by Cassini, and one by Kirch.[44] Only after the completion of Bessel's star catalogue could the stellar coordinates to which the positions of all comets, planets, and satellites are necessarily referred finally be accepted as sufficiently reliable for the purpose of analysis.[45]

Encke's critical investigation of the motion of the comet of 1680–81 confirmed that Flamsteed's observational data were definitely the best, with those of Newton a close second; both were reliable enough to represent the motion to within 20 seconds in the two equatorial coordinates.[46] Despite the uncertainty of Kirch's single observation of 13 November 1680, it was valuable in that it lay well in advance of those others. A thorough examination of the tracts of Kirch, Dörffel, and Zimmermann by Encke and Wilhelm Olbers in a search for other reliable preperihelion observations merely served to confirm that nothing more suitable existed.[47] In a least-squares analysis of the selected data using the sophisticated theory developed by Carl Friedrich Gauss, Encke gives Kirch's observation one-half, and Cassini's observations one-third, of the weight accorded to those of Flamsteed and Newton.[48] He then found that the most probable parabola yielded almost as good a fit of the data as the most probable ellipse, with a hyperbola perhaps even marginally better. The elliptical representation favored by Halley was rejected, since it gave a significantly poorer representation of the most reliable observations.[49]

It would appear, therefore, that the comet of 1680–81 has paid us a visit that it may never repeat;[50] but the learned world will surely always remember it as one of the most celebrated of the many hundred comets recorded in history—not simply because of its brilliance, glowing nucleus, and lengthy tail, but also because it was the object of Newton's serious scientific attention. Through him, the first theory of cometary motion was born. Without it, Halley could never have recognized the periodic return of the comet that now bears his name.

NOTES

1. Georg Samuel Dörffel, *Astronomische Betrachtung des Grossen Kometen, welcher in ausgehenden 1680, und angehenden 1681 Jahr hochst verwunderlich und entsetzlich erschienen* (Plauen, 1681).

2. Angus Armitage, "Master Georg Dörffel and the Rise of Cometary Astronomy," *Annals of Science* 7 (1951): 303–15, includes a photograph of this woodcut.

3. Johann Hevelius, *Cometographia* (Danzig, 1668), esp. 149–64.

4. Ibid., 570–87, 66off. Hevelius's ideas are well summarized in Thomas Barker, *An Account of the Discoveries concerning Comets, with the Way to find their Orbits, and some Improvements in constructing and calculating their Places, etc.* (London, 1757), 3, 4.

5. Flamsteed to Towneley, 7 February 1680–81, Royal Society, MSS LIX.c.10, F.1.51.

6. Eric G. Forbes, *The Gresham Lectures of John Flamsteed* (London: Mansell, 1975), 20–34.

7. Giovanni Battista Riccioli, *Almagestum Novum* (Bologna, 1651), 2:11–12 (this discussion ends with the comet of 1618–19); Ioannes Regiomontanus, *De Comitae Magnitudine, Longitudineque Problemata 16* Nuremberg, 1531); Petrus Apianus, *Astronomicum Caesareum* (Ingolstadt, 1540).

8. His views on comets are to be found in the third of Flamsteed's Gresham College lectures, delivered on 11 May 1681. See Forbes, *Gresham Lectures*, 105–17.

9. The list of Flamsteed's micrometric measurements, sent with his letter to Towneley of 22 March 1680/81 (Royal Society, MSS LIX.c.10, F.1.52), has been published in Forbes, *Gresham Lectures*, 28. An extract from Flamsteed's letter to Halley, omitting his opinion of comets, their formation, motion, and so on, was printed in Francis Baily, *An Account of the Revd John Flamsteed* (London, 1835), 123–24. The missing details have since been supplied in *The Correspondence of Isaac Newton*, ed. H. W. Turnbull et al. (Cambridge: Cambridge University Press, 1959–77), 2:336–40.

10. This was conducted through the intermediary of James Crompton (1648–94), with whom Flamsteed had become acquainted during his student days at Jesus College, Cambridge. See note 15.

11. Edmond Halley, *Catalogus Stellarum Australium* (London, 1679) is the outcome of the St. Helena sojourn. Hevelius's account of Halley's Danzig visit between mid May and mid July 1679 is contained in his *Annus Climactericus* (Danzig, 1685). The dispute of Hevelius and Flamsteed is briefly discussed in

Eugene Fairfield MacPike, *Hevelius, Flamsteed, and Halley* (London: Taylor and Francis, 1937), 85–88; and in Forbes, *Gresham Lectures,* 34–39.

12. Gottfried Kirch, *Neue Himmels-Zeitung darinnen sonderlich und ausführlich von den zweyen neuen grossen in 1680. Jahr erschienenen Cometen . . .* (Nuremberg, 1681). This 144-page treatise contains two general maps showing the comet's progress through the constellations and three others indicating its changes in appearance and location with respect to neighboring bright stars.

13. Halley's letter from Paris of 22 January 1680/81 communicating these foreign observations is apparently no longer extant. The information was, however, imparted by Flamsteed to the Savilian professor of astronomy at Oxford, Edward Bernard, on 4 February 1680/81 (Bodleian Library, Oxford, MS. Smith 45, 45–47) and again three days later to Richard Towneley (Royal Society, MSS LIX.c.10, F.1.51).

14. Flamsteed's conclusion regarding the Earth's effect on comets is explicitly stated in his letter to Towneley of 7 February 1680/81 (Royal Society, MSS 243[F1], no. 51). See also John Flamsteed, "An account of Hevelius his Prodromus Cometicus, together with some Animadversions made upon it by a French Philosopher," *Philosophical Transactions of the Royal Society* 1, no. 6 (6 November 1665): 104–8, esp. 105.

15. Four letters written by Flamsteed to Crompton on 15 December 1680, 3 January, 12 February, and 7 March 1680/81 found their way into Newton's hands. They provoked the response referred to here and, somewhat more fully, in Forbes, *Gresham Lectures,* 31–34. All are published in Newton, *Correspondence.*

16. Newton to Crompton for Flamsteed, 28 February 1680/81, in *Correspondence* 2:341–42.

17. Newton to Crompton for Flamsteed, April 1681, ibid., 358–62, esp. 361.

18. Dated 12 April 1681, the draft letter is preserved in a collection of over sixty manuscript letters designated ADD 3979 in the University Library, Cambridge. The letter that was sent is Newton to Flamsteed, 16 April 1681, in *Correspondence* 2:363–67.

19. The diagram was enclosed with Flamsteed's fourth letter of 7 March 1680/81, in Newton, *Correspondence* 2:348–56. See note 15.

20. Ibid., 366.

21. This had already been published by John Wallis in his edition of *Jeremiae Horrocci . . . Opera Posthuma* (London, 1673) and in Robert Hooke's *Lectures and Collections* (London, 1678). It was subsequently reprinted in Wallis's *Opera Mathematica* (Oxford, 1693), 2:455–62.

22. "Appendix 3. Computations of Rectilinear Cometary Paths," in *The Mathematical Papers of Isaac Newton,* ed. D. T. Whiteside (Cambridge: Cambridge University Press, 1967–80), 5:524–31. Whiteside's tentative dating of this appendix as ca. October 1685 is inconsistent with his previous remark (ibid., 303) that these worksheets were composed by Newton "about spring 1681."

23. "From four observed positions of a comet crossing the sky with a uniform rectilinear motion, to gather its distance from the Earth and the direction of its motion, supposing the 'Copernican hypothesis,'" (ibid., 299–304).

24. Richard S. Westfall (*Never at Rest: A Biography of Isaac Newton* [Cambridge: Cambridge University Press, 1980], 394) assumes that Newton had solved the

mechanics of orbital motion for a planet circling the Sun around January 1680 but that he did not try to apply this knowledge to comets because they were different in nature.

25. Newton, *Mathematical Papers* 4:409; "Geometria Curvilinea," ibid., 420–505.

26. Ibid., p. 410, 413.

27. "Proposition I. Theorem I: The areas which revolving bodies describe by radii drawn to an immovable centre of force do lie in the same immovable planes, and are proportional to the times in which they are described" (*Sir Isaac Newton's Mathematical Principles of Natural Philosophy and His System of the World*, trans. Andrew Motte [1729], ed. Florian Cajori [Berkeley and Los Angeles: University of California Press, 1966], 1:40–42; hereafter cited as *Principia* [Motte-Cajori]); "Proposition XI. Problem VI: If a body revolves in an ellipse; it is required to find the law of the centripetal force tending to the focus of the ellipse" (ibid., 56–57).

28. *The Posthumous Works of Robert Hooke . . . containing his Cutlerian Lectures, and other discourses, read at the meetings of the illustrious Royal Society*, ed. Richard Waller (London, 1705), 149–85.

29. Propositions 12 and 13 of Newton's *Principia* (1687) demonstrate that an inverse square distance law of force likewise applies to both of these cases; see *Principia* (Motte-Cajori), 1:57–61.

30. Ibid., 507–12.

31. "The approximate determination of a parabolic cometary path," in Newton, *Mathematical Papers* 6:481–97.

32. Hooke, *Posthumous Works*, 153; Giovanni Domenico Cassini, *Observations sur la comète qui a paru au mois de décembre 1680. Et en janvier 1681. Présentées au Roy* (Paris, 1681).

33. Newton, *Mathematical Papers* 6:483.

34. James Gregory, "A Geometrical Exercise in the Measuring of Figures"; see Newton, *Mathematical Papers* 4:413. This alternative method was an application of Newton's method of finite differences for interpolating intermediate positions of the comet useful for producing an ephemeris; see *Mathematical Papers* 4:590–617.

35. "Revised Computation of the Elements of a Parabolic Cometary Orbit," in *Mathematical Papers* 4:498–507.

36. "Prop. XLI. Prob. XX: Cometae in Parabola moventis Trajectoriam ex datis tribus observationibus determinare" (*Mathematical Papers* 6:487–89).

37. A. N. Kriloff, "On Sir Isaac Newton's Method of Determining the Parabolic Orbit of a Comet," *Monthly Notes of the Royal Astronomical Society* 85 (May 1925): 640–56.

38. The historical evidence and computational technique on which Halley based this opinion have been examined and rejected by John Russell Hind, "On the Supposed Period Revolution of the Great Comet of 1680," *Monthly Notes of the Royal Astronomical Society* 12 (1851): 142–50.

39. William Whiston, *The Cause of the Deluge demonstrated: wherein it is proved that the famous Comet of A.D. 1680 came by the Earth at the Deluge, and was the Occasion of it* (London, 1714).

40. *Isaac Newton's Philosophiae Naturalis Principia Mathematica: The Third Edition (1726) with Variant Readings*, ed. Alexandre Koyré and I. Bernard Cohen (Cambridge: Cambridge University Press, 1972), vol. 2.

41. I. Bernard Cohen, *Introduction to Newton's "Principia"* (Cambridge, Mass.: Harvard University Press, 1971), 162. The other two reasons here stated are Newton's failure to solve the lunar theory and Kepler's problem of determining the exact relationship between a planet's true anomaly and the area of its elliptical orbit swept out by the radius vector in the same interval of time.

42. These changes are all contained in *Principia* (Motte-Cajori), 507–42; see p. 519 for the diagram.

43. Cassini (*Observations sur la comète*, 34–35) stresses this fact very explicitly in his classification of the observational data according to their accuracy.

44. Johann Franz Encke, "Versuch einer Bestimmung der wahrscheinlichsten Bahn dese Cometen von 1680. Mit Rücksicht auf die planetarischen Störungen während der Dauer seiner Sichtbarkeit," *Zeitschrift für Astronomie und verwandte Wissenschaften* 6 (Tübingen, 1818), 27–120, 129–80, esp. 36.

45. Friedrich Wilhelm Bessel, *Fundamenta Astronomiae pro Anno 1755 Deducta ex Observationibus Viri Incomparabilis James Bradley in Specola Astronomica Grenovicensi per anno 1750–1762 Institutis* (Königsberg, 1818).

46. This was the final result of the first section of Encke's "*Versuch einer Bestimmung*" (p. 120).

47. Kirch, *Neue Himmels-Zeitung;* Dörffel, *Astronomische Betrachtung;* Johann Jacob Zimmermann, *Cometo-scopia, oder Himmel-gemäser Bericht mit müglichstem Fleiss darstellende beedes die nach der Trigonometria Sphaerica, astronomische Calculation, als auch Astro-Theologische Aussdeuting dess mitten im Novembri 1680.sten Jahrs entstandenen und biss in den Anfang Februarij 1681 erschienenen grossen Wunder-Sterns und Cometens . . .* (Stuttgart, 1681). Encke also gave due consideration to another tract containing pre-perihelion and many other observations, namely Alessandro Marchetti's *Della natura delle comete . . .* (Florence, 1684), which, because of the three-year delay in its publication, was not known to Newton at the time he examined the other foreign data. Although Baron Franz Xavier von Zach (*Zeitschrift für Astronomie und verwandte Wissenschaften* 2 [Stuttgart, 1816], 100–123) had argued that Marchetti's data were accurate to within a few seconds of arc, Encke's own study led him to conclude that these data were, on the contrary, utterly useless.

48. Encke, "Versuch einer Bestimmung," 142.

49. Edmond Halley, *Tabulae Astronomicae* (London, 1749), contains his "Synopsis Astronomiae Cometicae qua Cometarum hactenus debite observatorum Motus in Orbe Parabolico repraesentantur. Eorumque qui annis MDCLXXX & MDCLXXXII fulsêre Post certas Periodos redeuntium, Motus in Orbibus Ellipticis accurato calculo subjiciuntur."

50. Brian G. Marsden's *Catalogue of Cometary Orbits*, 4th ed. (Cambridge, Mass.: 1982), lists the eccentricity of this comet's orbit as 0.999986, which agrees closely with several earlier estimates listed in J. G. Galle's *Verzeichniss der Elemente der bisher berechneten Cometenbahnen* (Leipzig, 1894), 13, thereby implying that the orbit is to all intents and purposes indistinguishable from a parabola.

SEVENTEEN

Edmond Halley:
His Interest in Comets

David W. Hughes

Edmond Halley was born on 8 November 1656 and died at the age of eighty-five on 25 January 1742. During his long life, not only was he a Captain in the Royal Navy and Clerk, Fellow, Council Member, and Secretary of the Royal Society, but he also held Britain's most important astronomical appointment, that of Astronomer Royal (from 1720 to his death), and one of the most prestigious positions in mathematics, that of Savilian Professor of Geometry at Oxford University (from January 1704 to his death). Halley was a giant among scientists and well worthy of being designated the second greatest British scientist of his time. His light today would shine even brighter if he had not lived in such close temporal proximity to Isaac Newton.

Arago in 1855 wrote, "Halley méritera de vivre dans la postérité comme un des savants qui ont le plus contribué aux progrès de l'astronomie. Son génie scientifique fut apprécié de bonne heure, parce qu'il était uni au plus noble caractère."[1] Dingle in 1956 said of Halley, "Never has such a man been born into an age so completely ready to receive him. . . . He epitomised within himself the whole scientific movement." Dingle also brought Halley, and all scientists, down to earth by saying, "There is not one of his scientific papers that might not have been written by another, and in time doubtless would have been so written, but it would have taken the whole Royal Society to produce them all."[2]

Bullard in 1956 concluded that Halley's forte was as an organizer of data. "Again and again he collects a mass of information of varying reliability, containing many errors and contradictions, and reduces it to order. He did this with the magnetic observations, with the tides in the Channel, with the comets, with the eclipse of 1715 and with the Moon's orbit. His remarkable work on the path of the great meteor of 1719 is of the same kind and so is his discussion of the trade winds."[3] Added to his collecting and correcting ability was however the deep desire to understand the science of the phenomena, coupled with an outstanding ability in two key fields of scientific endeavor: physics and mathematics.

Halley lived in the age of the scientific generalists, men who turned their minds and talents to all the interesting scientific problems of the day. In the astronomical realm, comets were well to the fore as "problem objects," the three remarkable comets which appeared in 1664, 1665, and 1680 attracting the attention of most men of science. Three cometary problems were writ large: (1) what was their physical form? (2) what orbits did they have? and (3) were they periodic or completely random? Halley spent very little time on the first problem. He was told the answer to the second by Isaac Newton, who also used the observations of the comet of 1680 to illustrate how orbital elements could be calculated; Halley in turn went on to use this technique to calculate the orbits of a further twenty-three comets. Problem 3, however, was a main concern of Halley's, and his solution of it made him the first man to prove that comets were periodic. He showed that the comets seen in 1531, 1607, and 1682 had very similar orbits and concluded that they were in fact the same astronomical object returning to the inner solar system every seventy-six years or so. He predicted that it would return again at the end of 1758, and this it did, about seventeen years after his death. In the words of Benjamin Martin (May 1759), "As it is the first comet which has been predicted, and has returned exactly according to that predication, it cannot but excite the attention and admiration of the curious in general, and fill the minds of all astronomers with a ravishing satisfaction, as it has, by this return, confirmed Sir Isaac Newton's rationale of the solar system, verified the cometarian theory of Dr. Halley and is the first instance of astronomy brought to perfection."[4]

This prediction proved true and was the first triumph of Newton's theory of universal gravitation and tolled the final death knell of Descartes's vortical theory (Fig. 17.1). The ultimate test of a hypothesis is its predictive capability, and the scientific world greatly admires people who make predictions and are subsequently proved to be correct. Halley will be forever remembered as the first person to predict the return of a comet. Already within a decade of the return, the comet was beginning to be referred to as Halley's Comet. The earliest record of this appellation was probably in a report by the abbé de LaCaille in 1765.[5] In 1769 Charles Burney wrote that "the Comet of 1759 is known throughout Europe by the name of Dr. Halley's Comet."[6] Although by 1835 the name was in general use, by 1910, regrettably, the large majority of Halley's other scientific work had been all but forgotten.

Elsewhere I have reviewed Halley's scientific career and scientific suc-

Figure 17.1. A copper medallion (11.1 × 8.9 cm) issued around 1780 showing Isaac Newton. The small comet hovering above his right shoulder is Halley's comet, depicted at its 1758–59 reappearance.

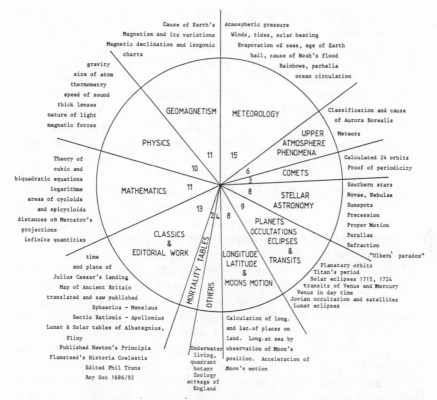

Figure 17.2. The percentages of Halley's professional life spent in various pursuits (after D. W. Hughes, "Edmond Halley, Scientist," *Journal of the British Astronomical Association* 95 [1985]: 193).

cesses and found that Halley spent a mere 3 percent of his scientific life studying comets (Fig. 17.2).[7] It is this 3 percent that I consider in this paper. In cometary science Halley was at the watershed: before him comets were omens and portents; afterward they were predictable astronomical phenomena.

COMETS BEFORE HALLEY

Aristotle thought that comets were atmospheric phenomena, mainly, it seems, because they were unplanetlike, having sporadic times of arrival and departure, following random tracks, being seen outside the zodiacal band of the sky, having tails, and "vanishing without setting, gradually fading above the horizon . . . without leaving a star." They were supposedly caused by vapors that rise from the Earth to accumulate at the top of the atmosphere; there they burned slowly, because if the combustion took place quickly, shooting stars would be formed. Comets were linked with meteorology: "when there are many comets the years are dry and windy."[8] Apparently the great comet of 371 B.C. occurred during a dry winter when the north winds prevailed, and the comet of 341–40 B.C. was in the sky when there were storms at Corinth. Aristotle regarded comets as weather signs indicating strong and dry winds. He thought the winds produced the comets, but this was soon reversed so that comets became progenitors of winds and thus spawned the consequences of winds, such as floods and fires. Prior to Aristotle some Babylonians regarded comets as extensive planets, permanent members of the solar system that were only visible from Earth when they came close. They were thought to be periodic, an opinion also held by the Pythagorean School. Others simply thought comets to be fires produced by a kind of eddy of violently rotating air.

Pliny notes that comets moved and changed their position with respect to the fixed stars. Seneca thought that their motions, like those of the planets, might be determined and predicted and added that "the time will come when those things which are now hidden shall be brought to light by time and persevering diligence. Our posterity will wonder that we should be ignorant of what is so obvious." Seneca also thought that comets were above (that is beyond) the Moon, and from their rising and setting he judged them to have something in common with the stars. Their form, he said, "is too beautiful to be thought accidental whether you consider their vastness or their brightness that surpasses in size and brilliance all other stars. Their appearance has in truth, an exceptional distinction; they are not cribbed and cabined within narrow bonds, but let loose to roam freely, to range over the region of many stars."[9]

Since people like to predict the future, most accepted Aristotle's ideas, and comets soon became astrological portents. The Elizabethan writer Leonard Digges, for example, wrote in 1576: "Cometes signifie corruption of the ayre. They are signes of earthquakes, of warres, of changying of Kyngdomes, great dearth of corne, yea a common death of man and beast."[10] The height of the comet dread was in the fifteenth and sixteenth centuries, when the skies abounded with large, bright comets visible to the naked eye. A roll call would read A.D. 1402, 1403, 1449, 1456, 1457 (two), 1472, 1500, 1506, 1531, 1532 (two), 1533, 1538, 1539, 1556, 1558, 1569, 1577, 1580, and 1582. This abundance encouraged people to make lists, the first printed one being by Antonius Mizaldus in 1544, in which a "resulting" disaster was carefully noted after each recorded comet.[11] Ludwig Lavater in 1556 produced a second list, and in 1668 Lubieniecki published a two-folio volume entitled *Theatrum Cometicum*, which listed accounts of 415 comets or supposed comets with concurrent events both good and bad.[12] Lubieniecki concluded that, as the good events apparently balanced the bad, comets had nothing at all to do with earthly happenings. Pierre Bayle in 1699 agreed.[13]

The comet of 1680 featured prominently in Halley's early life. The appearance of this large, bright comet produced a rash of pamphlets relating many superstitions in several countries of Europe (Fig. 17.3 shows a typical example). A medal was struck to commemorate the event, and the French *Journal des sçavans* (20 January 1681) even went so far as to discuss seriously a "comet egg" that was apparently laid by a "virginal" hen in Rome and had a picture of a comet on its shell.[14]

Unperturbed by all the astrological prognostications, astronomers still regarded comets as objects worthy of investigation. Regiomontanus (i.e., Johann Müller) and Bernard Walther measured the celestial coordinates of the bright comet of 1472 so well that Halley could subsequently use them to determine its orbit, and Girolamo Fracastoro in 1538 announced that comet tails always pointed away from the sun.[15] Independently and almost simultaneously Apian published the same conclusion, but he included a diagram (Fig. 17.4) that obviously made a great impression because he is usually credited with the European discovery of this fact.[16] The Chinese, however, were far ahead of both of them. Biot noted in 1843 that, on observing Halley's comet in late March 837, Chinese astronomers recorded in the Annals of the Tang dynasty: "En général, quand une comète (littéralement un balai) paraît le matin, alors elle est dirigée vers l'occident; quand elle paraît le soir, elle est dirigée vers l'orient. C'est une règle constante."[17]

It seems that many astronomers studied the comet of 1577. Tycho Brahe observed it from the island of Hveen, and in his German treatise on comets he explained how he attempted to determine the distance between the Earth and the comet and found that the head of the comet was more than four times as far from the Earth as the Moon.[18] This lower limit came from an inability to detect a diurnal parallax (a shift in the position of the object as seen against the celestial background caused by the observer's motion as the Earth spins). The diameter of the coma was calculated to be over three thousand kilometers, and the tail was five hundred thousand kilometers long and thirty-six thousand kilometers wide. Michael Maestlin came to similar conclusions. The distance measuring technique had previously been applied to the nova of 1572, which was also found to be superlunary. The astronomical community was shocked to realize that these fast-moving comets apparently traveled through space unimpeded by the crystalline spheres that were traditionally supposed to carry the planets around on their courses. Maestlin, like Brahe, thought that comets were transitory, created and destroyed by God at or near the time of their first and last appearances.

Kepler was curious about the vagaries of comets and began studying

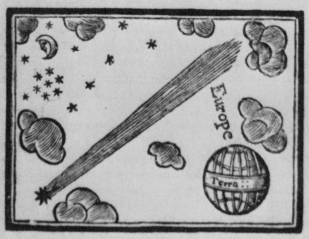

Figure 17.3. A pamphlet warning of the calamities to be expected after the appearance of the comet of 1680.

Figure 17.4. An Apian woodcut from Hevelius's *Cometographia* (1668) showing
the 1531 apparition of Halley's Comet, the tail of which is clearly pointing away
from the Sun. Notice that the zodiac is reversed, Cancer being on the left of Leo.
(Courtesy of the Crawford Library, Royal Observatory, Edinburgh.)

the problem in earnest around 1602. His views were given in a short German tract that he published in 1608 soon after seeing a comet in September 1607. Comets were thought to be illuminated by the Sun and not self-luminous. Their tails were believed to result from light refracted through their globular, glassy head and falling on material floating in the aether; they were supposedly a condensation of the all-pervading aether, a celestial "abscess" of impurities. Kepler suggested that space was as full of comets as the sea was of fish but only those that came close to Earth could be seen. The Sun's rays, on passing through the comet, forced out some of the cometary material to form the tail, which pointed away from the Sun. These rays eventually completely destroyed the comet. He added certain astrological details, including that contact between the tail and the Earth's atmosphere could add impurities and result in widespread mortality. Three comets appeared in 1618, and Kepler published a book on the subject in 1619.[19]

Unlike Brahe and Maestlin, both of whom embraced a geocentric cosmology, Kepler was a Copernican. The calculation of the comet's orbit and distance thus had to take into account the parallax exhibited by the comet owing to the movement of the Earth. Unfortunately, the limited data available to Kepler for the comets of 1607 and 1618 could be fitted to almost any theoretical orbit shape. Brahe and Maestlin thought that the comet of 1577 moved around the Sun in a circular orbit close to that of Venus (this comet displayed an apparent motion similar to Venus but with a somewhat greater maximum solar elongation). In their view, the Sun was moving too—in a circular, moonlike orbit around the Earth. Kepler apparently felt the closed elliptical orbits of the "enduring and devinely appointed planets" were not fitting for such transient objects as comets.[20] Why should an object that never returned to its starting point in the heavens have a closed orbit? Kepler was of the opinion that comets moved with regular varying speeds along straight lines. According to Ruffner, Kepler thought that comets were ignited, accelerated, and then slowed down rather like rockets, projected in all directions through the heavens but in straight-line trajectories. Meteors acted as another of Kepler's analogues.[21]

Pierre Gassendi, in his 1652 treatise on comets, had them moving along straight lines at constant speeds, and he also (going back to Seneca) considered them to be one of the everlasting works of nature. Gassendi unfortunately was content with just musing on comets and never submitted his ideas "to the numbers."[22] Giovanni Alfonso Borelli wrote to Father Stefano de Angeli on 10 February 1665 about the comet of 1664. Writing under the assumed name of Pier Maria Mutoli, he concluded that his orbital calculations made sense only if he adopted a heliocentric viewpoint and had the Earth moving. The resulting cometary orbit resembled an ellipse or a parabola. Pierre Petit decided that comets were

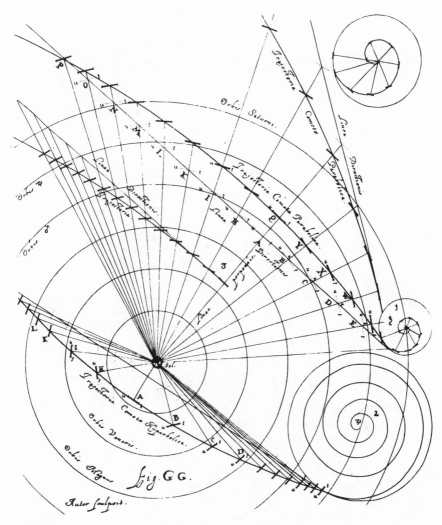

Figure 17.5. Hevelius's ideas as to the origin (planetary) and orbits (parabolae and hyperbolae) of comets, taken from his *Cometographia* (1668).

probably periodic and surmised that the comet of 1664 was the same as that of 1618 and that it might return in 1710.[23]

Hevelius had comets moving along lines which were "never exquisitely straight as Kepler and others would have it, but partly inflected and curved so that the concave side always faces the Sun."[24] Galileo had shown that projectiles move in parabolic tracks, and Hevelius thought that most comets behaved similarly. His ideas are illustrated in Figure 17.5, where comets, supposedly nonrotating disc-shaped bodies, can be

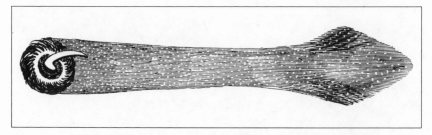

Figure 17.6. Hevelius's drawing of Halley's Comet as seen from Danzig on 8 September 1682 (new style), showing the luminous ray thrown out from the nucleus. Taken from his *Annus Climacterius* (1685).

seen being ejected from the planets. The change in the orientation of these discs apparently modified the motion of the comet. Thus the comet emitted by Saturn started with the disc perpendicular to the Saturn-comet line and then moved off with the disc perpendicular to the Sun-comet line. Hyperbolic and parabolic trajectories are tried. Hevelius carefully catalogued all historical records of comets in his *Cometographia*. To Hevelius, comets were agglutinations of atmospheric exhalation; while any planet could give birth to a comet, Jupiter and Saturn were the most likely parents because of their color and size. The planet's rotation, he suggested, throws the comet out at a tangent. Hevelius (1611–1687) observed the 1682 apparition of Halley's comet from Danzig and noticed a luminous ray thrown out from the nucleus into the tail. His drawing of the comet is shown in Figure 17.6.

Sir William Lower hinted in a letter of 6 February 1610 to Thomas Harriot that comets sometimes move in very eccentric ellipses.[25] When discussing the comet of 1652, Seth Ward, Savilian Professor of Astronomy at Oxford, declared that comets are probably "carryed round in Circles or Ellipses (either including or excluding the Globe of the Earth), so great, that the Comets are never visible to us, but when they come to the Perigees of those Circles or Ellipses, and ever after invisible till they have absolved their periods in those vast Orbs." Ward was worried that Gassendi's "unending straight lines" would make the universe infinite; his circles and ellipses thus "greatly reduced the immensity."[26] In 1678, Robert Hooke (1635–1703), a student of Ward's and Halley's associate at the Royal Society, published his lecture notes of 1665. He was obviously much interested in the comet of 1664 and inquired

> what kind of motion it was carried with? Whether in a straight or bended line? And if bended, whether in a circular or other curve, as elliptical or other compounded line, whether the convex or concave side of the curve were turned towards the Earth? Whether in any of those lines it moved

equal or unequal spaces in equal times? Whether it ever appears again, being moved in a circle or be carried clear away and never appear again, being moved in a straight or paraboloidical line?[27]

Hooke thought it was natural that the Sun's attraction should make the comet follow a closed orbit. He suggested also that the comet of 1664 might be a return visit of the comet of 1618. Hooke was convinced that, considering the accuracy of the cometary observations of those days, any number of theoretical ideas would fit. He was a great advocate of improving the observational data and then starting with a fresh theory. Dörffel, however, was the true forerunner of Newton.[28] He had, he said, a new "and still unripe" idea that might improve the hypothesis of Hevelius, which was that "the path of the motion of the 1680 comet was a parabola which had its focus at the centre of the Sun" (Fig. 17.7).[29] Comets, in particular their physical form, orbits, and possible periodicity, were astronomical concepts of considerable interest at the time of Halley's birth. Each new comet that appeared only fueled this interest.

COMETARY WORK DURING
HALLEY'S LIFETIME

Halley was born at his father's country house in Haggerston, an area that today is covered with the sprawl of London suburbia but then, in 1656, was a hamlet three miles northeast of St. Paul's Cathedral. His father also had a town house and business premises in Winchester Street, which was later demolished to be covered by the railways converging on London's Broad Street Station. According to John Aubrey (a contemporary gossip and antiquarian), "At 9 years old, his father's apprentice taught him to write, and arithmetique."[30] This was the time when bubonic plague had been raging in London for eighteen months, a time that culminated with the Great Fire of London in 1666. For a young boy learning to read, the possible sight of John Gadbury's prophecy (Fig. 17.8) would have been a frightening yet enthralling introduction to comets.

Halley's first contact with a cometary astronomer was probably with Hooke, whom he would have met at the Royal Society. Halley, age twenty-three, was elected Fellow on 30 November 1678, about the time that Hooke's book on comets was published. Soon after, Halley met a second cometary astronomer, Johannes Hevelius, when he went to Danzig on behalf of the Royal Society and possibly at the bidding of Flamsteed to "become personally acquainted with Hevelius, to study his instruments and observing technique at first hand and to consult him concerning the further advancement of astronomy."[31] Halley arrived in

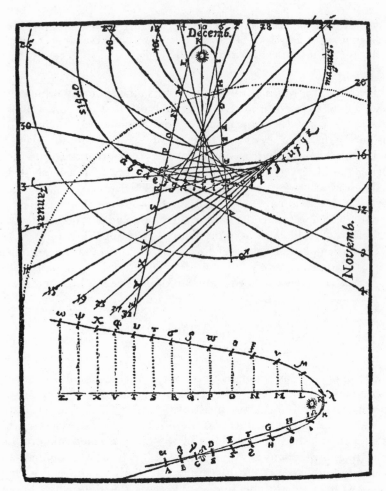

Figure 17.7. Magister Georg Samuel Dörffel saw the comet of 1680 in November before it became lost in the solar glare, and he anticipated its reappearance and continued observing the comet until it faded from his sight in February 1681. To estimate the path of the comet Dörffel first marked points a, b, c, etc. at four-day intervals along the Earth's orbit throughout the period of the comet's visibility. From there he constructed lines of sight to the comet: aA, bB, cC, etc. The positions of the comet, A, B, C, etc., were obtained by trial and error with the proviso that the comet's speed increased up to perihelion passage and decreased afterward. He guessed that the true orbit, α, β, γ, etc., was a parabola, with the Sun at one of its foci. Dörffel had no ideas as to what the orbital parameters were.

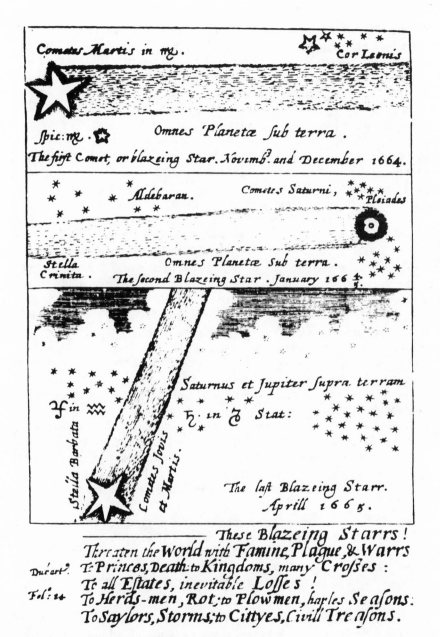

Figure 17.8. Gadbury's prophecies concerning the comet of 1664, one of which was that it threatened the world with plague. This was published in London in 1665 at the time of the Black Death, when Halley was about nine.

Danzig on 16 May 1679 and left in early July. What he thought about Hevelius's observing techniques is debatable, but it is hard to imagine that at some time in the two months they were together they did not discuss comets and the ideas that Hevelius put forward in his *Cometographia* of 1668.

MacPike reprinted a manuscript "Memoir of Halley," which was found in the Bodleian Library at Oxford and was apparently written in the mid 1740s by Martin Folkes, a contemporary of Halley and President of the Royal Society from 1741 to 1752. In this manuscript we read that Halley, who decided to make "the Tour of France and Italy, and to converse with the Eminent Astronomers and other Learned Men of those parts, set out for Paris, on the 1st December 1680, in Company with Mr. Nelson, well known by his religious writings: and I remember to have heard him say, he was on the road between Calais and Paris [he arrived in Paris 24 December 1680], when he first saw the Famous Comet of that year in its return from the Sun; he had already seen it in its going down to the Sun in the month of November before his setting out." [32] This comet passed perihelion on 18 December when it was only 0.006222 astronomical units (AU) from the Sun. It was, according to Mairan, "si remarquable par sa grandeur, & si terrible aux yeux d'un vulgaire." [33]

In Paris the comet was all the rage. Halley wrote from Paris to Robert Hooke on 15 January 1681: "The generall talk of the virtuosi here is about the Comet, which now appears, but the cloudy weather has permitted him to be but very seldom observed. Whatever shall be made publick about him here, I shall take care to send you, and I hope when you shall please to write to me you will do me the favour to let me know what has been observed in England." [34] Hooke was obviously interested in comets, having published data on the comet of 1677 in 1678. Halley apparently wrote to Flamsteed on 22 January; [35] Flamsteed's reply, written from Greenwich on 17 February 1681, includes the following:

> You tell me you have meditated upon comets and come to a result yet desire my thoughts as to the Philosophicall part of them. . . .
>   I conceave therefore that the Sun attracts all the planets and all like bodies that come within our Vortex, more or lesse according to the different substance of theire bodyes and nearenesse or remotenesse from him. [36]

Flamsteed went on to explain how the comet moved in straight lines except when "ye Matter of ye Vortex moved against it bent it into a Curve." He drew a picture of the comet moving toward and then away from the Sun without going around it (Fig. 17.9). "Ye Sun hee repells it as ye North Pole of ye loadstone attracts ye one end of ye Magnetick needle but repells ye other." He emphasizes in his letter to Halley: "My theory

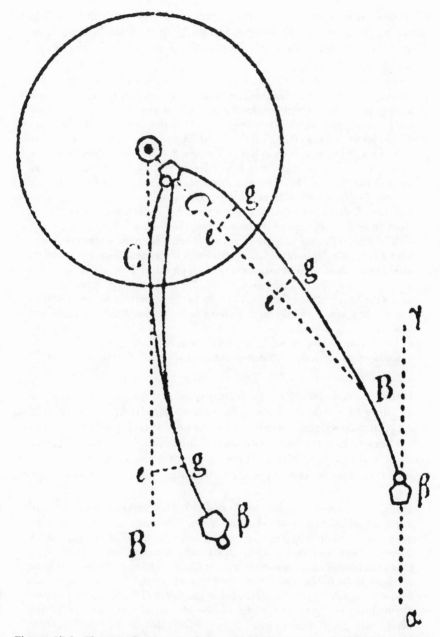

Figure 17.9. Flamsteed's picture of the orbit of the comet of 1680. Notice that the comet does not go round the Sun but is repelled from it, rather like two similar-polarity magnetic poles coming close together.

of motion differs very little from youres but to tell you the truth I have made no triall by calculation yet but by a large draught on paper."[37] Then follows a discussion of his ideas as to the physical nature of comets:

> As for the body of the Comet nothing better occures to my thoughts at present then that it may have beene some planet belonging formerly to another Vortex now ruined: for Worlds may die as well as men: that its naturall motion being destroyed its body is broke & the humid parts swim over ye rest yet so as some small peeces of ye solid part of ye Masse here & there lie out above them, this its ill defined figure & dusky light persuades me: which in my opinion was not much different from yt of ye obscure large spots in the Moone which are accounted the aqueous part of it; onely the greater distance of the Comet caused its colour to appeare lesse bright but with here & there some very small pointes of light which might be reflected from ye prominent tops of yet broken parts of solid matter. . . .
>
> The humid part of ye body of ye comet being outmost might cause it to have a large atmosphere: & from both when it was near ye Sun the violent action of his raies upon it might carry forth plentifull Steames of matter to a vast distance which caused ye tayle to appeare double the lenghth when neare the Sun it did to the lenght on its perigee where it lay most convenient to be seene & should on yt account have appeared longest. Conceave how yet smoke would appeare from a chimny in a moveing ship or ye steames from a drop of water let fall on a moved hot iron [and] you will apprehend the reason of ye deflection of ye tayle I thinke very naturally.[38]

Halley moved from Paris to Saumur, a town on the River Loire and from there he wrote to Hooke again on 29 May 1681. This was a long letter containing details about the books he was trying to obtain for the Royal Society Library and about such things as the methods whereby he compared the populations and sizes of London and Paris. About 20 percent of this letter is taken up with a discussion about the comet:

> Monsieur Cassini did me the favour to give me his booke of ye Comett Just as I was goeing out of towne; he, besides the Observations thereof, wch. he made till the 18 of March new stile, has given a theory of its Motion wch. is, that this Comet was the same with that that appeared to Tycho Anno 1577, that it performes its revolution in a great Circle including the earth wch. he will have to be fixt in about 2 yeares and halfe or that its diurnall motion of the perigeon 24'.5".2'".40'''' and that the diurnall motion is of the perigeon direct is 6".31''', the Radix of the Motion of Longitude & of the perigeon is Sagittarius 14°:00' to 1577 November 7ᵈ St. vet 6ʰ p.m. in Uraniburgi that the proportion of the perigeon distance to ye Apogeon is at 1−21½ the Northern Node 21° of Sagittarius fixt and the inclination 29°:15', this is the Sume of his Hypothesis and he says it will answer exactly enough to the Motions of the two Comets as likewise to that of April 1665;

I know you will with difficulty Embrace this Notion of his, but at the same
tyme tis very remarkable that 3 Cometts should so exactly trace the same
path in the Heavens and with the same degrees of velocity. I tryed but
without Success to represent the Observations by an equable Motion in a
right line. I made a theory to hit the first and last and two intermediate
Observations, but then the Latitudes differed a little too much and the rest
of the Longitudes would not hit right, especially at first where they differed 51'. it Semeth to me that the real motion was swifter at first then
afterwards when the body was not only to sight but really deminished.
your thoughts hereupon may serve to guide me in my Speculation. I am
yet resolved to try one bout with it, and it will be with a great deal of regret
that I shall be forced to give over. I believe the Observations of Mr.
Flamsteed are the best that are made of it. the instruments of the Obser-
vatiure here not being Compareable to his Sextans.[39]

Flamsteed's sextant is illustrated by Francis Place and was one of the best
instruments of the day.[40] It also acted as a model for Halley's 5.5-foot
sextant that he took to St. Helena in 1676.

Jean-Dominique Cassini ("who has been my very particular good
friend," as Halley said in the same letter to Hooke)[41] at the time of
Halley's visit to Paris was fifty-five years of age and director of the Observatoire de Paris. Cassini knew Halley by reputation and from reading his
Catalogues des Estoilles Australes, which had just been published in Paris in
1679. To Cassini the three comets of 1577, 1665 (April), and 1680–81
were simply three appearances of the same object. Although Halley was
not convinced of this, he still found the similarity of their tracks across
the celestial sphere and of their velocities remarkable. Maybe this sowed
the seed of his great endeavor and he later on tackled the problem of
calculating the orbits of twenty-four comets simply to see if any were periodic, as Cassini and Petit had proposed. Halley's cometary orbital calculations thus started in Paris, but he bypassed Hevelius's hyperbolae
and parabolae and regressed to the straight-line tracks suggested by
Kepler, and he also assumed a constant velocity.

Failure was inevitable and doubtless annoying. This annoyance was
probably exacerbated by the fact that Halley regarded himself an expert
when it came to the calculation of the orbits of astronomical objects. His
first research paper, for example, concerned the use of three (and only
three) observations of Jupiter and Saturn as a basis for calculating, both
geometrically and algebraically, the eccentricities and aphelion distances
of their orbits.[42]

The letter (to Hooke) quoted above shows that Halley would not be
easily persuaded to drop the comet orbit problem, but we do not know
whether Hooke did have any helpful suggestions. The 1680 comet caused
considerable excitement both in England and elsewhere. It was seen on

its way to perihelion, became lost in the Sun's glare, and then seen again on its way out. Isaac Newton thought the observations were of two different comets, but Flamsteed believed (correctly) that they were one and the same. The fact that the celestial tracks before and after conjunction showed drastic departures from the arc of a continuous great circle goes some way to explain Newton's dilemma. Newton did not really start thinking of comet paths before 1683–84, and Halley at this stage was confused about the cause of cometary motion. In a letter to Newton, Flamsteed wrote, on 7 March 1681: "Mr Halley thinkes the comet to be a body that has lost its principle of gravitation, and yet I perceive would have it attracted by ye Sun."[43]

In 1682, "Halley's comet" returned to the vicinity of the Sun. According to Flamsteed, the comet was first seen by his neighbors at Greenwich on the evening of 15 August and again on the next morning. His assistant saw it on the evening of the seventeenth,

> but because of the atmosphere foul with clouds I [Flamsteed] was unable to observe it until the 19th. Even then I could not do so with the sextant because part of the house came between it and the comet. However I examined its head with the 16ft long telescope and it appeared very meagre, but a thick tail emerged from it this being about 5 gr. long, and widely spread out and very thin around its end; at the 9th hour its direction was towards the head [?] of Ursa Major.[44]

Flamsteed recorded detailed observations of the comet from 20 August until 9 September. Halley saw it from Islington. He had returned from his grand tour on 24 January 1682 and had married Mary Tooke on 20 April. "Mr. Halley intending now to settle for some time at home resolv'd to persue his Astronomical observations, and having, in order to it, fixt the sextant he had at St. Helene, in a small Observatory he fitted up at Islington, where he then lived, he began a regular Course of Observations, of the Moon especially; on 7th November 1682 and carryed on the same to the 16th June 1684."[45]

Unfortunately, the comet appeared before 7 November, and presumably Halley's 5.5-foot telescopic-sighted sextant was not properly mounted when the comet was visible. His positional observations are thus rather crude, evidently naked-eye alignments, which could have been confirmed by positioning a hand-held piece of string to overlay the respective stars and the comet. They were jotted down in a small octavo-sized notebook, now in the archives of the Royal Greenwich Observatory, Herstmonceaux, and catalogued as Halley manuscript RGO 2/5 (the Observatory has nineteen Halley manuscript items in its collection). The book RGO 2/5 is bound roughly in vellum and originally appears to have been a college notebook (Halley attended Queen's College, Oxford, between 24 July 1673 and about October 1676). On the cover is written, in Halley's hand, "Edmond Halley his booke and he douth often in it Looke." Much of the book is filled with neatly written notes in both English and Latin on geometric conics (the language often changing haphazardly from line to line). There are many careful diagrams of parabolae, and the notes and diagrams were usually placed on alternate pages. The cometary observations are in Latin and were jotted down in the book some time after the work on parabolae; they appear on three pages and have in places been written over the original contents of the notebook. (The first of the pages referring to the comet is reproduced in Fig. 17.10).[46] Although Halley's 1682 comet observations were far too inaccurate to be used for orbital calculations, when the large sextant was properly erected the situation was much improved. To quote from a letter from Flamsteed to Hevelius: "Also Dr. Halley [orders me to greet you] whose observation of some comets lately observed at Islington near London where he now lives, I have included beside mine."[47] The reference to comets (plural) is puzzling, but the comet of 1683 was certainly visible between 24 July and 5 September of that year.

The next chapter in the history of Halley's interest in comets introduces gravity, the inverse square law, and the work of a new acquaintance, Isaac Newton (1642–1727). It also involves the ideas of his established scientific colleagues Robert Hooke and Christopher Wren (1632–1723). In universities in those days, the study of natural philosophy was usually based on René Descartes's *Principia Philosophiae* (1644). Here space was purely geometrical, and projected bodies continued to move at a uniform speed in a straight line. In 1666 Hooke realized that to keep a planet moving in its orbit required a radial force pulling it toward the Sun and not a tangential force pushing it from behind. By 1670 Hooke had cleverly linked this radial force with that of terrestrial gravity. Planets attract objects on their surfaces toward their centers as well as attracting other planets toward the same spot. But how does this force vary as a function of distance? Hooke hypothesized that an inverse square law explained this phenomenon. Wren also arrived at the inverse square law in 1677,[48] as did Halley, toward the end of 1683, by inference based on the assumption that the planets moved in circular orbits and that the square of their orbital period was proportional to the cube of the distance between the planet and the Sun. The words *inference* and *hypothesis* must be stressed, for neither Halley nor Hooke could explain why planets moved along ellipses.

In a letter to Newton dated 29 June 1686, Halley stated that in January 1684 he

came one Wednesday to town, where I met with Sr. Christ. Wrenn and Mr. Hook, and falling in discourse about it, Mr. Hook affirmed that upon the

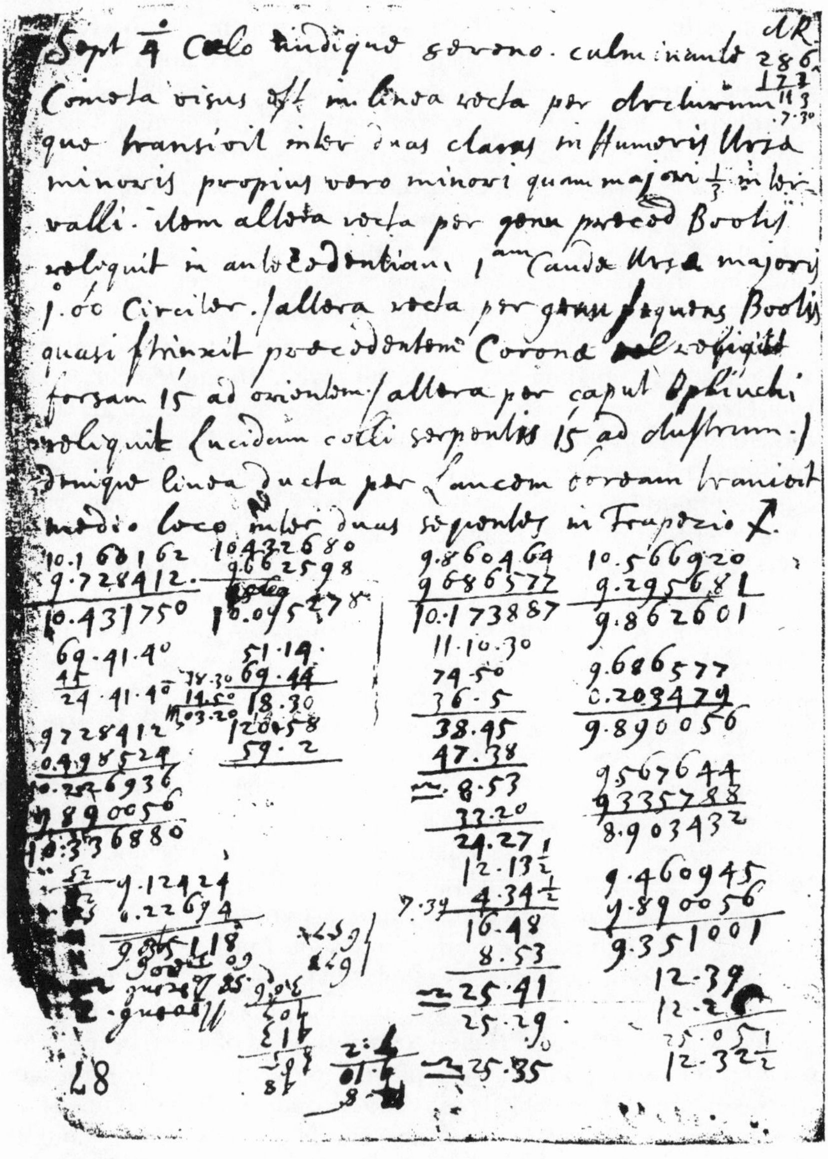

Figure 17.10. A page from Halley's notebook (RGO 2/5) on which his observations of the 1682 apparition of Halley's Comet are recorded. This notebook has been used haphazardly, with pages being filled at random and work often being recorded from back to front. On some pages notes are inserted upside down.

principle [of the inverse square law] all the Laws of the celestiall motions were to be demonstrated, and that he himself had done it; I declared the ill success of my attempts; and Sir. Christopher, to encourage the Inquiry said, that he would give Mr. Hooke and me 2 months time to bring him a convincing demonstration thereof, and besides the honour, he of us that did it, should have from him a present of a book of 40s. Mr. Hook then said that he had it, but that he would conceale it for some time, that others triing and failing, might know how to value it when he should make it publick, however I remember Sir Christopher was little satisfied that he could do it and tho Mr. Hook then promised to show it him, I do not yet find that in that particular he has been as good as his word.[49]

Several people were obviously worried about this problem; in fact, as Westfall suggests, "it was, indeed, the great unanswered question confronting natural philosophy, the derivation of Kepler's laws of planetary motion from principles of dynamics."[50] Halley had met Newton in 1682 when they talked about comets (Newton's observations of the comet of 1682 were as rough as Halley's). Seven months elapsed after January 1684 before Halley had the idea of consulting Newton at Cambridge about the inverse square law problem.

The August following when I did my self the honour to visit you, I then learnt the good news that you had brought this demonstration to perfection, and you were pleased, to promise me a copy thereof, which the November following I received with a great deal of satisfaction from Mr. Paget; and thereupon took another Journey down to Cambridge, on purpose to conferr with you about it, since which time it has been entered upon the Register books of the Society.[51]

Newton had already solved the problem and had been stimulated to study the subject by some correspondence he had had with Hooke in 1679. The best account of the visit comes from Abraham De Moivre, who made notes of Newton's experience:

In 1684 Dr. Halley came to visit him at Cambridge, after they had been some time together, the Dr. asked him what he thought the Curve would be that would be described by the Planets supposing the force of attraction towards the Sun to be reciprocal to the square of their distance from it. Sr Isaac replied immediately that it would be an Ellipsis, the Doctor struck with joy & amazement asked him how he knew it, why saith he I have calculated it, whereupon Dr. Halley asked him for his calculation without any further delay. Sir Isaac looked among his papers but he could not find it, but he promised him to renew it & and then send it him.[52]

Westfall dismisses the "charade of the lost paper."[53] Newton was simply not a man to give out results of his research without some thought. On checking his original solution he found that he did not obtain the correct answer (owing to confusion between the axes of the ellipse), so he started again. In November 1684 Edward Paget passed on to Halley Newton's reworked solution in the form of a nine-page treatise entitled *De Motu Corporum in Gyrum* (On the Motion of Bodies in an Orbit). Starting from simple dynamical principles, Newton showed that the orbit of a body under the influence of an inverse square law is a conic section (i.e., ellipse, parabola, or hyperbola); he also demonstrated that Kepler's second and third laws were a natural consequence of the inverse square law. Halley realized that *De Motu* "embodied a step forward in celestial mechanics so immense as to constitute a revolution."[54] *De Motu* was in such demand among the interested scientists that even the Astronomer Royal, Flamsteed, had to wait a month before he could see it.

We now come to the blossoming relationship between Newton and Halley, which led to the publication of the *Principia*. While Halley liked to say that he had been "the Ulysses who produced the Achilles," Westfall does not think that this is the case.[55] The request that led to *De Motu* produced just the right challenge to Newton to make him completely unsatisfied until he had solved the problem of the inverse square law in full. "As a student he had found the inverse square relation from Kepler's third law. Under Hooke's stimulus, he had extended the inverse square force to account for Kepler's first law. In August 1684, Halley evoked the same splendor anew and this time Newton surrendered utterly to its allure."[56] Newton told Flamsteed in January 1685, "Now I am upon this subject I would gladly know ye bottom of it before I publish my papers."[57] During 1685 he succeeded in proving rigorously that gravitational bodies like the Earth can be treated as if all their mass were concentrated at a point at the center of the globe.

The *Principia* was eventually finished and presented to the Royal Society on 28 April 1686; Edmond Halley, the newly appointed Clerk to the Society, had to report on it. On 22 May 1686 Halley announced that the Royal Society would publish the book and that he was to superintend the printing. On 2 June it was noted that Halley would finance the printing himself. Halley became embroiled in the debate between Newton and Hooke as to who had first thought of the inverse-square law, and Newton nearly went so far as to withhold the third book of the *Principia*, the one in which Newtonian gravitation is applied to the bodies of the solar system. Halley's tact averted this dire move. The *Principia* was published in July 1687, in Latin. According to De Morgan, Halley "made himself thoroughly master of its contents."[58]

In the *Principia* Newton, in discussing comets, had established that the "substance of theire bodyes," as Flamsteed had put it, did not matter.[59]

Comets and planets alike all move on conics under the influence of the
same inverse square law. Newton used the comet of 1680 as an example,
exactly the comet that had caused all the fuss while Halley was in Paris. It
must be stressed that Newton's *Principia,* apart from all other things, is a
formidable textbook on comets. During Halley's lifetime it was published
in three editions, those of 1687, 1713, and 1726. The third edition
(which was considerably extended compared to the first) was translated
by Andrew Motte, from Latin into English, and this was published in
London in 1729. As we are trying to assess the effect of the *Principia* on
Halley, we will concentrate on the first edition and especially Book
Three: *The System of the World.*

Lemma 4 shows that even though comets are more remote than the
Moon, they are still to be found in the planetary as opposed to stellar
regions, this being argued from observation of the variation in their direct and retrograde motions. The nearness of comets is confirmed by
noting that their luminosity varies as the fourth power of distance. Their
tails are caused by smoke arising from them. Newton recorded carefully
the variation of magnitude of the 1680 comet as a function of time.
Comets shine because they reflect sunlight, and their paths show that
"the celestial spaces are void of resistance."[60] Proposition 40 indicated
that the orbit of a comet was a conic section and that the Sun was at the
focus of the orbit.

Proposition 41 was one of the really major breakthroughs: to quote
Newton, it was the solution of "a Problem of very great difficulty."[61]
From three given observations it was shown how to determine the orbit
of a comet moving along a parabola. Newton used Flamsteed's observation of the 1680 comet (12 December 1680–5 February 1681) and added
some of his own observations taken between 25 February and 9 March
1681. The three observations specifically used were those for 21 December 1680 and 5 and 25 January 1681. Newton found that the orbit
had its ascending note in Capricorn 1°53' and an inclination of 61°20.33';
its perihelion was 8°38' from the node, and it had ecliptic coordinates of
longitude Sagittarius 27°43', latitude 7°34' south. The latus rectum of
the orbit was 236.8/10000 astronomical units (AU). The comet passed
perihelion on December $8^d00^h04^m$.

All this I determined by scale and compass . . . in a pretty large figure in
which, to wit, the radius of the Earth's orbit was equal to 16⅔ inches of an
English foot.

Lastly, in order to discover whether the comet did truly move in the orbit so determined, I investigated its place in this orbit partly by arithmetical
operations and partly by scale and compass. These predictions for 12, 29
December and 5 February and 5 March were compared with observations
and found to agree to a reasonable accuracy.[62]

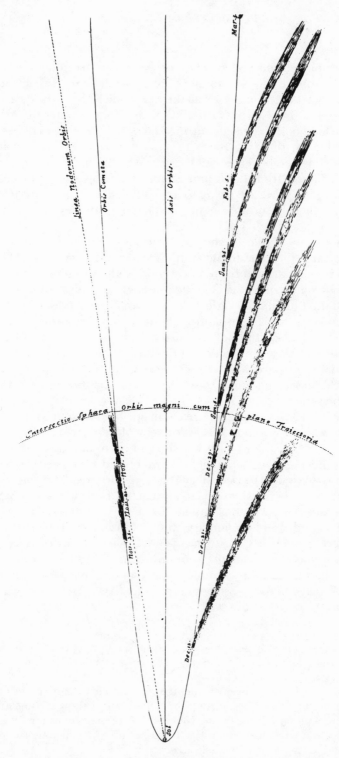

Figure 17.11. The orbit of the comet of 1680, as given by Newton in Book Three of his *Principia* (1st ed., 1687).

Figure 17.11 shows the orbit given by Newton and the observed development of the tail. Newton continues his work by discussing the physical nature of comets:

> Now if one reflects upon the orbit described, and duly considers the other appearance of this comet, he will be easily satisfied that the bodies of comets are solid, compact, fixed and durable, like the bodies of the planets; for if they were nothing else but the varpours or exhalations of the earth, of the sun and other planets, this comet in its passage by the neighbourhood of the sun, would have been immediately dissipated; for the heat of the sun is as the density of its rays, that is, inversely as the square of the distance of the places from the sun.[63]

Newton concluded that comet tails are "a very fine vapour which the head or the nucleus of the comet emits by its heat."[64] He explained why comets are brighter after perihelion than before and considered the variation of coma brightness as a function of the angle between the tail and the velocity direction of the comet. At the end of Proposition 41 Newton writes: "But as to the transverse diameters of their orbits, and the periodic times of their revolutions I leave them to be determined by comparing comets together which after long intervals of time return again the same orbit."[65] This is exactly the job that Halley undertook. Proposition 42 shows that one can move from a calculation of the parabolic orbital parameters to the calculation of the elliptical parameters, specifically the period and semimajor axis. And here the first edition of the *Principia* ends.

Halley was clearly impressed. He gave a six-page notice of the book in the *Philosophical Transactions of the Royal Society*, which ended: "It may be justly said that so many and so valuable philosophical truths are herein discovered and put past dispute were never yet owing to the capacity and industry of any one man."[66] After the *Principia*'s publication Halley busied himself with the routines of his job as Clerk to the Royal Society, including taking the minutes of the Council meetings and editing the *Philosophical Transactions*. It seems that Halley stayed as Clerk until February 1699, although his practical duties evidently ended in 1696.[67] Comets came to the fore around mid 1695, when Halley started calculating cometary orbital parameters using Newton's technique. To do so requires a catalogue of comet positions, and Newton was very helpful here too. According to Westfall, "Some time after 1680, he [Newton] systematically collected information on all recorded comets and classified them under a number of headings."[68]

Halley was with Newton early in August 1695, to quote Newton, "about a design of determining the Orbs of some Comets for me." In the

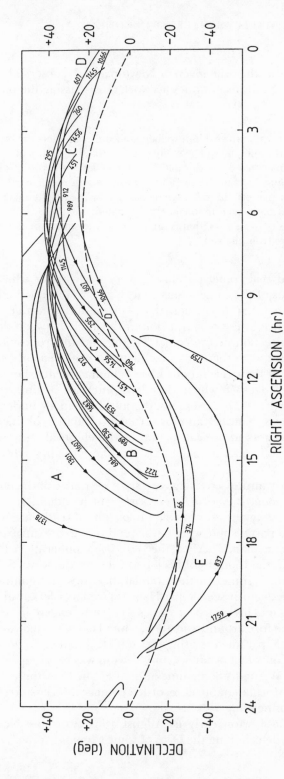

Figure 17.12. The visible paths of Halley's Comet across the sky for each of the apparitions in the last two thousand years. The five classes A, B, C, D, and E are defined in a paper by D. W. Hughes in "The Position of the Earth at Previous Apparitions of Halley's Comet," *Quarterly Journal of the Royal Astronomical Association* 26 (1985): 513.

next month Halley worked on the 1683 comet. Hevelius had communicated his observations of this comet to the Royal Society. Halley wrote to Newton on 7 September 1695, "Having gotten some little direction from a course Construction, I took the pains to examine and verifie it by an accurate Calculus, wherein I have exceeded my expectation, finding that a parabolic orb limited according to your Theory will most exactly answer all the observations Mr. Flamsteed and myself formerly made of that comet, even within the compass of one minute." Halley was less happy about doing the same job for the comet of 1664, since telescopic sights were not used for those observations. He also planned to work on the comet of 1680–81. Halley took on these orbital calculations willingly, "being desirous as far as you will permitt it, to ease you of as much of the drudging part of your work as I can, that you may be the better at leisure to prosecute your noble endeavour."[69]

On 28 September 1695 Halley wrote to Newton telling him that he had computed the orbits of the comets of 1683 and 1664 and was working on the comet of 1680–81. First, he found that there was a mistake in the celestial positions being used. Second, he realized that the orbit was elliptical and not parabolic. Third, and even more important, we come across Halley's own comet: "I must entreat you to procure for me of Mr. Flamsteed what he has observed of the comet of 1682 particularly in the month of September for I am more and more confirmed that we have seen that comet now three times since ye Yeare 1531, he will not deny it you, though I know he will me."[70] Flamsteed and Halley had fallen out, and thus he needed Newton to act as his agent.

It is not totally surprising that Halley suspected the comets of 1531, 1607, and 1682 as being three appearances of one and the same object. As can be seen from Figure 17.12, they certainly have very similar paths across the sky. By early October 1695 Halley had started to be concerned about the gravitational perturbations exerted on comets by planets. He asked Newton, "I must entreat you to consider how far a Comets motion may be disturbed by the Centers of Saturn and Jupiter, particularly in its ascent from the Sun and what difference they may cause in the time of the revolution of a Comett in its so very Elliptick Orb."[71] Halley worried about the transfer from a parabolic to an elliptical orbit for the 1680 comet and said to Newton, "perhaps Your sagacity may discover how to adjust the matter so as to remove the greatest part of those errours which upon severall attempts I found to hard for me."[72] A table comparing Halley's calculations with the observations is also given, which subsequently is reproduced in the second and third editions of *Principia*. Notice that right from the start of his calculation Halley had a clear picture of elliptical cometary orbits and that he used the parabolic (eccentricity equal to 1.0) assumption simply to ease his calculations.

By 15 October Halley had mastered the orbit of the 1664–65 comet and had come to the conclusion that Hevelius had "fiddled" his results slightly, "Hevelius to help his Calculations to agree with the hevens, had added 8 or 9 minutes to the places observed on the 4th 5th and 8th of December." Halley was very complimentary to Newton's hypothesis of cometary motion, saying that it "traces out its course as exact as the best Astronomical Tables can any of the planets, notwithstanding that this Comett [1664–65] came so near the earth as to encrease its visible velocity near tenfold."[73] On 17 October Newton replied to Halley stating that he agreed that the comet of 1680–81 moved in an ellipse but that he calculated a slightly different set of orbital parameters:

> You have made ye Orb of the Comet of 1664 answer Observation much beyond my expectation thô with double pains in calculating all the Observations anew. I can never thank you sufficiently for this assistance & wish it in my way to serve you as much. How far a Comets motion may be disturbed by Saturn & Jupiter cannot be affirmed without knowing the Orb of ye Comet & Times of its transit through ye orbs of Saturn & Jupiter. If in its ascent it passes through the Orbe before its heliocentric conjunction with ye Planet, the time will be shortened, if after, it will be lengthened, & the decrease or increase may be a day, a week, a month, a year or more; especially if the Orb be very excentric & ye time of ye revolution long.[74]

Halley's letter to Newton on 21 October 1695 is the herald of his famous 1705 paper. He tells how he had nearly finished calculating the orbit of "his" comet (1682), "and next you shall know whether that of 1607 were not the same." Moreover, "I am now become so ready at the findings a Cometts orb by Calculation, that since you have not sent the rulers as you wrote me, I think I can made a shift without them. And I intend as far as I can to limitt the Orbs of all the comets that have been hitherto observed, of all which I shall duly give you an account."[75] Halley was dispensing with Newton's old-fashioned geometrical procedures and using algebra instead.

Newton wrote to Halley in late October asking him to do some more calculations concerning the comet of 1680 so that he might put these in the *Principia*'s second edition. The cometary correspondence then dwindled as Newton became Master of the Mint (appointed 13 April 1696) and Halley moved to the Chester Mint as Deputy Comptroller, where he remained until it closed down in 1698.

Halley did not keep his new findings to himself but presented them to the Fellows of the Royal Society. These papers were recorded in the *Journal Book* of the Society:

> June 3, 1696. Halley produced the Elements of the Calculation of the Motion of the two Comets that appear'd in the Years 1607 and 1682, which

are in all respects alike, as to the place of their Nodes and Perihelia, their Inclinations of the plain of the Ecliptic and their distances from the Sun; whence he concluded it was highly probable not to say demonstrative, that these were but one and the same Comet, having a Period of about 75 years; and that it moves in an Elliptick Orb about the Sun, being when at its greatest distance, about 35 times as far off as the Sun from the Earth. [This refers to the comet that afterwards became known as Halley's comet.]

July 1, 1696. Halley read a Paper of his own wherein he gave the Elements of the Motion of the famous Comet of 1618, supposing it to move in a parabolicall Orb, which he had so fixt as to answer the Phenomena of that Comet, and he concluded that it had gone within the Orb of Mercury. But by reason of the Courseness of the Orbservations left us, it was not possible to reconcile all of them, but he had founded his Calculus on such of them as seem'd best circumstanced and most certain.[76]

Between 1698 and 1705 Halley busied himself with the first and second Atlantic voyages, the charting of the English Channel, a visit to Trieste, Boccari, Vienna, Osnaburg, Hannover, and Holland, and applying for and being appointed to the Chair of the Savilian Professor of Geometry at Oxford. He also continued with his cometary studies, because the year 1705 saw the publication of his famous research paper on comets. It is not known when he finished his calculations of twenty-four orbits, but Gregory in 1702 indicated that they were completed by the publication date of his book; the reference in the paper to the comet of February 1702 indicates that it was written after this comet's appearance.

The paper was published three times in 1705. The first was a university publication from Oxford (the original manuscript of this is bound into the back of Halley's copy of Gregory's *Elementa Astronomiae*, now in the Cambridge University Library). Halley wrote to Charlett (the Warden of New College, Oxford) on 23 June 1705: "I return you many thanks for your repeated favours as well in what relates to my house, wherin I must esteem you my greatest benefactor, as for your kind endeavours to give reputation and value to my small performance about Comets, which no wais deserves a place in your Catalogue, or to bear the badg of the Theatre."[77] The *Synopsis* had the privilege of bearing the imprint of the Sheldonian Theatre, the official seal of the Oxford University Press. Second, it was published as a slightly enlarged version (still in Latin), entitled *Astronomiae Cometicae Synopsis* in the *Philosophical Transactions* (24 : 1882–99), planned for March 1705 but evidently appearing late. And third, it appeared in an English version of the Oxford paper entitled *A Synopsis of the Astronomy of Comets,* printed for John Senex in London in 1705 (Fig. 17.13). This version is also reproduced in *Miscellanea Curiosa* ([1708] 2 : 321–44).[78]

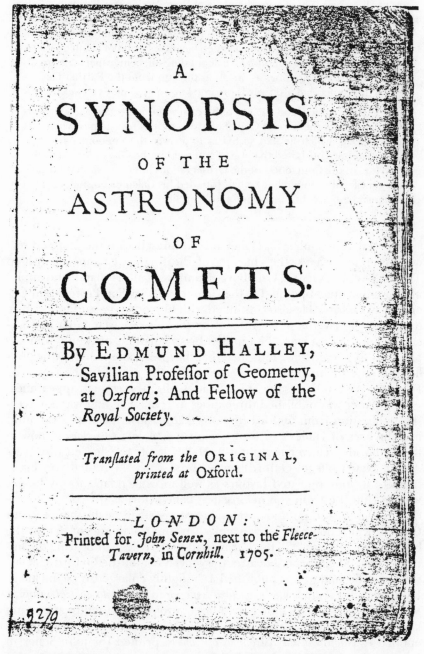

A
SYNOPSIS
OF THE
ASTRONOMY
OF
COMETS.

By EDMUND HALLEY,
Savilian Profeſſor of Geometry,
at *Oxford*; And Fellow of the
Royal Society.

Tranſlated from the ORIGINAL,
printed at Oxford.

L O N D O N :
Printed for. *John Senex*, next to the *Fleece-
Tavern*, in *Cornhill.* 1705.

Figure 17.13. The title page of the original English-language version of Halley's
Synopsis (1705).

A SYNOPSIS OF THE ASTRONOMY OF COMETS

Halley starts this paper with a brief review of cometary astronomy, touching mainly on the work of Seneca, Tycho, Kepler, Hevelius, Cassini, Flamsteed, and Newton. As we said earlier, the calculation of the orbit of the comet of 1680 given by Newton in the *Principia* acted as the springboard of Halley's work:

> Wherefore (following the steps of so Great a Man) I have attempted to bring the same Method to Arithmetical Calculation; and that with desired success. For, having collected all the Observations of Comets I could, I fram'd this Table, the Result of a prodigious deal of Calculation, which, tho' but small in bulk, will be no unacceptable Present to Astronomers. For these numbers are capable of representing all that has been yet observ'd about the Motion of Comets, by the Help only of the following General Table; in the making of which I spar'd no Labour, that it might come forth perfect, as a Thing consecrated to Posterity, and to last as long as Astronomy it self.[79]

Two tables are mentioned here. The first is a Table of the Elements (Fig. 17.14; see also Figs. 17.15 and 17.16), in which Halley discusses the twenty-four comets in detail. The first accurate observations of any comet (according to Halley) are those of Nicephorus Gregoras, a historian and astronomer from Constantinople, in A.D. 1337. The 1472 comet was observed by Regiomantanus, the 1577 one by Tycho, and the 1680 one by Halley and Newton. The comets of 1531 and 1532 were observed by Peter Apian, the 1556 one by Paulus Fabricius, and the 1596 one by Michael Maestlin—but they are "not so certain as the rest."[80] The 1684 comet was only seen by Blanchinus and the 1698 one only by the Parisian observers.

Halley then goes on to draw some conclusions:

> By comparing together the Accounts of the Motions of these Comets, 'tis apparent, their Orbits are dispos'd in no manner of Order; nor can they, as the Planets are, be comprehended within a Zodiack, but move indifferently every Way, as well Retrograde as Direct; from whence it is clear, they are not carry'd about or mov'd in Vortices. Moreover the Distances in their Perihelium's are sometimes greater, sometimes less; which makes me suspect, there may be a far greater Number of them, which moving in Regions more remote from the Sun; become very obscure, and wanting Tails, pass by us unseen.[81]

Since none were found with hyperbolic velocities, Halley thought it highly probable that the comets move on elliptical orbits and thus return

The Astronomical Elements of the Motions in a Parabolick Orb of all the Comets that have been hitherto duly observ'd.

Com. An	Nodus Ascend.	Inclin. Orbitæ	Perihelion	Distan. Perihelii à Sole	Log. Dist. Perihelii à Sole	Temp. æquat. Perihelii	Perihelium à Nodo
1337	♋ 24.21. 0	32.11. 0	♉ 7.59. 0	40666	9.609230	June 2. 6.25	46.22. 0 Retrog.
1472	♓ 11 46.20. 0	5.20. 0	♈ 15.33.30	54273	9.734584	Feb. 28 22.23	123.47.10 Retrog.
1531	♏ 19 25. 0	17.56. 0	♑ 1.39. 0	56700	9.753583	Aug. 24.21.18	107.46. 0 Retrog.
1532	♊ 20.27. 0	32.36. 0	♊ 21. 7 0	50910	9.706803	Oct. 19 22.12	30.40. 0 Direct.
1556	♌ 25.42. 0	32. 6.30	♌ 8.50. 0	46390	9.666424	Apr. 21.20. 3	103. 8. 0 Direct.
1577	♉ 25.52. 0	74.32.45	♐ 9.22. 0	18342	9.263447	Oct. 26 18 45	83.30. 0 Retrog.
1580	♈ 18.57.20	64.40. 0	♑ 19. 5.50	59628	9.775456	Nov 28 15.00	90. 8.30 Direct.
1585	♋ 7 42 30	6. 4. 0	♈ 8.51. 0	109358	0.038856	Sep. 27 19.20	28 51.30 Direct.
1590	♊ 15.30.40	29.40.40	♋ 6.54.30	57661	9.760882	Jan. 29. 3.45	51.23.50 Retrog.
1596	♌ 12.12.30	55.12. 0	♋ 18 16. 0	51293	9.710058	Full 31.19.55	83.56.30 Retrog.
1607	♉ 20.21. 0	17. 2. 0	♋ 2.16. 0	58680	9.768490	Oct. 16. 3.50	108.05. 0 Retrog.
1618	♊ 16. 1. 0	37 34 0	♈ 2.14. 0	37975	9.579498	Nov. 29 12.23	73.47. 0 Direct.
1652	♊ 28.10. 0	79.28. 0	♉ 28.18.40	84750	9.928140	Nov. 2.15.40	59.51.20 Direct.
1661	♊ 22.30.30	32.35.50	♉ 25.58.40	44851	9.651772	Jan. 16.23 41	33.28.10 Direct.
1664	♊ 21. 4. 0	21.18.30	♋ 10.41.25	102575	0.011049	Nov. 24.11.52	49.27 25 Retrog.
1665	♊ 18.02. 0	76.05. 0	♊ 11 54.30	10649	9.027309	Apr. 14. 5.15	1.56 7.30 Retrog.
1672	♑ 27.30.30	83.22.10	♈ 16.59. 30	69739	9.843476	Feb. 20. 8.37	109.29. 0 Direct.
1677	♑ 26.49.10	79 03 15	♉ 17.37. 5	28059	9.448072	Apr. 26.00.37½	99.12. 5 Retrog.
1680	♐ 2. 2. 0	60.56. 0	♑ 22 39.30	00612¼	7.787106	Dec. 8 00. 0	9.22.30 Direct.
1682	♑ 21.16.30	17.56. 0	♋ 2.52.45	58328	9.765877	Sept. 4.07 39	108.23 45 Retrog.
1683	♑ 23.23. 0	83.11. 0	♊ 25.29 30	56020	9.748343	July 3. 2 50	87.53.30 Retrog.
1684	♑ 28.15. 0	55.48.40	♊ 28.52. 0	96015	9.982339	Mai 29.10.16	29 23 00 Direct.
1686	♒ 20.34.40	31.21.40	♐ 17.00.30	33500	9.511883	Sept. 6.14.33	86.25.50 Direct.
1698	♒ 27.44. 1	11 46. 0	♑ 0.51.15	69129	9.839606	Oct. 8.16.57	3 7. 0 Retrog.

This Table needs little Explication, since 'tis plain enough from the Titles, what the Numbers mean. Only it may be observ'd, that the *Perihelium* Diſtances, are eſtimated in ſuch Parts, as the Middle Diſtance of the Earth from the Sun, contains 100000.

Figure 17.14. Halley's table of the orbital elements of twenty-four comets. All are assumed to be parabolic (i.e., eccentricity equal to 1.0), and in fact twenty-one nearly are, the sole exception being Halley's Comet (1531, 1607, and 1682). The elements given in the table are specifically illustrated for the comet of 1682 in Figure 17.15. The orbits are shown in Figure 17.16.

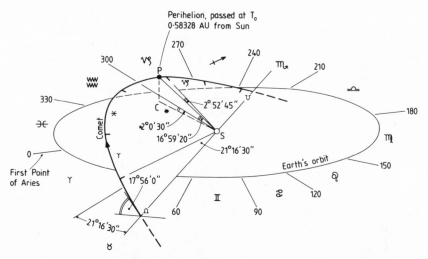

Figure 17.15. The inner portion of the orbit of Halley's Comet in 1682, to illustrate the parameters given in Halley's table of cometary elements (Figure 17.14).

to the Sun. As he put it, "The Space between the Sun and the fix'd Stars is so immense, that there is Room enough for a Comet to revolve." Halley even goes so far as to tell us why he constructed the table—and consequently spent all this time working on cometary orbits: in order "That whenever a new Comet shall appear, we may be able to know, by comparing together the Elements, whether it be any of those which has appear'd before, or not; and consequently to determine its Period, and the axis of its orbit, and to foretell its Return." [82]

We have already seen that around 1696 Halley came to the conclusion that the comets of 1607 and 1682 were one and the same. By 1702–5 he had added the comet of 1531 to this list and had recorded "that in the year 1456, in the summer time, a comet was seen passing retrograde between the earth and the sun, much after the same manner, which tho nobody made observations upon it, yet from its period and manner of its transit, I cannot think different from those I have just now mention'd." [83] We now come to Halley's (and astronomy's first) prediction of a cometary return. Rigaud notes that in the 1705 Latin version of the *Synopsis* Halley wrote, "I can undertake confidently to predict." [84] The English translation of that year was more trepidatious: "Hence I dare venture to foretell, that it will return again in the Year 1758. And if it should then return we shall have no reason to doubt but the rest must return too." [85] One of the reasons for Halley's trepidation is illustrated in Table 17.1. The comet's period had changed by fifteen months between 1531–1607 and 1607–82, and the inclination by 54 minutes of arc. The fact, how-

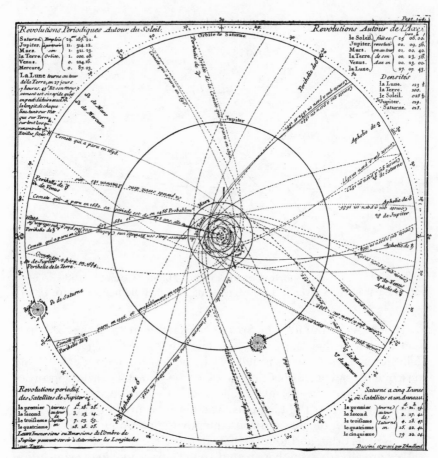

Figure 17.16. The orbits of the twenty-four comets in Halley's table, taken from Pierre C. Le Monnier, *La théorie des comètes* (Paris, 1743), 144.

ever, that Jovian perturbations of Saturn can change Saturn's period by thirteen days per orbit helped Halley to convince himself that the changes in orbital parameters of his comet from apparition to apparition were only to be expected.

Halley continued to work on comets, and a later version of the *Synopsis* was written just before 1715.[86] In the last version of the *Synopsis*, printed posthumously, he wrote: "When I had carefully searched into the Catalogues of ancient comets and discovered that three others had preceded the aforesaid three, manifestly in the same order, and at like intervals of time (viz. in the year 1305 about Easter, in the year 1380 the month unknown, and lastly in the month of June 1456), I began to be much more confirmed in my former opinion."[87] (We should note in

TABLE 17.1. *Orbital Elements of Halley's Comet*
(extracted from Fig. 17.14)

Date of perihelion passage	Interval	Longitude of node	Argument of perihelion	Inclination	Perihelion distance (A.U.)
1531, Aug 24.89		Tau 19°25'	107°46'	17°56'R	0.56700
	76.143 yr.				
1607, Oct 16.16		Tau 20°21'	108°05'	17°02'R	0.58680
	74.885 yr.				
1682, Sept 4.32		Tau 21°16'30"	108°23'45"	17°56'R	0.58328

NOTES: *Tau* refers to the Taurus region of the ecliptic, *R* stands for retrograde.

passing that only the June 1456 comet *was* actually Halley's comet.) He still worried about perturbations, realizing that the comet had been accelerated by Jupiter in 1681. In foretelling its reappearance, he wrote: "It is probable that its return will not be until after the period of 76 years or more, about the end of the year 1758, or the beginning of the next."[88] This prediction was amazingly accurate, considering that it was recovered on 25 December 1758 and passed perihelion on 13 March 1759. Halley went on to calculate the elliptical orbital parameters for the 1607 and 1682 comets with great care and immediately noticed that because of the retrograde motion the orbit was precessing, as was to be expected from Book Three, Proposition 14, of the *Principia*. Later on in the paper he made that much quoted prediction: "You see therfore an agreement of all the Elements in these three, which would be next to a miracle if they were three different Comets; or if it was not the approach of the same Comet towards the Sun and Earth, in three different revolutions in an Ellipsis around them. Wherefore if according to what we have already said it should return again about the year 1758, candid posterity will not refute to acknowledge that this was first discovered by an Englishman."[89]

It did return, and he was duly acknowledged. But what of the other comets in his table? "We do not have the same evidence that any other Comets have returned, as we have in this of ours of the year 1682. But if any arguement may be drawn from the equality of periods, and from similar phenomena, that wonderful comet which appeared in the year 1680, was one and the same with that of 1106."[90] Similarities were also noted with the comets of A.D. 531 and 44 B.C.; Halley thought that "it is not therefore unwarrantable to believe" that these were apparitions of the same comet, a comet with a period of 575 years.[91] Unfortunately, he was wrong; Newton's (1680) comet has a period of about 9,400 years. Another periodic comet of the time was that of 1661, which was thought to have a period of 129 years and to be the same comet as that of 1532. It wasn't. All three are illustrated in Figure 17.17.

A major part of the *Synopsis* was taken up by Halley's General Table and a detailed description of how this table was derived. It gives the mean angular rate of motion of the radius vector of a body moving in a parabolic orbit as a function of the body-focus-perihelion angle. As all parabolas are similar curves, the data in this table can simply be scaled according to perihelion distance to apply to all comets. The table is clearly an adjunct to the instructions given by Newton in the *Principia*. From three cometary positions Newton showed how parabolic orbital elements could be calculated. Given these, Halley's General Table enabled one to "compute the apparent place of any one of the forementioned comets for any given time," and Halley goes into all the details and gives examples of how to do so.[92]

The General Table essentially records the solution to Barker's equation, which, following Roy,[93] can be written:

$$\tan\frac{\theta}{2} + \frac{1}{3}\tan^3\frac{\theta}{2} = 2\left(\frac{GM_0}{P^3}\right)^{\frac{1}{2}}(t - T_0)$$

where θ is the angle comet-sun-perihelion point at time t, G is Newton's constant of gravitation, M_0 is the mass of the Sun, T_0 is the time of perihelion passage, and P is the *semilatus rectum* ($= q(i + e)$, where q is the perihelion distance, i is the inclination, and e is the eccentricity). Halley was also mindful of the fact that the velocity of a comet in a parabolic orbit was $(2GM_0/r)^{\frac{1}{2}}$, where r is the distance between the comet and the Sun, and that this velocity was $\sqrt{2}$ times that of an object moving in a circular orbit around the Sun of radius r.

The final version of Halley's paper ends with some general comments. The author is so impressed with the way the elliptical and parabolic orbital theory fits the observations that he throws down a challenge:

> Let now the Patrons of Vortices and an absolute Plenum, try whether according to their Hypotheses, they can delineate the path of this Comet, through nine whole Signs and for the space of about four months, and whether any other Curve, or any other law of motion sensibly different from ours, can exhibit with the like certainty the peculiar curvature of its path, and its velocities so very differently increased and diminished. If they cannot do this, let them at last leave off trifling, give themselves up to the study of truth, and swear according to the Motto of our Royal Society, *Nullius in verba.*"[94]

Figure 17.17. The frontispiece of William Whiston's *Astronomical Lectures, read in the public schools of Cambridge* (1715: R. Senex, London). Three "periodic" comets are shown, but only one, Halley's Comet, is correct. These three "periodic" comets stayed firmly entrenched in the astronomical literature until about 1825, when P/Encke and then P/Biela were added.

The final version of the *Synopsis* was written between 1715 and 1717, was sent to press in 1717, and was not published until after Halley's death. It contained a new section on elliptical cometary orbits. Using Kepler's third harmonic law (the square of the sidereal period equaling the cube of the semimajor axis, a), Halley calculated a for P/Halley and the eccentricity. He also concluded that Jovian perturbations were responsible for the temporal variation of the argument of perihelion, the longitude of the nodes, and the inclination.

Let us return briefly to Halley's first table (Fig. 17.14), which, to quote him, was "the Result of a prodigious deal of Calculation."[95] Elsewhere I give a step-by-step guide to the probable methods that Halley used (unfortunately we are not told exactly *how* he calculated orbits).[96] How accurate was Halley? We can answer this question comparing his results with those presently accepted and printed in Marsden's catalogue.[97] Out of his twenty-four calculated orbits, five can be classified as being of poor accuracy: those for 1337, 1472, 1596, 1686, and 1689 (interestingly, the first two and last two in his list). Of the remaining nineteen, seven are of good accuracy and the remainder are of average accuracy. Halley's best seven give a reasonable indication of the exactness of his method. These comets were observed between 1661 and 1684, and for their orbits Halley was calculating perihelion distances to ±0.00078 AU, inclination to ±0.27°, arguments of perihelia to ±0.065°, times of perihelion passage to ±0.080 day, and longitudes of ascending nodes to ±0.093°. For the other nine comets the results were on average twelve times less accurate. We can conclude from these values that the results given by Halley in his main table (Fig. 17.14) are quoted to a much greater accuracy than is justified. His longitude of ascending node is quoted to about the nearest minute of arc when they are at best accurate to about 6 minutes of arc. Times of perihelion passage are quoted to the nearest minutes when they are at most accurate to the nearest 120 minutes. Halley happily quotes perihelion distances to an accuracy of about 1 part in 50,000—when he is working at best only to an accuracy of 1 in 700! It is obvious that Halley enjoyed using six-figure logarithms and did not like losing figures when quoting his results, even when these figures were far from significant.

He was not alone, for the very concept of significant figures would be something completely foreign to Halley and other scientists of his period. As M. A. Hoskin puts it, "Everyone of the day divided 1 by 3 and wrote down 0.33333 . . . . . for as much space as they had room for."[98] This practice lasted well into the late eighteenth century. Halley was, however, mindful of the importance of accuracy, for example noting that good observations of the transit of Venus across the Sun's disc would yield "a way by which the vast distance of the Sun may be correctly estimated to within one five hundredth part of its amount."[99] Halley in his

Synopsis simply quoted all his results to the same number of figures, and the only hint of their varying reliability came when he wrote:

That our Five first Comets, (the Third and Fourth observ'd by Peter Apian, the Fifth by Paulus Fabricus) as also the Tenth seen by Maestlin, if I mistake not, in the Year 1596 are not so certain as the rest; for the Observations were made neither with fit Instruments, nor due Care, and upon that Account are disagreeing with themselves, and can by no means be reconcil'd with a regular Computation. The Comet which appear'd in the Year 1684 was only taken Notice of by Blanchinus, who observed at Rome: And the last, which appear'd in the Year 1698 was seen only by those at Paris, who determin'd its course in a very uncommon Way. This comet was very obscure; and, altho' it mov'd swift, and came near enough our Earth; yet we, who are wont to be curious enough in these Matters, saw nothing of it. For want of Observations I have left out of the foregoing Catalogue, those two remarkable Comets which have appear'd in this our Age, one in November, in the Year 1689 the other in February in the Year 1702. For they directing their Courses towards the Southern Parts of the World, and being scarce conspicuous here in Europe, met with no Observers capable of the Business. But, if any one shall bring from India, or the Southern Parts, an accurate Series of requisite Observations, I will willingly fall to work again, and undergo the Fatigue of representing their Orbits in Numbers, as I have done the rest.[100]

It must be remembered that the main purpose of Halley's first table was to allow the parameters to be used in the production of an ephemeris, a set of cometary celestial coordinates over a specific time interval. This would in turn enable astronomers to sift out unreliable observations and check to see if future comets had been seen before. Cometary observational data that span only a short time interval might hinder these aims. Examples of the first of these tasks are given in the 1715 *Synopsis*.

How long did it take Halley to calculate his twenty-four cometary orbits? We can only put forward an educated guess. I think that each orbit would have taken him a week, taking into consideration the accuracy he attained. Allowing for him speeding up as he became more proficient, I would estimate that the whole table represents about twenty weeks' work, "a prodigious deal of calculation" indeed.[101] Why only twenty-four? While twenty weeks of orbital calculations would seem to be enough for anyone, the answer is much simpler. Of the 425 comets that had been seen before the year 1700, only 24 had been observed well enough (i.e., had an accurate series of celestial coordinates spanning a time interval of at least a few weeks), to merit the efforts of calculating their orbit.

In the later version of the *Synopsis* Halley joins the ranks of the catastrophists. The 1680 comet, he reports, came so near the path of the Earth, that had it had come towards the Sun thirty one days later than it did, it had scarce left our globe one Semi-diameter of the Sun towards the North: And without doubt by its centripetal force (which with the great Newton I suppose proportional to the bulk or quantity of matter in the Comet), it would have produced some change in the situation and species of the Earth's Orbit, and in the length of the year. But may the great good GOD avert a shock or contact of such great Bodies moving with such forces (which however is manifestly by no means impossible), lest this most beautiful order of things be intirely destroyed and reduced into its antient chaos. But of this by the bye.[102]

Halley also evoked comets as a probable responsible agent for the biblical Flood. In the *Philosophical Transactions* he discusses Robert Hooke's suggestion that the Noachian deluge resulted from a shifting of the Earth's poles, which caused the biblical lands to come under the bulging waters of the Earth's equator.[103] Halley, however, had shown that the Earth's poles move extremely slowly and that, if Hooke was right, this hypothesis would increase the theological time scale unreasonably. So the blame was placed on a comet. At a Royal Society meeting on 12 December 1694

Halley read an account of his Hypothesis for explaining the strange changes that seem to have hapned in the superficiall parts of the Earth: which he shewed might be made out, by supposing the Choc of some Comet or other great body, striking against the Earth after any sort. This would produce a new Axis and poles of Diurnal Rotation, and a new length of the Day and year, but, above all, so great an agitation of the Waters as may account for all these strange marine things found on ye Tops of hills and deep underground. He supposed that the Caspian Sea might have been the depression occasioned by such a Collision, and the that extreme Cold of the Nor West parts of America may be occasioned by those parts having once been the North Pole of the World.[104]

His main paper on the subject was not published until 1725, the delay of thirty years being probably due to apostatical concern.[105]

CONCLUSIONS

I am left in no doubt that Edmond Halley was a great astronomer and a great scientist. Comets were objects of considerable interest and the cause of much scientific effort and speculation at that time. Halley was in the thick of this. His involvement is summed up in Table 17.2, together with important events in his life. Why was he interested in comets and

TABLE 17.2. *Edmond Halley, His Life and His Comets*

Date	Age	Rulers	Life	Comments
1656 1665 1668	0	Commonwealth	Born 29 October (8 Nov. n.s.).	Publication of Gadbury's *De Cometis;* Lubie- niecki published *The-* *atrum Cometicum;* Hevelius published *Cometographia.*
1673	17		Went up to Queen's Col- lege, Oxford.	
1676	20		Nov.—sailed to St. Helena.	
1678	22		28 Nov.—Fellow of Royal Society.	Publication of Robert Hooke's *Cometa.*
1679			Visited Hevelius—ar- rived 26 May; left end of July.	
1680	24	Charles II	1 Dec.—set out for Paris; arrived 24 Dec.	Saw the great comet of 1680 when between Calais and Paris; dis- cussed comets with Flamsteed and Cassini.
1682	25½		20 April—married Mary Tooke. Set up a small observatory in Islington.	"Halley's Comet" discov- ered at Greenwich, 15 Aug. Halley obtained only rough positions, 16 Aug.–9 Sept.
1683	27			Used 5.5 ft. sextant at Islington to observe comet of 1683 (August).
1684	28		Became friendly with Newton; visited him in August. Received *De Motu,* a revolution in celestial mechanics.	"Joy and amazement" on being told that comets move in ellipses.
1685	29	_____	Became Assistant Secre- tary of Royal Society. Edited *Phil. Trans.* for next 7 years.	
1687	31	James II	Published 1st edition of *Principia.*	A formidable textbook on comets giving de- tails of how to calcu- late the orbit of the comet of 1680.

(continues)

TABLE 17.2. *(continued)*

Date	Age	Rulers	Life	Comments
1691	34	William & Mary	Tried and failed to get the Savilian Chair of Astronomy at Oxford.	
1694	38	_____		Discussed cometary collisions at Royal Society.
1695				Calculation of cometary orbits and much contact with Newton.
1696	39½	William	Late summer, appointed Deputy Comptroller of the Chester Mint (held for 2 years).	3 June, 1 July—read paper at R.S. that gave the orbital elements of the comets of 1607, 1682, and 1618.
1698	42		19 Aug.—commanded the *Paramore* and voyaged for 2 years measuring magnetic variation.	
1702		_____	Wrote "Synopsis."	
1704	47		8 Jan.—appointed Savilian Professor of Geometry at Oxford; held Chair until his death.	
1705	49	Anne		Published "Astronomiae Cometicae Synopsis," three times, twice in Latin (Oxford), and in *Phil. Trans.* 24, 188–99, once in English (London). Published "Synopsis of Cometary Astronomy" in *Miscellanea Curiosa*, vol. 2, 321–44.
1713	57		3 Nov.—became Secretary of Royal Society.	*Principia*, 2d ed., published with extended comet section. Published account of Kirch's observation of the 1680 comet, *Phil. Trans.* 29, 169.

(continues)

TABLE 17.2. *(continued)*

Date	Age	Rulers	Life	Comments
1715/6	60			Published extended version of "Synopsis" in Gregory (1715) and Whiston (1716). Became more convinced of periodicity.
1716				Wrote final version of "Synopsis."
1717		George I		Published an account of a small telescopic comet in *Phil. Trans.* 30, 721. Sent final version of "Synopsis" to press.
1720	62½		9 Feb.—appointed as Astronomer Royal	
1724				Met J.-N. Delisle and encouraged him to check his comet tables. Calculated comet position for Newton.
1726		_____		*Principia*, 3d ed., published.
1739				Reexamined orbit of comet of 1531.
1742	85	George II	Died 14 Jan.	
1752				Publication of Halley's astronomical tables, which included last version of "Synopsis," edited by John Bevis.

specifically in their orbits? We must remember that Halley was a skilled mathematician and that his first foray into scientific publication, at the impressive age of nineteen, concerned the solution of a planetary orbit problem.[106] The appearance of the "wonderful" comet of 1680, when Halley was in his early twenties, must have also been a trigger. It would have been galling for a young man freshly introduced to the exalted circles of astronomy, meeting with Hevelius, Hooke, Cassini, Flamsteed, and Wren, to realize that his attempts to explain a comet's orbit by a straight line were completely futile. Halley realized that first-class observations were needed and was probably disappointed that his sextant was not yet assembled in 1682 when "his" comet came by. His sextant *was* in use in 1683, and he took an accurate set of positional observations of the comet of that year.

At twenty-eight Halley became friendly with Newton, a man for whom he never lost his admiration. Newton drew back the veil of mystery. Imagine Halley's "joy and amazement" at being shown that comets really move on elliptical paths around the Sun, the Sun being at the focus. *De Motu* and *Principia* went even further. Only three good, temporally spaced, observations were needed to calculate the five parabolic orbital elements of a comet. Newton showed the world how to do it, using the comet of 1680—Halley's Paris comet—as an example. Newton was obviously delighted when Halley in 1695 helped him by calculating the orbits of other comets. The calculation provided Halley with just the sort of mathematical task he liked: the methodical, meticulous reduction to order of a large mass of data. Halley had read the speculations put forward by Petit, Hooke, and Cassini as to the periodicity of comets; but after 1696 he needed to speculate no longer, he could then prove them right or wrong. To this end he calculated the orbital parameters of twenty-four comets. Out of these, three were definitely successive apparitions of the same comet, having a period of about 75.5 years. Halley predicted that it would return in 1758. Any new comet could also be compared with his table to see if that comet had appeared before; if it had, its next return could be foretold.

Halley was the first astronomer to prove that comets were periodic. As predicted, "his" comet did return in December 1758 and by popular acclaim was named after him. Out of the twenty-four comets in his 1705 table only one was truly periodic. Scientists had to wait until 1822 before the reappearance of comet Encke (a comet that orbits the Sun every 3.3 years) added the second periodic comet to the list.

NOTES

1. François Arago, "Des changements d'aspect présenté par la comète de Halley," *Astronomie Populaire* (Paris, 1855), 3:367.

2. H. Dingle, "Edmond Halley: His Times and Ours," *The Observatory* 76 (1956): 117.

3. Sir Edward Bullard, "Edmond Halley (1656–1741)," *Endeavour* 15 (1956): 189.

4. Benjamin Martin, *Miscellaneous Correspondence; A Section of His General Magazine of Arts and Sciences,* 4 vols. (1759–64), 3:97–98.

5. Nicolas L. de la Caille, *Mémoires de mathematique et de physique tirés des registres de l'Académie royale des sciences, de l'année 1759* (Paris, 1765), 522–34.

6. Charles Burney, *An Essay towards a History of the principal Comets that have appeared since the Year 1742* (London: Printed for T. Becket and P. A. De Hondt, in the Strand, 1769), 53–72.

7. D. W. Hughes, "Edmond Halley, Scientist," *Journal of the British Astronomical Association* 95 (1985): 193.

8. Aristotle, *Meteorology*, Book 1.

9. Seneca, *Quaestiones Naturales*, Book VII, chaps. 24–32.

10. Leonard Digges, *Prognostication Everlastinge*, 2d ed. (London, 1576).

11. Antonius Mizaldus, *Cometographia* (Paris, 1544).

12. Ludwig Lavater, *Cometarum Omnium Fere Catalogus* (Zurich, 1556; updated and translated into German, 1681); Stanislaw Lubieniecki, *Historia Universalis Omnium Cometarum—Theatrum Cometicum* (Amsterdam, 1668).

13. Pierre Bayle, *Lettre où il est prouvé que les comètes ne sont point le présage d'aucun malheur* (Cologne, 1682; 3d ed., Rotterdam, 1699).

14. G. F. Chambers, *The Story of Comets* (Oxford: Oxford University Press, 1910), 110, discusses the medal; on the "comet egg," see P. Lancaster Brown, *Halley and His Comet* (Poole, Eng.: Blanford Press, 1985), 90.

15. *Scripta . . . J. Regiomontani de Torqueto, Astrolabio armillari, Regula Magna Ptolemaica, Baculoque, Astronomico, & observationibus Cometarum . . .*, ed. J. Schoener (Nuremberg, 1594); see C. Doris Hellman, *The Comet of 1577: Its Place in the History of Astronomy* (New York: Columbia University Press, 1944), 81. Girolamo Fracastoro, *Homocentrica* (Venice, 1538).

16. Peter Apian, *Practica auff duz 1532 Jar* (Landshut, 1531).

17. M. E. Biot, *Comptes rendus, Académie de sciences* (Paris, 1843), 16:751.

18. Angus Armitage, *Edmond Halley* (London: Nelson, 1966), 163. For a full treatment of sixteenth-century ideas concerning comets, see Hellman, *The Comet of 1577*.

19. Johannes Kepler, *Three Tracts on Comets* (Augsburg, 1619).

20. Ibid., 93–94.

21. J. A. Ruffner, "The Curved and the Straight: Cometary Theory from Kepler to Hevelius," *Journal for the History of Astronomy* 2 (1971): 178.

22. Pierre Gassendi, "Syntagma philosophiae, Liber V, 'De Cometis & Nouis Sideribus,'" in *Opera Omnia* (Lugdvni, 1652), 1:706–10.

23. Pierre Petit, *Dissertation sur la nature des comètes* (Paris, 1665).

24. Johannes Hevelius, *Cometographia* (Danzig, 1668).

25. Chambers, *Story of Comets*, 48.

26. Seth Ward, *De Cometis* (Oxford, 1653).

27. Robert Hooke, *Letters and Collections* (London, 1678).

28. Georg Samuel Dörffel, *Astronomische Betrachtung des Grossen Cometen, welcher in ausehenden 1680, und angehenden 1681 Jahr höchst verwunderlich und entsetzlich erschienen* (Plauen, 1681).

29. Angus Armitage, "Master Georg Dörffel and the Rise of Cometary Astronomy," *Annals of Science* 7 (1951): 303.

30. John Aubrey, *Brief Lives*, ed. A. Clarke (Oxford, 1898), 282.

31. *Correspondence and Papers of Edmond Halley*, ed. Eugene Fairfield MacPike (London: Taylor & Francis, 1937), 41, 42.

32. Ibid., 4, 5.

33. Ibid., 18.

34. Ibid., 48.

35. *The Correspondence of Isaac Newton*, vol. 2, ed. H. W. Turnbull (Cambridge: Cambridge University Press, 1960), 336, 339.

36. Ibid., 336, 337.

37. Ibid., 337, 338.

38. Ibid., 338, 339.

39. Halley, *Correspondence and Papers*, 51.

40. Derek Howse, *Francis Place and the Early History of the Greenwich Observatory* (New York: Science History Publications, 1975).

41. Halley, *Correspondence and Papers*, 49.

42. Edmond Halley, "Methodus directa et geometrica, cujus ope investigantur aphelia, eccentricites, proportionesque Orbium Planetarum primariorium . . . ," *Philosophical Transactions of the Royal Society* 11 (1676): 683.

43. Newton, *Correspondence* 2:351.

44. John Flamsteed, *Historia Coelestis* (London, 1712), Book 1, pt. 3, p. 109.

45. Halley, *Correspondence and Papers*, 5.

46. D. W. Hughes and A. Drummond, "Edmond Halley's Observations of Halley's Comet," *Journal for the History of Astronomy* 15 (1984): 189.

47. Flamsteed to Hevelius, 9 October 1683, Royal Greenwich Observatory MS. 1/42, fol. 16ov.

48. Richard S. Westfall, *Never at Rest: A Biography of Isaac Newton* (Cambridge: Cambridge University Press, 1980), 402.

49. Newton, *Correspondence*, 2:442.

50. Westfall, *Never at Rest*, 396, 402, 403.

51. Newton, *Correspondence* 2:442.

52. Abraham De Moivre, Memorandum, University of Chicago Library, Joseph Halle Schaffner Collection, MS. 1075-7.

53. Westfall, *Never at Rest*, 403–5.

54. Ibid., 404.

55. De Moivre, Memorandum, University of Chicago Library, Schaffner Coll., MS. 1075-7.

56. Westfall, *Never at Rest*, 405.

57. Newton, *Correspondence* 2:276.

58. Augustus de Morgan, *Cabinet Portraits of British Worthies* (London, 1847), 12:5.

59. Newton, *Correspondence* 2:337.

60. *Isaac Newton's Mathematical Principles of Natural Philosophy and His System of the World*, trans. Andrew Motte (1729), ed. Florian Cajori (Berkeley and Los Angeles: University of California Press, 1962), 497.

61. Ibid., 504.

62. Ibid., 512.

63. Ibid., 521.

64. Ibid., 522.

65. Ibid., 532.

66. Edmond Halley, *Philosophical Transactions* 16 (1687): 291f.

67. Eugene Fairfield MacPike, *Hevelius, Flamsteed, and Halley* (London: Taylor & Francis, 1937), 54.

68. Westfall, *Never at Rest*, 395.

69. *The Correspondence of Isaac Newton*, vol. 4, ed. J. F. Scott (Cambridge: Cambridge University Press, 1967), 169, 165.

70. Ibid., 4:172.
71. Ibid., 4:173.
72. Ibid., 4:174.
73. Ibid., 4:176, 177.
74. Ibid., 4:181.
75. Ibid., 4:182.
76. Halley, *Correspondence and Papers*, 238.
77. Ibid., 125.
78. P. Broughton, "The First Predicted Return of Comet Halley," *Journal for the History of Astronomy* 16 (1985): 123, lists all the editions of the *Synopsis* from 1705 to 1759.
79. Edmond Halley, *A Synopsis of the Astronomy of Comets* (London: Printed for John Senex, 1705), 6.
80. Ibid., 19.
81. Ibid., 20.
82. Ibid., 20, 21.
83. Edmond Halley, "Astronomiae cometicae synopsis," *Philosophical Transactions* 24 (1705): 1897.
84. S. P. Rigaud, *Correspondence of Scientific Men* (Oxford, 1841), 1:34.
85. Halley, *A Synopsis* (1705), 22.
86. This version was printed in David Gregory's *Elements of Astronomy* (1715), vol. 2, and in William Whiston's *Sir Isaac Newton's Mathematick Philosophy more easily demonstrated with Dr. Halley's account of Comets illustrated* (London: John Senex, 1716); see also Colin A. Ronan, *Edmond Halley: Genius in Eclipse* (London: Macdonald, 1969).
87. Edmond Halley, *Astronomical Tables with Precepts both in English and Latin* (London, 1752), Oooo3.
88. Ibid., Rrrr2.
89. Ibid., Ssss[1].
90. Ibid., Ssss2.
91. Ibid., Ssss3.
92. Halley, *A Synopsis* (1705), 15.
93. A. E. Roy, *Orbital Motion*, 2d ed. (Bristol: Adam Hilger, 1982), 89.
94. Halley, *Astronomical Tables*, Tttt3, Tttt4. The motto *Nullius in verba* is taken from Horace, *Epistolae* 1.i, line 14, the complete line reading: *Nullius addictus jurare in verba magistri* ("Not committed to swearing by the words of the master"; i.e., we reject authority as a source of truth).
95. Halley, *A Synopsis* (1705), 6.
96. W. Hughes, "Edmond Halley: His Comets and His Mathematics," *Bulletin of the Institute of Mathematics and Applications* 21 (1985): 146.
97. B. G. Marsden, *Catalog of Cometary Orbits* (Enslow, N.J., 1983).
98. M. A. Hoskin, private correspondence with author, 9 April 1985.
99. Edmond Halley, "Methodus singularis qua Solis Parallaxis sive distantia a Terra, ope Veneris intra Solem conspiciendae, tuto determinari poterit," *Philosophical Transactions* 29 (1716): 454.
100. Halley, *A Synopsis* (1705), 19.
101. Ibid., 6.

102. Halley, *Astronomical Tables*, Tttt4.

103. Edmond Halley, "An Account of some Observations lately made at Nuremberg by Mr P. Wurtzelbaur, showing that the Latitude of that Place has continued without sensible alteration for 200 Years last past . . . ," *Philosophical Transactions* 16 (1687): 403.

104. Halley, *Correspondence and Papers*, 234.

105. Edmond Halley, "Some Considerations about the Cause of the universal Deluge . . . ," *Philosophical Transactions* 33 (1725): 118.

106. Edmond Halley, "Methodus directa et geometrica," 683.

EIGHTEEN

The First International Halley Watch: Guiding the Worldwide Search for Comet Halley, 1755–1759

Craig B. Waff

In his lecture before the 25 April 1759 public assembly of the Paris Academy of Sciences, Jérôme Lalande opened with the declaration: "The Universe sees this year the most satisfying phenomenon that Astronomy has ever offered us; unique event up to this day, it changes our doubts into certainty, & our hypotheses into some demonstrations."[1] He was speaking, of course, about the year's premier astronomical event— the appearance of a comet that appeared to fulfill Edmond Halley's bold prediction that one would appear about 1758 or 1759 with orbital elements similar to those of comets observed in 1682, 1607, 1531, and possibly before. Halley, who had laboriously calculated the elements of these comets and had discerned their similarity, had speculated that the comets seen in these earlier years were one and the same and that, if so, this celestial object traveled in a highly elliptical retrograde orbit about the Sun with a period of about seventy-five or seventy-six years. Halley's prediction of a return appearance of such a celestial body was virtually without precedent, and by the late 1750s many commentators argued that the return of the comet at the appointed time would be one of the strongest vindications of Isaac Newton's theory of universal gravitation.

If such an interpretation was to be successful, however, the comet had to be recovered at the earliest possible moment and observed over the longest possible interval of time to ascertain most clearly its orbital similarity with those seen in 1682, 1607, and 1531. Such a task was no easy matter. By the mid eighteenth century the timing of other relatively rare astronomical events, such as solar and lunar eclipses and the transits of the planets Mercury and Venus across the face of the Sun, could be predicted within a few minutes of their actual occurrence, and the location in the sky of the heavenly objects involved, which were seen almost daily, could be pinpointed without difficulty. (Traveling to the proper location on Earth to observe such phenomena, however, did often have its difficulties.) Comets, in contrast, unlike the Moon, Sun, and planets, had up to then made unexpected appearances and had always been observed over a period of only a few months or less; their orbital paths were consequently known with little certainty. Furthermore, even Halley in making his prediction had recognized the unevenness in the periods of revolution of this supposedly recurrent comet. The date of its expected return to perihelion, as well as the moment when it might be recovered by earthbound eyes, was thus highly uncertain. In the late 1750s, astronomers and other interested individuals in many countries responded in a variety of ways to this challenge, and their efforts to facilitate the sighting of the expected comet at the earliest possible moment (detailed below), as well as to observe it throughout its apparition in 1758–59,[2] constitute what may well be considered the "first international Halley watch."

EDMOND HALLEY'S
SYNOPSIS OF THE ASTRONOMY OF COMETS

Because comets had never been seen beyond the inner region of the solar system, astronomers were unable to track such objects over a long enough interval of time to determine strictly by observation if they, like the planets, traveled in closed orbits around the Sun. In the first edition of his *Principia* (1687), however, Isaac Newton had demonstrated (Prop. 40, Book Three) that comets, like planets, must move in conic sections with foci in the center of the Sun. Newton thus foresaw the possibility of a closed elliptical orbit for some comets, but he offered no examples. It was Halley who undertook the task of calculating, by geometrical construction, orbital elements for twenty comets that he considered the best observed, and of examining these elements for similarities that might indicate that a comet had appeared more than once to earthbound observers and that it consequently traveled in a closed orbit around the Sun.

Halley's first intense period of investigation of cometary motion appears to have begun around August 1695, when he visited Newton at Cambridge to determine for the latter the orbits of several comets, including those seen in 1664–65, 1680–81, 1682, and 1683.[3] Even before he undertook detailed calculations of the comet of 1682, Halley appears to have been struck by similarities in motion that this comet shared with those seen in 1531 and 1607; as early as 28 September he informed Newton that he was "more and more confirmed that we have seen that Comett now three times, since ye yeare 1531."[4] Further calculations strengthened this belief of Halley's, and at the 3 June 1696 meeting of the Royal Society of London the secretary recorded that

> Halley produced the Elements of the Calculation of the Motion of the two Comets that appear'd in the Years 1607 and 1682, which are in all respects alike, as to the place of their Nodes and Perihelia, their Inclinations to the plain of the Ecliptick and their distances from the Sun; whence he concluded it was highly probable not to say demonstrative, that these were but one and the same Comet, having a Period of about 75 years; and that it moves in an Elliptick Orb about the Sun, being when at its greatest distance, about 35 times as far off as the Sun from the Earth.[5]

An appointment as Deputy Comptroller of the Chester Mint (1696–98) and several sea voyages (1698–1701)[6] interrupted Halley's further work on comets over the next decade, so it was not until 1705 that he published his *Synopsis of the Astronomy of Comets.*[7]

The principal feature of this work was a table (see Fig. 17.14) listing orbital elements that Halley had calculated for twenty-four well-observed comets seen since 1337.[8] Near the end of his essay Halley remarked that he had considered the orbits of all these comets as parabolic. Such orbits, he said, were easier to calculate than the other conics, but if comets had such orbits in reality, astronomers had little hope of ever seeing them again: "upon which Supposition it wou'd follow, that Comets being impell'd towards the Sun by a Centripetal Force, descend as from Spaces infinitely distant, and by their Falls acquire such a Velocity, as that they may again run off into the remotest Parts of the Universe, moving upwards with such a perpetual Tendency, as never to return again to the Sun."[9] Halley argued, however, that the frequency of cometary appearances, plus the fact that none had ever been observed to move with a hyperbolic motion, made it probable that they traversed highly eccentric elliptical orbits, whose orbital elements would differ little from the parabolic ones that he had calculated. After noting the similarity of orbital elements of the retrograde comets seen in 1531, 1607, and 1682, he observed that "nothing seems to contradict" his belief in the identity of these comets

> besides the Inequality of the Periodick Revolutions: Which Inequality is not so great neither, as that it may not be owing to Physical Causes. For the Motion of *Saturn* is so disturbed by the rest of the Planets, especially *Jupiter,* that the Periodick Time of that Planet is uncertain for some whole Days together. How much more therefore will a Comet be subject to such like Errors, which rises almost Four times higher than *Saturn,* and whose Velocity, tho' encreased but a very little, would be sufficient to change its Orbit, from an Elliptical to a Parabolical one.[10]

Halley's belief that the three comets were one and the same was reinforced by one further piece of evidence: "in the Year 1456. in the Summer time, a Comet was seen passing Retrograde between the Earth and the Sun, much after the same Manner: Which, tho' no Body made Observations upon it, yet from its Period [i.e., seventy-five years before 1531], and the Manner of its Transit, I cannot think differently from those I have just now mentioned." Halley therefore declared that he would "dare venture to foretell, That it [the comet] will return again in the Year 1758"—that is, about seventy-six years after 1682.[11]

Halley promised to discuss the subject of cometary motions in a larger volume "if it shall please God to continue my Life and Health," and he in fact did so in a revised and much expanded version of the *Synopsis*, written sometime before 1719, that appeared in the posthumously published *Astronomical Tables* (Latin, ed., 1749; English ed., 1752; French ed., 1759).[12] Halley recalled that after the original (1705) version appeared he discovered in some catalogues of ancient comets that three other retrograde ones—seen in 1305 around Easter, in 1380 in an unknown month, and in June 1456[13]—had preceded at like intervals (seventy-five or seventy-six years) the three (1531, 1607, and 1682) that he had already suspected were the same comet. He also noted that he had subsequently developed a method, which he had applied to the 1682 comet, by which a highly eccentric elliptical orbit could be calculated. After comparing the observed position of the comets seen in 1531 (by Apian), 1607 (by Kepler and Longomontanus), and 1682 (by Flamsteed) with the positions generated from the computed orbit, Halley claimed that "it is manifest that two Periods of this Comet are finished in 151 years nearly, and that each alternately, the greater and the less, are compleated in about 76 and 75 years."[14] Anticipating that some might consider the inclinations and periods of the 1531, 1607, and 1682 comets to be too divergent to support the hypothesis that they were identical comets, Halley argued that the comet's close encounter with Jupiter in 1681 had increased both the comet's period and its inclination during the current revolution. (Implied but left unsaid was his evident assumption that previous variations in the orbital elements had been caused by close encounters of the comet with Jupiter and perhaps other planets during earlier visits to the inner solar system.) Halley consequently remarked that "it is probable that its return will not be until after the period of 76 years or more, about the end of the year 1758, or the beginning of the next."[15]

ONE COMET OR TWO?

As Halley had anticipated, the unevenness of the periods of this supposedly identical comet led some to doubt that "equality of periods,"

even if interpreted in a broad sense, could be counted as a reliable criterion for recognizing a new appearance of a previously seen comet. In his
treatise on the spectacular appearance of the comet of 1744, the Swiss
astronomer J. P. Löys de Chéseaux argued that attraction alone could
not produce substantial changes in a comet's orbital plane and its arrival
velocity. He suggested that the slight, but nevertheless real, resistance of
the solar atmosphere could alter the orbital elements of a comet passing
through it.

As for Halley's supposedly thrice-seen comet, Chéseaux felt that it was
"very possible & even rather probable" that the inequality of periods
could be explained by the presence of two comets, with identical and
constant periods, moving in the same orbit, with one comet *near* but not
quite at its aphelion at the same time that the other was at its perihelion.[16]
Calculating 151 years 10 days between the perihelion passages of the
supposedly identical comet seen in 1531 and 1682, he suggested that, if
this two-comet hypothesis was correct, the comet seen in 1607 would return after the same period of time and would consequently reach perihelion on 7 November 1758. If so, the comet would appear very brightly
in autumn and would pass near the Earth in mid September.

Chéseaux thus argued that "equality of periods" was a less reliable criterion for recognizing the same comet at different apparitions than such
other characteristics as the color, size, and light of the head, of the atmosphere, and of the tail, having regard of course to the different distances
from the Earth. He had to admit, however, that the comets seen in his
century seemed to differ in appearance from those observed in previous
centuries and that, with the exception of two or three, their orbital paths
bore little similarity to one another. The possibility remained that a
comet might change in appearance over the course of several apparitions, but Chéseaux thought this unlikely, because the fixed stars and the
planets, on whose nature the comets depended, had remained constant.
He concluded that similarities in orbital speed and in the figure and size
of the orbits were the surest marks of identity of a comet in its diverse
apparitions.[17]

Fourteen years later the two-comet theory again suffered from a most
unlikely area. Thomas Stevenson (d. 1764), a plantation owner on the
West Indies island of Barbados and a former Surveyor General of that
country, had observed the comet that had appeared in September and
October 1757, and he may also have observed a lunar eclipse in 1729.[18]
He suggested a two-comet theory, quite possibly without knowledge of
Chéseaux's speculations, in a 1758 letter to John Rotheram, who had just
returned to England after eight years in Barbados, where he had served
as a private tutor (1750) and subsequently as usher (1751–53) and later
master (1753–58) of the Codrington College grammar school.[19] Rotheram was able to arrange for an extract of this letter from his "inge-

nious friend" to appear in several London newspapers and magazines around late October 1758.[20]

In his letter to Rotheram, after listing the periods—151 years 74 days, 75 years 60 days, 76 years 53 days, and 74 years 323 days—that had passed between successive returns to perihelion of the supposedly identical comet in 1305, 1456, 1531, 1607, and 1682 (he called the interval 1305–1456 a double period, apparently to avoid discussion of the 1380 comet, whose exact perihelion date Halley had been unable to pinpoint), Stevenson observed that they seemed too variable to belong to any one comet, "how irregular soever we may suppose those bodies to be in their revolutions."[21] He was more inclined to believe that two comets were involved here, with one near its aphelion at the same time that the other was at its perihelion, and both having a period upward of 151 years. According to this supposition, it was the comet seen in 1305, 1456, and 1607 that was expected to appear shortly.

As for the suggested 1305 return, about which Halley had remarked only that a comet appeared at Easter, Stevenson pointed out that Easter in this year occurred on 11 April. Assuming that the comet would not be observed until at least ten days after it had passed perihelion, when it would be about 40° from the Sun and 825/1000 [AU?] from the Earth, he established 1 April as the perihelion date. Calculating that 302 years 198 days had elapsed between this date and 16 October 1607 (Halley's calculated perihelion date for that year's apparition), Stevenson took half this period (151 years 99 days) and added it to the latter date. By this means he derived a perihelion date of 23 January 1759 (old style) or 3 February (new style) for the forthcoming apparition.

In a late June 1759 letter to James Bradley, the English Astronomer Royal, Stevenson elaborated on his discomfort with Halley's single-comet theory:

> Dr Halley, from the near resemblance of the Comits Elements, was naturally induced to believe them one, & the same Comit; and in order to establish that Hypothesis, he endeavoured to Account for the difference of the time of their Periods, and Inclination of their Plans, from the atractions of Jupiter & Saturn. I cannot take upon me, to say any thing Contrary, to what is advanced, by so great an Astronomer, but must acknowledge my own ignorance, that I cannot apprehend if once Accelerated, how he was retarded, & after that Accelerated & retarded Alternately, according to the times of his Appearances recorded in History. . . . Again nor can I conceive, how the atraction of Jupiter or Saturn whos plans differ little from the plan of the Ecliptic; could increase the Angle of Inclination of the Comits Orbit, which is upwards of 17° for if you make the distance of either of the planets from the Suns Radius; the distance of the Comit from either of them (If Perpendicle) will become the Tang^t of the Angle of In-

clination of the two Plans; & Surely the shorter that Tang[t] is, the smaller the Angle of Inclination at the Sun, (the Common intersection of all the plans) will be.[22]

Such considerations led Stevenson to consider Halley's one-comet theory "more improbable (and is almost Impossible) Then that there should be two Comits, of nearly the same Elements."[23]

Stevenson then proceeded to detail a series of calculations that he thought would demonstrate to Bradley how his own theory was "much more consistent with the Heavens."[24] He first noted that he had determined the perihelion of the 1759 apparition (which he had just finished observing a few days earlier) to be 13 March, a date that in fact agreed with that determined by European astronomers. Halley had calculated a perihelion date of 16 October for the 1607 return, which implied a 1607–1759 period of revolution of 151 years 136 days. After asking Bradley to suppose that the comet's period was lengthened by only 4 days during each revolution, Stevenson then backtracked to the 1305 return. Referring to "the Plan of the Comits Orbit, Projected" (possibly a diagram, now lost, that accompanied the letter), Stevenson now argued that if the comet had passed through its perihelion point on 30 January 1305 (rather than on 1 April as he had claimed in his letter to Rotheram), then it would take 71 days for it to approach its closest point (perigee) to Earth, when it would be "the most Conspicuous"; this would explain why it was observed around Easter (11 April) of that year. By adding first 151 years 128 days, then an additional 151 years 132 (128 + 4) days, and then an additional 151 years 136 (132 + 4) days to this 30 January 1305 date, Stevenson obtained dates of 9 June 1456, 17 October 1607 (O.S.), and 13 March 1759 (N.S.) for successive perihelion passages—"a surprising agreement," he claimed, in the times of its period.[25]

Stevenson felt that his hypothesis was strengthened when one considered the inclinations of the 1531, 1607, and 1682 comets. Halley had made the first and third both to be 17°56′, "which shews them to be the same Comit," while making that of the 1607 comet to be only 17°2′, "almost a Degree Difference."[26] Stevenson believed that his hypothesis would be entirely established if Bradley determined the 1759 comet to have the latter inclination.

Stevenson mentioned one other argument for doubting Halley's seventy-five-year period for a single comet. "There is," he said, "some Analogy, between the Perihelion distance, and the time of the Comits Period." As an example he noted that the 1680 comet, whose period was the longest known, had the shortest perihelion distance of all comets observed. Stevenson remarked that other comets had nearly the same perihelion distance as those which Halley perceived to be one and the same, yet they had not been observed to return in intervals much longer than seventy-six years.[27]

The inequality of periods that concerned Chéseaux and Stevenson was interpreted quite differently by Nils Schenmark, a member of the Swedish Academy of Sciences. Noting that about seventy-six years had passed between the 1531 and 1607 returns, and about seventy-five years between the 1607 and 1682 returns, he suggested in 1755 that the period might be decreasing in an arithmetic proportion. On the basis of this hypothesis he derived a period of 73 years 228 days for the current revolution and hence a perihelion date of 19 April 1756.[28]

SOME EARLY EPHEMERIDES

With one exception (to be discussed below), no other commentators had the courage to hazard a fairly precise prediction of the perihelion date of the expected comet. A more cautious and practical approach was to develop a kind of comet ephemeris, a guide to where in the heavens the comet would most likely first appear during a given month of the year.

The first person to put this approach into practice was Thomas Barker (1722–1809), a grandson of William Whiston living in Lyndon, near Uppingham, Rutland, in England, and an author mainly of religious works. In a letter to Bradley dated 17 December 1754, he observed that the area of the sky where one should look for the comet "will be very different, according to the time of the year it comes; and its period is not sufficiently known to fix the month of its next perihelion." [29] Barker constructed twelve tables that gave the apparent path of the comet, with each table supposing the perihelion to occur in a different month of the year and, under these separate suppositions, naming the places where the comet would probably begin to appear. He explained how he determined these places:

> On a large sheet of pasteboard, I divided the circumference of a circle ten inches radius into degrees, for the magnus orbis. On the right point of the ecliptic and focal length I drew a parabola like that observed in 1682, round the sun, the center of the circle, and marked every fourth day's motion from the perihelion, and the line of its nodes. The co-sine of the comet's inclination set off on perpendiculars to this, towards the several points of the parabola, forms the projection of it, or points in the plane of the ecliptic, over which the comet is at any time perpendicular.[30]

From the twelve separate monthly tables Barker produced an additional table (Fig. 18.1) that indicated where in the heavens he believed the

A TABLE shewing where the Comet may be expected to begin to appear any Month.

Month		Scarce to be seen	Lat.	
January	end	Retr. between 30° & 15° ♐	Small increasing S.	7 Weeks after Perihelion
February	begin	30 & 15 ♑	Small N. or S.	a Month after Perihelion
March	end	30 & 0 ♒	Small N. decreasing	
April	begin	15 & 0 ♓	Small N. decreasing	2 or 3 Weeks after
April	end	Stat. 10 ♈ & 20 ♓	Small N.	
May	begin	middle ♈	} N.	about Perihelion
May	end	begin. ♉		1, 2, or 3 Weeks
June	begin	begin. ♉		
June	end	end ♉		
July	begin	begin. ♊	N. increasing	2 to 5 Weeks before
July	end	middle ♊		
August		end ♊		
September		Stat. 25 & 30 ♊	Small increasing N.	5 to 8 Weeks before
October		Retr. end ♊	Small S. or N.	2 Months before Perihelion
				2 or 3 Months
Novem.	begin	begin. ♊	Small S.	
Novem.	mid.	5 ♊ & 20 ♉		
Novem.	end.	begin. ♉ end. ♈		3 Months before Perihelion
Decem.	begin	begin. ♉	Small S. or N. very faint	11 to 14 Weeks
Decem.	end	begin. ♈		

350

Figure 18.1. Thomas Barker's table showing where he expected the comet might first become visible for any month of the year. (From "Extract of a Letter . . . concerning the Return of the Comet, expected in 1757 or 1758," *Philosophical Transactions* 49 [1755]: 350.)

Als de Comeet. den 14^{den} February in het *Perihelium* komt.

Op de Plaat den Weg B b.

Dagen	Langte g°. min.	Breedte gr. min.	Diftan- tie à ☉	Di- ftant. à ☉
Octob. 27 in ♊	20 0	4 35 Z	1 24	2 06
Nov. 6 ——	10 10	3 30	1 00	1 92
—— 16 in ♉	23 45	1 50	0 79	1 78
—— 21 ——	13 0	0 50	0 73	1 71
—— 26 ——	1 50	0 8 N	0 71	1 63
Dec. 1 in ♈	20 0	1 35	0 72	1 57
—— 6 ——	9 20	2 45	0 77	1 48
—— 11 ——	1 0	4 5	0 84	1 41
—— 16 in ♓	23 30	4 25	0 92	1 33
—— 26 ——	13 25	5 35	1 09	1 17
Januar. 5 ——	7 0	6 15	1 27	1 02
—— 15 ——	1 30	6 35	1 42	0 87
—— 30 in ♒	24 30	6 55	1 57	0 67
Febr. 19 ——	14 40	6 0	1 46	0 59
Maart 6 ——	7 5	3 15	1 15	0 71
—— 21 in ♑	27 30	2 0 Z	0 75	0 94
—— 31 ——	11 40	11 5	0 49	1 10
April 5 in ♐	26 25	18 35	0 39	1 17
—— 10 in ♏	29 15	27 20	0 33	1 25
—— 15 in ♎	26 45	30 20	0 37	1 33
—— 20 ——	5 20	27 10	0 47	1 41
—— 25 in ♍	23 15	24 5	0 60	1 48
Mey 5 ——	12 25	19 25	0 92	1 63
—— 15 ——	8 0	16 25	1 25	1 78
—— 30 ——	6 45	14 20	1 75	1 99

Wan·

Figure 18.2. Dirk Klinkenberg's table of expected positions of the comet, assuming a perihelion date of 14 February, 1757/58. Klinkenberg constructed eleven other similar tables, based on different hypothetical perihelion dates spread evenly throughout the year. (From "Kort berigt wegens eene Comete-sterre, die zich in den Jahre 1757 of 1758, volgens het Systema van Newton, Halley, en andere Sterrekundigen, zal vertoonen," *Hollandsche Maatschappij der Wetenschappen Verhandelingen* 2 [1755]: 288.)

comet would begin to be visible for any month of the year. This table proved to be quite popular. After first appearing, together with his letter to Bradley, in the 1755 *Philosophical Transactions* (the letter was read at the Royal Society on 20 March 1755), the table was printed anonymously in 1756 issues of the *Gentleman's Magazine* and the *Scots Magazine* and in full or abbreviated form in at least two English almanacs for the year 1758.[31]

Another early, nearly simultaneous effort of constructing a comet "ephemeris" was made in 1755 by Dirk Klinkenberg, a Dutch astronomer who had discovered the 1743 II and 1748 II comets. In a fashion similar to Barker he constructed twelve tables (Fig. 18.2) charting the expected path of the comet, with each table based on the supposition of a different mid-month perihelion return date (i.e., 15 January, 14 February, 16 March, etc.).[32]

FINDING THE COMET THE ILLUSTRATED WAY

Barker claimed that the diagram (Fig. 18.3) that he had drawn to compute the expected places of the comet could be used to test if a newly observed comet was the one expected: "One observation of a known comet will, on such a scheme, determine in some measure its whole course; for, from the earth's place, draw the observed longitude of the comet, where that cuts the projection of the parabola is the comet's place; to which if the observed latitude agrees, it confirms it: Then the other data being already known, and one place given, its whole course may be traced." The diagram could also be used, Barker pointed out, to find out whether a comet seen in the past but whose orbit was not well determined was identical to one of 1682: "for if an old comet was seen in August, in ♒ [Aquarius], or in ♋ [Cancer], with south latitude, or very bright in January, it cannot be the comet of 1682; but if in November in ♉ [Taurus], near the ecliptic, it may. It then remains to see, whether the rest of the description will agree with the course it would in that case take: if it does, as the account is more or less perfect, there is a greater or less probability of its being the same."[33] The underlying assumption for these tests was the premise that the comet in all its revolutions would follow virtually the same orbit. If, however, its motion was perturbed significantly at some point by a relatively close encounter with a planet, such tests might prove worthless or at best inconclusive.

Barker's diagam may have inspired a more elaborate one by the English science popularizer Benjamin Martin (1705–82).[34] Martin, who earlier had been a schoolmaster in Chichester and an itinerant lecturer and who in 1756 had established an instrument-making business in Lon-

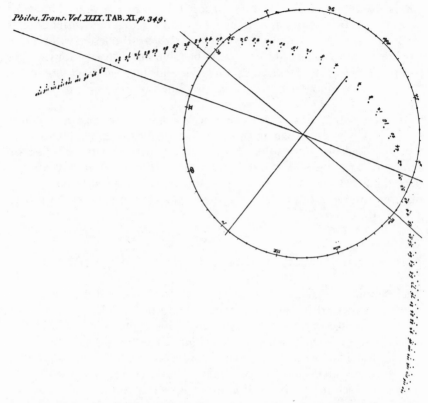

Figure 18.3. Thomas Barker's diagram in which he overlaid the apparent parabolic orbit of the comet over the nearly circular orbit of the Earth. (From "Extract of a Letter . . . concerning the Return of the Comet, expected in 1757 or 1758," *Philosophical Transactions* 49 [1755]: plate facing p. 349.)

don, published on 24 February 1757 a broadside (Fig. 18.4) that illustrated the orbit of the anticipated comet overlying the orbit of the Earth.[35] Those who purchased the broadside were informed by Martin that the conjecture that the same comet had been seen six times, in an apparent pattern of alternate intervals of seventy-five and seventy-six years, had been made very probable by the time of the appearance, the length of the period, the retrograde motion, the place of the perihelion and nodes, the perihelion distance, and the inclination of the orbit. As the last interval (1607–82) between apparitions had been seventy-five years, it was presumed that the current revolution would take seventy-six; therefore, the next appearance of the comet would probably be in 1758. Nevertheless, as the exact time of its appearance was uncertain, Martin "thought it expedient" that its orbit should be represented over a 145-day period,

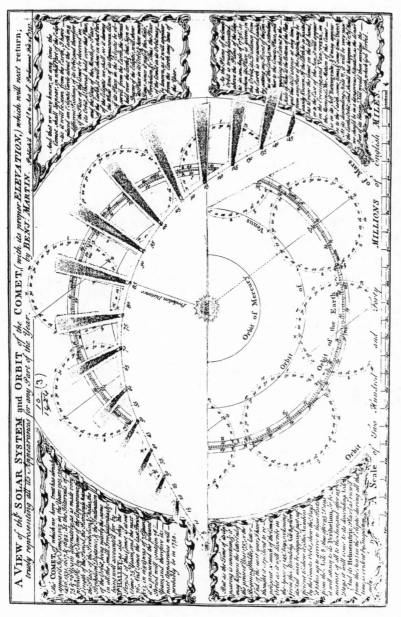

Figure 18.4. Benjamin Martin's broadside of 24 February 1757 illustrating the orbit of the comet overlying the Earth's orbit. (British Library Map Division.)

beginning at the point where the comet passed through its ascending node and where, according to Martin, "its Tail may be supposed just sufficient to shew it."[36] After 115 days the comet would reach its perihelion point, and 30 days later it would pass through its descending node. In order to show in what part of the ecliptic the comet would be seen as observed from Earth, Martin placed an "Ecliptic circle" around the Earth at eight different positions (each one 45 degrees from its neighbors) along its orbit. Under this arrangement,

> if the Place of the Comet be observed in its Orbit, a Thread held over that Place, and the Day of the Month, or Place of the Earth, it will shew in what part of the Ecliptic we shall see it during the Whole time of its Appearance. Also if its Place in the Ecliptic be observ'd from the Earth, the Thread held over the Earth & that Sign or Degree of the Ecliptic, will shew its Place in its Orbit, & how many Days since it pass'd the Node, Perihelion, & c. Thus the Place of the Comet in its Orbit may be known, as it will appear from the Earth any time of the Year.[37]

At the end of the text, printed along the margins of his broadside, Martin pointed out that the comet would be very near the Earth's orbit as it passed through its descending node; he cautioned: "should that happen the 12th of May we should be in a dangerous Situation, as the denser Parts of its blazing Tail would then envelope the Earth, which God forbid."

Newspaper advertisements for Martin's broadside often appeared together with notices of his forthcoming lectures. Martin undoubtedly used the broadside in his lectures devoted to comets (of which there were many in 1757–59), and it is quite likely that the lectures in turn stimulated sales of the broadside. In any case, his closing comment was reported widely and criticized by numerous commentators as irresponsible; as I have described elsewhere, it appears to have revived apprehensions among the English public, aroused earlier by the Methodist evangelist John Wesley, regarding the possible devastating consequences of a collision or close encounter of the expected comet with the Earth.[38]

Meanwhile, across the English Channel, comet maps of a different kind were being offered to the French public. T. Jamard, a member of the Roman Catholic Augustinian order at the Abbaye Royale de Sainte-Généviève in Paris, constructed a celestial map (Fig. 18.5) on which he represented the orbital paths of the comets seen in 1531, 1607, and 1682.[39] If one assumed with Halley that these comets were one and the same, the different paths for each apparition illustrated the effect of the annual parallax of the orbit of the Earth around the Sun. Jamard presented this map to King Louis XV on 17 April 1757 and to the Paris

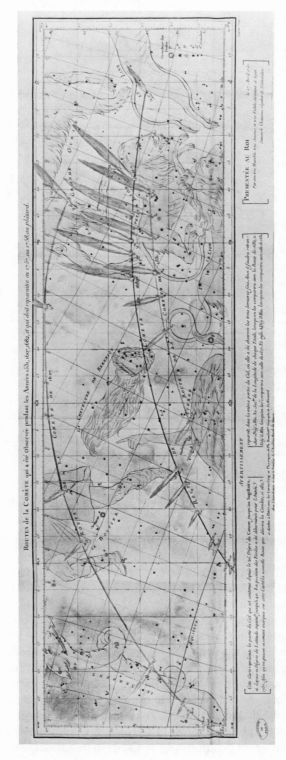

Figure 18.5. T. Jamard's celestial map (1757) representing the orbital paths of the comets seen in 1531, 1607, and 1682. (Paris Observatory archives.)

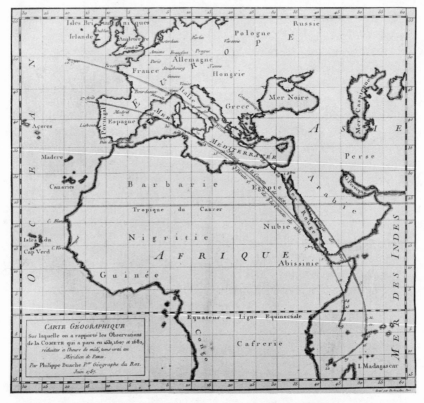

Figure 18.6. Philippe Buache's geographical map (1757) presenting "the places over which the comet, which one awaits in 1757 & 1758, has been directly vertical in the three last apparitions in 1682, 1607 & 1531." (Paris Observatory archives.)

Académie des Sciences shortly afterward. On the same day (14 May) that the map received a favorable evaluation from academicians Pierre Le Monnier and Alexandre-Gui Pingré, the academy received an accompanying memoir on the comet by Jamard.[40] This memoir also received a favorable review, again by Le Monnier and Pingré, on 8 June, and both were published, together with another map, this one by Philippe Buache (Fig. 18.6) within the next month.[41]

In the memoir Jamard stated that he believed, unlike Halley, that it was improbable that the comet's return would be delayed more than a year by the action of Jupiter; he therefore expected the comet to appear before the end of 1758. If the precise time of apparition was impossible to predict, one could, Jamard noted, at least announce the places in the heavens where it would appear and the route it would seem to take according to the different positions of the Earth in its annual orbit. Rather long and annoying calculations might be employed to determine these places (which an "étude d'obligation," Jamard claimed, prevented him from undertaking).[42] He pointed out, however, that nearly the same goal could be achieved by combining the known places of the comet's perihelion and ascending node, as well as the perihelion distance from the Sun, with the different places of the Earth on its orbit in the different months of the year. Under this procedure, Jamard then proceeded to make fourteen different assumptions (1 and 23 January, mid February, 20 March, 5 and 20 April, 20 May, 20 June, 22 July, 22 August, 22 September, 23 October, 22 November, and 21 December) regarding the perihelion date. For each situation he gave such information as the times and constellations in which the comet would be expected to appear and disappear, the intervening route it ought to take, its probable brightness, how long its tail might be, and the likelihood of discovery. For example, if the perihelion was assumed to occur on 1 January,

> one would be able to commence seeing it at the end of the month of November preceding toward the middle of the Sign of Capricorn; it will be at that time little elevated on the Ecliptic, rather distant from the earth, & would be able even to escape [observation], if the Astronomers do not bring much attention upon it. If one can discover it as early as the beginning of the month of November, it will appear larger and situated south of the Ecliptic in the last degrees of Aquarius; it will be exceedingly south; that which makes me believe one would be able to see it only toward the middle of the month. Its tail will be small, because it will not yet have passed its Perihelion.[43]

Like Martin, Jamard could not resist making one rather dramatic speculation. Noting that the comet would have a relatively close encounter with the planet Venus if its perihelion was around 5 April, he suggested that such an encounter might cause a sensible disturbance in the course of this planet.[44]

"COMET" SIGHTINGS

With the publication of these ephemerides and various pronouncements about the potential danger of comet-Earth collisions or close encounters, it is perhaps not surprising that several unusual phenomena seen in the skies in 1757 were quickly assumed to be comets, and in some cases as the one long expected. On 2 April, the *London Evening Advertiser* reported: "It is said that the comet which Sir Isaac Newton foretold would appear in the year 1757, was seen one night this week in the northern horizon."[45] Four days later, in Ireland, "A *Comet* was seen near *Clonmell* in the N.W. quarter: it appeared like a small Star, surrounded with a great light."[46] Whether these were sightings of genuine comets remains unclear; no professional astronomers confirmed them. On 3 June, navigators in the Greenland fishery became greatly alarmed with an appearance in the heavens that "some of them imagined might be the Comet so much talk[ed] of"; when the report of this event reached England, however, it was quickly interpreted to be a parhelion or mock sun.[47]

When an actual comet was independently discovered by several observers in mid September 1757—the first confirmed comet to be seen in seven years—there was naturally speculation as to whether it was the one whose return was expected. The comet was first seen in the morning sky by the amateur Christian Gärtner near Dresden on the eleventh, by Bradley at Greenwich on the thirteenth, and by Klinkenberg at The Hague on the sixteenth.[48] Bradley later recalled that "when I first discovered this Comet, it appeared to the naked eye like a dull star of the 5th or 6th magnitude; but viewing it thro' a seven-foot Telescope, I could perceive a small Nucleus (surrounded, as usual, with a nebulous atmosphere), and a short tail extended in a direction opposite to the sun."[49]

The first published reports on this object appeared near the end of the month. On 29 September, the *London Chronicle* and the *London Evening-Post* published identical dispatches reporting that it could be seen near the first-magnitude star Regulus at about four in the morning as "a small round blurry Spot without any tail."[50] Two days later, details of the comet's positions recorded at The Hague, Leyden, and other Dutch localities were published by the *Chronicle*, together with the observation, "Its Tail is scarce to be discerned without a Telescope."[51] The most embellished report, however, appeared the same day in *Read's Weekly Journal:* "By letters from Leyden, we have an account of the appearance of a Comet, in the signs Gemini and Cancer, the tail of which was computed 11 minutes in length, and of 5 Magnitude, and 'tis observed that this is the phenomenon predicted to appear in the latter end of this year, by the learned Dr. Edmond Halley, Regius, professor [sic] of Astronomy to King George the first, & c."[52] *Read's* speculative identification had some merit. Lalande later noted that this comet, when first seen in Holland on 16 September, had a position conforming to the orbit of the comet of 1682, if one assumed it was at that time forty-three days from perihelion.[53] Its subsequent course, however, indicated that it was moving in an entirely different orbit. At the end of the month, the English physician and astronomical enthusiast John Bevis, writing under the pseudonym "B. J.," observed:

> We are to hope for its true theory from the accurate observations, and no less correct calculations of our Astronomer Royal, to whose assiduity in looking out for the expected comet, we owe its discovery some weeks ago.

The motion of this by no means agrees with what the other should have at this time of the year, in the same part of the heavens; besides that is retrograde in its orbit, whereas there is great reason to think this is direct.[54]

Other astronomers soon shared Bevis's opinion. The comet of 1757 continued to be observed for the next month, with a final observation by Pezenas in Marseille on 27 October.

THE EPHEMERIDES OF
THE *BOSTON-GAZETTE* AND LALANDE

The appearance of the comet of 1757 renewed public interest in the *expected* comet and may have inspired the publication of new ephemerides to guide the search for it. In the British colony of Massachusetts, the citizens of Boston were kept well informed of the expected comet's likely whereabouts in a twelve-part, anonymously written "Account of the COMET's Orbit" that appeared serially in the *Boston-Gazette* newspaper between 31 October 1757 and 2 October 1758. The reason for the publication of this account was stated at the beginning of the first installment:

> THAT a COMET is expected about the year 1758, is a Thing that has been so often mention'd, and is indeed so generally known, that some may think it unnecessary to have any more said about it. But tho' it be known, it may not be generally attended to; and there is good Reason to remind People of it, because it is not at all improbable, that the Comet may pass unseen, if it be not carefully watch'd for. . . . To prevent, if possible, its escaping Observation, which would be a very great Disappointment to all Lovers of Astronomy, and to secure the earliest Discovery of it that we can, we propose to publish in our Paper, from Month to Month, an Account of the apparent Situation of the Northern Part of its Orbit in the Heavens, which is the only Part in which it has ever yet been seen.[55]

For each month, the position of the ascending and descending nodes, as well as some intermediate point of the comet's orbit, was given. A circle passing through these three points, the author of the ephemeris noted, "would be, near enough for the present Purpose, the Projection of the Orbit in the Heavens." The author was clearly aware of what would be the most difficult and most favorable times of the year to discover the comet:

> In the Month of February, the Comet's ascending Node will go forward from 19° to 27 of *Aries,* and the descending node from 6° to 22 of *Capricorn;* and the Latitude of the most Northern Part, which will be in the be-

ginning of *Pisces*, will not exceed 6 $\frac{1}{4}$°. The proper place to look for the Comet is a little to the Eastward of the Sun setting; and presently after Sun set, the proper Time for it. If the Comet should be now drawing near its Perihelion, the Probability of discovering it would be but small. For the Perihelion part of the Orbit lies now beyond the Sun, and within about 20° from him; so that by the Time the Evening Twilight is ended, this Part of the Orbit is set.[56]

On the other hand,

IN September, the Comet's ascending node is almost stationary, continuing about 27° of *Gemini;* and the descending Node goes forward from the 13th to the 29th of *Libra.* The Latitude of the Northern Part of the Orbit, which is in Conjunction with the Sun, will increase from 24° to 37°. The Comet may now be look'd for in the N.W. for about 2^h after Sunset; and in the N.E. long before Sunrise.

Should the Comet be now near its Perihelion, the Earth is in as [proper a] Situation for discovering it, as can be, because that Part of the Orbit, which is near the Perihelion, and in which the Comet is most likely to be seen, has about this Time of the Year, a great Latitude, and so passes at a great Distance from the Sun. In fact, all the Observations we have of this Comet in its several apparitions in the Years 1531, 1607, and 1682, were made between the 22d of *August,* and the 27th of *October.*[57]

During the twelve-month period in which this serialized "Account" appeared, the anonymous author felt compelled on two occasions to comment on comet "sightings" that had been reported elsewhere in the *Gazette.* As for the comet of 1757, which the paper reported had been seen in Barbados by Stevenson, the author argued, "The Circumstances of this Comet . . . do not agree with the Orbit of the other," that is, the expected comet. Later accounts from England and Holland confirmed him in this view.[58] As for an alleged sighting of a comet at the end of February 1758 in Venice and Rome, he insisted that "some Account of its situation and Course in the Heavens" was needed before one could pronounce whether it was the one expected. The *Gazette* writer was more inclined to go along with Halley's prediction that the anticipated comet would appear at the end of 1758 or the beginning of the following year. As that time was fast approaching when the last installment of the "Account" appeared, the author closed by expressing the hope that "all who have any Taste for Astronomy, will be very vigilant in their Endeavours to discover" the comet.[59]

Bevis and the *Boston-Gazette* writer were not the only commentators who dutifully informed the public that the comet of 1757, seen in September and October, was not the one expected. In an article in the November issue of the *Mémoires pour l'Histoire des Sciences & Beaux-Arts,* Lalande did likewise.[60] Perhaps to give hope to his disappointed readers, he pointed out that in November the Earth would be at a most favorable position for observers to perceive the expected comet. The orbits of the Earth and the comet most closely approached during this month, and if the comet at this time was at this point of its orbit, it ought to be easily seen. The conditions for recovering the comet would become less favorable in the subsequent few months, Lalande argued, both because the distance between the orbits would increase and because rainy weather often occurred in these months.[61]

Lalande claimed that astronomers were fully convinced by Halley that an identical comet was seen in 1305, 1380, 1456, 1531, 1607, and 1682 and that it would return shortly, even if possible faintness and great distance from the Earth, and perhaps even bad weather, prevented them from seeing it. The public, however, would not enjoy the same conviction: "it would place among the hazardous predictions a discovery that makes nevertheless so much honor to modern Physics. The Dissertations would be revived in the Colleges; the disdains among the ignorant; the terrors among the people, & 76 years would have to elapse before one would recover again the occasion to lift all these doubts."[62] Given this kind of public attitude, Lalande argued, one would be unable to bring too much attention to assuring its return, or to direct too many eyes to where it ought to appear, or to search for it too soon. He especially hoped that the inhabitants of the southern provinces, who enjoyed serene skies while Paris was shrouded in fog and clouds, would actively seek the comet.

The importance of recovering the expected comet was underscored by the lesser assurance astronomers had that other comets would return. Lalande pointed out that Halley's suggestion that the comets seen in 44 B.C. and A.D. 531, 1106, and 1680 might be identical had been subsequently disputed by Richard Dunthorne, who had discovered in the Cambridge University Library a manuscript entitled "De significatione Cometarum" which indicated that the comet of 1106 did not have the same orbital elements as that of 1680. Furthermore, Lalande noted, the similarity of orbital elements of two other comet pairs, those of 1532/1661 and 1264/1556, had led to some hope that they would return in, respectively, 1790 and 1848, but the absence of any known observations of earlier returns at the appropriate constant intervals (129 and 292 years in these cases) made these identifications far more tentative than the multiply observed returns of the supposedly identical comet of 1531/1607/1682.

In order to know where to look for the comet, Lalande argued, one had to determine how far from the Earth the comet could be perceived.

He pointed out that in 1531 it was perceived at one-half the Sun's distance from the Earth; in 1607, at one-third this distance; and in 1682, again at one-half. In the last case, it was very near perihelion, and consequently very luminous; yet if one had first seen it in October, it would have been more than two months from perihelion and consequently very faint. Lalande concluded that those who had the best view and were the most attentive ought to be able to perceive it when it came within two-fifths of the Sun-Earth distance. On this supposition he then gave the most likely places the comet would be located if it was first seen, respectively, on 1, 5, 10, 15, 20, and 25 November.

THE PERTURBATIONAL ANALYSIS OF CLAIRAUT

In his article Lalande recalled that Halley had based his prediction of a late-1758 or early-1759 return on the argument that the comet had been sensibly delayed by a close encounter with Jupiter in June 1681. Halley had made no mention of a subsequent post-perihelion encounter with Jupiter, at about the same distance, in November 1683, whose action, in Lalande's opinion, would have tended to destroy that of the June 1681 encounter,[63] nor had he remarked on a close encounter with Venus on 22 September 1682 at a distance one-seventh that of the Sun-Earth distance. It would be impossible to state anything about the complicated effects these encounters would have had on the comet's motion, Lalande concluded, without achieving a rigorous analysis—which, he announced, his fellow academician Alexis-Claude Clairaut had undertaken, beginning in June 1757, despite the "frightful" length of the calculations involved.[64]

Clairaut, Jean d'Alembert, and Leonhard Euler had each independently derived approximate solutions to the three-body problem in the late 1740s and had applied these to the theory of the Moon's motion, to the theory of the Sun's apparent motion, and to the theory of the perturbational effects that Jupiter and Saturn have on each other's motion.[65] In the first half of 1757 Clairaut had been involved in applying his own solution to the theory of the Sun's apparent motion.[66] Immediately after completing these determinations, he turned to a new subject that would dominate his life and those of some of his assistants over the next year. As he informed the English astronomer Gael Morris in September,

> Several months have been spent already since those [solar theory] determinations, But immediately after them, An enterprise much more fatiguing has engrossed my whole attention. It was the calculations of the perturbations which the Comet now expected has received from the Planets and

especially Jupiter's. The Theory of such perturbation is more cumbersome than the planet's, because of the Comet's Orb being so inclined, & its prodigious Excentricity. The algebr[a]ical abbreviations grounded upon the vanishing of many terms in the first case, having no room here. I thought at first of giving out the precepts which my Theory gave, to make the computations of those Perturbations, in order to leave the incumbrance of it, to the Astronomers that would be glad to calculate the time of the Comet's next apparition: Supposing that the inequality of her periods was only caused by the attraction of the Planets. Considering afterward that my precepts were very troublesom[e] to follow, & very easy to be ill-understood in some cases, & fearing that some error arising from it, spoiled the whole work, & disgraced the Theory, I have with the help of a friend undertaken the whole & am very near an end. Hitherto I have been so hard at work, as to neglect all correspondence, for fear the Comet got the start of me and appeared before the end of my calculations. Now I have time to breathe, for tho' I have not finished the whole enterprise, I am advanced enough to know I have sufficient time.[67]

The friend that Clairaut spoke of was Lalande, who many years later recalled the hardship involved in the calculations:[68]

The courage that this undertaking required is difficult to comprehend, if one does not know that during more than six months we calculated from morning to night, sometimes even at dinner, and that at the end of this forced work, I had a malady that changed my temperment for the rest of my life; but it was important that the result was given before the arrival of the comet, in order that no one would doubt the agreement between the observation and the calculations which served as the foundation of the prediction.[69]

Although both Clairaut and Lalande seemed reluctant to admit it at the time, they would not have dared undertake the enormous calculations invovled without the great assistance provided by the third member of their team, Mme. Nicole-Reine Étable de la Brière Lepaute, whom Clairaut later called *la savante calculatrice*.[70]

A detailed discussion of their work is beyond the scope of this paper, so only a summary of the main points of Clairaut's lecture at the 14 November 1758 public assembly of the Academy, at which their results were announced, will be given here.[71] Like Lalande, Clairaut remarked on the extraordinary public interest in the expected comet:

The Comet that one has awaited for more than a year has become the object of an interest much more intense than the Public puts ordinarily to the Astronomical questions. The true Amateurs of the Sciences desire its return, because there ought to result from it a very beautiful confirmation of a system, in favor of which almost all the phenomena testify. Those who are pleased on the contrary to see the Philosophers plunged into uncertainty and trouble hope that it will return not at all, & that the discoveries, as much from Newton as from his Partisans, would be found anew with the hypotheses that the sole imagination has given birth to.

Several persons of this last class triumph already, & regard a year of delay, which is due only to some announcements lacking any foundation, as sufficient for condemning the Newtonians.[72]

Clairaut declared that he would show that this delay, far from harming the system of universal gravitation, was a necessary result of it, and that a certain amount of additional time would pass before the comet appeared. After explaining in general terms the nature and extent of the effects of planetary perturbations on the comet, Clairaut concluded that during the current revolution, up to around 1751 when the comet returned to its mean distance, Jupiter had delayed the return by 518 days and Saturn by more than 100 days. He therefore predicted that the comet would reach perihelion around the middle of April 1759. Because his theory had predicted the lengths of the two previous revolutions to within a month, he set a possible similar margin of error for his prediction of the current one. Clairaut suggested that the comet could also be affected by means he had no way of calculating, such as unknown forces acting in the distant regions of the solar system that the comet traversed in the outer, unseen portion of its orbit. Such forces might arise from other comets or even from a planet too distant from the Sun to ever be perceived.

In mid March 1759 both Lalande and Pingré computed new ephemerides of likely places to look for the comet based on Clairaut's predicted perihelion date.[73] Lalande in fact gave such positions based on assumed perihelion dates of 1 and 15 March, 1 and 15 April, and 1 and 15 May. In all cases, he noted, the comet would pass quite near us, and would be past its perihelion, a "circumstance that always renders the Comets more brilliant, on account of this luminous trace or tail, that it acquires in the neighborhood of the Sun."[74] Pingré, like Lalande and Clairaut, stressed the importance of recovering the comet:

Although it appears to me easy to demonstrate that the system of Halley on the return of Comets would suffer no prejudice, when even the one that he has announced the return, for the beginning of this year, escaped our Observations, it is necesary to admit that this system [of Halley] will acquire a great weight of authority in the mind of others, if the event responds to the first prediction of the return of a Comet, that one has based on the general system of the universe. The Cartesians, the Newtonians cannot be indifferent on this phenomenon.[75]

Pingré recalled that he had searched unsuccessfully for the comet the previous November. He then discontinued his search for the next few months; as Lalande had demonstrated in his earlier letter, the positions of the Earth and the comet in their respective orbits would make it impossible to search for the comet with the naked eye up to the end of March. Now, however, a period of optimal viewing conditions was beginning. Furthermore, the time of Clairaut's predicted perihelion date was fast approaching. Pingré proposed to answer three questions: Will the comet be easy to see? Will it be visible for a long time? What precautions must be taken to prevent it from escaping our observations? On the basis of eleven different suppositions of the perihelion—3, 13, 23, 25, and 28 March; 2, 12, and 22 April; and 2, 12, and 22 May—Pingré gave eleven different positions and times where and when the comet might most likely be first perceived, as well as its subsequent course. Pingré developed his scenarios on the assumption that the comet might be first perceived by the naked eye as far away as one-half (rather than Lalande's two-fifths) the Sun-Earth distance. He gave two reasons: the extra attention brought by the first active search for a comet, and the fact that a first appearance by the comet during this period would be post-perihelion, when the light of its tail would make it recognizable at a greater distance.

DELISLE

At about the same time that Clairaut began his perturbational analysis of the comet, his academic colleague Joseph Delisle initiated his own approach to finding the expected comet at the earliest possible moment.[76] Rather than calculating the entire expected course of the comet under various hypotheses of perihelion date, this veteran astronomer argued that the emphasis should be limited to the moment when it ought first to appear, "because having once found it, one would be able to follow it by the observations & the calculation during the remainder of its apparition."[77] This moment of first appearance, both to naked-eye and telescopic observation, would occur a certain number of days before perihelion, when light from the Sun falling on it would be strong enough to make the comet perceptible from the Earth.

In order to make the best estimate of how soon before perihelion the comet could be seen, Delisle examined the previous apparitions of this supposedly identical comet. From Peter Apian's *Astronomicum Caesareum*

		LONGITUDE.	LATITUDE boréale.	LONGITUDE.	LATITUDE boréale.
Novembre..	1	♄ 15ᵈ 45′	24ᵈ 14′	♓ 28ᵈ 5′	17ᵈ 23′
	10	23. 50	17. 31	♄ 7. 25	14. 27
	20	♒ 1. 5	13. 27	15. 20	12. 13
Décembre...	1	8. 5	10. 34	23. 50	10. 21
	10	13. 25	9. 9	♒ 0. 5	9. 18
	20	19. 25	7. 55	7. 5	8. 23
Janvier.....	1	26. 5	6. 56	14. 35	7. 34
	10	♓ 0. 50	6. 21	20. 15	7. 7
	20	6. 20	5. 52	26. 20	6. 40
Février....	1	12. 55	5. 26	♓ 3. 25	6. 17
	10	✕ 17ᵈ 45′	5ᵈ 10′	✕ 8ᵈ 35′	6ᵈ 4′
	20	23. 5	4. 57	14. 25	5. 53
Mars......	1	27. 35	4. 48	19. 35	5. 47
	10	♈ 2. 15	4. 41	24. 25	5. 42
	20	7. 30	4. 36	♈ 0. 20	5. 39
Avril.....	1	13. 50	4. 34	7. 25	5. 39
	10	18. 5	4. 32	12. 25	5. 41
	20	23. 15	4. 34	18. 5	5. 47
Mai........	1	28. 55	4. 36	24. 5	5. 55
	10	♉ 3. 50	4. 42	28. 55	6. 6
	20	8. 25	4. 51	♉ 4. 50	6. 20
Juin......	1	14. 27	5. 3	11. 35	6. 41
	10	18. 50	5. 14	16. 35	7. 2
	20	24. 5	5. 32	22. 25	7. 30
Juillet.....	1	29. 25	5. 57	28. 50	8. 12
	10	♊ 3. 55	6. 21	♊ 4. 25	8. 54
	20	9. 5	6. 56	10. 50	9. 54
Août	1	15. 5	7. 53	19. 25	11. 31
	10	20. 25	8. 47	26. 5	13. 9
	20	26. 5	10. 12	♋ 4. 50	15. 54
Septembre..	1	♋ 2. 35	12. 52	18. 35	20. 39
	10	8. 25	15. 58	♌ 3. 35	25. 58
	20	16. 25	22. 28	♍ 0. 25	33. 59
Octobre...	1	♌ 1. 45	37. 25	♎ 16. 5	37. 19
	10	♍ 14. 35	62. 24	♏ 18. 25	31. 36
	20	♓ 25. 5	44. 38	♓ 11. 35	23. 40

Figure 18.7. Joseph Delisle's table of positions of the comet calculated at ten-day intervals, based on the supposition that it would be first seen either thirty-five or twenty-five days before reaching its perihelion. (From "Sur la Comète de 1759, ou le retour de celle de 1682," *Mémoires de l'Académie Royale des Sciences*, 1760 [pb. 1766]: 385–86.)

(1540) he learned that the comet of 1531 had been seen eighteen days before perihelion and that only six days later it had a tail longer than 15 degrees. The comet of 1607 had been first seen thirty-three days before perihelion; Delisle learned from Johannes Hevelius's *Cometographia* (1668) that three days later it had an exceedingly short tail, its head was not quite round, and though brighter than stars of the first magnitude, it had a pale and weak color. Delisle believed that if telescopes had been available at this time, the comet might have been seen as early as thirty-five days before perihelion. Unfortunately, for neither apparition was any information given on the size and figure of the comet at the time of discovery or how it was first perceived to be a comet. The comet of 1682, Delisle noted, first appeared, whitish and without a tail, twenty-four days before perihelion. He conjectured that at each apparition the comet might have been seen telescopically about a month before perihelion if a search had been undertaken in the place where it was at that time.

On the basis of the Earth's continuously changing position throughout the year and assuming a fixed orbit for the comet, Delisle then calculated at ten-day intervals where the comet would be on the suppositions that it would be first seen either thirty-five or twenty-five days before reaching its perihelion. He gathered these data in a table (Fig. 18.7), which he publicly announced in November 1757.[78] The data points were also plotted on a celestial map and when connected formed two ovals (Fig. 18.8).[79] It was along arcs connecting identical days on these two ovals that Delisle instructed his assistant Charles Messier to look for the comet. But what could one conclude if the comet first appeared on a certain day but not along that day's arc? Several explanations were possible: "it would have been a mark where its points were badly placed, or that there was some change in the motion of the Comet since the last apparition; or finally that it would have been able to come from the fact that it was a new, unexpected comet that was found by chance in the vicinity of the place where the comet predicted by M. Halley would be able to appear."[80] Delisle pointed out that his tabulated positions had not been calculated rigorously but rather by mechanical operations that he considered sufficient for indicating *approximately* where to search for the comet each day.

THE RECOVERY OF THE COMET

The comet eventually identified as the one predicted by Halley was first observed on the evening of 25 December 1758 by the German amateur astronomer Johann Georg Palitzsch (1723–88), a prosperous farmer

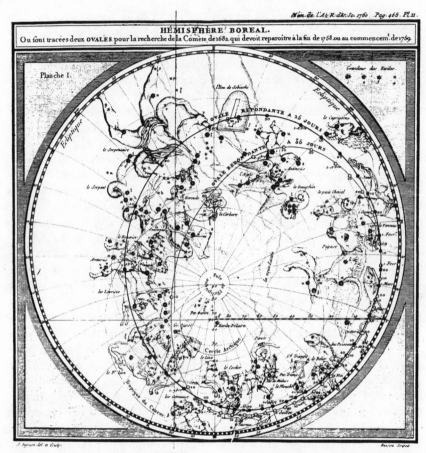

Figure 18.8. Delisle's celestial map on which the thirty-five and twenty-five data points are connected to form two ovals. (From "Sur la Comète de 1759, ou le retour de celle de 1682," *Mémoires de l'Académie Royale des Sciences*, 1760 [pb. 1766]: plate II, facing p. 465.)

living in Prohlis, a small town near Dresden in Saxony.[81] Whether he made use of any ephemeris to facilitate his discovery remains unclear, but he was certainly aware that a comet was expected.[82] In an account of the discovery published in a Dresden newspaper by his friend Christian Gotthold Hoffmann, a local official, Palitzsch remarked:

> Following my fatiguing habit of wanting to observe as much as possible all that occurred in Nature, and especially the remarkable celestial events, I examined the stars on the 25th of December about six o'clock in the evening with my 8-foot Telescope. The constellation of the Whale presented

itself well, and it was also the epoch when the announced Comet ought to approach and show itself. It thus came to pass for me the indescribable pleasure to discover in the Fish, not far from the marvelous star of the Whale [the variable star Mira Ceti], a nebulous star never perceived there before. To tell the truth, it is found between the two stars marked ε and δ on Bayer's Uranometria, or O and N on Doppelmayer's map.

The same observation, renewed on the 26th and 27th, confirmed my supposition that it was a comet; because from the 25th to the 27th, it had effectively moved from the star O toward the star N.[83]

Palitzsch made no attempt to identify this newly discovered comet as the one expected. Hoffmann, who observed it on 27 December, however, suggested that it might be the same as the one observed by Hagecius in 1580.

The first person to claim publicly the comet's identification with the one expected was the anonymous author of a small pamphlet, *Anzeige daβ er im Jahre 1682. erschienene und von Halley nach der Newtonianischen Theorie auf gegenwärtige Zeit Vorhervekundigte Comet wirklich sichtbar sey; und was derselbe in der Folge der Zeit für Erscheinungen haben werde von einem Liebhaber der Sternwissenschaft*, published in Leipzig on 24 January 1759.[84] The author, most likely Gottfried Heinsius, a professor of mathematics at the University of Leipzig, had heard of Palitzsch's and Hoffmann's observations and immediately suspected the object they had seen was the expected comet.[85] After performing a theoretical analysis (probably based on the orbit of the 1682 comet) of where the comet would likely appear, the pamphlet writer observed it himself with a three-foot telescope on 18 and 19 January at positions predicted by his theory. After reporting these sightings, the author devoted the rest of his essay to a fairly accurate description of the comet's expected positions and appearances over the next few months.

Meanwhile, in Paris, Messier, guided to some degree by Delisle's map, independently discovered the comet on the evening of 21 January 1759, after a search lasting more than a year. Although he claimed that the comet was approximately at the position indicated on the map for a first-apparition date of 21 January, Messier clearly extended his search along the arc for this date beyond the confines of the ovals. Messier in fact speculated that if Delisle had taken looser limits on how soon the comet might be seen with a telescope before perihelion, he might have discovered the comet much earlier. Messier continued his pre-perihelion observations through 14 February, but he was forbidden by Delisle to announce his discovery until after the comet rounded the Sun and was recovered, during the morning of 1 April, at a position that strongly indicated an orbit similar to the ones seen in the previous apparitions. Co-

incidentally, news of Palitzsch's discovery, apparently delayed by the
Seven Years' War then raging, arrived in Paris the same day.[86] By then,
however, the comet had been independently recovered by observers in
the Caribbean and elsewhere in Europe.

CONCLUSION

The recovery of Comet Halley at the earlist possible moment during its
first return to perihelion following Halley's work was clearly desirable
but difficult to achieve. The principal difficulty was the unequal periods
of revolution for the comets seen in 1682, 1607, 1531, 1456, and possibly
earlier that Halley was claiming to be one and the same. Although most
astronomers accepted Halley's suggestion that the differences in period were due to perturbations in its motion caused by close encounters
with various planets, others remained uncomfortable with the unprecedented magnitude of the apparent changes—a year or longer—in period (by contrast, the periods of the planets varied by only a few days).
The two-comet theories proposed by Chéseaux and Stevenson, however
improbable they might seem today, were reasonable explanations at the
time for the multiple appearances of comets that had obvious similarities
in various orbital elements (such as inclination and distance from the
Sun at perihelion) but whose apparent periods, though grossly similar
(about seventy-five or seventy-six years), still varied to an unprecedented
extent and in a seemingly alternating fashion. After the first extensive
analysis of the perturbations in the motion of Comet Halley, undertaken
by Clairaut and his associates, revealed that such variations could be
naturally explained, these theories became unnecessary.

For the majority of mid-eighteenth-century astronomers, the apparent inequality of periods posed a practical problem never before considered. If the identity of the expected comet with those seen in 1682, 1607,
1531, and earlier was to be established clearly, its observation over the
longest possible interval of time, and hence its recovery at the earliest
possible moment, were essential. The apparent inequality in periods,
however, implied an uncertain date for the return of the comet to its
perihelion point in the late 1750s. This situation, coupled with the comet's
changing visual appearance as seen from Earth (due to then little understood physical causes and the rapidly changing Earth-comet distance), in
turn made the date of its first sighting by earthbound eyes highly uncertain. Although their precise methods varied, most commentators overlaid the orbit of the 1682 comet onto the orbit of the Earth and endeavored to make informed estimations of how soon and how well the comet
might be seen for the various configurations of the known positions of

the Earth and Sun and the supposed positions of the comet at different times of the year.

Although such exercises may have contributed only to a minor extent to hastening the recovery of the comet, their value to astronomers and to the public (for whom some of the ephemerides were clearly designed) should not be underestimated. By considering the many variables that influenced the potential visibility of the comet, the makers of the ephem-erides were able to present a reasonable idea of the comet's possible whereabouts for a given time of the year and thus prevent needless, and potentially discouraging, searches at times when, and in areas of the heavens where, the comet could not possibly be seen. Such familiarity may have speeded the determination that the comet seen in 1757 (as well as one observed in 1758) was not, and the one discovered by Palitzsch and Messier in the winter of 1758–59 indeed was, the comet so eagerly expected.

NOTES

1. Lalande, "Mémoire sur le retour de la Comète de 1682, observé en 1759, avec les Élémens de son orbite pour cette dernière apparition," *Mémoires de Mathematique et de Physique, tirés des Registres de l'Académie Royale des Sciences*, 1759 (pb. 1765): 1.

2. I am currently preparing for publication a chronological collation of all known observations of the comet made during the 1758–59 apparition.

3. In his letter to Flamsteed dated 14 September 1695, Newton recalled that "when I received your last Mr Halley was with me about a designe of determin-ing the Orbs of some Comets for me." (*The Correspondence of Isaac Newton*, ed. J. F. Scott [Cambridge: Cambridge University Press, 1967], 4: 169).

4. Halley to Newton, 28 September 1695, ibid., 172.

5. In *Correspondence and Papers of Edmond Halley*, ed. Eugene Fairfield Mac-Pike (London: Taylor and Francis, 1937), 238.

6. For details of the latter, see Norman J. W. Thrower, ed., *The Three Voyages of Edmond Halley in the "Paramore," 1698–1701*, Hakluyt Society Publications, 2d ser., vol. 156 (London, 1981).

7. Edmund Halley, *A Synopsis of the Astronomy of Comets* (London: John Senex, 1705). In the same year the essay also appeared in Latin both as an Oxford pam-phlet and in the *Philosophical Transactions of the Royal Society* 24 (March 1705): 1882–99, under the title "Astronomiae Cometicae Synopsis." For a list of the many subsequent publications of this essay, see Peter Broughton, "The First Pre-dicted Return of Comet Halley," *Journal for the History of Astronomy* 16 (1985): 123–33, esp. 124. The origin of the essay is briefly discussed by Michael Hoskin, "The First Edition of Halley's 'Synopsis,'" ibid., 133. For a detailed discussion of the essay, see S. P. Rigaud, *Some Account of Halley's Astronomiae Cometicae Synopsis* (Oxford: S. Collingwood, 1835).

8. Halley, *Synopsis*, 7.

9. Ibid., 20.

10. Ibid., 21–22.

11. Ibid., 22.

12. Ibid., p. 22. Both the Latin and English editions of the *Astronomical Tables* were edited by John Bevis. I have used the latter, *Astronomical Tables with Precepts both in English and Latin for computing the Places of the Sun, Moon, Planets, and Comets* (London: William Innys, 1752), in which the "Synopsis" is printed on signatures Llll3–Tttt4.

13. As noted above, Halley had in fact mentioned the 1456 comet in the 1705 version of the "Synopsis." He may perhaps have subsequently discovered a better account of it, leading him to narrow its return from "Summer time" to "June."

14. Halley, *Astronomical Tables*, sigs. Ooo03–Ooo04. In the revised "Synopsis," Halley presented an extensive account of the observations of 1531, 1607, and 1682; for the three earlier suggested apparitions (1305, 1380, and 1456), however, he provided no information other than the dates, and he did not specify the catalogues that he consulted. While the identification of the 1456 comet as an apparition of Comet Halley was verified by Pingré, later investigators demonstrated that the two previous apparitions occurred in 1301 and 1378.

15. Ibid., sigs. Rrrr[1]–Rrrr2.

16. J. P. Löys de Chéseaux, *Traité de la Comète qui a paru en décembre 1743 & en janvier, février, & mars 1744* (Lausanne and Geneva: Marc-Michel Bousquet, 1744), 45.

17. Ibid., 44–47.

18. His observations of the comet were reported in the *Boston-Gazette and Country Journal*, no. 139 (28 November 1757): 2; an observation of a lunar eclipse made in Barbados by "Mr. Stephenson's Brother" was published in the *Philosophical Transactions* 36, no. 416 (November–December 1730): 440–41.

19. For further information on Rotheram, see William Prideaux Courtney's article on him in the *Dictionary of National Biography*, ed. Leslie Stephen and Sidney Lee (Oxford: Oxford University Press, 1897), 17:299–300; and Frank J. Klingberg, ed., *Codrington Chronicle: An Experiment in Anglican Altruism on a Barbados Plantation, 1710–1834* (Berkeley and Los Angeles: University of California Press, 1949), 89–90, 109, 114–15.

20. "Extract of a Letter from Thomas Stevenson, Esq.; in Barbadoes," *Lloyd's Evening Post and British Chronicle* 3, no. 199 (25–27 October 1758): 406–7; also in *London Chronicle; or, Universal Evening Post* 4, no. 286 (26–28 October 1758): 413, and *London Magazine; or, Gentleman's Monthly Intelligencer* 27 (November 1758): 564. Stephen Skinner and I have discussed the life and work of Stevenson in our "Tales from the First International Halley Watch (1755–59): 2. Thomas Stevenson of Barbados and his Two-Comet Theory," *International Halley Watch Newsletter*, no. 10. (1 September 1987): 3–9.

21. See note 20.

22. Stevenson to Bradley, 30 June 1759, Royal Greenwich Observatory, MS. 3/43:8, fols. 316r–317v.

23. Ibid., 316r.

24. Ibid.

25. Ibid., 316r, 317r.

26. Ibid., 317r.

27. Ibid.

28. Nils Schenmark, "Om den Cometens återkomst til vårt Planet-systeme, som syntes år 1682," *Kongl. [Svenska] Vetenskaps-Academiens Handlingar*, 16 (July–September 1755): 216–24; a German translation appears as Nic. Schenmark, "Von der Wiederkunft des Kometens, der sich 1682 gezeiget hat, in unsere Planetenwelt," *Der königlich-schwedischen Akademie der Wissenschaften Abhandlungen* 17 (July–September 1755): 216–23.

29. Thomas Barker, "Extract of a Letter of Thomas Barker, Esq.; to the Reverend James Bradley, D.D. Astronomer Royal, and F.R.S. concerning the Return of the Comet, expected in 1757, or 1758," *Philosophical Transactions* 49, pt. 1 (1755): 347–50, with plate facing p. 349; quote p. 347. Barker later published *An Account of the Discoveries concerning Comets, with the Way to find their Orbits, and some Improvements in constructing and calculating their Places. For which Reason are here added New Tables, fitted to those Purposes; Particularly with regard to that Comet which is soon expected to return* (London: J. Whiston and B. White, 1757), which I have not seen. See also an additional letter of his to Bradley, dated 8 December 1755, in *Miscellaneous Works and Correspondence of the Rev. James Bradley*, ed. S. Rigaud (Oxford: Oxford University Press, 1832), 491–92, and the letter cited in note 63.

30. Barker, "Extract of a Letter," 348.

31. "Precepts for determining, from one single Observation, the whole apparent course of the expected Comet, with directions in what part of the Heavens to look for it every Month in the Year," *Gentleman's Magazine and Historical Chronicle* 25 (September 1756): *413, with plate facing p. 414; also in *Scots Magazine* 18 (November 1756): 550. "A Definition of Comets, with Precepts to determine their Place and Course in the Heavens," last two pages in *Merlinus Liberatus. Being an Almanack For the Year of our Redemption, 1758 . . . By John Partridge;* and "Precepts for determining from one single Observation the whole apparent Course of the Comet, expected in this Year 1758; with Directions in what Part of the Heavens to look for it every Month in the Year. Being communicated to the Author by an ingenious Hand," first three pages after ephemeris in *Merlinus Anglicus Junior: or, The Starry Messenger For the Year of our Redemption, 1758 . . . By Henry Coley;* both almanacs were printed by R. Reily for the Company of Stationers and released to the public in November 1757.

32. D. Klinkenberg, "Kort berigt, wegens eene Comeet-sterre, die zich in den Jahre 1757 of 1758, volgens het Systema van Newton, Halley, en andere Sterrekundigen, zal vertoonen," *Hollandsche Maatschappij der Wetenschappen Verhandelingen* 2 (1755): 275–318, with two plates following p. 318. My nonfamiliarity with the Dutch language prevents me from making any further comment on this paper, or on the anonymous "Bedenkingen over den Komeet of Staartster, waar van de Wederkomst eerlang verwagt wordt," *Uitgezogte Verhandelingen uit de nieuwste Werken van de Societeiten der Wetenschappen in Europa*, 2. deel, 7. stukje (1757): 492–506, or Jan Schim, "Aenmerkingen over den Loop der Staertster, die eerlang verwagt wort, en in 't Jaer 1682 verscheenen is," *Hollandsche Maat-*

schappij der Wetenschappen Verhandelingen, 4 (1758): 490–505, with plate facing p. 504.

33. Barker, "Extract of a Letter," 349.

34. For further biographical information on Martin, see John Millburn's two books *Benjamin Martin: Author, Instrument-Maker, and "Country Showman,"* Science in History, no. 2 (Leyden: Noordhoff International, 1976) and *Benjamin Martin: . . . Supplement* (London: Vade-Mecum Press, 1986).

35. Benjamin Martin, *A View of the Solar System and Orbit of the Comet, (with its proper Elevation,) which will next return; truly representing all its appearances for any Part of the Year.* A copy of this rare broadside is held by the British Library Map Division under shelfmark *10.(3.).

36. Ibid.

37. Ibid.

38. Craig B. Waff, "Comet Halley's First Expected Return: English Public Apprehensions, 1755–58," *Journal for the History of Astronomy* 17 (1986): 1–37.

39. T. Jamard, *Routes de la Comète qui a été observée pendant les années 1531, 1607, 1682, et qui doit reparoître en 1757, ou 1758, au plûtard* (1757). Copies of the map are held by the British Library Map Division (shelfmark K.1.81.1.) and the Observatoire de Paris archives (shelfmark A4-10, piece 42c,15).

40. T. Jamard, *Memoire sur la Comète qui a été observée en 1531, 1607, 1682, & que l'on attend en 1757, ou au plûtard en 1758. Présenté a l'Académie Royale des Sciences avec une Carte céleste, sur laquelle sont tracées les Routes de cette Comète dans ses trois dernières apparitions* (Paris: Quai de l'Horloge de Palais, 1757). Copies of this memoir are held by the British Library Map Division (shelfmark K.1.81.3.), the Bibliothèque Nationale in Paris (shelfmark V.7991), and the Observatoire de Paris archives (shelfmark A4-10, piece 42c,15).

41. Philippe Buache, *Carte géographique sur laquelle on a rapporté les Observations de la Comète qui a paru en 1531, 1607 et 1682, réduites à l'heure de midi, tems vrai au Méridien de Paris* (June 1757). In an "Avertissement" within Jamard's memoir, it is noted that "one has proposed to present on this Geographical Map the places over which the Comet, which one awaits in 1757 & 1758, has been directly vertical, in the three last apparitions in 1682, 1607 & 1531." The purpose of this map remains unclear. For the Academy's reception and review of Jamard's map and memoir, see Académie Royale des Sciences, *Procès-verbaux* 76 (14 May, 8, June, and 9 July 1957): 325, 339, and 463. Jamard presented a printed copy of the memoir to the Academy on 9 July.

42. Jamard, *Memoire sur la Comète,* 8.

43. Ibid.

44. Ibid.

45. *Evening Advertiser,* no. 479 (31 March–2 April 1757): [3], col. 3.

46. *Gentleman's and London Magazine: and Monthly Chronologer* (Dublin) 24 (issue for April 1757): 214.

47. *London Chronicle: or, Universal Evening Post* 2, no. 102 (23–25 August 1757): 190, col. 3. The extract from one of the navigator's journals, as reported by the newspaper, read as follows: "That, at Midnight, on Friday the 3rd of June last, in 77 Deg. 30 Min North Latitude, the Weather being clear, they observed the Sun to be very bright, and encompassed with a luminous Circle, coloured like

the Rainbow, at the Distance of 10 Degrees from his Body. After this they had dark close Weather; and, at Four in the Morning, the Appearance of a bright Sun broke out to the Eastward, about 60 Deg. above the Horizon, accompanied with a broken Halo or Semicircle, distant from it 11 Deg. the Back of which was turned towards the true Sun, and from this Halo issued a Tail or Stream of Light, extending 50 Degrees in Length towards the North."

48. J. Bradley, "Observations upon the Comet that appeared in the Months of September and October 1757, made at the Royal Observatory," *Philosophical Transactions* 50 (1757): 408–15; Dirk Klinkenberg, "Observations on the late Comet in September and October 1757; made at The Hague," ibid., 483–88. For other observations of this comet, see Pingré's memoir (note 61 below). For a discussion of its orbit, see C. Wirtz, "Die Bahn des Kometen 1757," *Astronomische Nachrichten* 201, no. 4806 (6 July 1915): cols. 109–26.

49. Bradley, "Observations upon the Comet," 408.

50. *London Chronicle* 2, no. 117 (27–29 September 1757): 310, col. 2; also in *London Evening-Post*, no. 4664 (27–29 September 1757): [3], col. 2.

51. *London Chronicle* 2, no. 118 (29 September–1 October 1757): 313, col. 1. An identical report was published at the end of October in the *London Magazine; or, Gentleman's Monthly Intelligencer* 26 (issue for October 1757): 514.

52. *Read's Weekly Journal, or British-Gazetter*, no. 3946 (1 October 1757): [3], col. 3.

53. Lalande, "Lettre au sujet de la Comète dont on attend le retour," *Mémoires pour l'Histoire des Sciences & Beaux-Arts*, November 1757, 2850.

54. Bevis's letter, dated 29 September 1757, was one of two that appeared in "Curious Accounts of the present Comet," *Gentleman's Magazine and Historical Chronicle* 27 (issue for September 1757): 392–93. It also appeared in *Gentleman's and London Magazine* 26 (issue for September 1757): 443.

55. "Account of the COMET's Orbit," *The Boston-Gazette, and Country Journal*, no. 135 (31 October 1757): [1], col. 1; no. 140 (5 December 1757): [1], col. 1; no. 145 (9 January 1758): [1], col. 3; no. 148 (30 January 1758): [2], col. 3; no. 153 (6 March 1758): [3], col. 1; no. 157 (3 April 1758): [2], col. 3; no. 161 (1 May 1758): [2], col. 3; no. 165 (29 May 1758): [3], col. 1; no. 170 (3 July 1758): [3], col. 2; no. 174 (31 July 1758): [1], col. 3; no. 178 (28 August 1758): [3], col. 1; no. 183 (2 October 1758): [1], col. 3. The first two installments were also published in the *New York Mercury*, no. 275 (21 November 1757): [1], col. 1; no. 279 (19 December 1757): [2], col. 3. I have reprinted all twelve installments in my "Tales from the First International Halley Watch (1755–59): 1. Boston Waits For and Watches the Comet," *International Halley Watch Newsletter*, no. 9 (1 September 1986): 16–26. In this article I have argued that the most likely compiler of the "Account" was John Winthrop, the Hollis professor of mathematics and natural philosophy at Harvard and a later observer of Comet Halley in 1759.

56. *Boston-Gazette*, no. 148 (30 January 1758).

57. Ibid., no. 183 (2 October 1758).

58. Ibid., no. 140 (5 December 1757); no. 145 (9 January 1758).

59. Ibid., no. 165 (29 May 1758).

60. Lalande, "Lettre au sujet de la Comète dont on attend le retour," *Mémoires pour l'Histoire des Sciences & Beaux-Arts*, November 1757, pp. 2850–63; also

in *Mémoires de Trévoux*, December 1757, 502–11. The latter journal, published in Amsterdam, reprinted articles from the former. Lalande's letter was dated 15 October 1757.

61. His pessimistic assessment for this period was shared by Pingré, who, in a lecture read at the public assembly of the Académie des Sciences held on 12 November 1757, remarked: "As for the expected comet, I have said above that its apparition is perhaps questionable; it is not that I recall any doubt on its return, but the clouds, the bad weather, may they not at all hide it from view? There is besides an extremely disfavorable case for discovering it, if it passes by its perihelion on 23 January or ten or twelve days before or after. If it is at perihelion toward the end of February, in March & April, it will be very beautiful . . . ; but even in this supposition, it may appear only for a few days; it soon reaches the southern pole of the ecliptic. In these different circumstances, it may escape us; the surest [method] would be without doubt to search for it with instruments, but for that it would be necessary to know correctly the time of its passage, & it is that which it is not too easy to guess." Pingré expressed hope that Clairaut's theoretical research and calculations would help pinpoint an approximate time for the comet's return to perihelion. See Pingré, "Mémoire sur la Comète qui a paru en cette année 1757," *Mémoires de l'Académie Royale des Sciences*, 1757 (pb. 1762): 97–107, esp. 107.

62. Lalande, "Lettre au sujet de la Comète," 2052.

63. In a letter to the editor dated 15 August 1758 and published in the *London Magazine; or, Gentleman's Monthly Intelligencer* 27 (September 1758); 463–64, Thomas Barker pointed out that "Dr. Halley, in his Astronomical Tables, remarks, that the comet of 1682, having passed in its descent not remote from Jupiter, might possibly be in some measure affected by its attraction. But it is remarkable, that both Saturn and Jupiter were then so situated, that the comet approached them, both in coming down to, and going up from the Sun; as the four calculations I have subjoined will shew. The masters of the doctrine of gravity can best judge, whether such large bodies would at that distance sensibly alter the comet's orbit and present period."

64. Lalande, "Lettre au sujet de la Comète," 2858–59.

65. See Craig B. Waff, "Universal Gravitation and the Motion of the Moon's Apogee: The Establishment and Reception of Newton's Inverse-Square Law, 1687–1749" (Ph.D. diss., Johns Hopkins University, 1976); Curtis A. Wilson, "Perturbations and Solar Tables from Lacaille to Delambre: The Rapprochement of Observation and Theory," *Archive for History of Exact Sciences* 22 (1980): 53–304; and idem, "The Great Inequality of Jupiter and Saturn: From Kepler to Laplace," *Archive for History of Exact Sciences* 33 (1985): 15–290.

66. Clairaut, "Mémoire sur l'orbite apparente du Soleil autour de la Terre, en ayant égard aux perturbations produites par les actions de la Lune & des Planètes principales," *Mémoires de l'Académie Royale des Sciences*, 1754 (pb. 1759): 521–64. This paper was read at the Academy on 9, 13, and 23 July and 14 December 1757 (Académie Royale des Sciences, *Procès-verbaux* 76 [14 May, 8 June, and 9 July 1757]: 463, 465, 487, 640).

67. Clairaut to Gael Morris, 16 November 1757, Royal Society, Letters and Papers, vol. 3, no. 274. The portion of this letter dealing with the comet has been

published as Appendix 1 (pp. 263–64) in René Taton, "Clairaut et le retour de la comète de Halley," in *Arithmos-Arrythmos: Skizzen aus der Wissenschaftsgeschichte. Festschrift für Joachim Otto Fleckenstein zum 65. Geburtstag*, ed. Karin Figala and Ernst H. Berninger (Munich: Minerva, 1979), 253–74. Clairaut gave Morris permission to read the letter, which was written in English, at a meeting of the Royal Society, and this was indeed done on 22 December 1757 (Royal Society, Journal Book, vol. 23, pp. 19–21).

68. One who chose to avoid such hardship was d'Alembert, who admitted that "the dislike that I have for the great calculations kept me from searching the disturbances that Jupiter and Saturn ought or may cause at this Comet; but I have no doubt that they influence it" (d'Alembert to Frisi, 20 November 1758, in *Memorie appartenenti alla vita ed agli studj del Signor Don Paolo Frisi*, ed. Pierre Verri [Milan: Giuseppe Marelli, 1787], 84–85).

69. Lalande, *Bibliographie astronomique; avec l'histoire de l'astronomie depuis 1781 jusqu'a 1802* (Paris: Imprimerie de la Republique, An XI [1803]), 678.

70. The most extensive biographical account of Lepaute is Lalande's obituary of her in his *Bibliographie astronomique*, 676–81. Lalande there claims that Clairaut, who never married, omitted mentioning her in his 1760 book on comets because "this judicious, but weak, scholar" had complied with the demands of an envious female friend who, in Lalande's opinion, "had some pretentions without any kind of knowledge." Lalande, however, made no mention of Lepaute either in his lecture (note 1) to the 25 April 1759 public assembly of the academy, and referred to her only as "M^{de}. L. P." in his "Histoire de la Comète observée en 1759," *Connoisance des Temps pour l'année 1761* (1759), 214. He did, however, mention her by name (p. 110) in the *Tables astronomiques de M. Halley* (Paris: Durand, 1759). See also W. T. Lynn, "Madame Lepaute," *Observatory*, 24 (February 1911): 87–88; and Elizabeth Connor, "Mme. Lepaute, an Eighteenth-Century Computer," *Astronomical Society of the Pacific Leaflets*, no. 189 (November 1944).

71. Clairaut, "Memoire sur la Comete de 1682, addressé à MM. les Auteurs du Journal des Sçavans," *Journal des Sçavans*, January 1759, 38–45. This was reprinted (with some footnotes added) in Clairaut's *Théorie du mouvement des Comètes, dans laquelle on a égard aux altérations que leurs orbites éprouvent par l'action des Planètes. Avec l'application de cette Théorie à la Comète qui a été observée dans les années 1531, 1607, 1682 & 1759* (Paris: Michael Lambert, [1760]), iv–xiv.

72. Clairaut, "Memoire sur la Comete de 1682," 38.

73. Lalande, "Lettre au sujet de la Comète dont on attend le retour," *Mémoires pour l'Histoire des Sciences & Beaux-Arts*, April 1759, 1 : 924–31; also in *Mémoires de Trévoux*, 43 (May 1759): 97–102. Pingré, "Lettre de M. Pingré, Bibliothecaire de Ste. Génevièvre, de l'Académie Royale des Sciences, au sujet de la Comète dont on attend le retour," *Mémoires pour l'Histoire des Sciences & Beaux-Arts*, April 1759, 2 : 991–1008; also in *Mémoires de Trévoux* 43 (May 1759): 137–48.

74. Lalande, "Lettre au sujet de la Comète," 926.

75. Pingré, "Lettre," 991.

76. For an extensive discussion of Delisle's support of Halley's cometography, see Simon Schaffer's "Halley, Delisle, and the Making of the Comet," Chapter 14 in this volume.

77. "Lettre de M. de l'Isle, de l'Académie Royale des Sciences, &c., à l'Auteur du Mercure, sur le retour de la Comète de 1682, contenant les premières Observations qui en ont été faites à Paris, avec l'explication de la méthode dont on s'est servi pour la découvrir," *Mercure de France,* July 1759, 1 : 146–75, esp. 148–56; quote p. 149. Messier repeated Delisle's description in his "Histoire & Observations du retour de la Comète de 1682, découverte à l'observatoire de la Marine à Paris, le 21 Janvier 1759, vers les six heures du soir, dans la constellation des Poissons, observée jusqu'au 3 Juin," *Mémoires de l'Académie Royale des Sciences,* 1760 (pb. 1766): 380–433, esp. 383–89.

78. On page 2869 of the November 1757 issue of the *Mémoires pour l'Histoire des Sciences & Beaux-Arts* is listed a brochure by Delisle entitled *Recherche du lieu du Ciel, où la Comète prédite, par M. Halley, doit commencer a parôitre; avec une Table des longitudes & latitudes des points du Ciel, où l'on doit la chercher pendant une année entière, à commencer du premier Novembre 1757.* Although this notice indicated that the brochure could be found at the shop of "Buttard, rue S. Jacques, à la Vérité," it seems apparent, from later remarks by other Parisian astronomers, that the brochure was never published; no surviving copies are known. A large quantity of Delisle's manuscripts on "Recherches sur le retour de la comète de 1682" do, however, exist in the archives of the Observatoire de Paris. For a list of these manuscripts, see Josette Alexandre, "La comète de Halley à travers les ouvrages et manuscrits de l'Observatoire de Paris," *Isis* 77 (March 1986): 79–84.

79. The table and map were published by Messier in his "Histoire & Observations du retour de la Comète de 1682," 385–86 and pl. II (preceding p. 465).

80. "Lettre de M. de l'Isle," 155.

81. The most extensive biographical accounts of Palitzsch are Lose, *Schattenrisse edler Teutschen* (Halle, 1784), 3 : 193–240; and Friedrich Theile, *Johann Georg Palitzsch: Ein Lebensbild* (Leipzig: Louis Genf, 1878). Siegfried Koge is preparing a new biography for publication in 1988, the two hundredth anniversary of Palitzsch's death. For the present, see Koge's "Der 'Sterngucker in Pruhls': Entdecker des Halleyschen Kometen 1758," *Astronomie und Raumfahrt* 29, Heft 2 (1984): 32–36.

82. The only pre-1759 German-language aid for finding or tracking the comet of which I am aware is a translation of Martin's broadside (see note 35). This translation was recently reprinted in G. A. Tammann and Philippe Veron, *Halleys Komet* (Basel: Birkhäuser Verlag, 1985), 202.

83. Christ. Gotthold Hoffmann, "Nachricht von dem Cometen, welcher seit dem 25. Dec. 1758. gesehen wird," *Dreßdnische Gelehrte Anzeigen auf das Jahr 1759,* 2. Stück, cols. 17–22, esp. 19–20. I am grateful to Siegfried Koge and the Staatsarchiv in Dresden for supplying me with a photocopy of this account. Much of it is transcribed in Ritter Olbers, "Einige Bemerkungen über den berühmten Halleyschen Kometen," *Astronomisches Jahrbuch für des Jahr 1828* (1825): 144–50, esp. 144–48.

84. The copies of the pamphlet (published by Bernhard Christoph Breitkopf) that I have seen are held by the Stanford University Library and the Crawford Library at the Royal Observatory, Edinburgh. The type is set differently and variant emblems are used in these two copies, indicating that two print-

ings of the pamphlet were made; there are also minor spelling differences between the two copies. The essay was republished in the *Hamburgische Magazin* 22, 3. Stück (1759): 313–25 and the *Dreßdnische Gelehrte Anzeigen auf des Jahr 1759*, 7. Stück, cols. 97–112.

85. In his letter to Leonhard Euler, dated 21 April 1759, Heinsius reports that he observed the comet with a three-foot telescope on 18, 19, 22, and 27 January. He also admits authorship of an unspecified writing on the comet that almost certainly is the Leipzig pamphlet. An abstract of this letter is included in A. P. Juskevic and E. Winter, eds., *Die Berliner und die Petersburger Akademie der Wissenschaften im Briefwechsel Leonhard Eulers.* Teil 3 (Berlin: Akademie-Verlag, 1976), 120–21. The editors of this letter incorrectly identify the comet paper that Heinsius refers to here as his "De Cometa pro Proximo Anno 1758 Expectando," which was read to the St. Petersburg Academy on 31 October 1757.

86. Messier, "Histoire & Observations du retour de la Comète de 1682," 390–92, 420.

Index

Compositor: G&S Typsetters, Inc.
Text: 10/12 Baskerville
Display: Baskerville
Printer: Edwards Brothers, Inc.
Binder: Edwards Brothers, Inc.